BIBLICAL ARCHAEOLOGY IN FOCUS

BIBLICAL ARCHAEOLOGY IN FOCUS

Keith N. Schoville

Introduction by Menahem Mansoor

BAKER BOOK HOUSE
Grand Rapids, Michigan

Library of Congress
Catalog Card Number:
78-62914

ISBN: 0-8010-8112-2

Printed in the United States of America

Illustration Credits

Aleppo Museum, 222, 235

American Schools of Oriental Research, Bulletins of, 296 (bottom), 476 (top and bottom), 477 (bottom), 483, 491 (top and bottom)

Ashmolean Museum, 178

Biblical Archaeologist, 139, 141, 243, 244, 278, 281, 286 (bottom, left, and top, right), 296 (bottom), 300, 316, 319, 444 (top)

Biram, A., Nelson Glueck School of Biblical Archaeology, 350 (top)

The British Museum, 56, 84, 138 (top, right), 179, 182, 183, 199, 201, 259, 423 (top)

Brooklyn Museum, 58

Millar Burrows, 451

Richard L. W. Cleave, 348 (bottom), 364, 380, 430 (top and bottom, left), 440, 467 (bottom), 477 (top)

Doubleday and Company (from *Near Eastern Archaeology in the Twentieth Century*), 286 (bottom right and top left), 373

Hammond, Inc., 50, 68, 71, 155, 266

Hebrew Union College Biblical and Archaeological School, Jerusalem, 108, 109, 110, 111

Iraq Museum, 193 (top)

Israel Colour Slides Co., 441, 444 (bottom)

Israel Department of Antiquities and Museums, 340

Israel Exploration Journal XVIII, 414

Israel Museum, Jerusalem, 304, 449, 450, 455 (top), 461

Israel Office of Information, 308, 311

Jordan Tourist Department, 486 (right)

Kathleen Kenyon, 32, 47, 398, 405

Levant Photo and Design Service, 70, 493

Lock and Whitfield, 85

The Louvre, 86, 180, 240

Matson Photo Service, 55 (bottom), 267, 326, 467

John McGovern, 185 (top), 187 (bottom), 190, 198, 200, 202 (bottom left and right), 207

Metropolitan Museum of Art, 148, 149

Ernst Meyer, 87

Museum of Fine Arts, Boston, 225

Museum Haaretz, Tel Aviv, 64 (left)

National Aeronautics and Space Administration, 265

Oriental Institute, 104, 132 (bottom, right), 181, 189, 191, 202 (top, left), 204, 205, 206, 211 (Erich F. Schmidt), 212 (top), 215 (top), 255 (top), 258, 453, 485

Palestine Archaeological Museum, 457, 467 (top)

Charles Pfeiffer, 430 (middle, left)

Photo Archives photographiques, Paris, 138

Photo Sport, Beirut, 249 (bottom)

Photographic Media Center, University of Wisconsin, 42, 117 (top, right), 139, 141, 243, 244, 278, 281, 286, 294, 300, 316, 319, 342 (George C. Whipple), 373, 387, 391, 395, 444 (top), 455 (bottom), 460, 491 (top, bottom)

Pontifico Instituto Biblico, 35, 43, 46, 97, 137 (bottom), 187 (top), 193 (bottom), 208, 211, 212 (bottom), 215 (bottom), 220 (top), 223, 226, 234, 249 (top and middle), 260, 261, 262 (bottom and middle), 263, 375 (bottom), 376 (top), 379, 423 (bottom), 469, 482, 486 (left), 489, 490

Praeger Publishers, Inc. from *Science in Archaeology,* 65

G. P. Putnam's Sons from *Archaeological Encyclopedia of the Holy Land,* 64

Religious News Service, 247

Claude F. A. Schaeffer, 242

Keith N. Schoville, 23, 37, 39, 45, 105, 114 (top), 255 (bottom), 262 (top), 263, 296 (top), 299, 334, 339, 344, 348 (top), 350 (middle and bottom), 352, 356, 358, 372 (bottom), 375 (top, middle), 406 407, 411 (top, left and bottom), 420 (bottom right and left), 422, 430 (right), 433, 434 (top), 435, 442, 443, 455 (middle), 457 (bottom, left), 470, 471, 474

Staatliche Kunstsammlungen, Weimar, 82

Carl A. Stapel, 80, 114 (bottom), 115 (bottom), 117 (bottom), 140 (top), 331, 356, (middle), 360, 363

University of Chicago Press from Palais Royal D-Ugarit II, Pl. VII, 239

University of Pennsylvania Museum, 48

The University Museum, Philadelphia, 185 (bottom), 330, 332, 333

Trustees of the Wellcome Trust, 420 (top), 429

This work is dedicated
to the memory of the late
CHARLES F. PFEIFFER
distinguished scholar,
author, teacher, editor,
and staunch friend of the
Department of Hebrew and Semitic Studies

Contents

Preface 9
Introduction 11

PART ONE Understanding Biblical Archaeology

1 **The Dimensions of Biblical Archaeology** 15
- Defining *Archaeology* 16
- Defining *Biblical* 16
- The Temporal Dimensions of Biblical Archaeology 26
- The Spatial Dimensions of Biblical Archaeology 65

2 **The Development of Biblical Archaeology** 79
- Period of Pious Pilgrims—Third Century A.D.-1799 80
- The Treasure Hunters—*circa* 1800–1890 84
- Biblical Archaeology Becomes a Science—1890-World War II 87
- The Modern Era of Biblical Archaeology—1948-Present 91

3 **Money, Men, Methods, and Materials** 95
- Money 95
- Men 98
- Methods 103
- Materials 112
- Interpretation 119

4 **The Development of Writing** 127
- Communication by Gestures, Motions, and Objects 128
- Pictures, Pictograms, and Ideograms 129
- Syllabic Writing 136
- Alphabetic Writing 139

5 **The Bible and Archaeology** 153
- The Limitations of the Bible 154
- The Limitations of Archaeology 156
- The Peculiarities of the Archaeologist 159

PART TWO A Survey of Significant Sites and Finds Outside the Holy Land

6 **Mesopotamia** 173
- Nippur 175
- Ur 181
- Uruk 186
- Babylon 188
- Nuzi 192
- The Assyrians 195
- Nineveh 198
- Nimrud 200
- Khorsabad (Dur-Sharrukin) 204
- Ashur 207
- Persia (Iran) 208
- Pasargadae 210
- Persepolis 211
- Hamadan 213
- Susa 213

7 **Asia Minor and the Hittites** . . . 219

8 **Syria and Lebanon** . . . 231
- Mari 232
- Ugarit 236
- Ebla (Tell Mardikh) 242
- Byblos 247

9 **Egypt** . . . 253
- Tell el-Amarna 258
- Sinai 261
- Pe-Rameses and Pithom 262
- Thebes 264
- Elphantine 268

PART THREE A Survey of Significant Sites Within the Holy Land

10 **Ai** . . . 277

11 **Arad** . . . 285

12 **Ashdod** . . . 293

13 **The Bar Kochba Discoveries** . . . 303

14 **Beer-sheba** . . . 315

15 **Tell Beit Mirsim** . . . 323

16 **Beth-shan** . . . 329

17 **Caesarea** . . . 337

18 **Dan** . . . 347

19 **Gezer** . . . 355

20 **Gibeon** . . . 363

21 **Hazor** . . . 371

22 **Herodion** . . . 379

23 **Jaffa** . . . 385

24 **Jericho** . . . 391

25 **Jerusalem** . . . 401

26 **Lachish** . . . 419

27 **Masada** . . . 429

28 **Megiddo** . . . 439

29 **The Dead Sea Scrolls and Qumran** . . . 447

30 **Samaria** . . . 465

31 **Shechem** . . . 473

32 **Transjordan** . . . 481
- Teleilat el-Ghassul 482
- Bab edh-Dhra' 483
- Petra 483
- Heshbon 487
- Dibon 488
- Amman 489
- Jerash 491
- Zarethan 494
- Succoth 495

Index . . . 499

Preface

The writing of a book is an emotional experience. In the preparation of *Biblical Archaeology in Focus* I have, in a very real sense, poured a part of my life into its production. So I send it forth to you with mixed emotions. It is a relief to have completed a consuming task, but a certain anxiety remains. I am concerned that the work will accomplish the purpose for which it was prepared, that it will help you to acquire an informed overview of the archaeological enterprise. I feel much like a parent who has prepared a surprise party for a child, then hovers in the background anxiously hoping that the results will please. In short I hope that the treatise is a treat for you. And, although I regret that some of the book is already outdated, this is beyond my control; archaeological work of significance that is currently going on cannot be included. We can only record the past.

The format of this book is based on experience gained while teaching courses on biblical archaeology to both graduate and undergraduate students at the University of Wisconsin-Madison during the past decade. It has been arranged so that one can read the introductory material in the first five chapters and then study information on those archeological sites that are most attractive to the individual. For classroom instruction or for individual research, I have suggested topics for further investigation and have included useful bibliographic information for each site or chapter. The basic material presented in the text is intended to stimulate interest in acquiring further knowledge, according to individual interests, and I wanted you to be able to pursue those interests easily. *Biblical Archaeology in Focus* should mark the beginning, rather than the end, of an interest in the subject.

I would like to acknowledge some of the people who have made this work possible. If it were not for the activities of the archaeologists, many of whom I have named but far more who remain unnamed, neither this book nor the hundreds of others that are listed in the bibliographies would have been written. I have been fortunate to be able to draw upon the experiences and wisdom of a broad range of men and women who have excavated and published. I have benefited considerably from my students and colleagues at the University of Wisconsin-Madison in the Department of Hebrew and Semitic Studies, and particularly from my mentor and friend, Dr. Menahem Mansoor. A substantial part of the sections on the story of writing and the Dead Sea Scrolls have benefited from his work. I am also grateful for the continuing support of the Wisconsin Society for Jewish Learning, true friends of the department.

The publisher, Baker Book House, has been both patient and helpful. I am grateful for the assistance of Betty De Vries, the technical editor, and the other members of Baker's staff. I must mention especially Cornelius Zylstra, editor (now retired), and his successor, Dan Van't Kerkhoff. Both have given me a great deal of encouragement. Particularly supportive to the enterprise from its inception was the late Dr. Charles E. Pfeiffer, to whose memory this work is dedicated. To the most deserving, my wife, Merrlyn, goes my gratitude for her patience while I labored at what must have seemed an unending task.

Keith N. Schoville
June 1978

Introduction

Many books on biblical and Palestinian archaeology have been published during the last decade and one wonders whether another book on the subject is justified. Professor Keith N. Schoville's *Biblical Archaeology in Focus* has many unique features that will not only justify its appearance but will also make real contributions to this important discipline. Our author has in mind the importance of a balanced presentation of archaeological research for college and seminary students in particular and for the layman in general. He presents his information in simple, yet scholarly, language that the reader will have no difficulty in understanding. This is particularly important in view of the manner in which discoveries are reported in the popular press. Despite their usefulness for stirring and maintaining public interest in archaeological research, as we have witnessed in the case of the Dead Sea Scrolls, the Tutankhamun treasures, and very recently the Ebla discoveries, these reports are frequently inaccurate and sensationalized and often plagued by overstatement. It is therefore of paramount importance to present accurate and balanced information. To do this is not an easy task, since the author must provide a basis for understanding how archaeology developed as well as its nature today.

A balanced presentation will lead the reader to appreciate the complex elements that interact in archaeological research—geography, politics, money, ancient texts and artifacts, and more. The archaeologist himself should be presented as an individual who pursues his obsession with the ancient past under conditions that most of us would find intolerable, carrying on research at considerable sacrifice of time, money, and energy. It is true that archaeology unearths documents and artifacts, yet, however revealing and interesting they may be, they are not enlightening in themselves alone. Conclusions must be drawn from them. For that purpose the archaeological data must be observed during the process of discovery, classified, correlated, and interpreted, with the use of all possible scientific aids and tools. Many a biblical scholar strives to reach objective conclusions based on these data, although even at best no human scholar can help avoiding his own subconscious, personal bias. On the other hand, we know of scholars who deal with the problems with deliberate bias in which their personal approaches and theories are involved, resulting in chaotic, unscientific, and at times even fantastic conclusions. One example is the case of the Dead Sea Scrolls. So the reader must be made aware that while archaeological discoveries must be interpreted, there are limits beyond which the data should not be pressed in terms of illuminating, illustrating, or confirming the Bible. Within those limits, however, both recent and older discoveries should be incorporated in a balanced interpretation that treats the Bible with the respect which it merits.

I have closely followed the development and writing of *Biblical Archaeology in Focus* and, in my opinion, it presents a balanced view of the subject since it is the product of an effective and experienced teacher and public speaker. A knowledgeable scholar who has traveled extensively in Bible lands over the past decade and who has participated in careful archaeological research at Tell Dan in Israel, Professor Schoville spent five years in the preparation of this book. The extensive bibliographies at the end of each chapter, the recommended readings, and the questions for discussion and further research greatly enhance the text which may well become a standard reference work in the field.

Menahem Mansoor

Part One

Understanding Biblical Archaeology

1

The Dimensions of Biblical Archaeology

"More has been learned about the Bible in the last century than in all the previous centuries of its existence," according to a publicity brochure for a recent series of Bible commentaries. Allowing for a certain amount of advertising hyperbole, the statement still rightly emphasizes the dramatic advances, which have been made in recent years, in our understanding of the life and times of the biblical peoples and of the languages and texts that comprise the Bible. These new insights and advances in knowledge have been the direct result of intensive archaeological research during the past century in the lands of the Bible, and they are a part of the current phenomenon of worldwide interest in archaeological research that involves both the amateur and the professional archaeologist. Around the world the search continues for new evidence of human culture in past ages. The purpose of the activity is the recovery of the story of mankind, and implicit in that quest is the assumption, shared by all humanistic disciplines, that the story of man's past contains empirical wisdom and knowledge that has significance for the problems of the present and of the future.

Biblical archaeology is concerned with the recovery of an extremely significant part of mankind's story. It is archaeological research in the lands of the Bible—the ancient Near East—focused on the biblical period. Such a statement about biblical archaeology is deceptively simple, for it veils a subject far more vast and complicated than the general public or the beginning student may suspect. Since biblical archaeology is but one facet of a far broader enterprise, an understanding of the place archaeology fills in man's search for knowledge is important both for an appreciation of the discipline's continuing contributions to the story of man in general and for the understanding of the Bible in particular. A later chapter will treat the nature of modern archaeology and the history of its development, while this chapter will focus primarily on the implications of the term *biblical.* It seems appropriate at the outset of this study, however, to provide a workable definition of archaeology. Definitions are often the curse of the student and the bane of the teacher, but without a general agreement of terminology, the learning process is necessarily hampered.

Defining Archaeology

A search of existing literature will produce numerous definitions of archaeology ranging from "the scientific study of material remains of past human life and activities," from a currently popular dictionary, to the candid assessment of the British scholar P. R. S. Moorey in *Archaeology, Artifacts and the Bible,* who stated frankly that "archaeology is the study of durable rubbish." Other definitions of the word include "the study of the material remains of man's past"; "the study and historical interpretation of *all* the material remains that vanished civilizations have left in the ground"; and "the study of the things men made and did, in order that their whole way of life may be understood." Not to be outdone, the author suggests that archaeology is the systematic recovery, analysis, and interpretation of the surviving evidence of human activity.

Reducing to a single sentence an enterprise that reaches around the world is appropriate only if the sentence is expanded so as to draw out some of the implications of meaning that are hidden therein. This will be done later in the chapter "Money, Men, Methods, and Materials."

Defining Biblical

A definition of the term *biblical* might seem unwarranted to the reader, but there are ramifications to the word that ought to be clearly understood, and it has been the experience of the author in the classroom that the information which follows has been helpful to the student.

The word *biblical* itself is derived from "Bible," which in turn is the Anglicized form of the Greek word *biblia* ("books"). The

Greek form is traceable to Byblos, the name of a Phoenician port city famed in antiquity for its commercial role in papyrus trade. (Byblos was derived from the earlier name *Gebal.*) Since papyrus was one of the important writing materials used by the ancients, the name of the city noted for the papyrus trade was easily adopted for the Greek word for book. The use of the word *Bible* to signify a collection of sacred books is traceable to approximately A.D. 400; the adjective *biblical* developed later from the noun.

Inherent in the name *Bible* is the concept that the Book is in reality a collection of books, although this truth is often overlooked. The Bible is a veritable library comprising the national literature of ancient Israel and the literature of its ethnic and spiritual descendants, the first-century Christians. Modern biblical scholars generally assume that this literature is the remnant of what was at one time a much larger corpus. The Bible itself gives some support to this view, for it mentions histories of both the kings of Israel and the kings of Judah (I Kings 14:19, 29, etc.), the book of the Wars of Yahweh (Num. 21:14), the book of Jashar (Josh. 10:13 and II Sam. 1:18), and a collection of laments (II Chron. 35:25). Other works of Jewish literature from a later period have survived outside the collection of texts in the Bible. These are known as the Apocrypha and the Pseudepigrapha, and they have endured the ravages of times largely because Christians were interested in them and used them. The recent discovery of the Dead Sea Scrolls suggests that during Israel's earlier period there were many additional documents, documents that no longer survive.

Viewed as a collection of literature, the Bible contains a diversity of literary materials composed in vivid narrative and poetry and marked by varieties of parallel expression. Historical narrative comprises the major part of the prose sections of the collection, particularly the historical books from Joshua to II Chronicals and also the material in Ezra-Nehemiah. A large part of the Torah, or Pentateuch, as the first five books of the Bible are frequently called, contains legal materials, particularly a part of Exodus and the bulk of Leviticus, Numbers, and Deuteronomy. The books of Ruth and Esther are short stories, and similar short stories have been incorporated in some of the larger books. Popular lore is expressed in a number of parables and fables (cf. Judg. 9 and II Kings 14:9), dreams and their interpretations (Gen. 28 and 41), and etiological explanations of the origins of names and places. Prophetic literature, consisting primarily of prophetic oracles but also including historical and biographical information, comprises an important and distinctive literary type. The prophetic works tend to be written in poetic style more often than in prose. Wisdom Literature, which is made up of collections of proverbs and maxims similar to collections of the sayings of sages discovered in Egypt and Mesopotamia, is the basis for the entire books of Proverbs and Ecclesiastes. Collections of psalms, prayers, hymns, songs and lamentations are among the most significant types of poetry found in the biblical literature.

The books of the Apocrypha were a part of the Septuagint, the first translation of the Hebrew Bible into another language. It was used initially by Greek-speaking Jews living in Alexandria in the third century B.C., and it subsequently included a number of works which are not in the Hebrew Old Testament. These books consisted in part of additions to certain books of the Bible; for example, Susanna, Bel and the Dragon, and the Song of the Three were additions to the Book of Daniel, and there were pious additions to the Book of Esther. Other apocryphal works were associated with the names of ancient personages; for example, Esdras is related to the canonical Book of Ezra. Two romantic novels, Tobit and Judith, are a part of the Apocrypha, along with historical books—I and II Maccabees—and wisdom literature—the Wisdom of Solomon and Ecclesiasticus (often called the Wisdom of Jesus son of Sirach). Baruch and additional short compositions—the Letter of Jeremiah, the Prayer of Manasseh, and II Esdras—are also included in the Septuagint. These works comprise an important bridge of literary materials between the Old and the New Testaments and between the Old Testament and the later rabbinic writings.

Additional apocryphal works that were not incorporated into the Septuagint have survived, including the *Book of Jubilees,* the *Book of Enoch,* and others. The *Genesis Apocryphon,* discovered among the texts from the Dead Sea caves, is of the same literary type. Another group of documents known as the Pseudepigrapha ("False Writings") was neither a part of the Old Testament nor of the Apocrypha. These works were attributed to ancient personages, for example, Adam, Enoch, and Moses; this explains the term by which they have come to be known. They were composed originally in Hebrew, Aramaic, and Greek between 200 B.C. and A.D. 200, and they are of great historical interest.

The New Testament, too, contains a variety of literary types. The first five books, the four Gospels and the Acts of the Apostles, are historical in character. The Gospels relate the sayings and activities of Jesus, but they can hardly be considered biographical since they deal almost exclusively with the last two or three years of his life. The Acts of the Apostles is actually a sequel to the third Gospel, Luke, and it outlines the expansion of the early church westward from Palestine to Rome within a period of approximately thirty years from the death of Jesus. Apart from the Book of Revelation, which is also called the Apocalypse of St. John and which is similar in literary type to a number of other works from the same era called apocalypses, the remaining New Testament books consist of letters. Thirteen of these epistles bear the name of Paul; four of these are addressed to individuals and nine are addressed to churches. The Letter to the Hebrews is anonymous, but it is traditionally ascribed to the apostle Paul. One letter was written by James, probably the brother of Jesus, one by Jude, two by Peter, and three that bear no name have traditionally been attributed to John, for they bear certain affinities to the Gospel of John.

The Bible is a collection of individual works, but down to the present they have been available as independent works or as smaller collections. Copies of the first five books of the Old Testament, for example, are available bound together. The Psalms, the Twelve (Minor) Prophets, and the Five Scrolls (*Megillot*) are often found as individual volumes. The Five Scrolls consist of the Song of Songs, Ruth, Lamentations, Ecclesiastes, and Esther, five books which play a part in the commemoration each year of the Jewish festivals of Passover, Shavuoth, Ninth of Ab, Succoth, and Purim, respectively. The Apocrypha, too, is available as a single volume, although its individual books are interspersed among the other books in Catholic editions of the Bible (cf. the chart of the canon on p. 25), and occasionally they may be found in Protestant Bibles collected and bound together between the Old and the New Testaments. The New Testament books are available, also, as individual books, such as the Gospels, Acts, and so on.

The process of collecting and binding these varied works together began in Christian circles during the second century A.D. when the codex, the book form, began to displace the scroll. This change had its beginnings in non-Christian circles, perhaps as early as the first century B.C. While early Christian writers no doubt employed the scroll as well as the codex, the great New Testament manuscripts such as Vaticanus and Sinaiticus, which date to the fourth century, are all of the codex form. Manuscripts of the Hebrew Bible, on the other hand, composed two distinct groups. Those intended for use in the synagogue and for public reading were required to be hand-copied on a scroll. This practice of using the more venerable form in public worship has continued to the present. Copies of the text in the codex form for use in private and at home, however, began to be used at an early date.

Both Christian and Jewish Bibles began to be reproduced in printed form with the development of the movable type printing press. The famous Gutenberg Bible was printed from 1450 to 1456 by Johann Gutenberg; it was a reproduction of the Latin Vulgate version which had been translated from the original Hebrew and Greek by Jerome in the fourth century. The first complete Hebrew Bible was published in 1488 in Italy by the Soncino Press, although portions of the Bible had been printed in Hebrew prior to that time. The most famous Hebrew printed Bible, however, was that of Jacob Ben Chayyim, printed by Daniel Bomberg at Venice in 1524–25.

The Bible reached the English-speaking world in the vernacular primarily through the heroic efforts of William Tyndale, but he was unable to complete his work of translation and publication, for he was put to death as a heretic as a result of his efforts to get the Scriptures into the hands of the masses in a language they could understand. The first complete printed English Bible was that of Miles Coverdale, published in 1535, in which he incorporated much of Tyndale's translation of the New Testament and of the Pentateuch. Thus, by the early sixteenth century a technological development had made it possible to easily reproduce copies of the Bible which were virtually free from error and relatively inexpensive. This was a very significant advance over the production of hand-copied manuscripts, as that process involved an ever-present factor of human error.

An amazing feature of the transmission of the text of the Bible, however, was the incredibly small number of errors that had crept into the text in the long period of hand-copying prior to the development of the printing press. This was particularly true of the Hebrew Bible. The first printed Hebrew Bible was based on the Masoretic Text, a name that is often abbreviated simply to MT. The MT was the culmination of the work of several generations of Jewish scholars at work in Tiberias, along the western shore of the Sea of Galilee, from approximately the seventh through the ninth centuries. The word *masora,* from which the term *masoretic* is derived, signifies "tradition," and the Masoretes were devoted to the idea of conserving the traditional pronunciation of the Hebrew text which they had received. The text itself, consisting of consonants, had been fixed, according to the tradition, during the days following the destruction of the second temple; that is, after the destruction of Jerusalem by the Romans in A.D. 70. The text was fixed by comparing several scrolls, and the process of copying the consonantal text was so carefully controlled by the Jewish scribal tradition of meticulous checking, including the counting of the number of verses and of the number of consonants in a book, that it had been transmitted virtually free of error to the Tiberian Masoretes. This exacting work had assured the preservation of the consonantal text, but the pronunciation of that text was open to change because the vowels were not adequately indicated. It was the Masoretes' determination to preserve the correct pronunciation of the text for liturgical purposes that motivated them to develop a system of marks which were placed above, within, and below the consonants and which were intended to assure the correct vowel sounds, the proper accentuation, and the correct syntactical division of the text. Along with this system of marks, the Masoretes compiled multitudinous notes about features of the text and entered these notes in the margins of the Bible. Thus they established a final, authoritative text, the *textus receptus* ("the received text"), culminating a movement that had begun centuries earlier to establish a normative text. A measure of the success of the scribes and the Masoretes in their work has been provided by the discovery of the Dead Sea Scrolls. This discovery has given us copies of parts of the Bible over a millennium older than previously known texts. These provide a basis for comparison with the MT.

The concept of the Bible as a one-volume collection of the surviving remnant of what was once a much larger mass of literature is an inadequate and unsatisfactory explanation of the development of the Bible, however, for the literature survived in part because the people who treasured and copied the texts considered them to be in a very real way sacred, a revelation from God. They were a source of knowledge about God, about his relationship to the community of believers, and about his will for them. The study of the Bible cannot be separated from concepts of revelation, inspiration, and canon. The scope of this book, however, does not allow for a full development of this aspect of the word *Bible,* nor of its derivative, *biblical,* but the reader ought to have an awareness of these concepts.

Contemporary views of inspiration and revelation, modified by cultural and theological factors, can generally be arranged along a continuum. At one extreme is the view of inspiration by dictation, according to which God, the initiator and active agent of revelation, transmitted his word and his will to selected writers who were so overwhelmed by the divine activity that their human personalities were completely sublimated to that of the divine. His words have in reality become their words. The other extreme denies the existence of God and, therefore, divine revelation. These extremes are balanced by more moderate views that allow room both for the revealing activity of God within and through human personalities and experiences and for the retention of the individuality of the writers. The personality of the inspired human writer, in these moderate views, is expressed in the written work along with the revelation of the divine. Whatever the current views of the reader, an investigation of the subject should prove very stimulating and rewarding. For the purpose of this study, however, it is important to note simply that behind the development of a canon of sacred scripture lies the concept of inspiration and revelation.

The Bible was canonized gradually. The oral traditions of hoary antiquity about Abraham and the other patriarchs and the activities of Moses, Joshua, and the judges of the early tribal period, the period of the amphictyony or tribal confederacy prior to the establishment of the monarchy, were all imbued with a certain sanctity, for these traditions testified that God had communicated with men in the past. In the period of the United Monarchy the revealing activity of God continued, particularly to King David and his son Solomon. In the same period prophetic activity was evident, and this impetus became more pronounced in the period of the Divided Kingdom. The prophets spoke out in the name of the Lord and, beginning with Amos, the revelations that came to them were recorded. These were probably kept by and transmitted through faithful disciples, but, in the opinion of many scholars, the first written work to receive widespread recognition as the "authoritative Word of God" seems to have been a scroll found in the temple about 621 B.C. It was this document which played a significant role in stimulating the reforms of Josiah, king of Judah (II Kings 22:8f.). The antiquity of the scroll has been a matter of scholarly controversy with opinions ranging from attributing it to Moses to assigning its composition to nameless scribes contemporary with the time of its discovery. The assumption is that the scroll comprised most of our present Book of Deuteronomy.

The destruction of the city of Jerusalem and the subsequent deportation of the bulk of the population, including particularly the religious and political leaders, produced a cultural shock that shattered the foundations of the nation. It is apparent that a substantial quantity of literature had existed in Judah prior to the deportation to Babylon. No doubt some of that literature was lost during the conflict, but the literature that survived the trauma of the Babylonian captivity did so because of its national and spiritual significance. Depending on one's point of view, the survival of the literature was either accidental or providential. During the years of exile, the captives were giving feverish attention to the causes of the national catastrophe and the implications of that disaster for their faith. By the time of Ezra, in the late fifth century B.C., the Torah could be read as the authoritative rule of life for the Jerusalem community (Ezra 7). A number of works written during the exile (for example, Ezekiel) and after the exile were considered as further revelations from God, but later tradition held the view that inspiration ceased in the time of Ezra. By the early second century, B.C. three categories of books were considered inspired to some degree—the Law, the Prophets, and the Writings. The prologue to the Greek translation of Ecclesiasticus, a book in the Apocrypha originally written about 180 B.C. but translated in approximately 132 B.C., mentions "the law, the prophets, and the other books of our fathers." It seems the movement which was to culminate in the establishment of a tripartite Jewish canon was well underway at that time. It is probable that no work that was to ultimately enter the Jewish canon postdates the Maccabean revolt which began about 168 B.C., and it can be argued that every work in the Writings, the last group to attain canonical status, was written well before that revolt. Here scholarly opinion varies. Readers who are interested in the problems of dating biblical works should consult the discussions in recent commentaries.

Samaritan priests with their cherished "Abisha Scroll" of the Pentateuch.

"Canon" is a Grecized form of the Semitic word *qaneh,* meaning "reed, measuring rod." The English words *cane* and *cannon* have the same origin. In Greek the word came to be used metaphorically to signify a rule or standard. The development of the canon as a list of standard inspired books proceeded from the Torah to the Prophets and finally to the Writings. The Torah, the Law, was considered as the only authoritative scriptures by two early Jewish sects, the Samaritans and the Sadducees. The Prophets were accepted as authoritative scripture by the other Jewish sects at the turn of the era, and the Writings, a conglomerate of works containing religious and nationalistic sentiments of varying dates, also were largely considered scripture. (This was particularly true of the Psalms.) The Dead Sea Scrolls have produced evidence of an open-ended view of inspiration in the Qumran sect, analogous to a similar view that was held within early Christianity. The author of the Temple Scroll wrote as one authoritatively inspired, and the canon of the church incorporates those Christian writings which were believed to have been inspired by the Holy Spirit.

The canon of the Hebrew Bible was essentially closed as the result of decisions reached by the rabbis at the Council of Jamnia about A.D. 90, although certain books among the Writings were disputed for a number of years afterwards. It would be incorrect, however, to assume that these men arbitrarily set the canon. Theirs was the culminating step in a process of selection that had begun far earlier and involved the consensus of the community of devout believers. A combination of factors was involved in the process, including the inherent literary beauty of the individual books, their nationalistic appeal or their compelling spiritual power, and their association with inspired men of old, particularly the prophets. Other factors were at work to bring the fixation of the canon at that particular time. The loss of the central sanctuary with the destruction of Jerusalem in the revolt against Rome had cut off from Judaism the unifying force of the cultic activities associated with worship at the temple. The survival of Judaism now depended upon its one remaining spiritual possession—the sacred books. It was important for all, then, to specify what books were to be included in the Bible. Furthermore, since the growing Christian movement, which posed a different kind of threat to Judaism, used a Greek translation of the Bible that included such questionable books as the Apocrypha, a different and distinctive canon was of value. So a combination of political, cultural, and religious factors led to the establishment of the canon. The church adopted the Jewish

The Bible Canons

TRIPARTITE HEBREW CANON

THE LAW (*Torah*)
Genesis (*Bereshith*)
Exodus (*Shemoth*)
Leviticus (*Wayyiqra*)
Numbers (*Bemidbar*)
Deuteronomy (*Devarim*)

THE PROPHETS (*Nevi'im*)
Joshua (*Yehoshua'*)
Judges (*Shophtim*)
Samuel (*Shemuel*—two books)
Kings (*Melachim*—two books)
Isaiah (*Yesha'yah*)
Jeremiah (*Yirmeyah*)
Ezekiel (*Yehezkel*)
Hosea (*Hoshea'*)
Joel (*Yoel*)
Amos (*'Amos*)
Obadiah (*'Ovadyah*)
Jonah (*Yonah*)
Micah (*Mikhah*)
Nahum (*Nahum*)
Habakkuk (*Habakkuk*)
Zephaniah (*Zephanyah*)
Haggai (*Haggay*)
Zechariah (*Zekharyah*)
Malachi (*Mal'akhi*)

THE WRITINGS (*Ketuvim*)
Psalms (*Tehillim*)
Proverbs (*Mishlei*)
Job (*'Iyyov*)
Song of Songs (*Shir Hash-shirim*)
Ruth (*Ruth*)
Lamentations (*'Eikhah*)
Ecclesiastes (*Koheleth*)
Esther (*'Ester*)
Daniel (*Daniel*)
Ezra (*'Ezra*)
Nehemiah (*Nehemyah*)
Chronicles (*Divrei Hayyamim*—two books)

ROMAN CATHOLIC CANON

OLD TESTAMENT
(with *Apocrypha*)
Genesis
Exodus
Leviticus
Numbers
Deuteronomy
Joshua
Judges
Ruth
I Samuel
II Samuel
I Kings
II Kings
I Chronicles
II Chronicles
Ezra
Nehemiah
Tobit
Judith
Esther
I Maccabees
II Maccabees
Job
Psalms
Proverbs
Ecclesiastes
Song of Songs
Wisdom
Sirach
Isaiah
Jeremiah
Lamentations
Baruch
Ezekiel
Daniel
Hosea
Joel
Amos
Obadiah
Jonah
Micah
Nahum
Habakkuk
Zephaniah
Haggai
Zechariah
Malachi

NEW TESTAMENT
St. Matthew
St. Mark
St. Luke
St. John
Acts
Romans
I Corinthians
II Corinthians
Galatians
Ephesians
Philippians
Colossians
I Thessalonians
II Thessalonians
I Timothy
II Timothy
Titus
Philemon
Hebrews
St. James
I St. Peter
II St. Peter
I St. John
II St. John
III St. John
St. Jude
Revelation

PROTESTANT CANON

OLD TESTAMENT
Genesis
Exodus
Leviticus
Numbers
Deuteronomy
Joshua
Judges
Ruth
I Samuel
II Samuel
I Kings
II Kings
I Chronicles
II Chronicles
Ezra
Nehemiah
Esther
Job
Psalms
Proverbs
Ecclesiastes
Song of Solomon
Isaiah
Jeremiah
Lamentations
Ezekiel
Daniel
Hosea
Joel
Amos
Obadiah
Jonah
Micah
Nahum
Habakkuk
Zephaniah
Haggai
Zechariah
Malachi

NEW TESTAMENT
Matthew
Mark
Luke
John
Acts
Romans
I Corinthians
II Corinthians
Galatians
Ephesians
Philippians
Colossians
I Thessalonians
II Thessalonians
I Timothy
II Timothy
Titus
Philemon
Hebrews
James
I Peter
II Peter
I John
II John
III John
Jude
Revelation

canon for its Old Testament, but while it retained the books of the Apocrypha they were relegated to a secondary place in the list of inspired works. For the Old Testament, then, the close of the first century saw the fixation of the consonantal text and the establishment of the canon in the form which has continued to the present time. The final steps in the process of canonization were completed with the definition of the authoritative books of the New Testament by the close of the second century A.D.

The Temporal Dimensions of Biblical Archaeology

Archaeology today is a quest for the story of mankind that extends across the face of the world. On every continent, men and women are pressing the search for evidence, probing every period of man's existence from a time as recent as the last century all the way back into the dim recesses of time. Where does the biblical period fit into this continuum of time? The late William F. Albright, a leading biblical scholar of this century, defined the temporal scope of biblical archaeology as extending "from about 9000 B.C.E. to about 700 C.E., a few generations after the Arab conquest. Of course this does not mean that remains of earlier or later date are without significance, only that in such ancient and modern times we soon reach periods of diminishing returns for biblical research."

The limits of biblical archaeology as outlined by Albright lie on both sides of the line that divides time into prehistory and history, with the development of writing marking the watershed between the two. A system of writing, man's greatest invention, was being developed almost simultaneously by approximately 3500 B.C. in the two great river valleys that produced the earliest civilizations in antiquity—the Nile in Egypt and the Tigris-Euphrates in Mesopotamia. The distinction between historical and prehistorical times, however, varies around the world and among differing peoples. Even in modern times there are a few small groups of people who have yet to enter into the historical period, for their cultures have not yet adopted a system of writing.

In the Bible, the Book of Genesis divides easily into two main sections: primeval history, covering the materials in the first eleven chapters, and the story of the patriarchs, covering chapters 12–50. In the opinion of E. A. Speiser, author of *The Anchor Bible Commentary on Genesis,* everything that precedes the story of the patriarchs is a broadly conceived preface, a prelude to the particular story with which the rest of the Pentateuch is concerned. The difference is underscored by the scope of the two subdivisions of Genesis. The patriarchal narratives take up four-fifths of the entire book, yet they cover only four generations of a single family. Primeval history, on the other hand, has the whole world as its stage, and its time span reaches back all the way to creation. In other words, primeval history seeks to give a universal setting for what is to be the early history of one particular people. Conceivably, then, one could include all periods of prehistory as well as the appropriate historical periods under the rubric *biblical archaeology*. In fact, British archaeologist Dame Kathleen Kenyon in her excellent book, *Archaeology in the Holy Land,* broadened the traditional scope of Palestinian archaeology to include periods earlier than the historical era.

Just as the author of Genesis prefaced his account of the lives of the patriarchs with an outline of anterior time, the student of biblical archaeology will find it helpful to acquaint himself with some of the changes that took place in the development of human culture during those archaeological and historical periods that preceded the patriarchal period. In this way the biblical peoples and events can be seen in a more realistic perspective than would otherwise have been possible. The following survey of human culture and history is based on the general conclusions of scholars who work closely with the archaeological data. They are to be taken provisionally, of course, for in archaeology as in other disciplines unanimity among scholars can hardly be expected. It is out of the heat of scholarly controversy that new understanding is forged; however, there is a broad general agreement on the sequence of cultural development and on the suggested dates. The main periods are delineated primarily on the basis of significant technological changes; these are then further subdivided into phases. Consult the accompanying charts for a schematic view of the periods.

The Paleolithic Period BEFORE 10,000 B.C.

Louis S. B. Leakey, the famous British anthropologist, believed that he had recovered some of the earliest remains of man from the Olduvai Gorge in northern Tanganyika. At that Central African site, in debris associated with the skeletal remains of *Zinjanthropus,* he discovered the earliest known forms of pebble-tools. These artifacts consisted of primitive stone tools shaped by other than natural forces. The only other place in the

Archaeological

PREHISTORIC AGES

DATE	ARCHAEOLOGICAL PERIOD
Prior to 10,000	Paleolithic (Pre-Cave Culture)
10,000–8000	Mesolithic (Cave Culture)
8000–5500	Neolithic Prepottery
5500–4000	Neolithic Pottery
4000–3100	Chalcolithic

HISTORIC AGES

	DATE (B.C.)	Archaeological Periods	PALESTINE (CANAAN)	EGYPT
CANAANITE (Bronze) Age	3100–2000	Early Bronze	Egyptian and Mesopotamian influences. Urban settlements mainly in Plains (Gezer) and Jordan Valley (Beth-yerah); some also in Hills (Ai).	United Kingdom. Old Kingdom (Dynasties III–VI). Pyramids and Temples. Beginning of Middle Kingdom (Dynasties XI–XII).
	2000–1550	Middle Bronze (Patriar-chal Age)	Strong political and cultural ties with Egypt. Small city-states of Western Semites (based on the feudal rule of patriarchal chiefs). Hyksos invasion. Age of the Patriarchs: Abraham, Isaac, Jacob and Joseph. Immigration from Mesopotamia (Ur-Haran) and descent into Egypt.	Middle Kingdom (Dynasty XII). Second Intermediate Period including Hyksos rule. Dynasties XV–XVI. Liberation of Egypt (Dynasties XVII–XVIII).
	1550–1200	Late Bronze	Egyptian conquest of Canaan. Their administration based on Canaanite petty kingdoms. Penetration of Israel and Syria by Semitic nomads. The Exodus. Beginning of Israelite invasion of Canaan. Collapse of Egyptian domination. Establishment of the kingdoms of Edom, Moab, the Amorites and Ammon. Moses and Joshua.	New Kingdom (Dynasties XVIII–XIX). Tell el-Amarna Period. Egyptian imperialism.
ISRAELITE (Iron) Age	1200–900	Iron Age I	Invasion of the Sea Peoples. Complete conquest of Canaan by the Israelites. Period of the Judges: Deborah, Gideon, and Samuel. The United Monarchy: Saul, David, Solomon. The struggle with the Philistines. Political expansion of Israel at its peak.	End of New Kingdom (Dynasties XIX–XX). Dynasty XXI.
	900–600	Iron Age II	Divided Monarchy: Kingdoms of Judah and Israel. Fall of Samaria (722). Egypt and Assyria-Babylon compete for rule of the country.	Libyan and Nubian rule (Dynasties XXII, XXIII, XXV), Assyrian conquest. Revival under kings of Saite (Dynasty XXVI)
PERSIAN (Iron) Age	600–330	Iron Age III	Nebuchadnezzar conquers Jerusalem; Babylonian Captivity. Beginning of the Diaspora. THE PERSIAN EMPIRE Cyrus takes Babylon (539). Organization of Persian administration under Darius I. Persian conflict with Greece. The Return from Captivity. Building of the Second Temple and the walls of Jerusalem. Ezra and Nehemiah. Rule of the High Priests and the "Great Assembly" at Jerusalem.	Cambyses conquers Egypt (525). Jewish military colony in Egypt (Elephantine).

and Cultural Charts

MESOPOTAMIA	SYRIA	ASIA MINOR	CULTURAL FEATURES	PRINCIPAL PALESTINIAN SITES
Early Kingdoms of Sumer (Kish, Ur-Haran, Akkad, Assyria and Elam).	Eblaite culture (Old Canaanite).		Organized kingdoms in Egypt and Mesopotamia. Early law codification in Mesopotamia. International trade. Epic literature (Gilgamesh, etc.) in Mesopotamia. Dramatic, religious, and didactic literature.	Beth-yerah, Beth-shan, Arad, Ai, Gezer, Dothan, Jericho, Megiddo, Tell el-Farah, Tell Beit Mirsim
Expansion of Western Semites. Temporary rise of Assyria. First Babylonian Dynasty: Hammurabi, the lawgiver. Conquest of Babylon by Hittites. Rise of Cassite Dynasty.	Expansion of Amorites (Western Semites). Cultural centers at Ugarit and Byblos.	Rise of the Hittites.	Beginnings of alphabetic writing in Canaan and Sinai. Establishment of urban centers with improved fortifications; metal arms and implements; Hyksos introduce horse and war chariot into Canaan and Egypt.	Megiddo, Nahariya, Gezer, Hazor, Dan, Jericho, Shechem, Tell el-Farah, Tell Beit Mirsim, Tell el-Ajjul
Cassite Period. Rise and fall of Middle Assyrian Empire.	Rise and decline of Kingdom of Mitanni.	Rise and fall of New Hittite Empire.	Strong Egyptian influence. Cuneiform alphabetic script at Ugarit (Mythological literature).	Beth-shan, Beth-shemesh, Tell Beit Mirsim
	Most flourishing periods in the history of Ugarit and Byblos.		Intensive trade with Cyprus and general influence of the Aegean culture. Hellenic (Doric) invasion in Greece. Moses: the Ten Commandments—Birth of the Hebrew nation.	Tell Abu Hawam, Tell el-Farah, Lachish, Megiddo, Hazor, Gezer, Jericho
Rise of Assyria under Tiglath-pileser I. Arameans and Chaldeans cross the Euphrates and invade Mesopotamia.	Small Hittite kingdoms in the North. Rise of the Arameans. Phoenician coastal cities flourish: Byblos, Sidon, Tyre.	Destruction of Hittite Empire. Phrygians in Northwestern Asia Minor.	Organization of Israelite State. Economic prosperity; mining; foreign trade. Diffusion of alphabetic writing.	Beth-shan, Beth-shemesh, Megiddo, Jerusalem, Tell Abu Hawam, Tell en-Nasbeh, Tell Beit Mirsim, Tel Qasile, Gezer, Gerar, Gibeah, Dan
Peak of Assyrian power; fall of Assyrian Empire; fall of Nineveh (612).	The Aramean and Hittite kingdoms subdued by Assyria.	Eastern Asia Minor within orbit of Assyrian conquests. Western Asia Minor becomes part of Greek world.	Development of arts of warfare. Phoenician and Aramean influences; Phoenician colonies in Western Mediterranean. Aramaic becomes official language throughout Assyrian Empire. Height of Judean and Israelite culture. The Prophets.	Jerusalem, Samaria, Beth-shemesh, Gezer, Lachish, Megiddo, Dan, Hazor, Gerar, Tell Beit Mirsim, Tell Qasile, Tell Jemmeh, Beer-sheba, Arad
			The last of the pre-exilic prophets: Jeremiah. Influences from East (Persia) and West (Greece). Post-exilic prophets.	Ashkelon, Gezer, Lachish, Jerusalem, Tell Deir 'Alla, Tell el-Hesi, Tell Jemmeh

world where examples of similar pebble-tool artifacts have been discovered is in the Holy Land at Ubaidiyah, a site in the Jordan Valley south of the Sea of Galilee. Before his death, Leakey had been at work on the Ubaidiyah site. Here in the same general occupational layer that contained the pebble-tools, the oldest skull fragments of *Pithecanthropus* yet discovered in the Near East were recovered. For the period of prehistory, then, Palestine, the classic country of biblical archaeology, is also becoming a major center for anthropological research.

Such meager evidence as exists for these ancient peoples has been gleaned mainly from open-air sites and from the terraces of ancient river beds. During this age man did not yet live in caves, so the label *Pre-Cave Culture* seems appropriate.

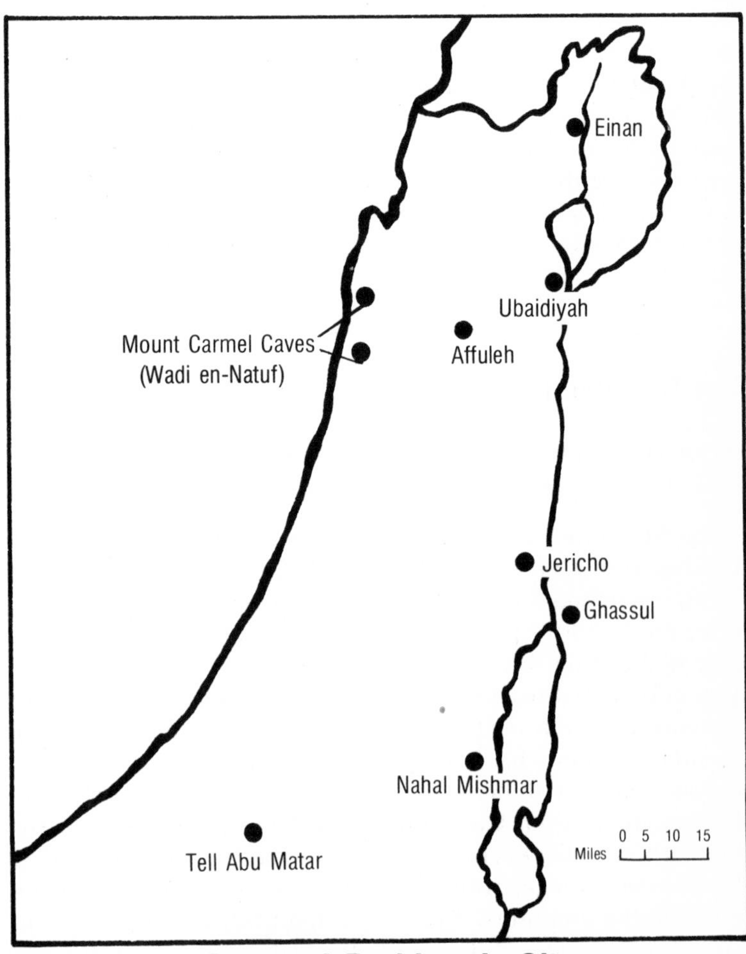

Selected Prehistoric Sites

The Mesolithic Period CIRCA 10,000–18,000 B.C.

Pre-Cave culture was succeeded by a cave culture in Palestine. As a result of excavations in caves of the Mount Carmel range, this cave culture is now known in some detail. The caverns excavated contained a number of skeletons of early man along with stone handaxes and fishhooks, and a number of rudimentary sickles. Changes in climate may have been responsible for the shift from life in the open to the shelter of caves. The later phases of the Carmel cave culture, during the Upper Mesolithic period, beginning about 9000 B.C., have produced evidence that a more sophisticated economy was developing. This Natufian culture, named after the caves of the Wadi en-Natuf in which the evidence was found, was based on hunting and food-gathering, but the development and use of the mortar and pestle along with the flint-bladed sickle suggest the possibility that man had begun to produce his own food through sowing and reaping. There is also some evidence that animal domestication began during this period. Here, too, the earliest evidence of art in the Palestinian area was discovered in the form of shell pendants, necklaces, and bones carved to represent animals. These decorative elements appear to have had no purpose other than the satisfaction of aesthetic tastes.

The Neolithic Period CIRCA 8000–4000 B.C.

(NEOLITHIC PREPOTTERY: 8000–5500 B.C.)
(NEOLITHIC POTTERY: 5500–4000 B.C.)

The Mesolithic, or Middle Stone Age, with its Natufian culture began to give way to the Neolithic, or New Stone Age, in the eighth millennium B.C. Revolutionary developments characterize the Neolithic period; in fact the foundations of civilization were laid during this age. These changes were wrought over a span of time that reached down to the fifth millennium B.C. The evidence for the transition from the Mesolithic to the Neolithic period in Palestine has been produced primarily by the spade of Kathleen Kenyon in her excavations at Jericho. She has shown a definite connection, based on the evidence of similar flint and bone artifacts, between the culture of the Natufian hunters of the Carmel caves (as well as similar sites scattered across Palestine) and the prepottery Neolithic community at Jericho. On the basis of the carbon-14 dating of charcoal remains from the earliest structure at Jericho, it is evident that by 9000 B.C. man, the

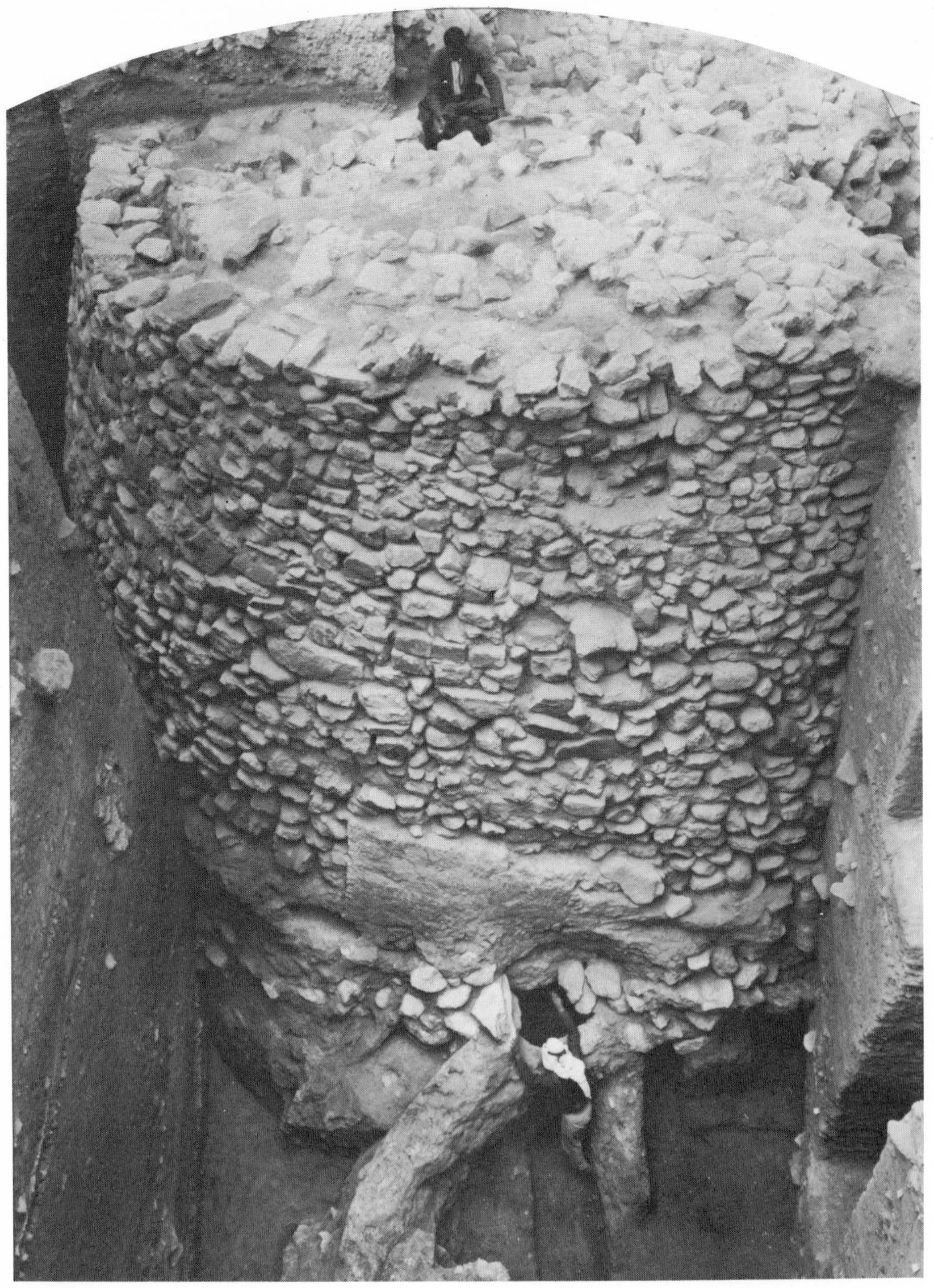

The great tower of the earliest Neolithic period, ca. 8000 B.C. The man who is on the top is looking down the staircase. The entrance into the interior of the tower is marked by the man at the bottom entrance of the staircase. The interior staircase is very steep.

wandering hunter, was undergoing a transition to settled communities. Once the foundations of civilization were laid by the establishment of village life and an economy based upon agriculture, they served to further stimulate the changes in man's life and material culture which were to follow. Miss Kenyon has noted:

> Once man is settled in one spot, the rest follows. He has leisure to develop skills, and a sedentary life means that he can burden his household with their products, with the results of his handicrafts and his arts. A community life grows up, which is the basis of civilization. It is no longer a case of one family group against nature, including other family groups; man gains the security of living in an increasingly large group, and in the give and take of group life he sacrifices some of his primitive freedoms in return for his security; the give and take becomes systemized into the regulation of customs and ultimately laws, and a communal organization emerges.

It was during the Neolithic era, then, at Jericho and at other sites in Palestine, in Anatolia, and in Mesopotamia, that man was beginning to raise grain (emmer wheat, barley, flax), domesticate animals (sheep, goat, cow, pig, and ass), spin and weave animal and vegetable fibers into cloth, and produce pottery. Archaeologists have found it convenient to divide the period into two phases: Prepottery Neolithic and Pottery Neolithic.

The earliest forms of pottery appear at Jericho by about 5500 B.C. In Kenyon's view, the archaeological evidence makes it likely that this technological advance was introduced by newcomers to the area, immigrants from an area not yet identified but probably to the north in Syria. But whether the technique was developed locally or imported, the vessels simply replaced earlier utensils made of stone, reeds, and leather. The pottery was of a coarse nature, made of rather gritty clay in which considerable quantities of straw had been mixed, and its soft and crumbly nature indicated that it had been fired at a low temperature. This suggested to the excavator that the craft of pot-making had not progressed very far. It had, however, ushered in a technological feature that was destined to serve as the archaeologist's most valuable dating tool.

Archaeologists have yet to work out satisfactorily the sequence of culture for the Pottery Neolithic period. This is due to the lack of consecutive sequences of both architecture and artifacts. The main outlines for the period are drawn from a tentative sequence of materials found at sites scattered from Galilee in the north to the Negev in the south. The evidence suggests that at this time Israel and Jordan were both thickly occupied with unfortified villages peopled by diverse groups. In time copper was introduced into this culture, and the Chalcolithic period began, the period of copper-stone culture.

The Chalcolithic Period CIRCA 4000–3100 B.C.

Evidence from Tell Halaf in northern Mesopotamia indicates that copper began to be used in that area by as early as the second half of the fifth millennium; its appearance in Palestine, however, is not attested before about 3500. At Ghassul, a site just a few miles northeast of the Dead Sea, and at Tell Abu Matar in the Negev south of Beer-sheba, copper implements have been found. At the Beer-sheba site a metal-working complex was uncovered in a context that has been dated by the carbon-14 method to the thirty-sixth to thirty-third centuries.

Evidence from a number of other Chalcolithic sites supports that obtained from Ghassul and Beer-sheba to indicate that life in that era involved a nomadic village mode of existence. Carved ivory figures representing humans indicate that the people had short skulls and long noses, features which suggest ethnic kinship with the inhabitants of Anatolia, the area in which copper technology had begun at a much earlier date. There is evidence, too, of trade. The artistic ability of the inhabitants is indicated by the ivory carvings, the fine incised stoneware, and the remnants of plastered walls with intricate painted geometric designs discovered at Ghassul. A number of interesting clay ossuaries shaped like little houses are connected with the Chalcolithic culture. The bones of the dead were given a secondary burial in these containers; they are of interest now because they are suggestive of the religious views of the culture and because they provide a graphic example of the probable appearance of the houses of the living.

The copper artifacts associated with the Chalcolithic culture were not used for common everyday activities, it appears, for they were produced in the form of mace-heads, axe-heads, and scepters, which were most likely used for ceremonial purposes. During the period when archaeologists were searching for additional scrolls in the caves along the Dead Sea, a totally unexpected cache of 429 copper articles from the Chalcolithic period came to light in a cave in the Nahal Mishmar. In the upper level of the cave were found materials from the period of the second temple and from the Bar Kochba era. In the lower strata of the same cave mace-heads, scepters, crowns, axes, and

Typical Chalcolithic pottery from Ghassul.

Geometric designs created in fresco discovered at Ghassul.

adzes were excavated. It is possible that the objects were once used in a sanctuary of the Chalcolithic period which was discovered a few miles away near En Gedi.

The Chalcolithic culture seems to have disappeared from Palestine during the thirty-second century B.C., leaving a major break in the occupational history of the area. Despite the relatively limited period of the culture in Palestine, from about 3500 to 3200, most scholars refer to the fourth millennium as the Chalcolithic period.

The Early Bronze Age CIRCA 3100–2000 B.C.

The next major archaeological epoch has been designated the Bronze Age, even though true bronze did not appear in Palestine until the second millennium. It is also called the Canaanite Age, for the land of Palestine began to be populated by a new people who had a characteristic Mediterranean long skull (dolichocephalic) in contrast to the earlier brachycephalic types. As the chart indicates, the Bronze Age is arranged in a sequence from Early Bronze to Middle Bronze and through Late Bronze, covering a period of two millennia.

The Bronze Age Sequence in Palestine

BRONZE AGE (Canaanite)		3100–1200 B.C.
Early Bronze (EB)	3100–2000	
EB I 3100–2800		
EB II 2800–2600		
EB III 2600–2300		
EB IV 2300–2000		
Middle Bronze (MB)	2000–1550	
MB I 2000–1900		
MB II 1900–1550		
Late Bronze (LB)	1550–1200	
LB I 1550–1400		
LB II 1400–1200		

The Canaanites were a part of the peoples designated Amurru by the Sumerians and Akkadians of Mesopotamia. These were the Amorites of the Bible. The name designated those people who lived in the territory west of the Euphrates River (including Syria and Palestine) and spoke dialects of the northwest branch of the Semitic family of languages. The incursion of Canaanites into the area of Palestine had begun by about 3200 B.C. On the basis of differing cranial types, contrasting burial practices, and the appearance of new pottery forms without antecedents, it is evident that the new culture introduced into the area in the Early Bronze Age had no connection with the culture of the preceding era. The Early Bronze Age witnessed a sudden burgeoning of the population concurrent with the establishment of numerous villages. Many of these were destined in the course of time to become major Palestinian tells. The several phases of the Early Bronze period are based on the changing pottery inventory and variations in burial practices, but the essential continuity of the culture suggests that there were successive movements into the area of peoples who differed very little from one another and were quickly absorbed into the existing population.

A remarkable feature of the era was the rapid transition from life in unwalled villages to the fortification of these settlements. Subsequently further expansion led to the development of fortified towns on a number of the sites. The trends toward urbanization and toward massive fortifications should be seen against the backdrop of the development of the great centers of civilization in the same period—Egypt to the west and Mesopotamia to the east. The tendency toward town-planning, architectural design, and sophisticated building seems to have been imported from the eastern center of civilization. The early defenses were constructed of mud-brick, but these were soon followed by stone embankments thrown up against them. Within the walls residential buildings were constructed along with at least one temple and other public buildings. The defensive measures were intended as security against a foe. Egypt was the most

A section of the Early Bronze defensive wall at Arad.

likely villain, for the Egyptians of the early dynasties exhibited a universal hostility toward Palestine. It is unclear whether the political structure found to be best suited to build and maintain these walled urban centers was the city-state form that predominated in Mesopotamia and in the Middle and Late Bronze eras, or a more-or-less unified kingdom. The security of the walled towns was not sufficient, however; for at the close of the Early Bronze III period in the twenty-fourth century, not one city was extant in the country.

The Middle Bronze Age CIRCA 2000–1550 B.C.

The destruction of the urban centers of the Early Bronze Age was not the work of the Egyptians. The majority of scholars place the responsibility on another of the recurring waves of Amorites from the semiarid fringes of the northern Syrian desert. Successive waves of these nomadic Semites apparently washed across the land and spilled into the delta region of Egypt, ushering in the first intermediate period of Egyptian chronology (ca. 2200–2000 B.C.). In Palestine the period designated Early Bronze IV reflects a reversion on the part of the population to a nomadic or seminomadic mode of existence, apart from the former urban centers that now lay in ruins. The subsequent period, Middle Bronze I, represents a gradual sedentarization of the newcomers.

In Genesis the Amorites are located in the hill country. A millennium later, at the time of the Israelite conquest, the population base, now known as Canaanite, has shifted to the plains and valleys (Num. 13:29; Josh. 5:1; 10:6). There they occupy major walled cities. The reversion to town life began in the Middle Bronze II A period, apparently under the combined stimuli of elements within the Canaanite Amorite population buttressed by still later waves of Amorites. Contacts with Phoenician coastal cities also contributed to the urge to urbanize. In the opinion of G. Ernest Wright, the settlements of Middle Bronze I were "very fragile towns that were just beginning to be established before they were quickly snuffed out by the second major Amorite wave beginning in MB II A." William G. Dever, on the other hand, suggests that the abrupt termination of Middle Bronze I "may be explained as easily by an abandonment of most sites as it is by the hypothetical 'destruction' posited by some scholars." At any rate, Lapp, Dever, and Kenyon agree that there was a disjunction with virtually no continuity between the two periods.

Patriarchal history begins with the Middle Bronze II period. This is not to imply that contemporary written records of the lives and the activities of the patriarchs exist outside the Bible, but simply that the archaeological evidence from the Central Mesopotamian Valley, from Palestine, and from Egypt fits remarkably well with the biblical traditions when they are laid alongside one another. The arrival of Abraham in Canaan can be posited in the period from approximately 2000 to 1800 B.C., placing him in the land near the close of the Middle Bronze I era or during the first phase of the Middle Bronze II period (MB II A), circa 1850–1750 B.C.

Cyclopean wall of ancient Shechem. Mount Gerizim, the holy mountain of Samaritan tradition, is in the background.

The Bible pictures Abraham journeying from Haran in Mesopotamia to the land of promise, arriving first at Shechem in the central highlands. From there he travels by stages through the area southward, finally concentrating his residency and activities in the hill country to the south and particularly in the Negev. Culturally he does not seem to be out of place; to the contrary, he fits into the society quite easily. At the same time, he does maintain contact with the land of his origin, and his family contracts matrimonial ties with their relatives who continue to reside in Mesopotamia. These traditions have received illumination from the archaeologist's spade during the twentieth century.

The personal names of the patriarchs and the names of the places with which they are associated fit well in the Middle Bronze I–II period. The Execration Texts discovered in Egypt contain long lists of place names and the names of leaders in the area of Canaan in the twentieth and nineteenth centuries. These names are predominantly good Northwest Semitic (Amorite) names of the same type that are attested in the Mari documents from Mesopotamia which date to the eighteenth century. The texts from Mari on the Euphrates and from Nuzi, a site east of Mari in the area near Paddan-Aram, also bear witness to the cultural traditions associated with the patriarchs.

Archaeology has also revealed something of the extent of commercial activities that existed in much of the Bronze Age. Goods flowed along trade routes between major centers in Anatolia, Mesopotamia, Egypt, and the islands of the eastern Mediterranean Sea. Palestine provided an important land bridge through which passed commercial routes that connected the Nile Valley and the Asian centers of commerce, and along these routes donkey caravans plied their trade throughout the Bronze Age. According to Mesopotamian documents, the Amorites of Syria and Central Mesopotamia were actively engaged in caravaneering. The wealth of Abraham in silver and gold as well as cattle, his considerable resources in available manpower (cf. Gen. 14), his origins among the Amorites of Mesopotamia, and his continuing contacts with caravan centers in that region all support the view that Abraham may have been a successful caravaneer. William F. Albright has argued for this idea, and he has pointed to further substantiating data produced by Nelson Glueck. Glueck mapped by surface survey the patterns of settlement in the Negev region. His work has been supplemented by both Yohanan Aharoni and Beno Rothenberg so that the caravan routes that crossed this area and through north-central Sinai are now known. Approximately a distance of one day's journey by donkey separated the settlements, and their occupation ended near the close of Middle Bronze I. Since an occupational gap of nearly a millennium left the area empty until near the end of the Late Bronze Age, the feeding stations and support systems necessary for donkey caravaneering were not available in a later period. At the latest, Abraham must have been in the land by 1800 B.C., the Middle Bronze II A period.

Middle Bronze II A marked the resurgence in Palestine of sedentary life and the beginning of the development of urban centers following the long interlude of unsettled, seminomadic conditions that had characterized the preceding era. Excavations reveal that villages began to appear once more, and a number of the major tells, including Shechem, Hazor, Megiddo, Lachish, Tell Beit Mirsim, and Tirzah (Tell el-Farah), were reestablished as walled cities. The population density was on the increase, with the native elements receiving reinforcements from the north and the east. The newcomers brought with them new pottery forms produced with advanced techniques. In contrast to earlier primarily hand-formed ceramics, the new wares were produced almost wholly on the potter's wheel. The carinated bowl of this period, with its sharply angular features, was characteristic of the attempt to produce a less expensive pottery substitute for a more costly metal prototype. The addition of either a red or white slip followed by high burnishing added to the attractiveness of the ware. Bronze weapons were also introduced into the Palestinian area at this time in the form of spears, daggers, and bronze axe-heads.

The discovery of Egyptian statues and inscribed stones from the twelfth dynasty of the Middle Kingdom period at sites along the major international routes, including Megiddo and Gezer, indicates the interest and influence of Egypt in the area during the Middle Bronze II A period. The discovery of Egyptian scarabs, furniture, and alabaster jars of this period at Jericho indicates the pervasive Egyptian influence well into the interior of Palestine. At the same time, the political turmoil in Mesopotamia during the Isin-Larsa era, subsequent to the fall of Ur (ca. 2000 B.C.), helps to explain the migration into the area of new people who brought with them advanced knowledge and a high degree of technological skill. What has been said above is by no means the entire cultural picture of Middle Bronze II A, but it is sufficient to indicate the beginnings of the basic Canaanite culture in Palestine which was destined to persist with only minor changes throughout the remainder of the Bronze Age. It was, in fact, a part of a fairly homogeneous culture that extended from the southern fringe of Anatolia southward along the Mediterranean littoral and into the Sinai Peninsula.

The developments of the Middle Bronze culture that had begun in Middle Bronze II A were expanded dramatically during the Middle Bronze II B phase (ca. 1750–1650). Egypt had entered a period of decline, labeled the second intermediate period, which was marked by a loss of influence in Asia and the division of political power at home. This decline was caused in part by the waves of West Semites who flooded Syria, Palestine, and the eastern delta region. At Tanis, a major political center that controlled the eastern delta, a dynasty of rulers came to power who were referred to by the Egyptians as the Hyksos, "rulers of foreign lands." In Palestine, archaeological evidence indicates that the Hyksos had established a major center at Hazor, just north of the Sea of Galilee. Here and at numerous other sites in Palestine a new defense structure began to appear in the form of mighty ramparts of earth, called *terre pisée,* which were thrown up around the cities. These were then topped with brick walls. They may have been developed as a defense against the battering ram and the siege tower. Other cultural features, including the appearance of new pottery types along with continuing manufacture of the older forms, suggest that the appearance of the Hyksos did not constitute a conquest of Canaan; rather, the newcomers appear to have infiltrated the area and to have amalgamated easily with the native population. To the Egyptians the Hyksos were foreign Asiatics; to the populace of Canaan they seem to have been simply an integral part of the population.

It is probable that the story of Joseph's rise to power in Egypt should be connected with the Hyksos period. As a Semite among Semites, this could easily have occurred, and it appears that the Hyksos maintained a basis of support in Canaan as well as in the delta. Egyptian products flowed into the area from the economic exploitation of the riches of Egypt. The people of Palestine prospered and reached a density of population and economic and artistic heights that were not attained again in the area for more than a millennium.

Beyond Canaan itself during this period, the Hittites were establishing themselves as the major power in Anatolia, while to the southeast the Hurrian kingdom of Mitanni was preparing to appear on the scene. The important city of Ugarit, situated at the northern extremities of the Canaanite area, already had trade connections with these peoples and with the inhabitants of the lower Mesopotamian Valley. Another feature of the times was the spread of the Akkadian language as the vehicle of literary and diplomatic communication, but already in the area of Canaan the first steps toward the development of an alphabetic script and system of writing were being taken. In time the new system would displace the earlier, more cumbersome syllabic form; it would become the vehicle for transmitting the religious concepts of both Canaanites and Israelites.

Constructed approximately 1650 B.C., this Middle Bronze II glacis was discovered at Gezer.

The final phase of the Middle Bronze Age may be connected with the appearance of a number of Indo-Aryan and Hurrian names alongside Semitic and Egyptian names among the later Hyksos pharaohs. Middle Bronze II C saw the development of further modifications in the fortifying of a number of sites in Canaan. At Gezer a tremendous wall in the "Cyclopean" style was erected, similar to one of the same period excavated at Shechem. Slightly later this was further reinforced with a glacis, a sloped surface of fill covered with crushed chalk *(terre pisée)* at a 45° angle, laid up against the vertical wall. Similar installations appear at sites throughout the area, for example, at Dan, Hazor, Megiddo, and Jericho. On a number of sites fortified temples were also built about this time. It has been suggested that a conquering class of chariot warriors became the dominant force in this period, establishing themselves as the rulers of the major cities, and that some of the defensive features were due to their innovations.

The Late Bronze Age CIRCA 1550–1200 B.C.

Middle Bronze II C gave way to the first phase of the Late Bronze Age when Amosis, the first king of the eighteenth dynasty of Egypt, rose up and expelled the Hyksos from his land (ca. 1550 B.C.), ushering in the era of the New Kingdom in Egyptian history. The Egyptians were not content, however, merely to reconquer their land. They swept across Palestine and through Syria in a series of almost annual campaigns until they reached the west bank of the Euphrates by 1500 B.C. in the reign of Thutmosis I. So ferocious was the Egyptian assault on the Hyksos fortress cities that every major site in Palestine suffered destruction at that time, and a number of these remained unoccupied for a considerable period thereafter.

The Egyptian domination of the Canaanite area that began with the expulsion of the Hyksos was destined to continue throughout the Late Bronze Age, but in the earliest phase, Late Bronze I (ca. 1550–1400), the Egyptian policy was aimed at the reconquest and subjugation of the Syro-Palestinian city-states. Subsequently, the rather closely-knit political structure that has been posited for the Hyksos period was replaced by a less dangerous (from the Egyptian point of view) arrangement, whereby each petty king was subject to the pharaoh. Egypt's main interests in the area were essentially twofold: to reap the economic benefits available in the form of timber, minerals, agricultural products and tribute, and to establish a buffer against the threats of the growing Hittite power in Anatolia and the strong kingdom of Mitanni on the Middle Euphrates. Accordingly, the pharaohs pursued a policy of benign neglect, permitting minor alliances between the city-states. Egypt even allowed internecine conflicts in this period as long as the flow of tribute remained uninterrupted and no threat of international proportions developed.

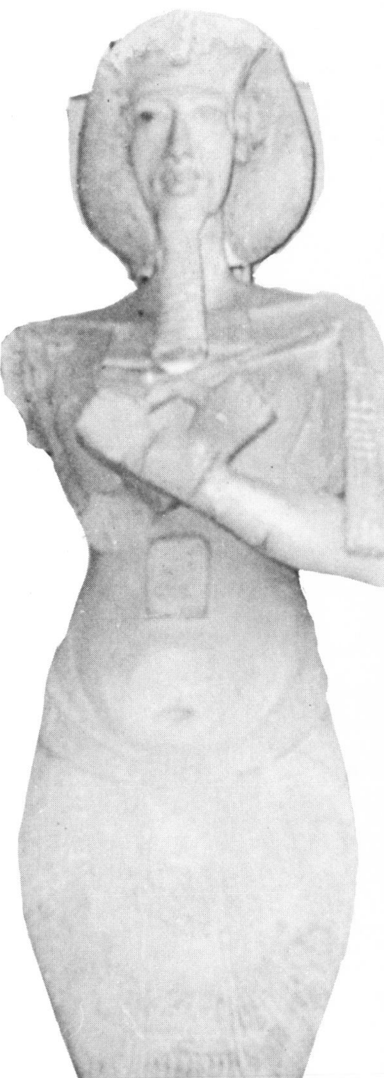

Statue of Akhenaten, pharaoh of the Amarna period.

The constant drain on the resources of the area due to Egyptian exploitation and the petty rivalries among the Canaanite rulers combined to bring about a steady decline in the quality of the material culture throughout the Late Bronze Age. Early in Late Bronze I, however, a rather unique red-and-black painted pottery called bichrome ware was in use. It has been found in sites on Cyprus and along the Mediterranean littoral from Ras Shamra in the north to Tell Ajjul in the southern coastal plain. Imported wares from Cyprus and the Mycenaean area which appear in excavations indicate the extent of international trade that developed in the Late Bronze Age; nevertheless, when the artifacts of the period are compared with equivalent materials from the preceding Middle Bronze II culture, the decline in the quality of the Late Bronze culture is apparent.

Late Bronze II A (ca. 1400–1300) spanned the Amarna Age of Egypt. The conquering pharaohs of the eighteenth dynasty had amassed wealth and power, extending Egyptian control over territories from Nubia in Africa to the banks of the Euphrates in Asia, but during the subsequent Amarna Age the pharoahs, particularly Amenhotep III (ca. 1402–1363) and his son and successor, Amenhotep IV (Akhenaten, ca. 1363–1347), turned from the paths of conquest to the more peaceful and pleasurable pursuits of employing the wealth of Egypt to build palaces and temples, decorating them with revolutionary art forms. As a result of this benign neglect, during the Amarna period Egyptian dominance of the Canaanite area declined, but the correspondence between the Egyptian sovereign and his underlings, the petty kings of Canaanite city-states, which was recovered from Tell el-Amarna in Egypt has provided important evidence of the political conditions in Canaan during this period.

The archaeological evidence for the date of the exodus points to the final phase of the Late Bronze Age, Late Bronze II B (ca. (1300–1200). The Amarna era had ended with the reign of Tutankhamun (ca. 1346–1337), and the nineteenth dynasty was established by Ramses I (ca. 1302). That line of pharoahs continued under his successors to approximately 1200 B.C. The early pharaohs of the dynasty were confronted by the threat of the Hittite empire in Syria, but the vigorous military action of Ramses II early in his lengthy reign led to a settlement between the two powers. A parity treaty was signed (ca. 1286 B.C.); copies of the treaty have remarkably survived in both Egypt and Anatolia.

Ramses II was somewhat of a megalomaniac; the magnificent, world-renowned temple at Abu-Simbel was only one of his many building projects, for ruins of statues depicting him in heroic proportions still dot the landscape from Upper Egypt to the delta. The exodus of the Israelites under the leadership of Moses most likely occurred early in his reign. The archaeological evidence for this view includes the date of the establishment of the store-cities mentioned in Exodus, the reappearance of a sedentary population in Transjordan, the destruction layers datable to the general period which have been discovered in a number of Palestinian tells, and the mention of Israel in the Merneptah Stele.

The reign of Ramses II extended from about 1290 to 1223; he was succeeded upon his death by his son Merneptah. The Israelites were employed by the Egyptians in the building of the royal store-cities—Pithom and Ramses according to the biblical account—and it was from this area that they set forth on the journey into the wilderness. The biblical city Ramses was apparently founded by Seti I, father of Ramses II, but mainly built and named by the latter. It was located at either Tanis or Qantir in the northeastern region of the delta. The exodus undoubtedly took place while these cities were being erected.

The late Nelson Glueck's surface survey of ancient sites in Transjordan, carried out in the years from 1932 to 1947, determined that the reestablishment of sedentary occupation in that area began about 1300 B.C. After a lengthy period of minimal human habitation which began in the Middle Bronze Age, the kingdoms of Edom and Moab had progressed to the extent that they were able to impede the advance of the Israelites through their territories prior to the Israelite invasion of Canaan. The first references to these Transjordanian kingdoms in Egyptian sources come from the nineteenth dynasty. Since Edom and Moab were not firmly established until about 1300, it seems unlikely that they could have hindered the Israelites prior to that time.

There is evidence that a number of Palestinian sites, for example, Beth-el, Debir (Tell Beit Mirsim), Lachish (Tell ed-Duweir), and Hazor, were destroyed in the last half of the thirteenth century. This may be connected with the Israelite conquest of Canaan. The excavator of Hazor, Israeli archaeologist Yigael Yadin, has stated that "the greatest contribution of the excavations to Old Testament study is related to the vexed problem of 'Joshua-Judges.' The excavations have shown in a decisive manner that the great Canaanite city [Hazor] was destroyed by fire, and was never rebuilt, in the second part of the thirteenth century B.C. . . . This destruction must be attributed to the one described so minutely in the book of Joshua." Unfortunately, the evidence from all the excavated sites is not so conclusive. At both Jericho and Ai archaeological research has failed to produce any substantial evidence that the sites were occupied and fortified at the time of the thirteenth-century Israelite conquest, and it is possible that destruction layers on the numerous sites that might be attributable to Joshua's forces may have been caused by Egyptian reprisals, inter-city warfare, or even the Sea Peoples. Despite these problems, the destruction layers frequently are convincing, for they agree with the textual evidence in the Bible, and the ensuing occupation is materially different from and inferior to that which precedes it, a feature that is best

Biblical Hazor.

explained by the intrusion of the seminomadic Israelite conquerors.

The stele of Pharaoh Merneptah commemorated his victory over an invading force of Libyans who were supported by early contingents of the Sea Peoples, infiltrating settlers from the fringes of Anatolia and the Aegean Sea who would later pose a massive threat to his successors. The stele with its hymns of victory was set up in Merneptah's mortuary temple at Thebes. Near the close of the inscription he also described the subjugation which he had imposed on the inhabitants of Syria and Palestine, and here is recorded the oldest extrabiblical reference to Israel yet discovered: "Israel lies desolate; its seed is no more." By approximately 1220, then, Israel was a force to be reckoned with in the land of Palestine. Allowing for a forty-year period for the Israelite experience in the wilderness, we must date the exodus at no later than 1260 B.C.

The Merneptah Stele. The name "Israel" appears near the bottom of the stele.

Iron Age I CIRCA 1200–900 B.C.

The Israelite exodus from Egypt and the subsequent conquest of the land of Canaan at the close of the Late Bronze Age must

The Iron Age Sequence in Palestine

IRON AGE (Israelite)		1200–330 B.C.
Early Iron (Iron I)	1200–900	
Middle Iron (Iron II)	900–600	
Late Iron (Iron III)	600–330 (Persian)	

be seen against contemporary international developments if one is to acquire a realistic perspective of the events. The arrival of the mysterious Sea Peoples on the borders of Egypt had begun as early as the reign of Seti I, the father of Ramses II, but the aggressive activities of these wandering marauders were not limited to Egypt alone. Pouring out of the north and west, they were a mixture of peoples who were being forced out of their former homelands by a combination of circumstances that are not certainly known, but those whose origins are traceable to the Aegean area must have been moved by the pressures of the Dorian invasions. They attacked and destroyed Hattusas, the capital of the Hittites in Anatolia, the Amorite kingdoms in Syria, the major port city of Ugarit in northern Syria, and Pales-

"Sea Peoples" battling Egyptians, based on the relief at Medinet Habu.

tine as well. Pharaoh Ramses III of the twentieth dynasty defeated them decisively (ca. 1196 B.C.) in a great sea battle, and his exploits against the invaders were recorded on the mortuary temple and palace at Medinet Habu. The Egyptian documents name the Luka, Sherden, Danuna, Akawasha, Tursha, Sheklesh, Weshesh, Tjeckker, and the Peleset among the Sea Peoples. Scholars have suggested a number of correlations on the basis of these names. For example, the Sherden have been identified with Sardinia, the Sheklesh with Sicily, and the Tursha with the Etruscans, but the Peleset are of primary interest. Following the Egyptian victory, the Peleset occupied the coastal plain south of Jaffa, where they may have served the Egyptians as a buffer zone of mercenaries for the protection of Egypt's northeastern boundary. In the Bible they are known as the Philistines.

The Philistines brought with them the technological advance of iron metallurgy which marked the transition from the Late Bronze to Iron Age I. They may have acquired this knowledge from earlier contacts with the Hittites. According to the Bible, they effectively monopolized the iron-working industry so that the Israelites were at a disadvantage, able to use iron agricultural tools but unable to acquire iron weapons. Even as late as the beginning of the monarchy, only Saul and Jonathan possessed iron swords.

Another important innovation, the art of making hewn stone cisterns, which were then coated with an impervious layer of lime plaster, made it possible for the invading Israelites to establish a sizable population in the hill country apart from the few springs around which Canaanite cities had been established. This development permitted the collection and storage of an adequate supply of essential water. Consequently, a fundamental change in land use and a major shift in population resulted. Prior to the Iron Age, the population of Palestine was clustered primarily in the valleys and plains, separated by the intervening forested hills into small enclaves. In the Iron Age the settlement of large areas of the hill country occurred for the first time, and the reduction of the native forests was rapidly accelerated to provide areas for cultivation as well as for building purposes.

Iron I "spinning" bowl from Beth-shan (cf. Prov. 31:19).

The Israelite propensity to settle in the hills contributed in part to their survival, for Egypt was primarily interested in dominating the cities in the plains and valleys in order to protect the strategic highways through the land. The Philistines, too, were to become a serious threat to the Israelites only somewhat later. The period of the judges, however, was one of internal conflicts among the tribes and external threats from the east—the Moabites, Midianites, Ammonites, and Arameans.

During Iron Age I the area that had been previously dominated by the Canaanites was drastically reduced as the result of the incursions of Hittites and Arameans into Syria, of the Israelites into the hills on both sides of the Jordan River, and of the Philistines into the southern coastal plain of Palestine. Where once the Canaanites had flourished in a region that extended from the southern fringes of the Taurus Mountains in the north to the deserts of the Sinai Peninsula in the south, including the hinterland eastward from the Mediterranean coast, the remnant of the Canaanites who retained a separate identity was confined to a coastal area only one-tenth the original size. History identifies this Canaanite remnant as the Phoenicians. Near the close of the Iron I period they began to expand vigorously and to dominate the sea trade on the Mediterranean while simultaneously developing close ties with the Israelite monarchy under King David.

Philistine jug and crater with Mycenaean style decorations. Note the Egyptian influence in the lotus on the jug.

Archaeologically speaking, the cultural transition between the Israelites and the Canaanites is marked by the inferior quality of the material remains of the newcomers. The period of the judges has been described as an archaeological Dark Age, with scant traces of architectural remains and mundane artifacts, yet at a number of sites such as Tell Beit Mirsim, Beth-el, Shiloh, and Gibeah, sufficient remains attributable to Israelite occupation have been recovered to convey the general picture that one would expect. The newcomers, possessing little knowledge of the arts of settled life, produced poor imitations of Canaanite architecture and pottery. A predominant form of the eleventh century was the large store jar (pithos) with a collared rim made of a coarsely textured clay. Regional variations developed as the scattered Israelite settlements came under the local influences of their Canaanite and Philistine neighbors.

The ceramic evidence for Iron Age I includes the distinctive wares associated with the Philistines. Both the forms of the vessels and their decorations were a new element on the Palestinian scene. The major type of vessel was a deep crater, or two-handled bowl, and a second characteristic form was the jug. These were decorated with stylized birds, often drawn with their heads turned backward, preening their feathers. Geometric designs and friezes of spirals or groups of interlocking semicircles also appear on Philistine ware. The fact that the style and form of this pottery are akin to Late Helladic III C pottery from the Aegean area fits well with the biblical record indicating that the Philistines came from Caphtor (Crete). Philistine pottery is most abundant in excavations of the areas of Philistine settlement mentioned in the Bible—the coastal plain and the major valleys along the fringes of the hill country.

Another interesting feature of Philistine culture is the anthropoid clay coffins that have been found at several sites in association with the pottery. A stylized face has been carved on the lid of several such sarcophagi. By the late eleventh century, typical Philistine ceramics were no longer manufactured, apparently due to the forces of assimilation.

The Philistines and Israelites lived in close proximity for a century that was marked by only minor contentions, but in the last half of the eleventh century, the Philistines began a program of aggressive expansion that threatened the independent existence of the Israelite tribes. It seems likely that the Philistines were reacting to the threat of the Israelites who were becoming more firmly established and who were experimenting with a more centralized political system. It was the Philistine menace, perhaps more than any other one factor, that forced Israel to choose a king.

Samuel closed the period of the judges by anointing Saul as the first Israelite king. Saul, a *nagid* ("prince"), a charismatic leader, became *melek* ("king") on the day after his victory over the Ammonites (I Sam. 11:15). His rule was the monarchy in embryonic form. There was no central government; the tribes retained their own administrative autonomy. A dramatic and drastic change came with the reign of David, and, more particularly, with Solomon. Tribal boundaries were forsaken in his reorganization into administrative districts; the corvée, a form of forced labor for the state, was imposed; international relations were established, including the development of a diplomatic corps and marriage alliances with ruling houses in foreign states; a middle class of businessmen and landed property holders emerged; and the center of worship was shifted to Jerusalem, the capital city.

The kingdom of David and Solomon, the United Monarchy, spanned no more than three-quarters of a century, from about 1000 to 922 B.C. It was the only period in which the Israelites

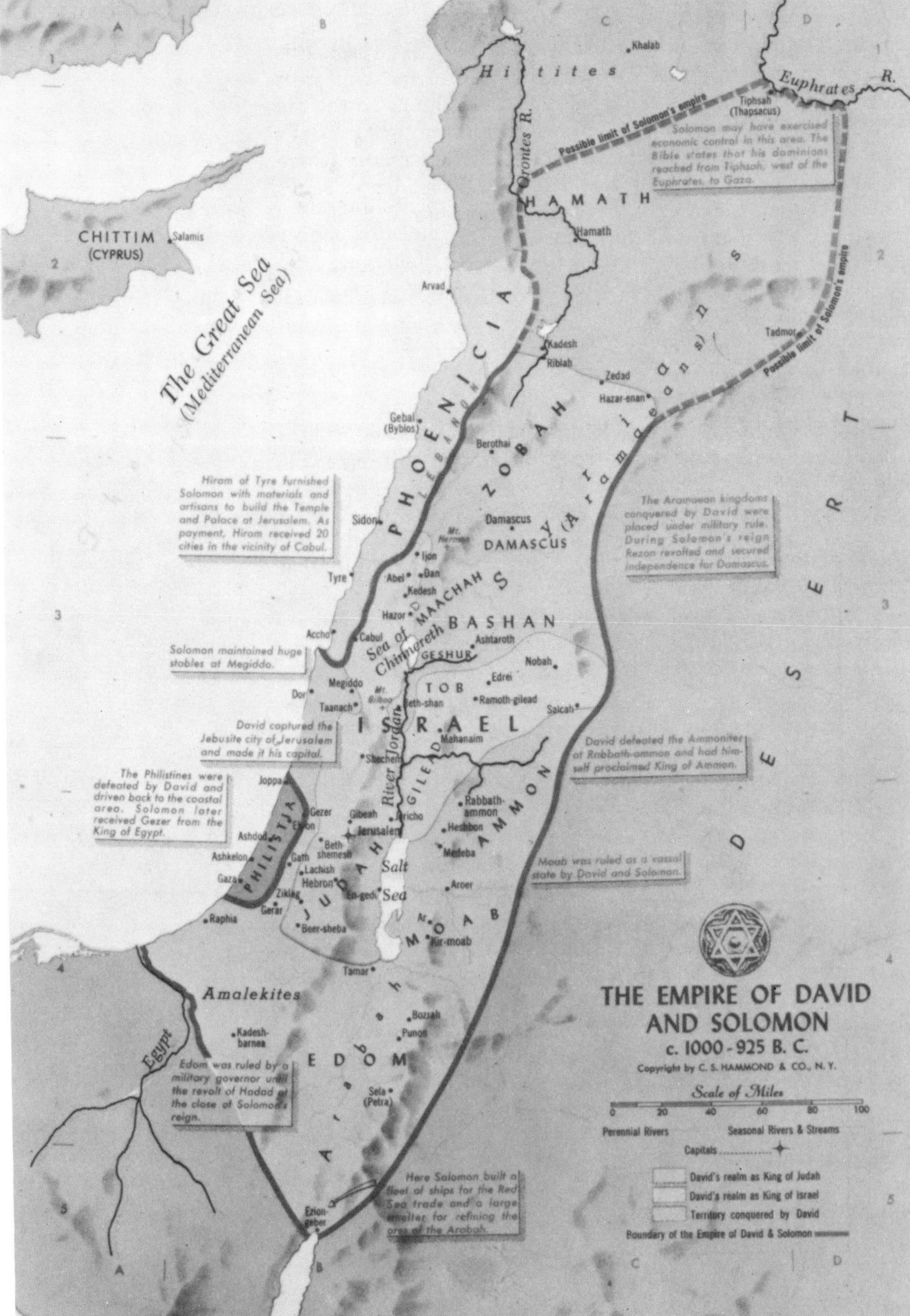
THE EMPIRE OF DAVID AND SOLOMON
c. 1000-925 B. C.
Copyright by C. S. HAMMOND & CO., N. Y.
Scale of Miles
0 20 40 60 80 100
Perennial Rivers
Seasonal Rivers & Streams
Capitals
David's realm as King of Judah
David's realm as King of Israel
Territory conquered by David
Boundary of the Empire of David & Solomon
The Great Sea
(Mediterranean Sea)
CHITTIM
(CYPRUS)
Salamis
Hittites
Khalab
Euphrates R.
Orontes R.
Tiphsah
(Thapsacus)
Possible limit of Solomon's empire
Solomon may have exercised economic control in this area. The Bible states that his dominions reached from Tiphsah, west of the Euphrates, to Gaza.
HAMATH
Hamath
Arvad
Kadesh
Riblah
Zedad
Hazar-enan
Tadmor
PHOENICIA
LEBANON
Gebal
(Byblos)
ZOBAH
Berothai
Hiram of Tyre furnished Solomon with materials and artisans to build the Temple and Palace at Jerusalem. As payment, Hiram received 20 cities in the vicinity of Cabul.
Sidon
Mt. Hermon
Damascus
DAMASCUS
(Arameans)
SYRIA
The Aramaean kingdoms conquered by David were placed under military rule. During Solomon's reign Rezon revolted and secured independence for Damascus.
DESERT
Ijon
Abel
Dan
Tyre
Kedesh
Hazor
MAACHAH
BASHAN
Accho
Cabul
Sea of Chinnereth
Ashtaroth
GESHUR
Nobah
Solomon maintained huge stables at Megiddo.
Megiddo
Dor
Mt. Gilboa
TOB
Edrei
Taanach
Beth-shan
Ramoth-gilead
Salcah
ISRAEL
David captured the Jebusite city of Jerusalem and made it his capital.
Mahanaim
David defeated the Ammonites at Rabbath-ammon and had himself proclaimed King of Ammon.
Shechem
River Jordan
GILEAD
The Philistines were defeated by David and driven back to the coastal area. Solomon later received Gezer from the King of Egypt.
Joppa
Gezer
Gibeah
Jericho
Rabbath-ammon
Ekron
Jerusalem
Heshbon
AMMON
Ashdod
Beth-shemesh
Medeba
Ashkelon
Gath
Salt Sea
Moab was ruled as a vassal state by David and Solomon.
Lachish
Gaza
Hebron
PHILISTIA
En-gedi
JUDAH
Aroer
Ziklag
Gerar
Raphia
Beer-sheba
MOAB
Kir-moab
Tamar
Amalekites
Bozrah
Punon
Kadesh-barnea
Egypt
EDOM
Edom was ruled by a military governor until the revolt of Hadad at the close of Solomon's reign.
Sela
(Petra)
Arabah
Here Solomon built a fleet of ships for the Red Sea trade and a large smelter for refining the ores of the Arabah.
Ezion-geber

were an important political power in the ancient Near East. This was due in part to the weakened condition of the two great centers of empire in Egypt and Mesopotamia and in part to the genius of David. As a political outlaw, toward the close of Saul's reign, David had taken refuge within Philistine territory where he acquired a knowledge of their arts of warfare. Upon Saul's death he became the ruler of the southern area of Judah, and his charismatic leadership soon brought the northern and southern tribes together under his control. His role as a man of war was but one aspect of his range of talents. He was in fact a political sage, religious reformer, builder of cities, poet, and musician. Upon his death, David left to Solomon an empire that extended from the Sinai Peninsula to the Euphrates River.

The accession of Solomon is now dated at about 961 B.C., based on a synchronism between the eleventh (or twelfth) year of Hiram of Tyre and the fourth year of Solomon. His reign was marked by penetrating and extensive Phoenician influences, and foremost among them was that of the monarchy itself. The

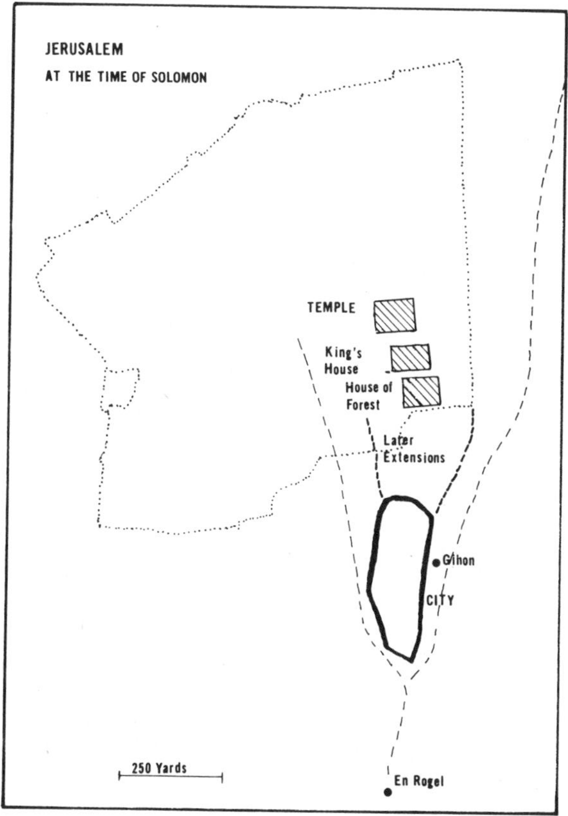

Bible records the injunctions of Samuel against the desire of the people to have a king like all the nations around them. The list of oppressive measures that they should expect the king to enact was not extraordinary; on the contrary, they were the normal prerogatives of Canaanite rulers, and Solomon employed them all. He established twelve new administrative districts that ignored the earlier tribal divisions. He established a state monopoly on trade, taking advantage of the overland trade routes that he controlled. His mercantile activities included importing horses from Anatolia for sale to Egypt, and the exploitation of the mineral wealth of the Arabah and the products of the Arabian peninsula to the south. Commercial relations with the Phoenicians enabled him to establish a seaport at Ezion Geber, a venture that provided Israel with access to the rich trade in spices and other exotic goods produced in areas to the south and east.

He employed the corvée to further his own extensive building programs. These included such magnificent buildings as the temple and palaces for himself and his numerous wives. The latter he acquired through extensive political alliances. In addition, he rebuilt and fortified a number of cities outside the capital, particularly Hazor, Megiddo, and Gezer, encircling them with casemate walls and providing them with well-constructed, three-chambered gates.

In contrast to the simple culture of peasants, represented by the pottery, tools, weapons, and architecture of the earlier part of the Iron I period, at the beginning of the monarchy there is evidence of many decisive and rapid changes in the style and methods of manufacture of the ceramic wares. The transition to a higher culture, toward which this evidence points, took place primarily during the reign of Solomon, and, as Kathleen Kenyon has noted, along with "a sudden rise in the standard of living the perfection in every kind of product is noticeable in archaeological excavations." Yet there was a contrast between the luxury of the major urban centers and the comparative poverty of the outlying districts. The oppressive measures of King Solomon were destined after his death to spark the rebellion which ended with the division of the kingdom.

Iron Age II CIRCA 900–600 B.C.

Iron Age II spans the years from the death of Solomon (ca. 922) to the destruction of Jerusalem in 587/6 B.C. It may be conveniently divided into two phases: (a) the time of the Divided Kingdom, with Judah in the south ruled from Jerusalem and Israel in the north ruled from Samaria, and (b) the period in which the kingdom of Judah continued alone following the Assyrian conquest of Samaria in 722/1 B.C. Jerusalem itself suffered a similar fate at the hands of the Babylonians in the sixth century. An additional phase, extending through the period of the Babylonian captivity to 538 B.C., is occasionally included in Iron II. That date marks the first return of the exiles to Jerusalem from Babylon under the new Persian regime. The period of the Babylonian captivity may also be placed in the Iron III period.

The policies of Solomon at both the national and the international level had brought the nation into a golden age of cultural and economic prosperity, but not without exacting a price from the populace. Toward the close of Solomon's reign one of his leading administrators, Jeroboam, fell from favor and fled to Egypt for refuge. Upon the death of the king, Jeroboam reappeared at Shechem as a spokesman for the northern tribes. Rehoboam, the son and successor of Solomon, had traveled to Shechem to seek the approval of the tribal leaders in the north to his accession to the throne. When he refused to ease the economic burdens that had been imposed upon the people by his father, and when he threatened to increase the oppression of his government, he found himself with barely half a kingdom. The northerners rejected his rule and chose for their king Jeroboam.

The Solomonic empire dissolved into three important kingdoms: Syria (Aram), Israel, and Judah. Much of the history of the Divided Kingdom era involves the intrigues and battles of these three with one another during the first phase of the period. At the same time, beyond the horizon to the east a specter began to rise which was to haunt these three small kingdoms and in the course of time sweep away Syria and Israel. That threat was the Mesopotamian empire of Assyria.

Dynastic changes were a notable feature of the history of the northern kingdom, Israel, until it was destroyed by Assyria in 722 B.C. In contrast the dynasty of David continued to rule in Judah. Omri established an important Israelite dynasty circa 876 B.C. Soon afterward he moved the capital from Tirzah to Samaria. Although the Bible devotes only a few lines to his reign, in Assyrian historical documents his domain is identified as the "land of Omri." He was succeeded by his son, Ahab, who married a Phoenician princess, Jezebel. Apparently under her influence, Ahab built a temple in Samaria for Baal, the Canaanite god. The atmosphere of his reign, marked as it was by religious syncretism, international intrigues, and social upheaval, was in part responsible for the surge of prophetic activity in Iron

Age II. Ahab's political power has been emphasized by Assyrian documents that record how he provided a force of two thousand chariots and ten thousand men toward a coalition that withstood the army of Shalmaneser III at the battle of Qarqar in 853 B.C.

When Jehu assassinated Jehoram, king of Israel, and mortally wounded Ahaziah, king of Judah, on the same day, he brought an end to the dynasty of Omri and established his own claim to the throne of Samaria. The Bible states that this was done with the approval of the prophet Elisha. By these violent acts Jehu has provided biblical scholars with an important synchronism for the chronology of the kings of Judah and Israel. The date for these events has been established at about 842/1 B.C., based on information from the dated annals of Shalmaneser III of Assyria.

Through the study of the Assyrian historical records and the discovery of written materials in Palestine from such sites as Samaria, Lachish, and, most recently, Arad in the Negev, archaeology has in the present century been shedding increasing light on the events of Iron Age II. The fortunes of both Israel and Judah fluctuated with the ebb and flow of Assyrian dominance of the area. Despite the extent of the kingdoms of Israel and Judah in the days of Jeroboam II and Uzziah, a period of affluence that witnessed the condemnation of the prophet Amos, a period of decline soon followed. Assyrian activity in the area led to the fall of Samaria, capital of Israel, in 722/1 B.C. Sargon II followed the standing Assyrian policy of deporting the upper strata of the population and importing foreigners to replace them. An Assyrian governor was also appointed over the conquered area.

The small kingdom of Judah continued under the leadership of the Davidic dynasty as a vassal state of the Assyrian empire. A revolt against Assyria, led by King Hezekiah, brought the forces of Sennacherib into Palestine in 701. Hezekiah's preparations for defense included the excavation of the famous water tunnel that connects the Gihon spring to the Pool of Siloam. Although the city was saved, heavy tribute was imposed, leaving the country in an impoverished situation. During the long reign of Manasseh (ca. 687–642), Judah followed a pro-Assyrian course. Young King Josiah, however, instituted a period of religious reform, political expansion, and anti-Assyrian policies. He was able to pursue an independent course largely due to the progressive disintegration of Assyrian power following the death of Ashurbanipal (633). The renaissance under Josiah was destined to be short-lived, for the next great world power was rising in the east, the neo-Babylonian empire of Nebuchadnezzar. By the year 597, his expansion into the west had brought him to Jerusalem, and on March 15/16 the city was captured. King Jehoiachin was deported to Babylon along with the leading citizens of his realm. A revolt against Babylon a short time later, in the days of the prophet Jeremiah, brought the armies of Nebuchadnezzar back to Jerusalem. The city was captured and razed in the summer of 587/6 B.C., and most of the remaining population was deported. Thus ended the kingdom of Judah and the period of the first temple.

Judean pottery, Iron Age II.

The pottery of Iron II reflects a gradual and continuous evolution of forms that are traceable back into the Canaanite culture of the Middle Bronze Age. Regional differences between the pottery of the north and the south are distinguishable, reflecting in part the political division. Moreover, phases of pottery through the period are discernible, but as G. E. Wright has observed, the changes in styles and fashions are so gradual in this period that dating within a period of less than a century is unfeasible. Interesting inscribed jar handles appear in this era, and at a number of sites have been discovered limestone pillar capitals which are the forerunners of the classic Ionic capital developed later in Greece.

An inscribed jar handle from Tell Beit Mirsim. The seal identifies the steward of King Jehoiachin (ca. 597 B.C.).

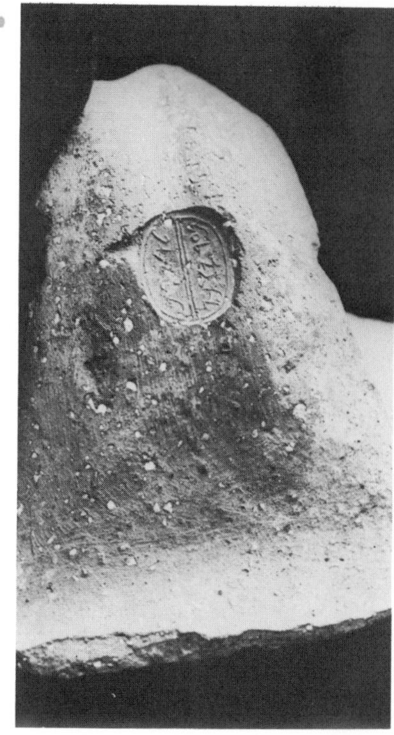

The Babylonian exile is depicted in somber tones in Psalm 137, yet the hardships seem to have been spiritual and intellectual rather than material. The "Jehoiachin Tablets," discovered by R. Koldewey in his excavations at Babylon early in the twentieth century, indicate the humane circumstances under which King Jehoiachin and his sons lived in exile. The Bible indicates that in the reign of Evil-Merodach, in the mid-sixth century B.C., Jehoiachin was elevated from prisoner to favored status in the royal court. This information, coupled with the large numbers of Jews who chose not to return to Jerusalem when Cyrus, king of Persia and conqueror of Babylon, permitted them to do so, indicates the acceptable conditions that the Jews found in the environs of Babylon.

At the same time, the very defeat and exile itself resulted in a period of intense spiritual and intellectual turmoil for the Jews. The work of the prophet Jeremiah prior to the destruction of Jerusalem and the work of Ezekiel in Babylon were a part of the broader search for religious meaning in the destruction of their homeland and temple. Accordingly, during the period much attention was afforded to what survived of the national literature. It is probable that the roots of the idea of the synagogue are traceable to the exile. The result among the Jews in Babylonia was the elimination of pagan practices, an emphasis upon monotheism, and a religious fervor for the Law.

Iron Age III CIRCA 600–332 B.C.

Iron Age III, or the Persian period, was ushered in with the fall of the city of Babylon to Cyrus, king of the Medes, in October, 539 B.C. Within a year of his conquest of the Chaldean empire, Cyrus had issued an edict permitting the Jews to return to their homeland and to rebuild the Jerusalem temple (Ezra 1:2–4; 6:3–5). He extended similar rights to other displaced national and ethnic groups, choosing to extend his rule by propaganda and diplomacy in contrast to the terror and force that had marked the Chaldean regime. The direct result of Cyrus' policy was the establishment of a small group of returnees in the environs of Jerusalem under the political leadership of a scion of the house of David, Sheshbazzar, and under the religious leadership of the high priest Joshua.

The returnees were faced with strong opposition from neighboring peoples. Local nobles from Samaria and Transjordan regarded the province of Judah as a part of their jurisdiction, having established a quasi-political control over the area and its population in the decades following the Babylonian conquest. This population was composed of the descendants of the poorer classes of Jews who had not suffered deportation, mixed with a smattering of neighboring peoples who had infiltrated the area and intermarried. A natural antagonism thus existed between the returnees, who were zealously religious, and the permanent inhabitants, whose efforts were primarily aimed at wresting a living from the rocky soil of the Judean hills. Despite these problems, the temple was rebuilt and rededicated by 515

The Cyrus cylinder.

B.C., an event that ushered in the era of the second temple. The prophets Haggai and Zechariah were actively involved in this development.

The period from the completion of the temple until the arrival of Nehemiah is very obscure, but before the close of the sixth century the political leadership of the community had passed to a series of high priests and, for reasons unknown, all connections with the Judean royal house had dissipated.

Nehemiah came with the authority of the Persian throne to rebuild the walls of the city and to institute needed social and religious reforms. Despite threats and ridicule from Sanballat, Tobiah, and Geshem, leaders of Samaria and Transjordan, Nehemiah fulfilled his purposes, establishing Jerusalem once again as a defensible city. Before the close of the fifth century, Ezra arrived in Jerusalem and carried out religious reforms that purged Judaism of a number of tendencies which had crept in and threatened its survival. Ezra is to be credited with the establishment of the Torah as the supreme authority and guide for normative Judaism. Little more is known about the political fortunes of the small Jewish enclave around Jerusalem from the time of Ezra until the arrival of the conquering Greeks nearly a century later.

The material remains of the Persian period are significant for illuminating an otherwise dark age. The massive destruction of Judah wrought by Nebuchadnezzar's forces is evident. The displacement of most of the population is indicated by the meager signs of occupation during the sixth century at excavated sites. Continued occupation seems to have occurred only in a handful of towns, mainly to the north. Thus, a gap in the pottery sequence occurred in the Persian period. The paucity of material remains indicates, too, that the resettlement of Judah was a very slow process. The area reoccupied was a strip in the highlands stretching from a few miles north of Jerusalem southward to the area of Beth-zur and Tekoa. The fertile valleys toward the Mediterranean Sea remained in other hands. The population by the close of the sixth century has been estimated at no more than twenty thousand. Not until the third century B.C. did the population reach its former level.

The artifactual evidence indicates that while the people were poor, the jewelry, coins (minted locally), and ceramic articles were executed with considerable technical skill and stylistic sophistication. Persian influences are exhibited in the artifacts, as would be expected, but in addition Phoenician and particularly Greek influences are very much in evidence. The Greeks had become increasingly competitive with the Phoenicians in

Mediterranean trade until in the sixth century numerous Greek trading posts had been established on the coasts of Egypt, Syria, and Palestine. Accordingly, Greek imports and local imitations increased at Palestinian sites thereafter.

Historical evidence for the situation in Judah around 400 B.C. can be found in the Elephantine Papyri, discovered near Aswan in Egypt in the late nineteenth century. When the Jewish military colony that produced the papyri wanted help in rebuilding their local temple, they wrote to the governor of Judah. After being refused assistance from Jerusalem, they also sent the request to the sons of Sanballat, the governor of Samaria.

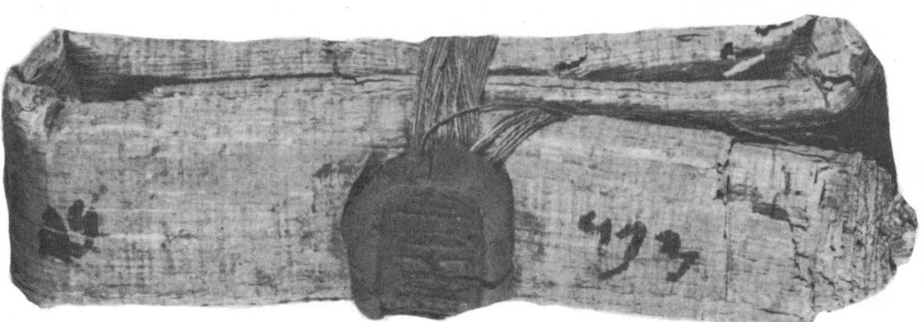

A folded, sealed papyrus document from Elephantine.

The reestablishment of a religious center at Jerusalem in the Persian period brought into being ties between the Jews of the Diaspora and Jerusalem. The religious and spiritual forces then set in motion were destined to provide a cohesive element in Judaism that still exists.

The Hellenistic Period CIRCA 332–63 B.C.

When the Persian empire fell to Alexander the Great, the Hellenistic period was ushered in. It was destined to continue until the arrival of the Romans in Palestine. Hellenism signifies Greek ideas and culture. Long before the conquests of Alexander, Greek ideas and wares were being disseminated along the eastern littoral of the Mediterranean Sea through commerce, but a powerful wave of influence followed the advance of the Macedonian's armies. The power of a foreign, technologically superior culture began to weaken the traditional disciplines of oriental life, replacing them with Greek modes of thought and activity. The tendency to assimilate Greek ways was particularly strong in Jerusalem among the upper-class citizens, the commercial and political aristocracy. In time, a reaction against Hellenism was to develop, leading finally to the Maccabean revolt.

Alexander died in 323 B.C., a victim of drink and disease. A period of conflict followed as his generals vied for parts of the disintegrating empire. By 300 B.C. Seleucus I had gained control of Syria, Persia, and Mesopotamia, while Ptolemy I ruled Egypt; both kings laid claim to Palestine, but Egypt had established its control over the area.

The Ptolemies established a benign policy toward their Palestinian territory. Judea was permitted to maintain self-government under the high priest, who combined religious and political authority. The major mark of Egyptian domination was the heavy tribute that was exacted. The Ptolemies initiated a tax-farming program whereby local appointees collected the taxes and forwarded them to the Egyptian authorities, with the local agent receiving a commission in return for his services. In this manner local aristocrats, including members of the high priestly family, came to have a vested interest in the Ptolemaic regime. They also developed a tendency to assimilate to the Greek way of life, and a Hellenizing party thus arose among the ranks of the wealthy and priestly aristocracy of Jerusalem.

Egyptian control of the area continued, despite Syrian claims, until Seleucus III reconquered Palestine in 198 B.C. The Syrian monarchs introduced no major changes of policy toward the Jewish people until the reign of Antiochus IV Epiphanes (175–163 B.C.). He moved to stamp out orthodox Judaism in 168 B.C. in reprisal for an outbreak of strife between the Jews who opposed Hellenization and the pro-Syrian Hellenizing party in Jerusalem. Antiochus' forces attacked the city and numerous citizens were slaughtered. Not content with this, he desecrated the sacred precincts of the temple, dedicating it to the worship of Olympian Zeus and instituting the sacrifice of swine on the altar of burnt offering in honor of the pagan god. Capital punishment was established for Jews who complied with such commandments as circumcision, and the books of the Torah were condemned to destruction. Jews were required to sacrifice to the Greek gods, and for this purpose altars were erected at a number of locations within the country. The result was the outbreak of the Maccabean revolt under the leadership of a priest named Mattathias from the village of Modin.

The leadership of the revolt soon passed to Judas, a son of Mattathias, and by 165 B.C. he had recaptured the temple precincts. The defiled holy place was duly cleansed and a ceremony of dedication to be perpetually observed was established. This was the institution of the Feast of Hanukkah. The conflict between the Hellenizing Jews, supported by the Syrians, and the Maccabees continued until 160 B.C. By that time the Maccabees had become powerful enough to establish the independent

The Hasmonean Dynasty (Maccabees)
(167–29 B.C.)

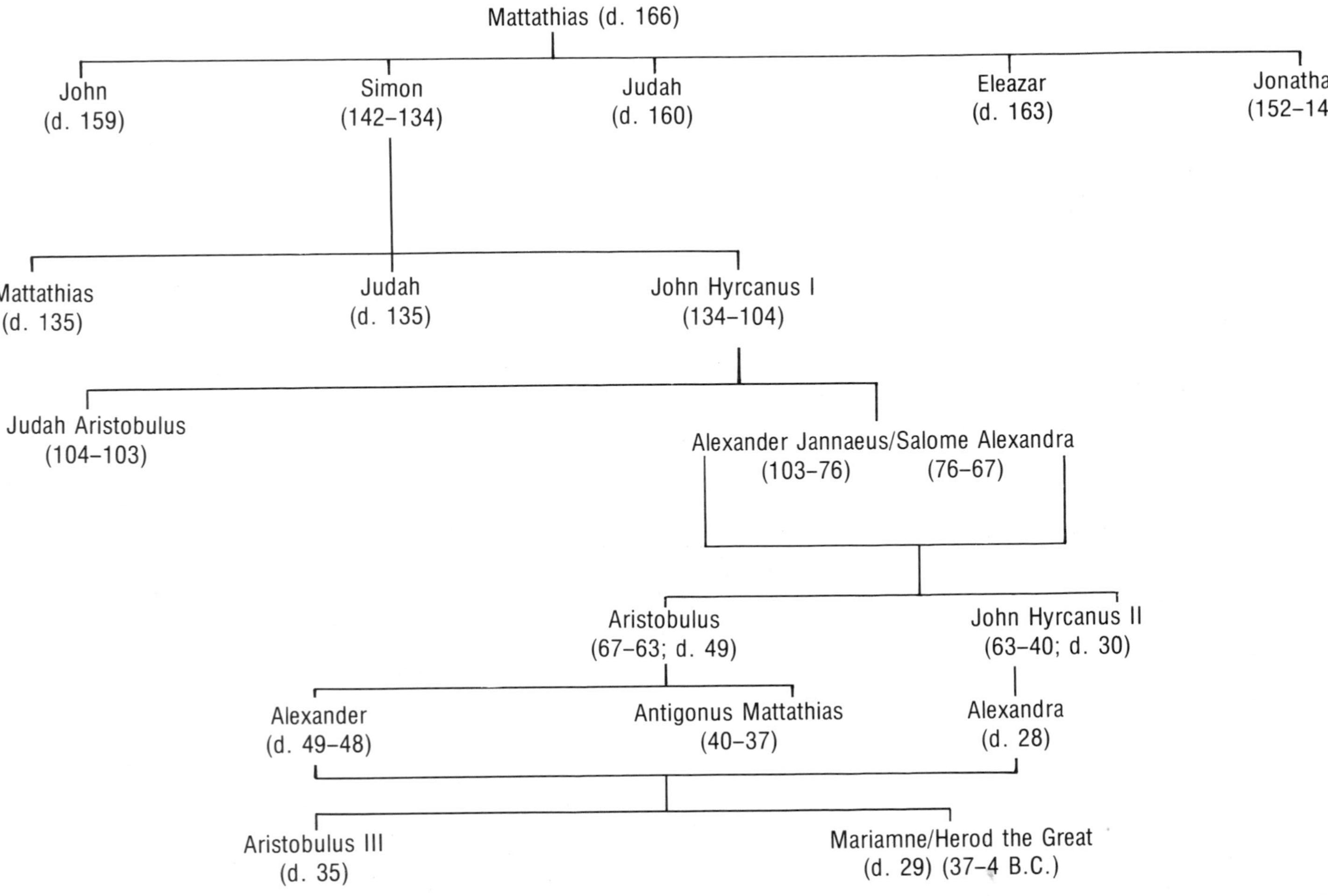

Hasmonean kingdom. With political control in his hands, Jonathan, successor to his brother Judas, also moved to acquire the high priestly office. Simon, the brother and successor of Jonathan, received confirmation as high priest with hereditary rights in 141 B.C., even though the office belonged by tradition to the Aaronide line of priests. The result was that his successors controlled both the political and religious authority, functioning as priest-kings apart from both the Aaronide and the Davidic lineage.

Due to fraternal struggles for power within the Hasmonean family, Roman forces who had gained control of Syria intervened. Under Pompey they occupied the city of Jerusalem in 63 B.C.

While the political changes that were discussed above were taking place, a number of significant features were developing in Judaism. The growth of a considerable colony of Jews in Egypt, particularly in Alexandria, who no longer were able to read the Scriptures in Hebrew led to the Septuagint, the Greek translation of the Old Testament. This occurred about 250 B.C., during the reign of Ptolemy II Philadelphus. From the fifth to the second centuries B.C., an emphasis in Jewish circles upon the individual and his destiny led to the growth of a school of thought concerned with wisdom. Ben Sira, one of the apocryphal literary works of the period, exemplifies the thought of a wisdom teacher. Other apocryphal and apocalyptic works were produced in the period from 200 B.C. to A.D. 100. During the period of Syrian domination, and even somewhat earlier, a reaction to the Hellenizing tendencies of the intelligentsia began. This reaction developed into the formation of a group of pious people called the Hasidim. In the early, more religiously oriented stages of the Maccabean revolt, the Hasidim supported the conflict; when the orientation later became more political, the Hasidim withdrew their active support. In the course of time they splintered into several sects, including the Pharisees and the Essenes. The Dead Sea Scroll community apparently had its roots in the circles of the Hasidim.

Although the archaeological evidence for the Hellenistic period is far from complete, good material evidence has been recovered from Marisa, Beth-zur, Samaria, Shechem, and Gezer. Generally speaking, the Hellenistic era introduced important changes in the material culture of Palestine as well as the philosophical and ideological changes previously noted. Items in common use such as lamps and pots changed radically. The manufacturing techniques employed finer clays fired at higher temperatures. Greek styles were imitated, and the walls of ves-

The Herodian Dynasty

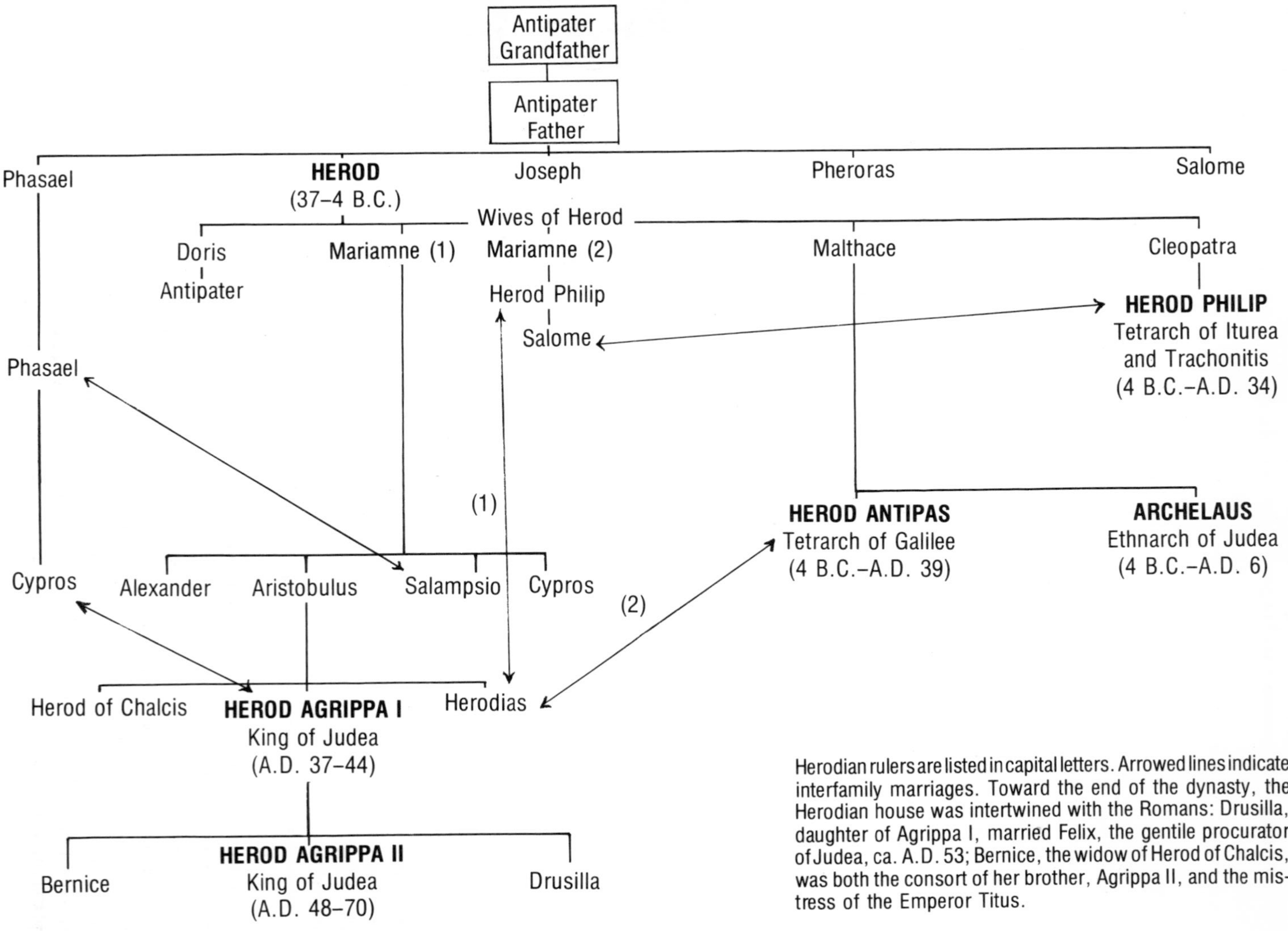

Herodian rulers are listed in capital letters. Arrowed lines indicate interfamily marriages. Toward the end of the dynasty, the Herodian house was intertwined with the Romans: Drusilla, daughter of Agrippa I, married Felix, the gentile procurator of Judea, ca. A.D. 53; Bernice, the widow of Herod of Chalcis, was both the consort of her brother, Agrippa II, and the mistress of the Emperor Titus.

sels tended to be thinner and more brittle. Architectural remains indicate an increasingly Hellenized style. Coins, both foreign and local, are a characteristic feature of the period. The simplicity of design on Maccabean coins is instructive, but they also exhibit increasing tendencies toward Hellenization. Numerous stamped Rhodian amphora handles indicate the desirability and availability of imported products. The transition to Roman dominance did not end the cultural patterns of the Hellenistic era; it only modified their expression.

The Roman Period 63 B.C.–A.D. 324

Once Rome had acquired control of Palestine, it did not relinquish its domination. The Roman general, Pompey, reduced considerably the Hasmonean territories, but he did entrust what was left to Hyrcanus II, a scion of the Judean royal house. Events led to Roman recognition of Herod the Great as king of Judea in 37 B.C., but his position was fraught with danger, for Rome was undergoing a period of political instability that witnessed a succession of rulers. Herod, with exquisite adroitness, managed to survive the turmoil by successfully transferring his allegiance to one after the other. His reign ended with his death in 4 B.C., shortly after the birth of Jesus. Herod secured his throne against Jewish dissidence by ruling with an iron hand and by assuaging hostilities with timely gifts. Upon his death his son, Archelaus, assumed the rule of Judea, Idumea, and Samaria. Another son, Herod Antipas, was given Galilee and Perea; a northern portion of Herod's kingdom fell to a third son, Herod Philip. When Archelaus failed to win the support of his subjects, he was deposed and Judea was reorganized into a Roman province. It was governed at first by a series of prefects. Agrippa I, the grandson of Herod, was appointed king over all the territories which had been ruled by his grandfather. His reign was brief (A.D. 41–44), ending with his death. Thereafter a series of procurators renewed the direct rule of Rome over Jewish affairs.

Typical pottery of the Herodian period.

Under the earlier prefects, relations between the Romans and the Jews had not deteriorated to the point of open rebellion; there is little evidence of political bloodshed prior to the time of Pontius Pilate (A.D. 26–36). But from Pilate onward disturbances, messianic aspirations, and political unrest threatened the stability of Roman Judea. Open rebellion broke out in A.D. 66, the beginning of the first Jewish revolt against the Romans. The conflict resulted in incredible suffering and bloodshed for

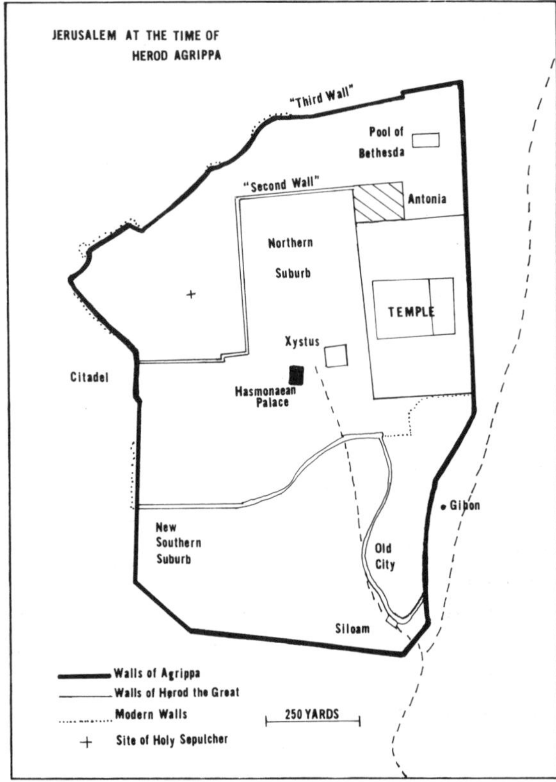

The "Judea Capta" coin depicting the victory of Vespasian over Jerusalem.

the Jews. Jerusalem and its temple were destroyed by Titus, son of the new emperor, Vespasian, in A.D. 70. A small remnant of the Jews took refuge on a rocky fortress near the Dead Sea. In A.D. 73, Masada fell and the revolt ended.

The moral, spiritual, and material devastation, which was a natural aftermath of the revolt, threatened the very existence of Palestinian Judaism and with it that of the Diaspora, which had always looked to Jerusalem for spiritual identity and direction. The destruction of the temple and its cultic rituals required drastic modifications of traditional Judaism. The task was taken up by Rabbi Johanan ben Zakkai. He established a community of scholars, Pharisaic sages, at Jamnia, an inland city near Joppa. Thus began the task of restructuring Judaism for existence without a state and without a temple.

Apart from the Pharisees, the only sect that survived the destruction of Jerusalem was the Christians. Those who had been in the city left it prior to the siege, fleeing to Pella in Transjordan. The church had already begun its expansionary movement into the Roman world before the revolt, and as a result it was becoming more and more a Gentile church. The aftermath of the revolt of the Jews against Rome was destined to lead to a widening gulf between Jews and Christians.

In 115–117 a widespread revolt of Jews in the Diaspora against the Romans occurred. This so-called war of Quietus touched Palestine, too, but the disruption was temporary and minor in nature. The accession of the Emperor Hadrian ushered in what seemed to be a new era for Palestinian Jewry. He acted favorably toward them and even promised to rebuild and return Jerusalem to them. He promised, also, to permit the rebuilding of the temple, but he changed his mind; Jerusalem was reconstructed as a pagan city and renamed Aelia Capitolina. Hadrian, during the later period of his reign, also introduced harsh measures, including the prohibition of circumcision. In 132 the second revolt of the Jews against Rome broke out. This conflict is also known as the Bar Kochba revolt, named after the central figure. Resolute as were the efforts of the Jews, they were doomed to failure, and the struggle for freedom ended with the death of the leader. A remnant of his forces found refuge in caves slightly west of the Dead Sea, there to die under Roman siege. Only in modern times have archaeologists recovered documents and artifacts from the caves—poignant remains that authenticate the final efforts of Jews in antiquity to politically possess Palestine, the land of promise, Canaan.

The Roman period through the end of the first century A.D. witnessed events whose implications for Western civilization are still vital. Recent discoveries in the Judean wilderness, particularly near Qumran at the northwest corner of the Dead Sea, have illuminated the multifaceted nature of Judaism in the period before the destruction of the temple. This period was crucial for Christianity, and the development of Christianity and of post-A.D. 70 Judaism was in part the result of factors present in the Roman period. A number of these factors will be dealt with later under the topic of Qumran and the Dead Sea Scrolls.

For the purposes of this text, our survey of the historical and archaeological periods will end at this point. History goes on, of course, and the subsequent eras (A.D. 324–640, Byzantine; 640–1099, Early Arab; 1099–1291, Crusades; 1291–1516, Mamluk; 1516–1918, Turk) are not without archaeological interest; they simply are not relevant to our understanding of the periods upon which our attention is focused.

The Spatial Dimensions of Biblical Archaeology

The term *biblical* carries with it connotations of space as well as of time. Although Palestine is by its very nature the center of interest, and although it is justly known as the land of the Bible,

Chronological Table

586 B.C.–

586/7	Destruction of Jerusalem by Babylonians; "Second Captivity"; End of the Kingdom of Judah
586–538	Exile in Babylonia
539	Conquest of Babylonia by Cyrus the Persian; End of Babylonian Empire
538	Cyrus's edict permitting the return of Jews to Judea; Beginning of the Jews' return to Jerusalem
445	Nehemiah rebuilds the walls of Jerusalem; Priestly theocracy in Jerusalem
333	Alexander the Great overthrows the Persian Empire and establishes Greek rule throughout the Near East
323	Alexander dies and his newly-founded empire breaks up into a series of rival Greek kingdoms. The Ptolemies rule in Egypt; the Seleucids in Syria, and the Antigonids in Macedonia
320	Ptolemy I conquers Jerusalem
285–246	Reign of Ptolemy II Philadelphus. Beginnings of the Septuagint (translation of the O.T. into Greek)
223–187	Antiochus III (The Great) of Syria annexes Palestine and makes it a province of the Seleucid Empire
200 B.C.–A.D. 100 (approx.)	Apocryphal and Apocalyptic Literature
187–175	Seleucus IV, beginning of Hellenistic infiltration, resisted by the Zadokite High Priest, Onias III
175–163	Reign of Antiochus IV (Epiphanes)
168	Antiochus begins his persecution of the Jews
165	Judas Maccabeus rededicates the Temple (Feast of Hanukkah)
163	Demetrius I reigns as King of Syria
160	Death of Judas Maccabeus. Independent Maccabean Kingdom established.
160–142	High Priesthood of Jonathan
145	Demetrius II reigns as King of Syria

# of Major Events

A.D. 200

142–134	High Priesthood of Simon
134–104	High Priesthood of John Hyrcanus (opposed by Pharisees)
104–103	Aristobulus I, High Priest and King
103–76	Alexander Jannaeus, High Priest, King, and conqueror
76–67	Alexandra's two sons, Hyrcanus II and Aristobulus II, fight over succession
63	Romans intervene and occupy Jerusalem. Roman rule begins.
37–4	Herod the Great; End of Hasmonean Dynasty. Birth of Jesus
c.30 B.C.–A.D. 45	Philo
27 B.C.–A.D. 14	Emperor Augustus
4 B.C.–A.D. 6	Archelaus, ethnarch of Judea and Samaria
6–15	Annas, high priest
26–36	Pontius Pilate, procurator of Judea. Death of Jesus; beginning of the Christian Church
c. 38–100	Josephus
40–50 (approx.)	The beginning of the New Testament literature
66	First Jewish revolt against Rome started by Eleazar Ben Hannais. Masada seized by Menahem. Murder of Menahem on Ophel
68	Destruction of the Essene community in the Dead Sea region by the Roman armies
70	The Romans led by Titus destroy Jerusalem and the Temple
73	Capture of the last stronghold, Masada, by the Romans
90	Synod of Yabneh (Jamnia). Canonization of the Hebrew Bible
132–135	Bar Kochba Revolt
1st–4th Centuries (approx.)	Apocryphal New Testament writings
200 (approx.)	Mishnah edited by Rabbi Judah, the Prince

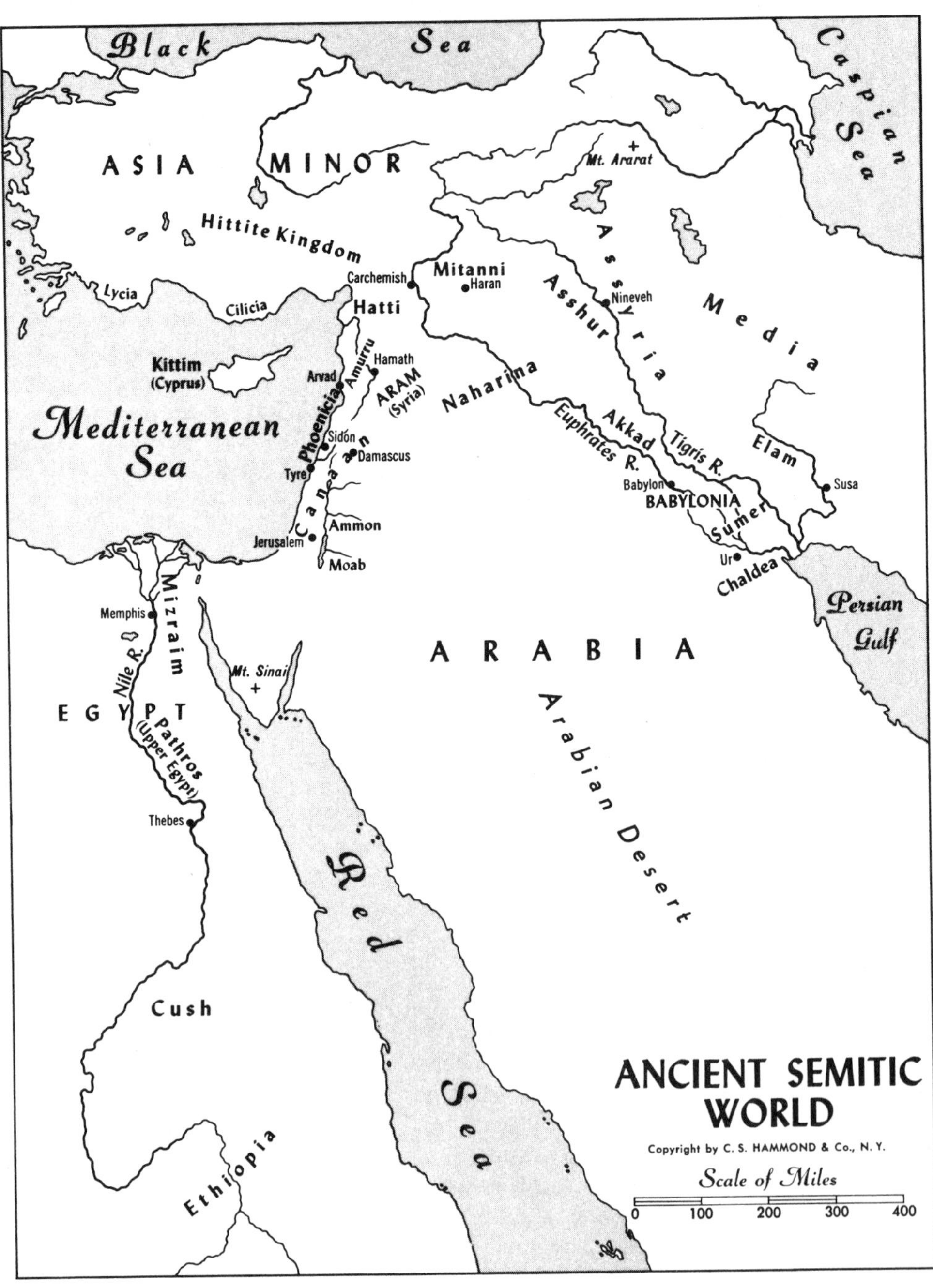
Black Sea
Caspian Sea
ASIA MINOR
Mt. Ararat
Hittite Kingdom
Assyria
Carchemish
Mitanni
Haran
Lycia
Cilicia
Hatti
Asshur
Nineveh
Media
Kittim (Cyprus)
Arvad
Amurru
Hamath
ARAM (Syria)
Naharina
Mediterranean Sea
Phoenicia
Sidon
Damascus
Tyre
Canaan
Akkad
Euphrates R.
Tigris R.
Elam
Susa
Babylon
BABYLONIA
Sumer
Ammon
Jerusalem
Moab
Ur
Chaldea
Persian Gulf
Memphis
Mizraim
Nile R.
ARABIA
Mt. Sinai
EGYPT
Pathros (Upper Egypt)
Arabian Desert
Thebes
Red Sea
Cush
Ethiopia
ANCIENT SEMITIC WORLD
Copyright by C. S. HAMMOND & Co., N. Y.
Scale of Miles
0 100 200 300 400

the spatial dimensions of the Bible extend to cover a far greater area. The geographical area implicit in the term *biblical* encompasses "all ancient lands from the Atlantic to India," in the view of the renowned biblical scholar William F. Albright. The region extends also from the southern fringes of Russia in the north to Ethiopia and the shores of the Indian Ocean in the south. It thus incorporates the two great centers of ancient civilization in the Nile and the Mesopotamian Valleys. Either directly or indirectly, excavations throughout this extensive area have illuminated various aspects of the Bible. An elementary acquaintance with the geography of the area is therefore essential for the student of biblical archaeology, for the Bible is replete with allusions to the geographical backdrop against which are played out the historical events that comprise the warp and woof of the narrative. The student should take advantage of a good historical atlas of the Bible in his studies. An atlas that combines maps of the physical features of the area with maps that indicate historical changes through the biblical period is preferable to an atlas of narrower scope. It should also include a descriptive text that connects the historical changes with biblical events and periods. The following description of the biblical world assumes the student has such an atlas at his disposal and is therefore limited to a summary.

Jerusalem, the city sacred to Jews, Christians, and Muslims alike, was the center of the inhabited world in the view of the early rabbis and Christian Fathers. In the sixth-century A.D. mosaic map in the Transjordanian church at Medeba, Jerusalem holds the central position. Jerusalem is set atop the central highlands at approximately 2500 feet above sea level. The central highlands, also known as the western hills, extend in a north-south direction the full length of Palestine and provide a natural separation between the coastal plain to the west and the Rift Valley to the east. The Rift Valley contains the Jordan River, the Sea of Galilee, the Dead Sea, and the Arabah. Beyond the valley to the east rise the hills of Transjordan, the eastern hills, which fall away eastward into the desert. Thus, the area divides naturally into five regions moving inland from the Mediterranean Sea from west to east: coastal plain, central highlands, Rift Valley, the hills of Transjordan, and the desert.

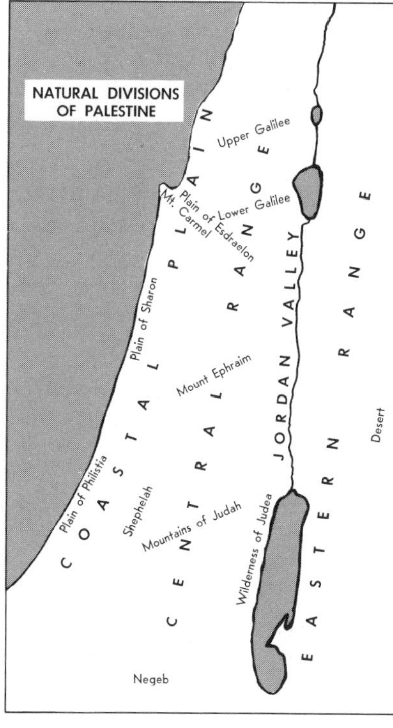

The entire area forms the southern extension of arable land which curves northward and easterly into the Mesopotamian Valley, the Fertile Crescent, as it was named by Sir Henry Breasted. The coastal plain extends northward from the Sinai along the Mediterranean coast to the border of modern Lebanon. It narrows progressively from a twenty-mile width near

Jerusalem as it is depicted in the sixth-century mosaic map at the church in Medeba, Jordan.

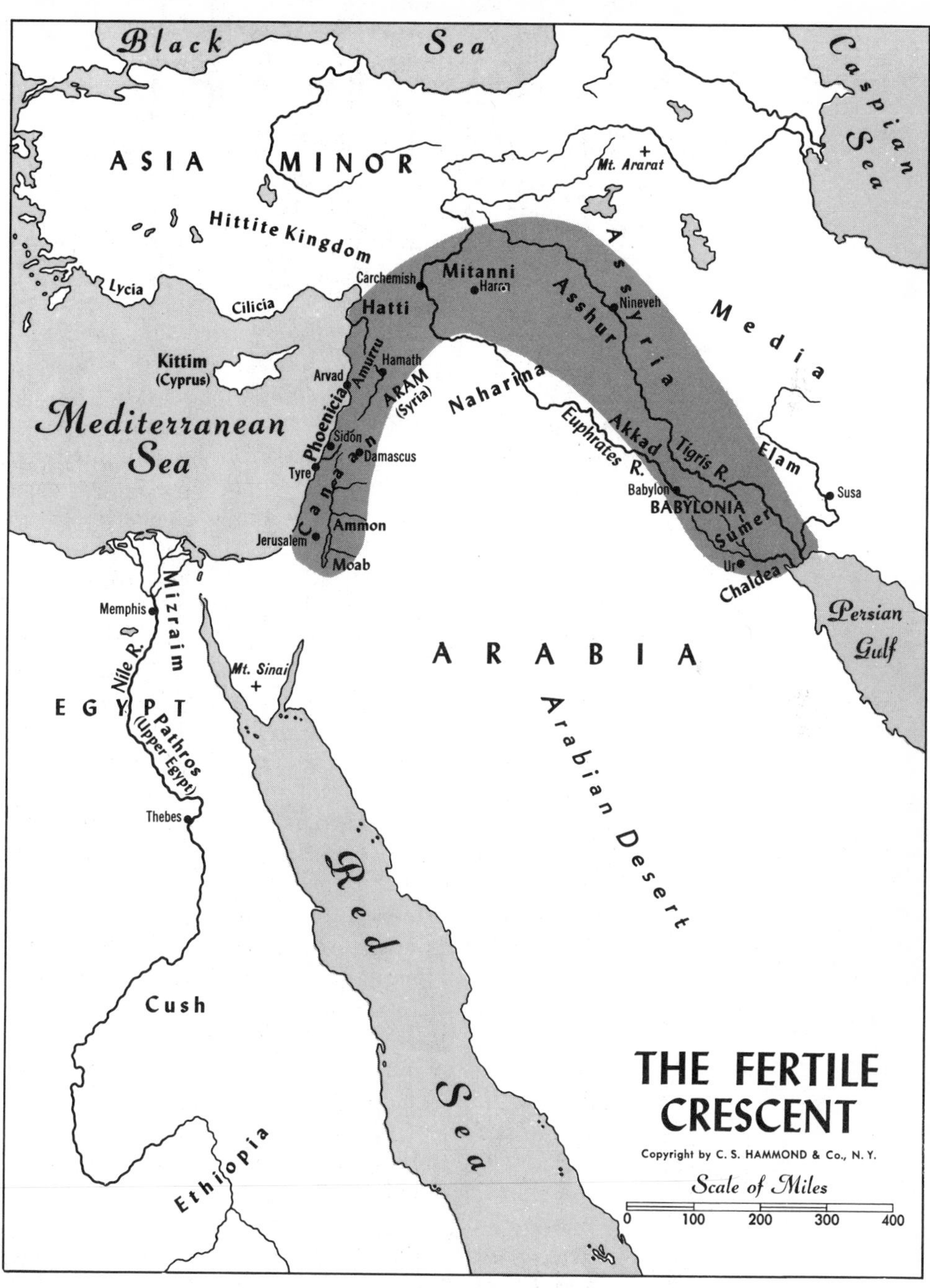
Black Sea
Caspian Sea
ASIA MINOR
Hittite Kingdom
Mt. Ararat
Assyria
Lycia
Cilicia
Carchemish
Mitanni
Harran
Hatti
Asshur
Nineveh
Media
Kittim (Cyprus)
Arvad
Amurru
Hamath
ARAM (Syria)
Naharina
Mediterranean Sea
Phoenicia
Sidon
Canaan
Damascus
Tyre
Euphrates R.
Akkad
Tigris R.
Elam
Susa
Babylon
BABYLONIA
Ammon
Jerusalem
Sumer
Moab
Ur
Chaldea
Persian Gulf
Memphis
Mizraim
Nile R.
Mt. Sinai
ARABIA
EGYPT
Pathros (Upper Egypt)
Arabian Desert
Thebes
Red Sea
Cush
Ethiopia
THE FERTILE CRESCENT
Copyright by C. S. HAMMOND & Co., N. Y.
Scale of Miles
0 100 200 300 400

Gaza on the Philistine Plain to twelve miles near Joppa, on the border of the Plain of Sharon, to less than two miles along the Plain of Dor south of Haifa. Mount Carmel, a northwesterly extension of the central highlands, interrupts the coastal plain where it meets the sea at the modern city of Haifa. North of Mount Carmel the Plain of Acco, some five to seven miles in width, ends abruptly at the white limestone cliffs of Rosh Hanikra, the ancient "Ladder of Tyre." Beyond this point narrow plains occur irregularly along the coast between the mountains that extend to the sea. This was the area which the Phoenicians occupied in antiquity. An extension of the Plain of Acco in a southeasterly direction parallel to and just north of the Carmel range connects to the Jordan Valley. This plain, known variously as the Plain of Jezreel and the Plain of Megiddo, bisects the central hills. The Galilee region lies to the north and the hill country of Ephraim (Samaria) stretches southward.

The hills of Galilee comprise one of four main regions into which the central highlands may be conveniently divided. Upper Galilee has heights reaching to nearly 4000 feet in the north to about 2700 feet further south. It is a southerly extension of the Lebanese mountains. Lower Galilee, in which Nazareth is nestled, does not exceed 2000 feet in elevation. This area is separated from Upper Galilee by a steep slope of from 1500 to 2000 feet in height. Further south, beyond the Plain of Jezreel, the hill country of Ephraim rises to elevations between 2500 and 3000 feet, with the southern area higher in elevation than the northern. No clearly delineated geographical features separate the hill country of Ephraim from the hills of Judea, but for convenience Jerusalem may be regarded as near the northern boundary of the latter. These hills rise slightly as one goes southward from Jerusalem to Hebron at about 3000 feet elevation, then some fifteen miles further south the hills fall away to the Negev, some 1500 to 1800 feet high. Further south beyond the Negev the Sinai massif rises to a height of nearly 9000 feet at Jebel Musa, the site of St. Catherine's Monastery.

To the west of the Judean hills, before one reaches the coastal plain, lie the low hills of the Shephelah, and to the east the land falls away rapidly into the forbidding wilderness of Judea, the desolate area in which the famous Dead Sea Scrolls were discovered. Here the terrain plunges into the Rift Valley along the Dead Sea, 1290 feet below sea level. Thus, a descent of over 3000 feet exists here within a distance of only ten to fifteen miles.

The awesome Rift Valley is a depression between two great geological faults. This cleft in the earth's surface begins in the plain between the Lebanon and Anti-Lebanon Mountains to the north and extends southward through Palestine, the Gulf of

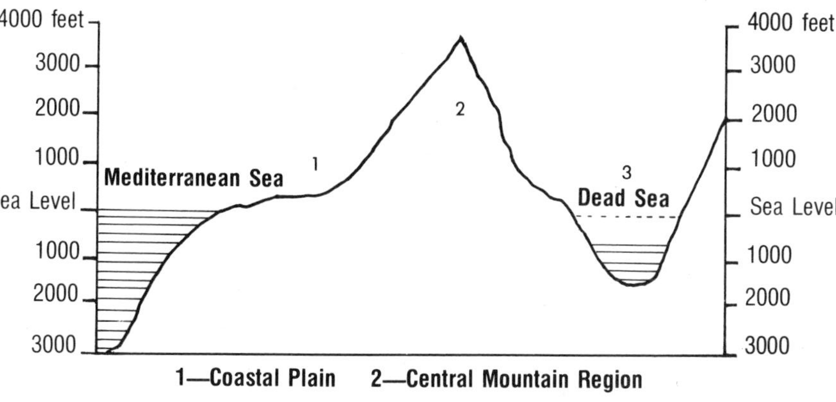

1—Coastal Plain 2—Central Mountain Region

3—Jordan Valley and Dead Sea

Eilat (Aqaba), and on into Lake Nyasa in Africa, a distance of 3,000 miles. (The Olduvai Gorge, site of the archaeological discoveries of Louis Leakey, is a part of this depression.) The Rift Valley in Palestine averages ten miles in width and varies in altitude from about 300 feet above sea level in the north to 1290 feet below sea level on the surface of the Dead Sea, the lowest point on earth apart from the ocean depths. Continuing southward, the elevation of the valley floor again increases to about 750 feet above sea level at the highest point in the Arabah before it descends again to sea level at the mouth of the Gulf of Eilat, the site of the biblical Ezion Geber. The Rift Valley can be conveniently divided into five areas—the Huleh Valley, the Sea of Galilee, the Jordan Valley, the Dead Sea, and the Arabah.

Extending southward from the base of Mount Hermon (9232 ft.), the Huleh Valley contained until recently an extensive body of water (Lake Huleh) along with surrounding swamps through which the upper Jordan River meandered. In modern times the river has been straightened and the swamps have been drained so that the present size of the lake is considerably reduced from its former size. South of the Lake Huleh region the Jordan flows swiftly down into the basin of the Sea of Galilee, 630 feet below sea level. The descent from 210 feet above sea level at Lake Huleh is made in a distance of ten miles.

The Sea of Galilee, thirteen miles long and seven miles across at its widest point, reaches a depth of almost 200 feet along its eastern shore where cliffs rise abruptly above it. The River Jordan flows through it to make it the only natural fresh-water lake in Palestine today.

The Jordan Valley proper extends southward from the Sea of

Galilee until it empties into the Dead Sea, approximately seventy miles further south. The name *Jordan* means literally "that which goes down," and the swift descent of the waters is slowed only by the torturous channel which they have carved out of the valley floor so that the actual course which the waters follow is three times longer than the distance by air. A low flat strip of dense jungle-like vegetation through which the river flows is called the Zor; the main part of the valley which stretches back to meet the hills on either side is called the Ghor.

As they empty into the Dead Sea, the waters of the Jordan bear a constant flow of dissolved minerals. The sea has no outlet, but the extremely high rate of evaporation maintains a uniform water level and a high concentration of salinity which prevents any form of marine life, hence its name. In the Bible, it is most frequently called the Salt Sea, but in the Roman period it was named the Sea of Asphalt. The sea, approximately forty-five miles long and ten miles across at its maximum width, is divided into two parts by the Lisan, a peninsula which extends into the sea from the eastern shore. North of the Lisan, the depth of the sea reaches 1200 feet which, when added to the surface level of 1292 feet below sea level, makes this one of the most astounding geological features on the face of the earth. To the south of the Lisan, the lake is only two to three miles across, and the depth is only thirty to thirty-five feet.

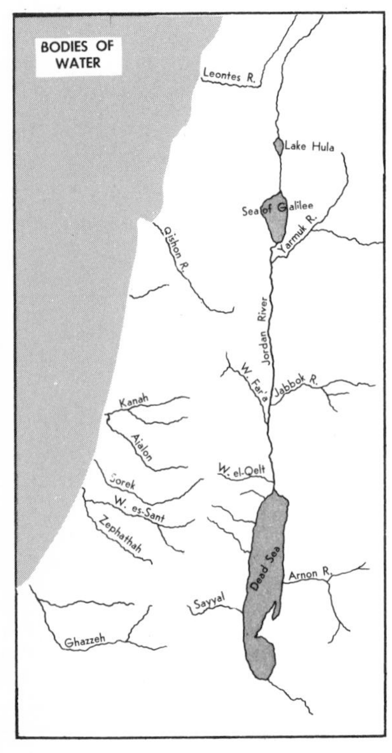

The Rift Valley from the Dead Sea southward to the Gulf of Eilat is called the Arabah. These 110 miles of valley floor lie between the mountains of the Negev to the west and of Edom to the east.

The Transjordanian hills which rise sharply from the eastern floor of the Rift Valley are broken into regions by wadis which penetrate into the valley from the east. These wadis are stream beds which are partially dry during most of the year but which during the rainy season may carry rapid, heavy flows of water. In the north, the Yarmuk enters the valley slightly south of the Sea of Galilee. It provides a natural boundry between the present states of Syria and Jordan, while in biblical times Bashan to the north was separated from Gilead to the south by the same wadi. Bashan, some 2000 feet in elevation, lies in the midst of an area of basalt caused by now extinct volcanoes. Its rich pasture lands fed the noted bulls of Bashan.

Gilead, a tableland higher and more rugged than Bashan, with heights approaching the 3000-foot level, is cleft by the Wadi Jabbok, now known as the Nahr ez-Zarqa. It enters the Rift Valley about midway between the Sea of Galilee and the Dead Sea, after flowing through an area that was occupied jointly in biblical times by the tribes of Reuben and Gad. The Ammonites also inhabited a part of the area. Rabbath-Ammon, their ancient capital, is now the modern city of Amman, Jordan.

No natural boundary separated the region of Moab from that of Gilead, but the northern boundary of Moab was generally eastward from the north end of the Dead Sea. Moab proper was divided into two parts by the Wadi el-Mujib, the Arnon of the Bible, which enters the Dead Sea midway along its eastern shore. Both areas consist of level tablelands with an elevation of 2000 to 2400 feet in the northern sector and up to 4000 feet in the southern.

The Wadi el-Hasa, the biblical brook Zered, which enters the Dead Sea at its southeastern corner, provided a natural boundary between Moab and Edom to the south. The mountains of Edom rise in places to a height in excess of 5000 feet. The King's Highway of the Bible traversed Bashan, Gilead, and Moab, and penetrated into Edom. From Edom another system of roads branched off. One led southward into the Arabian peninsula. Another led across the Arabah to the Negev and on to the city of Gaza. A third route followed the Arabah southward to the head of the Gulf of Eilat, then westward across the Sinai Peninsula to Egypt. Along the eastern fringes of the Transjordan hills the fertile land fades away into the forbidding deserts of Syria in the north and Arabia toward the south.

A combination of factors affects the patterns of rainfall and the supply of water so essential to life in Palestine—the geographical location, the prevailing winds, the landforms, and the geological substructures of the landforms.

The 30° north latitude line crosses Palestine just north of the Gulf of Eilat and extends through Cairo, Egypt. In the United States, the same line crosses northern Florida. The 32° line that crosses the hills of northern Galilee also crosses central Georgia. Most of the Holy Land lies in a subtropical zone with a modified Mediterranean climate, having a rainy season in the winter and a dry season in the summer. During the winter the prevailing winds blow out of the west-northwest across the Mediterranean, often producing violent thunderstorms, and then are forced upward by the mountains inland from the seashore. At other times easterly winds from the desert, the famous *khamsin*, flood the land with hot, dry air which scorches the countryside to a monotonous brown. The forces of nature contend for dominion over the land of Palestine, lying as it does between the desert and the sea. The pattern of rainfall tends to decrease from the north to the south and from the sea inland, averaging some thirty inches annually at Safad, in Upper Galilee, twenty-three

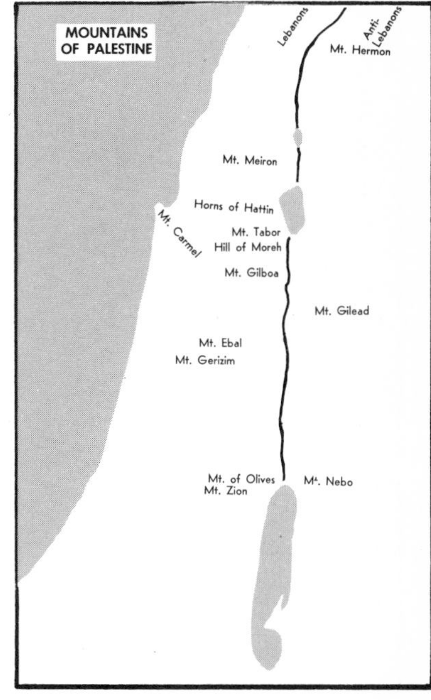

to twenty-five inches at Jerusalem, and eight to nine inches at Beer-sheba. Jericho, in the Jordan Valley, receives only four to six inches. Acco, along the northern seacoast, averages twenty-five to twenty-six inches; the Tel Aviv-Jaffa area, eighteen to twenty inches; and Gaza, fifteen inches. These local variations in rainfall are compounded by differences in altitude. (For example, though Jericho is at approximately the same latitude as Jerusalem, its extremely low altitude makes it an oasis in the desert, a northern extension of the desert conditions of the Negev into the Rift Valley. A few perennial springs in the area sustain life, for the rainfall is insufficient.) Marginal rainfall and rather severe fluctuations in annual rainfall combine to leave Palestine subject to droughts. The precariousness of life among the nomadic peoples along the desert fringes has produced throughout history a constant struggle for existence.

SUGGESTED TOPICS FOR FURTHER STUDY

1. The archaeology of prehistory in the lands of the Bible.
2. The development of the canon.
3. The rise of modern critical biblical scholarship.
4. The basic assumptions of modern biblical critics.
5. The ancient versions of the Bible—Greek, Syriac, Latin.
6. The development of the Masoretic Text.
7. The spectrum of views on inspiration and revelation.
8. History and historians—the changing concepts of what comprises history.
9. The idea of time.
10. The interrelationships between sedentarization and social organization.
11. The Sumerians—progenitors of Western civilization.
12. In the footsteps of Jesus—major routes in Palestine at the turn of the era.
13. The basic agriculture of ancient Palestine.
14. Water conservation and storage in ancient Palestine.
15. Investigate in greater detail one of the geographical regions of Palestine.
16. Investigate and sketch one of the chronological periods of biblical history.
17. Investigate one of the Iron Age kingdoms of Transjordan—Edom, Moab, Ammon, Aram.
18. Weather patterns in Palestine.
19. The nature of nomadism in the Near East.
20. Israelite adaptation of the hill country of Canaan to sedentary life.

RECOMMENDED READING

The works listed under the heading RECOMMENDED READING throughout this book are the most useful treatments, in the author's judgment. The FOR FURTHER READING entries provide additional sources for reading and research that will be useful for investigating the Topics for Further Study.

Albright, W. F., *From the Stone Age to Christianity* (Garden City, NY: Doubleday, 1957).

FOR FURTHER READING

General:

Useful articles on many of the topics mentioned in this chapter can be found in the following reference works:

Encyclopedia Judaica (Jerusalem: Keter, 1971).

The Interpreter's Dictionary of the Bible, ed. George A. Buttrick et al. (New York: Abingdon Press, 1962).

The New Bible Dictionary, ed. J. D. Douglas (Grand Rapids: Eerdmans, 1973).

Introductions to the Bible:

Anderson, Bernhard W., *Understanding the Old Testament* (Englewood Cliffs, NJ: Prentice Hall, 1975).

Archer, Gleason L., *A Survey of Old Testament Introduction* (Chicago: Moody Press, 1964).

Eissfeldt, Otto, *The Old Testament: An Introduction,* tr. P. Ackroyd (New York: Harper and Row, 1965).

Harrison, Roland K., *Introduction to the Old Testament* (Grand Rapids: Eerdmans, 1969).

Young, Edward J., *Introduction to the Old Testament* (Grand Rapids: Eerdmans, 1960).

The Bible as Literature:

Ackerman, James S., et al., *Teaching the Old Testament in English Classes* (Bloomington: Indiana University Press, 1973).

Beebe, H. Keith, *The Old Testament* (Belmont, CA: Dickenson, 1970).

Capps, Alton C., *The Bible as Literature* (New York: McGraw-Hill, 1971).

Freehof, Solomon B., *Preface to Scripture* (New York: Union of American Hebrew Congregations, 1964).

Gros Louis, Kenneth R. R., *Literary Interpretations of Biblical Narratives* (New York: Abingdon Press, 1974).

Henn, T. R., *The Bible as Literature* (New York: Oxford University Press, 1970).

Biblical History and Culture:

Bright, John, *A History of Israel* (Philadelphia: Westminster Press, 1959).

de Vaux, Roland, *Ancient Israel,* tr. J. McHugh (New York: McGraw-Hill, 1961).

Finegan, Jack, *Light from the Ancient Past* (Princeton: Princeton University Press, 1969).

Frankfort, Henri, *Before Philosophy* (Baltimore: Penguin, 1959).

Gray, John, *Archaeology and the Old Testament World* (New York: Thomas Nelson and Sons, 1962).

Kenyon, Kathleen, *Archaeology in the Holy Land,* third edition (New York: Praeger Publishers, 1970).

Noth, Martin, *The History of Israel,* tr. S. Godman, rev. P. R. Ackroyd, second edition (New York: Harper and Row, 1960).

Orlinsky, Harry M., *Ancient Israel* (Ithaca, NY: Cornell University Press, 1964).

Vawter, Bruce C. M., ed., *Background to the Bible Series,* twelve volumes (Englewood Cliffs, NJ: Prentice Hall, 1966–).

Biblical Geography:

Aharoni, Yohanan, *The Land of the Bible: A Historical Geography,* tr. A. F. Rainey (Philadelphia: Westminster Press, 1967).

Baley, Denis, *Geographical Companion to the Bible* (London: Lutterworth Press, 1963).

______, *The Geography of the Bible* (New York: Harper and Brothers, 1957).

May, Herbert G., ed., *Oxford Bible Atlas,* second edition (London: Oxford University Press, 1974).

Pfeiffer, Charles F., *Baker's Bible Atlas* (Grand Rapids: Baker, 1961).

2

The Development of Biblical Archaeology

Our definition of archaeology in the first chapter referred to the science as it stands today. Early usage of the word in the English language, however, referred to ancient history in general. This was in accordance with its derivation from the Greek, where it was synonymous with "ancient history." The noted archaeologist Père Roland de Vaux has noted that the prologue to the history of Greece by Thucydides, dealing with origins, was called "The Archaeology," while the history of Rome written in Greek by Denis of Halicarnassus bears the title *Roman Archaeology*. Josephus, who wrote the history of the Jews, entitled his work *Jewish Archaeology*. The Greek *archaios* ("ancient") and *logia* ("discourse, treatise of"), from which the English form ultimately derives, suggest this connotation. In the early eighteenth century, however, the term developed a meaning it did not originally bear—the systematic and descriptive study of antiquities.

When Sir Mortimer Wheeler, the renowned British archaeologist, was confronted with the question, "What in fact is archaeology?" he stated quite flatly, "I do not myself really know." His difficulty was not in giving a general definition, but in placing archaeology into a particular category of scholarly knowledge. The major source of that difficulty is to be found in the origins of archaeological research.

In one sense it can be said that interest in antiquities existed in antiquity; that is to say, in ancient times (as we construe them) man had an interest in his origins. When modern excavators

Cuneiform tablet, similar to thousands of others recovered at Nineveh from the Royal Assyrian Library.

came across the Assyrian libraries buried in Mesopotamia, they discovered that the Assyrians were indebted to literary collectors and librarians from the Old Babylonian times. The Babylonian collectors had themselves gathered Sumerian as well as Babylonian tablets into a library. The famous Royal Library discovered at Nineveh we now know had a long history. Part of it goes back to Tiglath-pileser III (744–727 B.C.). Sargon II (722–705) added many astrological works while his successor, Sennacherib (705–681), enlarged the collection and had it moved from Calah to Nineveh. In Nineveh Esarhaddon (681–670) added many mythological and historical documents. Then Ashurbanipal (669–627) enlarged the library into the magnificent collection that was discovered slightly more than a century ago. The monarch himself apparently mixed gentility with ferocity. According to A. T. Olmstead, he was schooled in both Akkadian and Sumerian, and on some of the documents he had inscribed: "In agreement with the original tablets and documents I caused copies of the Assyrian, Sumerian, and Akkadian to be written, compiled and revised in the chancellery of the experts, and as precious possessions of my royalty."

Jacquetta Hawkes has also called attention to a Thracian princess of the fifth century B.C. who made a collection of stone axes from prehistoric sites. Nebuchadnezzar's palace boasted an adjacent museum, containing statues, inscribed stones, and other relics from the past, and the last king of Babylonia, Nabonidus, much preferred the thrill of excavation to the pedantries of the monarchy.

These traces of "archaeological" interest from the ancient past mark man's universal characteristic of curiosity, but modern archaeology did not develop from such ancient activities. For our purposes we trace the rise of interest in biblical archaeology from the early travels of religious pilgrims to the Holy Land. For the sake of convenience, we can divide the development of biblical archaeology into four successive periods:

1) Period of pious pilgrims—third century A.D. to 1799.
2) The treasure hunters—circa 1800–1890.
3) Biblical archaeology becomes a science—1890 to World War II.
4) The modern era of biblical archaeology—1948–present.

Period of Pious Pilgrims

THIRD CENTURY A.D. TO 1799

During the early centuries of the common era devout Christians became interested in Palestine, the land of the origins of their faith, and many pilgrims made their way there to visit the places connected with the life of Jesus and the early activities of the apostles. Jewish interest in the historic homeland no doubt existed as well, but two tragic revolts against the Romans, one late in the first century and the other early in the second century A.D., resulted in a proscription, which lasted for several centuries, against Jews visiting Jerusalem. For Christian travelers, the road to the Holy Land became more accessible after the conversion of Constantine. St. Helena, the emperor's mother, was a pilgrim to the Holy Land early in the fourth century A.D., according to tradition, and she is said to have identified a number of sacred sites, but Eusebius of Caesarea (260–340) makes no mention of such a visit in his writings, nor does Bishop Cyril of Jerusalem (315–386), nor the Pilgrim of Bordeaux (ca. 333). The reports of the Pilgrim are among the earliest known records of a westerner's itinerary through the land. Eusebius left a record of his search for holy places in the *Onomasticon*, mentioning over one thousand place names. Of these, about one-third were given a definite location.

The expansion of Islam over Palestine in the seventh century slowed but never stopped the flow of pilgrims; however, few of the travelogues have survived until our day. The Crusades left Europe with a revived interest in the Holy Land, and the perceptive rulers of the area found it to their advantage economically to allow pilgrims to visit without a great deal of restriction. The freedom of access thus granted stimulated a gradual increase in the number of visitors to Palestine that has continued from medieval times until the present. The published accounts of the early visitors are of passing interest to the curious, but are hardly more than pious diaries, devoid of what might be called scientific interest.

In the fifteenth century an Italian merchant, Cyriac de Pizzicolli (b. 1391), became interested in ancient coins and works of art; he also was interested in copying inscriptions. He traveled in Egypt and Greece, and because he was careful to make systematic records and used an orderly method of investigation, he has been called by some the "father of archaeology." He died in the mid-fifteenth century, and his collections have been scattered.

A Dominican from Switzerland, Felix Schmidt, also known as Fabri, traveled to Palestine in 1480 and again in 1483. He explored the area from Jerusalem to Mount Sinai and made critical notes on locations. He also recorded observations on the customs of the inhabitants. His work evidences a new spirit of inquiry that distinguishes it from the usual medieval travel reports.

A German physician, Leonhard Rauchwolff (Rauwolf), visited Palestine in 1575, making notes on natural history and botany. A decade later Johann Zuallart indulged his interest in architecture and antiquities, producing a number of drawings. Then in the last years of the sixteenth century Johann van Kootwyck (Cotovicus), a Dutchman, visited the land and brought back accurate descriptions of a number of antiquities.

The most important seventeenth-century traveler to the Holy Land was an Italian nobleman, Pietro della Valle. He spent a decade traveling throughout the East, and his careful descriptions of his travels and of antiquities (published in 1650 as *Viaggi di Pietro della Valle il Pellegrino* with two other volumes published posthumously) profoundly stimulated European interest in the antiquities of the ancient world. Other important publications of the period came from the pens of the French Jesuit, Michael Nau, who visited Palestine in 1679, and the English Protestant cleric, Henry Maundrell, in 1703.

In this same period European travelers were penetrating the areas of ancient Mesopotamia and Persia. Both Rauwolf and della Valle had visited Mesopotamia, and there were others—Thomas Herbert, A. Daulier des Landes, and Jean-Baptiste Tavernier. But interest in the Holy Land continued to predominate. Bishop Pococke of England, in 1738, published more plans and drawings than any of his pilgrim predecessors, and they were the more significant in that he had gotten off the well-traveled routes on occasion. One of the most important publications was *Palaestina ex monumentis veteribus* (*Palestine Illustrated by Ancient Monuments*), put into print by the Dutch traveler, Adrian Reland. He had, probably for the first time in history, collected from known ancient and modern sources all the pertinent information about the antiquities of the Holy Land, digested this information critically, then published the results.

Johann Joachim Winckelmann
1717–1768

As important as were these increasingly critical studies of Palestinian antiquities, the eighteenth century also witnessed other currents of interest that were destined to contribute to the development of all archaeology. The Renaissance gave birth in Europe to a widespread interest in the fine arts of ancient Greece and Rome, particularly painted vases, sculpture, and the architecture of monumental ruins. But the recovery of art works of the classical world at first resembled little more than a treasure hunt, and destructive practices such as the use of ancient buildings as quarries for worked stone were commonplace. There was no concerted effort to use ancient works of art to develop a systematic understanding of the culture of the classical world. So things stood until the work of Johann J. Winckelmann

(1717–1768) who began to discriminate between artistic styles and to interpret the art of antiquity on a comparative basis. His work brought an order to the interpretation of ancient art that had previously been absent. For this reason Winckelmann has also been called "the Father of Archaeology," a title that fits only in terms of art and art history.

The eighteenth century saw the beginning, too, of what may be called modern archaeological excavations. These first organized efforts to excavate buried antiquities were initiated at Herculaneum (1738) and Pompeii (1748), two Roman cities that had been buried by the massive explosion of Mount Vesuvius, near Naples, in A.D. 79.

The close of the eighteenth century witnessed an event of singular significance when an officer of Napoleon's Egyptian expedition discovered a stone inscribed with Greek and two forms of Egyptian—demotic and hieroglyphic. Through the work of a brilliant French scholar, Jean François Champollion, the Rosetta Stone became the key to deciphering the ancient Egyptian system of writing. The stone, however, came into the possession of England as a trophy of war after the French capitulation at Alexandria in 1801. It was brought to the British Museum where it is still on exhibit.

Another stream of interest which was beginning in this period and which was later to contribute to the development of archaeology was the research into the great antiquity of man. John Frere, an Englishman, wrote a letter to the secretary of the Society of Antiquaries of London in 1797 in which he described the discovery of worked flints in a gravel pit. On the basis of the layers of soil above the stratum in which the flints were found, he reached the conclusion that they were from the remote past. The ideas of Frere were not widely circulated or accepted, however; it was the work of the Frenchman, Boucher de Perthes, that convinced the scholarly world of the great antiquity of man. His interests in the fossil and artifactual evidence began early in the nineteenth century and resulted in the publication of his conclusions in 1860 in a work entitled *De l'homme antédiluvien et ses oeuvres.* Two English scholars, Sir Joseph Prestwich and Sir John Evans, were impressed by de Perthes' work. They in turn convinced the learned world of man's great antiquity.

J. C. Boucher de Perthes
1778–1868

Two other ideas were developing concurrently with that of man's great age, and both were to contribute to archaeological theory and practice. These ideas were revolutionary geological theories about the extreme age of the earth, and a system of classifying materials into three ages—stone, bronze, and iron. The new approach to the geological record of the earth came through the work of such men as Sir Charles Lyell (1797–1875), who published his *Principles of Geology* in three volumes between 1830 and 1833. He taught that the earth's stratification was primarily the result of natural forces—changes in land and sea level and the work of rivers—rather than universal disasters and great floods. The three-age system of relative dating was first developed in Scandinavia. P. F. Suhm, in his *History of Denmark, Norway and Holstein* (1776), noted that tools and weapons from the area were at first made of stone, then of copper, and finally of iron. The work of S. Thorlacius (1802) and L. S. Vedel Simonsen (1813–16) furthered the acceptance of the three-age sequence for prehistory.

In 1859 the *Origin of Species* by Charles Darwin was published. His work stimulated the search for evidence of man's existence in the remote periods of time that were being recognized as a result of the new geology. Men began to think in terms of paleolithic (Old Stone Age) and neolithic (New Stone Age), two descriptive terms introduced by Sir John Lubbock in a book published in 1865. The evolutionary theory provided a new intellectual environment in which anthropology and its related discipline, archaeology, could flourish.

The Treasure Hunters

CIRCA 1800—1890

Claudius James Rich
1787–1821

The intellectual ferment that characterized Europe in the closing decades of the eighteenth century, which we have noted briefly above, continued into the succeeding century. Claudius J. Rich visited the ruins of Babylon in 1811, excavating a quantity of clay tablets, inscribed stones, and seals. His *Memoir on the Ruins of Babylon* stimulated the interest of scholars in the area and in the peculiar cuneiform tablets. Rich returned to Babylon in 1817, and his interests brought him to Nineveh and Nimrud in 1820 and to Persepolis in 1821. Paul E. Botta, a physician and the French consular agent in Mosul, began excavations on the mound of ancient Nineveh in 1842, but, failing to find anything of monumental size, turned to the site of Khorsabad, ten miles north. Here he discovered almost immediately huge sculptures from the ruins of the palace of Sargon II. With the aid of the French government, his activities continued and material began to flow to Paris and the Louvre. In 1845, Austen Henry Layard began excavations at Nineveh (which Botta had earlier abandoned). His discovery, almost immediately, of the palace of Ashurnasirpal II brought into the British Museum treasures superior to those discovered by Botta. That the search for

Mesopotamian antiquities was moved more by national pride than by scientific inquiry is evident in a transaction between the British Museum and Layard. Two thousand pounds was to be made available to Layard providing he "obtain the largest possible number of well-preserved objects of art at the least possible outlay of time and money." The search for the most auspicious finds and the haste involved led to the destruction of valuable materials, partly because the treasure hunters did not realize the value of the materials they were handling.

Austen Henry Layard
1817–1894

The Mesopotamian activity led to the discovery of many cuneiform texts, and as early as 1815 a German schoolteacher named Georg F. Grotefend deciphered Persian cuneiform as the result of a study which he had begun in 1802. His accomplishment received little notice in scholarly circles, however. As a result, progress in reading cuneiform was very slow until 1835. In that year Henry Rawlinson began the arduous task of copying the Behistun Inscription, a trilingual record of the exploits of Darius I. By 1846 Rawlinson had deciphered the Old Persian text and was progressing in the study of the Elamite and the Akkadian versions. Between 1846 and 1855 Rawlinson, Edward Hincks, and Jules Oppert succeeded in deciphering the Akkadian script; however, for twenty more years many scholars were not convinced that it could be read accurately.

Apart from advances in understanding ancient languages, however, little progress was being made in the mid-nineteenth century toward scientific excavation. In Palestine as in much of the ancient Near East, the search for museum antiquities predominated, but the paucity of such materials in the Holy Land led to other interests. Early in the century an interest in surveying the surface of the land developed. In 1805–07, Ulrich Seetzen explored Transjordan, discovering Caesarea Philippi, Gerasa (Jerash) and Amman. Johann Ludwig Burckhardt worked from 1801 to 1812, making three major contributions: the discovery of Petra, a careful recording of many Arabic place names, and the copying of certain inscriptions. His enthusiasm for Arabian exploration led him to become a Muslim, enabling him to visit sites and to copy inscriptions that were otherwise inaccessible. He is buried in a Muslim cemetery in Cairo.

Edward Robinson
1794–1863

The work of Edward Robinson and Eli Smith, his companion, in 1838 marked a significant advance in the topographical analysis of Palestine. They spent three months making a careful survey, noting the hour, compass point, and so on, of each place and landmark, and this on horseback. A contemporary who was also a researcher of topography wrote, "The works of Robinson and Smith surpass the total of all previous contributions to

Palestinian geography from the time of Eusebius and Jerome to the early nineteenth century." They were able to locate for the first time for Western scholarship scores of biblical sites. W. F. Albright called it a complete revolution in Palestinian exploration. Many times Robinson and Smith found that a town's ancient biblical name was still preserved in the site's modern Arabic designation.

The most comprehensive surface survey of western Palestine was conducted by C. R. Conder and H. H. Kitchener between 1872 and 1878. Six thousand square miles were surveyed and mapped at a scale of one inch to the mile. Only in recent years has their work been superseded by modern aerial techniques.

F. de Saulcy has been called the first modern excavator of a Palestinian site, but his work was of little permanent value due to his imprecise excavating methods. His excavations in 1850–51 and 1863 in the environs of Jerusalem preceded the first organized investigation under the Palestine Exploration Fund. This fund was established in 1865, and in 1867 Charles Warren was excavating in Jerusalem with its support. Excavations had begun, but they could hardly be called scientific; nevertheless, important discoveries were being made. Charles Clermont-Ganneau in particular, beginning in the 1870s, made many valuable finds. In 1871 he discovered the important inscription which prohibited Gentiles from entering the court of the temple,

Greek inscription from the time of Christ forbidding Gentiles to enter the inner recesses of the Herodian temple. This inscription was discovered by G. Clermont-Ganneau.

and he recovered and sent to the Louvre the Mesha (Moabite) Stone.

The stage was being set, however, for dramatic advances in archaeological research. Heinrich Schliemann began to dig at the site of ancient Troy in Asia Minor in 1870. He discovered that the mound was composed of layers of debris that remained from the destruction of ancient cities that had occupied the site. He did not make use, however, of any method of excavation by which the dating of the various layers could be determined. Wilhelm Dorpfeld joined Schliemann in 1882, and he continued the work after Schliemann's death in 1892. Although he brought order and planning into the excavation, he took no account of the pottery recovered. The value of painted pottery for ascertaining chronology had become evident to classical archaeologists by the 1880s, but since the primary interest was in ancient art, no attention was paid to unpainted sherds.

Heinrich Schliemann
1822–1890

The major breakthrough needed to place archaeological excavation on a firm scientific basis came in 1890 in Palestine. It involved careful technical observation of the debris layers being excavated and correlation of the pottery recovered with the sequence of the layers. Later, the man who transformed archaeology from a search for treasure to a concern with trash would write:

> In all ages there has been destruction for gold and valuables, and in the Renascence a ruthless seizure of marbles and stone work. To that succeeded destruction for the sake of art, excavations in which everything was wrecked for the chance of finding a beautiful statue. Then in the last generation or two, inscriptions became valued, and temple sites in Greece and in Egypt, and palaces in Babylonia, have been turned over, and nothing saved except a stone or a tablet which was inscribed. At last a few people are beginning to see that history is far wider than any one of these former aims, and that, if ever we are to understand the past, every fragment from it must be studied and made to tell all it can.

Biblical Archaeology Becomes a Science

1890 TO WORLD WAR II

The missing tool (a means of scientific dating) required for the accurate interpretation of archaeological finds was discovered and introduced into Palestinian archaeology by one man, Sir W. M. Flinders Petrie. Petrie (1853–1942) came from England to Egypt in 1880 to measure and study the pyramids of Gizeh. In the process he became enamored of the relics of Egyptian antiquity and during a long and fruitful career in archaeological research became a stellar Egyptologist. In the course of his exca-

Sir William M. Flinders Petrie
1853–1942

vations in the 1880s at Tanis, Naucratis, and Hawara, Petrie became convinced that, if enough attention were given to it, *unpainted* pottery could be just as effective an instrument for dating as the painted type used by classical archaeologists. Then, due to unstable conditions in Egypt, Petrie spent six weeks during 1890 excavating a Palestinian mound, Tell el-Hesi, near Gaza. Tell el-Hesi, which rises to approximately 120 feet above the surrounding plain, provided Petrie with a vertical section in which he could systematically observe and record the position of each characteristic potsherd in the excavation and correlate its position with architectural remains, the stratification, and other artifacts. He was able to correlate several strata with Egyptian dynasties, arranging thereby a fairly accurate relative chronology for the occupational history of the mound. The humble potsherd, the rubbish on the ground of any excavated site, was thus elevated to become the major implement in the archaeologist's hand in his attempts to pry open the vault of time.

In 1891, Petrie published *Tell el Hesy (Lachish).* Though this identification of the site has been proved in error, his report does emphasize the importance of stratigraphical excavation. Frank J. Bliss assumed the leadership of the work during 1891–93, continuing Petrie's methods and confirming his results. In 1901 Petrie published his principle of sequence-dating based on the changing forms of pottery. Thus, once the evolution in type of a particular class of pottery was established, a stratum in a tell could be dated relative to other strata on the basis of the forms of pottery associated with it. These two principles—stratigraphy and typology—are the basis for all modern scientific archaeological research.

Petrie had founded the British School of Archaeology in Egypt in 1895, and soon after a similar organization in Jerusalem. Other important schools of archaeology also came into existence near the turn of the century. The Dominican order had purchased property in 1893 for a building on the northern edge of Jerusalem. The Ecole Biblique et Archéologique was subsequently built on the site. In 1900 a cooperative venture was begun among the Americans. The American Schools of Oriental Research constructed a building on Saladin Road in Jerusalem in 1910 to house their activities. Today the complex bears the name of the Albright Institute of Archaeological Research. All these organizations are currently active in research.

In the decades between Petrie's pioneering work at Tell el-Hesi and the outbreak of World War I, the new techniques were applied and improved upon at numerous sites (and neglected at others). It was a busy period. Bliss and R. A. S. Macalister advanced the arts of stratigraphy and pottery dating at several mounds in the Shephelah, and then Macalister, attempting the impossible in his single-handed assault on Tell Gezer (1902–09), rather slighted them. The same problem of inadequate staffing and its corollary, inadequate attention to stratigraphy and pottery chronology, plagued German digs at Taanach and Megiddo between 1902 and 1905. The situation was at last remedied at Jericho in 1908–09 by the well-staffed German-Austrian expedition headed by Ernst Sellin and Carl Watzinger. This mission was able both to obtain good stratigraphical results and to publish them fully, though their system of pottery chronology was somewhat wanting. This was in part due to the inadequacy of comparative materials of established date and in part due to errors of interpretation by the major excavators. For example, Macalister had not recognized a long gap in occupation at the Gezer site. He therefore confused the dating of the pottery, for he assumed a continuous occupation. On the other hand, in 1908 a three-year campaign at Samaria was initiated under G. A. Reisner and C. S. Fisher. This effort was competently staffed and made significant advances in surveying and recording the finds in detail, both in drawings and in photographic records. (The first use of photographs to illustrate an archaeological report was probably by Alexander Conze of exacavations on Samothrace in 1873 and 1875.) But improvements in excavation techniques in the period before the war were not matched by clarifications in the chronology.

Following World War I, in the fifteen years from 1920 to 1935, archaeological excavation in Palestine proceeded on an unprecedented scale. Both the number of archaeologists present and the cooperation among them increased. Though errors were

This photograph of a Ptolemalion frieze was taken by Alexander Conze. His use of photography opened a new era in archaeological publications.

William Foxwell Albright
1891–1971

Nelson Glueck
1900–1971

made by some excavators, for the most part knowledge of the history of Palestine and the techniques for arriving at that knowledge were advanced on every hand. Perhaps the most signal of the technical advances was the firm establishment of the chronology of Palestinian pottery. This was due in large part to the work of William F. Albright from 1926 to 1932 during the excavations of Tell Beit Mirsim (possibly biblical Debir). The significance of Albright's contribution was emphasized by the distinguished Harvard scholar, G. E. Wright, who noted that the first volume of the Tell Beit Mirsim publication provided "a comparative study of Palestinian ceramics which, for the first time, plotted in writing the typological and stratigraphical evolution of the chief forms, while fixing their chronology within certain well-delimited periods." Though refinements continue to be made, Albright's chronology is still standard.

Of the myriad other excavations prior to the outbreak of hostilities in World War II, several are worthy of note. John Garstang, working at Jericho from 1929 to 1936, discovered an early culture termed prepottery Neolithic. At Samaria, a joint expedition led by J. W. Crowfoot both clarified Reisner's work and made many new discoveries. From 1932 until his tragic death at the hands of highwaymen in 1938, J. L. Starkey headed an important excavation at Lachish (Tell ed-Duweir). There was an attempt, beginning in 1925 and continuing through 1939, to make a complete excavation of Megiddo, one of the major mounds in Palestine. The concept was to remove the mound layer by layer, and a sizable quantity of material was removed, but, fortuitously, the attempt failed. The bulk of the site was left for the more advanced techniques of a later time. The progress of the Megiddo work was somewhat hindered by several changes of directors and the still-developing state of pottery chronology.

Additional excavations of this period could be noted, but only two further areas of interest will be mentioned. Palestinian archaeology has developed a concern not only with biblical history, but with prehistory as well. Thus, in 1928–34, Dorothy Garrod excavated a number of caves in Palestine which yielded important paleolithic and mesolithic finds, including among the latter the "Natufian" culture unearthed near Mount Carmel. Garstang's Neolithic finds at Jericho have been mentioned; more recent excavations at that site have produced new evidence of this culture and have connected its antecedents with the Mount Carmel finds. The Pontifical Biblical Institute sponsored excavations at Teleilat el-Ghassul, at the northeast tip of the Dead Sea, in 1929–38, where were found remains of a major Chalcolithic culture, now referred to as Ghassulian. Related prehistoric finds have now been made near Beer-sheba and Gaza; in addition, Chalcolithic remains have been found at En Gedi and in the Judean wilderness in the Nahal Mishmar.

The other area to be mentioned is the surface exploration of Transjordan undertaken by Nelson Glueck in 1933 and continued annually until 1946, when political circumstances prohibited his work in the area. It is interesting to note that Glueck developed an expertise in Palestinian pottery as a potsherd washer for W. F. Albright. On the basis of the sherds which he observed and collected, Glueck was able to infer the periods of occupation for the areas which he surveyed. This included a survey of the Negev area over a several year period beginning in 1946. The most intriguing discovery of his work is that for long periods of time these marginal regions were devoid of permanent settlers, and were given over to nomadic wanderers.

George Ernest Wright
1909–1974

The Modern Era of Biblical Archaeology

1948–PRESENT

Since the close of World War II, refinements and improvements in excavation techniques have continued to be made. Of primary importance has been the work of Dame Kathleen Kenyon at Jericho from 1952 through 1958, using stratigraphical techniques adopted from her teacher, Sir Mortimer Wheeler. The work at Shechem from 1956 to 1964, led by G. E. Wright, generated the project at Gezer, directed by W. G. Dever and then J. D. Seger, in the years from 1966 to 1973. The latter project employed an Americanized version of the Kenyon-Wheeler methodology, and it functioned as a practical school for aspiring archaeologists. Space does not permit mention of many other noteworthy projects which have been undertaken, but one cannot overlook the important manuscript and artifactual discoveries in the Judean wilderness (the Dead Sea Scrolls and others) as a landmark in biblical archaeology. Mention must be made, also, of the rise of a school of skilled Israeli archaeologists such as Yigael Yadin, Benjamin Mazar, Ruth Amiran, and others.

Kathleen Kenyon

One other noteworthy trend of post-World War II archaeology is the application of physical science techniques to the analysis of archaeological data. The carbon-14 method of dating organic materials is but one of a group of highly specialized techniques that include such procedures as neutron activation, thermoluminescence dating, and resistivity surveying. The biological sciences, too, are playing an increasingly important role in archaeological research, and this trend gives every evidence of continuing as modern man becomes more concerned about the ecology of the present compared to that of the past. The excavations at Caesarea Maritima are pioneering in the application of the computer and modern statistical methods to archaeological research.

This review of the development of modern biblical and general archaeology cannot pretend to be exhaustive. Many sites which are discussed in the following pages have not even been mentioned. The bibliography will indicate where further, more complete treatments may be found. It is hoped that what has been presented will provide an adequate background of the infancy and childhood, as it were, of the more mature archaeological methods referred to below.

SUGGESTED TOPICS FOR FURTHER STUDY

1. The influence of Constantine's conversion on European travel to Palestine.
2. The influence of Eusebius on the work of Edward Robinson.
3. European interest in the Holy Land as a result of the Crusades.
4. A profile of the travels of Pietro della Valle.
5. The rediscovery of Pompeii.
6. Johann J. Winckelmann—the father of archaeology?
7. The story of the Rosetta Stone.
8. Nineteenth-century England and the development of archaeology.
9. The treasures of the Louvre from the ancient Near East.
10. Ancient Near Eastern treasures in the British Museum.
11. Antiquities from the Middle East in the Berlin Museum.
12. The Behistun Inscription—its discovery, message, and significance.
13. Edward Robinson—topographer extraordinaire.
14. Highlights in the history of the Palestine Exploration Fund.
15. The discoveries of Charles Clermont-Ganneau.
16. The career of Sir Flinders Petrie.
17. W. F. Albright's influence on biblical archaeology.
18. Nelson Glueck—his surface surveys.
19. John D. Rockefeller's role in Palestinian archaeology.
20. Current trends in archaeology.
21. Recent archaeological discoveries.
22. A survey of leading American archaeologists.

RECOMMENDED READING

Albright, W. F., *The Archaeology of Palestine* (Baltimore: Penguin Books, 1954), pp. 23–48.

Avi-Yonah, M., *The Holy Land from the Persian to the Arab Conquest* (Grand Rapids: Baker Book House, 1966).

Ceram, C. W., *The March of Archaeology* (New York: Alfred A. Knopf, 1970).

Daniel, Glyn, *A Hundred Years of Archaeology* (London: Duckworth, 1967).

———, *Man Discovers His Past* (New York: Thomas Y. Crowell Co., 1968).

———, *The Origins and Growth of Archaeology* (New York: Thomas Y. Crowell Co., 1971).

———, *The Three Ages* (Cambridge, England: Cambridge University Press, 1943).

Hammond, Peter B., *Physical Anthropology and Archaeology* (New York: MacMillan Co., 1964).

Hawkes, Jacquetta, *The World of the Past* (New York: Alfred A. Knopf, 1963), pp. 3–104.

Mellaart, J., *The Neolithic of the Near East* (London: Thames & Hudson, 1975).

Oates, D. & J., *The Rise of Civilization* (London: Elsevier-Phaidon, 1976).

Williams, Walter G., *Archaeology in Biblical Research* (Nashville: Abingdon Press, 1965), pp. 23–35.

Wright, G. Ernest, "Archaeological Method in Palestine—An American Interpretation," *Eretz-Israel* (1969), pp. 120–33.

———, "The Phenomenon of American Archaeology in the Near East" in *Near Eastern Archaeology in the Twentieth Century* (essays in honor of Nelson Glueck), ed. James A. Sanders (Garden City, NY: Doubleday, 1970), pp. 3–40.

FOR FURTHER READING

Casson, Stanley, *The Discovery of Man* (London: H. Hamilton, 1939).

Heizer, R. F., ed., *Man's Discovery of His Past: Literary Landmarks in Archaeology* (Englewood Cliffs, NJ: Prentice Hall, 1962).

Hilprecht, H. V., ed., *Explorations in Bible Lands During the Nineteenth Century* (Philadelphia: A. J. Holman and Company, 1903).

Petrie, W. M. F., *Methods and Aims in Archaeology* (New York: MacMillan & Co., Ltd., 1904).

Pfeiffer, Charles F., ed., *The Biblical World: A Dictionary of Biblical Archaeology* (Grand Rapids: Baker, 1972).

3

Money, Men, Methods, and Materials

Money

Throughout its history, progress in archaeological research has been the result of the interplay between the factors of money, men, methods, and materials. One can reflect upon the early stages of archaeology, as we have done in the preceding chapter, and easily perceive that "there were giants in the earth in those days." Men like Edward Robinson, the explorer of the surface of Palestine in 1838, Heinrich Schliemann, the discoverer and excavator of ancient Troy from 1870 on, and Sir Flinders Petrie, who established the science of stratigraphy at Tell el-Hesi in 1890, worked virtually alone. These were individualists, either by choice or by necessity, who pursued their dreams, forging ahead of their contemporaries while they developed techniques that continue to be influential in current archaeology.

In the case of Schliemann we find a man who was independently wealthy; he simply financed his own expeditions. Few archaeologists have been so fortunate. All archaeologists find it easy to want to excavate a particular site. The fulfillment of the idea, however, even to a modest degree, requires enormous energy and conducive circumstances, not the least of which is ample funding for the project. The initial task of the archaeologist is to raise money, for without it site, tools, and workers cannot be brought together. Acquiring the financial backing for an expedition is doubtless the most disagreeable and the most necessary aspect of archaeology.

How are archaeological expeditions in the lands of the Bible financed? In the past, most excavations have been funded by educational institutions or by research organizations, with the funds ultimately coming from either private or public sources. The Palestine Exploration Fund was established in England in 1865. It has been one of the substantial and consistent underwriters of archaeological work in Palestine over the years. Its revenues derive largely from small donors. The remainder comes from more substantial individual grants. (Besides supporting excavations, the Palestine Exploration Fund financed the survey of western Palestine by C. R. Conder and H. H. Kitchener in 1872–78.) The support for the French Ecole Biblique et Archéologique operated by the Dominican order, comes from both government and church circles. German excavations have usually been supported by governmental and institutional funds. Wealthy individuals and families have supported archaeological work in the past. For example, John D. Rockefeller supported the Megiddo excavations and also supplied funds for establishing the Palestine Archaeological Museum in Jerusalem. The Rothschild family of France has long supported archaeological research. A recent project funded by them was the excavation of Hazor by Professor Yigael Yadin. The Corning Company provides an example of a business corporation that has supported archaeological research. Motivated in part by their interest in the manufacture of glass, they have supported excavations at ancient glassmaking sites in Palestine.

The financial undergirding of excavations in Palestine has been multinational in scope. In 1898 the Deutsche Orient-Gesellschaft was founded under the patronage of the German emperor. German expeditions have worked at Jericho, Megiddo, Taanach, and Shechem. In 1908 Harvard University began the excavation of Samaria. A wealthy American banker, Joseph Schiff, supplied the funds. Sir Charles Marston and Sir Henry Wellcome provided British funds for the excavation of Tell ed-Duweir, ancient Lachish, from 1932 to 1938. The University of Pennsylvania Museum supported the excavations at Beth-shan from 1921 to 1933. The American excavations at Megiddo (1925–39), while financed by Rockefeller monies, were carried out by the Oriental Institute of the University of Chicago. The American School of Oriental Research in Jerusalem was founded in 1900. It has played a significant role in numerous excavations, but it has normally been forced to operate with restricted funds. Projects at Tell en-Nasbeh, Tell Beit Mirsim, and Beth-shemesh

Tell ed-Duweir (biblical Lachish).

were carried out by the ASOR between 1926 and 1936, but most of the organization's efforts have been cooperative ventures with others. The Hebrew University opened in 1925. It has produced a number of important archaeologists. Noteworthy among the Israeli scholars was E. L. Sukenik, the father of Yigael Yadin and the purchaser of three of the original Dead Sea Scrolls. Another important Israeli institution is Tel Aviv University. Recently it fielded an expedition at Tell Seba, near Beersheba.

What has been said above substantiates the view of G. Ernest Wright that "money from pious, conservative, or fundamentalist sources has never played a very important role in archaeology. The major excavations have been sponsored by sources dominated by a broad humanistic interest." There is currently a trend, nevertheless, for increased financial and staff support derived from conservative circles. The excavations at Tell Dan are supported by a consortium of thirty-six institutions, and a number of these are theological seminaries or church-related institutions. This is but one example that can easily be multiplied. Evangelical involvement in archaeological research, both in the form of financial support and the work of active field archaeologists, has seldom been completely absent from Palestine. It is hoped that the trend toward the cooperation of those archaeologists who are motivated primarily by humanistic concerns and those moved by a deep religious interest will continue. Cooperation should result in benefits to both interest groups and bring continued progress in research.

Cooperative efforts are essential in the face of the worldwide scourge of inflation and its adverse effect on the archaeological enterprise in recent years. As early as the 1960s the excavations undertaken in Jerusalem by Kathleen Kenyon required the cooperative funding of the British School of Archaeology in Jerusalem, the Department of Antiquities of the Hashemite Kingdom of Jordan, the Palestine Archaeological Museum, the Ecole Biblique, the Royal Ontario Museum, the Commission des Fouilles of the French Government, the University of Toronto, Victoria University, the University of Trinity College, the University of St. Michael's College, Knox College, University College, McGill University, the Palestine Exploration Fund, the British Academy, the Russell Trust, Birmingham City Museum, the Ashmolean Museum, the Universities of Oxford, Cambridge, London, Glasgow, Durham, Liverpool, Sheffield, and Trinity College, Dublin, along with the National Geographic Society of America, Emory University (Georgia), the Southern Baptist Seminary (Louisville), the Pennsylvania Museum, the University of Sydney, the Australian Institute of Archaeology (Melbourne), the Otago Museum (New Zealand), and a number of private individuals. In short, it was an international effort.

Excavations at Caesarea are supported by a consortium of twenty-three institutions and organizations. Even with this broadly-based support the project employs volunteer laborers, college students who pay their own transportation costs in order to participate in the excavation. In addition, no staff member receives a salary from expedition funds, nor are they provided with transportation to and from Israel. Archaeologists today often pursue their interest at a considerable personal sacrifice.

Men

Apart from that most essential ingredient, money, the basic components of an archaeological expedition consist of a promising site, an available staff of workers, and the necessary equipment. A site may be an ancient necropolis, a cave, the remains of a solitary building complex, or any similar area exhibiting evidence of human occupation or activity. The usual site for excavation in the lands of the Bible, however, is a *tell*. A tell is a mound containing the debris of human occupation that has accumulated at a site, built up in successive layers over the centuries through a sequence of habitation, destruction, and reconstruction. Augmenting the debris of human activity is often a liberal measure of wind-blown sand and dirt, accumulated in those periods when the site was devoid of human occupation. Each tell came into existence because of the advantages which the site offered to its inhabitants. In the Middle East, two of the features that attract human settlement are a nearby perennial source of water and adjacent pasturage or fertile fields. A site may have been located adjacent to an ancient commercial route, or it may have been naturally defensible, or it may have commanded a strategic position. The same advantages that led to the initial occupation continued to draw later settlers. A long history of habitation could thus be established. Such tells are scattered over the face of the ancient Orient except for the Nile Valley. Egypt's long history of continuous culture within the safe confines of the river valley hindered the development of tells. Its history is recorded in tombs rather than tells.

The most attractive sites for excavation have been those with a direct connection to the Bible. A number of places mentioned in the Bible have retained their identity since antiquity. Jerusalem is a prime example of an unquestioned biblical site, but it is also an example of the restrictions such a site may impose on the archaeologist. Most of Jerusalem cannot be excavated now because of modern occupation. Sites have been tentatively identified upon the basis of similarities between the biblical description and the geographical surroundings. Beth-shemesh, located in the Wadi al-Ṣarar (which is most likely the biblical Valley of Sorek), is thus identified with Tell er-Rumeilah. The nearby Arab village of Ain Shems has preserved a part of the ancient name, although the location has shifted slightly from the tell proper. There are risks, therefore, in identifying a site solely on the basis of a modern name. Tell el-Jib provides an example of a site identified largely upon the basis of the similarity of the modern Arabic name. From jar handles which were recovered there, modern excavators have positively identified the site as ancient Gibeon. A number of sites have still not been definitely identified, including the location of the famous Philistine cities of Gath and Ekron; but in the past century and a half, beginning with the pioneering work of Robinson and Smith in 1838, literally hundreds of sites have been identified through surface surveys. In recent times aerial surveys have also contributed information on site identification. On the basis of these identifications, famous sites such as Megiddo, Jericho, and Samaria have been excavated.

A more recent trend has been the selection of sites on the basis of their potential for providing the specific kinds of information being sought by the archaeologist. For example, the Institute of Archaeology of Tel Aviv University has a particular interest in the royal city of the Israelite period at Tell Beer-sheba. Their interests in the Tell Masos excavations focus on the Middle Bronze Age enclosure. The work at Caesarea by the joint expedition mentioned above will throw light on the important Roman and Byzantine periods. Thus, particular sites may be selected for excavation in the hope of filling out the lacunae in the knowledge of specific periods.

Chance finds may lead to excavations. In Israel particularly, and to a considerable degree in the other modern states now occupying the area of ancient Syro-Palestine, construction of highways and buildings may lead to immediate "salvage" operations. The construction of a dam across the Euphrates River by the government of Syria led to a massive salvage effort very recently. In most salvage operations the construction is halted until the archaeologists have exploited the unexpected appearance of antiquities.

Easy accessibility may be a factor in the selection of a site for excavation. An expedition operating on a very limited budget would count this as a real advantage. Archaeology students at the University of Jordan began excavating Tell Siran early in 1972. The site is on the university's campus, so the costs of the project are relatively small.

Political factors may play a role in site selection. The Masada excavations were supported by the State of Israel, at least in part, in order to establish visible historical connections between the modern state and the band of heroic Jewish revolutionaries who died there in the Roman era. In a similar manner, the Hashemite Kingdom of Jordan has exploited the ruins of an Omayyad palace, located just north of Jericho and erected in A.D. 724, as evidence of the long-standing Arab connections with the area.

Political factors have also played a role in slowing archaeological work in the Bible lands. During the period from 1936 to 1952, Palestine was fraught with political unrest that eased only with the establishment of a cease-fire between the newly established State of Israel and the Hashemite Kingdom of Jordan. Little excavation could be accomplished during that period. As an aftermath of the Six Day War (1967), archaeologists who may desire to excavate in the occupied areas of the west bank of the Jordan River are intimidated. Arab spokesmen have vowed that any archaeologist who excavates in that area will thereafter be barred from excavating in any other Arab country. Archaeological activity is a national resource jealously guarded in the lands of the Bible.

From the foregoing discussion it is apparent that the reasons for the selection of particular sites for excavation are as varied as the people who excavate. One other motive for excavating should be mentioned, that is, in order to re-excavate. Dame Kathleen Kenyon has stated the rationale for re-excavation succinctly: "In Palestine the greater part of results of the major excavations before the First World War on sites such as Gezer, Samaria, and Jericho cannot be relied upon, and much revision is required of the results of the excavations between the two wars, though improvements in technique did result in sufficient information being provided for necessary reinterpretation." Re-excavation aims, therefore, at clarifying problems posed by previous expeditions.

Whatever the basic impetus may be, an individual, a small group of archaeologists, an institution, or a consortium of institutions may undertake an expedition. Permission for the project from the host government is essential, of course, and the supervision of the work by the state will follow. Governmental license does not guarantee easy access to the site, however. An extreme example of the difficulties that may be encountered in obtaining local permission to excavate a site can be found in Ovid R. Sellers's remarks about the 1957 excavation at Beth-zur.

> Negotiations for the use of the land were made by Emil Abu Dayeh. . . . These negotiations were complicated. In 1931 Khirbet et-Tubeiqa was community owned by residents of Ḥalḥul. The *mukhtar*, 'Abd el-Yusef, acted for the community and by his cooperation facilitated all arrangements, not only in designating the area to be dug but also in keeping amicable relations among the workers. Now three young *mukhtars* exercise authority in the area, and the hill is divided into individually owned plots. . . . Eventually arrangements were made with two owners for two plots. As work progressed we learned that a third owner was involved, and it was necessary to compensate him. A fourth owner had to be paid for parking our car on the corner of his land.

The recruitment of an adequate staff is an early item in the organization of an expedition, and the success of a project depends to a large degree on the quality of the people involved. The era when one or two men could assemble a crew of unskilled workers and excavate a site is gone. The refined techniques of excavation and analysis employed today require competence in and the control of every aspect of the work. The workers on a modern dig may be conveniently arranged into three categories: professional, semiprofessional (skilled), and unskilled. The Gezer staff provides a good example of the organization of a recent major expedition. The professional workers included: an executive committee (consisting of two members), a director, an associate director, four other field archaeologists, a photographer, a geologist, an administrative assistant, a consulting anthropologist, and consulting physicians. Among the semiprofessional staff were area supervisors and a foreman. The unskilled workers were largely student volunteers from the United States and Europe, with a few local wage earners. (The use of student volunteers to do the digging in place of paid local laborers marked a revolution in archaeological field work. It was first attempted at Tell Gezer on a major scale in 1965 at the instigation of G. Ernest Wright. The practice has spread rapidly since, and without such volunteer assistance many expeditions could not hope to continue their work at an optimum level.) The total personnel at work at any one time on the Gezer dig was approximately 125. By the close of the last season in 1973, literally thousands of people had participated in the Gezer project.

The tendency toward a greater diversity of talents and interests among core staff members is evident in the Joint Expedition to Caesarea Maritima. Included in an interdisciplinary team are paleobotanists, paleozoologists, an osteologist, a historical architect, a ceramicist, numismatists, anthropologists, an economist, a range of specialized historians, stratigraphers, a chemist, a physicist, a hydrologist, a geologist, computer scientists, and a number of technical specialists in such areas as photography and civil engineering. Few digs are so thoroughly staffed, but the dominant trend in archaeology in the Middle East is to employ more specialists in an attempt to wring as many data as possible from the material excavated.

Heinrich Schliemann wrote, "My instruments for excavating [Troy] were very imperfect: I had to work with only pickaxes, wooden shovels, baskets, and eight wheelbarrows." Today the properly outfitted expedition will include similar tools and equipment and much, much more.

For accurate measurement prior to and during excavation, surveying equipment is needed, including a transit theodolite, plumb lines, tape measures, line levels, and so forth. Trenching equipment for general digging will include picks, broad-bladed knives, crowbars, sledge hammers, shovels, hoes, mattocks, portable cranes, and occasionally even power shovels and bulldozers. Fine digging requires brushes, trowels, and small dental-type picks.

The removal of material from areas being excavated requires the "gufa," a discarded rubber tire which has been transformed into a pail. Pails for sherds are required along with a collection of paper bags and boxes as receptacles for small finds and larger artifacts. Wheelbarrows and, in some cases, small hand-operated railcars are used for transporting debris to the dump area.

Equipment for cleaning artifacts includes washing tanks, brushes, and pails. Careful recording requires cameras, film, and other photographic and developing equipment. Notebooks, tags, and nails for attaching tags to the strata are necessary in the squares being excavated. The drawing of sections (the perpendicular faces of the squares) requires string, a string level, scaled graph paper, pencils, pens and India ink, a plumb bob and an engineer's triangular scale. A journal must be kept, and a register of all individual finds that are to be retained is necessary along with the supplies for an index of small finds. Pottery drawing requires appropriate scaled drawing papers.

Putting an expedition in the field involves surface transportation—cars and trucks for the movement of personnel, equipment, and supplies to and from the site. The logistics involved in meeting the personal requirements of food, shelter, and hygienic living conditions for the staff of an expedition is itself a major undertaking, but only when the site is occupied with a competent staff and the proper equipment can the work of excavation begin. All the efforts of organization and preparation are aimed at that moment.

Methods

Before actual excavation begins, a contour map of the site is prepared. This map contains isometric lines which indicate the elevations above sea level. Surveying instruments are then used to lay out a system of grids, usually oriented along the north-south and east-west lines. In the process a bench mark (datum point) is established. This reference point is permanently marked with a cement post, steel pipe, or small rock outcrop, for all measurements must ultimately correlate to it. Any future excavations will also be able to relate to the bench mark. Normally the point will be identified as a measurement in reference to sea level.

Every director desires to obtain maximum results from the limited resources at his disposal. He must, therefore, select the most promising spots on the tell for excavation. Each of these spots is designated a *field.* On the basis of the master grid plan, each field is laid out in a series of squares (dimensions of five meters are common), but a one-meter balk, or wall of unexcavated material, is left between squares. A member of the core staff is assigned to each field. He is called a field supervisor. Within his field are several areas, with each area normally identical with a square. Each area will have its area supervisor. Under his direction six to eight workers can begin to remove the surface material of the first stratum, or layer.

A major decision confronting any excavation is the disposal of the excavated material, the location of the dump. Ideally, the dump will be close enough to the field for easy disposal of the unwanted materials but distant enough so that it will not interfere with the possible expansion of the field into an adjacent area of promise. The majority of archaeologists will testify that despite the care with which the dump site is chosen, as the excavation proceeds it often becomes evident that the dump has been lo-

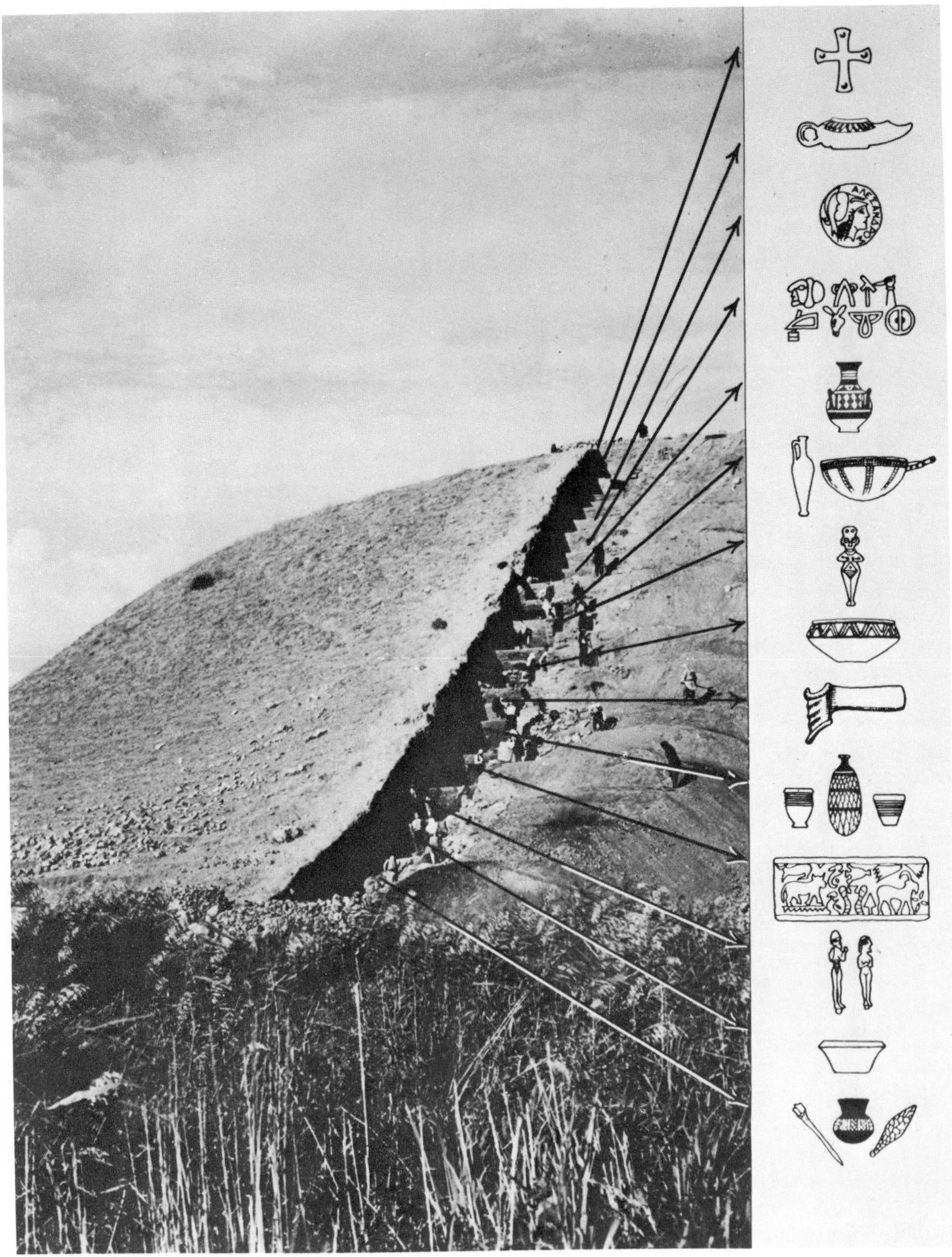

Step trench at Tell Jedeidah, Syria. The excavator of a tell is apt to find a series of civilizations superimposed on one another. At Tell Jedeidah fourteen distinct levels of occupation have been identified from 5500 B.C. to A.D. 600. Typical objects found on each level are shown on the right.

A typical dig scene. Note the variety of excavating tools and equipment.

Volunteer workers excavating at Gezer.

Evident stratification in a balk face.

cated in an inappropriate spot. In the history of archaeology more than one dump has been moved in order that the line of a city wall or the surface of a street can be properly investigated.

All competent archaeologists today use the stratigraphical method of excavating. Early archaeologists employed mainly mass excavation techniques, and a primary interest in architectural remains marked their work. The first steps toward the development of stratigraphical excavation in Palestine began with the work of Sir Flinders Petrie in 1890. At Tell el-Hesi he employed a step-trench method, assigning each workman to a level on one of the "steps" that comprised a trench which extended from the top of the tell to the bottom. By 1910 George A. Reisner and Clarence S. Fisher had developed excavation techniques that included accurate surveying, careful analysis of architectural remains, adequate photographic recording, and a carefully written record of the finds, but their methods were seldom systematically followed in pre-World War II excavations. Since that conflict, Palestinian archaeologists have turned to the system of excavation developed by the British archaeologist, Sir Mortimer Wheeler, and his illustrious student, Kathleen Kenyon.

The Wheeler-Kenyon method, based on the stratigraphical removal of debris within the controlled area of squares, focuses upon the vertical appearance of the balk surfaces. This contrasts with the earlier methods which were primarily oriented toward describing the architectural remains uncovered on the horizontal floor of the excavation. American archaeologists of the W. F. Albright-G. Ernest Wright school have joined to the British system of excavation a constant, careful analysis of the pottery as the excavation progresses. Stratigraphy and pottery analysis (typology) thus act as controls on each other, assuring more accurate information from the research.

In practice the area supervisor maintains a careful system of records for his square. This includes a daily top plan (a diagram drawn to scale of the appearance of the square's surface at the beginning of each day's work), daily note pages (containing sketches of the balk faces, a record of all objects found—including all baskets of pottery and the provenance of each—as well as a record of all official photographs taken, of all official plans drawn, and of all questions that may have occurred along with possible solutions), and locus lists. A locus is any distinct and recognizable feature which appears in the course of excavation. Such features (loci) may be surfaces of floors, layers of earth, ovens, walls, pits, and so forth. Every bit of material excavated in a square is associated with a locus and is appropriately numbered. Upon later analysis, adjacent loci can often be grouped into phases which are then assigned to strata. A stratum consists of occupational phases which have a common cultural association and are distinguishable from earlier and later strata by evidence of major destructions, gaps in occupation, or other clear stratigraphic features.

As the excavation proceeds, each locus is carefully excavated so as to avoid mixing with other loci. In order to anticipate the appearance of new strata, a small probe trench is cut into the square. The depth of a stratum can then be approximately determined, and the locus can be removed as the pickman carefully loosens the soil to the appropriate depth. The debris then can be removed by other workers. Pottery associated only with the stratum being excavated is collected and labeled. Isolated loci in a square are accurately located by measurement. Photographs are taken *in situ* and descriptive entries are made in the supervisor's records prior to the removal of such isolated items.

The sides of the square are kept perpendicular by trimming with a plumb bob and spirit level. The balks surrounding a square thus preserve in four sections the visual evidence of the excavated strata. Every stratum is carefully observed, distinguished by description, and labeled. Tags which identify the strata are numbered and on these tags is entered a descriptive word or two based on the distinguishing features of the particular stratum, such as the color, texture, and content of the soil. These tags are then attached to the balk walls with nails. Each section is studied and drawn to scale, providing a record of the appearance of the face of the balk. In this system the evidence will not be lost even though the balks may subsequently be removed. Later the information from all the squares and fields which are excavated can be correlated into a comprehensive picture of the occupational history of the site.

In theory this procedure sounds as simple as peeling the layers from an onion; in fact it is often complicated by intrusions which have disturbed underlying strata. Pits are one intrusive element that are the bane of the archaeologist's existence. These include storage pits, burial sites, postholes, and the like. Other disturbances have resulted from the construction of foundation trenches, from the robbing of stones for later construction, and from washouts. Stratification is seldom uniform or level. Few tells developed on level ground, and the practice in antiquity of filling in order to level an area often means irregularities in the strata. It is precisely because of the need to solve these types of problems that the system of stratigraphical excavation has developed.

Examples of Forms Used in the Gezer Excavations

Sample Top Plan

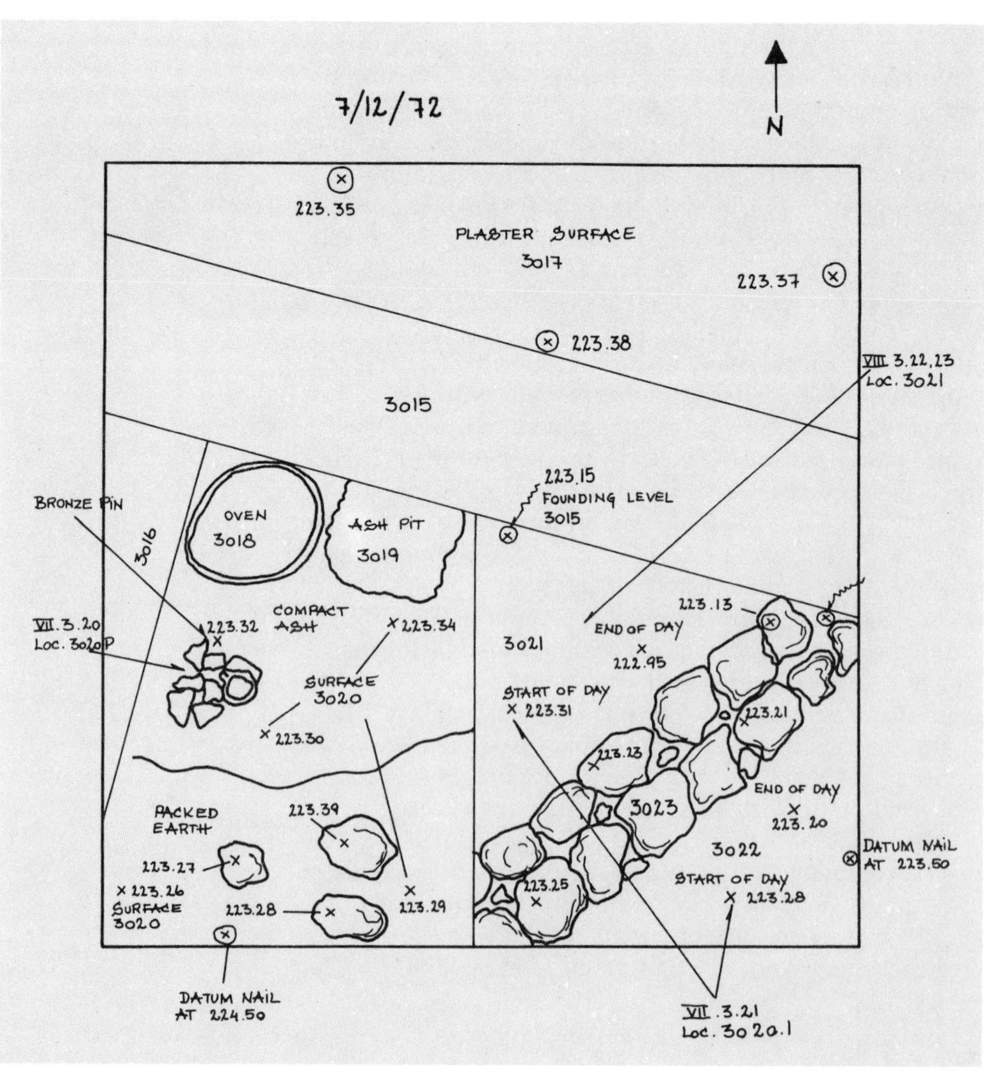

Sample Note Page

7/12/72

VII. 3. 20 LOCUS 3020. P. REMOVAL OF SMASHED POTTERY OVERLYING SURFACE LOC. 3020 ALONG EAST FACE OF WALL LOC. 2016 AND JUST SOUTH OF OVEN LOC. 3018. TOP LEVEL AT 223.35 (224.50−1.15)

VII. 3. 21 LOCUS 3020.1 PROBE THROUGH SURFACE 3020 IN SECTION SOUTH OF WALL 3015 TO SOUTH BALK. 2 METERS WHIDE FROM EAST BALK. FROM 223.31 (223.50−.19) AND 223.28 (223.50−.22). IN FINE COMPACTED AND LAMINATED SEDIMENTS 2.54 "GREYISH BROWN" 5/2 IN COLOR WITH TRACES OF GREY ASH AND CHARCOAL.

SPECIAL DATA LOCUS 3017. TRANSIT LEVELS ON SURFACE, WEST AT 223.35 (READING # 107), EAST AT 223.37 (READING # 108) AND SOUTH CENTER ALONG WALL 3015 AT 223.38 (READING # 109).

SPECIAL DATA LOCUS 3020.1 BRONZE PIN FOUND CA 25 CM. SOUTH OF OVEN 3018 AT 223.32 (224.50−1.18).

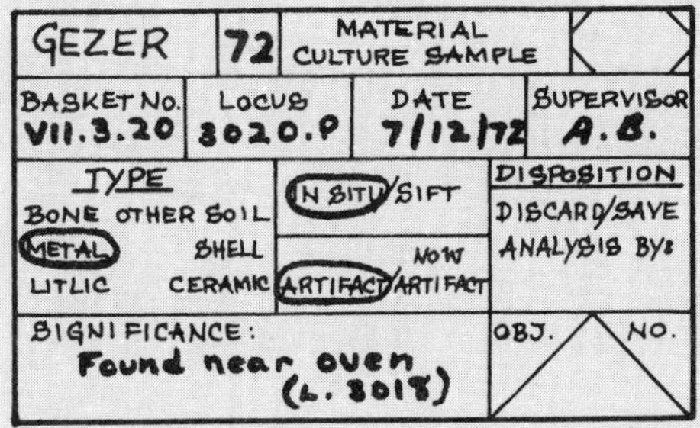

GEZER | 72 | MATERIAL CULTURE SAMPLE

BASKET NO.	LOCUS	DATE	SUPERVISOR
VII.3.20	3020.P	7/12/72	A.B.

TYPE: BONE, OTHER, SOIL, METAL (circled), SHELL, LITLIC, CERAMIC

IN SITU (circled)/SIFT

ARTIFACT (circled)/NON ARTIFACT

DISPOSITION: DISCARD/SAVE, ANALYSIS BY:

SIGNIFICANCE: Found near oven (L. 3018)

OBJ. NO.

SPECIAL DATA LOCUS 3020.1 REVEALS AN ALLIGNMENT OF STONES ACROSS SOUTH EAST CORNER OF THE AREA 3020.1 DISCONTINUED AT 223.20 (223.50 − 30) SOUTH EAST, AND 223.23 (223.50−.27) NORTH. STONES ASSIGNED AS LOCUS 3023, WITH SECTIONS NORTH AS 3021 AND SOUTH AS 3022.

VIII. 3. 22 LOCUS 3021 CONTINUING TO REMOVE "GREYISH BROWN" SEDIMENTS (NOW WITH LESS ASH AND CHARCOAL) IN SECTION BELOW LOC. 3020.1 NORTH OF LOC. 3023 FROM 223.23

SPECIAL DATA LOCUS 3023 NOW CLEARLY IS SEEN TO BE A WALL. QUESTION: ARE THE STONES PROTRUDING IN THE SOUTH WESTERN QUARTER PART OF A RELATED WALL SECTION?

VII. 3. 23 LOCUS 3021 CONTINUES VIII. 3. 22 FROM 223.17 (223.50 −.33).

Sample Field Report Section

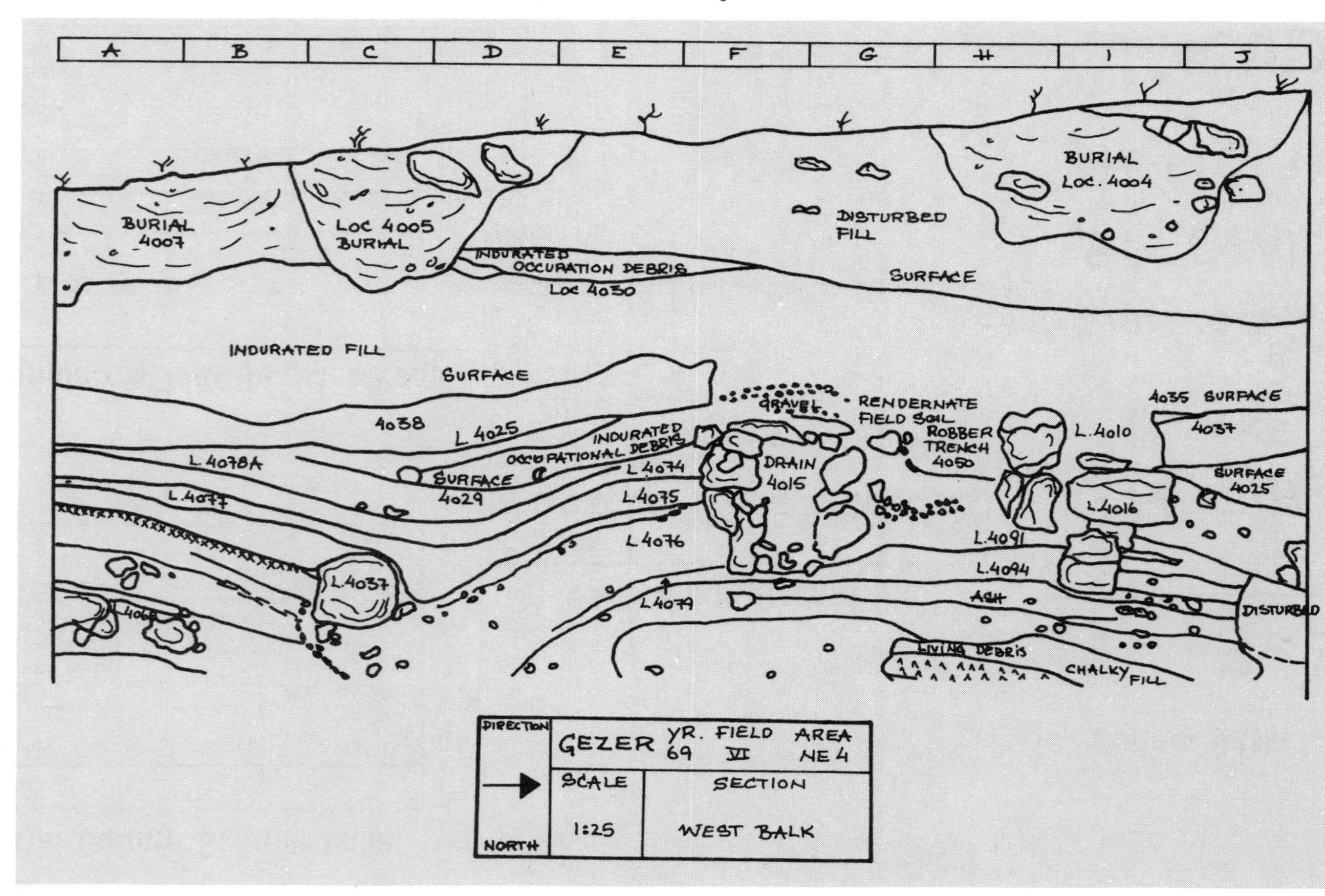

Material Culture Sample Label

GEZER		MATERIAL CULTURE SAMPLE	
BASKET NO.	LOCUS	DATE	SUPERVISOR
TYPE: BONE, OTHER SOIL, METAL, SHELL, LITLIC, CERAMIC	IN SITU/SIFT; NOW ARTIFACT/ARTIFACT		DISPOSITION: DISCARD/SAVE, ANALYSIS BY:
SIGNIFICANCE:			OBJ. NO.

Field Photo Record Slip

GEZER		FIELD PHOTOGRAPH	
FIELD/AREA	PRIME LOCUS	DATE TAKEN	SUPERVISORS
OTHER LOCI	FROM DIRECTION		COLOR
PURPOSE:			

Pottery Basket Tag

G 66 7/12/66
I. 6. 55
Loc. 6037
SPECIAL
HANDLING
"MEND"

Sample of Field Register Page

FIELD IV AREA 3

7/12-72

9.	L. 3001	HELL-ROM. MODERN. NS
10.	L. 3001	HELL-ROM. U.D. NS
*11.	L. 3002	ROMAN
12.	L. 3002	HELL-ROMAN

7/13-72

13.	L. 3003	HELL U.D. NS

We have described in an abbreviated form the adaptation of the Wheeler-Kenyon system by American archaeologists. These techniques have been widely employed with minor variations at sites such as Gezer, Shechem, and Tell el-Hesi since the resurgence of archaeological activity in Israel and Jordan in the 1950s. Essentially the same methods are used by the thriving school of Israeli archaeologists and the archaeologists of other nations under the scrutiny of the Israel Department of Antiquities and Museums. In Jordan, similarly, the Department of Antiquities encourages stratigraphical digging in the Wheeler-Kenyon tradition.

Materials

Archaeologists work solely with the *surviving* remains of human occupation. These remains may be generally classified into two categories: artifacts and epigraphs. Epigraphs are simply written materials. In contrast to the hundreds of thousands of inscribed clay tablets which have been recovered from Mesopotamia, archaeologists in Syro-Palestine count the discovery of written materials as an extraordinary event. These normally are inscribed stones, ostraca (pieces of broken pottery used as a writing surface), an occasional clay tablet written in cuneiform script, and, from later levels, coins. Rarely are papyrus, leather, or parchment fragments recovered, since they are organic materials subject to decomposition. Epigraphic materials dating to the biblical period which are discovered in Palestine may be written in Egyptian hieroglyphs, Akkadian cuneiform, or in one of the scripts of the Northwest Semitic languages—Canaanite (Old Hebrew), Moabite, Ammonite, or Aramaic. Written materials are the most desirable of finds, for they reveal something of the mind of ancient man to a degree that no common artifact can. They also provide valuable information for the comparative study of orthography, grammar, and vocabulary. The study of ancient texts, philology, is a complicated discipline practiced by specialists, and it is an integral aspect of archaeological research in the lands of the Bible.

Materials recovered in stratigraphical association (that is, in the same context) comprise an assemblage. An assemblage may contain artifacts, features, and nonartifactual material. Artifacts are man-made objects such as pots, jewelry, and tools. Artifacts are easily removed from the site as they are found. Features are objects with which man has worked, but which cannot be removed from the site without disassembling or completely destroying them. Fire pits, house foundations, walls, threshing floors, cisterns and silos are examples of features. These must be recorded in the field with accurate plans, cross-sectional drawings, and photographs before they are dismantled and removed. Nonartifactual materials include such things as animal bones, seeds, charcoal, shells, and ash layers. Such materials reveal information about the users even though they are not man-made. In the latest phase of the development of archaeology, interest in nonartifactual materials has increased considerably. Archaeologists are subject to trends, a common human trait, and the addition of specialists in paleobotany, paleozoology, and related disciplines to expedition staffs is doubtless a part of our modern interest in ecology. The work of these specialists with the nonartifactual materials may provide new information about the life of ancient man and suggest new directions for modern man.

Pottery is the most profuse artifact recovered by archaeologists in the lands of the Bible. The intimate relationship between ancient man and the earthen vessel is dramatically portrayed in the Book of Job where it is recorded that "he took a piece of broken pot to scratch himself as he sat among the ashes." So indestructible are potsherds that Job's sherd may still exist. While ceramic vessels are easily broken, and once broken they are fit only to be discarded, the pieces survive. Some of the larger pieces could have been used for scoops or for jar covers; others were used for writing surfaces; most were simply cast aside to be replaced by a new vessel. The availability of local clays and the ease of manufacture help account for the piles of sherds uncovered in Palestinian digs.

Man used stone vessels before he learned to make clay pots. The earliest forms of ceramic ware resemble the forms of contemporary stoneware. Clay was in use before pottery began to be made. The floors and walls of houses were sealed with it, and it was used to round out the corners of rooms. This made for easier cleaning of a domicile. Clay was also used for making mud-brick for building purposes in the prepottery Neolithic period. This usage of clay has continued, and mud-brick construction is still a feature of life in the modern Middle East.

About 5500–5000 B.C., the earliest pottery known was being made and used in ancient Jericho. It is easy to imagine an observant ancient man noting the effects of a cooking fire on his clay floor, and then, by a spark of genius, perceiving the possibility of producing hard utensils from pliable clay.

Ceramic vessels developed in two basic forms—the bowl and the jar. Bowls ran to a great variety of patterns and sizes. The largest, the banquet bowl, had four handles. Smaller

Modern potter at Hebron.

Clay plaque of the goddess Astarte.

modifications included bowls for serving wine and food, cups, ladles, and dippers. The jar was characterized by the narrow opening of the mouth. Wine, water, oil, and grains were kept in the largest storage jars. These were often round-bottomed, apparently for ease in tipping when the contents were being removed. Water pitchers, oil juglets, and even baby bottles were adaptations of this basic form. No matter what the form, Palestinian pottery was always functional. The primacy of function did not hinder the production of many aesthetically pleasing forms, however, as the illustrations in this text testify.

Pottery was produced solely by hand until the introduction of the potter's wheel in the third millennium B.C. At first a single wheel was used, but during the Middle Bronze Age a second, heavier flywheel was attached by a shaft to the smaller wheel upon which the clay was thrown. The flywheel could be turned by foot, leaving the hands free to form the vessel.

Ceramic technology through the centuries included more than household pottery. Clay figurines, particularly of the goddess Astarte, were produced throughout the biblical era. Incense burners and cultic masks were made of ceramic. Lamps, spindle whorls, loom weights, canteens (pilgrim flasks), and jewelry were manufactured from clay. Some of these clay products were molded rather than hand-formed or wheel-thrown.

The abundant fragments of pottery are often more eloquent than written records, and they are found on many sites for which no written records are known. The proportion of imported pottery to domestic ware can suggest the significance and the patterns of trade. The pottery also hints at the comparative wealth of the local economy. Population densities can be estimated on the basis of the quantity of discarded pottery at a site, but the most important value of pottery for the archaeologist is its use as a tool for dating.

The science of typology makes it possible to establish a pottery chronology. Ceramic typology is the classification and study of stylistic changes in pottery—its composition, decoration, and particularly its form—as it occurs in a mound from the earliest levels to the latest. Typological analysis is applied to other artifacts and features as well, but because pottery is the most abundant class of surviving artifacts it has come to play a dominant role in dating.

Typological studies are possible because of an innate and universal human characteristic—a propensity for style. Style is based on a group image of what is right, what is appropriate. Variations of style are permissible, but within limits acceptable to the group. In time styles do change, for popularity is a fleeting thing. Even so, a ceramic form, for example, a type of jug, will show changes over a period of time. These changes involve the rims of jars, the type and location of the handles, the thickness and form of the base, the addition and variation of decorations, burnishing or the lack of it, and the addition of glazes or washes. These changes in style permit the arrangement of pottery types into a series beginning with the initial appearance of a type at the site, through its rise to the height of popularity, and finally its disappearance. When the changing styles are correlated with the stratigraphy, a *relative date* can be established for the occupation of the tell. If some point of the relative sequence can be anchored to inscriptions, coins, or known events, an *absolute date* can be established and extended along the relative continuum. The correlation of similar ceramic typologies from other excavations in a region then establishes the dating of the area's cultural history. Absolute dates for biblical events prior to circa 960 B.C. are established primarily on the basis of Egyptian correlations. From the time of Solomon on a number of fixed dates can be established on the basis of synchronisms with extrabiblical records, particularly Assyrian and Neo-Babylonian annals.

Canaanite store jar (1.02m.).

The chronology of Palestinian pottery was established on a firm foundation by the pioneering work of W. F. Albright at Tell Beit Mirsim in the 1920s. Since that time further discoveries and refinements have so advanced the precision of ceramic dating in the area that most of the pottery from the biblical period is datable to within a century, and in some cases even more closely.

Students of archaeology are becoming aware of other dating methods which are based primarily upon the physical sciences. The best known of these is the carbon-14 method of dating. It was developed by Willard Libby of the Institute of Nuclear Studies of the University of Chicago in 1948. According to the principle involved, living organisms absorb radioactive carbon (C-14) from the atmosphere. After they die, the C-14 disintegrates at a known rate. By measuring the amount of C-14 remaining in a sample of organic material such as charcoal, the physicist can determine how long ago the organism lived. The process is complicated—the sample is purified, then heated into a gaseous form, and finally the amount of radiation is determined by a special Geiger counter. The half-life of C-14 is 5568 years, so a sample containing one-half the usual amount of C-14 would have lived 5568 years earlier, plus or minus a margin of two hundred years.

Middle Bronze II bowl (the angular shape is termed "carinated").

The fundamental assumptions on which this method is based

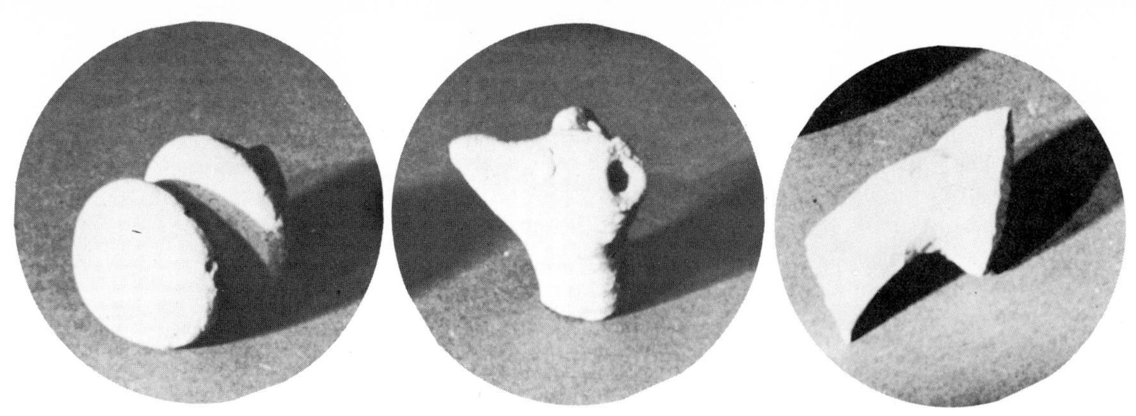

Characteristic pottery types from Chalcolithic to the Byzantine periods

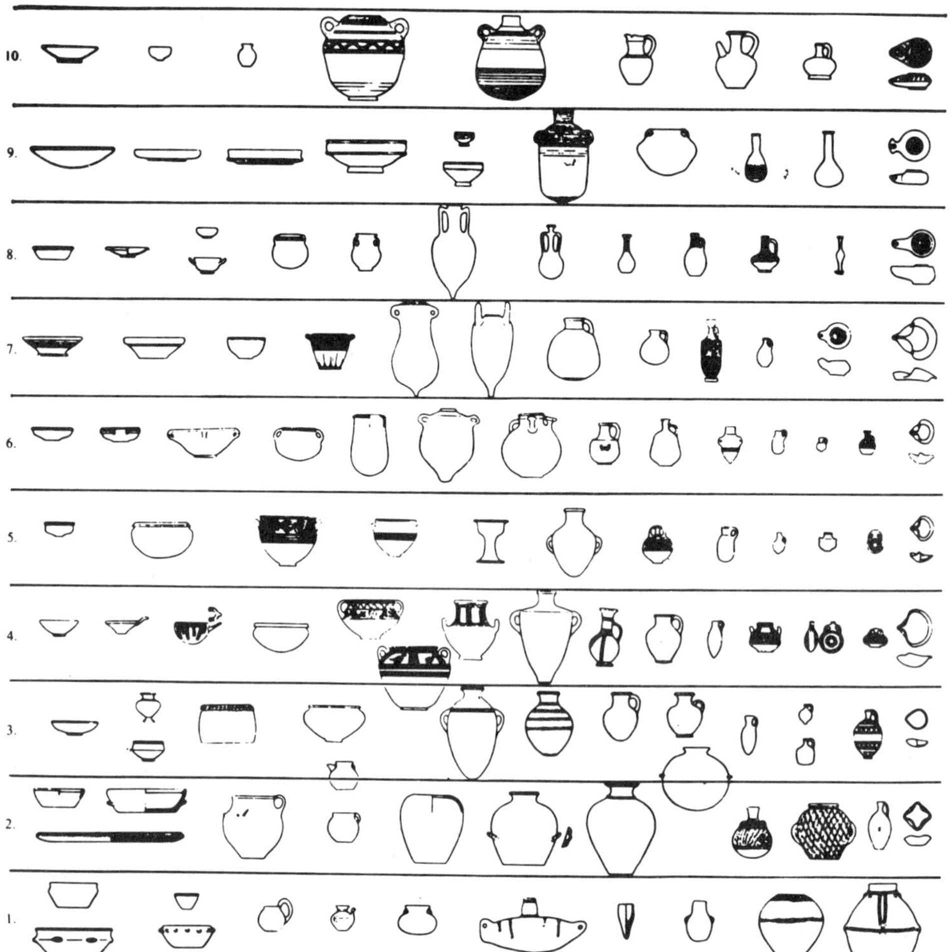

1. Chalcolithic period
2. Early Bronze Age
3. Middle Bronze Age
4. Late Bronze Age
5. Iron Age I
6. Iron Age II
7. Iron Age III
8. Hellenistic period
9. Roman period
10. Byzantine period

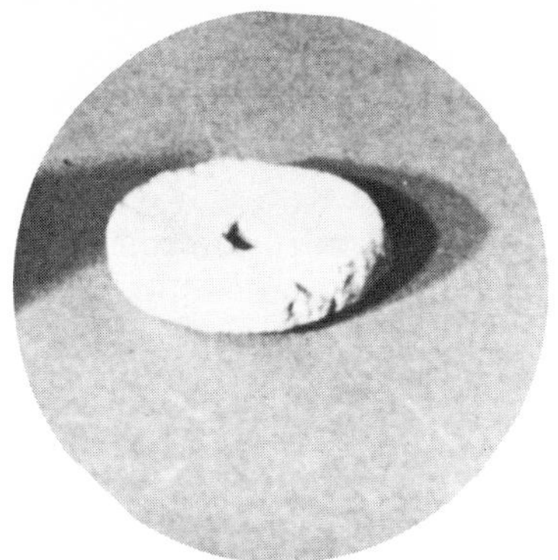

The versatility of ceramics. Left: clay rattle, animal head minus horns, inscribed jar handle from Gibeon. Above: spindle whorl.

Chart of the major dating methods and time zones to which each is applicable

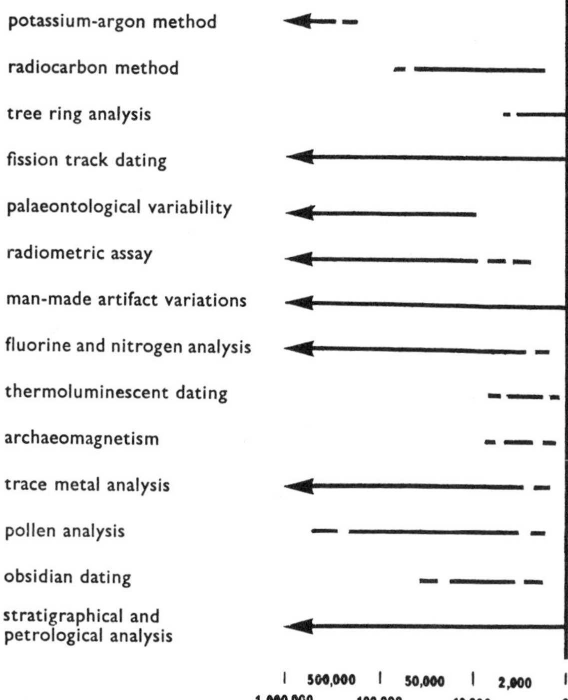

Typological changes in the oil lamp from the Middle Bronze I period through the Late Bronze periods (early to late, left to right).

are, however, a matter of scholarly controversy. It is not certain that the proportion of C-14 to C-12 (stable carbon) has remained constant, as has been assumed. The organic materials in a sample may also have been contaminated by the intrusion of secondary materials, for example, tree roots. Contamination is also possible during the removal of the sample from the site, during shipment, and during its preparation for the testing procedure. The established half-life figure has also been questioned recently, and the U.S. National Bureau of Standards has indicated that it is probably incorrect and will have to be revised. The revision will probably not alter greatly the previously published dates.

Potassium-argon dating is also based on a constant rate of radioactive decay—of potassium into the gas argon. The half-life of potassium has been reckoned at 1.3 billion years. By comparing the concentration of argon in a mineral sample to the total content of potassium, the time required for the potassium to produce the argon by radioactive decay can be computed.

Another technique is archaeomagnetism, the study of remnant magnetism in archaeological remains. Remnant magnetism is produced as follows: Certain oxides found naturally in clay lose their magnetism when heated above a certain point, as in the process of firing ceramic ware. Then, as the piece cools, the oxides are susceptible to a very stable remagnetization which is induced by the earth's magnetic field. A fired pot thus records in terms of magnetic direction and proportionate intensity the magnetic field of the earth at the time when and in the place where it was made. The data on the changes of the earth's magnetic field, in terms of direction and intensity, over the past few thousand years are presently very incomplete, but geophysicists are at work developing the system of archaeomagnetic dating from the accumulating information. A few experiments have arrived at dates within a fifty-year margin for samples that had previously been dated by archaeological content, historical records, or (less accurately) carbon-14.

Dating pottery by thermoluminescence is a technique in the early stages of development. It has been only partially successful, and it is not a routine procedure which can provide indisputable results. Pottery, like many natural minerals, has the property of storing energy by trapping electrons given off by radioactive impurities within its composition. When the ceramic ware is heated to a sufficiently high temperature, the trapped electrons are released in the form of light. This is known as thermoluminescence. In the course of time the pottery will again entrap radioactive particles. The longer the time that elapses, the more particles that will be trapped. To date such pottery, it is reheated and the light output is measured. The older the ware, the greater the amount of luminescence.

The study of tree rings as an archaeological dating tool is called dendrochronology. It was first employed by A. E. Douglass for dating American Indian ruins in the Southwest in 1929. This is still the area of greatest application for the method, although the techniques are being applied in many countries of the northern hemisphere. Tree-ring dating in the Middle East is in its infancy. The procedure calls for extensive regional cross-dating and the establishment of an accurate master chronology based on absolute dates. While progress in the development of this tool in biblical archaeology can be expected, political and economic factors in the lands of the Bible suggest that it will be slow.

It is apparent that these newer dating techniques will never play a predominant role in Palestinian archaeology. Pottery typology is still the least expensive, most readily available, and most precise (in general terms) dating technique available to the field archaeologist. The newer techniques are important for the supportive evidence they can provide to pottery chronology.

Interpretation

All the work of organization, all the expense, time, and effort invested in excavation are pointless without interpretation of the data produced and communication of those data to those who are interested. The scientific method requires observation, description, and explanation. Explanation in archaeological terms means interpretation and publication.

The interpretation begins in at least a preliminary way as the field archaeologist excavates. An attempt is made to schematize the occupational history of the site by correlating the stratigraphical and typological data which are being uncovered with known information about the history and cultural patterns of the region. This knowledge has been accumulated from previous excavations of sites in the same region. There is no necessity to confirm the previously published ideas of other archaeologists, for the new information being recovered may force reassessments of earlier views. Progress in archaeological research requires the critical appraisal of the data at hand rather than acquiescence to earlier opinions.

The initial task of interpretation is to identify the cultural phases of the site and to establish the chronological sequence. An American archaeologist, James Deetz, has described culture as a uniquely human system of habits and customs acquired by man through extrasomatic process, carried by his society, and used as his primary means of adapting to his environment. Societies do exist on the basis of patterns of learned behavior. Such phenomena as language, social organization, economic practices, and religious beliefs comprise interlocking patterns of behavior which are transmitted by the society through educative processes rather than through genetic or biological processes within the body of the individual. Culture is perishable, therefore, and cannot be recovered by means of the spade, for it consists of ideas and norms by which a society perceives itself. The archaeologist can attain a partial conception of a culture only as he perceives the relationships between the artifacts he recovers and the thought of the ancient makers. The material objects reflect in form and function the cultural patterns of the people who produced them. Cultural changes may be gradual over a lengthy period of time, or they may occur suddenly and drastically, as in the case of natural disaster or warfare with the displacement of the old population by a new group. The work of the interpreter is to observe these changes and to explain their significance with the most compelling hypothesis which can be generated. The hypothesis should integrate the material evidence and the textual evidence, both extrabiblical, when it exists, and biblical.

The work in the field in any one season does not permit the time needed for an in-depth analysis of the material remains. The season's activities are published, however, in a brief preliminary report. There is no coordinating center for such reports, although the Departments of Antiquities in both Israel and Jordan may publish some reports in their respective annuals. Preliminary reports may appear in popular journals, such as the *Biblical Archaeologist,* or in obscure newsletters. Under these circumstances finding the latest reports for a particular excavation can be difficult for the student, but bibliographies of Holy Land sites may be of some aid.

The initial hypotheses contained in preliminary reports must be tested and either substantiated or rejected in an expanded final report when the expedition has completed its field work. Such a report may fill several volumes. Information from each season's work, from the several fields excavated, and from each area must be digested and integrated into a concise publishable form. Hundreds of top and section plans must be reviewed. Box after box of pottery sherds must be reexamined and the initial analysis of type and form reconfirmed. The artifacts must be compared with similar types from earlier excavations in the same general region. A representative selection of significant sherds and small objects must be drawn to scale for illustrations in the final volumes. A unique object may require an examination of literature covering excavations throughout the Near East in search of parallel or similar characteristic features. Of the thousands of photographs taken at the site, only an appropriate few can be selected for publication. The costs of publication necessarily restrict the number used. Plans for buildings, defensive walls, and other significant structures and features must be drawn to scale. All this detail and more must be integrated with a text which interprets the data in terms of cultural sequences and historical changes. And this explanation should take into account the ideas and inferences presented in earlier archaeological reports about the same general area in which the site is located and the chronological periods which the excavation has revealed.

Obviously the process of publishing final reports is tedious and time-consuming. A common practice in the past has been for the director to assume the responsibility of preparing the final publication. A director is usually an archaeologist by avocation, earning his livelihood in some associated field. This leaves but a limited amount of time, usually during summers, for work on a final report. The result is a lag between the close of excavations and the publication of the final report that may extend from five to twenty years. The longer the lag, the longer colleagues are deprived of the information. The longer the lag, the less reliable the memory and the lower the quality of the final product. The only thing worse is a final report that is never completed. Besides the limitation of time, funds for final publication are ordinarily restricted and difficult to obtain. This activity does not have the glamour of excavating as a lure to potential financial donors. Despite these problems, final reports are published for the majority of excavations in the course of time. A recent hopeful trend has been to make the preparation of the final report a team effort of the core staff, but the problems of money and time still hamper the process of publication.

Interpretation is really an art, not a science. It is the area of least precision in archaeological research. In the post-World War II era, biblical archaeology has developed a more exact system of excavation and greater precision in recording the data than existed previously. But interpretation still involves the drawing of inferences based often upon the scantiest evidence.

The fragmentary nature of the evidence from the ancient Near East complicates the drawing of inferences. One reasonable estimate is that we have at hand less than 1/1000 of the potential evidence from antiquity. This figure is based on an admittedly optimistic projection that one-fourth of the material remains and inscriptions survived, that one-fourth of the available sites have been surveyed, that one-fourth of those sites have been excavated, that one-fourth of the excavated sites have been adequately examined, and that one-fourth of the materials and inscriptions have been published. In reality, hardly more than two hundred sites out of an estimated total of over five thousand in all of Israel and Jordan have been excavated. Less than fifty of these can be considered major excavations. In Mesopotamia less than 1 percent of the total sites have been excavated. No site has been totally excavated, except for rare sites such as Qumran and Masada. An estimated 1/400 of biblical Hazor has been excavated. Professor Yadin, the director of the Hazor expedition, has estimated that the complete excavation of the site at a normal pace would require eight hundred years. Seldom is more than 5 percent of a site excavated today. The bulk of the potential evidence remains buried.

The surviving remains from antiquity preserve only a tiny fraction of the full picture of ancient life, and even these fragmentary materials are mute as they are wrested from the soil. They speak only through informed, imaginative minds. The drawing of inferences involves the human element, and just as a literary or artistic work is in part an expression of the selfness of the artist, so the inferences drawn by an archaeologist are infused with his experiences and philosophy of life. What he is will tint his imagination and influence his judgments of what the evidence suggests. Yet the data are but meaningless curios without the subjective activity of interpretation. Historical reconstructions are necessary, but they are not identical with what the reality may have been. Hypotheses possess only varying degrees of probability, ranging from certain, to probable, to possible, to improbable, to impossible. The final *proof* of anything ancient must be confined to questions such as what kind of rock was used and how certain pottery was formed. Nevertheless, in the final analysis only the interpretation is useful, and it is most useful when it has undergone the critical appraisal of many scholars. That is why the publication of the data collected in an excavation and of the inferences drawn by the excavator is so vital. The inferences become fuel for the white heat of scholarly controversy. Scholarly consensus then establishes the highest level of probability for the most compelling hypothesis.

If the end result of archaeological research is such fragile cloth woven of fragmentary evidence and human subjectivity, one might question the value of the enterprise. What is the purpose of it all? The purpose is to acquire knowledge, to attain understanding, to comprehend the nature of man, and the story of man. For some it is also to comprehend more clearly the activity of God in history. And it is to acquire a degree of understanding about biblical man that is attainable in no other way. Archaeology has produced a stream of extrabiblical written sources for the study of ancient history. New light has been shed on the material culture of the ancient past. And the occupational histories of identified biblical sites have been laid bare for integration with the biblical references. The Bible and the People of the Book take on new, lively dimensions as a result of archaeological research. It is true that the research does not, indeed cannot, prove true the biblical traditions. The integrity of the Bible and of its statements of *faith* is established on the grounds of their own intrinsic merit. But archaeology can and does provide illumination, illustration, and, more rarely, confirmation of biblical statements of *fact*. Examples readily at hand are the illumination of the Canaanite religion derived from the texts excavated at Ras Shamra-Ugarit, the illustration of an Israelite "horned" altar recently recovered at Beer-sheba, and the confirmation of the presence of the exiled Judean king, Jehoiachin, in Nebuchadnezzar's capital, known from ration chits discovered in Babylon's ruins by Koldewey in this century. While archaeological inferences may occasionally pose problems (for example, the stratigraphical evidence does not confirm Joshua's conquest of Jericho), yet in no known instance of which the writer is aware has archaeology proven the Bible false. The value of the investment in men, money, and time is that knowledge has been acquired; the expanding interest in archaeological research in the last quarter of the twentieth century indicates that the quest for knowledge and understanding will continue.

SUGGESTED TOPICS FOR FURTHER STUDY

1. Archaeological research organizations in Palestine.
2. Surface surveys in the Holy Land.
3. Before the digging begins: problems in launching an expedition.
4. Stratigraphic excavation—the story of how it evolved.
5. The role of Samaria (Sebaste) in the career of Dame Kathleen Kenyon.
6. Contributions of Americans to archaeological methods before 1920.
7. A survey of written records from Mesopotamia that illuminate the Bible.

8. Methods of pottery manufacture.
9. Palestinian pottery in the patriarchal period.
10. Late Bronze Age Palestinian pottery.
11. Post-Solomonic Israelite pottery.
12. The story of carbon-14 dating.
13. William F. Albright's contribution to ceramic chronology.
14. The implications of artifacts for understanding culture.
15. A report on a post-World War II excavation of a biblical site.

RECOMMENDED READING

Albright, W. F., "The Impact of Archaeology on Biblical Research—1966" in *New Directions in Biblical Archaeology,* ed. D. N. Freedman and J. C. Greenfield (Garden City, NY: Doubleday, 1969), pp. 1–14.

Amiran, Ruth, *Ancient Pottery of the Holy Land* (New Brunswick, NJ: Rutgers University Press, 1970).

Boraas, Roger, "The Field and the Labs; Reflections from England" in *ASOR Newsletter* (no. 2), Aug., 1974.

Cross, Frank M., "W. F. Albright's View of Biblical Archaeology and Its Methodology," *Biblical Archaeologist* 36 (1973), pp. 2–5.

Deetz, James, *Invitation to Archaeology* (Garden City, NY: The Natural History Press, 1967).

Dever, William G., "'Biblical Archaeology'—or 'The Archaeology of Syro-Palestine'?" in *Christian News from Israel* (New Series) XXII, No. 1 (5), pp. 21–22.

Kenyon, Kathleen M., *Archaeology in the Holy Land,* third edition (New York: Praeger Publishers, 1971).

Lance, H. Darrell, *Excavation Manual for Area Supervisors* (Jerusalem: Hebrew Union College Biblical and Archaeological School, 1967).

Sanders, James A., ed., "Part I—Introduction" in *Near Eastern Archaeology in the Twentieth Century* (Garden City, NY: Doubleday, 1970), pp. 3–80.

Thompson, Henry O., "Science and Archaeology," *Biblical Archaeologist* 29 (1966), pp. 114–25.

Van Beek, G. W., "Archaeology" in *Interpreter's Dictionary of the Bible,* ed. George A. Buttrick et al. (New York: Abingdon Press, 1962), vol. 1, pp. 195–207.

Wheeler, Mortimer, *Archaeology from the Earth* (Baltimore: Penguin Books, 1954).

Woodall, J. Ned, *An Introduction to Modern Archaeology* (Cambridge: Schenkman Publishing Company, 1972).

Wright, G. Ernest, "Archaeological Method in Palestine—An American Interpretation," *Eretz-Israel (1969), pp. 120–33.*

———, "What Archaeology Can and Cannot Do," *Biblical Archaeologist* 34 (1971), pp. 70–76.

Yamauchi, Edwin M., "Stones, Scripts, and Scholars," *Christianity Today,* Feb. 14, 1969, pp. 8–13.

FOR FURTHER READING

*Albright, William F., *The Archaeology of Palestine* (Baltimore: Penguin Books, 1949).

Archaeology, Israel Pocket Library (Jerusalem: Keter Publishing House, 1974).

Archaeometry, Bulletin of the Research Laboratory for Archaeology and History of Art, Oxford University (1958-).

Bass, George F., *Archaeology Under Water* (London: Thames and Hudson, 1966).

The Biblical Archaeologist Reader, vol. 1, ed. G. Ernest Wright and David N. Freedman (Chicago: Quadrangle Books, 1961); vols. 2–3, ed. Edward F. Campbell, Jr., and David N. Freedman (Garden City, NY: Doubleday, 1964–70).

Biek, Leo, *Archaeology and the Microscope* (New York: Frederick A. Praeger, 1963).

Brill, Robert H., ed. *Science and Archaeology* (Cambridge: The MIT Press, 1971).

Brothwell, Don, and Eric Higgs, eds., *Science in Archaeology: A Survey of Progress and Research* (New York: Praeger Publishers, 1970).

*Ceram, C. W., *The March of Archaeology* (New York: Alfred A. Knopf, 1970).

Chaplin, Raymond E., *The Study of Animal Bones from Archaeological Sites* (New York: Seminar Press, 1971).

*Daniel, Glyn, *The Origins and Growth of Archaeology* (New York: Thomas Y. Crowell Co., 1971).

*Deetz, James, *Invitation to Archaeology* (Garden City, NY: The Natural History Press, 1967).

Forbes, Robert J., *Studies in Ancient Technology,* second edition, nine volumes (Leiden: E. J. Brill, 1964-).

*Franken, H. J., and C. A. Franken-Battershill, *A Primer of Old Testament Archaeology* (Leiden: E. J. Brill, 1963).

Freedman, David N., and Jonas C. Greenfield, eds., *New Directions in Biblical Archaeology* (Garden City, NY: Doubleday, 1969).

Hammond, Peter B., *Physical Anthropology and Archaeology* (New York: MacMillan, 1964).

Journal of Field Archaeology, Boston University Scholarly Publications, vol. 1, 1974.

*Kenyon, Kathleen M., *Archaeology in the Holy Land,* third edition (New York: Praeger Publishers, 1971).

Kitchen, Kenneth A., *Ancient Orient and Old Testament* (Chicago: Inter-Varsity Press, 1966).

Lapp, Paul W., *Biblical Archaeology and History* (New York: The World Publishing Company, 1969).

Limprey, S., *Soil Science In Archaeology* (New York: Seminar Press, 1972).

L'Orange, H. P., and P. J. Nordhagen, *Mosaics* (London: Methuen, 1966).

*recommended for general information

Matthews, S. K., *Photography in Archaeology and Art* (London: Baker, 1968).

Michael, Henry N., and Elizabeth K. Ralph, eds., *Dating Techniques for the Archaeologist* (Cambridge: MIT Press, 1971).

Moore, Charlotte B., ed., *Reconstructing Complex Societies* (Cambridge: American Schools of Oriental Research, 1975).

Nautical Archaeology and Underwater Exploration, International Journal of ed. Joan Du Plat Taylor, vol. 1 (London, 1972).

*Pfeiffer, Charles F., ed., *The Biblical World: A Dictionary of Biblical Archaeology* (Grand Rapids: Baker, 1972).

Pritchard, James B., *Archaeology and the Old Testament* (Princeton: Princeton University Press, 1958).

Sanders, James A., ed., *Near Eastern Archaeology in the Twentieth Century* (essays in honor of Nelson Glueck) (Garden City, NY: Doubleday, 1970).

Thomas, D. Winton, ed., *Archaeology and Old Testament Study* (Oxford: Clarendon Press, 1967).

Tite, M. S., *Methods of Physical Examination in Archaeology* (New York: Seminar Press, 1972).

Van Beek, G. W., "Archaeology" in *Interpreter's Dictionary of the Bible*, ed. George A. Buttrick et al. (New York: Abingdon Press, 1962), vol. 1, pp. 195–207.

*Wheeler, Mortimer, *Archaeology from the Earth* (Baltimore: Penguin Books, 1954).

Williams, Walter G., *Archaeology in Biblical Research* (Nashville: Abingdon Press, 1965).

Wilson, David, *The New Archaeology* (New York: Alfred A. Knopf, Inc., 1976).

*Woodall, J. Ned, *An Introduction to Modern Archaeology* (Cambridge: Schenkman Publishing Company, 1972).

4

The Development of Writing

Without written records, irrespective of the way they are put down on paper, with a ballpoint, a typewriter, or a computer, modern society as we know it simply would not exist. The concept *history* became possible only after man had invented a system of writing to preserve and record human endeavors by carving certain symbols in rock or on metal, and by writing on papyrus and clay tablets. The alphabet was the result of a three-thousand-year development starting with pictures conveying a message in a more or less ambiguous way, and ending in a system of writing in which each symbol tends to represent one sound or phoneme of the language in question. The word *alphabet* is derived from the Latin *alphabetum,* which in turn received its components from the Greek words for *A* (ἄλφα) and *B* (βῆτα), which represent the Phoenician (and Hebrew) words *aleph* and *beth.* The Phoenician (Canaanite) alphabet is a consonantal system of writing invented by the Semitic peoples who lived along the coast of the Mediterranean between the two great civilizations, Egypt and Babylonia. Although writing in more or less elaborate forms had existed for over two thousand years, the invention of the Semitic alphabet was a unique achievement in the history of human civilization. All alphabets used in the world today, about fifty, are derived from the Phoenician alphabet, which was invented about thirty-five hundred years ago.

In the history of writing, which is really the history of intercommunication among human beings, we can detect four stages of development, culminating in a universal alphabetic system:

1. Communication by gesture, motions, objects.
2. Pictures, pictograms, and ideograms.
3. Syllabic writing.
4. Alphabetic writing.

Communication by Gestures, Motions, and Objects

Since no actual writing occurred during this stage of communication among human beings, it is more accurate to define it as a period of prewriting. This does not mean, however, that modern man has outgrown these simple means of communication; on the contrary, we greet a person by raising our hat or waving an arm, and, of course, we still talk to others. We may tie a knot in a handkerchief to remind ourselves of an errand we have to do, or in a more general way, a flag is flown at half staff to honor a person who has recently died. For us, these form only a small portion of a much more comprehensive system of communication of which writing is the most important element. Primitive man had only these very simple means by which to make his thoughts known to others.

Prehistoric rock carvings and paintings which show animals and human beings in action have been discovered. These are considered primarily as art, although they probably also had magical or religious meaning. Undoubtedly, one of their functions was to communicate a message, either confirming an achievement in hunting or in battle, or providing directions to guide others in their activities. More is known about communication on this level in historic times. In a story told by Herodotus, the Greek historian, called the "father of history" (484–425 B.C.), knots in a cord served to count days. He related how the Persian king, Darius, when he was about to invade Scythia, gave a leather thong with sixty knots in it to the Greeks who were staying behind to defend a bridge over the Danube. He instructed them to untie one knot each day that he was away, and to remain at the bridge until all the knots were untied. In case the king had not returned by then, the Greeks would be free to go home. A more complicated system of knots was in use among the Incas of Peru during the sixteenth century when the Spaniards conquered the country. These *quipus* consisted of knotted cords attached to crossbars with other cords hanging from them. In addition to knots, different colors were used to indicate meaning. The knots and colors were a memory aid; if, in the course of time, people forgot what the *quipus* stood for, the record had lost its value, although it might still be regarded as a work of art. A similar way of recording facts was in use among the North American Indians who were skillful in weaving pictures of events in a belt. Here again, the beads themselves and their various colors had a certain meaning. These belts, or wampums, were carefully guarded by each tribe. The wampum that depicts the treaty between William Penn and the Indians, symbolized by an Indian and a white man holding hands, is well known. The white man is wearing a hat (a kind of trademark for white people in general). These examples suffice to show that memory and man's ability to interpret symbolic language are not a sound foundation for the building of a system of communication.

Pictures, Pictograms, and Ideograms

The insufficiency of the above ways of communication led to the invention of something more lasting, the use of pictures. This method was well known among the North American Indians and has been found at the earliest stages of the Sumerian and Egyptian writing systems that later developed into syllabaries. The advantages of the picture writing that was used by the North American Indians are that the simple drawings can be produced without much effort and that they do not offer too many difficulties to the "reader." At first the pictures bore much resemblance to reality; then they gradually became more stylized and more difficult to understand. When an Indian "wrote" an account of a hunting trip, he depicted the main character and all the significant people, animals, and objects he met on his way. Days were indicated by dashes. These accounts were to be regarded as a whole, with the individual pictures providing aids to piece the story together. Proper interpretation is not always easy; besides the necessity of being endowed with a good imagination, the "reader" must be well acquainted with the culture that produced the picture story. This is especially true of interpreting a historical account which consists of pictures drawn in a spiral form on a buffalo robe. This recording of historical events, one for each year, was begun by a Dakota Indian called Lone Dog. The first symbol was entered for the year 1800 and the tribe kept it up until 1871. For the first year, thirty (or thirty-one) short black lines stand for the killing of that number of Dakotas by Crow Indians. Black lines are always used to denote the number of Dakotas killed by enemies. The next year is represented by the head and body of a man covered with red spots, signifying that during that time many Dakotas died of smallpox. The decision of which event was the most important one for that year and thus should be entered on the robe was probably made by the council of old men and authorities of the tribe. At certain times the robe was exhibited to the members of the tribe for a lesson in history and the way to record it.

Picture writing had its problems. Not everyone seeing the pictures would arrive at the same story and not every artist would use the same pictures to convey a certain fact or idea. When many pictures had to be drawn, the artist eliminated much detail. A man would be drawn as a stick figure. The artist only had to add a spear to make a hunter out of him, a cripple was deprived of a leg, and an old man received a staff to lean on. Another simplification made it possible to represent many of the same objects with only one picture. One hunter with ten dashes under his feet symbolized ten hunters. A sun with seven dashes represented a week.

A problem for the picture writer was the representation of concepts like love, hate, and sorrow. They could not be depicted by simply drawing an object. The solution was found by combining two pictures to express an idea. Thus it became possible to depict the concept of weeping by drawing the picture for "water" above the picture for "eye." In the same way, the pictures for "woman" and "son" represented the concept of love; wife was represented by combining "woman" and "broom." Whenever the picture of an object was used for an abstract idea, the reader had to decide what was meant in the specific context. The picture of a pipe could stand for the object itself or for peace among North American Indians.

An example of picture writing in an entirely different part of the world, Mesopotamia, the land between the Euphrates and Tigris Rivers, is provided by a clay tablet found in the city of Uruk, the biblical Erech. It dates from a time when a people called the Sumerians dominated the southern part of the plain. This tablet is a ledger, written about 3100 B.C., one side of which is covered with small cases filled with signs for numbers in the shape of semicircles, and other symbols designating a name. The meaning is recorded on the other side of the tablet where we see five circles, four semicircles, and the heads of a cow and an ox. "Reading" this we conclude that the pictures stand for fifty-four ox-cows, or fifty-four cattle. This tablet, which is one of a limited number found, does not tell the same kind of story as the Indian pictures, but it represents the same stage in the development of writing.

An early example of Egyptian writing comes a little closer to our Indian story. It is found on the palette of Narmer, dug up at Hierakonpolis in Upper Egypt, and describes a historic feat that happened before 3000 B.C. On the large center field we see a king beating a conquered enemy. This is pure picture writing, showing the king proclaiming a victory over his enemies. The picture in the right top field corner is more complicated. It shows a falcon, a rope, a man's head, and an oval with six flowers on top. The falcon is a very common representation of the god Horus. The god holds the rope, which is coming out of the man's head, which in turn is attached to the oval object with the six flowers. Because the Egyptian word for flower (*kho*) also means "a thousand," there may be a symbolic element here. The picture may be read: "Horus brings to the pharaoh six thousand foreigners captured with their land."

For Indian writing this was the final stage of development; fortunately the Sumerians and Egyptians continued to develop more sophisticated writing systems, thus paving the way for the invention of the alphabet. In both writing systems pictures became simplified and standardized in much the same way, so the drawings for many familiar objects are similar in Egypt and Mesopotamia. The Sumerian sign for star (✳) is not basically different from the Egyptian (⚹) and the Hittite (⋇). Sumerian signs underwent some radical changes that made it impossible in most cases to recognize the underlying pictures. When much had to be written, the drawing became too time-consuming; as a result, the scribes left out many details. A further development consisted of turning all pictures around 90° counterclockwise with the result that they were all lying on their backs as it were. More simplification entered into the picture when instead of scratching the signs in clay, a writing tool made of a piece of reed with a triangular end, called a stylus, was introduced to make impressions on a clay tablet. Since the scribes did not want to move the clay tablet while writing, only a few basic strokes were used to make up the signs. These signs, called cuneiform from the Latin *cuneus* ("wedge"), can be horizontal (▷—), oblique (◿), or look like an eye (◁). The development from picture to abstract sign is clearly shown in the development of the sign for "sun." The sign started as ◯, then was turned around to ◁, first pictured in wedges as ⊲⊳, and finally looked like this ⊲. In order to express abstract ideas, the meaning of the original sign was expanded to include other desired meanings. A picture could now stand for "sun," a symbol which can be labeled a pictogram, or it could express the ideas *day, time, bright, light,* and others. In this case the sign is an ideogram. The result was that one sign could acquire so many

Early pictographic tablets from Uruk in Mesopotamia.

Pictorial origin of several cuneiform signs.

SUMERIAN | EARLY BABYLONIAN | LATE BABYLONIAN | ASSYRIAN

STAR
SUN
MONTH
MAN
KING
SON
PRINCE
LORD
HIS
REED
POWER
MOUTH
OX
BIRD
DESTINY
FISH
GARDENER
HABITATION

The Palette of Narmer. The obverse (below) contains a circular recess for grinding cosmetics. The reverse (right) depicts Narmer with mace in hand ready to smite an enemy.

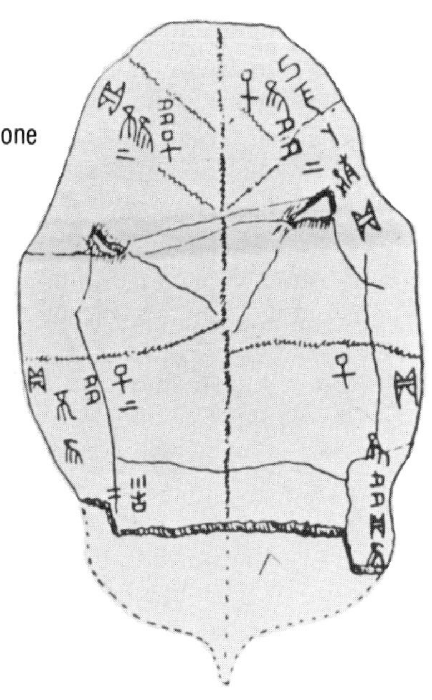

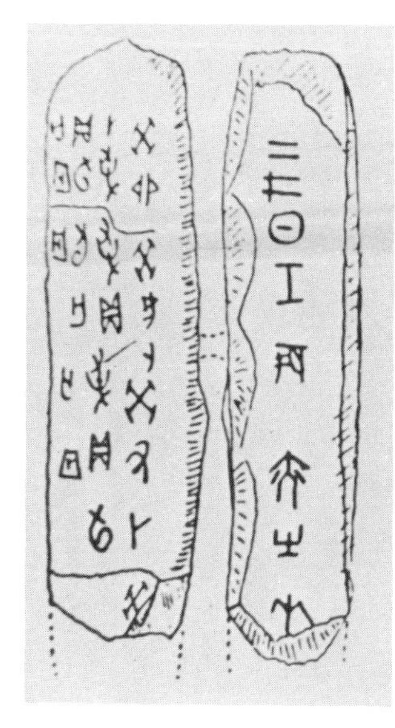

Chinese oracle texts on animal bone and tortoise shell.

Modern Chinese.

惟十又八年十又二月初
吉庚寅王才周康穆宮王
令尹氏友史趛典善夫克
田人克拜稽首敢對天子
不顯魯休揚用作旅盨惟
用獻于師尹朋友昏遘克
其用朝夕享于皇且皇且考其
口口口口降克多福眉壽永令
畯臣天子克其日易休無
疆克其萬年子子孫孫永寶用

meanings that it was difficult, even in context, to decide what the scribe intended to express. To alleviate this difficulty the scribes invented a number of signs that were placed before the word to indicate the meaning which the writer intended to express. Thus a certain sign before a word could indicate plurality, another might designate that the word is a royal name. These signs are called determinatives. They facilitated the reading of a text, but the large number of signs the Sumerians needed to write their language became very confusing.

The Egyptian picture writing, as shown on the palette of Narmer, developed along the same lines as Sumerian cuneiform, although the picture-character of the hieroglyphic signs was retained much longer. Pictograms were expanded into ideograms when the picture for "eye" no longer designated only an eye, but also expressed many other words which are in some way related to "eye," for example, to see, to watch, to be blind. The Egyptians had a remarkable sign for the word *king,* the picture of a bee, indicating that the capacity for organizing was thought to be more important than great strength. The Egyptians as well as the Sumerians felt the need to classify words with the help of determinatives, but in Egypt they were added after the words to which they referred. When a scribe wanted to indicate that the preceding word was a woman's name, the word was followed by the picture of an egg, as in the case of the name *Cleopatra,* which is attested in an Egyptian inscription.

Chinese is another language that started out with pictures, pictograms, and ideograms and finally developed a writing system where a sign stands primarily for a word. The old picture for "wood" looked somewhat like a tree with branches. A picture of a man on a cliff, representing danger, is an example of symbolism. The pictorial stage of this writing system is preserved in old inscriptions on animal bones, tortoise shells, bronze vessels, weapons, pottery, and jade. When pictograms developed into ideograms in the same way as had occurred in Sumerian cuneiform and in Egyptian hieroglyphs, the problem of one picture representing many concepts had to be solved. This was accomplished in the same way as in the other languages, but the terminology is different. Whereas the Sumerians and Egyptians used what we call determinatives, the Chinese used "keys." The sign *pa* has eight different meanings. When employed with the key denoting a plant, it means a banana tree; when employed with the key for "iron," it designates a war chariot; and with the key for "mouth" it conveys the meaning "cry."

In all these systems the same problem was apparent—the difficulty of distinguishing among the many meanings of a word-

An Indian rock drawing discovered in Michigan.

LITERARY HIERATIC OF THE TWELFTH DYNASTY (*Pr. 4, 2–4*), WITH TRANSCRIPTION

OFFICIAL HIERATIC OF THE TWENTIETH DYNASTY (*Abbott 5, 1–3*), WITH TRANSCRIPTION

LITERARY DEMOTIC OF THE THIRD CENTURY B.C. (*Dem. Chron. 6, 1–3*), WITH TRANSCRIPTION

Three forms of Egyptian writing: Hieroglyphic, Hieratic, and Demotic.

sign. Adding determinatives to ideograms was a big step forward, but it was not enough to end the confusion.

Syllabic Writing

A revolutionary advance took place when a picture was no longer associated with the object it represented, but with the sounds one heard, independent of the picture; in other words, when the principle of phonetization made its entry into the language. The Sumerian name *Kuraka* could be represented by three pictures—one for mountain, giving the sound *kur;* one for water, giving *a;* and one for mouth, giving *ka.*

The Egyptians also completely separated the semantic value of the object depicted from the sound it represented. An example is the word for draft-board ( )—*manet,* where "et" probably is the feminine ending. This word may also be used to write *mānet* ("she who remains"), and all the other words that are related to the verbal stem *moun.* The meaning "draft-board" was lost and became the phonetic sign for $m + n$, and could be used for all words that contained these letters in this order. This phonetic sign consists of two consonants; therefore it is called a bilateral sign. The Egyptians also developed alphabetic signs where one letter denoted a certain sound; these are called unilateral signs. An illustration of such a sound is the hieroglyph , which shows a mouth. As a pictogram it depicts the word *mouth.* The Egyptian word for it was *ro'* with a very weak final consonant indicated by the raised comma. The "o" was dropped and only the "r" remained. A third group of hieroglyphics consisting of three consonants, designated as trilaterals, is represented by the word for "beetle." It contains the consonants $h + p + r$.

At this stage the function of the signs, whether they were picturelike (Egyptian) or wedge-shaped (Sumerian), was to represent syllables, either a vowel plus a consonant, or the other way around. With this development the way was paved for the greatest feat in the history of writing systems—the alphabet.

Both Mesopotamian cuneiform and Egyptian hieroglyphs puzzled scholars for centuries, and at times it was thought to be useless to try to decipher these scripts. Thanks to persistent scholars, however, it is now possible to read languages written in both of these syllabic systems. Until the end of the eighteenth century not much progress had been made in deciphering cuneiform script. The breakthrough came when a German schoolteacher from Göttingen, Georg Friedrich Grotefend, accepted a bet that he could not decipher cuneiform script.

Georg Friedrich Grotefend
1775–1853

Grotefend set to work, utilizing his knowledge of ancient history and philology. He reasoned that the three languages occurring on his primary text, an inscription from Persepolis, conveyed the same message and that the one in the middle had to be Old Persian. He also knew that one of the other languages was Babylonian. In his studies he had learned that kings were referred to in formulaic phrases. Two passages seemed promising and he indeed found a phrase for "kings." By a process of elimination he discovered the names of the kings mentioned to be Darius and Xerxes. Grotefend succeeded in establishing sound values for thirteen cuneiform signs. However, when he presented his findings to the Göttingen Academy, the members could not believe that a young schoolteacher could have discovered something orientalists had puzzled over for centuries.

Henry Creswicke Rawlinson
1810–1895

An Englishman by the name of Rawlinson who went to India in the service of the East India Company spent a large part of his life transcribing, deciphering, and translating cuneiform texts. In Bombay he learned Persian, Arabic, and Hindustani in a very short time. He found his greatest challenge in an inscription spread over fourteen columns on a steep slope on Mount Behistun ("place of the gods"), twenty-two miles from Hamadan in Persia. When Rawlinson had translated a large part of the text he sent a report to the Asiatic Society in London from where the news spread to France.

Hieroglyphics appear on Egyptian pyramids, tombs, obelisks, and temples, where they were noticed and copied by medieval European travelers. It was not until 1798, however, with the finding of the Rosetta Stone during Napoleon's campaign in Egypt, that progress was made in deciphering the script. The Rosetta Stone, a slab of black basalt three feet nine inches high and two feet four inches wide, is inscribed with three bands of writing. The first is written in hieratic, a simplified form of hieroglyphics, the second in demotic, a cursive form of hieratic, and the third in Greek. A British scholar, Sir Thomas Young, identified the demotic words for "Ptolemy" and "king" and several conjunctions. By 1818 he had completed a hieroglyphic dictionary and five phonetic signs proved to be correct. After he had proved that the name in one of the ovals, which are called cartouches, was "Ptolemy," Young decided that it was impossible to make more progress in deciphering hieroglyphics and he gave up.

The Behistun Inscription.

The man who solved the problem was born in France in 1790. Jean François Champollion was not a very good student in school, but he excelled in languages. When he was twelve years old one of his teachers showed him his collection of Egyptian

The Rosetta Stone (3'7'' by 2'6'').

Jean Francois Champollion
1790–1832

antiquities, among them samples of hieroglyphics. The boy decided to decipher them and studied everything that would help him in this task. His command of Arabic became good enough to fool natives. Coptic, the language of Egyptian Christians, became more important to him than his native French. During the year he lived in Paris, Champollion worked on a Coptic dictionary and studied a copy of the Rosetta Stone in the Louvre. Jean and his brother were politically active against Napoleon, and after the emperor was banned to Elba they took part in a revolt to remove the Bourbons. Because of this activity, Jean lost his position as a teacher. However, this loss provided him with an opportunity to return to the problem of hieroglyphics. Champollion succeeded in translating the demotic text of the Book of the Dead into hieratic script and this again into hieroglyphics. Then he worked on the text of the Rosetta Stone. He found that there were 1419 Egyptian symbols compared to 468 Greek words. Thus each hieroglyph had to represent less than a complete word. The text contained several cartouches, all representing the same name. Young had already deciphered one of them as "Ptolemaios," but he had been unaware of the fact that vowels were not represented in the Egyptian writing system. Champollion made a more accurate translation—"Ptolms." In his search for more names the scholar found another royal name—*Cleopatra*—and several more occurrences of the name *Ptolemy*. By comparing the signs in the cartouches, Champollion found that the signs for the same letters matched. Now it was not difficult to decipher more Greek names. The question was, would his method work for Egyptian names also? This proved to be the case when Champollion succeeded in deciphering the name *Re m ss* (Ramses), and later *Thutmosis*. Not until some time afterward did it occur to Champollion that Egyptian civilization could now be made known to the world. Champollion, although in ill health, traveled for two years in Italy where he copied papyri collections in Florence, Turin, and Rome. In 1828 he led an expedition to Egypt, the country he knew so much about that it could have been his native land. On his return Champollion taught at the Collège de France where he continued until his death in 1832. The first chair of Egyptology in Europe was founded for him there.

Alphabetic Writing

The syllabic writing systems of Mesopotamia and Egypt did not develop into a system of alphabetic writing, although the Egyptians had a number of signs for single consonants which were used primarily for the transcription of foreign names. This potential alphabet was only an adjunct to the syllabic system of hieroglyphics, however, and in that system more than one symbol could be used to represent the same consonant. Until the development of the Canaanite alphabet nobody managed to invent a writing system in which one symbol stood for one consonantal sound.

Proto-Sinaitic inscription on a votive offering. (The signs read: TNT-'gift').

Exactly how the Canaanite consonantal alphabet system developed is unclear, but there is evidence that rudimentary forms of the signs were in use in the Middle Bronze Age. Several lines of development leading to the Canaanite alphabet have been

Cartouche from the Rosetta Stone containing the word *Ptolemy*.

Egyptian uniconsonantal sign list.

ʾ (aleph)
i, j (yod)
ʿ (aïn)
w
b
p
f
m
n
r
h
ḥ
ḫ (kh)
ẖ
s
ś
š (sh)
ḳ (q)
k
g
t
ṯ
d
ḏ

suggested. Inscriptions found in 1905 at Serbit el-Khadim in the Sinai Peninsula, not far from the coast of the Gulf of Suez and less than fifty miles from the traditional site of Mount Sinai, date to the period from 1800 to 1500 B.C. While the inscriptions, which are mainly funerary and votive in nature, have not been completely deciphered, the rudimentary signs are definitely alphabetic and recognizable as early forms of the Canaanite alphabet. They were probably written by Semitic miners who were either employed or enslaved by the Egyptians to work the turquoise mines in the area. Examples of similar alphabetic signs from the same general period have been recovered from a number of Palestinian sites. Very recently at Gezer several Middle Bronze store jars were found with what appear to be alphabetic signs scratched on their shoulders.

Early alphabetic inscription from Serabit el-Khadim.

Some enigmatic inscriptions from Byblos, tentatively dated to the close of the Early Bronze Age, may exhibit even earlier forms of alphabetic script, but the evidence is not conclusive. Another possible influence is the Cretan script. The island of Crete under the Minoan dynasty knew a period of prosperity from about 2000 B.C. until 1500 B.C. The Cretans employed two kinds of script; the older one, which has been designated Linear A, is mainly ideographic and has not yet been deciphered. The other one, known as Linear B, developed from Linear A during the fourteenth and thirteenth centuries B.C. It was deciphered by Michael Ventris, a British architect. Ventris found that Linear B was a syllabic system of a form of early Greek. Although some letters of the Semitic (Canaanite) alphabet show a close resemblance to a number of Cretan characters, no direct influence between Linear B and that alphabet can be shown.

An important discovery was made in 1929 in northern Syria at the site of the ancient city of Ugarit when archaeologists found tablets exhibiting eight different kinds of writing. All of these scripts were in use in the Late Bronze Age in Ugarit. One script looked like the cuneiform of Mesopotamia, but it proved to be alphabetic and was in principle quite like the linear Canaanite alphabet. A few years later a small clay tablet was found which listed the alphabet of Ugarit in order; thirty-two signs were used in the system, and they were written from left to right like Mesopotamian cuneiform rather than in the normal right to left direction of other Semitic alphabetic scripts.

6	5	4	3	2	1

Development of several signs in the Semitic alphabet. Top row: Proto-Sinaitic pictographs. Middle row: transitional forms, ca. 1200 B.C. Bottom row: Phoenician forms of the ninth century B.C. Letters shown are 1—*aleph* (ox), 2—*kaph* (palm of hand), 3—*mem* (water), 4—*ayin* (eye), 5—*resh* (head), and 6—*shin* (composite bow).

Another early inscription was found at Byblos on the sarcophagus of Hiram, a Phoenician king. Although the thirteenth century B.C. has been suggested as the date for this inscription, in which Hiram's son states that he made this sarcophagus for the eternal resting place of his father, it is more likely to be dated to the early tenth century B.C. The Hiram who was buried within it was quite likely the contemporary of David and Solomon. The script used was that of the Canaanite linear alphabet which is also known as the Phoenician alphabet. The Phoenicians comprised the remnant of the earlier Canaanites following the incursions of Arameans, Israelites, and Philistines into Canaanite territory in the Early Iron Age. Restricted thus to the Mediterranean coastlands, they turned their attention to the sea. They were bold sailors who knew the winds and the currents better than anyone else. As the traders of the Mediterranean world, they established colonies on the island of Malta and on the coasts of Africa and Spain, and trading stations in Italy and Greece. The Phoenician alphabet consisted of twenty-two symbols which were to become the basis for all subsequent alphabets.

The Phoenicians employed two related alphabets, one developed by the Tyrians and used mainly by the inland tribes, and the other used by the Sidonians. The Sidonian alphabet was used by the Jews until the captivity and survives in the modern Samaritan alphabet. The Tyrian branch was borrowed by the Greeks after the Trojan War. The most important Tyrian, or Moabite, inscription is found on the Mesha Stone, also known as the Moabite Stone, discovered in 1868 at Dibon, near the Dead Sea. The length of the inscription, the clear form of the letters carved in very hard material, and the definite date of the text make the Mesha Stone extremely important for the study of the language and the writing system. The contents are related in the first person by King Mesha of Moab who first tells how his country had been oppressed by the Israelites for forty years, from the time of Omri (876–869) until the reign of Omri's grandson, Jehoram (849–842). Then he relates the story of his insurrection against Israel, as told in II Kings 3, the outcome of which was that his army was defeated and his land laid waste. Mesha continues telling how he in turn defeated the Israelites, took the vessels of Jehovah, and dedicated them to his own god, Chemosh. This is followed by an account of the reconstruction of the cities, roads, walls, and palaces of his land. Finally, Mesha mentions a subsequent war against the Edomites.

Even older Phoenician inscriptions turned up on Cyprus in 1876. The longest one reads: "This vessel of good bronze was offered by a citizen of Carthage, servant of Hiram, king of the Sidonians, to Baal Lebanon, his Lord." The temple of Baal Lebanon must have been one of the "high places" mentioned in the biblical Book of Kings (in the record of Baal worship on Mount Carmel). The name of Baal Hermon is analogous to that

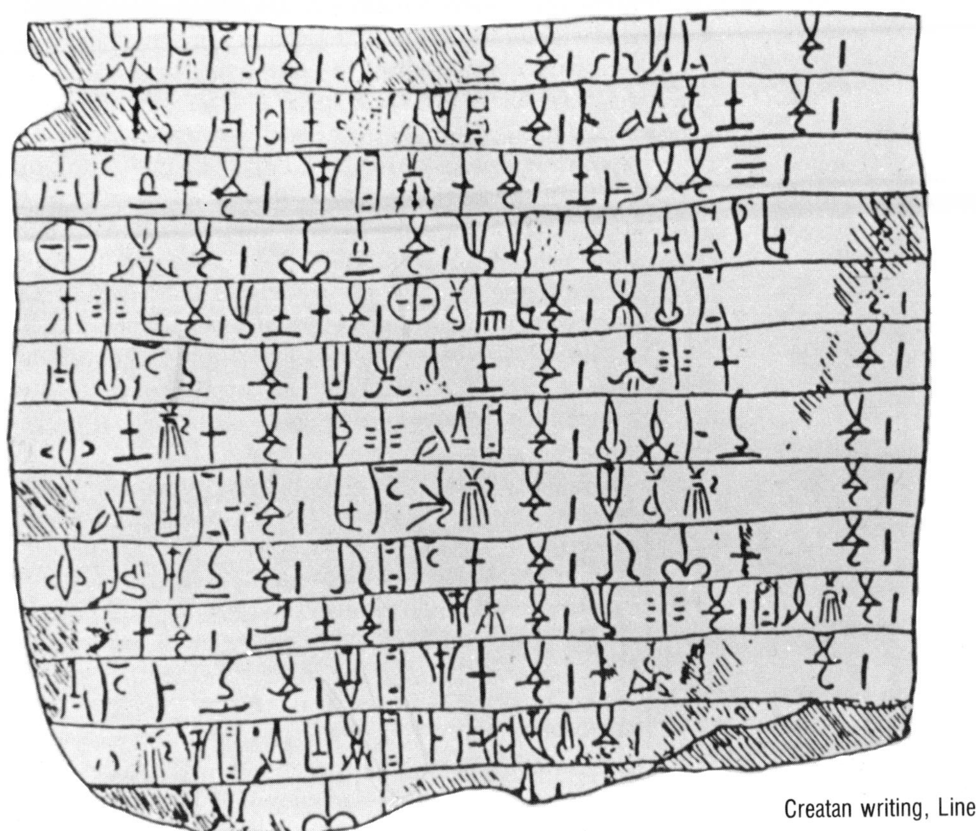

Creatan writing, Linear B.

A Phoenician inscription from Cyprus.

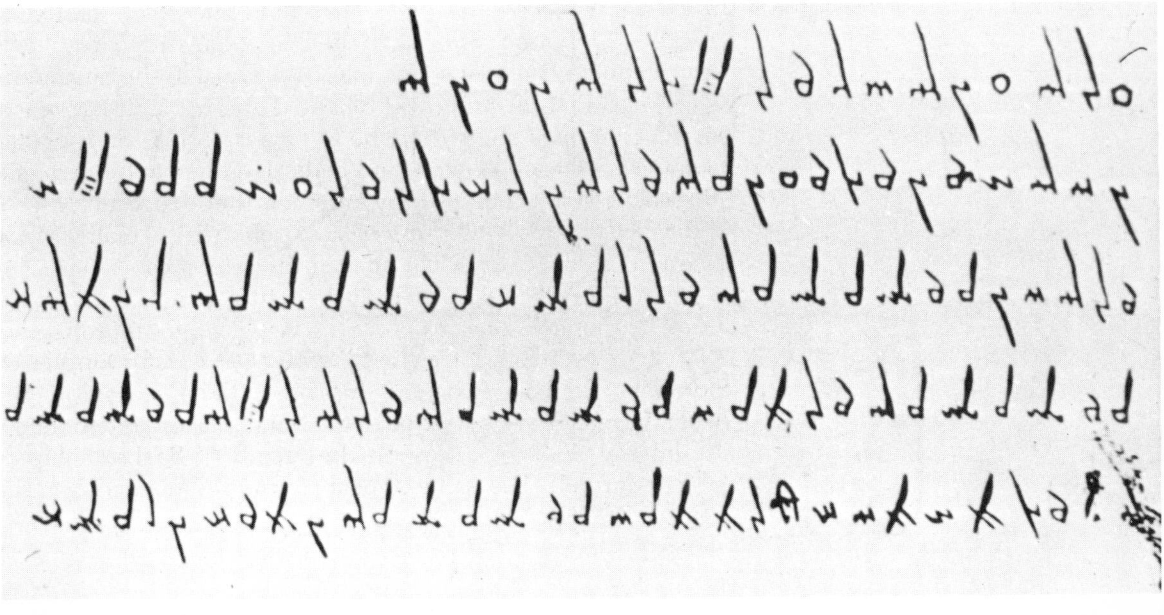

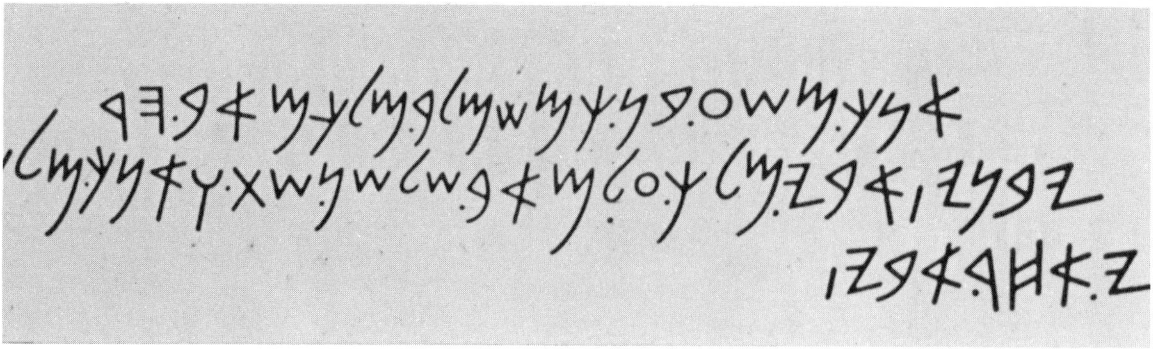

Part of the Moabite Stone.

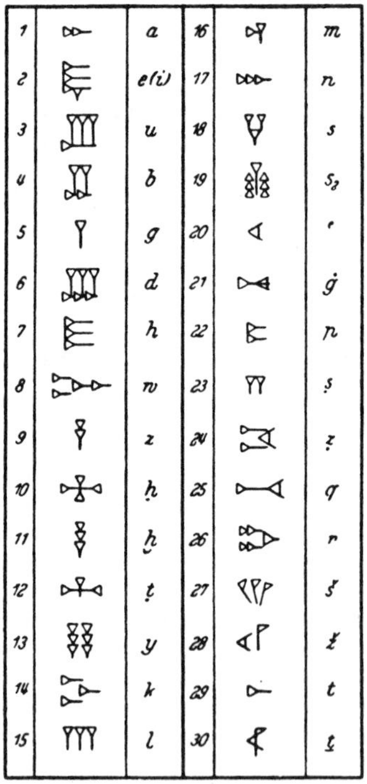

The Ugaritic alphabet. Above: the cuneiform characters with their alphabetic equivalent. Below: an example of Ugaritic writing.

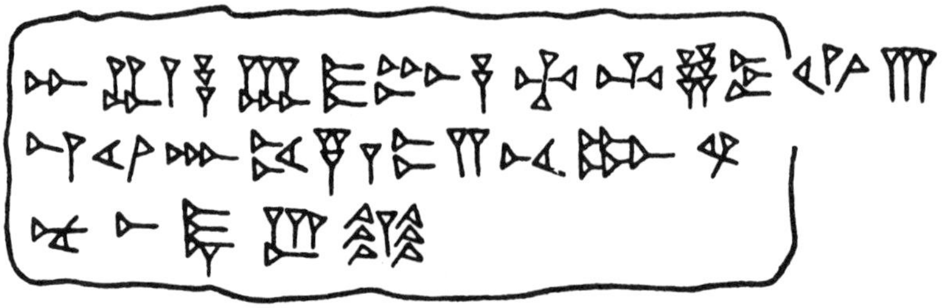

of Baal Lebanon. The name *Carthage* in the inscription does not refer to the Phoenician colony in Africa; it simply means "Newtown" and may denote a suburb of Tyre or Sidon.

The Sidonian version of the Phoenician alphabet is found in more inscriptions than the Tyrian one, all of them, however, dating from a later period. An important document occurs on the sarcophagus of Eshmunazar, king of Sidon, dating from the fifth or the beginning of the fourth century B.C. The twenty-two line inscription begins: "ASHMuN'AZaR MeLeK TSiDoNiM" (Eshmunazar, king of the Sidonians). The king speaks in the first person, relating that he and his mother have erected temples to Baal Sidon, Ashtaroth, and Ashnum. He beseeches the favor of the gods and prays that Dora, Joppa, and the fertile corn lands in the plains of Sharon may ever remain annexed to Sidon.

The Phoenician alphabet was adapted to the needs of different peoples. One of its modifications was called Aramaic, found first in the highlands of Aram (Syria) on the caravan routes from the West to Mesopotamia. The Jews brought it back with them from Assyria and, since Phoenicia was only a minor nation after Nebuchadnezzar had destroyed Tyre, Aramaic became the most important writing system in the area until the end of the second century B.C. The southern Aramaic branch developed into the square Hebrew alphabet and the northern branch into the modern Arabic alphabet with its extremely modified forms.

The Greek alphabet, also derived from the Phoenician writing system, became more important. Greece in the thirteenth and twelfth centuries B.C. was dominated by the Achaeans who had invaded Greece from the south. Rather than being a united country, Greece was divided into many city-states which often were at war with each other. Foreign trade was important. It has even been suggested that the Greeks did not attack Troy because of the beautiful Helen, but because their trade route to the Black Sea was under attack and had to be kept open. When the Greeks were invaded from the north by the Dorians, they were forced more and more to seek their fortunes on the high seas where they encountered the Phoenicians, both as friends and as foes. Early contacts between the two peoples had resulted from the establishment of Phoenician colonies on Greek soil.

Taking over a Semitic alphabet consisting of consonants only, because vowels are less significant to meaning than consonants in these languages, posed certain problems for an Indo-European language in which vowels are very important. Furthermore, Phoenician sounds differed from Greek sounds and thus certain changes had to be made. In due course, all problems were solved, and in the process the Greeks modified the forms of the Phoenician letters. The Greeks acquired the necessary vowels by converting unused signs from the Phoenician alphabet into vowel signs, for example, the consonantal sound of the Semitic *aleph* was simply dropped by the Greeks who used the sign to represent the vowel *a*. The other vowels were

Inscribed sherds from Corinth.

created in a similar manner. Since the Phoenician consonants did not match all the Greek sounds, some adaptations were necessary. There was *teth*, the Phoenician sound for an emphatic "t," that the Greeks did not need; therefore, they changed it into "th," *theta*. The *s*-sound posed a problem. The Phoenicians offered *samekh*, a sharp *s*-sound, *tsade* for "ts" (ca*ts*), and *shin* for "sh." The Greeks, who needed a symbol only for a soft "s," could choose any one of the three, and so they did. One group adopted the *tsade* under the name *san;* another group renamed *shin* to *sigma;* a third group preferred *samekh*, calling it *xi* and using it for "x." Now the Greeks had an alphabet in which the names of a number of the letters had meaning only in Semitic languages, where *aleph* means "ox" and *beth* stands for "house," whereas "ox" in Greek is *bous* and house is *oikos*. The final vowel on the names of the letters was probably added by the Greeks because of their dislike of final consonants other than "r," "s," and "n." The Greeks wrote from right to left, from left to right, and even in both directions, a phenomenon called boustrophedon, meaning "as the ox turns." The writing follows the path an ox takes when a field is plowed—one furrow is finished and the next one begins at the end of the first one. Since all asymmetrical letters have to be reversed in every other line, reading of boustrophedon writing is rather difficult.

Scholars do not agree about the time the Greeks took over the Phoenician alphabet. On the basis of inscriptions found, it may be concluded that the Greeks borrowed the Phoenician alphabet during the ninth century B.C. Although they did not invent the alphabet, the Greeks played an important part in the history of

Development of the Alphabet

Phoenician	Hebrew (square)	East Greek	Roman	minuscule	Cyrillic
	א aleph	Α alpha a	A A A	a	А
house	ב beth b,v	Β beta b	B	b	Б В
camel	ג gimel g	Γ gamma g	C G	c g	
gate	ד daleth d	Δ delta d	D	d	Д
?	ה he h	Ε e-psilon e	E	e	Е
nail	ו vav w	(F) digamma w	F	f	
weapon	ז zayin z	Ζ zeta dz	Z (late republic)	z	З
fish ?	ח heth h	Η eta e,h	H	h	И
?	ט teth th	Θ theta th	—		
hand	י yodh y	Ι iota i	I, J (xvi century)	i j	
palm	כ kaph k	Κ kappa k	K	k	К
goad	ל lamedh l	Λ lambda l	L	l	Л
water	מ mem m	Μ mu m	M	m	М
fish ?	נ nun n	Ν nu n	N	n	Н
support	ס samekh s	Ξ xi x	X (from West Gr.)	x	
eye	ע ayin	glottal stop Ο o-micron o	O	o	О
mouth	פ pe p	Π pi p	P	p	П
?	צ tsade ts		—	—	
monkey	ק koph k	(Ϙ koppa k*)	Q	q	
head	ר resh r	Ρ rho r	R	r	Р
tooth	ש shin s,sh	Σ C sigma s	S	s	С
cross	ת tav t	Τ tau t	T	t	Т
		Υ u-psilon u	U V W (medieval)	u v w	У
			Y (late republic)	y	
		Φ phi ph	—	—	Ф
		Χ chi ch	—	—	Х
		Ψ psi ps	—	—	
		Ω o-mega o		—	

*before a back vowel, o or u

Note: the Cyrillic alphabet contains a number of letters not shown here.

An Egyptian Hieroglyphic Alphabet
of 2500 B.C.

The signs were usually given the natural coloring of the objects they represent, in several hues. But they were often uniformly colored blue or green, especially on monuments containing religious texts.

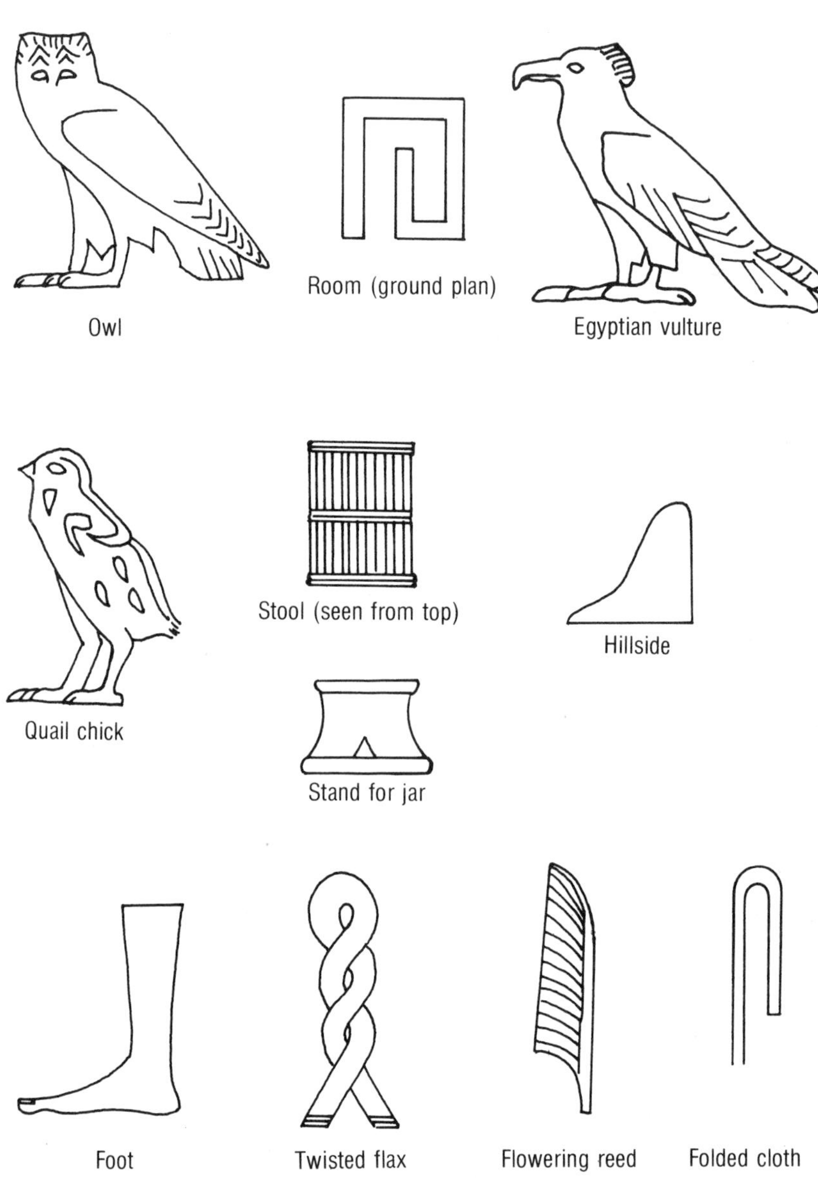

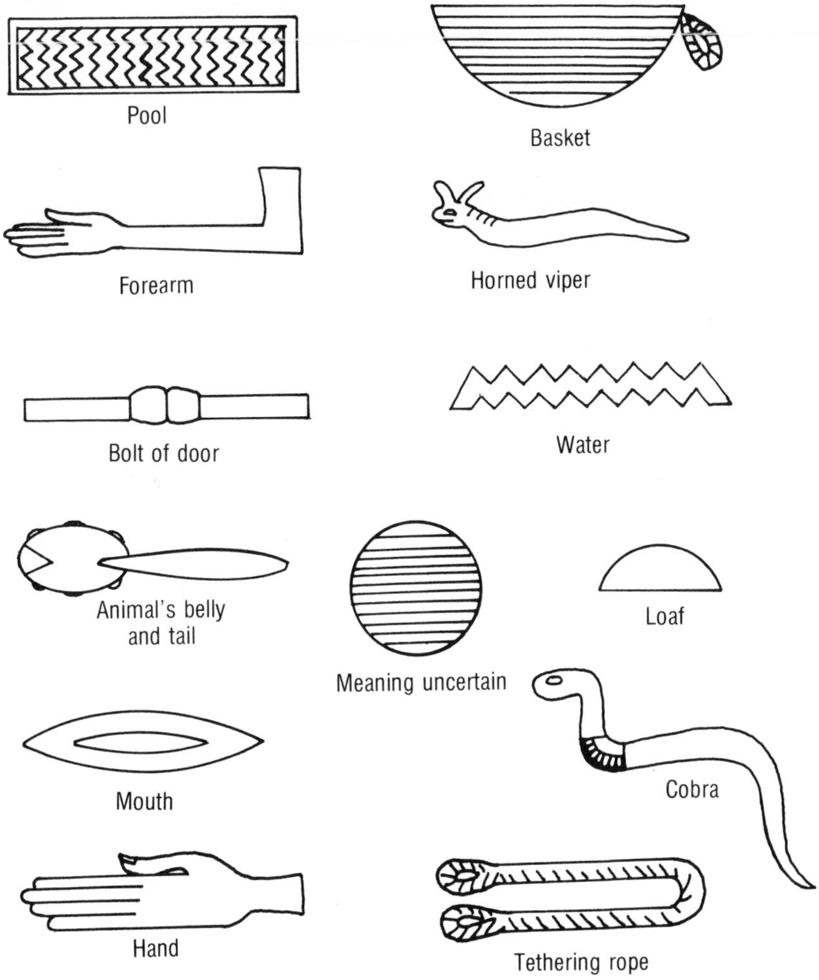

Pool
Basket
Forearm
Horned viper
Bolt of door
Water
Animal's belly and tail
Meaning uncertain
Loaf
Mouth
Cobra
Hand
Tethering rope

The following forms of the signs are simplified versions of those shown above. The Egyptians themselves sometimes used more detail, sometimes less:

3 (aleph)*
y
' ('ayin)*
w
b
p
f
h
emphatic h*
ch (as in Loch Lomond)
ch (closer to sh)
q (at back of throat)*
k
g
t
tch (as in catch)
m
n
r
z
s
sh
d
dj

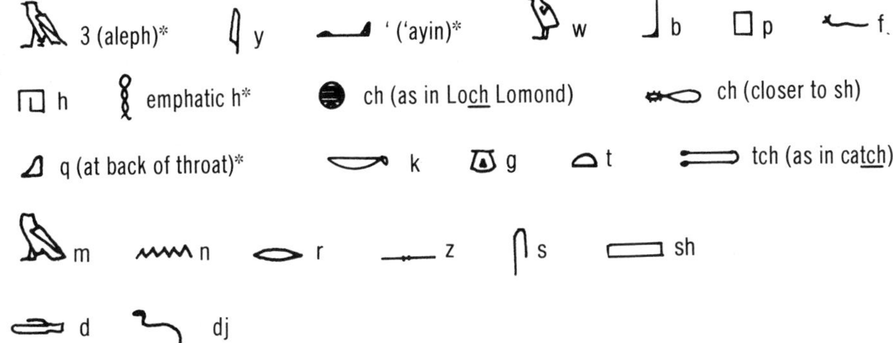

writing by adapting a Semitic writing system to an Indo-European language, thereby clearing the way for numerous peoples to write their language with a limited number of symbols. They showed their creativity in this process by using Semitic symbols they did not need for signs that were indispensable in their system, by adapting other signs to their needs, and by inventing additional symbols.

The most significant alphabet derived from the Greek is that of the Etruscans. The Etruscans played an important part in European civilization, providing the Romans with many of the institutions and cultural achievements for which they are famous. The gift of an alphabetic writing system is one of them. Etruscan inscriptions can be read (vocalized). However, since the language is unknown, understanding these inscriptions is in most cases impossible. The Romans also made some changes in the Etruscan alphabet to make it suitable for the writing of their own language. Our own system of writing is a further development of the Roman script.

SUGGESTED TOPICS FOR FURTHER STUDY

1. The pictograph as an early form of writing.
2. The inventor of writing—Egypt or Sumer?
3. The first thousand years of writing—from Sumerian to Akkadian.
4. The development of determinatives in Egypt and in Mesopotamia, and a comparison.
5. The history of the Chinese writing system.
6. The story of the modern deciphering of the Egyptian hieroglyphics.
7. The modern deciphering of Akkadian.
8. Pre-alphabetic writing systems of Crete, Greece, and Cyprus.
9. The names of the letters of the Semitic alphabet and their meanings.
10. Study the different directions in which Greek and Semitic alphabets and syllabaries were written.
11. Explore the way the Roman alphabet developed into our alphabet.
12. The forms of the letters of the Semitic alphabet in the time of Moses.
13. The references to written communication in the Hebrew Bible.
14. The role of the scribe in the ancient world.
15. Writing as a means of religious and political power over people in antiquity.

16. The implements and surfaces used for writing in the biblical period.
17. Writing as a means of recording compared to writing as a means of creativity (the production of literature).
18. The Moabite Stone and other early inscriptions discovered in Palestine.
19. The scroll and the temple—an investigation of the relationship between writing and temples in the ancient world.
20. The relationship between speech and writing.

RECOMMENDED READING

Chiera, E., *They Wrote on Clay* (Chicago: University of Chicago Press, 1955).

Cleator, P. E., *Lost Languages* (New York: The John Day Company, 1959).

Coogan, Michael D., "Alphabets and Elements," *BASOR* 216 (1974), p. 61.

Diringer, David, *The Alphabet* (London: Hutchinson of London, 1968).

———, *Writing* (London: Thames and Hudson, 1962).

Gelb, I. J., *A Study of Writing* (Chicago: University of Chicago Press, 1952).

McCarter, P. Kyle, "The Early Diffusion of the Alphabet," *Biblical Archaeologist* 37 (1974), p. 54.

Mercer, Samuel A. B., *The Origin of Writing and Our Alphabet* (London: Luzac, 1959).

Millard, A. R., "The Practice of Writing in Ancient Israel," *Biblical Archaeologist* 35 (1972), p. 98.

Ogg, Oscar, *The 26 Letters* (New York: Thomas Y. Crowell, 1971).

FOR FURTHER READING

Albright, W. F., *Archaeology and the Religion of Israel* (Baltimore: The Johns Hopkins Press, 1942).

———, *From the Stone Age to Christianity* (Garden City, NY: Doubleday, 1957).

Birch, S., *An Introduction of the Study of the Egyptian Hieroglyphics* (London, 1857).

Budge, E. A. Wallis, *The Book of the Dead* (London: K. Paul, Trench, Trubner & Co., Ltd., 1899).

———, *The Rosetta Stone* (London: The Trustees of the British Museum, 1929).

Burrows, M., *What Mean These Stones?* (New Haven: The American Schools of Oriental Research, 1941).

Champdor, A., *The Book of the Dead* (New York: Garrett Publications, 1966).

Champollion, J. F., *Monuments de l'Egypte et de la Nubie* (Paris: Firmin Didot Fréres, 1835–45).

Contenau, G., *Manuel d'Archéologie Orientala IV* (Paris: A. Picard, 1947).

Cooke, G. A., *A Textbook of North-Semitic Inscriptions* (Oxford: Clarendon, 1903).

Cross, F. M., "The Origin and Early Evolution of the Alphabet," *Eretz-Israel* (Jerusalem, 1967).

Diringer, David, "The Alphabet in the History of Civilization" in *The Role of the Phoenicians in the Interaction of Mediterranean Civilizations,* ed. William A. Ward (Beirut: American University of Beirut, 1968), pp. 33–41.

Doblhofer, E., *Voices in Stone* (London, 1961).

Driver, G. R., "Semitic Writing" in *The Schweich Lectures 1944* (London: Oxford University Press, 1948).

Gardiner, A. H., and T. E. Peet, *The Inscriptions of Sinai* (London: Egyptian Exploration Fund, 1919).

Gurney, O. R., *The Hittites* (London and Baltimore: Penguin Books, 1952).

Harden, Donald, *The Phoenicians* (London: Thames and Hudson, 1962).

Hooke, S. H., "The Early History of Writing" in *Antiquity* (Gloucester, England: 1937).

Kramer, Samuel Noah, *History Begins at Sumer* (Garden City, NY: Doubleday, 1959).

______, *The Sumerians* (Chicago: University of Chicago Press, 1963).

Lansing, Elizabeth, *The Sumerians* (London: Cassell, 1974).

Legge, G. F., *The History of the Transliteration of Egyptian* (London: Cambridge University Press, 1902).

Martin, W. J., *The Origin of Writing* (Jerusalem: Forum [Jerusalem radio airgraph digest paper, Dec. 16, 1943]).

Mercer, Samuel A. B., *The Pyramids Texts* (New York: Longmans, Green, 1952).

Moorhouse, A. C., *Writing and the Alphabet* (London: Cobbett Press, 1946).

Oppenheim, A. L., *Ancient Mesopotamia: Portrait of a Dead Civilization* (Chicago: University of Chicago Press, 1968).

Wemyss, S., *The Language of the World: Ancient and Modern, The Alphabets* (Philadelphia, 1950).

5

The Bible and Archaeology

The preceding chapters contained a broad spectrum of ideas about the Bible, archaeology, and archaeologists. Before continuing on to survey various sites and finds, this chapter will present several ideas intended to enable the reader to gain a more balanced perspective of the many and varied relationships that comprise the total archaeological enterprise.

The need for a proper perspective is evident when one realizes how reports of archaeological discoveries are presented to the general public in the popular press. A good example of this phenomenon is provided by the recent discoveries at Tell Mardikh, the site of ancient Ebla, in Syria. In one newspaper account the discovery of the Ebla tablets is said to have shed new light on the history of the Jewish people. This statement is attributed to Professor Giovanni Pettinato, the language expert who first read the texts. In fact, even if one considers that the history of the Jewish people began with the patriarch Abraham, the Ebla texts predate the patriarchs by half a millennium. Another bit of information that was included in the newspaper account of the discovery was the value of the tablets ($15,000,000) when they are in fact invaluable. Another report mentioned a king of the Eblaite dynasty named Ebrum, and immediately the name was associated with Eber, one of Abraham's progenitors. By way of contrast, one may read Pettinato's reports where it is noted that the *resemblance* of the Eblaite name to the Eber of Genesis 10:21 is "truly surprising."

The Eblaite report illustrates how the popular press, in their search for the sensational, far too often treat probabilities as facts and possibilities as certainties. The public, which remains largely uninformed about the real nature of archaeological research and which is therefore ill-equipped to interpret newspaper accounts of archaeological discoveries, does not realize the fragile nature of the "assured results" of archaeological research. But what may suffice for the general public is unacceptable for the beginning student in biblical archaeology or the interested layman.

Archaeological research is a uniquely human activity. It is man attempting to piece together the story of mankind from meager clues which he has been able to recover. In biblical archaeology, three factors are involved in the process of recovering the story—the Bible, archaeology, and the archaeologist—and each of these has its own peculiarities and limitations that affect the total phenomenon that we call archaeological research, including the final results.

The Limitations of the Bible

We suggested above that the Bible may be viewed as the surviving literature of ancient Israel, a literature that contains diverse elements of prose and poetry, proverbs and parables, prophetic oracles and historical narrative. But the Bible is more than simply literature. It contains history, but it is history viewed from a theological perspective. It is a history of the activities of God in the affairs of men. The Bible has survived because of the implications of its theological statements rather than the significance of its historical account of the affairs of men. It has survived despite its antiquity because it has spoken meaningfully to man through the centuries. It has spoken with meaning to those who possessed and transmitted it because it was accepted as the Word of God by those communities of faith who treasured it. At the same time, the Bible does contain history, and these historical records must be open to the same kind of examination as that to which any other ancient historical record may be subjected.

In a sense, then, the Bible contains two kinds of truth—statements of faith and statements of historical fact. Statements of faith contained in the Bible, including theological explanations of historical events, such as the cause of the withdrawal of Sennacherib's forces from the siege of Jerusalem in the time of Hezekiah (II Kings 19:35, 36), are not susceptible to the same type of inquiry as are the records of historical happenings and persons. Archaeological research cannot be used to "prove the

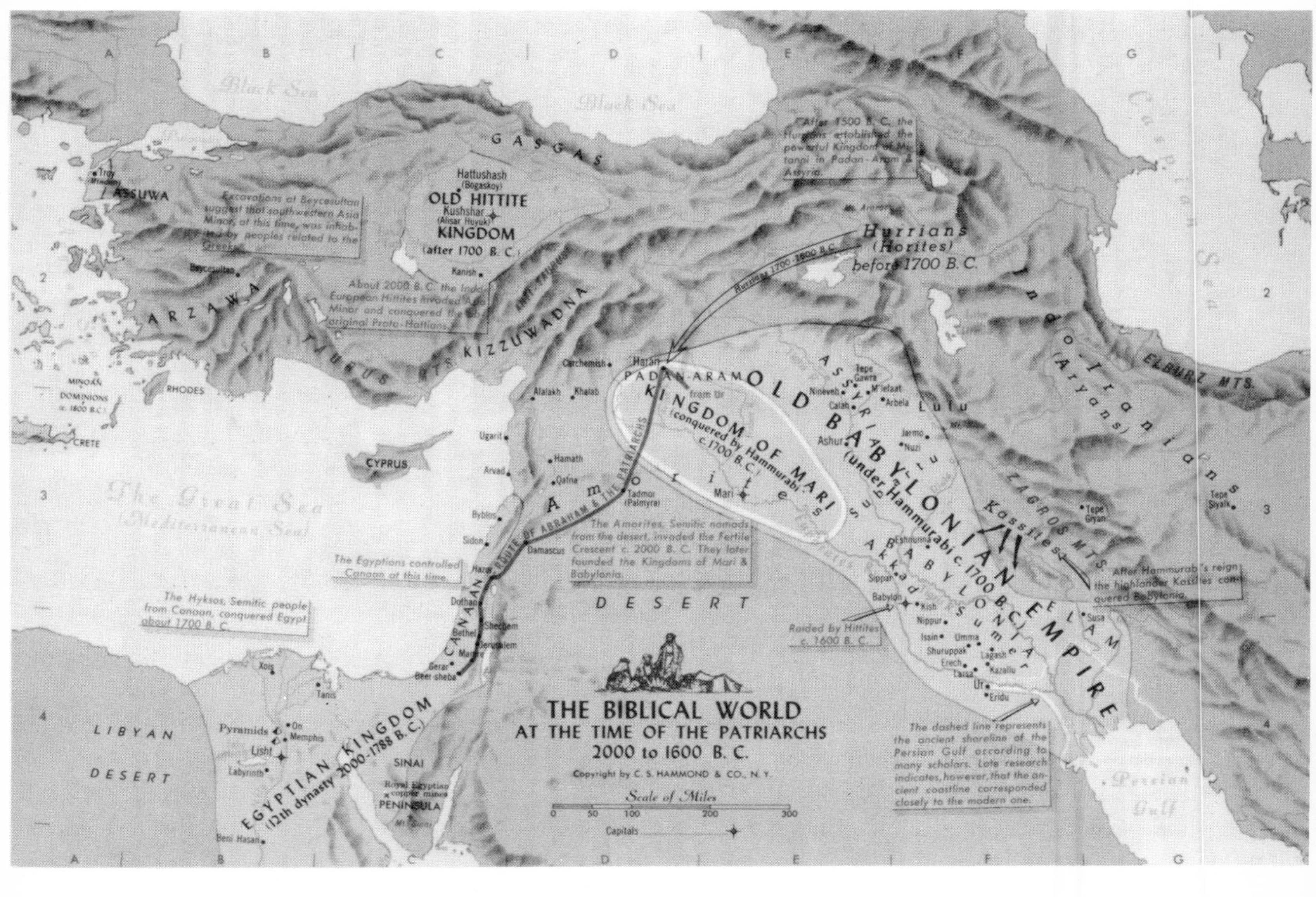
THE BIBLICAL WORLD
AT THE TIME OF THE PATRIARCHS
2000 to 1600 B. C.
Copyright by C. S. HAMMOND & CO., N. Y.
Scale of Miles
0 50 100 200 300
Capitals
Black Sea
Caspian Sea
The Great Sea (Mediterranean Sea)
Persian Gulf
GASGAS
Hattushash (Bogaskoy)
OLD HITTITE KINGDOM (after 1700 B. C.)
Kushshar (Alisar Huyuk)
Kanish
Troy
ASSUWA
Excavations at Beycesultan suggest that southwestern Asia Minor, at this time, was inhabited by peoples related to the Greeks.
Beycesultan
ARZAWA
About 2000 B. C. the Indo-European Hittites invaded Asia Minor and conquered the aboriginal Proto-Hattians.
TAURUS MTS.
KIZZUWADNA
MINOAN DOMINIONS (c. 1800 B.C.)
RHODES
CRETE
CYPRUS
After 1500 B. C. the Hurrians established the powerful Kingdom of Mitanni in Padan-Aram & Assyria.
Mt. Ararat
Hurrians (Horites) before 1700 B. C.
Hurrians 1700-1600 B.C.
Indo-Iranians (Aryans)
ELBURZ MTS.
Tepe Siyalk
Tepe Gyan
ZAGROS MTS.
Kassites
After Hammurabi's reign the highlander Kassites conquered Babylonia.
Carchemish
Haran
PADAN-ARAM
from Ur
KINGDOM OF MARI (conquered by Hammurabi c.1700 B.C.)
Mari
Alalakh
Khalab
Ugarit
Hamath
Arvad
Qatna
Tadmor (Palmyra)
Amorites
ROUTE OF ABRAHAM & THE PATRIARCHS
Byblos
Sidon
Damascus
Hazor
The Amorites, Semitic nomads from the desert, invaded the Fertile Crescent c. 2000 B. C. They later founded the Kingdoms of Mari & Babylonia.
The Egyptians controlled Canaan at this time.
CANAAN
Dothan
Shechem
Bethel
Jerusalem
Mamre
Gerar
Beer-sheba
The Hyksos, Semitic people from Canaan, conquered Egypt about 1700 B. C.
DESERT
OLD BABYLONIAN EMPIRE (under Hammurabi c.1700 B.C.)
ASSYRIA
Tepe Gawra
Nineveh
M'lefaat
Calah
Arbela
Lulu
Jarmo
Nuzi
Ashur
Eshnunna
BABYLONIA
Akkad
Sumer
ELAM
Sippar
Babylon
Kish
Nippur
Isin
Umma
Shuruppak
Lagash
Erech
Larsa
Kazallu
Ur
Eridu
Susa
Raided by Hittites c. 1600 B. C.
The dashed line represents the ancient shoreline of the Persian Gulf according to many scholars. Late research indicates, however, that the ancient coastline corresponded closely to the modern one.
Xois
Tanis
Pyramids
On
Memphis
Lisht
Labyrinth
Beni Hasan
LIBYAN DESERT
EGYPTIAN KINGDOM (12th dynasty 2000-1788 B.C.)
SINAI PENINSULA
Royal Egyptian copper mines
Mt. Sinai

Bible'' in terms of statements of faith. As Nelson Glueck, one of the great American archaeologists of this century, has indicated:

> The Bible is first and foremost a theological document, whose single and unifying purpose (however disparate the component parts of its total mosaic may be) is to portray the nature of God as the God of Israel, of all mankind, of the entire universe, and to explain what worship of Him involves.
>
> Those people are essentially of little faith who seek through archaeological corroboration of historical source materials in the Bible to validate its religious and spiritual insights.

The Bible, as a religious work, needs no proof of its inspiration and authenticity. Its truth is timeless and eternally valid, one evidence of which is its continuing influence on world culture right down to the twentieth century.

It is important to realize, at the same time, that archaeological excavations have produced ample evidence to prove unequivocally that the Bible is not a pious forgery. Thus far, no historical statement in the Bible has been proven false on the basis of evidence retrieved through archaeological research. But with equal frankness it must be noted that there is a lack of evidence from excavations to corroborate some of the historical statements in the Bible. For example, archaeology has found no evidence of walls in Late Bronze Age Jericho which could substantiate the account of the conquest of that city by Joshua and the Israelites.

The Limitations of Archaeology

Competent contemporary archaeologists work with three basic processes in mind—careful stratigraphic excavation, exact and meticulous recording, and comparative interpretation. These procedures are followed as a result of a primary premise, that an object and its significance for history can be understood fully only when it is studied in its archaeological context, that is, in the environment in which it was found, including the other items found in association with it. The activities of excavating, recording, and interpreting are carried on by individual archaeologists in connection with specific sites. Paul Lapp has poetically portrayed this relationship as ''a love affair between an archaeologist and an ancient ruin.'' A site, as the object of an archaeologist's devotion, can be as puzzling and unpredictable as one's beloved, in turn both tantalizing and demoralizing the lover.

One of the limitations of archaeology is the plethora of sites that have not yet attracted a lover. There are over five thousand ancient ruins in what is now Israel and Jordan, leaving aside for the moment the sites in the other areas of the ancient world. Most of the Palestinian sites are tells, and of these only a few hundred have attracted excavators. Of the excavated sites, only about thirty have been the scenes of major excavations; the remainder have consisted of small-scale soundings, emergency clearances, or salvage operations. It is important to be aware, also, that even the major excavations have left most of their sites untouched. It is apparent, then, that almost 98 percent of the major ruins of Palestine remain untouched by an expedition. In other words, in comparison to the miniscule amount that has been recovered, a massive amount of data remains untouched, despite nearly a century of excavations.

Another extenuating factor in biblical archaeology is the problem that many of the major excavations were carried out prior to 1936, before the development of some of the more sophisticated techniques that have been employed in excavations since the end of World War II. The results of earlier excavations may be suspect, therefore, and in some cases tells that were excavated when stratigraphic excavation was in its infancy have become the focus of recent re-excavations. Megiddo, Jericho, Shechem, Gezer, and the famed Tell el-Hesi are among these sites which have been re-excavated recently in order to clarify the work of the earlier excavations. Undoubtedly the final results of other earlier excavations will be reevaluated in the future through similar operations.

Unlike an experiment in chemistry or physics which can be repeated again and again with identical results as long as the conditions of the experiment are controlled, each archaeological site is unique. And once a part of the tell is disturbed, that part, that experiment, cannot be exactly repeated. Each site is unique even though there are basic similarities in Palestinian tells in the same region. The singular attributes of a tell are present when the archaeologist comes to it. Each is more or less eroded. Later cultivation may have disturbed important evidence on one tell but not on its neighbor. The condition of the layers of debris will depend upon whether they were laid down in peace or in war, and on whether they have been disturbed by subsequent inhabitants who dug pits, foundation trenches, silos, or reservoirs. One tell may have suffered one or two major gaps in occupation while another will have been occupied continuously. Thus the condition of the occupational layers will determine whether the process of stratigraphic excavation will be simple or complex.

Another problem in archaeological research is the problem of stratigraphical excavation. The recognition of the importance of careful stratigraphical excavation had developed slowly and erratically among archaeologists since the days of Petrie's work at Tell el-Hesi. No field of human endeavor advances smoothly, without regressions and tangents that are eventually abandoned, and this is true of the development of modern archaeology. In addition, the application of a generally approved method will be altered in a specific situation according to the predilections of the individual. In archaeology as in other fields, different individuals do things differently, and if any statement can be made about archaeologists generally it is that each one is strongly individualistic. Therefore no self-respecting individual will feel constrained to excavate his site according to an absolute standard that has been imposed upon him by an exterior source. In stratigraphic excavation, the flair of the individual must out; the restraints under which he works are largely self-imposed, although every archaeologist is to some degree subject to peer pressure.

The exact and meticulous recording that is required in modern archaeological research is also subject to manifold variations. No two excavations are going to employ, among other things, exactly the same recording forms, and the emphasis upon meticulousness will vary from dig to dig, again because archaeology is a distinctively human enterprise and because directors of digs are notoriously individualistic. The recognition of the importance of careful observation and recording did not occur overnight but underwent a sporadic development. Initially the interest of archaeologists was primarily in observing and recording architectural plans, particularly of monumental buildings such as temples and palaces. The recording and analysis of pottery forms were not completely neglected, but it was only through the industry and genius of William F. Albright and his work at Tell Beit Mirsim in 1926, 1928, 1930, and 1932 that pottery recording and analysis became the key to chronology in Palestinian tells. The methods of analyzing pottery and publishing the results are still undergoing evolution. Only occasionally are sherds profiled by cutting them with a ceramic saw so that a clean, sharp surface is observed and recorded.

The importance of recording debris stratification was first recognized by George A. Reisner in Palestine. As an Egyptologist, Reisner excavated at only one Palestinian site (Samaria) during 1909–10, but his attention to the study of debris was extraordinary for the time. The post-World War II interest in the rock and soil of debris strata was primarily the result of the work of Kathleen Kenyon, whose excavations at Jericho and Jerusalem influenced Palestinian archaeologists widely but not uniformly.

Photography has been employed as an aspect of recording archaeological excavations for over three quarters of a century, but in different ways and for different purposes with varying degrees of effectiveness. In the last decade a growing interest in the recording of ecological data has developed among archaeologists. This has been a worldwide phenomenon which has had its effect upon biblical archaeologists as well. Anthropological archaeologists have developed techniques for the collection and recording of such data in their attempts to enlarge our knowledge of man's existence in the prehistoric periods. But these techniques have not been adopted everywhere in current excavations in Palestine, nor is there any uniformity in practice.

A realistic view of the strengths and weaknesses of current archaeological research should include, then, the relative infancy of the discipline in terms of the number of sites excavated in comparison with the number of potential sites, the actual amount of work done at the excavated sites in comparison with what remains to be done, and the nature of the materials recovered—those materials, predominantly of an inorganic character, that have survived the toll of time. That view of current archaeological research must also take into consideration the misinformation that has resulted from past inadequacies in excavating and recording techniques, misinformation that is slowly being eradicated or corrected by more recent, technically superior, excavations. These limitations indicate the importance of the idea of "the present level of information." There must always be an open-ended quality to archaeological research which permits and encourages whatever changes in the understanding of old data the new data may require.

The Peculiarities of the Archaeologist

As we have indicated, the Bible has a singular historical viewpoint and archaeology as a discipline has its limitations. Nevertheless, it must be acknowledged that the most enigmatic element in the interrelationships involved in archaeological research is the archaeologist himself. Without a doubt, Palestinian archaeologists are extraordinary individuals. In support of this declaration, one needs but to consider what the pursuit of archaeological research in Syro-Palestine demands of the individual. He is compelled to leave the circle of family, friends, and associates at home to travel thousands of miles across land and sea to indulge his compulsion. As a result, he is forced to interrupt other interests and responsibilities in favor of archaeology, and this can place excessive strains especially on family relationships. (There are few archaeologists who can afford the cost of transporting their families with them to an archaeological excavation.) Such separations and strains have destroyed marriages. In addition, the absence of the archaeologist from home occurs during the most pleasant time of the year for the inhabitants of western Europe, Britain, Canada, and the United States, the areas from which come most of the foreign archaeologists who work in Israel and Jordan. Summer is the normal season for archaeological expeditions in Palestine, because rain is unlikely to hamper the operation at that time. So the archaeologist spends his summer working on a hot, dry, desolate mound, attempting to wrest whatever bits of information he can from the dust of the past.

Again, the extraordinary character of the archaeologist is evident when one observes that, almost without variation, archaeologists have earned advanced degrees that entailed long years of concentrated study (the majority hold earned doctoral degrees). Often he (or she) is a professor in a college or university who spends the greater part of the year in the pleasant and placid setting of academia, but the compulsion to dig is powerful enough to lead him to forsake the comforts and convenience of normal living circumstances at home for the frequently harsh surroundings of camp life.

Another factor that indicates the unusual qualities of the archaeologist is of an economic nature. Few archaeologists earn a living as field archaeologists; for most the activity costs rather than pays. There are excavations where staff members receive no more than transportation, food, and shelter in exchange for their contribution of labor and expertise. The initiator of an expedition faces the awesome economic task of raising the necessary financial backing for the project. This requires exceptional audacity, for he must convince people who control capital funds that the money should be used for digging rather than for more profitable investments. The effort also requires extreme tenacity, for the search for funds must continue in the face of disheartening refusals until some benefactor is found. The organizer also bears the primary responsibility for negotiating with the host country for the authorization to excavate, for obtaining the supplies for excavation, and for providing local transportation arrangements, shelter, and food for the expedition. Finally, the responsibility for the preparation of preliminary and final reports is his. Final reports are published as books, but inasmuch as they are technical publications for a small market they do not earn large royalties. It is a rare individual who can write a popular account of an excavation and realize a profit from his efforts.

The archaeologist is an extraordinary individual who is, at the same time, inevitably a product of his times. The world in which he grew up and in which he functions has left its indelible mark upon him, and it affects not only what he is particularly interested in, in terms of his archaeological activities, but also how he understands and interprets what he finds. The general validity of this idea can be recognized by noting that Palestinian archaeology has gone through several phases in which the predominant interests of the investigators have undergone gradual modification.

The first major involvement of an American in Palestine was the research of Edward Robinson, who came to Palestine in 1838 along with his friend and former student, Eli Smith. The intellectual world in which Robinson lived was only beginning to feel the development in Germany of the critical study of the Bible. Robinson himself had received training in Semitic languages and in biblical history and geography under leading German scholars, but there can be no doubt that Robinson and the vast majority of American and European scholars were devout churchmen. They assumed the veracity of the biblical information, both the historical data and the statements of faith. Robinson was an active biblical scholar who taught at Andover Theological Seminary and Union Theological Seminary in New York while his traveling companion, Eli Smith, was a missionary in Lebanon. There can be no doubt, then, that the prevailing influence of the Bible in Western society in the nineteenth century permeated Robinson and other investigators of the lands of the Bible in that period. These early explorers were intent upon identifying the places in Palestine of which they had read in the Bible. Attempts at identification continued in the later surveys of Conder and Kitchener, G. Schumacher, and others, but in the post-World War II period there has been a decline in the activity of establishing the location of biblical sites, in part because many sites have been identified and in part because other more compelling interests have arisen.

The earliest excavations in Palestine were those of F. de Saulcy, beginning in 1850. An impetus toward excavation resulted with the establishment of the Palestine Exploration Fund in 1865, which was in part inspired by the interests in excavation which were popular among the English gentry at that time. Charles Warren did excavate in Jerusalem toward the end of that decade, but the fund maintained an equal interest in topographical surveys, underwriting the Conder and Kitchener work. And despite the discoveries of Schliemann at Troy, many of the Palestinian mounds went unrecognized as more than natural formations. After the work of Petrie at Tell el-Hesi in 1890, the interest in excavating Palestinian sites quickened and continued until the outbreak of World War I caused a cessation of archaeological activities. One of the main problems that the archaeologists of the period faced was establishing an artifactual chronology so that their finds could be dated. This was a problem despite the establishment by Petrie of the fundamental principles of stratigraphic excavation and typological sequence-dating, but as W. F. Albright has indicated, "The net gain in improvement of technique was much greater than the gain in chronology and historical interpretation. In fact, the archaeological chronology of Palestine was in some respects more obscure in 1914 than it had been two decades earlier."

It is difficult to ascertain a direct line of correlation between the predominant interests of the world in which the pre-World War I archaeologists grew up and worked and the interest in chronology. The Western world of the last half of the nineteenth century, however, had experienced a multitude of revolutionary ideas. (1) The burgeoning influence of German biblical criticism, which incorporated Hegelian philosophy and the idea of the evolutionary development of biblical religion, jeopardized many traditional views of the Bible. (2) An array of mechanical implements that promised to ease human drudgery considerably was being developed. (3) New advances were being made in transportation and communication. (4) From the debris of Mesopotamian mounds cuneiform documents that were useful for illuminating the history of ancient empires contemporary with the Bible were being recovered. One can be certain that these and other developments stimulated the thought and activities of Palestinian archaeologists.

Archaeological activity began again in 1920 under the benevolent gaze of the British mandate government and continued unabated until 1936 when the activity was slowed by the outbreak of internal disorders in Palestine between Arabs and Jews. W. F. Albright arrived in Palestine in 1920 and was active throughout the period. His genius established the chronological framework for Palestinian archaeology on the basis of a careful analysis of pottery typology which he worked out in detail through his excavations at Tell Beit Mirsim between 1926 and 1932. Thus in the period under discussion Albright and other archaeologists pursued an interest in refining and using the ceramic chronological tool in their excavations. It was a period of international cooperation and interchange which was no doubt due to the influence of the League of Nations concept.

The three most significant American archaeologists of the twentieth century, Albright, Nelson Glueck, and George Ernest

Wright, were active both before and after World War II. All three had received training in the liberal scholarship of the day, which had resulted from the earlier and continuing critical study of the Bible, predominantly by German scholars. Albright said of himself, "I must admit that I try to be rational and empirical in my approach, [but] we all have presuppositions of a philosophical order." The same statement could be applied as easily to Glueck and Wright, for all three were deeply imbued with theological perceptions which infused their work. Albright, the son of a Methodist missionary, came to see that much of German critical thought was established upon a philosophical base that could not be sustained in the light of archaeological discoveries. He always maintained a vital and sympathetic interest in the implications of archaeological research for the study of the Bible, believing in the primacy of logical reasoning and the value of the systematic collection of factual data while treating the Bible with the same respect that other ancient documents received. Nelson Glueck was Albright's student. In his own explorations in Transjordan and the Negev and in his excavations, Glueck worked with the Bible in hand. He trusted what he called "the remarkable phenomenon of historical memory in the Bible." He was the president of the prestigious Hebrew Union College-Jewish Institute of Religion and an ordained rabbi. Wright went from the faculty of the McCormick Theological Seminary in Chicago to a position in the Harvard Divinity School which he retained until his death. He, too, was a student of Albright. There can be little doubt that these three men set the tone for American archaeology in Palestine from the end of World War I until the present decade. Their efforts were aimed toward understanding the Bible (and biblical faith) over against its setting in the ancient world. In this effort they were joined by many sympathetic students and associates.

It may come as something of a surprise to the reader, then, to learn that in recent years a considerable controversy has arisen among American archaeologists who work in the lands of the Bible over the appropriateness of the terminology *biblical archaeology*. We have noted elsewhere how Albright conceived of biblical archaeology—as covering the ancient world from Spain to India and from the Sahara northward to the Urals and stretching across time from 9000 B.C. to A.D. 700—though he considered that even these limits were flexible. The remains of earlier or later date were not without significance; they were simply at a point of such limited returns that they could safely be placed outside the interests of biblical studies.

Interestingly enough, the archaeologists who are questioning the old terminology are younger men. Paul Lapp, a "third generation" archaeologist of the Albright school, whose brilliant career ended tragically in an accidental drowning in 1970, purposely avoided the terminology. In his opinion, the term should be restricted to the archaeology of the biblical period just as Roman archaeology is the archaeology of the Roman period. At the same time, Lapp did not deny the legitimacy of biblical archaeology as a subject but he did reject the idea that a mastery of biblical archaeology was sufficient qualification for excavating in Palestine.

Both Lapp and his colleague, William Dever, were protégés of G. Ernest Wright, and both were directors of the American School of Oriental Research in Jerusalem, an institution which now bears the name The William Foxwell Albright Institute of Archaeological Research in Jerusalem. Dever has argued forcefully for the rejection of the expression *biblical archaeology* and in favor of *Syro-Palestinian archaeology* because of the rise of a number of independent, secularly orientated "national schools" of Palestinian archaeology. These schools, of which the Israelis' are the most vigorous, are divorced from traditional biblical and theological interests and utilize the Bible largely as a document of national history. Further, Dever has called attention to the broadening scope of archaeological activity in Palestine to include both the prehistorical and postbiblical periods, with a simultaneous broadening of interests to include anthropological studies, cultural history, and the investigation of ancient ecologies. Moreover, the development of volunteer programs in field work has involved affluent and mobile Western youth who are fascinated with Israel but little interested in Jewish or Christian concerns with the "Holy Land." Finally, modern field methods and techniques, including methods of excavation and analytical procedures derived from the natural sciences, are hardly uniquely applicable to the biblical period alone. It is Dever's view, therefore, that "for the first time in its history, Syro-Palestinian archaeology is becoming an autonomous discipline, no longer merely an adjunct of biblical studies."

The underlying influences which have led to this controversy are open to speculation. It is clear that for one group of active archaeologists the adjective *biblical* no longer seems adequate, although it has known a long and useful life up to the present time. The theological implications of the term may be an irritant to those who suppose that the philosophical presuppositions of a "scientific" age are more valid than the philosophical presuppositions that are connected with the Bible. At any rate, the word *biblical* connotes a relationship to the Bible while *Syro-*

Palestinian speaks of a region; neither term sufficiently and succinctly describes the totality of archaeological research in the area. It may be, however, that the declining influence of the Bible in much of Western society has contributed to the reduction in value of its adjective and that the evidence for this decline has indirectly surfaced in the current controversy.

It also seems apparent that younger Palestinian archaeologists have been influenced by the work of American anthropological archaeologists as well as by the research of Israeli and European prehistorians in Israel. In addition, archaeologists along with other thinking people have become increasingly aware of serious problems of worldwide scope—overpopulation, the threat of technology to ecology, and the concomitant problem of world food supplies. It is only natural, therefore, for their research to be focused upon similar problems in the world of ancient peoples. Another factor that may have contributed to the scholarly discontent with the older terminology is the advance in methods of excavation and the analysis of artifactual evidence, along with the increased employment of special techniques deriving from the physical sciences. All these post-World War II developments have raised archaeological research in Palestine to a higher level of sophistication than was realized previously. With a concurrent rise in the prestige of the discipline, the older descriptive phrase may appear shopworn and inappropriate.

(While the controversy continues, the employment of the term *biblical archaeology* in this work is an indication that the Albright definition has been adopted rather than the terminology proposed by the dissidents. *Biblical* is the more general term and can be applied to all discoveries within the time-space limits of Albright's definition that have a bearing upon biblical materials. *Syro-Palestinian* is too narrow for our purposes.)

At this point it is appropriate to return to the third process in modern archaeological research—interpretation. It is obvious that careful stratigraphic excavation and meticulous recording deal with tangible artifacts that are meaningless until they are interpreted. It is equally obvious that this is the most subjective aspect of the entire enterprise because of the incomplete and fragmentary nature of the surviving remains and, especially, because of the complexity of the human element, the interpreter. Interpretation has been called an art, with the interpreter as the artist, and as with an artist, the interpreter brings all that he or she is to the task, including his educational background, his experiences in life, his philosophical presuppositions, and in biblical archaeology his views about the Bible.

Despite the subjectivity that permeates the process, the interpretation of archaeological data is an absolute necessity, if any meaning is to be derived from the activity, as well as the ultimate end towards which the work proceeds. The fragmentary nature of the evidence requires that inferences be drawn, that hypotheses be presented. There are archaeologists who believe that their task is solely to present the evidence which they have excavated, leaving the task of interpretation to other specialists. Fortunately these comprise a small minority whose interests are in perfecting archaeological methodology rather than in comprehending history. The majority of Near Eastern excavators, by contrast, pursue an on-going interpretation of the materials they are excavating while the field work is in progress. This approach permits changes in interpretation of the material as the new data come to the surface. Such in-the-field interpretation is grounded in a thorough knowledge of comparative materials from earlier excavations as well as of the extant historical sources for the area in which the archaeologist is working. The final publications of most excavators will contain a detailed interpretation of the material remains of a site and whatever correlation to written sources may have been perceived. In Palestine the correlations are primarily made with the Bible, but of necessity they are almost invariably hypothetical. The archaeologist presents a hypothesis that in his judgment best explains the available data. This hypothesis is open to further modification or rejection upon the basis of later discoveries or as a result of the critical comments of fellow archaeologists. Interpretation, then, is an explanation of probabilities or possibilities. Interpretations of archaeological data in terms of the Bible must be recognized as uncertainties.

When one contemplates the peculiarity of the Bible as a historical work, the limitations of archaeology, and the uniqueness of the individual archaeologist, one may be tempted to question the value of this entire enterprise. By way of defense it can be stated that in spite of the imponderable features which we have noted, genuine progress has been made in our understanding of the Bible and of biblical history as a result of archaeological research in the lands of the Bible.

For one thing, the entire ancient world in which the biblical events occurred has been opened before our eyes. Ancient Sumer, whose existence was not even guessed previously, is now recognized as the fundamental civilization of the biblical world. Its contributions in terms of technology and thought have been traced into subsequent cultures—Akkadian, Old Babylonian, Assyrian, Babylonian—which were intimately connected with the history of ancient Israel. Similar information has been revealed about the ancient Egyptians, the Canaanites, and other peoples on the fringes of Israel's existence. The knowledge that has been gained of these peoples includes their languages and writings, their literature and art, their institutions, religions, and history, at least in part.

Archaeological research has established the identity of literally hundreds of places—in Mesopotamia, Persia, ancient Canaan, and Egypt—that are mentioned in the Bible. Furthermore, the discovery of thousands of historical texts in Egypt and Mesopotamia has enabled scholars to work out the historical chronology of the ancient world in considerable detail. Historical synchronisms have been established for dating the accession of Solomon (ca. 961 B.C.), the accession of Jehu, the Israelite king (842/1 B.C.), the fall of Samaria (722/1 B.C.), and the first capture of Jerusalem (March 15/16, 597 B.C.). These dates in turn provide a framework for the chronology of the kings of Israel and Judah. For those periods in which no synchronisms have been discovered, a relative chronology has been worked out in considerable detail based upon pottery dating techniques.

In contrast to our present state of knowledge concerning biblical chronology, in the seventeenth century Archbishop Ussher of Dublin used information from the Bible to work out a chronological table which placed the creation at 4004, the flood at 2348, Abraham's birth at 1996, and the exodus at 1491 B.C. But Ussher did not take into account, for example, that such a figure as "forty," which is found repeatedly in the Scriptures, was simply a way of rounding off a generation of human life. He could not effectively account for the reigns of various kings over a fraction of a year. Biblical writers simply did not leave sufficient information for the construction of an accurate table of dates; archaeology can and does clarify many points of biblical chronology.

Archaeology has provided material evidence that illuminates life in biblical times. Through the excavation of biblical sites a great deal has been learned of the nature and development of ancient architecture. The form and content of houses, palaces, temples, stables, and city walls and gates are now quite well known. We have a much clearer picture of what Solomon's temple looked like because Canaanite temples which have been excavated exhibit the same general plan.

Much more could be said about the illumination of religious ideas and practices of the ancient world, ideas and practices against which the prophets spoke. The archaeologist has uncovered ancient literatures with which the biblical literature can be compared and contrasted, and even the story of the development of writing has been wrested from the ancient soil so that we now know for a certainty that Moses lived in a literate society.

Archaeology has provided illumination, illustration, and occasionally confirmation of biblical data, but its primary contribution has been illumination. For many years to come archaeological research will no doubt continue to illuminate the Bible, thanks to that extraordinary individual to whom we here extend our word of commendation, the archaeologist.

SUGGESTED TOPICS FOR FURTHER STUDY

1. Collect and critically compare a selection of newspaper reports on archaeological discoveries and later reports in professional journals.
2. Investigate the nature of modern historiography.
3. Collect biographical information on a famous American archaeologist and write a brief character sketch.
4. Investigate the controversy over the term *biblical archaeology*.
5. Investigate the similarities and differences between the interpretation of archaeological data and the interpretation of a biblical text.
6. Collect information and write a short essay on the problem of interpreting the "Solomonic stables" at Megiddo.
7. Write an essay on what archaeology can and cannot do.

RECOMMENDED READING

Albright, W. F., *History, Archaeology and Christian Humanism* (New York: McGraw-Hill, 1964).

Dever, William G., *Archaeology and Biblical Studies: Retrospects and Prospects* (The Winslow Lectures at Seabury-Western Theological Seminary) (Evanston, 1973).

Frank, Harry T., *Discovering the Biblical World* (Maplewood, NJ: Hammond Incorporated, 1975).

Gray, John, *Archaeology and the Old Testament World* (New York: Harper and Row, 1965).

Kitchen, K. A., *Ancient Orient and Old Testament* (Chicago: Inter-Varsity Press, 1966).

Lapp, Paul W., *Biblical Archaeology and History* (New York: The World Publishing Company, 1969).

Williams, Walter G., *Archaeology in Biblical Research* (New York: Abingdon Press, 1965).

Wright, G. Ernest, *Biblical Archaeology*, revised edition (Philadelphia: Westminster Press, 1963—PB abridged edition).

FOR FURTHER READING

Albright, William F., "The Impact of Archaeology on Biblical Research—1966" in *New Directions in Biblical Archaeology,* ed. David N. Freedman and Jonas C. Greenfield (Garden City, NY: Doubleday, 1969), pp. 1-14.

Burrows, Millar, *What Mean These Stones? The Significance of Archaeology for Biblical Studies* (New Haven: The American Schools of Oriental Research, 1941).

Cross, Frank M., Jr., "W. F. Albright's View of Biblical Archaeology and Its Methodology," *Biblical Archaeologist* 36 (1973), pp. 2-5.

de Vaux, R., "On Right and Wrong Uses of Archaeology" in *Near Eastern Archaeology in the Twentieth Century,* ed. J. Sanders (Garden City, NY: Doubleday, 1970), pp. 64-80.

Dever, William G., "'Biblical Archaeology' or 'The Archaeology of Syro-Palestine'?" in *Christian News from Israel* (New Series) XXII, No. 1 (5), pp. 21-22.

Frank, Harry T., *Bible Archaeology and Faith* (Nashville: Abingdon Press, 1971).

Kitchen, K. A., *The Bible in its World* (Downers Grove: Inter-Varsity Press, 1978).

Lapp, Paul W., "Palestine Known but Mostly Unknown," *Biblical Archaeologist* 26, 1963, pp. 121-34.

______, *The Tale of the Tell,* ed. Nancy L. Lapp (Pittsburgh: The Pickwick Press, 1975).

Rowley, H. H., "Archaeology and the Old Testament" in *The Rediscovery of the Old Testament* (Philadelphia, 1956).

Unger, M. F., *Archaeology and the Old Testament,* third edition (Grand Rapids: Zondervan Publishing House, 1962).

Wiseman, D. J., "Archaeological Confirmation of the Old Testament" in *Revelation and the Bible,* ed. C. Henry (Grand Rapids: Baker, 1958), pp. 299-316.

———, (ed.), *Peoples of Old Testament Times* (London: Oxford University Press, 1973).

Wright, G. E., "Historical Knowledge and Revelation" in *Translating and Understanding the Old Testament,* ed. H. T. Frank and W. L. Reed (Nashville: Abingdon Press, 1970).

———, "The 'New' Archaeology," *Biblical Archaeologist* 38, 1975, pp. 104-115.

______, "What Archaeology Can and Cannot Do," *Biblical Archaeologist* 34 (1971), pp. 70-76.

Yamauchi, Edwin M., *The Stones and the Scriptures* (Leicester: Inter-Varsity Press, 1973).

———, "Stones, Scripts, and Scholars," *Christianity Today,* Feb. 14, 1969, pp. 8-13.

Part Two

A Survey of Significant Sites and Finds Outside the Holy Land

6

Mesopotamia

The word *Mesopotamia* is derived from the Greek expression meaning "the land between the rivers." The rivers, of course, are the Euphrates and the Tigris, both of which issue from the mountain recesses of Armenia in eastern Turkey. The valleys through which these rivers flow broaden into a single plain north of the Persian Gulf, and here the earliest centers of civilization developed by approximately 3100 B.C., the beginning of the Early Bronze Age. From one of these centers, the city of Ur, the patriarch Abraham was to begin his trek to the land of promise over a millennium later.

The contacts of biblical personalities with this area and the pervasive influence of Mesopotamian culture upon the rest of the ancient world make an archaeological study of this area essential to the study of the Bible. The Bible records contacts between the People of the Book and Mesopotamia in three particular periods—prehistorical, patriarchal, and post-Solomonic. The contacts existed at two levels—literary and personal. The biblical accounts of the creation, the flood, and the tower of Babel, which are recorded in the first chapters of Genesis, are similar to literary compositions which have been recovered from Mesopotamia, although the nature of the relationships is still a matter of scholarly dispute. The remainder of Genesis portrays the movement of Abraham from southern Mesopotamia to the area of Haran, then on to the land of Canaan, but it also mentions the invasion of the Jordan Valley by four kings from

Mesopotamia. And the son and grandson of Abraham both obtained wives from Haran, so continuing contacts with the patriarchal homeland are indicated for two or three generations after Abraham's journey to Canaan. Save for the mention of the fact that Othniel, the first judge, rescued Israel from the king of Mesopotamia, Cushanrishathaim, the biblical writers do not again indicate contacts with peoples beyond the Euphrates until after the death of Solomon.

The first direct contact between Assyria, the major power of Mesopotamia in the Iron Age II period, and Israel occurred in the time of King Ahab, but it is not mentioned in the Bible. The inscriptions of Shalmaneser III, however, record the battle of Qarqar on the Orontes River in 853. Among the confederacy that opposed Shalmaneser's Assyrian army was King Ahab. The first biblical mention of a Mesopotamian ruler during Iron Age II is probably in II Kings 13:5. The savior mentioned in this text is apparently an allusion to Adad-nirari III. The first direct reference to an Assyrian king is to Pul, Tiglath-pileser III, in II Kings 15:19; thereafter the interaction of Assyrian monarchs and the kings of Israel and Judah becomes an increasing concern of the biblical writers. Eventually the infrequent contacts led to the Assyrian conquest of Israel and domination of Judah. The Babylonian empire succeeded that of Assyria, and the Babylonian conquest of Judah resulted in the exile of the bulk of the survivors from their homeland. The Babylonian exile immersed the Jews in the river of Mesopotamian culture, and these cultural contacts continued during the period of the Persian empire despite the reestablishment of a Jewish religious and cultural center at Jerusalem by the close of the sixth century.

What is known of Mesopotamian prehistory and ancient history has been wrested from its soil during the last century and a half. Beginning with the first excavations of Claudius Rich at Babylon in 1811, European and American expeditions have probed numerous sites in the land of the two rivers. Some of these have been identified with places mentioned in the Bible; others were not mentioned in the biblical records, but have provided important literary and artifactual evidence for the establishment of the cultural sequence of the area. Out of a large number of excavated Mesopotamian sites, we have selected a limited number on the basis of their value for biblical studies. Other sites, possessing their own inherent significance, are of tangential interest to our purposes.

True civilization, marked by the development of urban centers, began in Mesopotamia at the beginning of the Early Bronze Age. Over five millennia separate the development of

Sumerian culture in the southern area of the Tigris and Euphrates valleys from the earliest form of village life yet discovered—Jericho in the eighth millennium B.C. (the Neolithic Age). Man's shift from hunting and food-gathering toward the domestication of animals and the practice of agriculture developed slowly through these years. The developments have been traced on the basis of evidence excavated at a number of sites ranging from northern to southern Mesopotamia—Tell Hassuna, Tell Halaf, Ubaid, Uruk, and Jemdet Nasr. These names in turn designate the cultural types represented at each site, providing a sequence of development from about 6000 to 3000 B.C.

Evidence from the seals, the pottery, and linguistic elements of preliterary inhabitants of southern Mesopotamia points to the predominance of the Ubaidians from the early fifth millennium to the middle of the fourth. The Ubaidian culture included such diverse aspects as beautifully decorated polychrome pottery, the use of brick for building, monumental structures in the form of early temples, and the importation of metals, semiprecious stones, and wood. The Ubaidian base was to be transformed into the first urban culture by the infusion of other ethnic elements—the Subarians from the north, the Elamites from the east, the Amorites from the west, and the Sumerians from the south. The Subarians apparently dominated all Mesopotamia toward the close of the Ubaidian period, but by 3100 B.C. the southern sector of the valley came under the control of the Sumerians. These intruders soon transformed the cultural elements of their predecessors into the first true civilization. And, as Samuel N. Kramer noted, "history begins at Sumer," for the Sumerians developed the system of cuneiform writing that ushered in the historical period.

Sumerian civilization centered on the area known in the Bible as "the land of Shinar." It was made up of a number of city-states in the broad valley between modern Baghdad and the Persian Gulf, an area of about eight thousand square miles. Among these cities was Nippur, the site to which we shall first turn our attention because of its value for comprehending the rise of Sumerian culture in the period before the time of Abraham.

Nippur

Nippur, modern Nuffar, is located approximately one hundred miles southeast of Baghdad. American scholars, in the period following the Civil War, were becoming more and more intrigued with the work of French, English, and German scholars, both in the deciphering of cuneiform texts and the excavation of Mesopotamian sites. In 1887 the University of Pennsylvania sent the Reverend John Peters at the head of an expedition to Nippur. Peters, an educated but inept individual, possessed a certain disdain for Asians. He encountered such difficulty negotiating with the Turkish officials for a permit to excavate that the expedition did not arrive at the site until January of 1889. Having successfully completed his arrangements with the central government, Peters failed to take into consideration the advisability of going through customary formalities with local sheiks prior to initiating the excavations. He thereby established a hostile environment that culminated in the destruction of the expedition camp by fire after only two months of actual excavation.

The following year Peters returned a wiser man. This time he was careful to placate both the local leaders and government officials with appropriate gifts. By mid-February he had struck one of the richest stores of cuneiform tablets ever found. (Unfortunately, almost a half century passed before they were to be studied systematically by S. N. Kramer.) The work was resumed in 1893 with John H. Hayes as the field director, and Herman V. Hilprecht of the University of Pennsylvania soon succeeded Peters as the director. The initial excavation was continued until 1900.

Excavations at Nippur were resumed in 1948 in a joint expedition under the direction of Donald E. McCown. The University Museum of Philadelphia and the Oriental Institute of Chicago were the cooperating institutions. Excavations were carried on in alternate years from 1949 to 1958.

The excavations indicate that Nippur was established by the fourth millennium B.C. in the Ubaid period. Early in the dig a map of the ancient city was discovered, inscribed on a clay tablet. It proved to be a valuable guide for subsequent excavations; of particular importance on the map was the plan of a temple.

The temple proved to be that of Enlil, the chief god of the Sumerian pantheon. The city was never a major political center of Sumer, but it is now known that the influential Enlil temple made it the recognized religious and cultural center for all of Sumer. Since kingship came down from the gods, each Sumerian ruler felt compelled to seek the favor of Enlil upon his reign. Enlil's sanctuary, the *Ekur* ("mountain house"), was therefore maintained by and embellished with gifts from a long sequence of Sumerian kings. As a result, the inscriptional materials from the sanctuary provide important evidence for the establishment of Sumerian dynastic chronology.

Along with the remains of the Enlil sanctuary and its ziggurat, a temple dedicated to Inanna, his consort, was also excavated. She was the "Queen of Heaven," and later came to be identified with the Babylonian Ishtar. Another small temple that has not been identified with a particular god was also uncovered. Apart from the temples, the scribal quarter of the city has yielded nearly forty thousand clay tablets, some four thousand of which are literary texts.

Upon reflection, it seems strange that we have been discussing a city (Nippur) and a people (the Sumerians) whose historical existence was undreamed of little more than a century ago. The recovery of the history of Sumer, which had been lost for over two thousand years, is a fascinating story worthy of a book-length exposition. We can only outline it briefly here.

The story begins with the recovery of cuneiform tablets in the mid-nineteenth century by the early excavators of *northern* Mesopotamian sites such as Nineveh, Nimrud, and Khorsabad. When Akkadian had been deciphered so that the tablets could be read, scholars found that contrary to expectations not all the tablets were written in the Akkadian language. Even though the cuneiform script was the form of writing upon all the tablets, a small number could not be read. In 1869 the French scholar, Jules Oppert, proposed that the unknown language be called Sumerian, for an oft-repeated royal title in the Akkadian texts was "king of Sumer and Akkad." Oppert's suggestions were

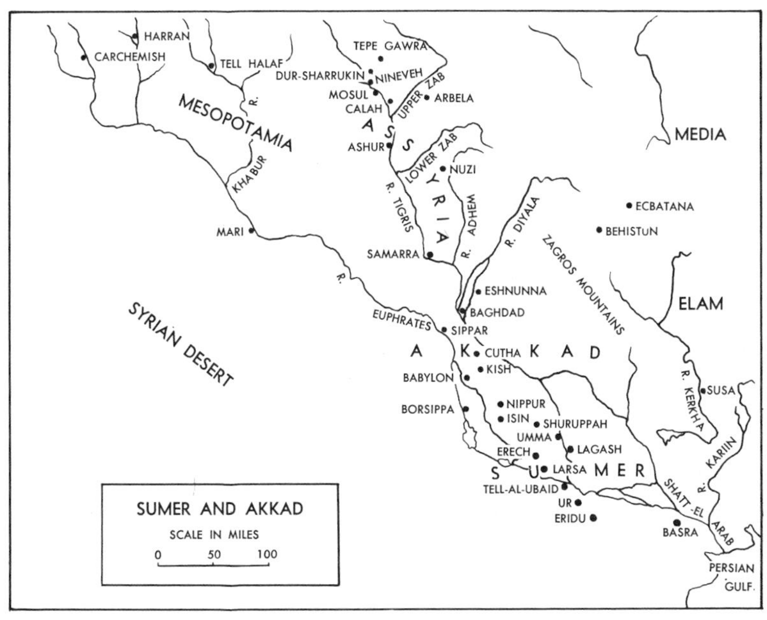

ignored until, toward the end of the nineteenth century, excavations at sites in southern Mesopotamia proved him right. Tablets by the thousands, dating to 2500 B.C. and earlier and written only in the Sumerian language, were recovered. Thanks to bilingual texts from the libraries of the Assyrian monarchs, the initial deciphering of Sumerian proceeded to the point that in 1914 the first Sumerian grammar could be published. It was only a matter of time, then, until Sumerology became a branch of studies separate from Assyriology.

Using literary evidence Sumerologists have been able to reconstruct a tentative history of Sumer. The first phase, circa 3100–2900 B.C., was marked by the development of writing, the invention of bronze, and the rise of the first true cities. Because of this last element, the period has appropriately been characterized as one of urban revolution. The name *Jemdet Nasr,* derived from the site that provided the first evidence of these developments, has been applied to the period.

The next major period, the early dynastic, consisted of several phases that occupied the centuries between 2900 and 2300 B.C. Sumerian traditions with strong affinities to the biblical story of the flood provide a useful point of separation between the Jemdet Nasr and early dynastic periods. In a list of antediluvian kings, Eridu is identified as the first city to which kingship was lowered from heaven. The first Sumerian ruler, Alulim, was followed by seven additional preflood kings who ruled variously at Eridu, Badtibira, Larak, Sippar, and Shuruppak. (The fifth ruler, Dumuzi, later was elevated to divine status in Mesopotamian mythology.) The last of the preflood kings was Ubar-Tutu, ruler of Shuruppak (modern Fara in southern Iraq). He is the Mesopotamian equivalent of Noah, for he constructed a vessel under divine guidance and survived the flood. Ubar-Tutu's name lived on in other forms—Ziusudra, Atarhasis, and, in the *Gilgamesh Epic,* Utnapishtim ("he has found [everlasting] life").

There is ample evidence of substantial floods at numerous sites in southern Mesopotamia. However, correlation of the material evidence of the flood layers cannot be used to establish the authenticity of the biblical flood. The flood layers at the various sites date to different periods. The flood deposit at Shuruppak does fit well with the Sumerian literary traditions, however, providing thereby a certain confirmation that a deluge did intervene between the Jemdet Nasr and early dynastic periods.

The Sumerian King List includes names of both preflood and postflood rulers.

The postdiluvian Sumerian King List indicates that kingship was again lowered from heaven to the city of Kish, and interestingly, at this site the evidence for a major inundation coincides with that of Shuruppak. The first ruler of postflood Kish was a

Part of the Gilgamesh Epic which contains an account of a flood with remarkable similarities to the biblical flood.

certain Etana. He was followed by twenty-two kings of Kish before the kingship was transferred to the city of Uruk. The fifth ruler of the first dynasty of Uruk was the legendary Gilgamesh. This extraordinary individual became the hero of numerous adventures in later Mesopotamian literature. The Sumerian King List documents eleven different cities that at one time or another were the centers of political authority in Sumer from the time of the flood until the accession of Hammurabi. As we have noted above, each Sumerian king sought the stamp of divine approval upon his royal authority from the Nippur priests and scribes. The Sumerian King List is one of the significant documents recovered in the Nippur excavations, and it has provided the main basis for establishing early Mesopotamian chronology. Probably the Nippur hierarchy maintained the authoritative document which the Americans discovered.

In the twenty-fourth century B.C., the political control of Sumer was wrested from Lugalzagesi of Uruk by Sargon of Akkad, a Semite. This marked the beginning of the next major

The victory stele of Naram-Sin of Akkad.

phase in Mesopotamian history—the Akkadian—which continued from about 2300 to 2100 B.C. Sargon established his capital at Agade in Akkad, the northern sector of Sumerian hegemony, and ruled from there for a period of approximately a half century. His reign was marked by extraordinary military and administrative achievements, for he conquered most of western Asia and dominated other areas as far afield as Egypt and Ethiopia. He instituted in Sumer the principles of dynastic succession and of empire in contrast to the older loose federation of city-states. His rule and that of his successors were marked by a broad range of cultural innovations.

The most notable ruler of the Akkadian dynasty after Sargon was his grandson, Naram-Sin, who styled himself with the revolutionary expression, "King of the four quarters (of the world)," and even as "god of Akkad." This last title may be indicative of a self-image that led Naram-Sin to commit the unimaginable act of destroying the holy Sumerian city of Nippur and disdainfully plundering the sacred temple of Enlil. Soon after, Naram-Sin met defeat at the hands of the Gutians, a semibarbaric people from the mountains of Iran. Their devastating incursions laid waste Sumer, and under Naram-Sin's successor Agade itself was destroyed, bringing an end to the Akkadian empire.

In the wake of the Gutian invasions, a reversion to the earlier city-state system occurred, and Lagash became the primary city of Mesopotamia. The most significant governor of Lagash was Gudea, and his peaceful pursuits set the stage for a renaissance of Sumerian culture which reached its apex in the so-called third dynasty of Ur (ca. 2100–2000 B.C.), a dynasty established by the remarkable Ur-Nammu. A politic ruler, Ur-Nammu rebuilt the temples of Enlil and Ninlil in Nippur, thereby winning the allegiance of the Nippur priesthood. Accordingly, he was given the title *King of Sumer and Akkad*.

The third dynasty of Ur ended with incursions of Semites called Amorites in the north and an invasion of Elamites from the east. The latter captured Ur and carried its last king away captive. Thereafter a rather chaotic two-and-a-half centuries witnessed the debilitating rivalries of the cities of Isin, Larsa, and Babylon as they vied for control of Sumer and Akkad. The close of the Sumerian era of Mesopotamian history came with the rise to power of Hammurabi of Babylon by the mid-eighteenth century B.C.

As a result of the varied Mesopotamian excavations late in the nineteenth and early in the twentieth centuries, thousands of clay tablets from Sumer came to rest in European, Asian, and

American museums. This dispersion of texts slowed the work of scholars for many years, but in the last four decades considerable progress has been made in assembling transcriptions of texts, in translating, and in interpreting. The earliest Mesopotamian documents still await deciphering. Slightly later materials consist primarily of economic and administrative texts by the thousands and votive texts by the hundreds, but very few literary texts have been excavated from the early dynastic period. The earliest literary tablets yet excavated date to about 2400, but the preponderance of Sumerian *belles lettres*—myths, epics, hymns, laments, wisdom literature—dates to the first half of the second millennium B.C. It is assumed that some of these were ancient oral traditions long before they were inscribed on clay tablets.

It is now known that even though the Sumerian language was being displaced by Akkadian subsequent to the Sumerian renaissance, the Mesopotamian scribes studied and copied the earlier Sumerian literature with meticulous care for centuries. Sumerian literature became the classics of antiquity and the model for the compositions of later authors. As Samuel N. Kramer, the noted Sumerologist has stated, "The ideas and ideals of the Sumerians—their cosmology, theology, ethics, and system of education—permeated, to a greater or lesser extent, the thoughts and writings of all the peoples of the ancient Near East. So, too, did the Sumerian literary forms and themes—their plots, motifs, stylistic devices, and aesthetic techniques. To all of which, Palestine, the land where the books of the Bible were composed, redacted, and edited by the Hebrew men of letters, was no exception." The Sumerian literature promises to provide illuminating parallels to the biblical literature as the research of Sumerologists continues.

The Taylor Prism, containing the annals of Sennacherib, the Assyrian king who besieged Jerusalem in the days of Hezekiah.

Ur

The location of Ur was lost in the mists of history for centuries, but it always survived in the memories of Bible readers because of its connection with the patriarch Abraham. In Genesis 11:31 is recorded the tradition that Abram set out from Ur of the Chaldees for the land of Canaan. The site of Ur was first visited by a westerner when W. K. Loftus visited it in 1850 while he was enroute to Warka. Ur is situated on the right bank of the Euphrates in southern Iraq, 220 miles south of Baghdad. However, the river which in antiquity flowed adjacent to the city now has shifted six miles away. The remains of the ancient ziggurat dominated the area which Loftus examined, providing the only visible surface evidence of ancient habitation. The brick of the tower had been mortared with pitch when it was constructed in the third dynasty of Ur, so the modern name is Tell el-Muqayyar ("the Mound of Pitch").

Loftus was followed in 1854 by another Englishman, J. E. Taylor, an official at Bosra, who had been sent by the British Museum to investigate the ruins further. He dug at the corners of the temple tower and discovered foundation deposit boxes in which were clay cylinders covered with cuneiform writing. These, however, were not read until 1856 when Henry C. Rawlinson was able to decipher them and to determine that they dated to the last king of Babylon, Nabonidus (556–539 B.C.). The texts reveal that Nabonidus restored the ziggurat which had ori-

The Standard of Ur, a two-sided wooden plaque depicting scenes of war on one side, scenes of peace on the other. Discovered by Sir Leonard Woolley.

ginally been erected by Ur-Nammu and his son. Since the Nabonidus inscriptions called the structure "The Ziggurat of E-gish-shir-gal in Ur," the identification of the site was established. Taylor also excavated a large building to the south of the ziggurat, which later was identified as a government building, but the excavations soon ceased due to two factors—no pieces desired by museums were discovered, and the site was difficult to reach.

Near the end of World War I the British Museum once again turned its attention to Ur. R. C. Thompson made a few soundings on the site in 1918. Soon after, H. R. Hall excavated at Ur and at Ubaid four miles away. His discovery of a temple at Ubaid in which there was inscriptional evidence of the historicity of the first dynasty of Ur, which had previously been considered semilegendary, confirmed the testimony of the Sumerian King List and opened a new era of interest in Mesopotamian history.

The major excavator of Ur was Sir Leonard Woolley, who began a series of excavations in 1922 that were jointly sponsored by the British Museum and the University Museum of Pennsylvania. These continued annually until 1934. Woolley was a remarkably able excavator. An idea of the measure of the man can be acquired in connection with one of his most spectacular discoveries, the royal tombs of Ur. He discovered the

tomb area in the fall of 1922 while determining the location of the sacred temple area (*temenos*) through a series of probes, but rather than pursue the excavation of tombs that were producing golden artifacts, Woolley turned his attention to other areas and returned to the cemetery only after a period of four years. He explained his actions later, citing two compelling factors that convinced him to refrain from immediate excavation of the tombs:

> We had a force of very wild Arab tribesmen, few of whom had ever handled tools before; they were completely ignorant, had no idea of what good workmanship was, were reckless and of course

> dishonest. Moreover we were ignorant too. The archaeology of Mesopotamia was in its infancy and there was no means of dating the small objects that come out of graves. . . . So I stopped work on "the gold trench" and . . . waited until four years' experience had equipped us better for the task.

In that four-year period he was able both to train his workmen and sketch out the Sumerian chronology. Woolley actually found two cemeteries in the same area, one superimposed over the other. On the evidence of cylinder seals recovered in the context Woolley dated the upper (more recent) cemetery to the time of Sargon of Akkad. The lower "royal tombs" contained hoards of rich artifacts fashioned in gold, silver, and lapis lazuli. The tombs were joined by massive death pits, containing the remains of what Woolley believed were members of the deceased king's court. These deaths had not been violent, and, since numerous cups were found beside the skeletal remains, it may be assumed that they took poison so that they might join their sovereign in the sleep of death.

The death-pit of Ur. Here Woolley excavated the evidence of a mass burial in antiquity.

The ruins of the ziggurat of Ur.

An artist's restoration of the ziggurat of Ur-Nammu at Ur.

The ziggurat of Ur, which first attracted the attention of explorers, has now been dated to the third dynasty of Ur. It was built during the reigns of Ur-Nammu and his successor, Shulgi, about 2100 B.C. Architecturally, it was a pyramid consisting of three massive steps atop which a sanctuary was built. The core of the Ur ziggurat was made of mud-bricks, but the brick of the exterior courses had been fired. This innovation and the use of bituminous mortar explain the remarkable preservation of the structure. The great ziggurat at Ur became a prototype for the construction of later Mesopotamian temple towers.

Perhaps the most fascinating of Woolley's discoveries was evidence of a tremendous flood which had inundated Ur, and presumably much of southern Mesopotamia, leaving a bed of clay which at one point reached a depth of eleven feet. He associated the preflood materials with the last phase of the Ubaidian culture and the postflood materials with the earliest phase of the Uruk culture. He connected this evidence with the statements about the flood which were recorded in the Sumerian

A golden flower headdress and other jewelry excavated at Ur.

King List, and he also perceived a connection between the Sumerian tradition of the flood and the biblical flood. As we have noted above, the interpretation of the Ur evidence has been modified by the results of other Mesopotamian excavations, particularly at Shuruppak and Kish. At present the literary evidence appears to correlate more adequately with the evidence of a flood that occurred at the beginning of the early dynastic period (ca. 2900 B.C.).

Ur had a prehistory of nearly two millennia which was followed by a historical period of about the same span of time. The life of the city slowly ebbed away between the fourth century B.C. and the turn of the era, probably because of the recurring problem of the need for a navigable waterway. Cyrus, the Persian monarch, left inscriptions that indicate that he was the last official builder of Ur. The city then faded into history until the spade of archaeologists disturbed its dust in this century.

Nothing that could be connected with the story of Abraham was found in the excavations, but the splendor of the Sumerian culture which he left as he traveled to Canaan has been revealed. It is evident that the patriarch turned his back on a rich, sophisticated society in response to the divine imperative.

Uruk

Modern Warka hides the remains of Uruk (the Erech of the Bible), one of the largest and most important cities of ancient Sumer. The ruins of Uruk are forty miles north of Ur. The site was visited by W. K. Loftus in 1850. Henry C. Rawlinson was an occasional visitor in the years from 1851 to 1855, but actual excavations were carried out by the Deutsche Orient-Gesellschaft in three expeditions: 1912–14, 1928–39, and 1954–59.

Uruk was one of the earliest Sumerian cities, having been established in the late fifth millennium B.C. Apart from the references to the city in Genesis 10:10 and in Ezra 4:9, where we are told that men of Erech were settled by the Assyrians in the cities of Samaria, the archaeology of Uruk is particularly significant for light shed upon the story of writing.

The German excavators recovered hundreds of pictographic tablets dating to the late fourth millennium B.C. These were the forerunners of the well-known cuneiform syllabic texts from Mesopotamia.

Uruk is also connected with the *Gilgamesh Epic.* The historical Gilgamesh was the most noteworthy ruler of the first dynasty of Uruk in the immediate postflood period. Stories about Gilgamesh which were embellished with legendary and mythologi-

The ziggurat of Uruk.

A view of the ruins of Babylon.

cal elements comprised an important part of Mesopotamian literature.

Babylon

The ruins of ancient Babylon lie scattered over the Iraqi terrain some fifty miles south of modern Baghdad. A branch of the Euphrates flows nearby, but the stream once divided the city and was bridged by an engineering wonder of the ancient world.

In antiquity, the city's commercial viability was based on its position at the hub of land and water routes. Now the inhabitants of the region live provincial lives around the settlement of Hillah, a few miles from the site of Babylon.

The story of the tower of Babel and the association of the city with the storied King Nebuchadnezzar were twin magnets that drew Western travelers to the site as early as the twelfth century A.D. The first significant account of the site was published by Pietro della Valle as a result of his visit in 1616. The inhabitants of Hillah at that time called one of the mounds in the area Babil, but in the course of time this identification was to be proved incorrect. Excavations identified the true site as a composite of mounds south of the Babil mound.

Robert Koldewey, the excavator of Babylon.

A minor excavation was carried out at Babylon as early as 1784 by J. de Beauchamp, but C. J. Rich's excavations in 1811 and again in 1817 were of greater significance, for they received a more detailed publication. In 1850, A. H. Layard, the great excavator of Nineveh, was attracted to the site, but his efforts were cut short when political conditions in the area became dangerously unstable. A French expedition worked at the site from 1852 to 1854, but little of value was accomplished. The great excavator of Babylon was destined to arrive in 1899. His name was Robert Koldewey, and he was sponsored by the Deutsche Orient-Gesellschaft (German Oriental Society). Koldewey continued his work at Babylon until 1917, when the vagaries of World War I brought his efforts to a halt. For a brief period in 1955–56, Heinrich Lenzen carried out minor excavations at Babylon, and the Iraqi Department of Antiquities has carried on the work of restoration in recent years so that the modern traveler can appreciate by means of the impressive ruins the grandeur of Babylon of old.

The Babylonian creation epic, *Enuma elish*, portrayed Babylon as the first city. According to this piece of pious political propaganda, the rebel gods whom Marduk (the king of the gods) had subdued built the city with its sanctuary complex, the Esangila, in his honor. The earliest mention of the city is probably in a date formula of Sharkali-sharri (ca. 2175 B.C.). The name is definitely mentioned in texts of the third dynasty of Ur. By the beginning of the Middle Bronze Age, Babylon had become the capital of a small, independent Amorite kingdom. The sixth king of the first dynasty of Babylon came to the throne in 1792. Hammurabi was destined to become one of the best-known figures in antiquity. The law code that bears his name is but one aspect of his genius, for he extended his control and organizational abilities over southern Mesopotamia and northward to Mari on the Euphrates and in the region south of Ashur on the Tigris. The dynasty ended in 1595 when the marauding Hittite monarch, Mursilis I, laid waste to the city. This event brought to a close the first great period in the city's history, the Old Babylonian.

By 1500 B.C., the city was under the control of the Cassites, a people from the Zagros mountains to the east. The Cassite dynasty lasted for half a millennium until their rule was broken by the rising power of Assyria. A subsequent dynasty included Nebuchadnezzar I (ca. 1100 B.C.), the namesake of the most famous ruler of Babylon, Nebuchadnezzar II, but nothing noteworthy is known of the city for centuries until the rise to power of Nabopolassar (625–605 B.C.).

Babylon reached its second zenith in history during the Neo-Babylonian era, a period of less than a century during which Nabopolassar, his son Nebuchadnezzar, and their successors conquered and ruled most of Asia. Nebuchadnezzar absorbed the former Assyrian territories after the crucial battle of Carchemish in 605 B.C. He ascended the throne in the same year and continued his rule until his death in 562. Before he died, he reconstructed Babylon into one of the most beautiful cities in the world, embellishing it with palaces, temples, and the famed hanging gardens.

In 556 B.C., a new dynasty was established by Nabonidus. His son, Bel-shar-usur, was regent when the city fell to Cyrus the Great in 539 (cf. Dan. 5, 7, 8). The Persians ruled Babylon until 331 when it fell to the armies of Alexander the Great. His plans to rebuild the city to its former greatness were abandoned after his death. His successor, Seleucus I, founded Seleucia on the Tigris a short distance away. Gradually the population shifted to the new city so that by the turn of the era only a few astronomers and mathematicians remained in Babylon. The abandoned city came to know the stark fulfillment of the words of the prophet Isaiah (13:1–22).

The archaeological and textual evidence indicates that

The stele bearing the Code of Hammurabi.

Detail of the Hammurabi stele.

Nebuchadnezzar's Babylon covered one thousand acres which were bisected by the Euphrates. The older (eastern) part of the city contained the monumental buildings—royal palaces and temples. A double-wall defense system encircled the city. It was over eighty-five feet thick and eleven miles long. The outer walls were approximately twenty-five feet wide, and they were reinforced with towers every sixty-five feet. An outer moat added to the defenses. The eight city gates were named after deities—Marduk, Ninurta, Urash, Sin, Adad, Enlil, Shamash, and Ishtar. The Ishtar Gate was the best known. It was decorated with enameled bricks, lapis-lazuli tiles, and colored bulls and dragons in relief. The gate opened onto a processional way that led past the hanging gardens and Nebuchadnezzar's palace, the temple of Ishtar, and the temple complex of Marduk, and to the temple of Ninurta.

The greatness that was Babylon's has partially been revealed by the archaeologist's spade. Of even greater significance are the epigraphic materials that throw new light upon the historical events surrounding Nebuchadnezzar's conquest of Judea and the fall of Jerusalem in 597 B.C. The Babylonian Chronicle, which is now in the British Museum, covers the history of the major events in the years 626–622, 610–594, 556, 555–539 B.C. (The

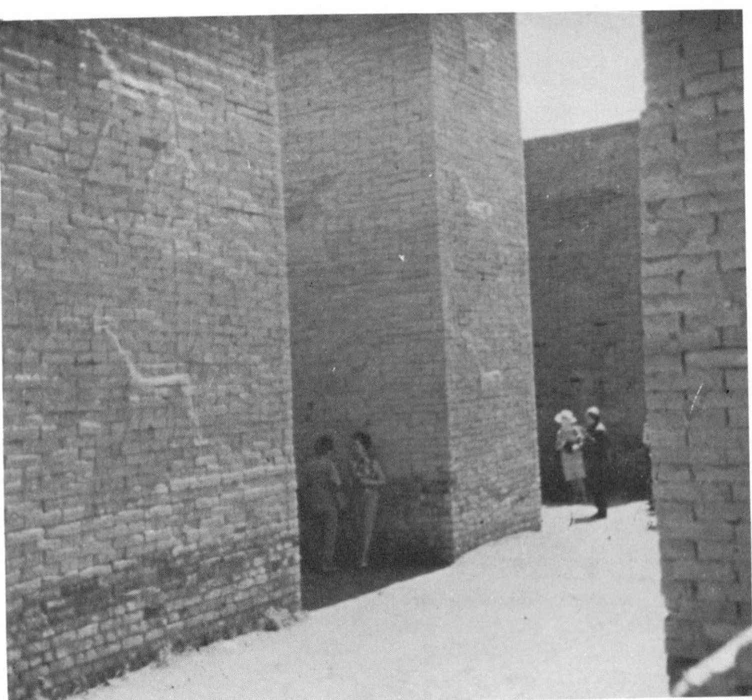

The ruins of the Ishtar gate.

An artist's reconstruction of the Ishtar gate in the time of Nebuchadnezzar.

missing years were recorded upon tablets that have not been recovered.) Of particular significance is the account of the capture of Jerusalem after a siege that ended on "the second day of the month Adar" (March 15/16, 597 B.C.). (Cf. II Kings 24:10–17.) The chronicle also records the conquest of Babylon by Cyrus of Persia in 539 B.C. (Cf. Isa. 44:24–28; 45:1–6.) This account is corroborated by the Cyrus Cylinder, an inscribed clay vessel found at Babylon which gives the Persian account of the capture. In the ruins of a storeroom near the palace of Nebuchadnezzar, Koldewey found a number of tablets which had been ration lists. Four of the tablets bear the names of Jehoiachin, who is identified as "king of Judah," and his sons, and refer to monthly rations of oil allotted to Jehoiachin. The tablets illuminate the references to Jehoiachin's capture and imprisonment in II Kings 24:12; 25:27ff. The tablets date to approximately 592 B.C.

Thousands of cuneiform texts have been recovered from Babylon, but many remain unpublished. The texts include inscribed bricks, foundation cylinders, business documents, letters, chronicles, administrative texts, and some legal texts. Surprisingly though, the important law code of Hammurabi was not recovered from the ruins of Babylon. It was found at Susa where it had been taken by an Elamite raider in the twelfth century B.C. French archaeologists discovered the engraved stele in 1901–02. It is probable that it had originally stood in the temple of Shamash at Sippar.

Nuzi

A half century ago, Nuzi was a nondescript place named Yorghan Tepe, a few miles southwest of Kirkuk in Iraq, with no apparent value for biblical studies. The place is not mentioned in the Bible.

In 1925, however, Edward Chiera of the Oriental Institute began excavations at the site and recovered approximately a thousand cuneiform tablets from the ruins of what proved to be a wealthy businessman's home. The tablets recorded the business affairs of the family during the fifteenth century B.C. Included on the tablets was the name of the town—Nuzi. These discoveries stimulated further excavations sponsored by the University Museum of Pennsylvania, Harvard Semitic Museum, the Iraq Museum, and the American Schools of Oriental Research. The directors of these excavations, which ended in 1931, included Chiera and Robert H. Pfeiffer during the first two seasons and Richard F. S. Star during the last two.

The Nuzi excavations revealed the ruins of a temple exhibiting

Bronze coat of mail from Nuzi, dating from the second millennium B.C.

Site of the Nuzi excavations.

seven phases, a palace with some painted rooms, a private residential sector, much pottery, and many small objects. But the significance of Nuzi lies in the thousands of clay tablets which were recovered from the debris of the fifteenth-fourteenth-century Hurrian town, even though the city had had a brilliant phase centuries earlier during the time of Sargon of Akkad, when its population had been predominantly Semitic. At that time it had borne the name *Gasur*. The Hurrians (biblical Horites) were a non-Semitic people that established colonies across northern Mesopotamia and even into Palestine in the late third and early second millennia B.C. In the Late Bronze Age the Hurrian state, Mitanni, of which Nuzi was a province, vied with the Egyptians and the Hittites as a major power. Mitanni was absorbed into the Hittite empire and the rising empire of the Assyrians by the close of the Late Bronze Age.

The Nuzi documents are written in Akkadian but with a generous sprinkling of Hurrian words, so that the texts have a value for reconstructing the language of the Hurrians. The tablets were excavated from both private and public archives, and some of them provide records that cover four to five generations of the same family. They are of particular interest to students of the Old Testament because they record social customs that are very similar to those recorded in the Bible in connection with the patriarchs; significantly, these tablets come from the same general area of Mesopotamia as the family of Abraham. Even though the tablets were written two to three centuries after the patriarchal period, it can be assumed that the customs of Nuzi had a history that extended well back into the Middle Bronze Age.

The texts throw new light, for example, upon the peculiar note in Genesis 15:2, 3, that Eliezer of Damascus was Abraham's first heir. It is now evident that the childless Abraham had adopted Eliezer either as a guarantee that he would have someone to tend him in his old age or as a surety for borrowing capital funds from Eliezer. Sarah gave her handmaid to Abraham, an act which we now know was quite within the customs of her environment, even though it may seem strange to us. The transfer of Esau's birthright to his brother Jacob (Gen. 25:31–34) is in keeping with at least two examples from the Nuzi tablets. Numerous other parallels to biblical customs have been noted—the significance of the father's blessing, the possession of the household gods and the attendant implication of property ownership, and collective public responsibility for a crime. No doubt these customs were widespread throughout the society of that day, so it is not necessary to posit a direct influence of

Hurrian law and customs upon the people of the Old Testament, whether in Palestine or in Mesopotamia. The texts do, however, illuminate and substantiate the patriarchal customs in particular and establish them authentically within the general time frame of the patriarchal era—the Middle Bronze Age.

Finally, the Nuzi texts provide several references to the *Habiru* who sold themselves into slavery. Apparently a part of the fifteenth-century population of Nuzi were Habiru. The relationship of this term to the word *Hebrew* will be amplified below in connection with the Amarna age.

The Assyrians

Apart from the probes of Claudius Rich which were mentioned above, the first major Mesopotamian excavations were carried out at sites that are north of Babylonia, along the Tigris River, in the territory which was occupied in antiquity by the Assyrians. These Semitic people first surface in historical records in the time of Sargon of Akkad, who was the first king of Sumer and Akkad to extend his authority into the area to the north. The Assyrians, however, may have been inhabitants of the area much earlier. The name of the people is derived from the name of their national god, Ashur, and the name also designated the early capital of the Assyrians. Later tradition remembered the earliest kings as "those who dwelt in tents," suggesting that they derived from Amorite stock. The Amorites ("westerners") were nomadic people who erupted from the regions of the Syrian desert from time to time and flowed into the more settled surrounding regions. The pattern of Amorite assimilation and amalgamation with the sedentary populations was repeated again and again, bringing the infusion of new stock into the populations of the Fertile Cresent.

The first independent Assyrian state developed in the aftermath of the collapse of the third dynasty of Ur, shortly after 2000 B.C. The available evidence suggests that the political power of Assyria was quite limited at that time, but Assyrian merchants established a number of trading colonies in distant Central Anatolia that thrived in the century from 1900 to 1800. Over ten thousand cuneiform tablets associated with Assyrian caravans and commercial activities have been recovered from sites in Turkey at Kültepe, Boghazköy, and Alishar. These so-called Cappadocian texts document Assyrian business activities and provide illumination about the Hattic peoples, the native inhabitants of the area that was later to be dominated by the Hittites.

This brief flourish of Assyrian independence was followed by an eclipse lasting from about 1850 to 1350, during which a succession of weak rulers was content to function under the title *Governor of the City of Ashur.* The period was marked by the domination of the Assyrians by the Babylonians and the Mitannians.

When the Hurrian kingdom of Mitanni began to wane in the fourteenth century, Asshur-uballit I (ca. 1362–1327) moved to establish Assyria as a significant power. He was a contemporary of Suppiluliumas, the Hittite king, and of Amenophis IV (Akhenaten), the pharaoh of the Amarna period in Egyptian history. Asshur-uballit assumed the title *King of the Land of Assyria,* and he established the pattern of dynastic succession from father to son in contrast to the earlier predominant pattern of brother to brother. From the beginning of this Middle Assyrian period on, the Assyrians and the Babylonians came to be linked together in a relationship somewhat akin to that which later existed between the kingdoms of Israel and Judah during Iron Age II.

The close of the Bronze Age was marked by a period of political turmoil throughout the ancient world that affected Assyrians as well as other ethnic groups, but of the several contending centers of power in Egypt, Anatolia, and Mesopotamia, Assyria was destined to be the major survivor. Under Tiglath-pileser I (ca. 1115–1077), the Assyrians began a period of expansion by means of conquest and coercion that eventually brought Assyria dominance over an area stretching between Persia to the east and the Mediterranean to the west, central Anatolia to the north, and Egypt to the south.

By the mid-ninth century B.C., the Assyrian menace had appeared on the eastern horizon, posing a direct threat to a number of small Syro-Palestinian kingdoms that included Israel and Aram (Syria). In an inscription of Shalmaneser III (ca. 859–825) which records the clash between a coalition of opposing forces and the Assyrian army, Ahab of Israel is identified as one of the leaders of the opposition. His ground forces and chariots comprised a major contingent in the battle of Qarqar, on the Orontes River, in 853. Later, Israel succumbed to Assyrian pressure. On the famous Black Obelisk of Shalmaneser, which was discovered at Calah, King Jehu is depicted paying tribute to the Assyrian monarch. The date was Shalmaneser's eighteenth year—841 B.C.

Although the biblical account does not specifically mention Adad-nirari III, the reference to a "deliverer for Israel" in II Kings 13:5 is probably an allusion to him. A stele of Adad-nirari has been found which records the receipt of tribute from Jehoash of Israel, along with others, in the year 796.

Israel and Judah were able to expand their territories and commercial interests in the days of Jeroboam II and the prophet Amos due to a succession of ineffective Assyrian kings. Tiglath-pileser III (744–727), however, launched a period of Assyrian recovery that continued under his successors. Assyrian dominance in the Near East was re-established, and, in the process, the kingdom of Israel was obliterated. In extant inscriptions Tiglath-pileser III mentions receiving tribute from a number of vassals, including King Azariah of Judah and Menahem of Samaria (Israel). Before the end of his reign, this Assyrian monarch suppressed the expansionary activities of Pekah of Israel (II Kings 15:29). Israelite rebellion brought siege and ultimately destruction to Samaria at the hands of Shalmaneser V. His successor, Sargon II, claimed the victory, and well may have been in charge of the besieging army. The fall of Samaria occurred in the days of Isaiah, but Judah did not feel the conquering might of Assyria until Sargon's successor, Sennacherib, invaded Judah in 701 upon the refusal of King Hezekiah to pay the expected tribute (cf. II Kings 18:13ff.). Jerusalem was not captured, but Judah came under the heel of Assyrian domination and submitted to the payment of tribute.

Manasseh, Hezekiah's son, ruled for fifty-five years (ca. 696–642), largely by submitting to the sovereignty of Esarhaddon (681–670) and Ashurbanipal (669–627?). Esarhaddon magnified his prestige by conquering Egypt, but Ashurbanipal (the "Asnapper" of Ezra 4:9ff.) is remembered in modern times primarily for the great library which he collected in his capital, Nineveh. During his reign Josiah came to the throne of Judah.

The prophet Jeremiah lived during the years when the Assyrian empire was collapsing. Ashurbanipal's successors were unable to hold the empire together, and, with the rise of an independent Babylon under the rule of Nabopolassar (626–605), a series of battles ensued that brought the final destruction of the major Assyrian cities—Ashur, Khorsabad, Calah, and Nineveh—by 612 B.C. The Egyptian forces under the leadership of Pharaoh Necho moved to assist their overlords, the Assyrians, but they were hindered at the battle of Megiddo in 609, the battle at which Josiah was fatally wounded. Necho's forces met the army of Nebuchadnezzar II, Nabopolassar's son, at the decisive battle of Carchemish in 605; the Assyrian and Egyptian effort was crushed. The triumphant Nebuchadnezzar succeeded his father to the throne in the same year, and Babylon succeeded Assyria as the dominant world power.

Nineveh

The numerous references to Nineveh in the Bible are an indication of its role as one of the oldest and greatest cities of Mesopotamia and as the capital of Assyria when that empire was at its height. The site is located on the east side of the Tigris River, just opposite modern Mosul. In 1820 C. J. Rich, who was an agent of the British East India Tea Company, visited Mosul and spent four months sketching a plan of the mounds across the river. He suspected that these were the ruins of Nineveh, and he collected a number of tablets and inscriptions, none of which he nor anyone else was able to read. The site is comprised of two large mounds, Kuyunjik and Nebi-Yunus (the latter name is connected with the tradition of the prophet Jonah), which lie within the ruins of walls whose perimeter is approximately eight miles. Nebi-Yunus is partially occupied by a village, but the northern mound has been left desolate since the destruction of Nineveh in 612 B.C.

In 1842 Paul Emile Botta came to Mosul as the French consular agent, and, stimulated by the earlier reports of Rich, he began excavating the Kuyunjik mound. A few months of work without discovering significant monumental art convinced him, however, to shift his efforts from Nineveh to Khorsabad (Dur-Sharrukin) ten miles north. There he met immediate and spectacular success. Austen Henry Layard (later to be knighted) arrived in Mosul in 1845. He excavated at Nimrud (Calah), twenty miles south of Nineveh, and made discoveries of spectacular palaces and bas-reliefs, but in 1849 he turned his attention to Kuyunjik, to the very spot that Botta had abandoned just a few years earlier. Layard's excavations in 1849–50 revealed the palace of Sennacherib and the famous Taylor Prism, which records the annals of Sennacherib, including his siege of Hezekiah's Jerusalem. In the spring of 1850 Layard and his assistant, Hormuzd Rassam, made their most significant find—thousands of clay tablets representing the library of Ashurbanipal.

Ruins of Nineveh.

This famous library was collected by Ashurbanipal "in order that he might have that which to read." He had been educated in both Akkadian and Sumerian, and some of his bookmarks state: "In agreement with the original tablets and documents I caused copies of the Assyrian, Sumerian, and Akkadian to be written, compiled and revised in the chancellery of the experts, and as precious possessions of my royalty." His library was to provide a key to the understanding of the whole Assyrio-Babylonian civilization. The transfer of the discoveries of Layard to the British Museum was destined to stimulate still another expedition to Nineveh.

The last half of the nineteenth century saw several British excavators at work on the site, but this was in the period when stratigraphical excavation was in its infancy. The activities of George Smith, however, are worthy of notice. Smith had been a banknote engraver who whiled away his free time at the British Museum. He became enamored of the study of cuneiform and learned to read it. In time he was appointed to a position in the Egyptian-Assyrian section of the museum, and, while deciphering some of the texts which Layard and Rassam had discovered at Nineveh, he came across a portion of the story of Gilgamesh. The story tells of this ancient hero who goes in search of the secret of life eternal, a secret possessed by Utnapishtim, the survivor of a great flood. Unfortunately, as Smith came to the crucial part of the story, the text was incomplete, for the concluding portion had been broken off. The *London Daily Telegraph* sent Smith to the site of Nineveh in 1873 to find, if possible, the missing fragments of the story. The amazing thing is that he was successful in his search. In addition, he found tablets containing the Mesopotamian creation epic, the *Enuma elish,* which he published in 1876.

The stratification of the ninety or more feet of debris at Nineveh has been clarified by R. Campbell Thompson and others, particularly in the years 1927–32. The archaeological evidence indicates that occupation began by 4500 B.C. The earliest pottery is of the Hassuna type; it is followed at a depth of eighty-two feet by Ubaidian pottery, indicating early connections with the Sumerian civilization to the south. An inscription of Naram-Sin of the Akkadian period has been recovered at the site. The Code of Hammurabi mentions Nineveh as the site of a temple dedicated to Ishtar, the Sumerian Inanna, and a temple of the goddess was discovered at Kuyunjik. Statues of Ishtar of Nineveh were sent as prized gifts to Egypt by the kings of Mitanni. Another important temple of Nineveh was dedicated to the god Nabu, patron of writing, the arts, and science. This may in part explain Ashurbanipal's interest in collecting a great library in the city.

The ruins of palaces built by Tiglath-pileser I (1115–1077), Ashurnasirpal II (884–859), Sargon II (722–705), and Sennacherib (705–681) all testify to the intermittent function of Nineveh as a royal city of Assyria, a role it shared with the cities of Ashur, Nimrud (Calah), and Dur-Sharrukin. However, the city was established as the permanent capital during the reign of Sennacherib. His impressive constructions include a magnificent palace, embellished with bas-reliefs of the siege and capture of Judean Lachish, an aqueduct that brought fresh water from the hills thirty-five miles distant, and the city walls. All these and more made Nineveh "an exceeding great city."

Bas-relief of a lion hunt from the palace of Ashurbanipal at Nineveh.

Nimrud

Nimrud's location, twenty miles south of Nineveh, was noted earlier. At one time the Tigris ran adjacent to the western edge of the city, but its bed has now shifted two miles further west of the tell. The complex of ruins spreads over nine hundred acres which are encircled by a massive mud-brick wall nearly five miles long. An acropolis, Fort Shalmaneser, covering sixty-five acres and separated from the adjacent city by its own wall, occupied the southwest corner of Nimrud.

The ruins of Nimrud.

The city is mentioned in Genesis 10:11 under the name *Calah*, which is derived from the Assyrian name for the city, *Kalbu*. The name *Nimrud* possibly was derived from the name of the Sumerian deity, Ninurta or Nimurta, to whom the city was dedicated in ancient times.

Excavations at the site began with A. H. Layard who worked here and alternately at Nineveh from 1845 to 1851. His excavations were confined primarily to the acropolis where he discovered the royal quarters of Ashurnasirpal II (884–859). Ashurnasirpal selected Calah as his royal headquarters at the beginning of his reign and carried out an extensive rebuilding program. His residence has been described as "one of the most beautiful palaces of antiquity." The rooms were wainscoted throughout with alabaster slabs nearly seven feet high and carved with reliefs depicting the triumphs of Assyria in war. The reliefs were inscribed with appropriate explanatory texts. The palace also boasted huge carved stone figures—winged bulls, lions, and *lamassu* (the familiar part animal, part human figures)—and a grand throne room. Layard and subsequent excavators uncovered the palaces of Shalmaneser III, Tiglath-pileser III, Esarhaddon, and Ashurbanipal also. The ziggurat, a temple complex known as the Ezida, and several temples have been cleared. The two major temples were dedicated to Ninurta and to Nabu.

Excavators who followed Layard include W. K. Loftus (1854–55), Hormuzd Rassam (1854 and 1878), George Smith (1872–73), and M. E. L. Mallowan, who directed a series of thirteen campaigns from 1949 to 1963. The work of Mallowan and his associates was vital to the recovery of the stratigraphy of the site,

Portal-relief figure from the palace of Ashurnasirpal at Nimrud.

The Black Obelisk of Shalmaneser III.

for the earlier excavators worked in the era before adequate archaeological techniques had been developed.

The history of Nimrud has now been traced from prehistoric times to its destruction at the end of the Assyrian empire. Some evidence also exists for minor occupation into Hellenistic times. The most important materials from Nimrud consist of the annals of the Assyrian kings of Iron Age II, and a collection of administrative letters and reports. These have illuminated the relationships between mighty Assyria and the petty kingdoms of western Asia, including Israel, Judah, and the Aramean kingdom of Damascus in the latter half of the eighth century B.C.

Layard's most significant discovery may well have been the Black Obelisk of Shalmaneser III, a limestone stele which depicts the exploits of Shalmaneser in a series of bas-reliefs which have been carved into the stone with accompanying explanatory texts. One of the panels depicts Jehu, the king of Israel, kissing the feet of Shalmaneser as Israelite officials bearing tribute to the Assyrian ruler stand behind their king. It has been established that this event occurred in 841 B.C. This event provides an important point for synchronizing the reigns of the kings of Israel and Judah, for Jehu attained power through a *coup d'état* which resulted in the deaths of both Joram of Israel and Ahaziah of Judah (II Kings 9–10).

The annals of other Assyrian kings of this period were carved in the pavement of the entrance to temples, on the wainscoting of palaces, and on commemorative stones. A sandstone stele of Ashurnasirpal marked the completion of his first "five-year plan" to beautify Calah. It includes a description of the principal buildings and of the surrounding botanical and zoological gardens. The text states that much of the labor for the project was provided by Syrian slaves. In a passage reminiscent of Sol-

Partial reconstruction of an Assyrian palace at Nimrud.

Jehu of Israel, from the Black Obelisk of Shalmaneser III discovered in the northwest palace at Nimrud.

Carved ivory cherubim of Phoenician workmanship discovered in the northwest palace of Nimrud.

omon's dedicatory activities at the completion of the Jerusalem temple, Ashurnasirpal describes the great ten-day feast which he gave for visiting dignitaries and the people of the district. The number of guests that were hosted totaled 69,574. On the basis of this figure it is possible to estimate the total population for the district around Nimrud at no less than 100,000. When the equivalent populations of other contemporary Assyrian cities are added to this number, it is apparent that Assyria could field overwhelming forces. A docket from Fort Shalmaneser records the inspection of 36,242 bows, and bowmen probably comprised no more than one-third of the forces. It is probable, then, that the Assyrians had an army of 100,000.

In contrast to the size of Assyria's forces, Menahem of Israel could not have fielded more than 60,000 men. This estimate is based on the passage in II Kings 15:19f. which states that Menahem of Israel paid one thousand talents of silver as tribute to Tiglath-pileser III at the rate of fifty shekels per man (1 talent = 3000 shekels). Fifty shekels was the market price for a premium slave in Assyria at that time.

The Assyrian account of the conquest of Samaria and the deportation of its inhabitants had been recovered from a number of inscribed prisms which Sargon had executed. These have been recovered at Ashur and Nineveh, and similar texts were found at Khorsabad. A similar prism recovered at Nimrud states that 27,290 prisoners were carried away into exile, and that he settled other people in the restored city, placing them under the authority of a district governor. In numerous other ways, the discoveries at Nimrud of materials from Iron Age II have illuminated the biblical account to a remarkable degree, supporting the historical information in the Bible and providing supplementary records.

Two horses' heads in a relief from the palace of Sargon at Khorsabad.

Khorsabad (Dur-Sharrukin)

Sargon II assumed the Assyrian throne in 721 B.C. He completed the decimation of Samaria and the siege of Tyre which his predecessor, Shalmaneser V, had initiated. The capture of Ashdod by Sargon is mentioned in Isaiah 20:1. In 1963 this historical reference in the Bible was corroborated when the Israeli archaeologist, Moshe Dothan, discovered an inscription of Sargon at Tell Ashdod. Between military expeditions to the west, Sargon found time to move his capital from Ashur to Calah to Nineveh and, finally, to a site ten miles north of Nineveh.

Sargon's newly constructed capital was initially named Dur-Sharrukin ("Sargonsburg"). The ruins of Dur-Sharrukin were destined to be known as Khorsabad, however, for they came to be associated with a Sassanid hero named Khosroes.

Paul E. Botta began digging the ruins of Khorsabad in 1843. He quickly came upon the ruins of Sargon's palace, and from it he extracted exquisite examples of Assyrian art. When drawings of these arrived in Europe, they became the objects of intense popular interest. Botta prepared a shipment of the monumental blocks of stone carved with reliefs, and such was the state of archaeology in this period that he cut some of the stones into six pieces for ease of handling. Furthermore, the first shipment sank to the bottom of the Tigris when the rafts upon which it was being carried down to the Persian Gulf overturned in treacherous rapids. Botta's activities at Khorsabad were halted when the French government transferred him to a different post. His successor, Victor Place, did succeed in shipping a number of pieces to Paris which still remain a part of the display of Assyrian materials at the Louvre.

The work of Victor Place continued from 1851 to 1855. He determined the floor plan of the palace and found important cuneiform documents along with additional artifacts of a domestic nature. The dust of Khorsabad was not disturbed again by the spade until Edward Chiera of the Oriental Institute of the University of Chicago began excavations in 1929. He reexamined the ruins of Sargon's palace and discovered an important "King List" before the excavation was completed in 1935. The list has been important in the establishment of the chronology of the Assyrian dynasties. Through comparative studies this

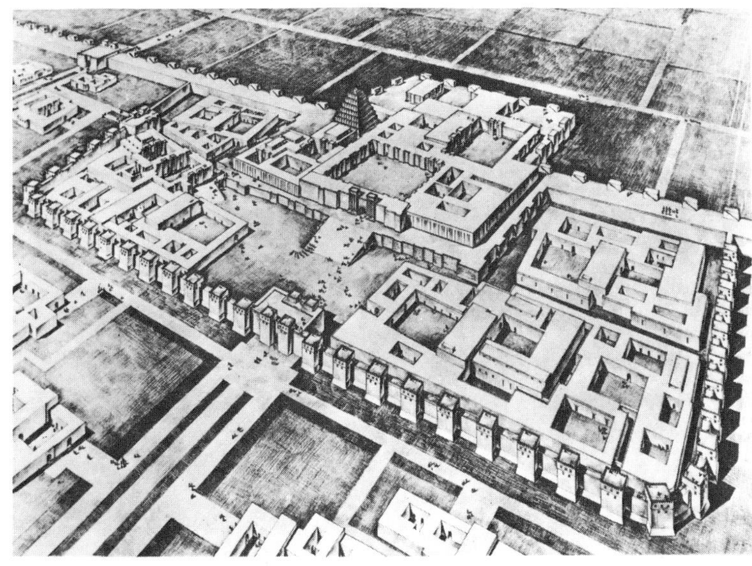

Artist's reconstruction of the Khorsabad palace of Sargon II.

Artist's restoration of painted plaster decoration in a house at Khorsabad. Sargon and one of his officers stand before a god.

chronology in turn contributes to the establishment of the chronology of the kings of Israel and Judah.

Ashur

Ashur, the titular capital of the Assyrians, occupied a low bluff on the west bank of the Tigris River a few miles north of the mouth of the Little Zab River. The site, which bears the modern name of Qalat Sharqat, is strategically located sixty miles south of Mosul at the gateway into Babylonia to the south. The Tigris pierces the natural barrier of the Hamrin mountains at this point.

Ruins of Ashur viewed from atop the ziggurat.

The soil of Qalat Sharqat was first disturbed by Austen Henry Layard in 1847. His early efforts were followed by the further probes of Hormuzd Rassam and Victor Place. Rassam identified the site as Ashur in 1853 when he discovered two cylinders of Tiglath-pileser I which mentioned the name of the city. The major excavations at the site, however, were carried out by a German expedition under the direction of Walter Andrae and Robert Koldewey from 1903 to 1914.

Ashur may have been colonized by Sumerians in the early third millennium B.C., but the basic population was Semitic. Sumerian influence is evident in the plan and the statuary of the ancient Ishtar temple. Before Assyria emerged as an independent state early in the Middle Bronze Age, Ashur was dominated by the Sumerians, then by the Sargonic kings of Akkad, and finally by the Neo-Sumerians. The German archaeologists were able to chart the monumental buildings as a result of their excavations and the discovery of a group of cultic texts that listed and described the temples of the city. The major sanctuaries included the Anu-adad temple with its twin ziggurats, dating to the twelfth century B.C.; the ziggurat of Enlil, which was rededicated to Ashur in the Middle Bronze period; the adjacent Ashur temple; and two additional temple complexes dedicated respectively to Ishtar and Nabu and to Sin and Shamash. Palaces and residential and mercantile areas were also excavated. The defenses of the city consisted of a wall system which included thirteen gates. Between the outer and an inner wall on the southern side of the city, an open space was excavated which contained two rows of inscribed stones arranged in parallel fashion. The inscriptions of one of the rows commemorated the Assyrian kings from approximately 1300 on, and the other row honored the leading government officials whose names were used to designate the activities of a particular year. This method of employing the names of high officials to desig-

The ziggurat at Ashur. The Tigris River is in the background.

nate the events of a particular year has produced the "eponym list."

Besides the cultic texts and the inscribed stelae mentioned above, the excavators of Ashur recovered an Assyrian version of the Mesopotamian creation epic. While Marduk, the patron god of Babylon, is exalted in the *Enuma elish,* the god Ashur is highlighted in the Assyrian account, which dates to about 1000 B.C. Also discovered were two damaged tablets which contain an Assyrian law code similar to the earlier Babylonian Code of Hammurabi. The Assyrian laws appear to be more severe than those of the Babylonians.

Ashur suffered a fate similar to that of the other capitals of the Assyrian empire. The city was captured by the armies of the Medes and the Babylonians in 614 B.C., two years before the fall of Nineveh.

Persia (Iran)

Biblical connections with Persia are limited to the exilic and postexilic periods; the books of Chronicles, Ezra, Nehemiah, Esther, Ezekiel, and Daniel contain numerous references to the great empire of the Persians. The Medes, a people closely related to the Persians, lived in the same general area to the east of the Mesopotamian Valley. They are mentioned as descendants of Japheth in the "Table of Nations" (Gen. 10), and the name recurs in II Kings 17, in Isaiah, in Jeremiah, and in several of the postexilic books noted above.

The Iranian plateau knew a long history of fragmentation before the establishment of the Persian empire in the sixth century B.C., but the Medes and Persians were destined to dominate almost all of the civilized world until late in the fourth century when the empire collapsed under the onslaught of the conquering Macedonian, Alexander the Great. The Medes were first mentioned in Assyrian documents during the reign of Shalmaneser III (858–824). At that time Assyria was apparently able to dominate them, but only with difficulty. Sargon II did send a group of the ill-fated captives from Samaria into exile in "cities of the Medes" (II Kings 17:6; 18:11), but in 612 B.C. a coalition of Scythians, Medes, and Babylonians destroyed the Assyrian capital at Nineveh, and the Medes acquired control of a portion of the eastern area which Assyria had dominated. The Persians, who had been vassals of the Assyrians, then came under the hegemony of Media, but by 550 B.C. the Median ruler, Astyages, was defeated by the Persian leader, Cyrus the Great. From this Medo-Persian base Cyrus went on to establish the Persian empire.

Cyrus was a descendant of an illustrious predecessor named Achaemenes, so the empire is frequently referred to as the Achaemenid empire. The conquests of Cyrus brought famed Babylon under his control in 539 B.C., and consequently the Jews in exile in Babylon came under Persian control. Cyrus introduced a revolutionary approach to the treatment of his subjects by permitting the peoples who had been captured and exiled by his Assyrian and Babylonian predecessors to return to their homelands. The Persian magnanimity extended even to the restoration of local shrines. Under these humane policies, those Jews who so desired were permitted to return to Jerusalem. This Persian humanitarianism was apparently the result of the strong influence of the Zoroastrian religion upon Persian thought, although it is much debated whether or not the Achaemenid monarchs were devotees of Zoroastrianism. It is known, however, that the symbol of Ahura Mazda is frequently found in association with royal Persian remains, and in Zoroaster's teaching this god represented the embodiment of goodness, wisdom, and truth. The historical information about Zoroaster (Zarathustra) is quite fragmentary, but he appears to have lived during the sixth century when the foundations of the Persian state were being laid.

The Jews who returned to Jerusalem established a small enclave as a part of the satrapy "Beyond the River (Euphrates)," but they continued under Persian authority until the time of Alexander the Great. In line with their general policies, the Persians permitted the reconstruction of the ruined Jerusalem sanctuary. The second temple was constructed between 520 and 515 B.C. The early years of the small Jewish community were fraught with dangers posed by political enemies from the surrounding areas who threatened to destroy the settlement. The leadership of Ezra and Nehemiah, both of whom acted under the authority of the central government, succeeded in thwarting the dangers. They also imposed vital social and religious reforms upon the population of Jerusalem and the neighboring area.

The books of Chronicles, Ezra, Nehemiah, Esther, and Daniel (in part) in the Old Testament and Tobit, I and II Esdras, the Additions to Esther and to Daniel in the Apocrypha are associated with the two-century period of Persian rule. Sections of Ezra and Daniel were written in Aramaic, a phenomenon that underscores the growth and influence of that language after the Persians adopted it as the diplomatic medium for their realm. Aramaic was destined to displace Hebrew as the predominant language of Palestinian Jews by the turn of the era. Jewish Palestinian Aramaic had its counterpart in Christian Palestinian Aramaic, and in the course of time a substantial deposit of Aramaic was indelibly impressed on the Talmud.

Archaeological research in Iran, as throughout the world, is not restricted to a single period of time, but for our interests we will note the activities that relate specifically to the period of the Persian empire, for it is in the remains of this era that we find correlations to the Bible. Our attention will focus upon Pasargadae, Persepolis, Hamadan, Susa, and the famed cliff bearing the Behistun Inscription.

Pasargadae

Pasargadae was the early capital of the Persia of Cyrus the Great. It is located in an elevated valley in the southwestern sector of Iran. Here Cyrus had won a decisive victory over the Median armies, and here he built a palace in whose ruins has been found the oft-repeated inscription, "I am Cyrus, the King, the Achaemenid."

The main features of the site include the citadel area, the palace, the sacred precincts, and the tomb of Cyrus. Although these ruins were often visited and described by earlier travelers, the first archaeological soundings were carried out only in the first decade of the present century by E. Herzfeld. Later, Sir Aurel Stein drew plans of the site, and in 1935 E. F. Schmidt made an aerial photographic survey. A five-year program of excavation was undertaken in 1949 by Ali Sami, who was then

Director of the Archaeological Institute at Persepolis. The most recent excavations were conducted by David Stonach, the Director of the British Institute of Persian Studies in Tehran from 1961 to 1963.

The tomb of Cyrus the Great at Pasargadae.

The ruins of Pasargadae have yielded the earliest known Persian bas-reliefs. One of them is the carving of a winged human figure that embellished a doorway. The tomb of Cambyses II, the son and successor of Cyrus, is located in the area of the palace, and Cyrus' tomb stands a short distance from the ruins of the city. According to tradition, Alexander the Great visited the tomb. No inscription is now evident on the structure, but the classical writer, Strabo, mentions an inscription which read, "O man, I am Cyrus, the son of Cambyses, who founded the Empire of the Persians and was king of Asia. Grudge me not therefore this monument." When David Stonach examined the tomb, he found a much-eroded winged disc which had previously gone unnoticed. The winged disc, a symbol of Ahura Mazda, is suggestive of Cyrus' religious beliefs.

Persepolis

The ruins of Persepolis, some fifty miles south of Pasargadae, are beyond doubt the most spectacular ruins of the Persians. The city was established by Darius the Great (522–485 B.C.) who had a massive terrace constructed on three levels of a spur of a mountain. Upon this the city was built and the capital was moved to Persepolis from Pasargadae. To Persepolis each year representatives of all the varied peoples which comprised the empire came to pay homage and to bring tribute to the King of Kings. The occasion was probably each spring at the time of the ancient New Year festival.

Silver drachmae of Alexander the Great from the treasury of Persepolis.

One part of the complex is the Apadana, the Hall of Audience of Darius the Great. One scholar has estimated that it could accommodate some ten thousand people. The Apadana and the other palaces and public buildings were destroyed by Alexander the Great. When he captured the city and transferred the riches to Ecbatana, the transfer required ten thousand mules and five thousand camels, according to the ancient writer, Plutarch. The magnificent architectural remains and the numerous small finds, including a gold foundation tablet of Darius I which bore a trilingual inscription and was found beneath the Apadana, all testify to the wealth and beauty of Persepolis, the city of the Persians.

The archaeological investigation of Persepolis through scientific excavations began in 1931. The expedition of the Oriental

The Apadana at Persepolis. This relief from the stairway shows Babylonians and Syrians bringing tribute.

Early Persian bas-relief.

Panoramic view of Persepolis.

Institute of the University of Chicago, directed at first by Ernst Herzfeld and then by E. F. Schmidt, continued until 1939. The Iranian Archaeological Service continued to excavate in the 1940s with André Godard and Ali Sami the successive directors of the work. A restoration program has also been established under the direction of Giuseppe and Ann Gritt Tilia, Italian specialists in restoration; both the excavations and restoration continue through the Iranian Archaeological Service.

Hamadan

Hamadan was known in antiquity as Ecbatana, and during the Persian period it functioned as a summer capital. Archaeological investigation has been restricted to salvage and occasional finds, however, because of modern occupation of the site. The Iranian Archaeological Service has begun clearing operations at the northern outskirts of the city, but so far scientific excavations have hardly begun. Incidental finds which are now mainly in the Teheran Museum include two small foundation tablets, one of silver and one of gold, gold drinking vessels, and jewelry. Most of these objects were discovered by illegal diggers.

The Book of Tobit records how Tobias, his dog, and the angel Raphael stopped on their journey to stay in Ecbatana with Raguel, a cousin of Tobias' father. The site also contains the traditional tomb of Esther and Mordecai; it is still being exploited by the local residents as an attraction for pilgrims and tourists. Other than these traditions and the fragmentary bits of the buried glory of the Persian capital that have occasionally surfaced, Hamadan still holds captive its historical secrets.

Susa

Susa is situated on a plain in southwestern Iran where it once functioned as a capital city and as a treasury of the Persians. It is also known as Shushan. Excavations have been going on at Susa longer than at any other Iranian site. W. K. Loftus identified the site and sank trial trenches there in 1854. It is the French, however, who are the excavators of Susa. Marcel and Jane Dieulafoy began work in 1884; then in 1897 Jacques de Morgan led the first of the annual winter excavations that have been conducted since by the French Archaeological Mission.

The four main mounds are known as the Acropolis, the Apadana, the Royal City, and the Artisans' City. The Acropolis has yielded evidence of a sequence of habitation from the fourth millennium B.C. to Islamic times. The early Susa material has provided a fairly well-established chronology for the comparative study of materials from other early Iranian sites. The Acropolis also contained the main citadel of the Elamites, who were powerful enough in the thirteenth century B.C. to occasionally dominate the city-states of Mesopotamia to the west. It was during this period that the famous diorite stele inscribed with the law code of Hammurabi was carried away to Susa as a trophy of conquest. In 1901, de Morgan discovered the stone in three parts on the Acropolis.

The Apadana, as at Persepolis, is a vast artificial platform which was constructed as the base for the palace of Darius I. Darius' reign is referred to by the prophets Haggai and Zechariah. The Apadana at Susa predates that at Persepolis. Darius' palace was decorated with glazed multicolored tiles with reliefs representing the king's bodyguard of bowmen, called the Immortals. These life-size reliefs are now in the Louvre.

The Royal City sector was examined by a deep probe of Roman Girshman which revealed approximately fifteen layers of occupation. These extended from the Islamic back to the Elamite period. The earliest Elamite period reflected a surprisingly high degree of urban planning.

Queen Esther lived in the magnificent palace at Shushan. In the ruins of the palace two foundation tablets were found in 1970, one written in Babylonian and the other in Elamite and both giving the same information. The texts are essentially a repetition of the content of previously discovered inscriptions. Darius the Great gives his ancestry, describes how he built his palace and where the workmen and the materials came from, and praises the god Ahura Mazda. The foundations were dug to bedrock, and for a base rubble and gravel were packed to a depth of forty cubits. The Babylonians manufactured both sun-dried and kiln-fired bricks, and the Assyrians brought cedar from Lebanon. Gold came from Sardis and from Bactria, and semiprecious stones from what is now a part of Russia. Silver and ebony came from Egypt, and ivory from Ethiopia and India. An idea of the splendor of the palace can be obtained by reading the Book of Esther.

The tomb of Daniel has also been traditionally associated with Susa. A conical white, sugar-loaf structure across the Shaur River from the site of Susa has been the destination of Muslim pilgrims for centuries. When they first arrived in Susa in the seventh century, the Arabs claimed they found Daniel's coffin on the Acropolis. The Sultan Sanjar is said to have commanded that the coffin be encased in an outer shell of crystal and sus-

An air view of the mound of Susa.

Restoring the ziggurat at Susa.

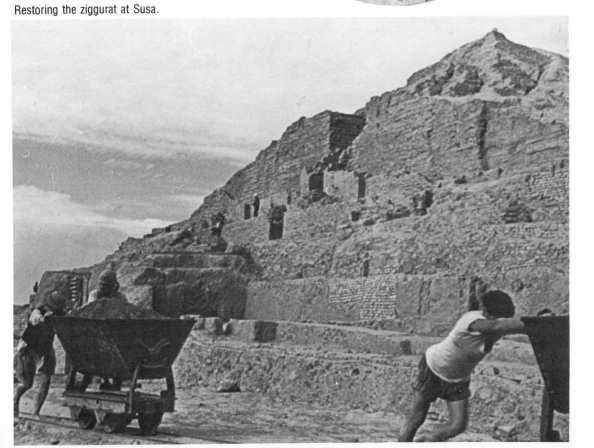

pended by iron chains from the middle of a bridge spanning the river as a means of settling a dispute between the inhabitants of the two parts of the city. Each group desired the coffin in their sector because it was thought to bring good fortune wherever it resided. The shrine is believed to date to the twelfth century, but it has undergone occasional rebuilding through the centuries.

The excavations in Iran have produced no material evidence of biblical characters such as Nehemiah, who served the king of Persia in the Shushan palace, but have shown the wealth and the splendor of the Persian kings during whose reigns they lived. And the composite nature of the Persian empire has been emphasized by reliefs found in the Persian capitals which testify to the breadth and diversity of peoples that the Achaemenid rulers controlled.

SUGGESTED TOPICS FOR FURTHER STUDY

1. Cultural horizons in Mesopotamia from 6000 to 3000 B.C.
2. An overview of the literature of Sumer.
3. A comparison of the *Enuma elish* and the Genesis account of creation.
4. The religious ideas in ancient Mesopotamian culture.
5. The Amorites.
6. The excavations at Ur.
7. Ziggurat and sanctuary in Mesopotamia.
8. A comparison of the *Gilgamesh Epic* and the story of the Genesis flood.
9. The archaeology of Babylon.
10. Patriarchal traditions and the Nuzi texts.
11. The basis of Assyrian military might.
12. Famous battles from Assyrian annals.
13. The library of Ashurbanipal.
14. The excavations at Nineveh.
15. The excavations at Khorsabad.
16. Mesopotamian law codes compared to the Mosaic laws.
17. Assyria as seen by the prophets.
18. Persian connections with biblical history.
19. The environment of the Babylonian exile.
20. Recent archaeological activities in Mesopotamia—Iraq.

RECOMMENDED READING

Finegan, Jack, *Light from the Ancient Past,* vol. 1 (Princeton: Princeton University Press, 1959).

Hallo, W. W., and W. K. Simpson, *The Ancient Near East: A History* (New York: Harcourt Brace Jovanovich, Inc., 1971), pp. 1–183.

Pritchard, James B., ed., *The Ancient Near East,* vols. 1 and 2 (Princeton: Princeton University Press, 1958 and 1975).

Thomas, D. Winton, ed., *Archaeology and Old Testament Studies* (London: Oxford University Press, 1967), pp. 39–101.

———, *Documents from Old Testament Times* (New York: Harper Torchbook, 1961), pp. 3–117.

Wright, G. E., ed., *The Bible and the Ancient Near East* (Garden City, NY: Anchor Books, 1965), pp. 265–99; 327–68.

FOR FURTHER READING

Cambridge Ancient History, revised edition of volumes I and II (Cambridge University Press [currently appearing in fascicles]).

Ellis, Richard, *A Bibliography of Mesopotamian Archaeological Sites* (Wiesbaden: Otto Harrassowitz, 1972).

Grayson, A. K., *Assyrian Royal Inscriptions,* I–II (Wiesbaden: Otto Harrassowitz, 1972, 1976).

Kramer, Samuel N., *The Sumerians: Their History, Culture, and Character* (Chicago: University of Chicago Press, 1964).

Larue, Gerald A., *Babylon and the Bible* (Grand Rapids: Baker, 1969).

Lloyd, S., *Foundations in the Dust: A Story of Mesopotamian Exploration* (Harmondsworth: Penguin Books, 1955).

Luckenbill, D. D., *Ancient Records of Assyria and Babylonia* (Chicago: University of Chicago Press, 1926).

Moscati, S., *The Face of the Ancient Orient* (Garden City, NY: Anchor Books, 1962).

Olmstead, A. T. E., *History of the Persian Empire* (Chicago: University of Chicago Press, 1959).

Oppenheim, A. L., *Ancient Mesopotamia* (Chicago: University of Chicago Press, 1964).

Orlin, Louis L., *Ancient Near Eastern Literature* (Ann Arbor: Campus Publishers, 1969 [a useful bibliography]).

Pallis, S. A., *The Antiquity of Iraq* (Copenhagen: Munkgaard, 1956).

Pfeiffer, Charles F., ed., *The Biblical World* (Grand Rapids: Baker, 1966).

Pritchard, J. B., ed., *Ancient Near Eastern Texts Relating to the Old Testament,* third edition; *The Ancient Near East in Pictures Relating to the Old Testament,* second edition; *The Ancient Near East: Supplementary Texts and Pictures Relating to the Old Testament* (Princeton: Princeton University Press, 1969).

Roux, G., *Ancient Iraq* (Harmondsworth: Penguin Books, 1966).

Saggs, H. W. F., *The Greatness That Was Babylon* (London: Sidgwick and Jackson, 1962).

Sumer, the Journal of Archaeology and History in Iraq.

7

Asia Minor and the Hittites

Among the peoples mentioned frequently in the Old Testament are the Hittites, but the textual passages in which the name occurs do not give us any idea of their origin or character. Thus we learn that Abraham bought the cave of Machpelah from Ephron the Hittite (Gen. 23:10; 25:9; 49:29; 30; 50:13); that Esau took Hittite women as his wives (Gen. 26:34; 36:2); that a man who had been spared in the destruction of Luz went to the land of the Hittites and built another city called Luz (Judg. 1:26); that the Hittites lived in the hill country of Judea (Num. 13:29); that Ahimelech, a contemporary of David, was a Hittite (I Sam. 26:6), as was Uriah the husband of Bathsheba (II Sam. 11; 12:9, 10; 23:29; I Kings 15:5; I Chron. 11:41). The Hittites are listed twenty-two times among the peoples who inhabited the land before the coming of the Israelites, ranking second only to the Canaanites. Ezekiel tells the people Israel, "Your mother was a Hittite, and your father an Amorite" (Ezek. 16:45). In other references the Hittites seem to be a foreign power, as when Solomon engages in trade with the Hittites (II Chron. 1:17) and includes Hittite women in his harem (I Kings 11:1), or when the Hittite allies of Israel cause panic in the Syrian forces (II Kings 7:6, 7).

None of this prepared scholars for the revelation that the Hittites had been a major power in the Middle East in the second millennium B.C. Egyptian records revealed that the kings of the eighteenth dynasty had been in contact with a country called

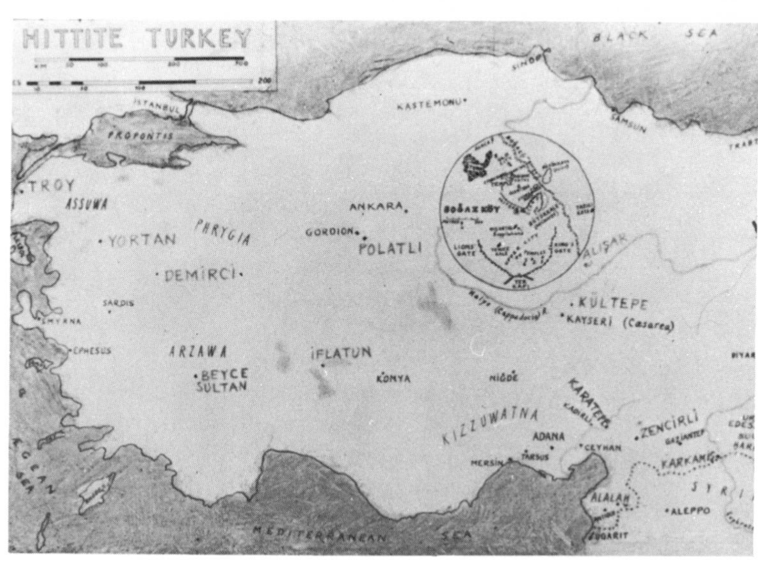

Kheta, which had opposed Ramses II at Kadesh on the Orontes. The name *Kheta* seems to be connected with the "Land of Hatti," a phrase which in the records of Tiglath-pileser I (ca. 1100 B.C.) refers to Syria.

Archaeological evidence of the Hittite kingdom accumulated gradually in the nineteenth century. In 1876 and 1880 A. H. Sayce, in papers presented to the Society of Biblical Archaeology, called attention to a hitherto unknown form of hieroglyphic writing found on basalt rocks at Hama and Aleppo and associated with rock carvings in Turkey—at Ivriz, Alaja Hüyük, Boghazköy, and Yazilikaya. By far the most important site for the understanding of Hittite culture is Boghazköy.

Lion orthostat gate at Boghazköy.

First visited in 1834 by a Frenchman, Charles Texier, Boghazköy became the focus of attention when in 1893–94 Ernest Chantre, another Frenchman, found there some fragments of clay tablets inscribed in a cuneiform script, examples of which had already been found in the Amarna correspondence. The German Assyriologist, Hugo Winckler, began excavations at Boghazköy in 1906, on behalf of the Ottoman Museum at Istanbul, with funds supplied by the Deutsche Orient-Gesellschaft. He excavated there in 1906–07, 1911, and 1912; excavations were resumed in 1931 by K. Bittel for the Deutsche Orient-Gesellschaft and except for a twelve-year interruption caused by World War II have continued to date.

Boghazköy—the modern name of the site, meaning "gorge village"—lies within the great bend of the Halys River, about a hundred miles east of Ankara, where the plateau of the Anatolian highlands begins to break down toward the Black Sea. The ancient Hittite capital, the city of Hattusas, is situated on a high spur, with valleys on three sides, a natural fortress. The site covers an area of about four hundred acres; about two miles away is the shrine of Yazilikaya ("Inscribed Rock"), a natural rock recess into which bands of bas-relief carvings have been incised.

To Winckler's expedition, the ruins of Hattusas soon yielded about ten thousand cuneiform tablets. Since some were written in Akkadian, scholars were immediately able to identify the tablets as the royal archives of the Hittite kings of the fourteenth and thirteenth centuries B.C. Most of the tablets, however, were in the unknown cuneiform script, which scholars immediately set about deciphering. Already in 1902 a Norwegian Scholar, J. A. Knudtzon, had suggested that the language had Indo-European affinities. This was confirmed in 1915 by the Czech scholar, B. Hrozný, who published the first sketch of the grammar in that year. His analysis of the grammar has proved sound; however, his assignment of vocabulary meanings was too often based on hasty etymological surmises. A study by F. Sommer provided the necessary corrective in 1920. The deciphering of the Hittite cuneiform, mainly by a group of German scholars, has been brought to a point where all but the most archaic inscriptions are fairly intelligible.

The deciphering of the hieroglyphic script—which proved to be a different though related language—proceeded more slowly, because no major bilingual text was available until 1947. Then an expedition led by H. T. Bossert, Director of the Department of Near Eastern Studies at the University of Istanbul, discovered

Hittite hieroglyphs.

Stele of Teshub, the Hittite storm god.

a bilingual inscription at the late Hittite fortress of Karatepe.

Among the other important sites in the reconstruction of Hittite culture have been Alishar, excavated by H. H. von der Osten; Tarsus in Cilicia, excavated by an American expedition under Professor Hetty Goldman; Kültepe and Karahüyük, excavated by Professor Tahsin Özgüç; and Alaja Hüyük, excavated by Dr. Hamit Kosay.

As a result of all these efforts, the history of the Hittite peoples has been fairly well reconstructed. The Hittites known to us through history took their name from the original inhabitants of the country they came to dominate. These earlier people, now called "Hattians" to distinguish them from the invaders, spoke a non-Indo-European language, Hattic, a few traces of which have been preserved: personal and place names in inscriptions from Cappadocia (central Anatolia) dating to the Middle Bronze period, and certain formulas in Hittite cultic texts. There is not enough of the language left to allow scholars to connect it to any known language group. The artifacts left by this people show them to have been outstanding craftsmen; it has been conjectured that their society was matrilineal, and that the strong position of the queen in the otherwise heavily patriarchal Hittite society and the prominence of a goddess in the state pantheon were cultural features taken over from this indigenous population, which continued to exist under the rule of the Hittite invaders.

Indo-European elements began to come into the area at least by the beginning of the second millennium B.C. The exact relation between Hittite and the other branches of the Indo-European family has not been established. Hittite was at first thought to belong among the "satem" languages, then assigned to the "centum" group, then recognized as an entirely separate branch of the Indo-European family; some think it may have been the first language to branch off from the parent stem, but that is not certain. The greater part of the vocabulary is of non-Indo-European origin. Probably around the same time as the Hittites, speakers of two closely related languages, Luwian and Palaic, entered the area. Luwian was subdivided into several dialects, one of which was the so-called hieroglyphic Hittite. One of the dialects of Luwian became the Lycian of classical times. Palaic is known only from the cult of one deity; all that can be said of it is that it does indeed belong to the Indo-European family.

The presence of these elements about 1900 B.C. is attested by cuneiform records, the so-called Cappadocian texts, left by Assyrian traders who arrived in Anatolia at that time, and found

Ruins at Kültepe, an Assyrian trading center in Hittite territory.

especially at Kültepe. Among the names recovered from these records are those of Anittas and his father Pitkanas. A dagger inscribed with the name of Anittas was also found at Kültepe. An anachronistic inscription from 1300 B.C. records what purports to be Anittas' own account of his exploits. After subduing the rival cities, including Hatti, he ruled the Cappadocian plateau from Kanesh (perhaps to be identified with Kültepe).

No Hittite king claimed Anittas as his forebear. They traced their lineage to King Labarnas, founder of the Old Kingdom (ca. 1740–1460). His son, Hattusilis I, was the first to rule from Hattusas; his exploits included the crossing of the Taurus mountains into Syria. Around 1600 King Mursilis I destroyed Babylon, ending its first dynasty, the dynasty of Hammurabi. On his return to Hattusas, however, he was assassinated by a relative, Hantilis, and a period of decline, aggravated by invasions of the Hurrians, set in.

The Hurrians, known in the Old Testament as the Horites, were a very widespread people who flourished from the middle of the third to the middle of the second millennium B.C. They are found as far east as Nuzi and as far south as central Palestine. (It has been conjectured that the Jebusites of Jerusalem were Hurrians.) Their original home was Armenia, and their language was akin to the ancient Armenian language, Urarti; it may be that the Caucasic language family, which survives today, is distantly related. Their chief political accomplishment was the establishment of the Mitanni kingdom, which became one of the main rivals of the Hittite empire. Its center was in the Middle Euphrates Valley, in the vicinity of Haran. The capital of Mitanni has not been found, but in the mid-second millennium they dominated Assyria, as the records at Nuzi show. From a few terms preserved in Hittite texts, having to do with horse training, it seems that the Mitanni kingdom too had an Indo-Aryan ruling caste. A large part of its significance lies in its role as the transmitter of culture borrowed from Mesopotamia to the Hittites. In religious texts from Boghazköy there are a great many passages in Hurrian.

In 1525 B.C., the Hittite kingdom was reconsolidated by King Telepinus. His chief accomplishment was to proclaim a precise law of succession and a set of rules for the conduct of kings and nobles. These rules were observed down to the last days of the Hittite empire and contributed a great deal to stability. When in the thirteenth century a king died without leaving a legitimate heir, the son of a concubine, Urhi-Teshub, was duly allowed to succeed to the throne. His reign of seven years, which seems to have been unsatisfactory, was brought to an end by a *coup détat* organized by his uncle Hattusilis. The latter, however, found it necessary to issue a document justifying his action. This testifies to the existence of a certain political conscience. In war, too, the Hittites were relative gentlemen. A city which did not surrender was razed, but its inhabitants were only taken away as serfs, not slain or tortured. The Assyrian delight in cruelty is completely absent from Hittite records.

After King Telepinus, there is a period for which records are incomplete. A new dynasty was founded by Tudhaliyas II, who also became the first king of the Hittite empire. The greatest king of the empire was Suppiluliumas, who acceded to the throne in 1380. During his time the Hittites subdued the Mitanni kingdom and also conquered Syria, imposing tribute on Ugarit. The eminence of King Suppiluliumas I is shown in the story of the appeal made to him by Ankhesenamun, the widow of King Tutankhamun, that he send one of his sons to marry her, as she did not find a suitable consort among the Egyptians. The king did not know if her request was serious, but when it was repeated in tones of desperation, he sent one of his sons, Prince Zannanza, to Egypt. But upon his arrival there, Prince Zannanza was waylaid and slain on the orders of a courtier named Ai, who then ascended the throne and married the queen. This was no doubt the marriage from which Ankhesenamun had thought to save herself by her appeal to the king.

Perhaps the height of Hittite glory was the battle of Kadesh on the Orontes in 1285 B.C. The Egyptian account of the battle is boastful in tone, but it seems clear that the Egyptians were checked and the Hittites were even able to advance. In 1269, under Hattusilis II, a treaty was concluded between the Hittite and Egyptian empires as equals. Each side drew up its own version of the treaty and sent it to the other; both versions have been preserved.

One of the most studied aspects of Hittite history is the documentary evidence of trade and diplomatic incidents with a nation referred to as Ahhiyawā or Ahhiyā. The hypothesis has been advanced that this was the country of the Achaeans, that is, Mycenaean Greece. There is also evidence of contact with Troy. But the identity of the names cannot be established with certainty.

The Hittite empire ended abruptly with the incursion of the Sea Peoples. Hattusas was destroyed about 1200 B.C., and the Hittite monopoly on iron technology was broken. It is probable that the Philistines, one of the Sea Peoples, acquired a knowledge of ironworking through these contacts.

Harmatite head of a king, perhaps a Hittite ruler. Workmanship suggests north Syrian origin.

Hittite kingdoms persisted for about five centuries in the former southeastern provinces of the Hittite empire. The Assyrian records show kings with Hittite names in Syria and the Taurus area. These are presumably the "kings of the Hittites" referred to in II Kings 7:6 and in II Chronicles 1:17. Many of these kings erected stone monuments with Hittite hieroglyphs, but the inscriptions are brief and uninformative. Most of the little that we know of these kingdoms is pieced together from the records of their neighbors. It seems, though, that the Hittites of the neo-Hittite kingdoms were not the direct descendants either of the Hittite empire or of its vassal states. With the exception of Carchemish and the three cities of the Tyanitis, all the names are new. The hieroglyphic Hittite of the inscriptions is actually a dialect of Luwian, which seems to have been at home in the Kizzuwatna province in the region of Cilicia, though a few examples of it have been found in Boghazköy. It is thought that after the invasion of the Sea Peoples, Syria was overrun by people from Kizzuwatna, or perhaps another Hittite province.

The neo-Hittite kingdoms in Syria managed to establish a balance of power with the Aramean nomads who settled to the south; for a time both enjoyed prosperity, as evidenced by the amount of the tribute paid to Assyria. But the growing strength of the Assyrian empire, and its adoption of a policy of outright annexation, eventually doomed them. The last of the neo-Hittite kingdoms, Kummukhi, was annexed in 709.

The overall pattern of society in the Hittite empire can be described as feudal. The kingdom was under a single sovereign, but the nobles, especially the king's kinsmen, the "Great Family," had numerous privileges. It was a ruling caste superimposed

Rock-carved Hittite figures.

on a native population; however, the ordinary citizen was free and even the serfs retained some rights. Numerous fragments of law codes have been found.

Most of the subject kingdoms were ruled by native vassals. The vassal king was sovereign within his own territory, but he had to abstain from treating with any foreign powers. In return for an oath given to the king and to his successors in perpetuity, he was guaranteed protection from other great powers.

The form of these treaties has been a point of major interest, especially to some Old Testament scholars who see it as a prototype of the covenant between God and Israel. The Hittite treaties consisted usually of six parts: (1) a preamble naming and giving the titles of the Great King, author of the treaty; (2) a historical prologue consisting of an enumeration of the past benefits conferred on the vassal by the sovereign; (3) the stipulation of the obligations incurred by the vassal in return for these favors; (4) a provision for the safekeeping and proclamation of the oath (usually a copy made of some precious metal was deposited in the temple and on certain occasions read publicly); (5) a list of the gods called to witness the treaties; (6) blessings in case the treaty was kept and curses in case it was broken. The Hittites placed some confidence in the sanction of the oath and in the "gratitude" of the vassal; unlike the Assyrians they did not take hostages to insure the keeping of the treaties.

In a somewhat similar manner, the Decalogue is prefaced with the words, "I am the Lord thy God, who brought thee out of the land of Egypt, out of the house of bondage." This brief formula corresponds to sections (1) and (2) of the Hittite treaties. The first stipulation of the Decalogue ("Thou shalt have no other gods before me") is similar to the vassal's promise not to treat with other lands. The vassal also swore not to murmur against the king and to keep peace with other vassals—this is also the burden of much of the covenant between God and Israel. In the stipulations of the Decalogue the I-Thou form is used, as it was in the historical section of the Hittite treaties. The formula of curse and blessing is found in Deuteronomy 28 and elsewhere. Traces of the form can also be found in the covenant described in Joshua 24, where the benefits conferred by the Lord on his people are enumerated at greater length. Particularly interesting in this account are Joshua's words: "Ye are witnesses against yourselves that ye have chosen you the Lord, to serve him. And they said, We are witnesses" (v. 22). The agreements made at Sinai and at Shechem contrast sharply with the covenant made with Abraham, in which it is God who promises to do certain things.

How directly the Hittite form influenced the Israelites is not certain. Whether or not one ascribes significance to the fact that the earliest preserved Hittite treaty is with a band of Habiru ('Apiru) engaged in military service with the king depends on whether or not one identifies the Habiru with the later Hebrews. However, the form of the treaty is not unique to the Hittite empire; by its very nature, it was international and probably came ultimately from Mesopotamian sources. Agreements of this kind were made with the Syrian peoples and with Egypt, and similar treaties have been found in Ugarit. The important thing is that the parallels between the material in Exodus, Deuteronomy, and Joshua, and the treaty form most often found in Hittite documents, are one piece of evidence for the ancient origin of these accounts in the Bible. The treaties of later times, under Assyrian hegemony, have a very different form.

The reconstruction of Hittite history has not solved all of the difficulties relating to the mention of this people in the Old Testament. With a fair degree of confidence it can be said that the Hittite kings with whom Solomon had dealings were the neo-Hittites of Syria. But what of the Hittites of the hill country of Judea? The records do not indicate that Hittite power ever spread to Palestine. There is one record from Boghazköy to the effect that under Mursilis II (ca. 1330 B.C.) Hittites from Kurustamma entered the "land of Misri," that is, territory under Egyptian control. But it is not certain that they settled in Palestine nor does it seem likely that they were sufficiently numerous to form an important ethnic element. Moreover, all the Hittites named in the Bible had good Semitic names, except perhaps Uriah, for which a Hurrian etymology has been suggested. It is possible that at one time the original Hattians gave their name to this entire area of the world, in which case the term *Hittite* would mean no more than "native." Another explanation proposed is that the name *Hittite* may sometimes represent a scribal error for "Horite" (Hurrian) or "Hivite"—the three names differ in Hebrew only by a single letter. As the Hurrians are known to have penetrated into central Palestine, this explanation is perhaps the most plausible.

SUGGESTED TOPICS FOR FURTHER STUDY

1. The Hittites in the records of Egypt.
2. Hittite sites: Boghazköy, Yazilikaya, Karatepe, Kültepe.
3. The structure of the Hittite language.
4. The "Thousand Gods of the Land of Hatti."
5. Hittite law and the structure of Hittite society.
6. The Hurrians and Mitanni.
7. The deeds of King Suppiluliumas.
8. Feudal treaty and the Old Testament covenant.
9. Archaeological evidence of the late Hittite kingdoms.

RECOMMENDED READING

Gurney, O. R., "Boghazköy" in *Archaeology and Old Testament Study*, ed. D. Winton Thomas (London: Oxford University Press, 1967), pp. 105–16.

______, *The Hittites* (Baltimore: Penguin Books, 1964).

"The Hittites" in *The Biblical World*, ed. Charles F. Pfeiffer (Grand Rapids: Baker, 1966), pp. 290–94.

"The Hittites" in *The Interpreter's Dictionary of the Bible*, ed. George A. Buttrick et al. (New York: Abingdon Press, 1962), vol. 2, pp. 612–15.

Mendenhall, George E., "Covenant Forms in Israelite Tradition" in *The Biblical Archaeologist Reader*, #3, ed. Edward F. Campbell, Jr., and David N. Freedman (New York: Anchor Books, 1970), pp. 25–53.

FOR FURTHER READING

Akurgal, E., *The Art of the Hittites* (London: Thames and Hudson, 1962).

Bittel, Kurt, *Hattusha: The Capital of the Hittites* (New York: Oxford University Press, 1970).

Contenau, G., *La Civilisation des hittites et des hurrites du Mitannai*, second edition (Paris: Payot, 1948).

Garstang, J., *The Hittite Empire* (London: Constable, 1929).

Goetze, A., "The Cultures of Early Anatolia," *Proceedings of the American Philological Society* 97, no. 2 (1953).

———, *Das Hethiter Reich* (*Der alte Orient*, Band 27 [Leipzig, 1928]).

———, "Kleinasien" in Müller, *Handbuch der Altertumswissenschaft* III.I, iii, second edition (München, 1957).

Güterbock, H. G., "Hittite Mythology" in *Mythology of the Ancient World*, ed. S. D. Kramer (Garden City, NY: Doubleday, 1961).

———, "Hittite Religion" in *Forgotten Religions*, ed. V. Ferm (New York: New York Philosophical Library, 1950).

Sommer, F., *Hethiter und Hethitisch* (Stuttgart: W. Kohlhammer, 1947).

Excavation Reports:

Bittel, Kurt, "Reports of Excavations at Boghazköy," *Mitteilungen der Deutschen Orientgesellschaft* LXX–LXXVIII (1932–39) and LXXXVI (1953) ff.

———, *Die Ruinen von Boghazköy* (Berlin and Leipzig: W. de Gruyter & Co., 1937).

———, and R. Naumann, *Boghazköy-Hattusa I. Architektur, Topographie, Landeskunde und Siedlungsgeschichte* (Stuttgart: Kohlhammer, 1952).

———, et al. *Yazilikaya*, Deutsche Orientgesellschaft, Wissenschaftliche Veröffentlichung No. 61 (1941).

Ozgüc, T., "Excavations at Kültepe, Level II Finds," *Belleten* XIX (1955).

von der Osten, H. H., *The Alishar Hüyük. Seasons of 1930–32*, University of Chicago Oriental Institute Publications XXVIII, XXIX, XXX (1937).

———, *Discoveries in Anatolia, 1930–31*, University of Chicago Oriental Institute Publication XIV (1933).

———, *Explorations in Central Anatolia. Season of 1926*, University of Chicago Oriental Institute Publication V (1929).

———, *Explorations in Hittite Asia Minor, 1927–29*, University of Chicago Oriental Institute Publications VI and VIII (1929–30).

For further listings of excavation reports up to 1955 see Seton Lloyd, *Early Anatolia* (1936), pp. 213–19. For recent work see the annual "Summary of Archaeological Research in Turkey" in *Anatolian Studies (Journal of the British Institute of Archaeology at Ankara)*.

8

Syria and Lebanon

The archaeological treasures of Lebanon, and particularly Syria, still await extensive exploration, despite the fact that a number of important sites have been excavated since the beginnings of modern archaeological research. This has been due, at least in part, to the changing political circumstances in the area since the outbreak of World War I. Before that time, the area was a part of the Turkish empire, and any efforts to pursue archaeological research under that regime were subject to the vagaries of local and state politicians. The obstacles were imposing. With the establishment of the mandate system after the war, the area now occupied by Syria and Lebanon came to be administered by the French, just as Palestine to the south was mandated by the League of Nations to British control. French scholars have dominated the archaeological work in the area, even after the end of the mandate period and the establishment of the modern states of Syria and Lebanon in 1944. The modern governments, particularly Syria, have been engrossed in solving political and economic problems and have relegated the work of archaeologists to a minor role.

The decade of the 1970s has thus far witnessed such internal dissension in Lebanon that little archaeological work has been accomplished, and the immediate future does not look promising. In Syria, however, the building of a dam across the Euphrates, with the subsequent creation of a large lake which threatens to cover many ancient sites, has led to a hasty attempt

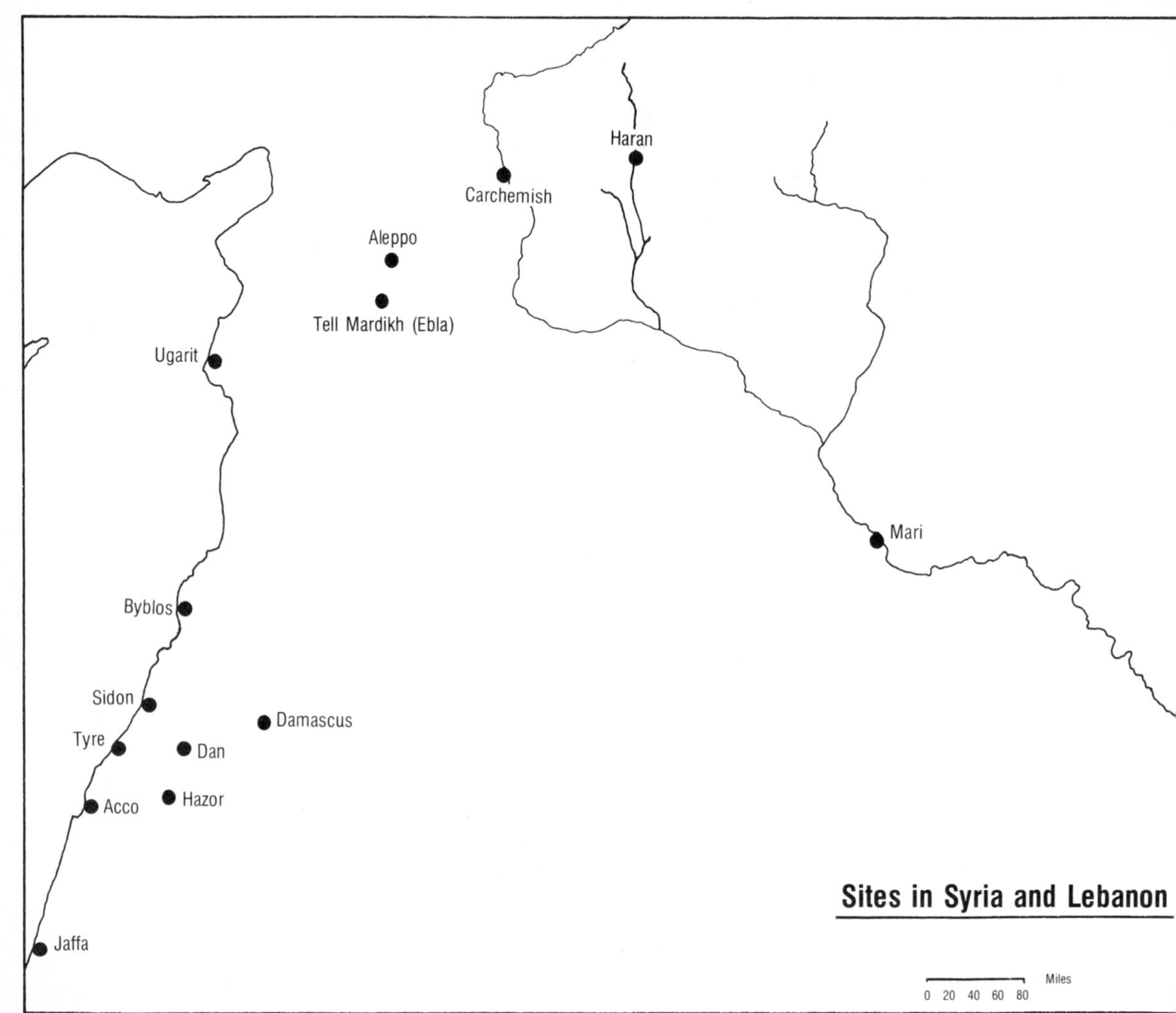

to recover whatever history of the sites in the area to be inundated may be salvageable. And with the recent important discoveries at Tell Mardikh, south of Aleppo, and the improved relationships between Syria and the governments of Western Europe and the United States, the outlook for archaeological research in Syria has brightened considerably.

We shall restrict our survey of sites in Syria and Lebanon to a few of particular significance—Mari, Ugarit, Ebla, and Byblos.

Mari

Mari was an important political center in northern Mesopotamia in the third and early second millennia B.C. Cuneiform texts from Sumer as early as 2500 B.C. as well as Old Babylonian references from the time of Hammurabi had revealed to scholars the importance of Mari decades before its location was established. The ancient city has now been identified with Tell Hariri, which is located some fifteen miles north of the Iraqi border and less than two miles west of the Euphrates River. This position in antiquity permitted Mari to benefit commercially from the intersection of the caravan routes that led from southern Mesopotamia to the Upper Euphrates and the route that led westward to the Mediterranean coast.

Tell Hariri first aroused the interest of archaeologists in 1933 when Bedouin discovered a headless stone statue as they searched the ruins for building stone. The French authorities instituted an excavation in that same year under the direction of André Parrot. Except for a period during World War II, the excavations have been continuous.

According to the evidence, Mari was founded in the late fourth millennium B.C.; the earliest buildings have been dated to about 3200. That a high level of art and culture was reached at Mari prior to 2500 B.C. is evident from the remains of a ziggurat and several temples dated to this period. Two of these temples were particularly important—one dedicated to the god Dagon, in which the earliest list of the Mari pantheon came to light, and a second dedicated to the goddess Ishtar. In some of the sanctuaries were found inscription-bearing statues of local kings and lesser dignitaries. The names of these leaders suggest that the population of the area was basically Semitic, even though the artistic representations indicate that the culture of Mari was heavily influenced by Sumerian elements.

Statues of deities discovered at Mari.

Tell Hariri was definitely identified with Mari by inscriptions that were found in the temple of Ishtar in 1934. Since the population of Mari was predominantly Semitic, as was the population of Canaan (including the biblical patriarchs), the cultic practices at Mari are important. The temples of the city were built in the form of houses, for the gods were thought to need structures for their habitation similar to those of men, only more grand. Similarly, Solomon's temple in Jerusalem was known as the "house of Yahweh." The temple of Ninni-Zaza had a *maṣṣebah,* a standing stone stele, and the temple of Dagon had two *asherim* (wooden poles) erected upon stone altars which were used for libation offerings. Both the *maṣṣebah* and the *asherim* were features of Canaanite religious centers, as the Bible indicates. The altars of Mari were for the most part built of earth, a practice in line with that of Israel (cf. Exod. 20:24), and the sacrificial animals at Mari were sheep and goats.

Mari experienced a second period of greatness in the early

Excavations at Mari.

Statue of a fertility goddess excavated at Mari.

second millennium B.C., concurrent with the period of the patriarchs in the Bible. The outstanding architectural discovery of this period is the royal palace of Zimri-Lim, a contemporary of Hammurabi, king of Babylon (and his friend until Hammurabi chose to conquer Mari, ca. 1759 B.C.). The palace covered an area of eight acres and contained over three hundred rooms and courtyards which were connected by a series of hallways. A part of the palace was set aside for administrative offices, and the archives of this complex have yielded some twenty-five thousand cuneiform tablets. These include economic, legal, and diplomatic texts which have extraordinary importance for casting new light upon patriarchal origins, for the Bible establishes the patriarchal roots in this general region. Thus far, only about one-fifth of the texts have been published.

Zimri-Lim had close connections with the west. His queen was from Aleppo, and he had personally visited Yamhad, the territory west of Aleppo, and Ugarit. There are references in the Mari documents to Byblos, on the Phoenician coast, and to the Canaanite cities of Hazor and Laish (biblical Dan). Political and economic emissaries from Mari were in contact with Hazor and Laish, and shipments of tin, a metal used in the making of bronze, were made to them.

The Mari texts have given scholars new insights into the social relationships of the area. One of the legal tablets contains an adoption contract in which the eldest adopted son is assured of receiving a double portion of the inheritance, a practice that was known in biblical law (Deut. 21:15–17). Correspondence from the Mari archives deals in part with local uprisings which were incited by the Habiru, and one of the tribal groups that receive frequent mention is the *Bene-Yamina* (the "Sons of the South"). The name is the equivalent of the biblical "Benjaminites." These nomadic peoples apparently migrated from the south (southern Mesopotamia), and according to one text they made a treaty with another tribe in the temple of the god Sin at Haran. Both Haran and Nahor are mentioned in the texts as cities subservient to Mari. Another group is known as the *Aramu* (Arameans). The equivalent of the name *Laban* also is attested in the texts. In the Bible Laban is known as an Aramean (Gen. 25:20), and the biblical formula, "A wandering Aramean was my father," need no longer be considered as an anachronistic element from Iron Age II that was imposed on a text from the twelfth century B.C. The designation has now been shown to have had a much earlier existence.

Numerous linguistic expressions and cultural concepts found in the Bible are also exhibited in the documents from Mari. The treaties between tribes in the Mari territory were sealed with a symbolic act, the ritual slaughter of a young ass. The background of the biblical expression "to cut a covenant" is now clear in the light of the Mari expression, "to cut the ass (of a covenant)." The cuneiform equivalent of the Hebrew word *judge* appears in the Mari documents. The primary connotation is not judicial; rather, the judge in the Mari documents is entrusted with governorship and rule, as were the biblical judges. Numerous other expressions in the Mari texts have West Semitic consonantal equivalents—"to wait," "to inherit," "to kill." These are not employed in standard Babylonian.

Statue of the great singer, Ornina of Mari (third) century B.C.).

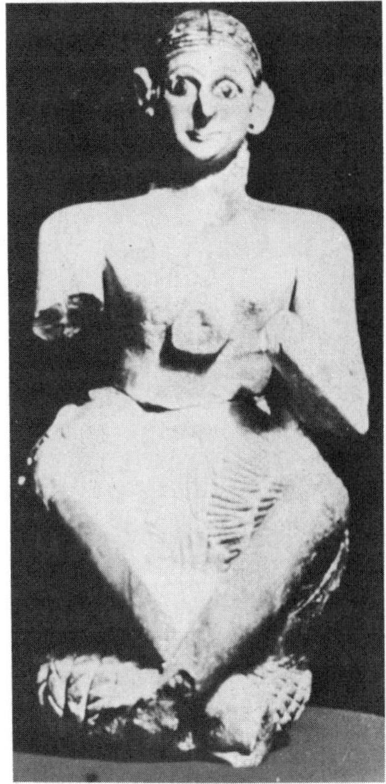

Several of the Mari texts reveal striking similarities to biblical prophetic texts. A god (especially Dagon) reveals himself spontaneously to a diviner-prophet, and, speaking in the imperative, sends the diviner with a message to the king. The formula, "[Being] God, I send you, so that you may speak to Zimri-Lim in these words," is strikingly similar to the way in which God sends forth the biblical prophet (cf. Ezek. 2:4). Such consciousness of prophetic mission has not been observed in any other texts from Mesopotamia. Even though biblical prophecy rises far higher than the Mari prophetic material, in terms of social and ethical concerns as well as of the perception of the universal in religious thought, the presence of a consciousness of prophetic mission in the midst of West Semitic tribes in a period several centuries earlier than the rise of biblical prophecy provides a new perspective for viewing the prophetic phenomenon.

As scholars continue to study the extraordinary riches of Tell Hariri, both textual and artifactual, they will doubtless continue to contribute to our understanding of the world of the patriarchs. The tedious task of transcribing and translating and studying the thousands of Mari tablets that await the scholar's touch should provide a continuing stream of illumination of the Bible for decades in the future.

Ugarit

In the spring of 1928, a Syrian peasant who was plowing near the coast of the Mediterranean Sea, seven miles north of Latakia, discovered an ancient tomb that lay just beneath the surface of his field. He removed the pottery from the tomb, and within a short time his discovery had come to the attention of local authorities who then notified the Director of Antiquities of the French mandate government, Charles Virolleaud. Virolleaud launched a preliminary investigation of the discovery in which it was noticed that the roof of the tomb was constructed in a corbeled fashion similar to the design of tombs of the Mycenaean culture that had been discovered earlier on the isle of Crete. This information, together with the indication that the field contained additional tombs, provided sufficient impetus for further investigation. An archaeological expedition under the direction of Claude F. A. Schaeffer arrived at the site in late March of 1929.

The newly discovered necropolis was partially explored during the first six weeks of the investigation, but the results were disappointing. The number of tombs that were found, however, indicated that a sizable community had existed somewhere in the area, so the archaeologists turned their attention to a small hill located approximately a mile to the south, which the local populace called Ras Shamra ("fennel head"), after the aromatic shrub that grew profusely across it. Ras Shamra proved to be a tell sixty-five feet high which covered some seventy acres. The ruins of a small harbor town were also discovered less than a mile away on the shore of the small bay Minet el-Beida ("White Harbor"). Although the bay is inadequate for modern shipping, it had served the needs of the craft of antiquity.

The Ras Shamra excavations met with immediate success. Monumental ruins of civic buildings and royal palaces began to appear, along with a profusion of pottery and occasional bronze articles. All these remains indicated that the city which had occupied the site had been very rich in material culture. Later it would be proven that the tell contained the remains of the ancient city of Ugarit, which was known to have existed in the area from references in the Amarna letters of Egypt and the political

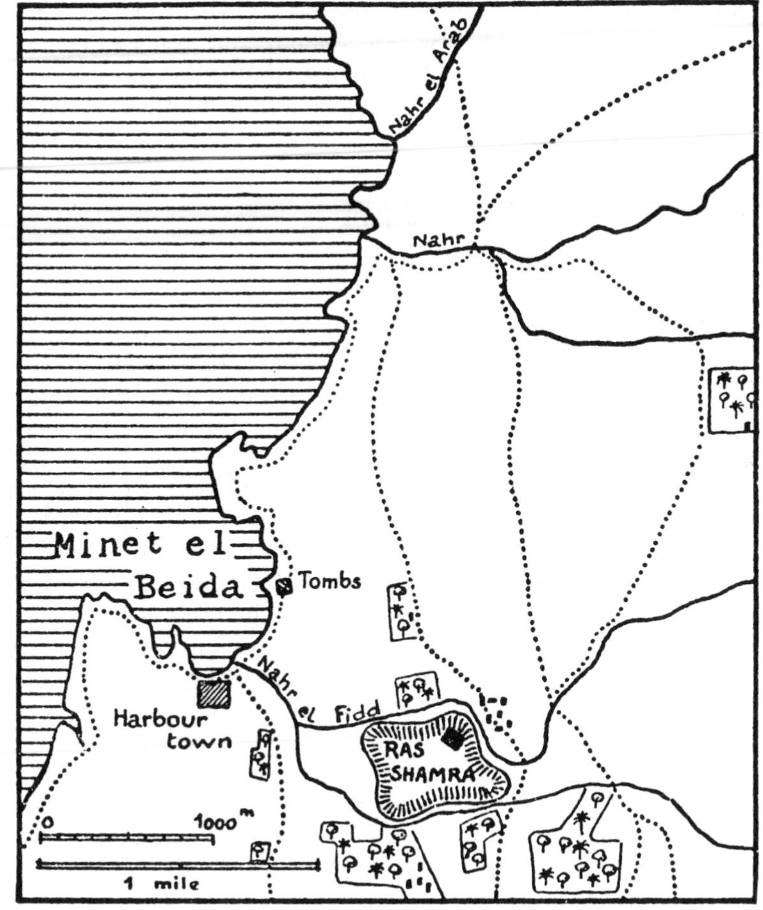

Ras Shamra and vicinity.

correspondence from Mari though its exact location had previously gone undetected. The extraordinary discovery of the first season, however, was of a number of clay tablets inscribed in a cuneiform script which the discoverers described as "indecipherable for the moment," even though they were well acquainted with Akkadian.

It was evident to Schaeffer and his colleagues that the language of the texts was not the familiar writing of Mesopotamia. The contents of the tablets could be determined only by deciphering the script. Fortunately, the process of deciphering was one of the shortest on record. The first tablet was recovered on May 14, 1929. By June 4, 1930, a partial deciphering had been published by a German scholar, Hans Bauer, whose work was based in part upon the earlier preliminary findings of Charles Virolleaud, the French scholar who was given the responsibility for publishing the texts. The work of Virolleaud and Bauer was supplemented by that of another Frenchman, Edouard Dhorme, so that by October, 1930, the cuneiform script was recognized as alphabetic (in contrast to the cuneiform of Mesopotamia which is syllabic in principle), and as containing less than thirty signs. The script had been used to write a Semitic language akin to Hebrew, the language in which the Old Testament was written.

In the course of subsequent seasons, additional texts were discovered in several archives of the complex of temple and palace buildings on the acropolis of the tell. The number of tablets has increased to a veritable library of administrative and religious texts. The tablets are inscribed in the alphabetic cuneiform script of Ugaritic (as the language has come to be known), and in cuneiform Akkadian, Sumerian, Hittite, Hurrian, Egyptian hieroglyphs, Hittite hieroglyphs, and in the linear Cyprio-Minoan script. These varied writing systems give the impression of a cosmopolitan society, an impression which has been substantiated by the richness of the artifactual material recovered in the course of a long series of seasons (the thirty-third campaign was fielded in 1972) which was interrupted only by World War II. Goblets and vases, including imported wares from the Aegean world, statuary, finely carved ivories, jewelry (some of gold), seals, bronze implements and more attest to the richness of the wealthiest Canaanite city known. Ugarit's wealth was largely due to its advantageous location. The fact that Ugarit was adjacent to a small harbor town on the Mediterranean permitted easy access to Cyprus and the Aegean islands to the west. Moreover, the city was located on a road that ran along the coast from Egypt to Asia Minor with another trade route branching to the east and south through Aleppo, to Mari on the Euphrates, and to Babylon further south. Ugarit became an important transit center in the movement of Cypriote copper, and bronze was produced in Ugarit. Like other Phoenician cities, Ugarit delivered timber to Egypt, and Ugarit produced the purple dye for which the Levantine coast was known throughout antiquity, as great heaps of murex shells at the site mutely testify. The dye was a product of a Mediterranean mollusk.

Schaeffer's excavations at Ras Shamra have revealed five major periods of occupation at the site. Flint and bone implements from level five are associated with the prepottery period of Neolithic times. Level four corresponds to the Chalcolithic era; painted pottery associated with the Halafian period of Mesopotamian culture was found at this level. The third level has been dated to the last half of the third millennium B.C., when the city was destroyed by fire; the subsequent reoccupa-

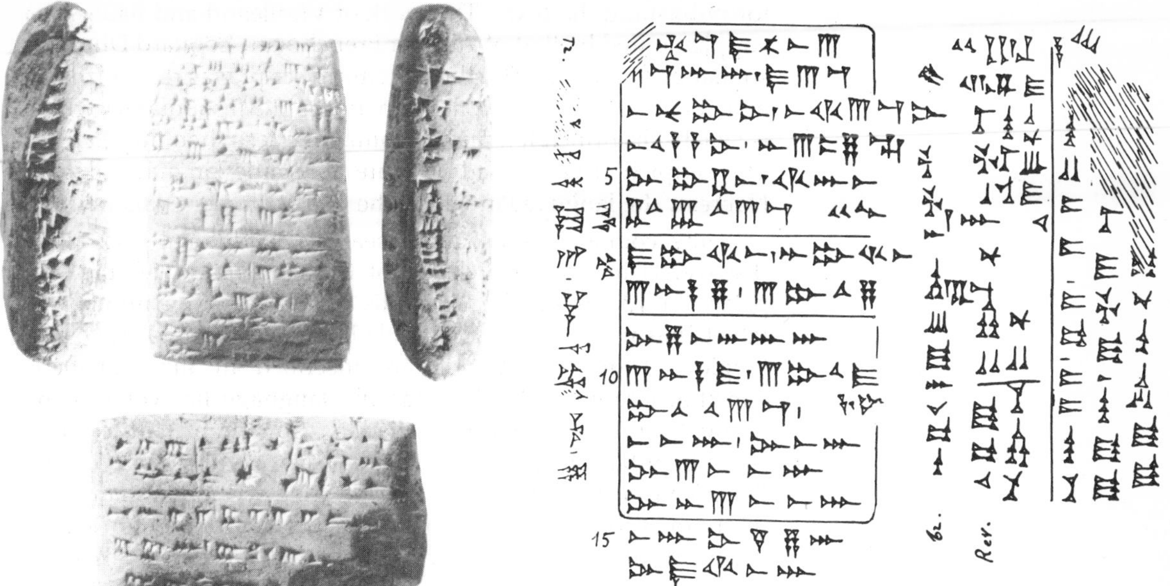

Private letter found in the royal palace of Ugarit with transcription. The alphabetic cuneiform text, RS 16.265, was recovered in room 73.

tion continued to approximately 2100 B.C. Khirbet Kerak ware was associated with the last phase of level three. The upper two levels (ca. 2100–1500 and 1500–1200 B.C.) are of predominant interest because the city bore the name *Ugarit* through this period. It is probable that the myths and legends contained in the literary texts were originally created by the inhabitants of level two, but the extant texts are to be dated to level one, the last level of occupation and the period in which Ugarit reached the heights of its literary and cultural achievements. The city came to an end with a violent destruction that has generally been attributed to the waves of Sea Peoples that spread across the Mediterranean world in about 1200 B.C.

The archaeological evidence from the tell has corroborated the indications of the first tomb that foreign influences had been at work in the area. Business records indicate economic ties with Egypt, Cyprus, Crete, and the Phoenician cities to the south, such as Byblos, Tyre, Acco, Ashdod, and Ashkelon. Ugarit also maintained a delicate balance in diplomatic circles in the Late Bronze Age, confronted as she was by the conflicting spheres of influence of the Egyptians to the south, the Hittites to the north, the Hurrian kingdom of Mitanni to the east, and, to a lesser degree, the weakened centers of power in Mesopotamia to the southeast. Royal correspondence discovered in the palace archives of Ugarit indicates that Niqmad II sent golden articles and other items to the Hittite king, Suppiluliumas (ca. 1375–1335 B.C.). At the same time Niqmad also maintained an alliance with Egypt.

The royal palace of Ugarit proved to be an impressive ten thousand square yards in extent, and it was made of finely cut stone. Nearby, in the highest part of the city, were uncovered the temples of Baal and Dagon. These sanctuaries provide the earliest evidence (until the recent discoveries at Ebla) of the tripartite Canaanite temple, a design which preceded the similar arrangement of Solomon's temple in Jerusalem. The outer court with the great altar has an adjacent inner court or hall, and within this hall is the innermost shrine, the most holy place. A number of stones with inscriptions and reliefs of gods were also found in these temple ruins. Both the temples and the palace yielded caches of tablets. Generally speaking, the palace texts are administrative in nature while the temple texts are literary and religious.

The administrative texts include economic tablets and lists of products, people, and provincial towns and villages. Some private royal correspondence has been found as well as diplomatic letters. From the administrative texts some insight has been obtained into the social organization of the kingdom of Ugarit and particularly into the nature of the institutional monarchy in the Late Bronze Age. A comparison of these data with the concept of kingship which is found in the literary texts which date to the Middle Bronze Age, particularly the story of King Keret, provides scholars with a view of the evolution of kingship in a Canaanite setting prior to the establishment of the Israelite monarchy. There is evidence of administrative practices similar to those which Solomon introduced in Israel. For example, the organization of the kingdom of Ugarit was along administrative rather than tribal divisions. Solomon apparently adopted the corvée, that is, forced labor for the state, from Canaanite precedents. The population of Ugarit and its environs was organized by localities, and by professions or guilds. But there was also an alien class of residents at Ugarit known as Habiru. As we have seen elsewhere, this class of society was widespread in the ancient world (cf. the discussion in the section on Egypt).

Ugaritic storm god. This limestone stele from Ugarit depicts Baal with a raised club in his right hand. He is leaning on a spear in his left hand. The top of the spear is in the shape of lightning, or a sacred tree.

The Ugaritic texts testify to a number of social conventions that were also found in ancient Israel, including rituals of death and mourning, slavery for debt, and the practice of blood revenge. Of even greater interest, however, are the legends and myths of Ugarit. There are two legendary epics about the ancient kings, Keret and Danel, and mythological texts about the gods of Ugarit—Baal and Anath; Kathir-and-Khasis, the divine smithy of the pantheon who bore a compound name; El, the patriarch of the gods; Athtart; Mot, the god of sterility and death; Yam, the sea-monster god, and others. These religious texts have provided the first genuine extrabiblical information that we have about Canaanite religious ideas and practices, and they have given scholars a plethora of comparative data with which to examine the biblical material.

The myths and legends of Ugarit permit us to glimpse the conceptions of the supernatural that infused Canaanite life and thought and to observe their cultic rites and practices. The Canaanites were polytheists, and their gods are primarily deified aspects of nature. Further, the pantheon at Ugarit was a community of husbands and wives, fathers and sons, brothers and sisters, who engaged in internecine conflicts, built houses, held banquets, and engaged in sexual relations. The sexuality of the gods and the fact that they were born are regular features of pagan thought. Thus the gods were seen as a part of the universe; they did not transcend the cosmos. In contrast to this view, the Israelite concept of deity in its fullest manifestation was of a supreme being who was not created, who was without sex or sexual activity, and who was greater than and apart from the cosmos which he had created. Images of the Canaanite gods were fashioned in human form; the Israelite God was not to be depicted in human form.

The texts from Ras Shamra also reflect the widespread use of both myths and magic in the ancient world. The myths about the gods seem to have been created for use at annual festivals as a means by which man might influence the gods to act favorably toward him and to provide for his material needs. Magic also played a role in the thought and practices of the inhabitants of Ugarit. Its purpose was to activate powers that transcended those of the gods so that the gods might be forced to act benevolently. Both the Law and the Prophets, by contrast, denounce the use of magic as a pagan deviation in which the Israelite was not to participate.

Despite the differences in concept between Israelite and Canaanite religion, a number of striking similarities did exist. The chief god of Ugarit was El. This is a common Semitic word for deity, but it is also used in the Bible for God and occurs in the ancient name *El-Shaddai,* which is normally translated as "God Almighty." The word for "priest" is the same in both cultures, and corresponding terms occur for "altar," "gift," "vow," "to sacrifice," and "to offer up." The same types of sacrificial animals also are stipulated, particularly the ox and the sheep; moreover, they are to be whole and unblemished. These

The ivory carving on the box found in a tomb at Ugarit depicts the Ugaritic goddess of fertility.

similarities may be attributed in part to the common Semitic background of both the Canaanites and the Israelites. There is no evidence of direct borrowing of the Canaanite cult by the Israelites, and Israel was warned in the Law (Lev. 18:3) not to adopt the customs of the Canaanites. Israel did adopt, however, the language of Canaan, and herein lies the most realistic explanation for the similarities which were noted above.

The task of publishing the Ras Shamra texts remains unfinished, and as recently as 1973 approximately sixty additional tablets were accidentally uncovered near Ras Shamra by a bulldozer. The future of Ugaritic studies holds the promise of making further substantial contributions to our understanding of the biblical language and literature, of the social and religious practices of the Canaanites into whose territory the Israelites came, and of the milieu of the ancient world at the close of the Late Bronze Age when the nation of Israel was being born.

Ebla (Tell Mardikh)

Tell Mardikh is an exceptionally large mound, covering 140 acres and rising some fifty feet above the surrounding area. It is situated in northern Syria on a plateau halfway between the modern cities of Hama and Aleppo.

In 1964 scholars at the University of Rome decided to carry out an archaeological excavation in Syria, and the directorship of the effort was given to a youthful professor, Paolo Matthiae. Against the judgment of older colleagues, he chose to excavate Tell Mardikh. Since the beginning of his work, thirteen seasons had been spent on the site through October of 1976.

The excavations at Tell Mardikh did not produce spectacular results from their inception; rather, long years of labor with minor finds characterized the seasons until 1968. In that year Matthiae discovered a statue upon which was inscribed a dedicatory message of King Ibbit-Lim, lord of the city of Ebla, to the goddess Ishtar. This discovery permitted the identification of the tell with the ancient city of Ebla. Mesopotamian records had previously revealed the existence of such a city-state, and it was known that Ebla had come into repeated conflict with the empire of Akkad and that Naram-Sin of Akkad (2230–2174 B.C.) had put it to the torch. The discovery of the statue spurred the excavators to renewed energy and anticipation.

Part of the Tell Mardikh (Ebla) archive discovered in 1975.

The next major discovery at Tell Mardikh occurred in 1974 when forty-two tablets of the Ebla archive were discovered. In 1975, however, approximately fifteen thousand tablets were unearthed, and the 1976 season produced an additional five thousand. This is the largest archive from the ancient Near East thus far discovered that dates to the third millennium B.C. It exceeds the total of Mesopotamian texts from the same general period by four times.

Apart from the important archives, which will be described in more detail below, the excavations have revealed that ancient Ebla was the center of a great Syrian culture which had heretofore gone unrecognized. The kingdom of Ebla had preceded that of Yamhad, whose capital was at Halab (Aleppo) and whose apex was reached in the Middle Bronze Age (ca. 1800–1700 B.C.). There was an imposing earthen rampart at Ebla in the period of the kingdom of Yamhad, although the relationship of the city to Yamhad is unclear. The rampart is similar to those associated with the Hyksos in Palestine, though its initial construction has been dated to Middle Bronze I, which is somewhat earlier than those discovered further to the south. However, the Ebla of Early Bronze IV is the city connected with the archives.

In the Early Bronze Age Ebla was divided into two sectors—an acropolis and a lower city. The acropolis contained four building complexes, including the palace of the city, the palace of the king, the stables, and the palace of the servants. This composite administrative center bore the name *e-MI-SITA* ("Governorship"). The lower city was subdivided into four quarters which corresponded to the four gates to the city: the gate of the city, the gate of Dagon, the gate of Rasap, and the gate of Sipiš. One of the texts contained a description of the layout of the city, and this has been used effectively by the excavators. Due to the size of Tell Mardikh, however, only a small portion of the total surface has thus far been disturbed.

Reception room of the Tell Mardikh palace (podium for the royal throne is lower left).

The building in which the archives were found is adjacent to, but outside the citadel on the western slope of the acropolis. It has been designated Building G. It was an administrative building which contained an ornate audience hall which was connected to the palace on the acropolis by a stairway that was embellished with decorations. The audience hall itself contained a podium for the royal throne. Remnants of carved wood that were apparently panels from chairs were recovered. Human figures of exceptional workmanship were included in the carvings, and they suggest that Ebla and its culture may have made valuable contributions to the artistic traditions of southern Mesopotamia.

The audience hall was apparently the place where foreign commerce delegations were received and where fees were exacted. That the audience hall had such functions has been deduced from the contents of the documents which were preserved in the archives in adjacent rooms. A large number of them are lists of textile deliveries to dignitaries of the city and to representatives of other cities. Other texts contain records of tribute and taxes, mostly in silver and gold, which were received by high dignitaries of the state.

Four of the Ebla tablets. Note the excellence of the scribal skill.

The citadel contained a temple which was dedicated to the goddess Ishtar. It was tripartite in form, in some respects similar to the form of Solomon's temple, and it is now the earliest remains of a sanctuary of this design. Another single-room temple was found in the lower city. This structure was similar in plan to the "fortress temple" which was discovered at Shechem in Palestine.

The forty-two tablets that were discovered in 1974 proved to be primarily of an administrative nature, dealing with metals, wood, and textiles. One text, however, was of a different character, for it contained a listing of personal names. It may have been a school exercise tablet. The largest part of the documents discovered the following year was also economic and administrative. These included lists of rations for the palace personnel (one tablet indicates that eleven thousand functionaries were employed as personnel of the palace); rations of bread, beer, wine, and oil for messengers enroute to friendly cities; offerings for the temples; lists of tribute paid to Ebla by various states; and the names of cities, functionaries, and personnel of the entire state. These texts often deal with agriculture (especially with various kinds of wheat and barley), viticulture, cattle husbandry, textiles, wood, precious stones, and metals.

A significant subgroup of the economic texts deals with international trade. This subgroup details the materials traded and provides information about the people and places for which the goods were destined. The main items of international commerce were textiles and metals. These tablets are also conspicuous in terms of their extraordinary physical size. Some contained as many as sixty columns and three thousand lines of text. One text alone contained two hundred fifty geographical names, and the entire group permits one to gaze upon the vastness of Ebla's commercial horizons and to see its refined commercial techniques.

A second group of texts is lexical in nature. Besides school exercises, there are lists of animals in general, of fishes and birds, personal names and professions, and lists of places that might be termed geographical atlases. The nomenclature is all closely bound to Mesopotamian terminology, and the arrangement of the lists is akin to alphabetical order, with the formative elements of a word determining its position in a list.

A third group of texts is described by the epigrapher as historical and historical-juridicial in nature. These include royal ordinances, edicts, state letters, lists of cities subject to Ebla, assignments of prebends (an endowment from the state for temple or clergy), and records of state marriages. This group also includes international treaties the most significant of which is that between Ebla and Ashur concerning the legal arrangements for a commercial center. The juridical texts deal with contracts to buy and sell, the partitioning of goods, and so forth.

The fourth group of texts is classified as literary. Numbering twenty in all, they contain stories with a mythological background, hymns to divinities, incantations, and collections of proverbs. The mythologies deal with Mesopotamian deities, such as Enki and Enlil, as well as Utu and Inanna. There is some indication that Mesopotamian gods such as Marduk, Nabu, and Tiamat had their origins in the West Semitic regions. The compositions in this group touch on such themes as creation and a flood; however, these compositions appear to be more closely related to the Babylonian myths than to the stories in Genesis.

A final category of texts has been labeled linguistic. They consist of syllabaries for use in learning Sumerian, some grammatical texts with verbal paradigms in Eblaite (a newly-discovered language to be discussed below), and, finally, bilingual word lists in Sumerian and Eblaite—the earliest bilingual word lists known. One hundred fourteen of the linguistic tablets are bilingual word lists. They contain, all told, about twenty-five hundred Sumerian words with their Eblaite equivalents.

Professor Giovanni Pettinato of the University of Rome has been given the responsibility for the paleographic study and publication of the tablets from Tell Mardikh. Eighty percent of the texts were written in Sumerian, but the remainder are written in a heretofore unknown language which Pettinato has labeled "Paleo-canaanite," because of its strong affinities with the Northwest Semitic family of languages. The language of Ebla is also called Eblaite. The Eblaite language was written with the script employed in writing Sumerian, but the language is definitely not Sumerian for the bilingual lists clearly demarcate the two.

The Paleo-canaanite language of Ebla has shown striking affinities with Ugaritic and with Phoenician as well as Hebrew, all of them manifestations of the Canaanite language. Among the extraordinary discoveries in the texts written in Eblaite is the identification of patriarchal-type names: *ab-ra-mu* (*'abram/ 'abraham*), *is-ra-ilu* (*yisrael,* Israel). These name types antedate the Middle Bronze II period, with which the patriarchs have ordinarily been associated, by half a millennium. Other biblical name types that occur in the texts are: *e-sa-um* (Esau), *da-'u-dum* (David), and *mi-ka-ya* (Micah). The bilingual tablets exhibit numerous linguistic expressions akin to Hebrew, such as the words for "desire," "first-born," "to eat," "king," and "mother." Other tablets contain place names of Canaan—Hazor, Megiddo, Acco, Gaza, *Urusalima* (Jerusalem)—and also the Cities of the Plain recorded in Genesis—Sodom, Gomorrah, and Zoar. The name of Abraham's city, Haran, occurs in the texts, as does the name of a city called Ur in the vicinity of Haran.

It is important at this early stage of discovery and deciphering that the finds at Tell Mardikh be kept in proper perspective. Many cases of texts still await cataloguing, and Pettinato has studied only a few tablets thoroughly. While his scholarly credentials are impeccable, he and the scholarly world anxiously look forward to the publication of the texts and the process of scholarly dialogue which will eventually establish an interpretative consensus about the implications of the texts for biblical studies. What is certain is that the discoveries at Tell Mardikh have opened up a new chapter in the study of the ancient world, a chapter which holds the promise of illuminating the biblical accounts of the patriarchs and the prepatriarchal era of Genesis 1–11.

Byblos

The site of ancient Byblos, the Gebal of Ezekiel 27:9, was unknown to Westerners until it was identified by Ernest Renan in A.D. 1860. The ruins are located atop a cliff not far from the Lebanese village of Jubayl, approximately twenty-five miles north of Beirut. The name of the village is actually an Arabic form of the ancient Gebal, which means "hill" or "bluff."

Below the acropolis lies the ancient harbor. Egyptian vessels used this port from the dawn of history as the closest anchorage to the famed cedars of Lebanon which grew atop the mountains only a few miles inland from the coast. The timber, of course, was highly desired by Egypt, a land that is practically devoid of trees. For over fifteen hundred years the forests of Lebanon supplied the Egyptians with wood for the construction of temples, palaces, and ships (including sacred and funerary boats). By the twelfth century B.C., the Egyptians began to feel the competition of the Assyrians for the wood of Lebanon. Tiglath-pileser I sought wood from the region in order to build temples for the gods Anu and Adad. The voracious appetites of subsequent Assyrian rulers for Lebanese timber is poetically underlined by the prophet Isaiah who depicted the trees of Lebanon rejoicing at the death of the king of Babylon, a reference some scholars believe applies to Assyria.

One of the few remaining cedars of Lebanon.

The cedars of Lebanon were highly prized by Israel's kings. When Solomon built the temple, he was supplied with cedars of Lebanon by his ally, Hiram of Tyre (I Kings 5:15–24). The logs were rafted along the coast to a harbor near Jaffa (II Chron. 2:15). The same procedure was followed centuries later with the construction of the second temple, when the forests belonged to the king of Persia (Ezra 3:7). The famed forests of Lebanon have been reduced through the centuries until fewer than four hundred of the cedars of Lebanon remain.

The excavation of Byblos was initiated by Pierre Montet in 1921–24. The work was continued thereafter by Maurice Dunand. According to a local tradition, the city was the oldest in the world, having been built by the god El. The French excavations have uncovered an unbroken series of debris levels that prove the great antiquity of the site. At the bottom of the tell atop virgin soil have been found human remains and artifacts that date to the Neolithic period. This earliest phase was displaced near the end of the fourth millennium B.C. in the Chalcolithic period by two successive phases. The new settlement was an urban culture, with new styles of architecture, including the construction of temples, and a protective wall around the city. One of the earliest temples in the Syro-Lebanese area was built around 2800 B.C. and dedicated to Baalat Gebal (The Lady of Gebal). Another built in the same era was dedicated to the god Resheph. These sanctuaries underwent several reconstructions through the centuries until they were finally incorporated into Roman temples.

We mentioned above the interest of Egypt in the lumber of Byblos. Egyptian interest in the city can be traced back to around 3000 B.C. in the form of a cylinder seal of the Thinite era of Egyptian history that was found beneath the floor of a temple of later date. Another important find was the Palermo Stone, which records the shipment of cedar wood to Egypt under Snefru, the founder of the fourth dynasty. The text states that forty ships loaded with cedar logs had come from Gebal.

The end of the third millennium B.C. saw the destruction of Byblos and the incursion of a new element. Many scholars connect this disruption with the Amorites, who have also been blamed for the first intermediate period in Egyptian history and simultaneous disruptions in Palestine and in parts of Mesopotamia. The city was rebuilt, and one can assume that the old and new elements of the population amalgamated. From this period on, metalworking became a significant part of the city's economy. The Middle Bronze Age also witnessed increasing cultural influences from the Aegean islands. One interesting discovery which Dunand connects with this period is a group of texts in a script that has until the present remained undecipherable. These enigmatic texts from Byblos were written on two bronze tablets, four spatulae, and three stones. Other scholars contend that the dating for these texts should be moved ahead to the end of the Bronze Age or the beginning of the Iron Age.

In the aftermath of the first intermediate period, Egypt renewed contacts with Byblos. The name appears in the Execration Texts, a fact which suggests that the relations between the rulers of Byblos and the pharaohs of Egypt were not always friendly. Byblos was ruled by local kings from the close of the Early Bronze Age until the arrival of Alexander the Great. Surprisingly, the names of twenty-nine of these rulers have been recovered from inscriptions at Byblos. One of the best-known rulers was Rib-Addi, who ruled during the Amarna period of Egyptian history. Over fifty of his letters were found in the Amarna correspondence. In them he constantly emphasizes his loyalty to the pharaoh, Akhenaten, while he pleads for help against his enemies, who are also enemies of Egypt.

Four royal tombs of the Middle Bronze Age were discovered intact. Two contained stone sarcophagi, and all of them had a rich display of grave goods—gold jewelry, pottery, alabaster

Byblos. Above: ca. 2000 B.C. temple. Right: ca. 1700 B.C. Canaanite temple.

Roman amphitheater at Byblos.

vases, silver and bronze objects, and carved ivory plaques. In 1923 the excavators discovered the sarcophagus of King Ahiram. A famous early Phoenician funerary inscription appears on the lid. Dated to circa 1000 B.C. or slightly later, the inscription can be translated as follows:

> The coffin which Ittebaal, son of Ahiram, king of Byblos, made for his father as his eternal abode. And if any king or any governor or any general attacks Byblos and exposes this coffin, may his scepter of authority be broken, his royal throne be overthrown, and may peace flee from Byblos; and as for him, may a vagabond (?) obliterate his inscription.

Apart from its intrinsic historical importance, the inscription is invaluable for the information which it provides of early Phoenician orthography and grammar.

Dunand has stated that in the Late Bronze Age private dwellings "desert the acropolis." The meager Iron Age remains that have been recovered are connected with the sanctuaries that continued in use. It is probable that the remains of residential structures of the Iron Age lie beneath the modern village to the north.

SUGGESTED TOPICS FOR FURTHER STUDY

1. Other Syro-Lebanese sites: Baalbek, Alalakh (now in Turkey), Hamath, Carchemish.
2. The story of the Phoenician expansion into the western Mediterranean.
3. A view of Phoenicia through the lens of Egyptian documents.
4. The history of Syrian city-states in Iron Age I–II.
5. Mari—the City of Zimri-Lim.
6. New light on the patriarchal era from the ruins of Mari.
7. The pantheon of ancient Ugarit.
8. Did the Phoenicians really sacrifice children to their gods?
9. A summary of the legends of Ugarit.
10. Ugarit in the Late Bronze Age—its diplomatic connections.

RECOMMENDED READING

"Byblos" in *The Biblical World,* ed. Charles F. Pfeiffer (Grand Rapids: Baker, 1966), p. 154.

Gray, J., "Ugarit" in *Archaeology and Old Testament Study,* ed. D. W. Thomas (Oxford: Clarendon, 1967), pp. 145–70.

Kapelrud, A. S., "Gebal" in *The Interpreter's Dictionary of the Bible,* ed. G. A. Buttrick (New York: Abingdon Press, 1962), vol. 2, pp. 359–60.

———, "Ugarit" in *The Interpreter's Dictionary of the Bible,* ed. G. A. Buttrick (New York: Abingdon Press, 1962), vol. 4, pp. 724–32.

Lewy, H., "Mari" in *The Interpreter's Dictionary of the Bible,* ed. G. A. Buttrick (New York: Abingdon Press, 1962), vol. 3, pp. 264–66.

"Mari" in *The Biblical World,* ed. Charles F. Pfeiffer (Grand Rapids: Baker, 1966), pp. 363–64.

Mendenhall, George E., "Mari" in *The Biblical Archaeologist Reader,* ed. D. N. Freedman and E. F. Campbell, Jr. (Missoula, MT: Scholars Press, 1964), vol. 2, pp. 3–20.

Parrot, A., "Mari" in *Archaeology and Old Testament Study,* ed. D. W. Thomas (Oxford: The Clarendon Press, 1967), pp. 136–44.

Pettinato, G., "The Royal Archives of Tell Mardikh-Ebla," *Biblical Archaeologist* 39 (1976), pp. 44–52.

Rainey, Anson F., "The Kingdom of Ugarit" in *The Biblical Archaeologist Reader,* ed. D. N. Freedman and E. F. Campbell, Jr. (Garden City, NY: Anchor Books, 1970), vol. 3, pp. 76–99.

"Ugarit" in *The Biblical World,* ed. Charles F. Pfeiffer (Grand Rapids: Baker, 1966), pp. 591–96.

FOR FURTHER READING

General:

The following journals may be consulted for articles containing information on ancient Syria and Lebanon:

American Journal of Archaeology, Annual of the American Schools of Oriental Research, Antiquity, Berytus, The Biblical Archaeologist, Bulletin of the American Schools of Oriental Research, Bulletin du Musée de Beyrouth, Journal of the American Oriental Society, Journal of Near Eastern Studies, Syria.

Albright, William F. *Yahweh and the Gods of Canaan* (London: The Athlone Press, 1968).

Harden, Donald, *The Phoenicians* (London: Thames and Hudson, 1962).

Wright, George E., ed., *The Bible and the Ancient Near East* (Garden City, NY: Anchor Books, 1965).

Byblos:

Albright, W. F., *The Archaeology of Palestine* (Baltimore: Penguin Books, 1954).

Dunand, M., *Byblia grammata* (Beyrouth: Ministére de l'education nationale et des beaux-arts, 1945).

______, *Fouilles de Byblos,* two volumes (Paris: P. Geuthner, 1937–54).

Dussaud, R., "Byblos et la mention des Giblites dans l'Ancien Testament," *Syria* IV (1923), pp. 300 ff.

Montet, Pierre, *Byblos et l'Egypte,* two volumes (Paris: P. Geuthner, 1928–29).

Mari:

Preliminary reports of the excavations appear in *Syria* XVI (1935) and later volumes. See also A. Parrot, *Les fouilles de Mari. Rapports préliminaires des campagnes I à X* (1933–55), ten parts, (Paris: P. Geuthner, 1933–1955). Final publications appear as:

Parrot, A., *Mission archéologique de Mari,* vols. I–IV (Paris: P. Geuthner, 1956–68).

The archives are being published in a series of volumes under the direction of A. Parrot and G. Dossin as *Archives royales de Mari.*

Malamat, Abraham, "Mari," *Biblical Archaeologist* 34 (1971), pp. 2–22. Consult his excellent bibliography on p. 22.

Ugarit:

Reports of the excavations at Ras Shamra have appeared in *Syria* X (1929) and thereafter. The texts have been published primarily in *Syria, Revue d'assyriologie,* and *Comptes Rendus, Academie des Inscriptions et Belles-lettres.*

Other sources of information on Ugarit and the Old Testament include *Biblica, Harvard Theological Review, Israel Oriental Studies, Journal of the American Oriental Society, Journal of the Ancient Near Eastern Society of Columbia University, Journal of Northwest Semitic Languages, Journal of Semitic Languages, Ugarit-Forschungen, Vetus Testamentum,* and *Zeitschrift für die Alttestamentliche Wissenschaft.*

Caquot, A., M. Sznycer, and A. Herdner, *Textes Ougaritiques,* vol. 1, *Mythes et légendes: introduction, traduction, commentaire* (Paris: Les éditions du Cerf, 1974).

Driver, G. R., *Canaanite Myths and Legends* (Edinburgh: T. & T. Clark, 1956).

Fisher, L. R., ed., *The Claremont Ras Shamra Tablets* (Rome: Pontificium Institutum Biblicum, 1972).

———, *Ras Shamra Parallels,* vol. 2 (Rome: Biblical Institute Press, 1975).

Ginsburg, H. L., "Ugaritic Myths and Legends" in *Ancient Near Eastern Texts,* ed. J. B. Pritchard (Princeton: Princeton University Press, 1955), pp. 129–49.

Gordon, C. H., *Ugaritic Literature* (Rome: Pontifical Biblical Institute, 1949).

———, *Ugaritic Textbook* (Rome: Pontifical Biblical Institute, 1965).

Gray, J., *The Canaanites* (London: Thames and Hudson, 1964).

———, *The Legacy of Canaan, Vetus Testamentum* Supplement V, second edition (1965).

———, "Texts from Ras Shamra" in *Documents from Old Testament Times,* ed. D. W. Thomas (Edinburgh: Thomas Nelson and Sons Ltd., 1958), pp. 118–33.

Kapelrud, A. S., *The Ras Shamra Discoveries and the Old Testament,* tr. G. W. Anderson (Norman: University of Oklahoma Press, 1963).

Nougayrol, J., *Le Palais Royal d'Ugarit,* ed. C. F. A. Schaeffer, vol. III (1955), vol. IV (Paris: Impr. nationale, 1956).

Pfeiffer, C. F., *Ras Shamra and the Bible* (Grand Rapids: Baker, 1962).

Pope, M., *The Story of Decipherment. From Egyptian Hieroglyph to Linear B* (London: Thames and Hudson, 1975), pp. 117–22.

Virolleaud, C., *La Légende de Keret, Roi des Sidoniens* (Paris: P. Geuthner, 1936).

———, *La Légende phénicienne de Danel* (Paris: P. Geuthner, 1936).

———, *Légendes de Babylone et de Canaan* (Paris: Dépôt: Libr. A. Maisonneuve, 1949).

———, *Le Palais Royal d'Ugarit,* ed. C. F. A. Schaeffer, vol. II (1957), vol. V (Paris, 1965).

9

Egypt

The beginnings of the story of Egypt are lost in the mists of time, but certain stages of prehistoric development have been charted by archaeologists on the basis of excavations in predynastic cemeteries whose names have been assigned to the various periods—Badarian, Amratian, Gerzean, and Semainean. The evidence suggests that at approximately the same time the Sumerians were establishing an early civilization in the valley of the Tigris and the Euphrates Rivers, the Egyptians were emerging along the banks of the Nile as the first national state.

The Egyptians had developed a system of writing shortly before the unification of Upper and Lower Egypt, either through an indigenous development or, as appears more likely, through contacts with the Sumerians. Among a number of slate palettes from this early period is the Narmer Palette, picturing Narmer wearing alternatively the crowns of Upper and Lower Egypt engraved with his name. It is probable that Narmer's successor, Hor-Aha, more commonly known as Menes, was the first pharaoh of the first dynasty. The history of ancient Egypt follows a continuum after this event, beginning about 3000 B.C. until the time of Alexander the Great. This historical continuum was divided into a system of thirty-one dynasties by an Egyptian priest named Manetho, a contemporary of the Macedonian conqueror. Modern scholars divide Egyptian history into a sequence of major eras interspersed with intermediate periods: early dynastic (ca. 2850–2615), Old Kingdom (ca. 2615–2200), first intermediate (ca. 2200–2000), Middle Kingdom (ca. 2000–1725), second intermediate (ca. 1725–1550), New Kingdom (ca. 1550–1100), third intermediate (ca. 1100–700), Ethiopian and Saitic (ca. 700–525), late dynastic (Persian, Ptolemaic—ca. 525–330).

Ancient Egypt existed almost in splendid isolation, drawing sustenance from the bosom of the Nile with its lifegiving annual inundations, and protected by the surrounding deserts. However, she maintained a vested interest in the land of Canaan throughout her history because this area provided a buffer zone separating her from other powerful peoples to the north and east. Furthermore Canaan, including the whole of the area now occupied by Syria, Lebanon, Israel, and Jordan, was a vital source of products which the Egyptians desired and which they were unable to produce in sufficient quantities to satisfy the needs of their population; for example, olives, timber, wool, wine, and minerals. Evidence of Egyptian contacts with Canaan begins with pottery discovered in Palestine bearing the name of Narmer, and continues through the biblical period with a profusion of stelae, seals, scarabs, and statues.

Evidence of contacts between southern Palestine and Egypt in the Old Kingdom period includes Egyptian artifacts from the ruins of the Early Bronze Age city of Arad in the Negev. The first intermediate period was a period of disintegration and disruption in the social and political life of Egypt that was apparently in part connected with disturbances in Canaan. The destruction of many Canaanite cities in the period from approximately 2200 to 2000 has been connected with the Amorite incursions; in fact, the entire ancient world seems to have suffered lengthy disruptions in this period. Subsequently, Egypt entered its golden age, the Middle Kingdom era, and simultaneously biblical events began to be played out in the land of Canaan with the arrival of Abraham, probably sometime during the nineteenth century.

An Egyptian document of this period, the "Story of Sinuhe," is an illuminating account of a courtier who fled Egypt at the death of the Pharaoh Amenemhet (ca. 1960), crossing into Palestine where he spent many years of his life before returning to his homeland. Apart from its inherent literary value, the story provides a description of the land of Canaan at the time when the patriarch was arriving. From the same general period, an important wall painting has been discovered in the tombs of Beni Hasan, which were cut out of rock and located 169 miles south of Cairo. One of the paintings depicts a group of thirty-seven Asiatics who had made a commercial trip to Egypt. The hieroglyphs mention "Ibsha," the leader, as the "ruler of a foreign country." The painting provides an authentic portrayal of the

Painting from the tomb of Khnem-hotep at Beni Hasan depicting the Canaanites entering Egypt during the nineteenth century B.C.

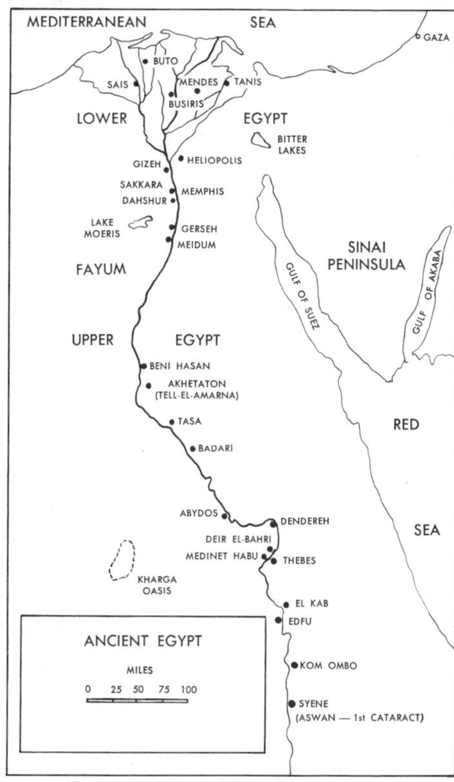

View of the Nile River at Cairo.

dress and appearance of Semites in the patriarchal age, and the donkeys and their cargo illustrate some aspects of Canaanite culture. This painting in the tombs of Beni Hasan also illuminates the biblical account of the movement of Abraham between Canaan and Egypt.

The Execration Texts consist of inscribed potsherds, clay figurines, and bowls. Written in hieratic script they contain imprecations and curses against actual or potential enemies of Egypt. As a form of sympathetic magic, they were apparently broken or buried in order to activate the written curses against the enemies, primarily Libyans, Nubians, and Asiatics. The first texts recovered were at Thebes, and these and subsequent discoveries have provided lists of personal and place names. For example, the names of Ashkelon, Jerusalem, Shechem, Hazor, Tyre, Acco, and Byblos occur. The names of the Asiatic rulers are thoroughly Semitic and of a type similar to those of the Hebrew patriarchal period.

The second intermediate period comprises the two centuries from 1750 to 1550. It is often called the Hyksos period, from an Egyptian word denoting "foreign rulers," because much of Egypt was controlled during this period by a succession of Asiatic pharaohs. The period ended with the expulsion of the Hyksos by Ahmose, the first pharaoh of the eighteenth dynasty. (The Hebrew name *Moses* is derived directly from the *-mose* element found in the names of several pharaohs of the Late Bronze Age.) The history of the period has been pieced together from fragmentary evidence recovered from Egyptian literary sources. Despite arguments to the contrary, there seems little reason to doubt that there was a connection between the rapid rise of Joseph, an Asiatic, to a position of power and the establishment of the Hyksos regime (Gen. 41). The restoration of Egyptian authority under Ahmose, with the subsequent enslavement of the descendants of Jacob, probably underlies the succinct statement of Exodus 1:8: "Now there arose up a new king over Egypt, which knew not Joseph."

It is evident from the information given above that much of what is known about Egyptian history derives from written material. Egyptian archaeology differs from that of Mesopotamia and Palestine, where the recovery of material evidence requires painstaking excavation, for in Egypt numerous remains are already above ground and readily available for study. Frequently the antiquarian in Egypt spends his time copying inscriptions on tombs and temples and studying reliefs and paintings which often contain accounts of the activities of the pharaohs. Excavations are more in the nature of clearing operations than the methodical excavation of mounds. The comparatively placid history of the Egyptian homeland, during which she was for long periods safe from the destructive incursions of conquering armies, hindered the development of genuine tells. Except for the monumental buildings, mud-brick and reeds comprised the normal building material. The annual flood of the Nile has obliterated the earlier sites within the flood plain.

Egyptian archaeology began with the arrival of Napoleon's armies in 1798, for he brought with him a contingent of scholars who set about drawing and describing antiquities and copying inscriptions, even though the peculiar hieroglyphs were not readable. The discovery of the bilingual Rosetta Stone in 1799 provided the key to deciphering them, as we have noted elsewhere. During the first half of the nineteenth century, industrious copying expeditions brought back to Europe a wealth of scenes and texts for scholars to study, but there was little excavation until 1850. In the three succeeding decades a Frenchman, August E. Mariette, dominated archaeological activities in Egypt. He was the founder of the Egyptian Museum, and he established regulations to protect Egypt from further plundering by foreign expeditions. He also set a pattern for the European domination of Egyptian antiquities which lasted until 1952. Mariette learned of his greatest error as he lay on his deathbed. He had thought no written records were to be found at the pyramids, but in 1881 Gaston Maspero discovered a lengthy text at Saqqara, the site of the oldest pyramids. In the last decades of the nineteenth century, Maspero was joined by the German, Adolf Erman, who clarified the study of the Egyptian language in its various periods, and by the young Englishman, Flinders Petrie, who was destined to revolutionize Near Eastern field archaeology.

In the twentieth century, George Reisner of Harvard worked in Egypt with great success. Reisner was also an important Palestinian archaeologist. James H. Breasted of the University of Chicago became America's great Egyptian historian, and the Oriental Institute recorded every known hieroglyphic inscription at Thebes, the ancient capital, under the guidance of H. H. Nelson.

To return to the sequence of Egyptian history and correlations with biblical events, the expulsion of the Hyksos introduced a new era called the New Kingdom period. The pharaohs succeeding Ahmose were not content until they had conquered all of Canaan, reaching the bank of the Euphrates River in the reign of Thutmosis III. (The accounts of his military successes are engraved on the walls of the temple of Karnak.) Destruction layers

Bust of Akhenaten.

Bust of Nefertiti, queen of pharaoh Akhenaten.

in many Palestinian mounds datable to this period starkly corroborate the Egyptian records. The land of Canaan came unmistakably under the control of Egypt in the Late Bronze Age.

The period from 1550 to 1200 was marked by an increase of diplomatic and political activity on a scale previously unknown in the ancient world. Egypt no longer could exist in splendid isolation, for centers of power were developing in Asia—the Hittites in Anatolia, Mitanni on the Middle Euphrates, Assyria in northern Mesopotamia, Babylonia to the south, and a conglomerate of city-states in Syro-Palestine. It was also a period marked by the mass migration of ethnic groups—Amorites, Canaanites, Sea Peoples—and in Palestine by increasing numbers of an ethno-social group called the *Hapiru*.

Tell el-Amarna

Illumination of the social and political situation in the land of Canaan in the Late Bronze Age, including the activities of the Habiru, has come from Tell el-Amarna in Egypt. The Amarna era in Egyptian history (ca. 1375–1350) is connected with Amenhotep IV, the "heretic pharaoh," who introduced new religious ideas in Egypt. He changed his name to Akhenaten ("the effective spirit of the Aten"—the sun disk), encouraged the sole worship of the Aten, and actively discouraged the worship of the other gods of Egypt, particularly the god Amun. Furthermore, he moved the political center of Egypt away from Thebes, the center of the cult of Amun, to a new site nearly 200 miles down river where he had a capital city erected. He named it Akhetaten ("the horizon of the Aten").

The modern name of the site is Tell el-Amarna, hence the name, the Amarna period. The only cuneiform tablets thus far discovered in Egypt were found in the ruins of this city in 1887. They constituted a part of the diplomatic correspondence between the Amarna pharaohs and the rulers of the major power centers of Asia—the Hittites, the Assyrians, the Mitannians, the Kassites, the Cypriotes—and the kings who ruled the city-states of Syro-Palestine. Of the more than 350 letters discovered, those from the Canaanite cities are of particular value, for they illuminate the unsettled political conditions that existed in the area prior to the exodus. Besides the names of ruling princes, the tablets provide a catalogue of place names, including such major Palestinian cities as Jerusalem, Gezer, Ashkelon, Shechem, and Megiddo—places also mentioned in the Bible.

Valuable information on the nature of the Canaanite language in the Amarna period has also been gleaned from the tablets.

Two of the Amarna letters.

While the Canaanite scribes wrote in Akkadian, the diplomatic language of the day, they often added after an Akkadian form the equivalent Canaanite word. It is from these Canaanite "glosses" that information about the contemporary Canaanite language can be gleaned. It is also worthy of note that even though the letters were written in a cuneiform script, Canaanite scribes of the period were familiar with several other writing systems including Egyptian hieroglyphics, the cuneiform alphabet known from Ugarit, and the linear alphabet from which our own ultimately derived.

The numerous references to the activity of the Habiru as a disruptive social element in Canaan comprise a facet of the Amarna letters that has received considerable scholarly attention. The name varies in form from *SA-GAZ* in the Sumerian language to *Habiru (Khabiru)/Hapiru/ʿApiru/ʿAbiru* in Akkadian. References to the class of people designated by the term have been found in texts ranging back into the Early Bronze Age from such diverse sites as Mari, Haran, Hattusas, Ugarit, Alalakh, and Amarna. These cover a geographical area that stretches the length and breadth of the ancient Near East. There can be little doubt that the name *Hebrew* derives from the term; just as certain is the evidence that throughout its history the word denoted a social class rather than an ethnic group. The Habiru were variously donkey caravaneers, mercenary warriors, highwaymen, herdsmen, and viticulturists. Often landless, they were a part of the lower classes of society, but in the Late Bronze Age in Canaan they had succeeded in associating themselves with Labayu, the ruling prince of Shechem. The threat which they posed to a number of the other cities in the region is a recurring theme in the Amarna letters.

Attempts to identify the Habiru mentioned in the Amarna documents with the Israelites of the exodus, however, seem ill-founded. The Hebrews of the Old Testament may have been Habiru, but not all the Habiru were biblical Hebrews. Most often the designation *Hebrew* in the Bible is applied to Israelites by outsiders, or by an Israelite speaking of himself or of his people to a foreigner. It does seem probable, nevertheless, that elements of native Canaanite Habiru amalgamated themselves with the invading Israelites during the conquest, swelling the number of the mixed company who had joined the descendants of the patriarchs in the exodus.

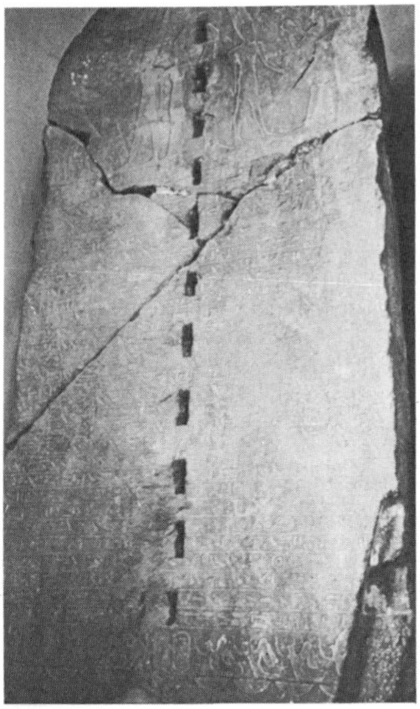

The modern name of the site of Akhetaten (Tell el-Amarna) is a misnomer; no tell developed, for after a brief period of occupation the city was abandoned soon after the death of Akhenaten. The tablets were discovered by a peasant woman who was digging out the decayed material of one of the buildings for use as a fertilizer. In the course of time the tablets that survived the misfortunes of careless handling and transport ended up in the British Museum, the Berlin Museum, and the Cairo Museum.

Flinders Petrie excavated at Tell el-Amarna in 1891, discovering numerous details of the city and a few more tablets. He was followed by a German expedition under the direction of Ludwig Borchardt between 1904 and 1914. In the aftermath of the First World War, the Egypt Exploration Society organized a lengthy series of excavations at the site, beginning in 1921. The directors included T. Eric Peet, Leonard Woolley, N. de Garis Davies, F. L. Griffith, and F. G. Newton.

The abjuration stele of Tutankhamun.

The Amarna era ended when the second successor of Akhenaten, Tutankh*aten,* changed his name to Tutankh*amun* (this signified his renewed allegiance to the god Amun as the chief deity). He also abandoned Akhetaten and moved his court to Thebes, the center of power of the priests of Amun. These actions effectively reversed the policies of his heretical predecessor. Tutankhamun reigned no more than eight years and died at the early age of eighteen. His tomb, filled with fabulous artifacts including a solid gold coffin, was discovered in 1922 in the Valley of the Kings near Thebes by Howard Carter after a search lasting eight years. The tomb of King Tut is the only tomb of the pharaohs of Egypt that has been found intact. The richness of the burial of this minor Egyptian ruler has been interpreted as an expression of gratitude from the priests of Amun for their return to power.

Sinai

The interest of Egypt in adjacent Asian territories in the Late Bronze Age has been highlighted by the discovery of a number of inscriptions at Serabit el-Khadim in the Sinai Peninsula. These Proto-Sinaitic inscriptions were discovered in the winter of 1904–05 by Petrie; a number of other expeditions have been made to the site since their discovery. The inscriptions are written in an early form of the alphabetic script. These Proto-Sinaitic inscriptions appear to have been carved into the rocks by Semitic slaves whom the Egyptians used to mine the turquoise deposits in the area. The mining activities began as early as 1600 B.C, so the inscriptions are usually dated around 1500.

Akin to the mining activities in Sinai are the copper mining ruins at Timna, some fifteen miles north of modern Eilat. Nelson Glueck called this complex "King Solomon's Mines," but Beno Rothenberg, who began to investigate the area in 1959, excavated an Egyptian temple dedicated to the goddess Hathor which stood adjacent to "Solomon's Pillars." Associated inscriptions make it evident that the mining activities were predominantly Egyptian and contemporaneous with the temple, which was erected at the close of the fourteenth century in the reign of Seti I. That the temple (and presumably the mines) continued to be used is indicated by gifts which were sent to it by Ramses II,

Proto-Sinaitic inscriptions from Serabit el-Khadim.

"Solomon's Pillars," near modern Eliat.

Merneptah, and Seti II. The sanctuary was eventually destroyed and abandoned in the twelfth century B.C., and the mines were not worked after this period until the Romans reopened them in the second century A.D.

As we have indicated earlier, the archaeological evidence supports a date for the exodus in the thirteenth century B.C., most likely during the reign of Ramses II. Ramses left an unprecedented mark upon Egypt. Relics of his reign lie scattered across the Egyptian landscape from the famed Abu-Simbel temple in Nubia to the Tanis temple in the delta, including monumental structures at Karnak, Abydos, and the Ramesseum at Thebes (his mortuary temple). The feats of this monarch in his conflicts with the Hittites and the subsequent treaty established with Hattusilis, king of the Hittites, are recorded in relief and hieroglyph on his temples.

Zoan (Tanis), in the northeast delta region (the scattered monuments name Ramses).

The mummy of Ramses II was recovered from a cave at Deir el-Bahri, near Thebes, by Emil Brugsch in 1881. Here it had been cast along with numerous other royal mummies in a second burial in an ancient attempt to thwart the activities of grave robbers. While a direct connection between Ramses and the exodus cannot be established, he is identified in the Bible as the builder of Pe-Rameses (Exod. 1:11).

Pe-Rameses and Pithom

No general agreement has been reached among scholars concerning the location of Pe-Rameses, but two sites in the northeastern delta within twelve miles of one another vie for this distinction—Qantir and Tanis. Qantir was excavated by Mahmud Hamza, and in the 1930 publication of the excavation

Late Bronze Egyptian temple ruins adjacent to "Solomon's Pillars."

appeared plans for a large palace as well as five ostraca bearing the name *Pe-Rameses*. Tanis, however, remains a strong candidate for the city. The site bears the modern name, San el-Hagar, but it has also been called Zoan and Avaris. This last name was used for the city several centuries before Ramses II when the Hyksos had established their capital there. Petrie began to excavate Tanis for the Egypt Exploration Fund in 1884, and a subsequent expedition under Pierre Montet spent a dozen years excavating in the ruins. Montet published his results in 1942 and 1951. The site has relinquished extensive temple ruins, statues, sphinxes, and engraved stones bearing the names of Ramses II and his successors.

Pithom is also mentioned in Exodus 1:11 in connection with the building activities of Ramses for which the Israelites provided forced labor. Two sites in the Wadi Tumilat in the eastern

Wadi Tumilat (possible site for Pithom and Succoth, cf. Exod. 1:11, 12:37).

delta are possible candidates for the city—Tell er-Retabah and Tell el-Maskhuta. Tell el-Maskhuta was excavated by Edouard Naville for the Egypt Exploration Fund in 1883. On the basis of his survey of the architectural remains and inscriptional evidence, he has argued strongly that the site is Pithom. Sir Flinders Petrie investigated Tell er-Retabah, publishing the results in 1906; he thought the site was the biblical Pe-Rameses. Alan Gardiner, however, has sifted the evidence from both sites and has come to the conclusion that Tell er-Retabah is the location of Pithom.

Thebes

Ramses II's son and successor, Merneptah, deposited a victory stele in his mortuary temple at Thebes on which was inscribed his successes in wars against his foes (ca. 1220 B.C.). Among the successes listed on the stele appears for the first time in an extrabiblical text the name *Israel*. The stele was discovered by Flinders Petrie and published in 1897. The discovery authenticated the presence of Israel in the land of Canaan by the close of the thirteenth century B.C.

The complex of buildings known as Medinet Habu at Thebes contains the mortuary temple of Ramses III (ca. 1198–1166). Ramses decorated the temple with reliefs and texts that testify to his exploits as a warrior. Of particular significance is the account of his victories over the Sea Peoples. The Sea Peoples have been mentioned earlier as a part of the extensive movements of people in the eastern Mediterranean area toward the close of the Late Bronze Age. Previous pharaohs as early as Thutmosis III had had to contend with the harassment of small bands of migrants who sought entry into the fertile Nile Valley. By the close of the thirteenth century B.C. the Sea Peoples had destroyed the Hittite capital and a succession of coastal cities in the Levant, including Ugarit. Ramses III was able to defeat the invaders on land and sea. Among the Sea Peoples who were repulsed by the forces of Ramses were the Peleset, who settled (or were settled by the Egyptians) along the southern coastal plain of Palestine by 1150 B.C. They are known in the Bible as the Philistines, and the Egyptian records have substantially supplemented the meager information about them contained in the Bible. Indications of the physical appearance, battle garb, and origin of the Philistines have been garnered from the Medinet Habu reliefs.

I Kings 14:25–28 records the invasion of Palestine by Shishak, king of Egypt, who threatened Jerusalem in the fifth year of Rehoboam's reign. The Judean monarch was forced to strip the

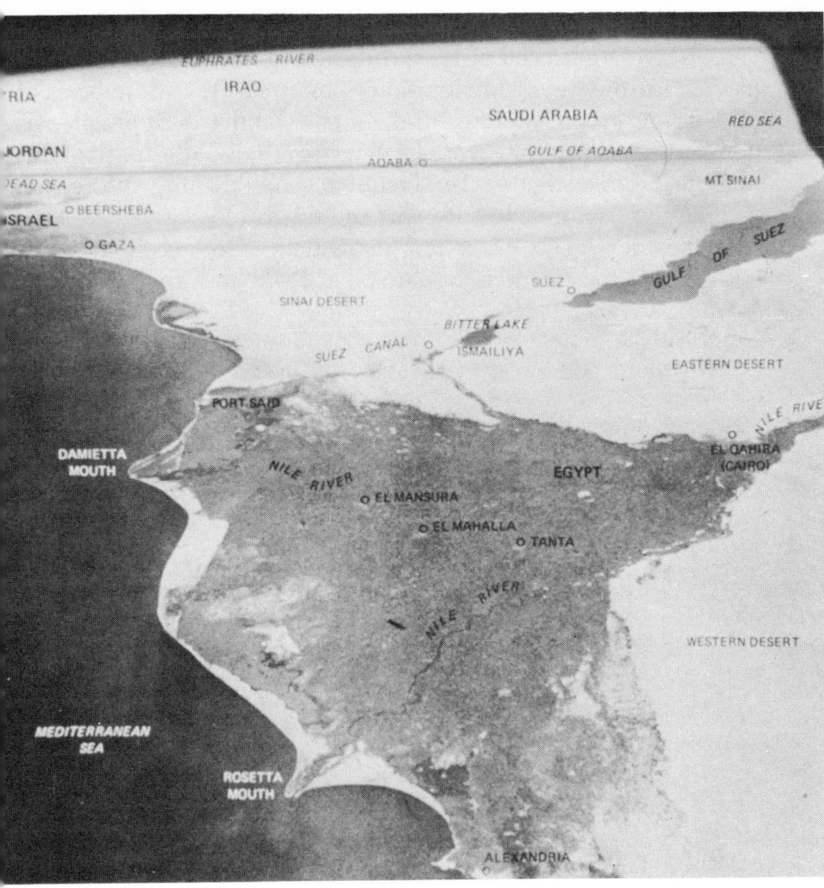

An astronaut's view of the delta, Sinai, and Palestine.

temple and the palace of Solomon of their treasures in order to buy Jerusalem's freedom from the threat. Shishak (Sheshonq I, ca. 940–915) had the details of his Palestinian campaign engraved on the walls of a building at the temple of Amun in Karnak. He claims to have captured in excess of 150 towns and cities. The excavations at Megiddo in part corroborated his claim, for a fragment of a triumphal stele which had been erected in the city was found by the excavators.

The sun of Egyptian splendor had begun to set with the twentieth dynasty, of which Ramses III was the outstanding leader. Despite the invasion of Shishak, the last ruler of the twenty-first dynasty, the kingdoms of Judah and Israel suffered relatively little in the way of Egyptian interference; the powers of Assyria and Babylon became their nemeses in the eighth and seventh centuries. Assyria so reduced Egyptian control in the delta that Ashurbanipal (668–626 B.C.) appointed vassals to rule that region, but Assyrian control was short-lived. The Babylonian

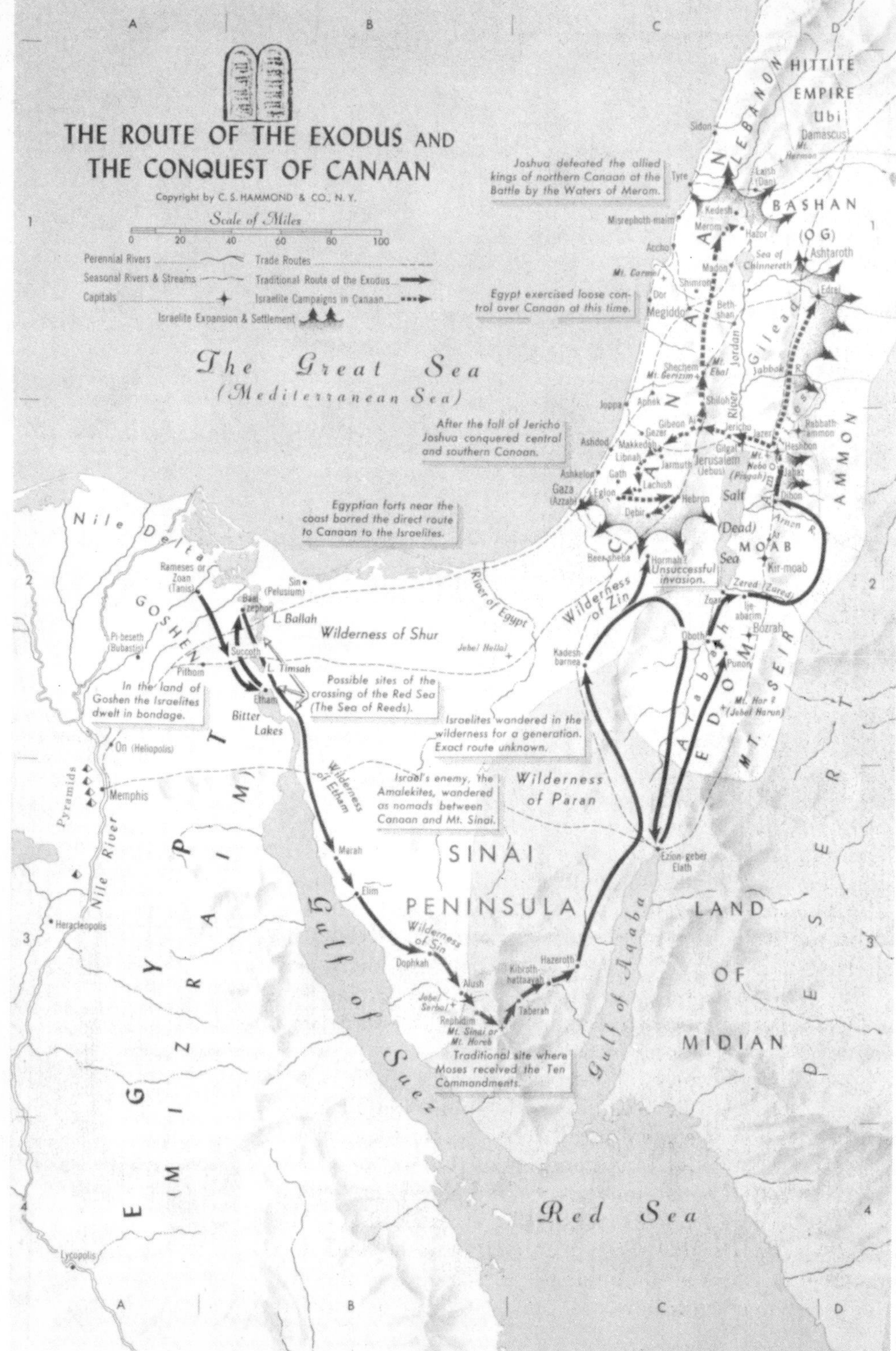

THE ROUTE OF THE EXODUS AND
THE CONQUEST OF CANAAN
Copyright by C. S. HAMMOND & CO., N. Y.
Scale of Miles
0 20 40 60 80 100
Perennial Rivers
Seasonal Rivers & Streams
Capitals
Trade Routes
Traditional Route of the Exodus
Israelite Campaigns in Canaan
Israelite Expansion & Settlement
The Great Sea
(Mediterranean Sea)
HITTITE EMPIRE
Ubi
Damascus
Sidon
LEBANON
Tyre
Joshua defeated the allied kings of northern Canaan at the Battle by the Waters of Merom.
BASHAN
(OG)
Ashtaroth
Kedesh
Merom
Hazor
Misrephoth-maim
Accho
Sea of Chinnereth
Madon
Shimron
Mt. Carmel
Dor
Megiddo
Edrei
Egypt exercised loose control over Canaan at this time.
Beth-shan
Jordan
Gilead
Jabbok R.
Shechem
Mt. Gerizim
Mt. Ebal
Joppa
Aphek
Shiloh
River
Gibeon
Ai
Jericho
Jazer
Rabbath-ammon
AMMON
After the fall of Jericho Joshua conquered central and southern Canaan.
Ashdod
Gezer
Makkedah
Libnah
Gilgal
Jarmuth
Jerusalem (Jebus)
Heshbon
Mt. Nebo (Pisgah)
Jahaz
Ashkelon
Gath
Lachish
Gaza (Azzah)
Eglon
Hebron
Salt
Dibon
Debir
Arnon R.
Egyptian forts near the coast barred the direct route to Canaan to the Israelites.
Nile Delta
Beer-sheba
Hormah
Unsuccessful invasion.
(Dead) Sea
MOAB
Ar
Kir-moab
Rameses or Zoan (Tanis)
GOSHEN
Sin (Pelusium)
Baal-zephon
L. Ballah
River of Egypt
Wilderness of Zin
Zoar
Zered (Zared)
Iye-abarim
Bozrah
Wilderness of Shur
Jebel Hellal
Pi-beseth (Bubastis)
Succoth
Pithom
L. Timsah
Kadesh-barnea
Oboth
Punon
EDOM
SEIR
Arabah
In the land of Goshen the Israelites dwelt in bondage.
Etham
Possible sites of the crossing of the Red Sea (The Sea of Reeds).
Bitter Lakes
Israelites wandered in the wilderness for a generation. Exact route unknown.
Mt. Hor (Jebel Harun)
MT. SEIR
On (Heliopolis)
Pyramids
Memphis
Wilderness of Etham
Israel's enemy, the Amalekites, wandered as nomads between Canaan and Mt. Sinai.
Wilderness of Paran
Nile River
EGYPT
(MIZRAIM)
Marah
SINAI PENINSULA
Ezion-geber Elath
Elim
Heracleopolis
LAND OF MIDIAN
Wilderness of Sin
Dophkah
Hazeroth
Kibroth-hattaavah
Alush
Jebel Serbal
Taberah
Rephidim
Mt. Sinai or Mt. Horeb
Gulf of Suez
Gulf of Aqaba
Traditional site where Moses received the Ten Commandments.
DESERT
Red Sea
Lycopolis

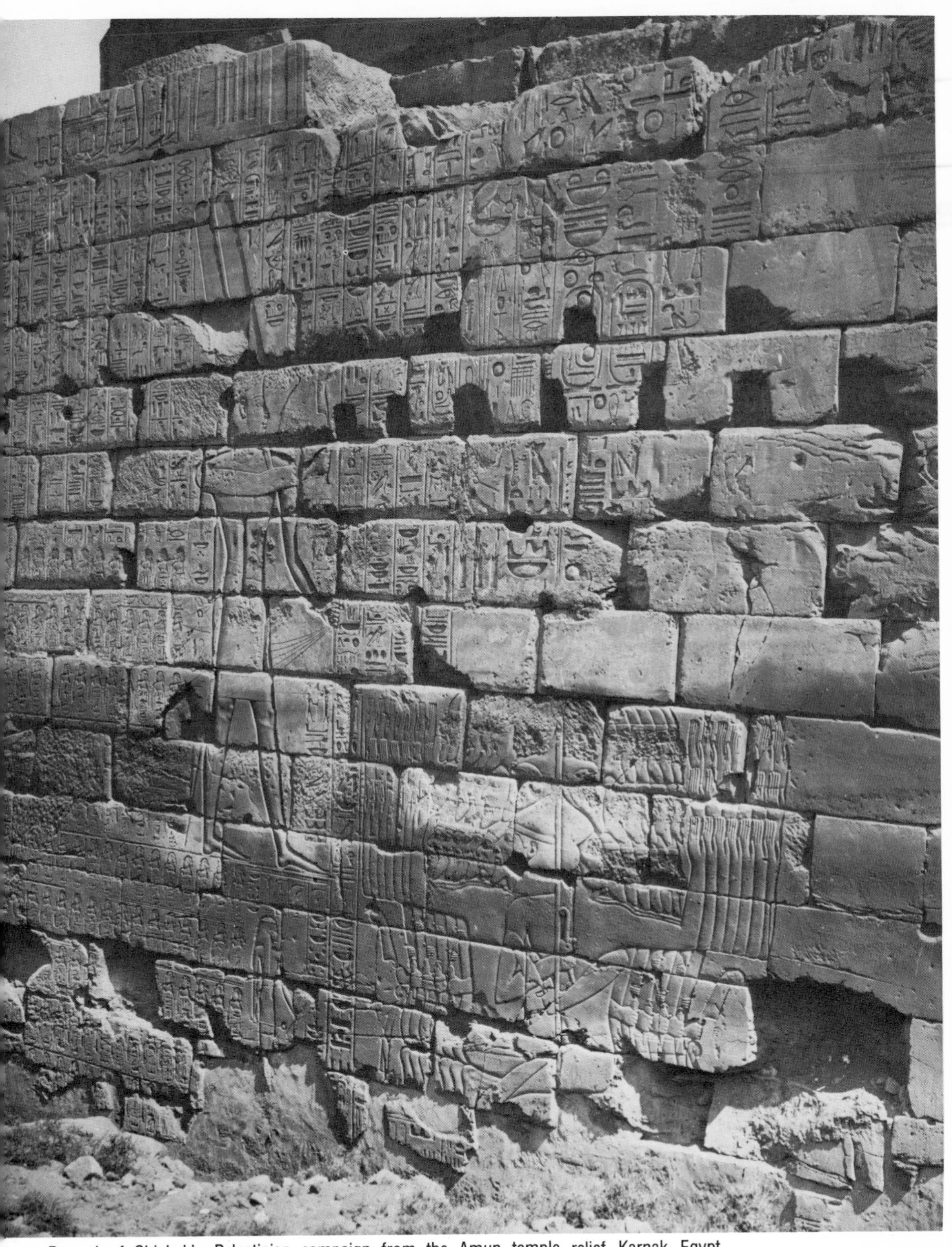

Record of Shishak's Palestinian campaign from the Amun temple relief, Karnak, Egypt.

threat to Assyria relieved Egypt of Assyrian control, and Egypt was able to re-establish her independence for well over a century, but the rise of the Persian empire resulted in the conquest of Egypt by Cambyses in 525 B.C.

Elephantine

The first cataract of the Nile is located at Aswan, and here, too, lies the island of Elephantine. In 1893 Charles E. Wilbour, an American student of Egyptian antiquities, purchased from an Arab woman the first of an extraordinary group of documents that are now known as the Elephantine Papyri. The papyri were written in Aramaic, the lingua franca of the Persian empire, and proved to be documents connected with a Jewish colony of mercenary soldiers (and their families) who had been in the service of the Egyptian and then the Persian governments. The colony had been established circa 650 B.C. and apparently lasted until circa 400 B.C.

The documents which Wilbour had purchased were carried to the United States; however, upon his death in 1896 the trunk containing the papyri was deposited in an attic where it reposed undisturbed until his daughter's death. As a part of her effects, the documents were bequeathed to the Egyptian Department of the Brooklyn Museum, and in 1953 they were published by Emil G. Kraeling.

Another group of papyri from Elephantine was acquired from dealers by A. J. Sayce and A. E. Cowley, and these were published in 1906. A third group of the documents was recovered in excavations on the island carried out by the Berlin Museum. These were published by Eduard Sachau in 1911.

The Elephantine Papyri have added significantly to our knowledge of Aramaic as it was used by this Jewish community in the same general period in which it was used in the writing of parts of the books of Ezra and Daniel. The documents are primarily legal papers—deeds, loan agreements, divorce papers—which illuminate the social intricacies of life in the community and provide important comparative materials for the study of the development of Jewish law and customs in the Persian period. Important letters and official correspondence comprise another aspect of the papyri. Of particular interest is an order given by the authority of Darius II in 419 B.C. in which the colony is directed to keep the Feast of Unleavened Bread. But the most enigmatic and revealing correspondence has to do with a temple of Yahu, that is, of Yahweh, that existed on Elephantine, for the law in Deuteronomy prohibited any altar except the one in Jerusalem. When the sanctuary was destroyed by a group of jealous Egyptians, the leaders of the Elephantine community wrote to the high priest in Jerusalem and to the

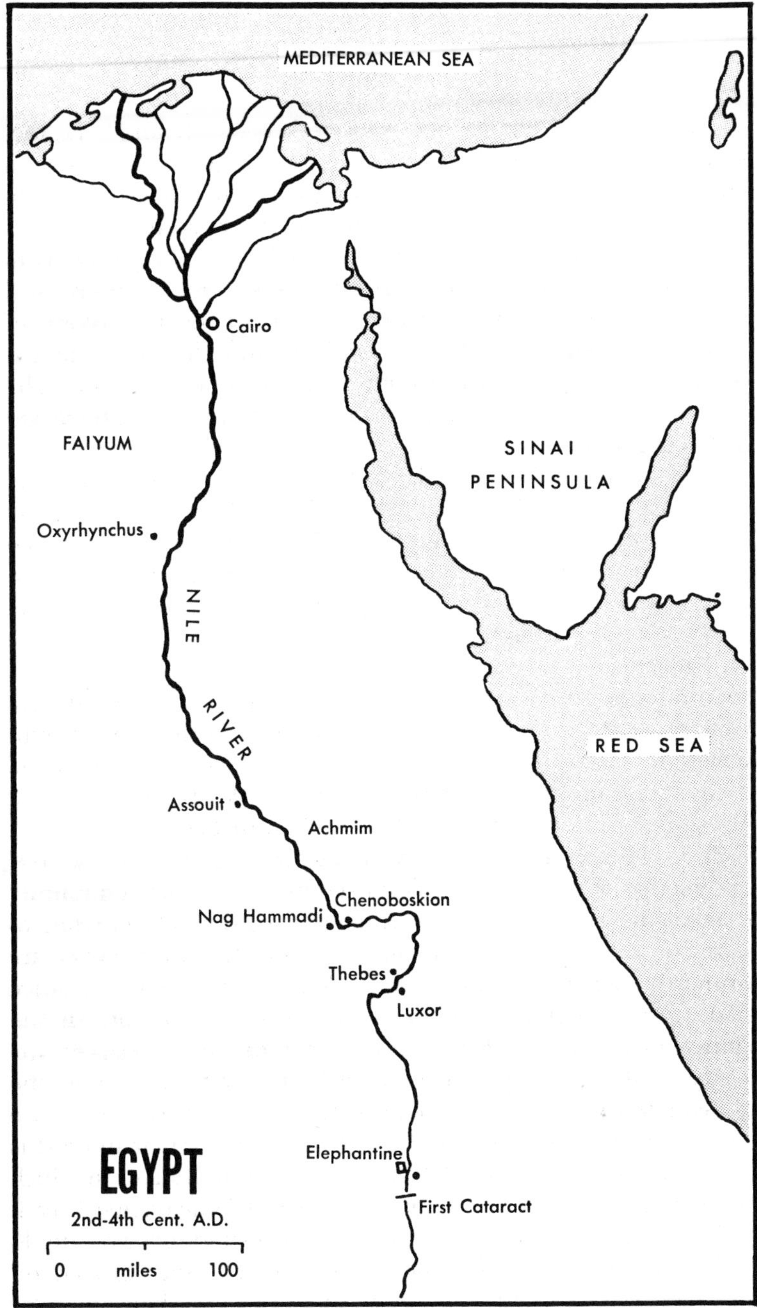

governor of Judah seeking authorization and assistance for its rebuilding. They also wrote to the authorities in Samaria. A memorandum from the governor of Judah to the Persian governor in Egypt supported the rebuilding of the temple, but there is no way of knowing with certainty that the temple was rebuilt.

Another unorthodox element of Elephantine Judaism was a tendency toward syncretism. The papyri which list contributions to the temple mention Yahu, but contributions were also made to Ishumbethel, Herembethel, and Anathbethel. The name *Anathyahu* also appears, combining the name of the Canaanite goddess, Anath, with the name of God. Such compound names may have been used only to emphasize certain qualities or aspects of Yahweh (Yahu), but even at that they deviate from the strict monotheism enjoined by the Bible.

The Elephantine Papyri provide a unique glimpse into the political, economic, social, religious, and corporate life of a Jewish community of the Diaspora contemporary with the period of Ezra and Nehemiah. The contrast between the reforms of those two stalwarts of the Bible and the life of the Elephantine community is striking.

We have been considering the implications of a few Egyptian discoveries that have illuminated the Bible and the People of the Book. As we have seen, Egypt's story has been pieced together primarily from three sources—tombs, temples, and papyri. The hieroglyphic inscriptions found in tombs and on temples dealt by and large with royal annals, affairs of state, and magical formulae by which to assure the welfare of the king in the hereafter. They were laboriously painted or incised on walls, columns, stelae, and sarcophagi. Papyrus, by contrast, provided a surface more suitable for longer compositions and more easily inscribed. As a result, this is the medium which has preserved for us what survives of Egyptian literature, as well as personal documents and communications such as the Elephantine Papyri.

Egyptian literature includes fiction, poetry, philosophy, medicine, astronomy, religion, and proverbs or wisdom. Thanks to the dry climate of Egypt and the preserving qualities of sand dunes, great amounts of papyrus have survived the toll of the centuries with the oldest extant papyrus dating to about 3000 B.C. Among the Egyptian documents in which thoughts and expressions similar to the Bible have been noted are: the "Story of Sinuhe," the "Tale of the Two Brothers," the "Report of Wenamon," and the "Instruction of Amenemope."

The "Story of Sinuhe" is set in the twelfth dynasty (ca. 1960 B.C.). It follows the adventures of an Egyptian courtier who has fled his beloved homeland out of a nameless fear and who finds refuge in the area of Syro-Palestine. Despite the prosperous new life which he establishes for himself in Asia, he longs for his homeland. Eventually he receives permission from the pharaoh to return to an honored place in the court and to the advantages of the traditional burial and funerary rites. To read the "Story of Sinuhe" is to read a literary masterpiece containing certain themes also found in the Bible; for example, in Asia Sinuhe obtains as his bride the eldest daughter of the man under whose protection he has come (cf. Moses in Exod. 2:15–21). He, like David (I Sam. 17), accepts the challenge to single combat with a warrior champion, and wins. The story also provides an Egyptian view of the land of Syro-Palestine, its inhabitants, and its customs in the period when it is assumed the patriarchs were migrating into the area.

The "Tale of the Two Brothers" begins as folklore and is soon transformed into mythology, for the story is really about two gods, Anubis (the elder brother) and Bata (the younger). The story begins in an Egyptian village, with the two brothers going out to the fields to cultivate each day. The elder had recently married, and his wife attempts to seduce the younger brother when he is sent to the house on an errand by her husband. When the younger brother refuses her advances, she unjustly accuses him before her husband. The younger brother flees, and the rest of the story is filled with magical elements like speaking oxen. The similarity between the opening episode of the story and the problems which Joseph confronted in Potiphar's house (Gen. 39:1–20) have been noted, and some scholars have even suggested that the Genesis account is based on the Egyptian myth. But the lack of similarity in the details of the story and the frequency of the theme in other literature make the suggestion difficult to accept.

The "Report of Wenamon" is a straightforward account of Wenamon's eventful trip to Byblos on a mission to obtain lumber from the prince of that Phoenician city. The lumber was needed for the construction of a barge for the god Amun-Re. The itinerary of Wenamon and the problems which he confronts illuminate the relationships between Egypt and her neighbors to the north in the period around 1100 B.C. Of particular interest is his contact with the Tjeckker people at Dor, where he is robbed. The Tjeckker are known from earlier Egyptian inscriptions as one of the Sea Peoples. Apparently they were settled along the Palestinian coast slightly north of the Philistines.

The "Instruction of Amenemope" is a part of the extant remains of Egyptian wisdom literature, consisting of moral teachings in the form of proverbs and wise sayings. Striking similarities between passages in this Egyptian work and the biblical Proverbs have been noted, and in particular Proverbs 22:17–24:22 is paralleled closely by the text of Amenemope. Borrowing on either side is impossible to prove, but the remarkable similarities indicate that the thoughts of the wisdom literature of the ancient Near East were not restricted by national boundaries.

These and similar documents from ancient Egypt came into the hands of Western scholars and institutions primarily through dealers in antiquities. The origin, actual dates of composition, and history of these documents are often in dispute. In contrast to these older documents, papyri from the Hellenistic (Ptolemaic) and Roman periods were often found after long, intensive search. Sir Flinders Petrie began the scientific search for papyri in 1899 when in excavations at Gurob in the Fayum he discovered mummy cases made of discarded papyri within the coffins of the Ptolemaic period. Digging in the cemeteries and trash heaps of Graeco-Roman settlements, Petrie and his successors recovered copies of known Greek classics as well as previously unknown literary works. In addition, the tons of papyri consisting of letters, tax receipts, inventories, contracts, and similar documents, written in the everyday language of the people, have provided invaluable resources for the study of Koine Greek, the language which the writers of the New Testament employed.

At Oxyrhynchus near the Fayum and at Chenoboskion were recovered two collections of papyri that are particularly important for the study of the history of early Christianity. B. P. Grenfell and A. S. Hunt discovered the manuscript known as the Logia or Sayings of Jesus in the rubbish heaps of Oxyrhynchus in 1897. In subsequent years, additional biblical and nonbiblical papyri were recovered at the site. The sayings purport to be the authentic words of Jesus, but they are tinged with ideas known to have been a part of Gnostic thought. They apparently date to the third century A.D., when the Gnostic problem still troubled the church.

The Chenoboskion papyri are also known as the Nag Hammadi Gnostic Texts. They were discovered by a local peasant in 1945 in a cemetery about sixty miles downstream from Luxor across the Nile from the village of Nag Hammadi. The thirteen codices comprise a library of Gnostic works written in the Coptic language but apparently translated from Greek manuscripts. Since knowledge of the Gnostic movement previously had depended upon references to Gnostic doctrines and teachers in the writings of the early church fathers, the Nag Hammadi Texts provide firsthand information on Gnosticism, and they will enable church historians to better assess the nature and substance of the Gnostic threat to Christianity in the second and third centuries A.D.

SUGGESTED TOPICS FOR FURTHER STUDY

1. The pyramids of Egypt—fact and fancy.
2. Who were the Hyksos?
3. The career of Pharaoh Thutmosis III.
4. The Sea Peoples and the end of the Late Bronze Age.
5. The Amarna letters—a survey of content and meaning for biblical studies.
6. Was Akhenaten a monotheist?
7. Who were the Habiru?
8. The discovery of King Tut's tomb.
9. The pharaoh of the exodus—an investigation of the problem.
10. The significance of Shishak's conquests for the interpretation of Palestinian archaeological sites.
11. King Josiah versus Pharaoh Necho—the political background of the conflict.
12. A survey of the legal documents from Elephantine.
13. Jewish temples (outside Jerusalem) in the Persian and Hellenistic periods.
14. Appraise the validity of the arguments concerning the influence of Egyptian literature upon the biblical writers.
15. The prophetic concept of Egypt against the backdrop of the history of Egypt in the prophetic period.

RECOMMENDED READING

"Egypt" in *The Biblical World,* ed. Charles F. Pfeiffer (Grand Rapids: Baker, 1966), pp. 207–18.

Gardiner, Alan, *Egypt of the Pharaohs* (Oxford: Oxford University Press, 1961).

Hallo, W. W., and W. K. Simpson, *The Ancient Near East: A History* (New York: Harcourt Brace Jovanovich Inc., 1971), pp. 185–298.

Thomas, D. Winton, ed., *Archaeology and Old Testament Study* (Oxford: Oxford University Press, 1967), pp. 3–35.

Wilson, J. A., "Egypt" in *The Interpreter's Dictionary of the Bible,* ed. George A. Buttrick et al. (New York: Abingdon Press, 1962), vol. 2, pp. 39–66.

Consult the helpful bibliographies in these works, and for added information on specific terms, such as the Elephantine Papyri, consult the articles and bibliographies in *The Biblical World* and *The Interpreter's Dictionary of the Bible.*

FOR FURTHER READING

For a list of periodicals relating to Egyptology, consult the bibliography in Hallo and Simpson's *The Ancient Near East,* pp. 308–09. The entire bibliography is up to date and useful. For a comprehensive bibliography of the history of archaeology in Egypt, consult Bratton's work, listed below, pp. 290–308.

Aharoni, Y., *The Land of the Bible: A Historical Geography,* tr. A. F. Rainey (Philadelphia: The Westminster Press, 1967).

Bratton, Fred G., *A History of Egyptian Archaeology* (New York: Thomas Y. Crowell Co., 1968).

Breasted, J. H., *Ancient Records of Egypt,* I–IV (Chicago: University of Chicago Press, 1906–7).

Cambridge Ancient History, revised edition (Cambridge: Cambridge University Press, fasc. 3, 1961; fasc. 5, 1962; fasc. 6, 1962; fasc. 10, 1962; fasc. 25, 1964; fasc. 27, 1965; fasc. 38, 1965; fasc. 52, 1966).

Ceram, C. W., *The March of Archaeology* (New York: Alfred A. Knopf, 1970).

Finegan, Jack, *Light from the Ancient Past* (Princeton: Princeton University Press, 1959).

Kitchen, Kenneth A., *Ancient Orient and Old Testament* (Chicago: Inter-Varsity Press, 1966).

Lichtheim, M., *Ancient Egyptian Literature* (Berkeley: University of California Press, I–II, 1973–76).

Orlin, Louis L., *Ancient Near Eastern Literature (A Bibliography)* (Ann Arbor: Campus Publishers, 1969).

Pfeiffer, Charles F., *Tell El Amarna and the Bible* (Grand Rapids: Baker, 1963).

Pritchard, James B., ed., *Ancient Near Eastern Texts Relating to the Old Testament,* third edition; *The Ancient Near East in Pictures Relating to the Old Testament,* second edition; *The Ancient Near East: Supplementary Texts and Pictures Relating to the Old Testament* (Princeton: Princeton University Press, 1969).

Ruffle, J., *Heritage of the Pharaohs* (London: Elsevier-Phaidon, 1977).

Simpson, William Kelly, ed., *The Literature of Ancient Egypt* (New Haven: Yale University Press, 1972).

Thomas, D. Winton, ed., *Documents from Old Testament Times* (New York: Harper & Row [Harper Torchbook], 1961).

Part Three

A Survey of Significant Sites Within the Holy Land

10

Ai

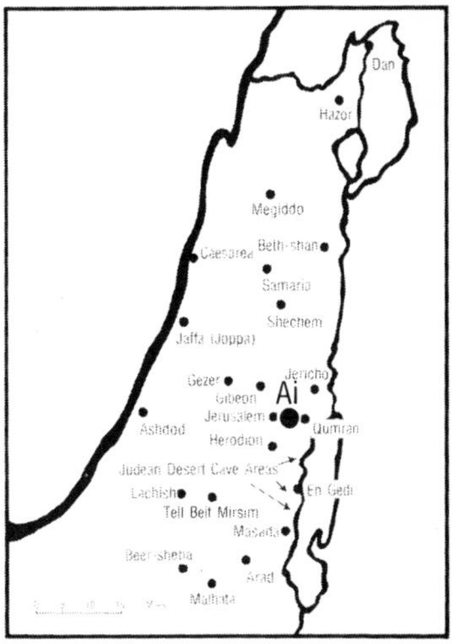

The biblical town of Ai, situated on a slope of the Judean hills at a site known as et-Tell, one mile southwest of Beitin, the biblical Beth-el, has been the subject of excavations under the direction of Judith Marquet-Krause and Samuel Yeivin in the thirties, and under Joseph A. Callaway in the sixties and early seventies.

Ai is mentioned in the Old Testament in Genesis 12:8, where we read that Abraham pitched his tent between Beth-el and Ai (Ha'ai) and built an altar to the Lord at the site. After his journey to Egypt the patriarch returned there (Gen. 13:3). More is told about Ai in the seventh and eighth chapters of the Book of Joshua, relating how the Israelite leader lost thirty-six men in his first attempt to conquer the city, but succeeded in capturing it after Achan, who had taken treasures from Jericho against the Lord's command, had been punished by death. The city was set afire and twelve thousand men and women were killed by the Israelites. The Israelite settlement that was established near the destroyed Canaanite city of Ai, called Aiath in the Book of Isaiah, was itself destroyed by the Assyrians during the seventh century B.C. (Isa. 10:28). After the Babylonian captivity, 223 men of Beth-el and Ai returned, according to Ezra 2:28 (Neh. 7:32 mentions 123). In Nehemiah 11:31 the returning exiles are designated as Benjaminites and the name of the city is given as A-i'ja.

The search for Ai was first undertaken from 1933 until 1935 by the Rothschild expedition under the direction of Judith

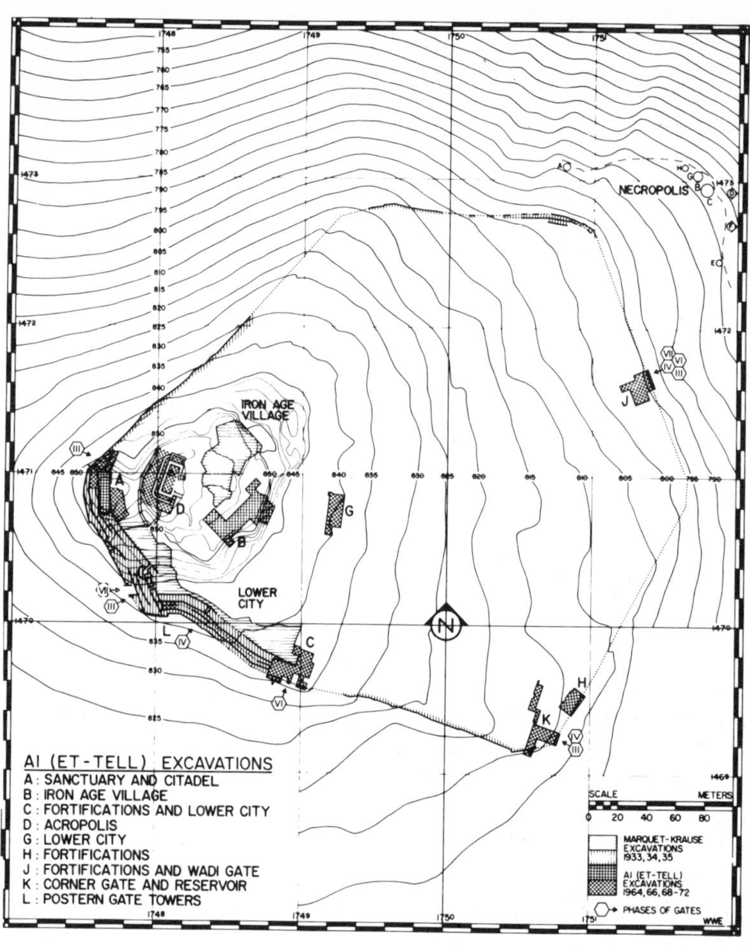

Plan of the Ai excavations.

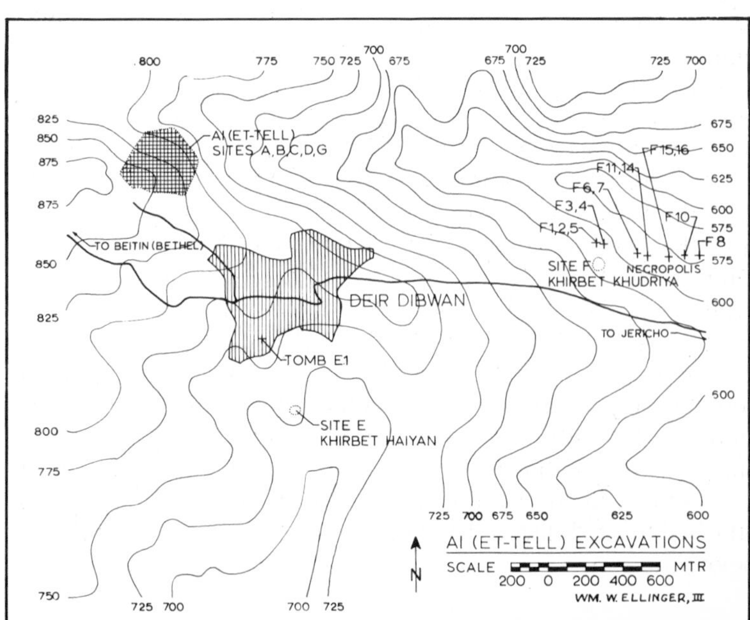

Regional plan of the Ai excavations.

Marquet-Krause and Samuel Yeivin; three levels of occupation in the upper city were excavated. This city was located on the eastern slope of the hill and dated from the Early Bronze Age. Parts of an elaborate defense system—a massive stone wall, twenty-five feet wide and twenty-nine feet high, joined to a semicircular tower—were uncovered. Inside the city a large palace with wooden pillars was laid bare. In an Early Bronze Age sanctuary, situated southwest of the acropolis upon which the palace had been built, alabaster bowls and ivory sacrificial objects were found. These evidences of Egyptian influence suggest that there were commercial relations between Egypt and Canaan during this era. The twenty-fourth or twenty-third century B.C. saw the destruction of Early Bronze Age Ai, with the city remaining in ruins until the Iron Age I period, when a pre-Israelite settlement was established at the site. This small unfortified village on top of the acropolis of et-Tell seems to have been the Ai conquered by Joshua.

Joseph A. Callaway directed operations at et-Tell from 1964 to 1972, excavating the Early Bronze Age city, completing the work of the Rothschild expedition, and finding new evidence of the Iron Age village and a Byzantine monastery. One of the most important discoveries of the Callaway expedition is a water reservoir twenty by twenty-five meters with a capacity of a thousand cubic meters. The bottom of this reservoir, the only one known to have been constructed in Palestine during the Early Bronze Age II period, was paved with flagstones set in red clay. Callaway also excavated nearby Khirbet Haiyan, which was occupied from Roman times through the Umayyad period. The oldest artifact found was a coin of Agrippa I; however, the earliest buildings date from the Byzantine period. The excavation of Khirbet Khudriya in 1966 showed that during the Byzantine period there had been a church near et-Tell. A number of tombs were also associated with the same period.

In contrast to the twenty-seven acres of the Early Bronze Age city, the Iron Age I settlement on the eastern slope of the hill near the uppermost terrace of the tell covered only three acres. On this site there is evidence of two closely related settlements. Walls, buildings, and floors shown signs of reconstruction during this period. The two distinct types of pottery found on this site, stone jars with long-collared rims and inverted concave cooking jars, do not appear together at any other site in the country. In addition, a libation bowl with eighteen closely spaced handles attached to the outer rim and wall was found. Two spouts in the form of animal heads, lions or bulls, were attached to a tubelike conduit built into the wall around the bowl below the rim.

The problem of definitely identifying the site of et-Tell as the biblical Ai has perplexed archaeologists and scholars for years. The excavations of Judith Marquet-Krause and Joseph Callaway reveal that there was no settlement in the area during the period in which the Israelites invaded Canaan. The identification of Ai with et-Tell itself was challenged by J. Simons and Yehezkel Kaufmann. Simons maintains that the words "beside Beth-el" in Joshua 12:9 indicate that Ai was nearer to Beth-el than the two miles that separate et-Tell from Beth-el. Kaufmann is convinced that the word *Ai* does not mean "ruin" but a "heap," denoting a pile of stones. Thus he rejects the idea that Ai was built over an ancient city. Other specific sites have been suggested as the biblical Ai, for example, Khirbet Haiyan, one mile south of et-Tell and Wadi Auja, the site of a popular infiltration route into the central hill country of Palestine. However, archaeological finds at these locations disprove these suggestions. To Hugues Vincent and other scholars, Ai was a military outpost. John Garstang concluded in the early part of the twentieth century that et-Tell and Ai were identical. Basing his opinion on the kind of ceramics found, he dated the fall of Ai in the sixteenth or fifteenth century B.C. William Albright believed that Ai fell to Joshua in the latter part of the thirteenth century, because of similar destructions of the cities of Tell Beit Mirsim, Lachish, and Hazor. Unfortunately, Garstang's and Albright's dating of et-Tell and the Israelite invasion do not hold water in the light of the findings of archaeological excavations at the site. Judith Marquet-Krause concluded that, since there was no settlement during the time of Joshua, the biblical account must be more legend than fact. But according to Callaway there is too much historical evidence to consider the story of the conquest a legend. He believes that Ai was subjected to a number of minor raids and that the final conquest was not military, but political and cultural, resulting in integration and assimilation with the invaders. Some scholars think it possible that the ancient city was taken by the Habiru who infiltrated the country during the Middle Bronze Age (1750–1550 B.C.) and who, according to the Amarna letters, were a complicating factor in Canaan during the Late Bronze Age. Some have suggested that an Iron Age city was conquered at a much later time, but the conquest was credited to Joshua. Others argue that this cannot be true, because a man of Joshua's stature would not have suffered defeat so easily. It may be possible, others have said, that the chroniclers, writing in a later age, confused the conquest of Beth-el, recorded in Judges 1:22–25, with Ai. It is clear that the archaeological evidence uncovered at et-Tell does not corroborate the biblical

Airview of Ai, viewed to the northeast.

Map of the Ai region (note the proximity of Beth-el to the west).

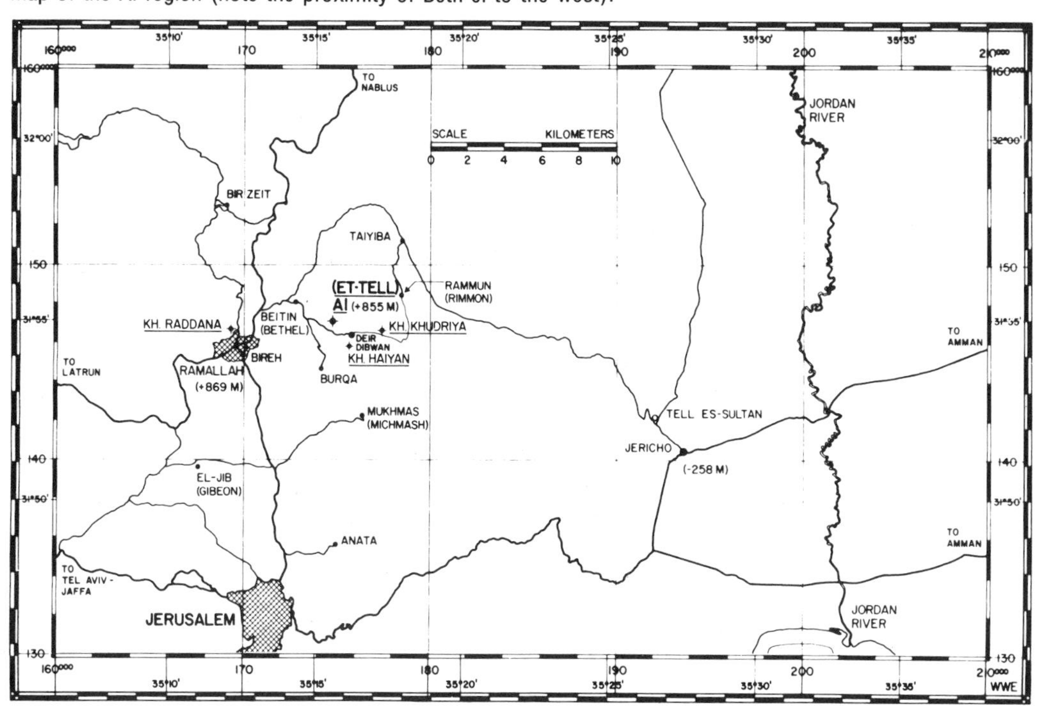

account, nor does it correlate well with the written sources. One must keep in mind that the site cannot be identified with certainty as the ruin of the city which Joshua conquered. Perhaps further evidence can be found which will resolve the problem.

SUGGESTED TOPICS FOR FURTHER STUDY

1. Archaeological excavations at et-Tell.
2. Conquest of Ai—fact or legend?
3. Joshua son of Nun—military leader or folk hero?
4. Beth-el and Ai.

RECOMMENDED READING

"Ai" in *The Biblical World,* ed. Charles F. Pfeiffer (Grand Rapids: Baker, 1966), pp. 25–26.

"Ai" in *Encyclopedia Judaica* (Jerusalem: Keter Publishing House, 1971), vol. 2, cols. 471–73.

"Ai" in *The Interpreter's Dictionary of the Bible,* ed. George A. Buttrick et al. (New York: Abingdon Press, 1962), vol. 1, pp. 72–73.

"Ai" in *The New Bible Dictionary,* ed. J. D. Douglas (Grand Rapids: Eerdmans, 1962), pp. 22–23.

Baker's Bible Atlas, ed. Charles F. Pfeiffer (Grand Rapids: Baker, 1972), pp. 89, 266.

FOR FURTHER READING

Albright, William, "Ai and Beth-Aven," *Bulletin of the American Schools of Oriental Research* 4 (1924), pp. 141–49.

———, "Archaeology and the Date of the Hebrew Conquest of Palestine," *Bulletin of the American Schools of Oriental Research* 58 (1935), pp. 10–18.

Callaway, Joseph A., "Ai," *Israel Exploration Journal* 19 (1969), pp. 236–39.

———, *The Early Bronze Sanctuary at Ai (et-Tell)* (London: Bernard Quaritch, 1972).

———, "Excavating Ai (Et-Tell): 1964–72," *Biblical Archaeologist* 39 (Cambridge, MA: American Schools of Oriental Research, 1976).

———, "New Evidence of the Conquest of Ai," *Journal of Biblical Literature* 88 (1968), pp. 312–20.

———, "News," *Palestine Exploration Quarterly,* July–Dec. 1969, p. 56.

———, *Pottery from the Tombs at Ai* (London: Bernard Quaritch, 1964).

———, "The 1964 Ai Excavations," *Bulletin of the American Schools of Oriental Research* 178 (1965), pp. 13–40.

———, "The 1966 Ai Excavations," *Bulletin of the American Schools of Oriental Research* 196 (1969), pp. 2–16.

———, "The 1968 Ai Excavations," *Palestine Exploration Quarterly*, Jan.–June 1970, pp. 42–44.

———, "The 1968–1969 Ai Excavations," *Bulletin of the American Schools of Oriental Research* 198 (1970), pp. 7–31.

11

Arad

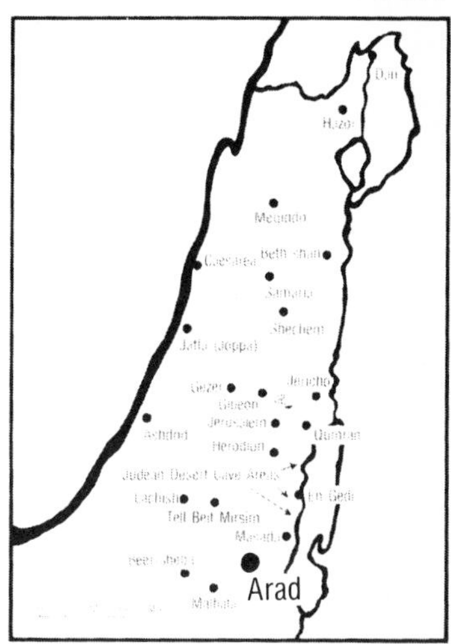

Arad, though seldom mentioned in the Bible, has yielded finds of great importance for biblical studies. The tell is located in the eastern Negev, about twenty miles northeast of Beer-sheba and fifteen miles west of the Dead Sea. There is little rainfall in the area, nor are there springs nearby. This lack of water appears to have been a constant problem, but Arad's location assured its continued existence. It was situated along one of the most important roads to the Arabah, Ezion-Geber, and Eilat, and at the southern border of Judah. Discoveries at the site indicate it served for a long period as a Judean fortress.

Arad is one of the more prominent tells of the eastern Negev and conforms to the location still known to Eusebius in the fourth century A.D. The identification with biblical Arad was confirmed when a Hebrew ostracon inscribed with the name of the city was found on the tell.

Excavation was begun contemporaneously with the founding of a modern city of Arad not far from the ancient site. Developers of the new city contributed generously to the excavation of the old one. Archaeologists from the Hebrew University, the Israel Department of Antiquities, and the Israel Exploration Society, in the main, conducted the excavations. Digging began in 1962 and continued to 1967; it was resumed in 1971–72. The work has focused on two separate areas of the tell which were occupied during two quite distinct periods. Ruth Amiran has been largely responsible for the excavation of the Early Bronze

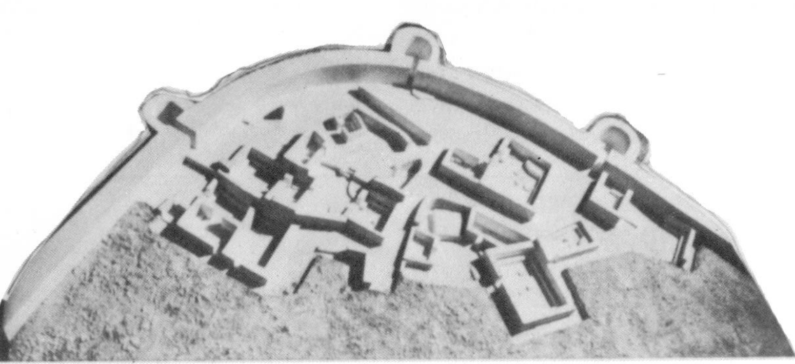

Model of a section of the Early Bronze Arad.

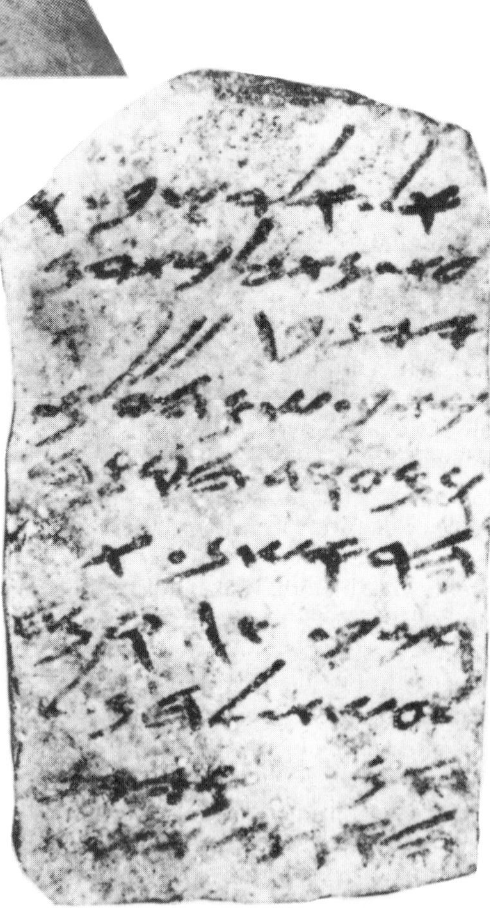

An Arad ostracon addressed to Eliashib, ca. 600 B.C. "To Eliashib, and now: Give the Kittim 3 baths of wine and write the name of the day. And from the rest of the first flour, let 1 ephah of flour be mixed to make bread for them. From the wine of the basins give. . . ."

The inner sanctum of the Arad sanctuary.

Age city on the large lower level of the tell. Yohanan Aharoni has directed the work for the Arad of the Israelite and later eras, atop the smaller citadel area to the east. An Arab settlement and fortresses of the Roman, Hellenistic, and Persian periods have been found on the site, but most interest attaches to the Bronze Age and Israelite levels.

Settlement at Arad began in the Chalcolithic period, in an open, scattered fashion (ca. 3400–3150 B.C.). Then late in Early Bronze I (ca. 3000–2900 B.C.) an unfortified village sprang up which grew during the Early Bronze II period (2900–2700) into a walled city enclosing nearly twenty-five acres. The city was constructed in an unusual way, evidencing, according to Amiran, a well-developed tradition of town planning in Canaan. Rather than building on top of a hill, the people of Arad put their houses on the inner slopes of a horseshoe-shaped ridge. The stone city wall was eight feet thick and situated on the peak of the ridge and across the shallow depression at the opening of the "horseshoe." This not only made the wall a good line of defense; it enclosed a city which sloped *down* toward its center. In this central depression, the builders made a large reservoir, so that all the rain water which fell on the city would run down into it for storage. Aharoni estimates that, even with the scant rainfall of the area, over ten thousand cubic meters of water would be available for collection each year—over two-and-a-half million gallons![1]

Other features of the Bronze Age city show careful planning. Semicircular towers project from the city wall every twenty or twenty-five meters. Both houses and public buildings display a typical, uniform architecture—the "broad room," that is, a single rectangular room with its entrance on the long side. Streets run parallel to the city wall, and the public buildings are located on the lower slopes, toward the center of the city. Temples and cultic objects, including an intriguing stele, have been found. Pottery finds indicate that Arad had trade connections with Egypt, and similarities in architecture, artifacts, and pottery have suggested that certain sites as far away as southern Sinai were outposts of the Canaanite civilization which flourished at Arad.

For all this, Bronze Age Arad was short-lived. It passed through four phases—an unfortified village, two phases of the walled city, and finally a town which apparently was also unfortified—within about two hundred years. Then it was abandoned for reasons still unknown. It remained abandoned

[1]*Israel Exploration Journal* 17 (1967), p. 237.

until the coming of the Israelites in the Iron Age. The site is thus *not* the Canaanite Arad mentioned in the Book of Numbers; Aharoni believes that the Canaanite Arad should be sought at nearby Tell el-Milḥ.

Israelite Arad began as a small, open village at the eastern end of the ancient site late in the eleventh century B.C., that is, at the end of the period of the judges. Aharoni believes its occupants were Kenites (Judg. 1:16). The Kenites were relatives of Moses and likely a clan of priests. They built a small sanctuary, with a high place and altar, on the site. Probably in the reign of Solomon, the strategically located settlement was converted to a small citadel only about fifty meters square, but very heavily fortified. Reservoirs within the fortress were filled from exterior sources, the water transported most likely in containers carried by donkeys. In the ninth century the Solomonic casemate wall was replaced by a solid wall thirteen feet thick, which in turn was converted to a casemate wall in the eighth century. From its founding to the end of the kingdom of Judah (587 B.C.), the citadel was destroyed and rebuilt six times. Each destruction is clearly delineated in the strata of the tell, an important aid to archaeologists. The most significant finds at Israelite Arad have been its ostraca and its sanctuary.

About two hundred ostraca—potsherds with writing on them—were found at Arad. Half of them are military supply records of the Persian period, written in Aramaic, and half of them are files from the archives of the royal citadel of the Judean kingdom. These Hebrew ostraca, including some deriving from every phase of the Israelite city, are of immense value for the study of the development of the Hebrew language and writing system during the biblical period. Even the many containing only a few visible letters contribute to the study of Hebrew writing.

The most important group of ostraca comes from the last phase of the Arad citadel and appears to be part of the official correspondence of a man named Eliashib. He apparently was in charge of the stores, or perhaps of the entire administration, of the fortress at this time (his seal was found in a room of the preceding stratum). The letters order him to provision certain people with quantities of flour, oil, and wine. Mentioned in the ostraca are "Kittim," evidently Greek mercenaries in the employ of the Judean monarchy. One letter from a subordinate intriguingly refers to "the matter you commanded me about: all is well. He is staying at the house of Yahweh" (that is, at the temple in Jerusalem).

Names mentioned in the Bible appear on ostraca which may be lots to be drawn for service in the sanctuary. Significantly, like a great many biblical names, several of the names on the ostraca have the element *-yahu,* reflecting the worship of Yahweh; but *none* of the names contain the element *-ba'al* ("Baal"). This is in sharp contrast to the situation at the contemporary Israelite capital of Samaria. Also, on one ostracon appears to be a previously unknown ancient Hebrew name for one of the months of the year, the month *Ṣaḥ*.

The discovery of an Israelite sanctuary at Arad, which came as a great surprise to all concerned, was made on the last day of the second season of excavations. That the small temple is in fact an *Israelite* temple and dedicated to Israel's God is proven by its general layout and contents, which conform to biblical descriptions of Moses' wilderness tabernacle and Solomon's temple, and by the fact that it was built at the same time as the earliest Israelite citadel at Arad and its history parallels what is known of the history of Judah.

The orientation of the temple is toward the west, like the tabernacle and Solomon's temple. The overall plan is also similar: an outer courtyard with a large altar for sacrifices; an inner courtyard or "porch," with bases for two pillars flanking the entrance to the next room, the Holy Place; three steps then lead up to the inner shrine, the Holy of Holies. The Holy of Holies at Arad contained two incense altars, a small "high place," and a sacred pillar. The large altar is made of unhewn stones (Exod. 20:25), and appears to have measured five cubits by five cubits (Exod. 27:1). The pillars correspond to those called Jachin and Boaz in Solomon's temple (I Kings 7:21; II Chron. 3:17).

The proportions of the Arad temple are different from those of the Jerusalem temple; for example, the Holy Place at Jerusalem was forty cubits long (east-west) and twenty cubits wide (north-south), while that at Arad, also measuring twenty cubits north-south, is much less than twenty cubits east-west. The Holy Place at Arad is a wide room, that at Jerusalem is a long room. Such differences may be partly due to the necessarily smaller size of the Arad temple.

In its historical development, the Arad temple presents interesting features. The Holy Place of the first phase of the temple is about one-and-a-half yards shorter than the Holy Place in later phases, and the altar likewise has sides about one foot shorter than the altar of later phases. It appears therefore that the standard of the cubit changed between the tenth and the ninth centuries B.C., from the older "common" cubit of about eighteen inches to the "royal" cubit of about twenty-one inches; the Holy Place and altar were enlarged to keep their measurements in cubits the same.

Furthermore, it may be noted that the temple was repaired and rebuilt with each destruction and rebuilding of the citadel as a whole. The locations of the Holy of Holies and the altar were never changed. But the altar appears not to have been used following the fourth phase of the citadel, though the rest of the temple remained. The temple itself was evidently deliberately eliminated in the building of the sixth citadel, a wall going right through the Holy Place. These facts would seem to coincide precisely with what the Bible tells us of the religious reforms of King Hezekiah and King Josiah of Judah: Hezekiah removed all altars to Yahweh except the one in Jerusalem (cf. II Kings 18:22); Josiah went further by removing the incense altars and high places (II Kings 23).

The Arad temple was built over the spot where the earlier (Kenite?) high place had been. Does its presence at Arad indicate an important place for the Kenites in Israelite religion? This is possible; but Aharoni attaches greater significance to the fact that Israelite and Judean royal sanctuaries now appear to have been built at the *borders* of the countries, with one in the center: Dan, Beth-el, and Gilgal, with Samaria in the center, for the Northern Kingdom; and Beer-sheba and Arad, with Jerusalem in the center, for the Southern Kingdom (cf. the references in Amos 5:5 and 8:14). This inference is significant both for biblical theology and for biblical archaeology, and it is to be hoped that further excavations, like Aharoni's at Beer-sheba, will shed more light on it.

SUGGESTED TOPICS FOR FURTHER STUDY

1. The history and significance of the Israelite sanctuary at Arad.
2. The Arad ostraca.
3. The history of the fortifications at Israelite Arad.
4. Arad and Early Bronze Age culture in Canaan.

RECOMMENDED READING

Aharoni, Yohanan, "Arad: Its Inscriptions and Temple," *Biblical Archaeologist* 31 (1968), pp. 2–32.

———, "Excavations at Tell Arad: Preliminary Report on the Second Season, 1963," *Israel Exploration Journal* 17 (1967), pp. 233–49.

———, "The Israelite Sanctuary at Arad" in *New Directions in Biblical Archaeology*, ed. D. N. Freedman and J. C. Greenfield (Garden City, NY: Doubleday, 1969), pp. 25–39.

———, "The Negev" in *Archaeology and Old Testament Study*, ed. D. W. Thomas (Oxford: Oxford University Press, 1967), pp. 384–403.

Amiran, Ruth, "The Beginnings of Urbanization in Canaan" in *Near Eastern Archaeology in the Twentieth Century*, ed. J. A. Sanders (Garden City, NY: Doubleday, 1970), pp. 83–100.

———, et al., "The Interrelationship Between Arad and Sites in Southern Sinai in the Early Bronze Age II," *Israel Exploration Journal* 23 (1973), pp. 193–97.

"Arad" in *Encyclopedia Judaica* (Jerusalem: Keter, 1971), vol. 3, cols. 243–49.

Mazar, Benjamin, "Arad and the Kenites," *Journal of Near Eastern Studies* 24 (1965), pp. 297–303.

FOR FURTHER READING

Aharoni, Yohanan, and Ruth Amiran, "Excavations at Tell Arad: Preliminary Report on the First Season, 1962," *Israel Exploration Journal* 14 (1964), pp. 131–47.

Amiran, Ruth, "Arad," *Israel Exploration Journal* 21 (1971), pp. 228–29.

———, "The Beginnings of Urbanization in Canaan" in *Near Eastern Archaeology in the Twentieth Century*, ed. J. A. Sanders (Garden City, NY: Doubleday, 1970), pp. 83–100.

———, "A Cult Stele from Arad," *Israel Exploration Journal* 22 (1972), pp. 86–88.

12

Ashdod

The city of Ashdod was in ancient times one of the five cities which comprised the heart of the territory of the Philistines. (The other four were Ashkelon, Ekron, Gath, and Gaza.) The site is located three miles from the seacoast, about halfway between Gaza and modern Tel Aviv-Jaffa. Nearby is the village of Isdud, preserving the ancient name; and not far away is the route of the highway which ran from Egypt northward as a link with Phoenicia, Syria, and Mesopotamia.

There can be little doubt that the tell near Isdud is the site of Ashdod, and modern excavation has produced a picture of the tell's history which corresponds with that of the great Philistine center. Archaeological work at Tell Ashdod was undertaken in 1962 as a joint effort of the Carnegie Museum in Pittsburgh, the Pittsburgh Theological Seminary, and the Israel Department of Antiquities. The director in 1962 and 1963 was David Noel Freedman; James L. Swauger directed the 1965, 1968, and 1969 seasons; and Moshe Dothan, who had served as archaeological director from the first, took over as director in 1970, 1971, and 1972.

The tell itself consists of both an upper (acropolis) and a lower city. The upper city was founded first, in the Middle Bronze II C period (ca. 1600 B.C.). Interestingly, nearby Tell Mor, which probably served as the seaport for Ashdod, was founded only a little later. The excavators speculate that both may have been founded in the last days of the Hyksos, as part of their general

Hellenistic pottery *in situ* at Ashdod, Gk. Azotus (cf. Acts 8:40).

defensive preparations against the resurgent native Egyptian leaders.

But the Egyptians did prove victorious, and in the Late Bronze Age Ashdod was a fortified site under their domination. Both locally made and imported Aegean (Mycenaean and Cypriote) pottery have been found in strata of this period.

The end of the Late Bronze Age saw the destruction of Ashdod, as of so many Palestinian sites. Shortly after 1200 B.C., a new group of people took over Ashdod, and from their pottery there can be no doubt that they were the Philistines.

And who were the Philistines? Where did they come from? The Bible states that they came from "the island of Caphtor" (Jer. 47:4; Amos 9:7), that is, from Crete, and in substance this appears to be correct. Archaeological discoveries have shed a great deal of light on Philistine origins and Philistine culture. One of the main sources is Egypt, where inscriptions tell of Late Bronze Age invasions and movements of "Peoples of the Sea," groups known as Sherden, Luka, Danuna, Akawasha, Tjeckker, and others, including a group called Peleset—Philistines. It appears that the second millennium B.C. was a time of great migrations of populations in the Middle East and surrounding areas. The Bible records one such set of migrations, that of the patriarchs, and later of the children of Israel first into and then out of Egypt. The picture as drawn by archaeology is on a broader scale. Early in the Middle Bronze Age there were movements of Semitic peoples—Amorites, including the patriarchs—in Mesopotamia and Canaan. Then came a migration of Indo-Aryan peoples southward from what is now southern Russia, pushing ahead of them and amalgamating with the Hurrians of the Caucasus area. These peoples pressed down into Syro-Palestine, and sent invaders plunging into Egypt. These invaders, known to the Egyptians as Hyksos, ruled there in the seventeenth century B.C. Further incursions from Europe in the Late Bronze Age brought disruption to the Aegean area and Anatolia and sent waves of displaced people from these places cascading down the Phoenician coast all the way to Egypt. These were the Sea Peoples, who appear under several pharaohs as invaders of Egypt. They also on occasion are referred to as mercenaries in the Egyptian army. The last set of disruptions brought about the collapse of the Hittite empire in Anatolia and the destruction about 1200 B.C. of its capital, Hattusas (Boghazköy), as well as of the city of Ugarit. They may also have precipitated the affairs at Troy sung of by Homer, and they brought the Philistines to Palestine.

The Aegean or southern Anatolian connections of the Sea

Part of an Egyptian relief showing captive Philistines (Medinet Habu).

Peoples are demonstrated in a variety of ways. The Akawasha are sometimes identified with the Achaean Greeks, and the Luka are Lycians. Ramses III was the last pharaoh to do battle with the Sea Peoples, specifically with the Peleset and Tjeckker. His inscription at Medinet Habu shows these people dressed in kilts and wearing feathered headdresses, both reminiscent of Late Bronze Age Cyprus. Other evidence for this connection has turned up at Ashdod, as we will see.

Ramses III settled (or was forced to settle) the Peleset and Tjeckker along the seacoast in southern Canaan. Thus it is that just at this time, the beginning of the twelfth century B.C., a new and distinctive type of pottery begins to be found precisely in the area known from the Bible as Philistine territory. This pot-

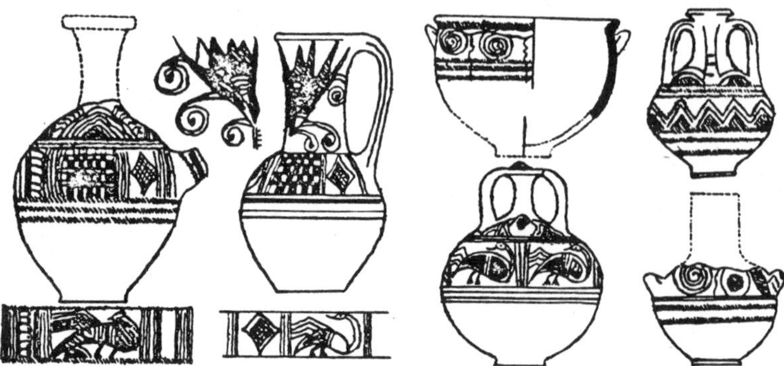

Philistine pottery from Palestine.

tery, too, has affinities with the Aegean area; its most striking feature is its beautiful, dark-painted decoration, with geometric designs and swans preening their feathers. This distinctive ware is found not only in the area immediately around the five Philistine cities, but also in adjacent areas of the Negev and Shephelah over which Philistine control was extended, and in cities farther away like Megiddo, which the Philistines also came to dominate. Little else is known of Philistine culture. Odd clay coffins with human features molded on the lids seem possibly to be a concomitant of occupation by Sea Peoples (cf. the section on Beth-shan); and the biblical notice that the Philistines knew the technology of iron, and kept it a close secret (I Sam. 13:19–21), may be confirmed by the finding of iron-smelting remains in Philistine-held areas. Nearly nothing survives of the Philistines' language. Their leaders are called *seranim* in the Bible, and this Philistine word may be connected with the Greek *tyrannos.* The words for Goliath's helmet (*koba'*) and for the box in which the Philistines sent gifts when they returned the ark of God (*'argaz*—I Sam. 6:8) may have Hittite connections. Goliath itself is a non-Semitic name, and may be Anatolian in formation, and the name of David's Philistine patron Achish (I Sam. 21:11; 24:10; etc.) may be the same as the Anchises mentioned by Homer.

The Philistines seem to have assimilated rapidly to Canaanite culture, probably abandoning their own religion and language in the process. All their gods which are known to us are Semitic (Dagon: Judg. 16:23; I Sam. 5:1–7; Baal-zebub: II Kings 1:2ff.; Ashtaroth: I Sam. 31:10), as are the names of later Philistine leaders, as known from Assyrian and other sources.

Philistine rule began in their five cities—Ashdod, Ashkelon, Ekron, Gath, and Gaza—but rapidly began to spread over southwestern Palestine. They thus posed the greatest threat to the Israelite settlers, beginning with the nearby tribe of Dan (cf. the literature on Samson, Judg. 13–16); they eventually came to absorb most of the energies of Israel's leaders in the latter part of the eleventh century B.C.—Samuel, Saul, and David. Archaeology confirms their growing hold over much of Palestine in this century, as witnessed also by I Samuel, despite periodic triumphs by Samuel and Saul. It was David who finally broke the power of the Philistines (II Sam. 5:17–25; 8:1), and after his time we hear no more of concerted Philistine action, only of the individual cities. David seems, in fact, to have taken elements of the former Sea Peoples into his service as loyal retainers—there is Ittai of Gath (II Sam. 15:18–22); the Cherethites (II Sam. 20:7), probably Cretans who lived in a certain portion of the Negev

(I Sam. 30:14); and Pelethites (II Sam. 20:7), a name which is perhaps a by-form of "Philistines." The evidence at Ashdod seems to confirm this picture of expanding Philistine domination followed by loss of power and assimilation.

As was noted above, the Late Bronze Age city of Ashdod was destroyed and a new settlement built early in the twelfth century B.C. There follow at least three strata (strata 13, 12, and 11), covering the twelfth and eleventh centuries, which are attributable to Philistine occupation. Above all, the characteristic Philistine pottery confirms this conclusion. Other finds at the site yield new information about the culture, religion, and origins of the Philistines.

In the earliest Philistine level was found some pottery which differs from the usual "Philistine" types, and which has close connections to Mycenaean III C 1 pottery known from Cyprus. This discovery adds weight to previous deductions about the immediate place of origin of the Sea Peoples, perhaps representing the pottery in use among the Philistines before they began manufacturing their own distinctive ware in Palestine itself. Yet even more striking than this was the discovery in the 1968 and 1969 seasons of seals inscribed with characters resembling the Cyprio-Minoan script of the thirteenth and twelfth centuries used in Cyprus and elsewhere in the eastern Mediterranean, including Deir 'Alla east of the Jordan (where some Philistine pottery has also been found) and Ugarit. This is the first written material to be found in a definitely Philistine context, and therefore the first archaeological evidence concerning the Philistine language. The seals date to the eleventh century B.C. Unfortunately, this writing system has yet to be deciphered, so that though we now have data which may bear on the language of the Philistines (although the presence of the seals in Philistine levels does not prove their inscriptions to be Philistine), exactly what those data are must await further developments!*

It should be noted that another piece of inscriptional material found at Ashdod, a potsherd with the Hebrew-Phoenician letters *(h)pḥr* ("[the] potter"?) scratched on it, suggests that at least by the eighth century the Philistine language, whatever its nature, had passed out of use at Ashdod and been replaced by a native Semitic dialect. Together with the evidence of the Semitic names of later Philistine rulers and of all known Philistine

*In the summer of 1966 the so-called Carian leather manuscripts from near Hebron came into the possession of the Department of Antiquities of the Hashemite Kingdom of Jordan. It has been suggested that the language of these documents is Philistine, but this supposition is far from certain. Cf. *Annual of the Department of Antiquities of Jordan* XV (1970), pp. 39–40.

Philistine citadel remains at Ashdod.

deities the material on this potsherd suggests there was a strong tendency to assimilate to the local Canaanite culture. (The "Ashododite" speech of Nehemiah 13:24 may well have been a local Semitic—Canaanite or Aramaic—dialect.)

Other interesting finds from the Philistine period at Ashdod include an intriguing group of small figurines. These feature extremely long necks and beak noses and, most strikingly, lower bodies stylized in the form of a four-legged table or couch. All the figurines are female, and there may be connections with Mycenaean mother-goddess figures depicted as seated on a chair. These figurines apparently represent a Philistine motif that persisted into the period of assimilation in later centuries, for a number of small broken offering tables of the ninth and eighth centuries show unmistakable resemblances to them, though none of these tables has been preserved with the upper (figurine) part intact.

Another object suggesting the continuation of some Philistine themes in a Canaanizing environment is one of the most appealing finds at Ashdod, a small terra-cotta libation stand with the figures of five musicians molded and carved on it. The musicians, with their droll, bulbous-eyed and large-nosed faces, are playing cymbals, pipes, a tambourine, and perhaps a lyre, and a procession of animals marches around the stand above them. They are reminiscent of both earlier and later figures at Ashdod, and the painted decoration on the stand, which was found in stratum 10, still shows characteristic Philistine features.

Stratum 10, however, is the level which attests to the end of the purely Philistine culture at Ashdod. It dates to the late eleventh-early tenth century B.C., and displays a complete changeover of material culture and building layout from the three preceding Philistine strata. No longer does the distinctive Philistine pottery appear; its place is taken by pottery types

Philistine ritual stand, decorated with four figures from Tell Qasile on the outskirts of Tel Aviv. The stand was discovered in 1972.

found elsewhere in Palestine at this period. There can be little doubt that this alteration is the result of the final victories of King David.

Yet the city of Ashdod continued, and even increased in size. It should be remembered that though Israelite kings broke the Philistines' hold over Palestine, the five Philistine cities themselves were never incorporated into Israelite territory, and periodic clashes continued until the autonomy of both was swept away by the great Middle Eastern empires (cf. I Kings 15:27; II Chron. 28:18; etc.).

In tenth-century Ashdod, a settlement outside the acropolis area already tentatively begun in the last Philistine period was enclosed by a wall, and by the ninth century this lower city had expanded to some size. A sacred area of the ninth and eighth centuries was found in the lower city, with an interesting group of cult vessels known as *kernoi*. These are hollow pottery rings with attachments in the form of cups and animal heads. Apparently they were for use in some ritual involving the pouring of a liquid into the cups and then out through the animal heads. From this period also come the above-mentioned offering tables which resemble the unusual table-figurines of the Philistine period. A continuing musical tradition is indicated by a small eighth-century figurine of a man playing a lyre.

In the eighth century, Philistia fell increasingly under Judean domination (II Chron. 26:6). Subsequently the region slipped under Assyrian control. Ashdod and the other cities were forced to pay tribute to the Assyrians, but not infrequently one or more of them would rebel against their overlord. Finally, in 712 B.C., Sargon II, according to both his own records and the Bible (Isa. 20:1), sent his commander-in-chief against Ashdod, captured it, and reduced it to an Assyrian province. These literary notices are confirmed by the discovery at Ashdod of a stele of Sargon II, commemorating his victory over a number of principalities. The stele is in three fragments, and much of it is missing, including any reference there may have been to Ashdod itself. Nevertheless, the stele's presence points to the historicity of the great king's conquest, and indeed the series of destructions and rebuildings of the gate of the lower city coordinates well with the successive conquests of the city by Uzziah (II Chron. 26:6), Sargon, and Nebuchadnezzar.

Ashdod never again regained its independence, continuing as first a Babylonian and then a Persian province. In Hellenistic times it became known as Azotus, and so it is called in the Books of the Maccabees and in the New Testament. After its conquest by the Hasmoneans, Ashdod gradually declined in importance, losing place to Azotus Paralius (coastal Azotus) to the west.

Philistine power in the Middle East was of brief duration, and their impact on world history virtually nil in comparison with that of Israel and Judah; their one enduring monument was their name, which became attached to the coastal area in which they lived and gradually to the whole country, for "Palestine" is derived from "Philistine."

SUGGESTED TOPICS FOR FURTHER STUDY

1. Israel and the Philistines.
2. Philistine origins—archaeological and literary evidence.
3. The culture and religion of the Philistines.
4. The Philistine cities after David.

RECOMMENDED READING

Burns, A. R., *Minoans, Philistines, and Greeks, B.C. 1400–900* (London: Dawsons, 1968).

Dothan, M., *Ashdod, a City of the Philistine Pentapolis," Archaeology* 20 (1967), pp. 178–86.

———, "Ashdod of the Philistines" in *New Directions in Biblical Archaeology,* ed. D. N. Freedman and J. C. Greenfield (Garden City, NY: Doubleday, 1969), pp. 15–24.

———, "The Musicians of Ashdod," *Archaeology* 23 (1970), pp. 310–11.

———, and D. N. Freedman, *Ashdod I, Atiqot* 7 (1967).

Greenfield, Jonas C., "Philistines" in *Encyclopedia Judaica* (Jerusalem: Keter, 1971), vol. 13, vols. 399–404.

Hindson, Edward E., *The Philistines and the Old Testament* (Grand Rapids: Baker, 1971).

Macalister, R. A. S., *The Philistines: Their History and Civilization* (London: British Academy, 1914; reprint: Chicago, 1965).

Mitchell, T. C., "Philistia" in *Archaeology and Old Testament Study,* ed. D. Winton Thomas (Oxford: Clarendon, 1967), pp. 404–27.

Wright, G. E., "Fresh Evidence for the Philistine Story," *Biblical Archaeologist* 29 (1966), pp. 70–86.

The yearly excavation reports by M. Dothan in the *Israel Exploration Journal* 18–22 (1968–72) should be consulted for the finds at Ashdod in the seasons after 1965 (see the *For Further Reading* section). At this writing, no publication volume for these seasons has appeared.

FOR FURTHER READING

Avi-Yonah, M., and M. Dothan, "Ashdod" in *Encyclopedia Judaica* (Jerusalem: Keter, 1971), vol. 3, vols. 695–97.

Dothan, M., "The Foundation of Tel Mor and of Ashdod," *Israel Exploration Journal* 23 (1973), pp. 1–17.

———, "Tel Ashdod," *Israel Exploration Journal* 18 (1968), pp. 253–54; 19 (1969), pp. 243–45; 20 (1970), pp. 119–20; 21 (1971), p. 175; 22 (1972), pp. 166–67, 243–44.

13

The Bar Kochba Discoveries

The Jewish revolt against Rome from A.D. 132 to 135 was not recorded in detail by any second-century historian, yet it was an extremely interesting and important event in Jewish history. It was the last fight for Jewish independence that took place in Palestine until the recent War of Independence in 1947–48, and one can speculate that the course of Jewish history might have been quite different had the revolt succeeded. Until now, the only information we had about the revolt and its leader Simon Bar Kochba was given us in the Talmud and in brief references in other works. It is possible that in the Talmud much legend has been woven in with the facts.

In 1951 and 1952, as a result of archaeological excavations, the first actual physical evidence of the revolt was found—several bundles of papyrus and leather which contained contracts and documents dating from about A.D. 132. Especially interesting was the discovery of two letters sent by Simon Bar Kochba, one of which was probably written or dictated by him, and contains his signature. All these discoveries were made in the Wadi Murabbaat caves in Jordan, about eighteen kilometers (eleven miles) south of Qumran, where the first Dead Sea Scrolls were discovered in 1947.

After the discovery and excavation of the Murabbaat caves, the area south of Qumran and further inland near En Gedi was explored. Expeditions were made to the area around En Gedi in 1953, 1955, 1959, 1960, and 1961; the archaeologists uncovered numerous manuscripts, tools, household articles, implements of

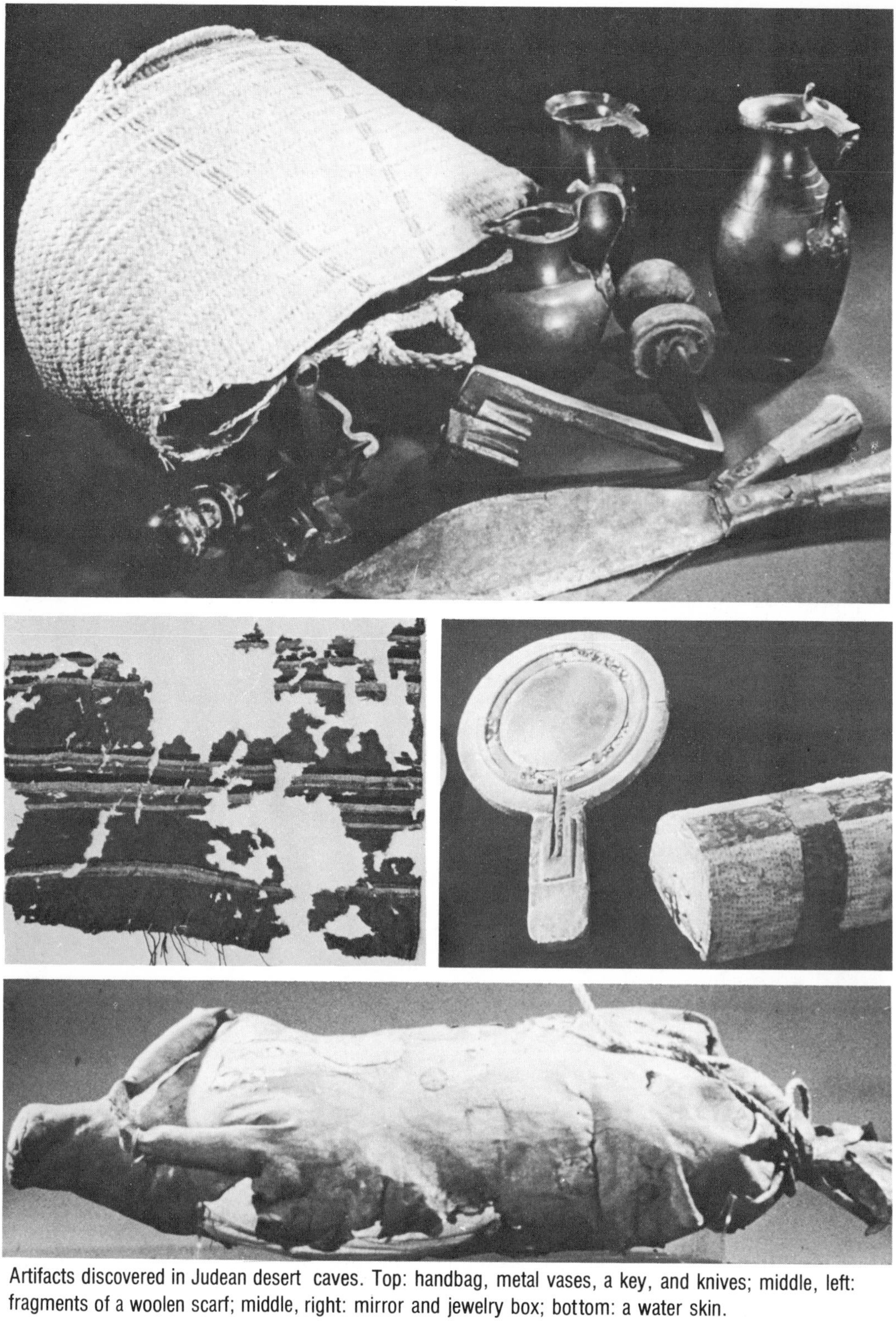

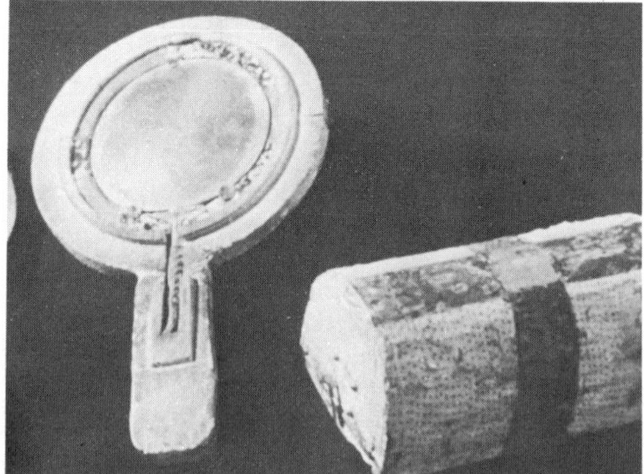

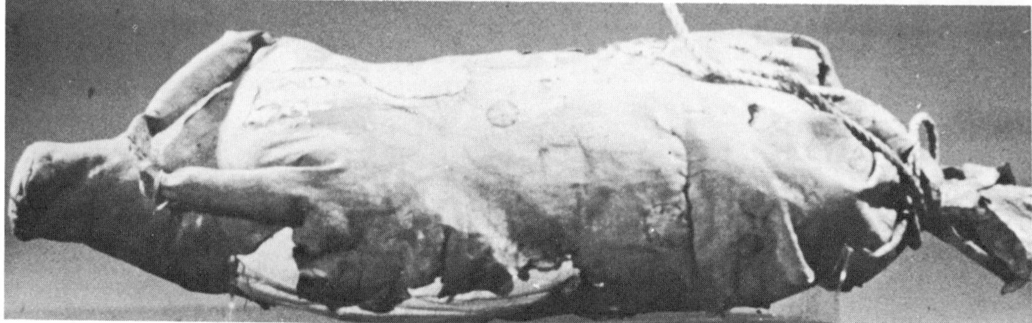

Artifacts discovered in Judean desert caves. Top: handbag, metal vases, a key, and knives; middle, left: fragments of a woolen scarf; middle, right: mirror and jewelry box; bottom: a water skin.

war, and many skeletons, all dating from the period of the second Jewish revolt against Rome. The finds in 1960 and 1961 were the first discoveries from this period to come out of the Israeli part of the Judean desert. The 1960 expedition yielded fifteen letters written to or by Bar Kochba as well as two parchment fragments of Exodus which were inserted in phylacteries and date from the first century. The expedition in 1961 yielded a great deal of material. Nearly fifty papyri and a number of tools, baskets, textiles, and so forth were found. The documents have been deciphered, and all are from the time of the second revolt or prior to it. Many are legal documents: bills of sale, contracts, and deeds. The complete story is to be found in Yigael Yadin's book *Bar Kochba,* published in 1971 (see the bibliography). All these finds serve to increase our knowledge of that obscure time.

Historical Background

The basic causes of the uprising in 132 can easily be surmised. Roman rule was harsh and oppressive and Judea's poverty made the severe burdens imposed on the people even more unendurable. Although the Emperor Hadrian began his reign with a benevolent attitude toward the Jews, he later refused to permit the rebuilding of the temple. Subsequently he decided to prohibit circumcision and the observance of the Jewish religion. This caused relations between Jews and the Roman government to become severely strained. They reached the breaking point with Hadrian's decision to rebuild Jerusalem as a heathen city, Aelia Capitolina. Such an explosive situation needed only a spark and a capable leader to ignite it.

Such a leader was found in Simon Bar Kochba, whose real name, we learn from letters which have been found, was Simon Bar Kosiba. He was proclaimed messianic king by Rabbi Akiba and renamed Bar Kochba ("son of a star"). In its early stages his uprising against the Romans was completely successful. The Romans were driven out of Judea, Jerusalem was captured, the sacrificial cult was apparently restored, the "Freedom of Israel" was officially proclaimed, and Jewish coins were once again struck.

However, in 133 the Romans counterattacked with an army of thirty-five thousand men under Hadrian and his commander, Julius Severus. Talmudic extracts suggest that they first entered Galilee, then fought actions for the Valley of Jezreel, Ephraim, and the Judean hills, and eventually retook Jerusalem. In 134–35 the Romans besieged Bar Kochba's last stronghold, Bethar, and gradually reduced the remaining hill and cave strongholds. Bethar fell to the Romans soon after, and Bar Kochba was killed. Virtually the whole population of Bethar was slaughtered, including school children who, according to an eyewitness account, were wrapped in their study scrolls and burned to death. Records speak of the destruction of fifty fortresses and 985 villages during the war, and of 580,000 Jewish casualties besides those who died of hunger and disease. As a result of the revolt, Judea fell into desolation, its population was annihilated, and Jerusalem was turned into a heathen city barred to Jews.

The First Discoveries

In 1950 and 1951 documents dating from the period of the revolt were found in two areas by Bedouin of the Ta'amireh tribe. In 1951 they brought to Jerusalem a group of manuscripts they had found the preceding summer in caves in the Wadi Murabbaat. In addition they brought other fragments which were described by scholars as coming from an "unknown source." It is now known that the material did in fact come from a cave north of Masada in Israeli territory.

The Wadi Murabbaat caves are situated about twenty-five kilometers southeast of Jerusalem. On the basis of the information given by the Bedouin, Father R. de Vaux and G. L. Harding, two archaeologists who had been working with the Dead Sea Scrolls from the very beginning, excavated the Wadi Murabbaat area in 1952. They found two letters addressed by Simon Bar Kochba to Yehoshua ben Galgola, and in 1953 they found a letter written to Bar Kochba from two officials of a Jewish community, as well as many other documents from about A.D. 125 to 135. Among these documents were real estate transactions, a bill of divorce, and contracts dealing with the renting of fields and guaranteed by the authority of Bar Kochba. Many of the documents found are published in Yadin's *Bar Kochba.*

One of the letters addressed by Simon Bar Kochba to Yehoshua ben Galgola was probably written in his own hand, as there is a resemblance between the script in which the text was written and that of the signature. The letter is signed "Simon, son of Kosibah," and reads as follows:

> Simon, son of Kosibah, to Yehoshua, son of Galgola, and to the men of Kephar Habbaruk, greetings. I take Heaven as witness against me [that] if anyone of the Galileans who are among you should be ill-treated, I will put fetters on your feet as I did to Ben-Aphlul.

There are many lacunae in the letter and the second sentence has also been translated: "I call Heaven to witness against me [that if] of the Galileans who are at your place there should be missing even a single one, I will put fetters on your feet, as Akiba [did] to Ben-Aphlul."

There is speculation as to who the Galileans were—Christians, or members of a Galilean sect that lived in the neighborhood of Khirbet Qumran, or Jewish refugees from Galilee. The ill-treatment they suffered can easily be explained if we assume that, as the food shortage (of which other documents inform us) grew harsher, non-Judeans received a biased treatment.

This letter acquaints us with the original form of the name on which the Bar Kochba of our sources is based. It confirms the fact that Simon was his first name, which until now had only been inferred from the name *Simon* on certain ones. The letter also shows that Hebrew was used at least for official letters, and demonstrates the influence of Aramaic on the Hebrew of this period.

The Israeli authorities had been suspicious for some time that Jordanian Bedouin had helped themselves to the contents of caves in Israel. To check these suspicions, Yohanan Aharoni of the Hebrew University set out with a unit of soldiers in 1953 and discovered a number of caves in the hills about one thousand feet above sea level. The parachutists found bat droppings and cigarettes, shreds of Bedouin clothing and firearms, in addition to some documents. In 1955, Aharoni led a new expedition to the wadi known as Nahal Hever. This area is slightly south of Wadi Murabbaat. The expedition found dozens of well-preserved skeletons of adults and children. Other finds in this area made it clear that this was one of the hideouts of the Bar Kochba rebels after they had been driven into the mountains by the Roman legions.

The tools, inscriptions, and documents found in 1955 showed that rather than surrender to the legionnaires who were besieging them, the rebels slowly starved to death in the caves after their supplies had given out. The Hebrew University, the Israel Exploration Society and the Government Antiquities Department, anxious to forestall further raids on the caves, sponsored an expedition in 1960 to follow up the 1955 expedition.

The 1960 Expedition

The time elapsing between the two expeditions was so great because the caves were extremely hard to enter and to explore, and the expedition was both difficult and expensive. The area was within easy shooting distance from Jordan, and no expedition was possible without an armed escort and helicopters. Prior to the expedition helicopters had to photograph the area, as the caves are in canyons as deep as four hundred yards and the caves along the cliff faces are not visible from the top. From the films the leaders of the expedition were able to decide which openings might be the mouths of caves.

The expedition was led by Yadin, N. Avigad, Aharoni, and P. Bar-Adon. The army provided the expedition with scouts and engineering and liaison units, in addition to equipment. To this force were added some tens of students and kibbutz members.

Artifacts discovered in the Judean desert caves in 1961.

One large cave in the Nahal Hever had three chambers which yielded several important finds. A burial niche was found in the third chamber: along the right-hand wall of the chamber, there was a collection of baskets overflowing with skulls, and in the far corner was layer upon layer of large mats covering human bones. Between the mats and the bones were a great many fragments of colored cloth. In the center of the niche was another burial basket covered by large pieces of colored cloth. These bones of three men, eight women, and six children were probably the remains of some of Bar Kochba's warriors and their families who died of starvation. In the first chamber of the cave, a woven basket containing Roman cult vessels was unearthed. In the basket were twelve jugs, a cult pan, three incense shovels, bowls, and a key. Some of the figures of Roman deities stamped on the handles appeared to have been deliberately rubbed out. These vessels were probably booty taken by Bar Kochba's fighters from a Roman camp before they were forced to flee to the caves (it is known that the Roman legions went into battle carrying all the equipment needed for ritual purposes, for sacrifices and libations).

Biblical Psalms and Bar Kochba's Letters

In the last few days of the expedition, several of the most important finds were made. The first of these was a scroll fragment of Chapter 15 and the beginning of 16 from the Book of Psalms. This fragment dates to about the second half of the first century A.D., and contains possibly the oldest extant version of these psalms. The text is identical with the Masoretic version. Very close to the end of the expedition another valuable find was made—fifteen Bar Kochba letters were found in a goatskin water bottle. Nine are in Aramaic, four in Hebrew, and two in Greek. The letters are in varying states of preservation, and some are in extremely good condition. One of the letters is inscribed on four wooden tablets and the rest are on papyrus.

The letter on wood consists of orders given by Bar Kochba to his adjutants; it is the first discovery in Israel of an inscription on wood from this period. The letter is signed Shmuel Bar Ami. As the signature is in a different handwriting from that employed in the body of the letter, we may assume that the signatory was not the writer of the letter, but rather served as Bar Kochba's adjutant, dictating letters to a scribe on his chief's behalf.

Of the papyri, which were opened by Professor Biberkraut of the Hebrew University, the first four turned out to be more letters from Bar Kochba. The first unfortunately was written on papyrus that had been used before. The original writing had been rubbed out with a wet sponge and the surface used again. In order to save the papyrus, this custom was widespread during this period throughout the East. The third papyrus, which measured about eight by twelve centimeters, contained inscriptions written in a firm and still distinct hand. In it, Shimon commands Yehonatan Bar Ba'yah to do whatever Elisha commands. We do not know who Elisha was.

Among the letters opened after these first four:

(1) One orders both Yehonatan and Masabala bar Shimon to send "Elazar Bar Hittah immediately" and to reap the benefits of the property of this man.

(2) Another letter tells Yehonatan and Masabala "to harvest the ripened wheat of the winter" and to send it to a specified person.

(3) Another letter, giving instructions to the same two men, confirms Yadin's belief that the letters belong to the period before the rebels took refuge in the caves, since it deals with such matters as crops, fields, and houses. This letter also establishes the fact that the rebel headquarters was at En Gedi, less than four miles north of Nahal Hever where the letters were found. In this letter, Bar Kochba writes:

> You, Yehonatan bar Ba'yah and Masabala bar Shimon, and people of En Gedi, are sitting in comfort, eating and drinking the property of the house of Israel, and are not concerning yourselves about supplies for your fellow brethren.

Yadin assumes that these letters were written while Yehonatan and Masabala ruled over an area which contained fields of wheat, and that upon taking refuge in the caves, they brought with them the letters of their commander, Bar Kochba. One letter deals with the *lulav* and *etrog,* ritual articles needed for the holiday of Succot. In the Greek letters we have Bar Kochba's name for the first time in Greek; it is spelled Kosiba or Koziba. All the letters confirm the rabbinic stories that Bar Kochba was a stern and ruthless commander. He was undoubtedly a pious man concerned just as much with religious observance as with his fight against the Romans. He may also have been a supreme egotist—he described himself as "prince over all Israel."

The 1961 Expedition

In 1961 an expedition led by the same four archaeologists went to explore the area further. They found nearly fifty papyri, together with numerous tools, household items, and women's possessions, as well as five door keys, one of them particularly large, which are believed to have been the keys of the En Gedi fortress which the rebels abandoned. The papyri were found in a leather pouch and a goatskin bag; one was rolled up inside a hollowed-out reed.

Three of the documents from the leather pouch are contracts in elegant Mishnaic Hebrew covering the lease of land in En Gedi by Bar Kochba through an administrator; they are dated "in the third year of Shimon Ben Kosiba, prince over Israel." Payment is detailed in Roman and Jewish money. The document from the reed is poorly preserved, and so only partly deciphered, but deals with the sale of a vegetable garden in En Gedi.

The bundle of papyri found in the goatskin water bag belonged to a woman named Babata, and pertained to her legal affairs—which were extensive and complicated, since she had had two husbands and was involved in property disputes and the guardianship of her fatherless son, Yeshua. Most of the thirty-five documents were in Greek, but some were in Aramaic and Nabatean. Their dates can be fixed with some precision. Typical of them is a contract regarding the guardianship of the orphan Yeshua, son of Babata, the daughter of Shimon. There were two guardians, a Jew and a Nabatean. Each signed his name in his own language. The contract is dated in the ninth year of the Emperor Hadrian, that is, A.D. 125. These documents clarify much about the legal system of the times, and explain many heretofore obscure references in the Talmud.

The 1961 expedition found skeletons in all the caves, mostly of women and children, a phenomenon suggesting the majority of the men had already been killed in battle outside the caves. Some of the skeletons were in wooden coffins, one of which, according to Avigad, was of a type not previously found in Israel.

Among the fragments of Hebrew and Greek papyri found by Aharoni's group were pieces of a scroll containing the Book of Jonah in Greek, in a text different from the Septuagint. Parts of the same scroll (which included the Minor Prophets) had been published in 1953 by P. Barthelemy without indication of their origin. It is now clear that they had been taken from this cave by Bedouin.

Equally important, but unrelated to the Bar Kochba period, was a spectacular find of objects from the Chalcolithic period (ca. 3500 B.C.) made by Bar-Adon. It has been described as of worldwide importance, providing a link with the civilizations of the same period in the Caucasus and Anatolia. Found were 429 objects, mainly of bronze and copper, ornamented with geometric patterns and beautifully sculpted ibex and deer and distinguished by extraordinary technical perfection and beauty. The study of the finds is not yet completed, and while certain of the objects can be identified, for example, mace-heads, chisels,

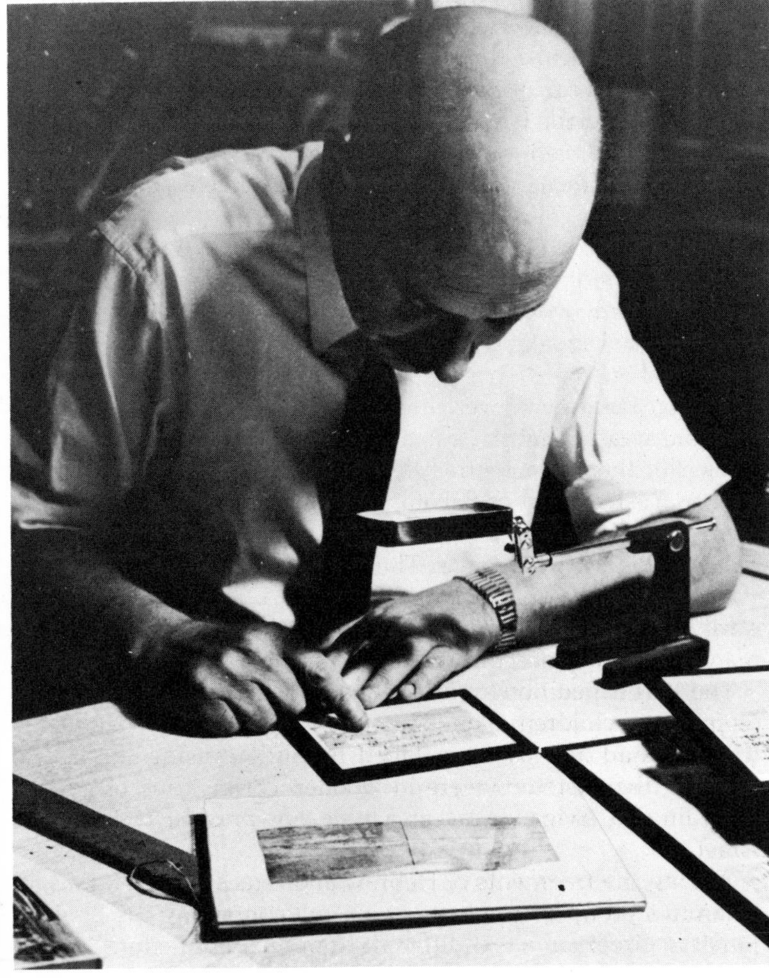

Yigael Yadin, Israeli archaeologist, examines one of the Bar Kochba letters.

axes, adzes and hammers, many are of a sort never before found, and even their purpose is unknown.

Significance of the Bar Kochba Finds

As a result of these expeditions, the world of Bar Kochba and his rebels is steadily being reconstructed. For the first time we have actual documents from that period. Before we had many legends but a paucity of historical facts.

We now know for certain that, after the rebels' capture of about fifty towns, they were crushed by Hadrian's troops under Julius Severus. He pushed them to their last refuge among the caves of the Judean wilderness by the Dead Sea. The Romans, knowing the caves were well-stocked with food and natural cisterns, sat down at both ends of the valleys leading into the cave areas and waited. Rather than surrender, the rebels stayed put, and died of starvation. This uprising was the last major revolt by the Jews against an established authority for eighteen centuries, until the Warsaw Ghetto revolted against the Nazis in 1943.

We learn from the letters that Bar Kochba's authority might have been a little weak in the provinces, and that he probably had his headquarters in the vicinity of Bethlehem. We also learn the importance of En Gedi as a port. Supplies must have come from the southern or eastern shores of the Dead Sea to En Gedi on the western bank, to be transferred inland to the troops fighting the Romans.

We learn of the religious fervor of the rebels from the record of their preparation for the holiday of Succot and from the fact that the garments found were made entirely of wool (strict Jewish observance forbids mixing animal and vegetable fibers in a garment). We learn of a new figure in Jewish history—Botniya Bar Miasa, who is given the name *Rabenu,* a name given in other sources only to Moses and Judah. Bar Miasa must have been a great spiritual leader, probably head of the Sanhedrin, about whom all records have been lost.

Yadin feels that the letters were written before the flight to the caves because some of them deal with the village of Tekoah which at the time of the last stand in the caves was already in Roman hands. Also the fact that some of the letters concern grain harvest indicates that the Jews still possessed some land when they were written. The collector of the letters must have prized them highly to have carried them along to the caves and deposited them among the women's belongings where they were not likely to be found by the Romans.

The many household items, personal items, war items, and documents give us much new and valuable information on how people lived in Palestine some eighteen hundred years ago. This was a period of Jewish history which until now was filled with many gaps for the historian and archaeologist.

SUGGESTED TOPICS FOR FURTHER STUDY

1. Bar Kochba and the causes of the second Jewish revolt.
2. Major finds of the Bar Kochba excavations.
3. Content and significance of the Bar Kochba letters.
4. The Bar Kochba finds and legal terminology in the Talmud.
5. Rabbi Akiba and Bar Kochba.

FOR FURTHER READING

Benoit, P., J. T. Milik and R. de Vaux, *Les Grottes de Murabba'at* (*Discoveries in the Judaean Desert II*) (Oxford: Clarendon, 1961).

Fitzmyer, Joseph A., "The Bar Kochba Period," *Saint Mary's Theology Studies* I (1962), pp. 133–68.

Fuks, A., "Aspects of the Jewish Revolt in AD 115–117," *The Journal of Roman Studies* 51 (1961), pp. 98–104.

Israel Exploration Journal 11 (1961) and 12 (1962). The entire issues are devoted to Bar Kochba finds.

Mansoor, Menahem, *The Dead Sea Scrolls* (Grand Rapids: Eerdmans, 1964).

Mantel, H., "The Causes of the Bar Kochba Revolt," *The Jewish Quarterly Review* 58 (1968), pp. 224–42, 274–96.

Raphael, Ch., *The Walls of Jerusalem* (New York: Chatto & Windus, 1968).

Ussishkin, D., "The 'Ghassulian' Temple in Ein Gedi and the Origin of the Hoard from Nahal Mishmar," *Biblical Archaeologist* 34 (1971), pp. 23–39, figs. 10–23 (on the Chalcolithic finds).

Yadin, Yigael, *Bar Kochba: The Rediscovery of the Legendary Hero of the Last Jewish Revolt Against Imperial Rome* (London: Weidenfeld and Nicolson, 1971).

______, *The Finds from the Bar Kochba Period in the Cave of Letters* (*Judean Desert Studies I*) (Jerusalem: Israel Exploration Society, 1963).

______, "New Discoveries in the Judean Desert," *Biblical Archaeologist* 24 (1961), Nos. 2 and 3.

______, "The Secrets in the Cliffs: The Discovery of the Bar-Kochba Letters," *The Atlantic Monthly*, Nov. 1961, pp. 129–35.

14

Beer-sheba

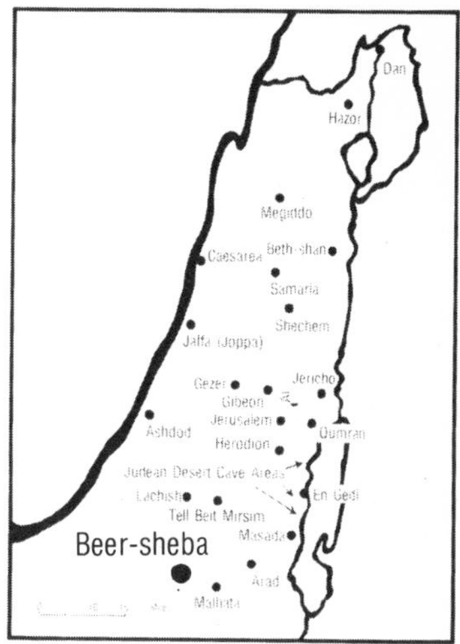

Tell Beer-sheba is situated about five miles east of the modern city of Beer-sheba. The Arabic name, Tell as-Sab[c], and the fact that it is the only true city-mound in the area confirm its identification as the biblical Beer-sheba. Surrounded by the Hebron and Beer-sheba wadis, the tell lies a few miles north of the Negev—the desert which divided Egypt and Israel in the time of the patriarchs. During the Israelite period, Beer-sheba formed the southern tip of the border and defined the expanse of the kingdom, as referred to in the biblical expression, "from Dan to Beer-sheba."

Soundings of the site were carried out in 1962 by R. Gophna on behalf of the Israel Department of Antiquities but the actual excavations were begun in 1969. The archaeological expedition began as an educational project by the Institute of Archaeology of Tel Aviv University, and was under the direction of Professor Yohanan Aharoni. These excavations are not to be confused with the work of J. Perrot at Tell Abu Matar, the site of a Chalcolithic village near Beer-sheba, from 1952 to 1954.

The ancient city of Beer-sheba figures in the Bible from the time of Abraham and Isaac who dug wells there and made alliances with Abimelech, the king of Gerar (Gen. 21:31; 26:33). Together Abraham and Abimelech pledged an oath and, as a sign of good faith, Abraham set aside seven ewes. From this incident the Bible explains the origin of the city's name, a combination of *Beer* ("well") and *sheba* ("oath" or "seven"). This is

Plan of Beer-sheba at the close of the sixth season of excavations.

Ancient well, excavated at Beer-sheba. Note the location on the plan of the tell.

also the place of the sanctified well near which Abraham planted a tamarisk tree and worshiped on the high place (Gen. 21:33). These wells are located near the dry river beds and most probably were reached by a tunnel from the city. So far, only the steps leading to the shaft of the tunnel have been uncovered in the eastern corner of the city. This entrance to the water system closely resembles those at Megiddo and Hazor.

The earliest occupation in the area is evidenced by Chalcolithic cave remains from the fourth millennium B.C., but the actual settlement of the tell appears to date only from the twelfth or eleventh century B.C. This premonarchial village may be identical with the one mentioned in connection with the judicial activities of Samuel's sons (I Sam. 8:2). The actual fortification of the site dates to the tenth century B.C., but the city underwent a destruction in that century, probably as the result of the Palestinian campaign of Pharaoh Shishak, and again the ninth century. The fortified tell suffered massive destruction about a century before the downfall of the kingdom of Judah, probably due to the campaign of Sennacherib against King Hezekiah. The city was not actually reconstructed thereafter; however, evidence of minor repairs to the city wall had been uncovered. Evidence in the surrounding area indicates that occupation continued into the Byzantine period. Occupation in the Persian period is supported by the Bible, for Beer-sheba and its villages are mentioned among the villages of Judah in Nehemiah 11:27. Evidently there were civilian dwellings scattered over an area near the tell and the wells, but the citadel itself was nothing more than a royal military post atop the tell.

The major efforts of the excavation concentrated on the Israelite period when the fortified city itself was first settled (ca. the tenth century B.C.). Tell Malhata and Tell Arad were also built in this period, and with Beer-sheba they formed a chain of fortifications on the desert border of the United Kingdom of the Hebrews. Because of its strategic position, one of the main concerns of the city dwellers of Beer-sheba was security, and the excavations have uncovered a carefully planned defense system. The fortifications include a rampart, six to seven meters high, which provided a full view of the entire surrounding area. It was constructed in the Hyksos manner, with layers of red wadi material, pebbles, and earth, and covered by a glacis or sloping bank of earth. A deep moat encircled the rampart, making the approach even more difficult. Beer-sheba was further strengthened by two kinds of city walls—the earlier Solomonic wall, a solid four meters thick, and a casemate wall partitioned into chambers. The latter was probably built by either Uzziah or

Hezekiah, eighth-century B.C. Judean monarchs. One reason for the strength of Beer-sheba's fortifications is noted in the Arad documents which indicate that the city served as the royal administrative center of the south.

In the Israelite period, Beer-sheba was encircled by one street which originated at the gate. The excavations uncovered the entire gate, which measured fourteen by seventeen meters with a four-meter-wide gateway. An incense altar was discovered in the open area of the gate, probably belonging to the *bamah* ("high place") of the gate entrance. A similar *bamah* was also found next to the gate entrance at Dan, establishing another link with Beer-sheba as a border city. The existence of such Israelite shrines is mentioned in the Bible. King Josiah attempted to purify the religion of Judah "from Geba to Beer-sheba," and he "broke down the high places of the gates that were at the entering in of the gate" (II Kings 23:8).

Two streets begin at the gate and lead to the raised area at the center of the tell. Here, it seems most probable, public buildings were erected, and the cultic nature of the finds reveals the presence of a sanctuary. In the debris of the buildings, Aharoni uncovered beads, amulets, ostrich eggs, a faience bowl and a number of bronze objects, including a form of the double crown of Egypt along with the figure of a goddess and a miniature sphinx. Another important find among these objects was a votive cylinder seal on which was depicted a deity with a worshiper standing before him. The inscription on the object has been the basis of an inference that the seal is of Aramaic origin, either from Syria or Transjordan in the ninth to seventh centuries B.C. In another area an Iron Age crater was discovered which bore the Hebrew letters *qdš* (*qodesh*), the word meaning "holiness." Perhaps this vessel once contained a worshiper's votive offering. Many zoomorphic vessels and figures of animals were among the finds, all associated with the ritual and cult practices of the Israelites at Beer-sheba.

An extraordinary find of the fifth season of excavations (1973) was a horned altar. Unlike the small horned altars, such as those found in the Megiddo and Tell Dan excavations, the Beer-sheba altar consisted of several ashlar blocks. These cut stones had been dismantled and reused in a repaired section of the storehouse complex on the tell. The four altar horns were found arranged one beside the other in the wall, three intact and the fourth broken. Other blocks of similar stone were found nearby, and in 1976 additional blocks were found so that almost the entire altar has now been recovered and reconstructed. The dismantling and reuse of the altar has been assigned to the reign

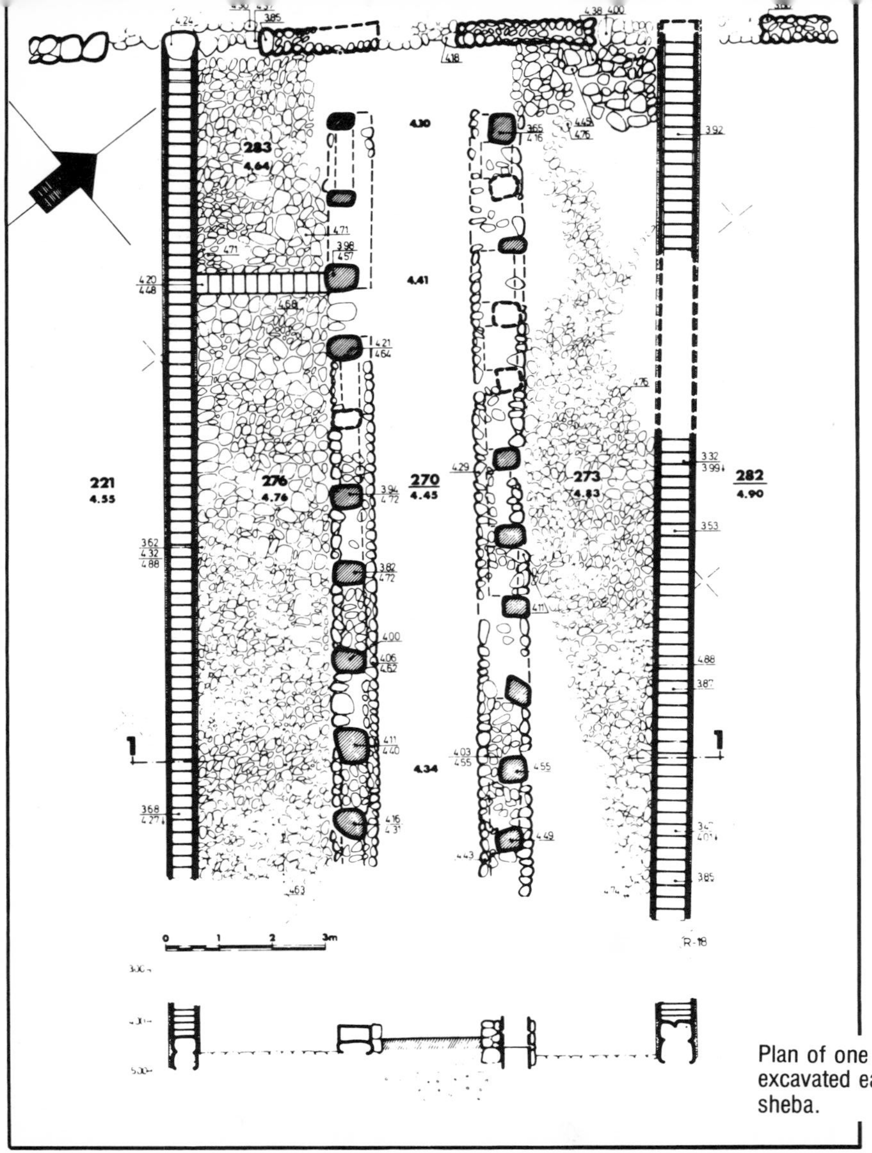

Plan of one of the storehouses excavated east of the gate of Beer-sheba.

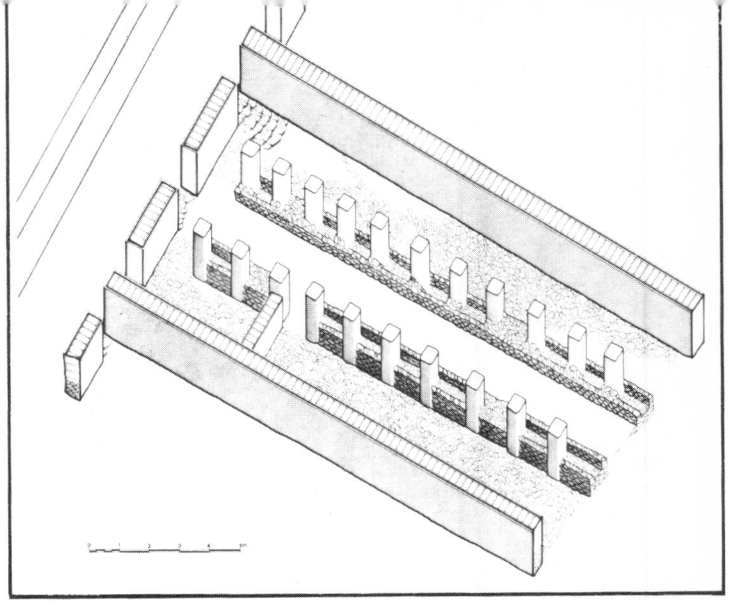

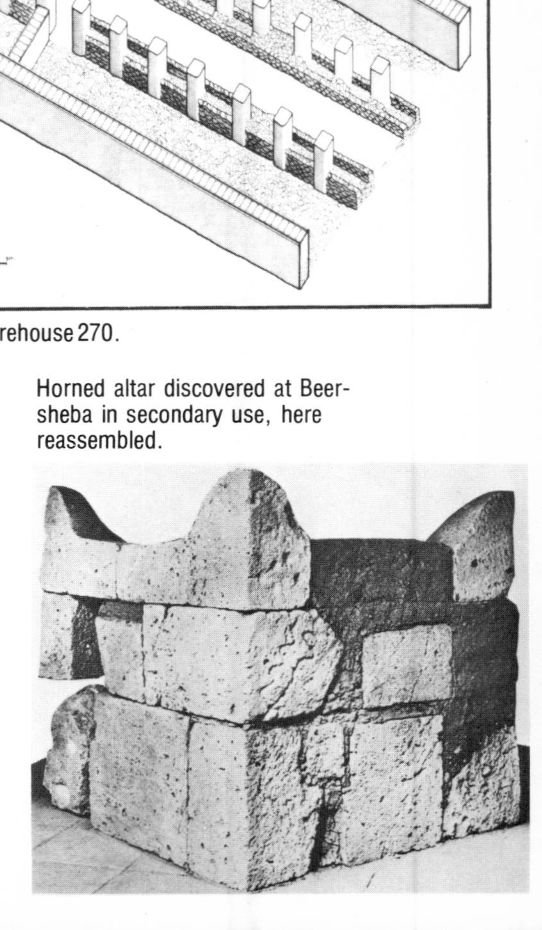

Isometric drawing of Storehouse 270.

Horned altar discovered at Beer-sheba in secondary use, here reassembled.

of Hezekiah, near the end of the eighth century B.C. II Kings 18:22 records that he instituted a reform which included the removal of altars outside Jerusalem and an insistence upon worship at the Jerusalem sanctuary alone. The large public building which the excavators uncovered in the northwestern corner of the city was probably the Beer-sheba temple.

In the light of the finds mentioned above, Aharoni suggested that the Beer-sheba temple served as a border sanctuary in the period of the monarchy as did the temple at Arad, which he also excavated. He has noted one important difference, however: the pagan nature of the cult objects uncovered at Beer-sheba shows a strong foreign influence, mainly Egyptian, in contrast with the finds at the Arad sanctuary which reveal a purer form of Israelite worship. The difference caused Amos to denounce the worship at Beer-sheba along with the deviant religious practices at Dan and Beth-el, the two northern border cities in which Jeroboam set up the golden calves (Amos 5:5; 8:14). This raises one of the major issues which has emerged from the excavations—the question of the role of these border sanctuaries in Israelite worship and history. The issue can be resolved only through further research.

SUGGESTED TOPICS FOR FURTHER STUDY

1. The Beer-sheba fortifications and the reasons for them.
2. The Beer-sheba discoveries and the history of Israelite religion.
3. Israelite border sanctuaries and Beer-sheba.
4. The "Capital of the Negev": Beer-sheba in the Bible.

RECOMMENDED READING

Aharoni, Yohanan, "Excavations at Tel Beer-sheba," *Biblical Archaeologist* 35 (1972), pp. 111–27.

———, "The Israelite Sanctuary at Arad" in *New Directions in Biblical Archaeology,* ed. D. N. Freedman and J. C. Greenfield (Garden City, NY: Doubleday, 1969), pp. 25–39.

"Beersheba" in *Encyclopedia Judaica* (Jerusalem: Keter, 1971), vol. 2, cols. 383–86.

"Beersheba" in *The Interpreter's Dictionary of the Bible,* ed. G. A. Buttrick (New York: Abingdon Press, 1962), vol. 1, pp. 375–76.

FOR FURTHER READING

Aharoni, Yohanan, "Nothing Early and Nothing Late: Re-Writing Israel's Conquest," *Biblical Archaeologist* 39 (1976), p. 55.

———, "Tel Beer-sheba," *Israel Exploration Journal* 19 (1969), pp. 245–47; 20 (1970), pp. 227–29; 21 (1971), pp. 230–32.

———, "Tel Beersheva," *Revue Biblique* 77 (1970), pp. 405–07.

Avi-Yonah, M., ed., *Encyclopedia of Archaeological Excavations in the Holy Land* (Jerusalem, 1975), vol. 1, pp. 74–89.

Beer-sheba I: Excavations at Tel Beer-sheba, 1969–1971 Seasons (Tel Aviv: Institute of Archaeology, Tel Aviv University, 1973).

Boyd, Bernard, "Excavations at Tell Beer-sheba, Israel, 1969–1970," *American Journal of Archaeology* 75 (1971), p. 196.

Gophna, R., "Beersheba," *Israel Exploration Journal* 13 (1963), p. 33.

Liphschitz, Nili, and Y. Waisel, "Dendroarchaeological Investigations in Israel, Tel Beersheba and Arad in the Northern and Eastern Negev," *Israel Exploration Journal* 23 (1973), pp. 30–36.

15

Tell Beit Mirsim

Tell Beit Mirsim is located about fifteen miles southwest of Hebron and fifteen miles northeast of Beer-sheba, near where the Judean hills and the lower-lying Shephelah run into the Negev wasteland.

In 1924, W. F. Albright came to the conclusion that the mound of Tell Beit Mirsim represents the remains of the biblical city of Debir, also known as Kirjath-sepher (Josh. 15:15). The size of the mound, its location, and the pottery strewn on its surface, as well as the fact that there seems to be no other tell in the vicinity which meets the requirements for Debir, all led him to this conclusion. In recent times this identification has been challenged by Galling, Kochavi, and others, who have located Debir elsewhere. Whether it is Debir or not, Tell Beit Mirsim does well exemplify the history of a town in southern Palestine from the end of the Early Bronze Age to the fall of the kingdom of Judah in 587 B.C.

The excavations at Tell Beit Mirsim were carried out in 1926, 1928, 1930, and 1932 by the American Schools of Oriental Research and Xenia Theological Seminary, under the direction of Albright and M. G. Kyle. The excavators kept in constant touch with other archaeologists working in Palestine, comparing finds and conclusions. The best techniques of the day, those of C. S. Fisher, were used, and Fisher himself was often consulted. The result was that the carefully reconstructed series of pottery types became the standard for Palestinian chronology, and the pottery-dating system was put on a firm footing. While no extraordinary finds were made at Tell Beit Mirsim, this establishment of the pottery chronology gave it an important place in the history of biblical archaeology.

The various occupational levels of the tell were all found to be clearly separated from one another by distinct layers of burning, which could usually be traced over most of the excavated area. This series of occupations and destructions made the stratification and history of the site all the easier to establish.

The town was founded about the twenty-third century B.C., in the Early Bronze III B period, and reoccupied in Middle Bronze I (ca. 1900 B.C.). In Middle Bronze II A (eighteenth century) a better-preserved occupation is found, with a thick city wall and at least one large house built on the "court" plan. This entails an enclosed court standing between the house proper and the street. This town was apparently destroyed by fire, but rebuilt by the same people.

Strata E and D at Tell Beit Mirsim represent the Hyksos period, Middle Bronze II B and C, from about 1700 to 1500 B.C. Here we find the typical Hyksos fortifications with stout revetments to the defensive walls. The town in this period was comparatively wealthy, owing to the expanding wealth of the Hyksos empire; a number of Hyksos scarabs were found. In stratum D (sixteenth century), a house of considerable enough proportions to be called a palace was uncovered; it was built on the "court" plan, with stables and storerooms apparently on the ground floor and living quarters on the second and third floors. The culture and religion of these people were illuminated by the finding of a carved snake goddess, evidently a fertility goddess, and a set of playing pieces consisting of five cones and five pyramids of blue faience and an ivory teetotum for use as a die. This level, the height of feudal Middle Bronze Age society at Tell Beit Mirsim, was completely destroyed in the late sixteenth century, apparently in the Egyptian reconquest of Palestine after their expulsion of the Hyksos. The site then lay in ruins, unoccupied, for perhaps as long as a century.

The town was not rebuilt until the fourteenth century. Its new inhabitants seem not to have included the very wealthy, Egyptian rule perhaps proving burdensome in its exactions. From this town (stratum C) come a number of Astarte figurines and, from a pit filled with the bones of sacrificial animals, a crudely carved stone lion along with a stone basin decorated with carved lions. The Canaanite cult in which these objects served is not certainly known; a building near the pit may have been its temple.

The tossing of the lion and lion basin into the refuse pit may possibly be attributed to the Israelites who captured and destroyed Tell Beit Mirsim late in the thirteenth century B.C. There follow two Iron Age strata, extending to the fall of Judah, each stratum divided into several phases. The three phases of stratum B are distinguished by an initial absence of Philistine pottery, then by an abundance of it for a fairly long time, and finally by its total disappearance. This indicates the unstable conditions in Palestine in the period from about 1200 to about 1000 B.C., as witnessed in the books of Judges and I Samuel. The actual occupational remains of stratum B are rather light, but the entire period is characterized by a great number of grain pits all over the mound; most of the pottery was found in these grain pits. They evidence the necessity of storing food in safe places during that insecure time (cf. Judg. 6:3–6, 11).

Stratum B was probably destroyed by Pharaoh Shishak in his raid about 918 B.C. The phase which followed it, stratum A, lasted over three hundred years, the remainder of the existence

An archaeologist examines an ancient dye vat at Tell Beit Mirsim.

of the Judean kingdom. The houses now typically had no court, but contained a single room on the ground floor with large stone pillars supporting a second floor and the roof. An outside staircase led to the upper (living) quarters. The town went through many rebuilding phases, the population gradually increasing to a maximum which has been estimated at between twenty-five hundred and five thousand persons.

Beit Mirsim at this time developed a specialized industry, the making of woolen textiles. The great sheep pasturage of the Negev spread to the south, and in the town were found great numbers of loom weights for the weaving of the spun wool into cloth. Dyeing facilities were also found, with cylindrical stone dye vats and other equipment similar to that still in use among the local people.

The quality of the buildings at Beit Mirsim declined as the kingdom of Judah itself declined around 600 B.C. From the last stage of the town's existence come two jar handles stamped with the seal of "Eliakim steward of Yaukin." Two similar objects have been found elsewhere in Judah; Yaukin is a shortened form of Jehoiachin (Hebrew *Yehoyakin* or *Yoyakin*), the king of Judah exiled by Nebuchadnezzar in 597 B.C. According to Albright, Eliakim was probably the man left in charge of the king's property after the latter went to Babylon. Compare Ziba the steward of Saul (II Sam. 9:9f.; 19:18, 30; the same Hebrew word—*na'ar*—is used of Ziba and on the Eliakim seal).

The final destruction of Tell Beit Mirsim apparently took place at the hands of Nebuchadnezzar's army in 587 B.C.

SUGGESTED TOPICS FOR FURTHER STUDY

1. The excavation of Tell Beit Mirsim and the development of biblical archaeology.
2. Tell Beit Mirsim and biblical Debir—a problem of identification.
3. Tell Beit Mirsim: the history of a town in Judah.
4. Textile manufacture in ancient times.

RECOMMENDED READING

Albright, W. F., *The Archaeology of Palestine and the Bible* (New York: Fleming H. Revell, 1932), pp. 63–126.

______, "Debir" in *Archaeology and Old Testament Study*, ed. D. Winton Thomas (Oxford: Clarendon, 1967), pp. 207–20.

______, *The Excavation of Tell Beit Mirsim*, vol. I, *Annual of the American Schools of Oriental Research* 12 (1932); vol. IA, *AASOR* 13 (1933); vol. II, *AASOR* 17 (1938); vol. III (with J. L. Kelso), *AASOR* 21–22 (1943).

Kochavi, M., "Khirbet Rabud = Debir," *Tel Aviv (Journal of the Tel Aviv Institute of Archaeology)* 1 (1974), p. 2.

Kyle, M. G., *Excavating Kirjath-sepher's Ten Cities* (Grand Rapids: Wm. B. Eerdmans, 1934).

FOR FURTHER READING

Avi-Yonah, M., "Debir" in *Encyclopedia Judaica* (Jerusalem: Keter, 1971), vol. 5, col. 1429.

16

Beth-shan

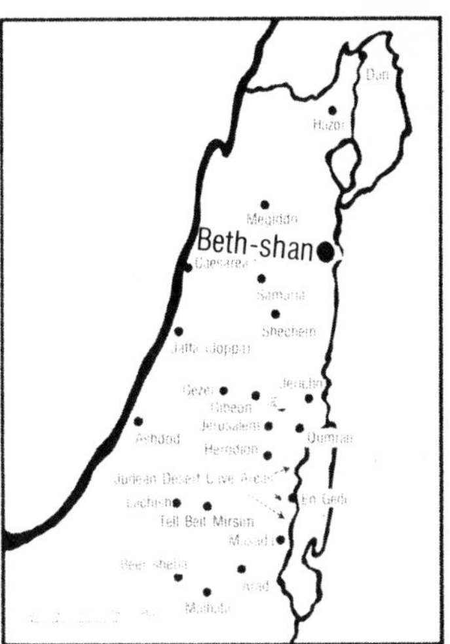

At the eastern end of the Vale of Esdraelon, approximately fifteen miles south of the Sea of Galilee and not too far from the Jordan River, stands Tell el-Husn, one of the most imposing city-mounds in the Holy Land. The nearby village of Beisan preserves the name of the ancient city which once stood on the tell—Beth-shan. At the foot of the tell flows the perennial River Jalud. The whole area is well-watered and very fertile, and in addition the site is located at the intersection of the ancient highways leading north to Syria and west to the seacoast and south to Egypt. It was, therefore, an important city at several times in antiquity.

The meaning of the name *Beth-shan* is not entirely clear. Shan, or Shean, may have been a deity; Beth-shan would then mean "House of Shan" (cf. Beth-el, "House of El [God]")—several temples have been found at Beth-shan, as we shall see. Shan then might perhaps be identified with one of the deities of these temples, though the town name is older than any of the temples.

Excavations at Beth-shan were carried out by the University of Pennsylvania Museum in 1921–23 (directed by C. S. Fisher), 1925–28 (Alan Rowe), and 1930, 1931, and 1933 (G. M. FitzGerald). Not all the mound was excavated in this project, which concentrated on the acropolis-mound at the tell's summit and on the cemetery north of the tell; nor were the results of the excavation ever completely published. In the 1950s and 1960s,

Stele of Ramses II discovered at Beth-shan.

N. Zori and S. Applebaum dug at Beth-shan for the Israel Department of Antiquities, but their work was directed mainly toward a later period than concerns us. Recently, Frances James has worked over some of the most important material from the Pennsylvania excavations, presenting a clarified picture of one period of the town's history.

Beth-shan's favored location brought about a settlement there in the Chalcolithic period, in the mid-fourth millennium B.C., and occupation continued into the Early and Middle Bronze Ages. No town wall has been found for any of Beth-shan's ancient phases, but erosion and the very steep sides of the tell may have caused the wall remains to slide to the bottom.

The most significant finds at Beth-shan come from the Late Bronze and Early Iron Ages, during much of which the city was under Egyptian domination. In fact, the city apparently served as an Egyptian military outpost and administrative center. We seem to see at Beth-shan a combination of Egyptian political hegemony and Canaanite cult, with very likely a garrison of mercenary soldiers recruited from among the Sea Peoples (Aegeans) who settled in Palestine after Egypt barely prevented them from taking over her homeland.

Above: an alabaster bowl with stand from Late Bronze Beth-shan. Below: Late Bronze zoomorphic vessel in the shape of a goat.

The Pharaoh Thutmosis III, by his own account, took Beth-shan in 1468 B.C. Thereafter we find abundant evidences of Egyptian presence in the city, including two victory stelae of Sethos I (late fourteenth century B.C.), telling of his defeat of certain local powers who attacked Beth-shan, and of his defeat of the Habiru ('Apiru), so well known from the Amarna letters as fomenters of trouble in Palestine, and connected by many with the Hebrews; a stele of Ramses II (thirteenth century), telling how in his ninth year he received the homage of Asiatic rulers at his Egyptian capital; a statue of Ramses III (twelfth century), perhaps commemorating his victory over the Sea Peoples; inscriptions of an important official of Ramses III, one Ramses-Wesr-Khepesh; and smaller objects of Egyptian origin.

Another interesting presence at Beth-shan is indicated by certain burials in the cemetery nearby. These burials were made in clay coffins of a peculiar type: the head end of the coffin's top consisted of a removable lid on which was formed a representation of a human face, often with stylized arms and headdress surrounding it. These coffins, of Egyptian derivation, are associated with twelfth-century pottery (the equivalent of Level VI of the tell itself). Elsewhere in Palestine, similar coffins are associated with the pottery typical of the Philistines, one of the groups of Sea Peoples defeated by Ramses III and settled by him in Palestine. We learn in I Samuel 31:10 that the Philistines, after defeating King Saul in the battle of Gilboa in the Vale of Esdraelon, displayed his body on the wall of Beth-shan. The finding of the distinctive coffins would seem at first glance to confirm the Philistines' presence at Beth-shan. Yet none of the well-known Philistine pottery has turned up at Beth-shan, with the coffins or elsewhere, and it may be better, with Frances James, to assume that since both the Bible and archaeology connect the Philistines almost entirely with *southern* Palestine, the Philistine enemy in I Samuel 31 probably represents a coalition of Philistines and some northern Sea Peoples (and perhaps Canaanites as well), all referred to by the Israelites under the single designation *Philistines*. The coffins at Beth-shan, then, probably indicate the presence there of Sea Peoples who were allied with, but not identical to, the Philistines. Most likely they served as mercenaries in the Egyptian army.

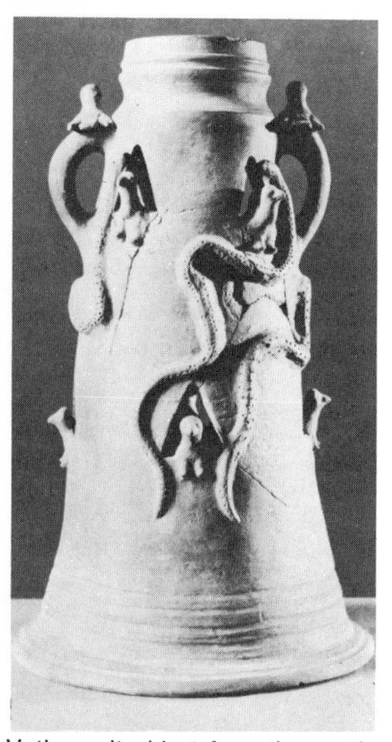

Votive cult object from the southern temple at Beth-shan.

The finds at Beth-shan include a series of temples apparently dedicated to Canaanite deities—though their worshipers seem often to have been Egyptians. In Level IX (late fourteenth century) a double shrine was found, one part with several altars and the remains of a sacred bull, and the other with a small sacred stone (*maṣṣebah*) and an Egyptian votive stele dedicated to the god Mekal, Lord (*baal*) of Beth-shan. The god is shown as bearded, with a tall conical headdress and two gazelle horns on his forehead. Another relief panel in the temple precinct shows two pictures of a large dog fighting a lion; the signification of this is not completely clear. In Levels VII and VI another temple was found, better preserved in Level VI than in VII, with two antechambers and a two-part main hall with two altars. In the Level VII phase, a votive panel was recovered showing a goddess with two horns and a high crown, perhaps the consort of Mekal; in Level VI was a life-size hawk wearing the crown of Upper and Lower Egypt, and a stele dedicated to "Antit Lady of Heaven and Mistress of All the Gods." In Level V two additional temples appeared, a southern one, built over the previous temple, but according to a different plan, and a northern one, which shows evidence of two distinct phases. These two phases, in fact, characterize all of Level V. Numerous cult objects were found in Level V, all in the earlier phase, most typically the hollow cylindrical stand decorated with snakes and birds; other snake representations were also found in this level. Apparently a fertility cult of Anath is to be understood.

As to the overall history of Beth-shan in this period, it should be noted that the above-mentioned stelae and a statue of a pharaoh were not found in their original settings (which would have been Levels VIII, VII, and VI of the archaeologists), but in a stratum of the eleventh-tenth century (the earlier phase of Level V). Furthermore, when found the stelae were overturned and the statue had had its head knocked off. This caused some confusion in the dating of the levels, and makes difficult the understanding of the history of Beth-shan during this time. James, after going over the remains from Levels VI, V, and IV, arrived at a reconstruction of the events of this period which seems plausible enough.

Level VI may be seen as a relatively brief stage to be dated to the twelfth century by the inscription of Ramses-Wesr-Khepesh. This is the period of the "Sea Peoples" coffins, of the Ramses III statue, and of two large buildings on the north side of the mound. Level VI ends about 1075 B.C., or even as early as 1100—very little typically Iron Age pottery has yet appeared.

When Level V was built, the earlier Egyptian stelae and statue were moved into it, showing that Egyptians or Egyptian sympathizers were still dominant in the town. This is the first phase of Level V, with the temples and cult objects, a phase which apparently lasted to the late tenth century B.C. The rather remarkable circumstance that the Egyptian monuments were in use as late as the age of David and Solomon may perhaps be explained by the Israelites' never having actually expelled the native inhabitants of Beth-shan (cf. Judg. 1:27, 28), not even when they took over the city sometime after Saul's death, and by David's permitting the Egyptianized state of affairs to continue there in order to foster good relations with Egypt. These relations remained good throughout Solomon's reign; it may be recalled that Solomon united his house with the Egyptian court by marriage (I Kings 3:1). On Solomon's death, however, the Pharaoh Shishak made a raid into Palestine and ravaged it. It may be that in retaliation for this the Israelites rudely put an end to the Egyptian presence at Beth-shan, and redid the whole city. The second phase of Level V lay above the overturned monuments and contained a gateway and rooms built in Israelite style. According to James the temples were transformed into administrative centers of a store city. This phase, begun at the end of the tenth century, persists till near the end of the ninth century when Beth-shan was destroyed in a holocaust.

A bowl from the Solomonic era discovered at Beth-shan.

Level IV reflects the return of a small, unimpressive Israelite settlement. It ended late in the eighth century, perhaps with the Assyrian conquest of Israel, and Beth-shan thereafter remained without inhabitants until the Hellenistic period—almost half a millennium. Only very slight cultic remains suggest the possibility of a shrine there in the Persian period.

In Hellenistic and Roman times, the town came to be called

Scythopolis, that is, "City of the Scythians" (though only by Hellenists; the natives still called it Beth-shan, as the Talmud and other sources attest). It has been thought that this name derives from the invasion of the Scythians, who swept through Syria and Palestine in the seventh century B.C., according to Josephus, and then presumably settled a colony at Beth-shan. This theory is now widely discounted, as is the Scythian invasion itself; in any case, we have seen that Beth-shan remained

Beth-shan today; the ruins of the Roman theatre of Scythopolis lie before the tell.

unoccupied during that time. It is more likely that the name derives from a settlement of Scythian contingents of Ptolemy II's army in the area about 254 B.C.

Scythopolis was a pagan city, both as to its Hellenized colonists and as to the native villagers, no doubt also soon Hellenized, who worked its fields. The first mention of Jews at Scythopolis is in II Maccabees 12:29f. Having with the rest of Palestine passed from Ptolemaic to Seleucid control by this time, Scythopolis evidently tried to remain neutral during the Maccabean wars. The city was taken by John Hyrcanus in 107 B.C., and the inhabitants were given the choice of converting to Judaism or leaving. To the Hasmoneans' disappointment, they left. Jewish settlers were moved in, and these remained even after the restoration of pagan control by Pompey in 63 B.C.

During the first revolt, in A.D. 66, the Jewish inhabitants of Scythopolis were apparently prevailed upon by their Gentile neighbors to join in resisting the Zealots; but, according to Josephus, the Gentile inhabitants played the Jews false, and a great massacre of the latter resulted. Yet in the ensuing centuries, a significant Jewish population remained at Beth-shan/Scythopolis, which became one of the great centers of textile production in the empire. Cloth goods from Scythopolis were valued throughout the Roman world. Earlier in the Roman era, Scythopolis had joined with nine cities east of Jordan to form the Decapolis, the League of Ten Towns mentioned in the New Testament and elsewhere. Being the only one of the ten west of the Jordan, it probably served as a trade link between the other nine and the Mediterranean seaports.

Archaeological remains from the Hellenistic and Roman periods at Beth-shan include a hoard of silver coins of Ptolemy II, a Greek or Roman temple, and a Roman theater. The theater was built around A.D. 200, and originally had a capacity of about eight thousand. A synagogue of the fourth century A.D. and a number of churches and monasteries in the vicinity accord with literary records in indicating the continued presence of both Jews and Christians in Beth-shan/Scythopolis.

SUGGESTED TOPICS FOR FURTHER STUDY

1. Canaanite religion at Beth-shan.
2. Beth-shan under the Egyptians.
3. Egypt and the Sea Peoples in Early Iron Age Palestine.
4. Problems of historical reconstruction at Beth-shan.
5. Scythopolis: a city of Greco-Roman Palestine.

RECOMMENDED READING

Avi-Yonah, M., "Scythopolis," *Israel Exploration Journal* 12 (1962), pp. 123–34.

FitzGerald, G. M., "Beth-Shean," in *Archaeology and Old Testament Study*, ed. D. Winton Thomas (Oxford: Clarendon, 1967), pp. 185–96.

Hamilton, R. W., "Beth-Shan" in *The Interpreter's Dictionary of the Bible*, ed. G. A. Buttrick (New York: Abingdon Press, 1962), vol. 1, pp. 397–401.

James, Frances, *The Iron Age at Beth Shan: A Study of Levels VI–IV* (Philadelphia: University Museum [Museum Monographs], University of Pennsylvania, 1966).

Thompson, H. O., *Mekal, the God of Beth-shan* (Leiden: E. J. Brill, 1970).

———, "Tell el-Husn—Biblical Beth-shan," *Biblical Archaeologist* 30 (1967), pp. 110–35.

FOR FURTHER READING

Applebaum, Shimon, "Where Saul and Jonathan Perished: Beth Shean in Israel—the Roman Theater," *Illustrated London News*, March 16, 1963, pp. 380–83.

"Bet(h)-Shean" in *Encyclopedia Judaica* (Jerusalem: Keter, 1971), vol. 4, cols. 757–58.

FitzGerald, G. M., "Beth-Shean" in *Archaeology and Old Testament Study*, ed. D. Winton Thomas (Oxford: Clarendon, 1967), pp. 185–96.

17

Caesarea

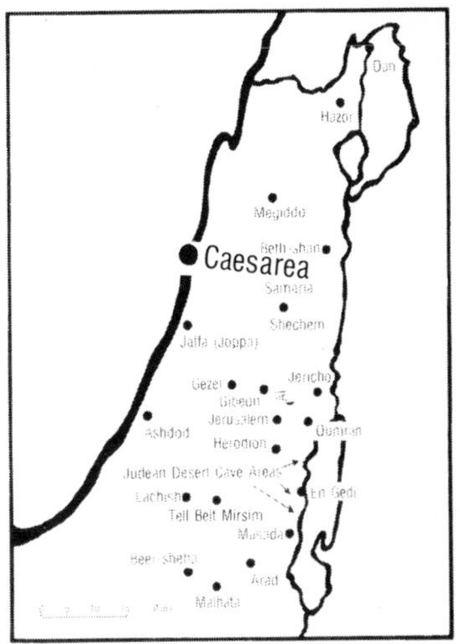

The ruins of Caesarea are located along the Mediterranean coast midway between the modern Israeli cities of Tel Aviv and Haifa. The history of the occupation of the site begins in the Persian period when the Phoenicians were given control of a part of the Palestinian coast. They built a fortification that is known in early Greek histories as Strato's Tower, a name that was derived from Abdashtart, the Sidonian king; during the Hellenistic era the town acquired a mixed population of non-Jews and Jews. The Romans acquired control of the whole of Palestine through the conquest of Pompey in 63 B.C.

Early in the reign of Herod the Great, the town was given to him by Caesar Augustus. Herod determined to construct a new city on the site to serve as the administrative center of the Roman provincial government in Palestine and to name it after his benefactor. Thanks to the account left to us by the Jewish historian Josephus, who must have known the city in its grandeur, we have a fairly detailed description of the city.

The construction of Caesarea Maritima, as it was called, required over a decade (from 22 to 10 B.C.). The ruins cover over eight thousand acres, making it the largest site in Palestine. In Herod's time Caesarea included all the major elements of a modern Roman city, with well-planned streets and an underground sewer system which was so constructed that the tides would clean it each day. Along with residential quarters, there was a royal quarter with palaces and a temple in honor of Augustus. Other monumental buildings included a theater, an amphitheater, and a hippodrome.

It was necessary for Herod's builders to provide an adequate water supply for the city inasmuch as the region has no natural springs nor nearby river, and the sandy soil made the building of reservoirs for the storage of rain water unfeasible. The system that was developed was an engineering marvel that included two aqueducts. One, carried on arches across the lowlands, brought water into the city from sources in the foothills of Samaria some ten miles distant. The water flowed initially through a long tunnel cut out of rock, in places over a hundred feet beneath the surface, before issuing into the aqueduct. This system underwent periodic repairs, and an inscription of the *Legio X Fretensis,* the Tenth Roman Legion, indicates one of the repairs was made by the legionnaires between the destruction of Jerusalem in A.D. 70 and the outbreak of the Bar Kochba revolt in 132. The second system was apparently added when the city's water requirements exceeded the capacity of the first aqueduct. A dam constructed across the Crocodile River (modern Zerqa) six miles north of the city created a lake approximately one mile wide and three miles long. From here the water was conveyed to the city by means of a ground level conduit which was protected by a vaulted roof. Recent excavations indicate that this system was constructed in the Byzantine period.

Another major engineering project undertaken by Herod's builders was the development of a seaport. The complex consisted of a north and a south harbor which were protected by two breakwaters, the northern one measuring 250 yards and the southern 600 yards. About forty acres of water were thus protected. In A.D. 130 the port was damaged severely by an earthquake; it fell into disuse in the late Byzantine period and is now heavily silted.

Caesarea, as a Roman provincial capital in New Testament times, had a mixed population of Jews and non-Jews. The Roman procurators, including Pilate, maintained their residence there, and the evangelist Philip (Acts 21:8) and the centurion Cornelius (Acts 10:1) lived there. The apostle Peter is known to have visited the city at least once, and the Book of Acts records several instances when the apostle Paul was in the city. Caesarea was the site of Paul's trial before Felix (Acts 23:23–33) and the port from which he sailed to Rome upon appealing his case to Caesar (Acts 25:11).

Caesarea had a sizable Jewish community during the first century of the common era, and the tensions between the community and their foreign overlords led to the outbreak of the first

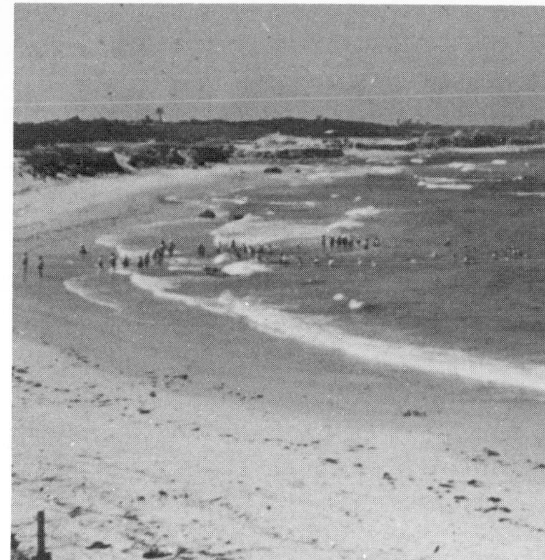

View of the southern harbor area of Caesarea today. Along this shore recent excavations uncovered the series of vaults, one of which contained the Mithraeum.

Part of the remains of the aqueduct at Caesarea.

mains of a Roman street.

revolt of the Jews against the Romans in A.D. 66. Vespasian was acclaimed emperor by the Roman legions stationed in Caesarea. In his pleasure, he raised the status of the city to that of a *colonia*. In the aftermath of the revolt, many of the captured Jewish Zealots were tortured and died in the prisons of Caesarea. The end of the ill-fated second revolt (Bar Kochba) in A.D. 135 brought additional suffering to the Jews, and according to tradition Rabbi Akiba was one of several Jewish leaders who were martyred in the hippodrome of Caesarea.

Caesarea was an important center of early Christianity in Palestine. Origen, an important third-century scholar, taught in a famous Christian school there which had a well-known library. His famous comparative textual work, the *Hexapla,* was destroyed along with the library upon the Moslem conquest. Eusebius, another early church father, who wrote an *Ecclesiastical History* and a work on Palestinian geography called the *Onomasticon,* was a fourth-century resident of the city. The Moslems held the city for 460 years until the arrival of the Crusaders who fortified an area of about thirty-five acres. Caesarea was destroyed in 1291 by the Moslems, when they put an end to Crusader rule in order to prevent a Christian resettlement. In modern times the members of kibbutz Sdot Yam have been working a large acreage of the soil that covers the extensive ruins.

Although Caesarea is one of the most important Palestinian sites for the study of the Roman and Byzantine periods, its investigation in modern times has been late and sporadic. The area was included in the Conder-Kitchener survey of western Palestine, and a map of the ruins with ground plans of the larger structures (of great use to later investigators) was prepared. In 1945, near the end of the British mandate, the Department of Antiquities made a small excavation at the site where a number of years previously the winter rains had uncovered a mosaic floor of a synagogue of the Byzantine period. The Israel Department of Antiquities and Museums carried out further minor excavations in 1951, when accidental finds stimulated the activity, and discovered a Byzantine street and church. M. Avi-Yonah of the Hebrew University excavated the remains of additional synagogues in the Jewish quarter in 1956 and 1962. A larger Italian expedition, directed by Antonio Frova, excavated the Roman theater from 1959 to 1961. In 1961 an extraordinary find was a stone that bore the three-line inscription: *Tiberieum/ [Pon]tius Pilatus/[Praef]ectus Iuda[eae]*—"Tiberius [the Roman emperor of the period]/Pontius Pilate/Prefect of Judea." This is the first archaeological evidence of Pilate, under whom Jesus was crucified, although there are references to him in the New Testament, Josephus, and the Roman historian Pliny.

In 1960 the E. Link underwater research team explored and measured the harbor facilities. During 1960 through 1963 an Israeli team, directed by A. Negev, excavated in the Crusader town and uncovered remains from the Crusader period back through the Arab and Byzantine eras to the Roman. In 1962 excavations at a Caesarean synagogue revealed part of a list of the twenty-four courses into which the Jerusalem priesthood was divided. The list specified the names of the courses and the cities in which the priests lived. The city of the eighteenth course was Nazareth.

The most ambitious program at the site was begun in 1971 by the Joint Expedition to Caesarea Maritima, under the direction of Robert J. Bull of Drew University. The expedition is made up of a consortium of schools which were granted an emergency license to excavate by Avraham Biran, who was then director of the Department of Antiquities. The emergency was created by the expansion of the banana plantations of the kibbutz and by the increase in the number of luxurious seaside villas that were being built in the area. Since 1971 the expedition has been in the field for six seasons, and has established itself as a major research project.

The expedition began with a firm commitment to excavate with a stratigraphical precision that had been lacking in the previous excavations on the site and to record the progress of the work and the artifacts with meticulous care. Among the advanced techniques which the Joint Expedition has employed is the use of aerial photography in color, black and white, and infrared. The photos have been used advantageously in the laying out of fields in the areas with the highest potential. Another piece of equipment that has been used enthusiastically and successfully at Caesarea is the magnetometer. With this instrument a careful measurement can be made of the variations in the magnetic field of the earth beneath, and it is possible to plot the locations of structures that are hidden beneath the surface. In the excavation procedures, eight-meter squares are used. The recording system includes the use of polaroid photography by each supervisor (the photos become an integral part of the daily records for each square) and the continuous drawing of the balks during the day as the work progresses. Daily top plans are also recorded for each square, and any new locus is described in terms of the scale of the Munsell soil color charts. In addition, all of the dirt is sifted as a matter of course. This procedure has enabled the expedition to recover many small objects, particu-

Theater inscription from Caesarea bearing the name of Pontius Pilate.

larly coins, that might otherwise have been lost. At Caesarea an attempt is also being made to program all of the artifacts for computerized analysis.

During the seasons through 1976, the Joint Expedition carried out excavations near the Byzantine esplanade, seeking to discover the main north-south street of the city. Two statues of the goddess of fortune (*Tyche*) have been uncovered in the area, but both are now little more than torsos. Further to the east, the plan of the hippodrome has been clarified. This large installation used for racing horses and chariots measured nearly 400 by 2000 feet. Along the seafront, between the amphitheater to the south and the Crusader city to the north, in an area in which a major public building of the Byzantine period had been discovered earlier by an Israeli probe, three inscriptions containing Romans 13:3 have been found. In addition, the area has produced over three thousand coins, eight gems, and over two hundred oil lamps. The coins, of course, provide valuable evidence for dating the strata in which they were found.

The marble medallion of the cult of Mithra discovered in the Mithraeum.

Perhaps the most unexpected discovery was uncovered in 1973 in a series of large vaults extending southward along and adjacent to the southern harbor. The entire complex doubtless served initially as warehouse facilities, but one of the vaults contained the first Mithraeum ever discovered in Palestine. A Mithraeum was a cultic sanctuary for the worship of Mithra, a popular mystery religion of the Roman and Byzantine periods. The installation included badly weathered paintings on the walls of the vault, plastered benches along three walls, and a central aisle; and centered at one end was a stone projection (the *bema*). The interpretation of the discovery as a Mithraeum was strengthened with the discovery of a white marble medallion that depicts major motifs of the cult of Mithra.

Additional fields have been opened by the expedition in the northern and southern suburbs. It is probable that some of the Hellenistic ruins in the north were a part of Strato's Tower. A survey of the architectural ruins throughout the site has resulted in a scale-drawn map of the city's remains. The investigation of the sewer system, which promised to provide a key to the layout of the streets, has been largely unproductive, in part because of the massive bulwark of sand that clogs the seaward openings and in part because of the profusion of later building remains that intrude to clog the Herodian sewers. Perhaps as important as any individual find has been the collection of a pottery corpus, obtained through carefully controlled stratigraphic digging, which will clarify the chronological typologies of Arab, Byzantine, and Roman pottery with a degree of precision that has been lacking until now.

Caesarea could be considered an important archaeological site in terms of the New Testament, so a word here about the archaeology of early Christianity may be appropriate, for as the reader is well aware, no separate category of New Testament archaeology has been incorporated into this work. One of the reasons for this is the limitations of space and purpose, but also it is difficult to justify the term *New Testament archaeology* in relationship to Palestinian sites. The expression naturally restricts itself to the first century A.D., and essentially to the last decades of the century when the New Testament documents were being written. At that point in the development of the church, Palestinian Christians were but one of a group of Jewish sects, particularly until the missionary work of Paul led to the development of a Gentile church located largely outside Palestine, and until the destruction of Jerusalem by the Romans isolated the largest community of Christians in Pella across the Jordan. One can hardly expect, therefore, that the artifacts of the first century would reflect a distinctive identifiable Christian culture.

At the same time, a number of the sites that have been included in our survey have produced material remains from the Herodian period and later, remains which illuminate the general period in which Jesus was born and reared and in which his first disciples lived. Among these one can mention Shechem, Samaria, Qumran, Jaffa, Jerusalem (particularly the recent excavations of B. Mazar), and Caesarea. No systematic, scientific excavations have been carried out at Bethlehem, where Jesus was born, or Nazareth, where he lived most of his life, but the identification of these places has been unquestioned because of the continuity of habitation and of tradition concerning them. The earliest church structures in Palestine were built in the Byzantine period (after A.D. 325). They commemorated the major sites connected with the life of Jesus, but there is no way of corroborating the authenticity of the traditions.

One site that might have been included in our survey as having a particular bearing on the life of Jesus is Capernaum. Partially excavated, it is located at Tell Hum on the north shore of the Sea of Galilee. The Franciscan order purchased the site in 1894, cleared away some of the ruins, and partly restored the ancient synagogue (1925). Contrary to the opinion of Father G. Orfali, who tried to prove a first-century date for the structure, it is evident that it dates to the second-third century A.D. (a time when many synagogues were built in Galilee). Therefore, it cannot have been the one in which Jesus taught, although the earlier structure may have stood on the same spot. More recent excavations have uncovered an octagonal Byzantine building

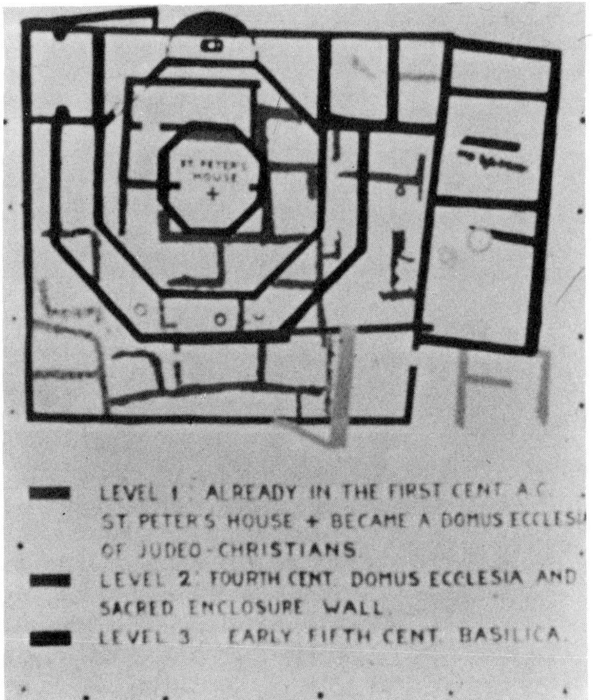

Schematic plan of the octagonal Byzantine house discovered in Capernaum.

which may have been a "house church" constructed over the site of the house of the apostle Peter. So the earliest evidence of Christian activity at Capernaum dates to the Byzantine era and is almost two centuries removed from the days of Jesus and the apostles. One can hope, of course, that the continuing stream of data being unearthed in the Holy Land will produce in the future earlier evidences of an identifiable Christian nature; the interested reader, in the meantime, will be able to find an array of documentary and artifactual evidence in extra-Palestinian sources and in Byzantine structures in Israel and Jordan that illuminate the history of Christianity from the second century on, but that evidence lies outside the scope of this book.

Suggested Topics for Further Study

1. A description of Herod's Caesarea.
2. Ancient Palestinian harbors exemplified by Caesarea.
3. A study of the religion of Mithra in the days of the Roman Empire.
4. The role of Caesarea in the development of the early church.
5. The role of Caesarea in the history of Palestinian Judaism.
6. The results to date of the joint expedition to Caesarea Maritima.

RECOMMENDED READING

"Caesarea" in *Archaeological Encyclopedia of the Holy Land,* ed. Avraham Negev (Jerusalem: Weidenfeld and Nicholson, 1972), pp. 73–74.

"Caesarea" in *The Biblical World,* ed. Charles F. Pfeiffer (Grand Rapids: Baker, 1966), pp. 162–64.

Fritsch, C. T., and I. Ben-Dor, "The Link Expedition to Israel, 1960," *Biblical Archaeologist* 24 (1961), pp. 50–59.

Holland, David L., "The Joint Expedition to Caesarea Maritima, 1971," *American Schools of Oriental Research Newsletter* 1 (1971–72).

______, "The Joint Expedition to Caesarea Maritima, 1971," *American Schools of Oriental Research Newsletter* 5 (1972–73).

Hopfe, Lewis Moore, and Gary Lease, "The Caesarea Mithraeum: A Preliminary Announcement," *Biblical Archaeologist* 38 (1975), pp. 2–10.

Howard, Cherie, "Discovery," *American Schools of Oriental Research Newsletter* 3 (1973–74).

Levine, Lee I., *Roman Caesarea: An Archaeological-Topographical Study* (Jerusalem, 1975).

Reifenberg, A., "Caesarea Maritima: A Study in the Decline of a Town," *Israel Exploration Journal* 1 (1950), pp. 20–32.

Yeivin, S., "Excavations at Caesarea Maritima," *Archaeology* 8 (1955), pp. 122–29.

FOR FURTHER READING

Avi-Yonah, M., "The Synagogue of Caesarea (Preliminary Report)," *Bulletin Rabinowitz* 3 (1960).

Barag, D., "An Inscription from the High Level Aqueduct at Caesarea, Reconsidered," *Israel Exploration Journal* 14 (1964).

Finegan, Jack, *Light from the Ancient Past,* vol. 2 (Princeton: Princeton University Press, 1959).

Fritsch, Charles T., ed., *Caesarea Maritima* (Missoula, MT: Scholars Press, 1975).

Frova, A., *Caesarea Maritima: Rapporto preliminare* (1959).

Hamburger, A., "A New Inscription from the Caesarea Aqueduct," *Israel Exploration Journal* 9 (1959), pp. 188–90.

Harrison, R. K., *Archaeology of the New Testament* (London: The English Universities Press Ltd., 1964).

Humphrey, John H., "Prolegomena to the Study of the Hippodrome at Caesarea Maritima," *Bulletin of the American Schools of Oriental Research* 213 (1974), pp. 2–45.

______, "A Summary of the 1974 Excavations in the Caesrea Hippodrome," *Bulletin of the American Schools of Oriental Research* 218 (1975), pp. 1–24.

Laeuchli, Samuel, "Urban Mithraism," *Biblical Archaeologist* 31 (Garden City, NY: Anchor Books, 1968), pp. 73–99.

Levine, Lee I., *Caesarea Under Roman Rule* (Leiden: E. J. Brill, 1975).

Riley, John A., "The Pottery from the First Session of Excavation in the Caesarea Hippodrome," *Bulletin of the American Schools of Oriental Research* 218 (1975), pp. 25–63.

18

Dan

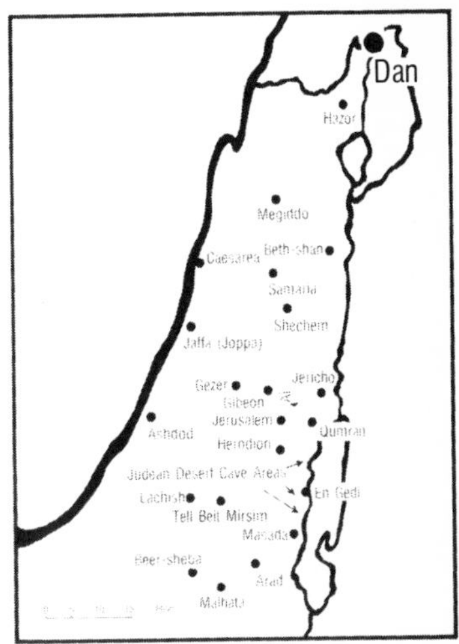

Tell Dan is located in the far north of Israel. The tell, some twenty-five miles north of the Sea of Galilee, lies at the foot of Mount Hermon, overlooking the Huleh Valley. At one of the main sources of the Jordan River, and on the trade route between Tyre and Damascus, the city was obviously in a position of importance for whoever controlled it. In pre-Israelite times it was known as Laish. After the conquest, Dan became the northernmost outpost of Israel; the expression "from Dan to Beersheba" came to be a fixed phrase meaning the whole of Israelite territory (II Sam. 24:2; I Kings 4:25; etc.). Its strategic position on the Israelite-Aramean border figures in the biblical history several times (I Kings 15:20; II Kings 15:29; etc.).

In postbiblical times, Dan is mentioned in the Talmud as only a small village. The site was not forgotten altogether, though. In the nineteenth century, Edward Robinson noted a mound whose Arabic name, Tell el-Qadi ("Mound of the Judge"), is an exact translation of the Hebrew name *Dan.* On the basis of the location and the name, the site was identified with the biblical city. This identification was widely accepted, and it has been essentially validated by subsequent excavations.

Archaeological investigation of the site was not begun until 1966, when Avraham Biran made soundings on behalf of the Israel Department of Antiquities. The tell itself is considerably higher at its rim than at its center; this was found to be due to a massive Middle Bronze Age wall and rampart system surround-

Part of the Dan high place. The monumental steps are to the right of the men.

General view of Dan, with the Jordan River flowing from the western edge of the site, monumental gate to the lower right.

ing the ancient city. Since then, Biran has continued the excavation each year, sponsored by the Department of Antiquities. Some additional support has also come from a consortium of American institutions in affiliation with the Nelson Glueck School of Biblical Archaeology, the Jerusalem school of Hebrew Union College-Jewish Institute of Religion.

The biblical record (Judg. 18) suggests that Laish was a quiet, sheltered, rather isolated spot when the tribe of Dan captured it. It apparently had not always been so. Burial offerings of the fourteenth century B.C. found by Biran included objects imported from Mycenae and Cyprus. And that there was prosperity long before the fourteenth century is indicated by an abundance of Early Bronze Age pottery. Moreover, Middle Bronze Age evidence from Tell Dan and elsewhere indicates that the city was a commercial center of some importance. A text in Akkadian from Mari mentions a consignment of tin shipped to "Wari-taldu [king] at Layish"—this confirms the biblical name of the city, and suggests it had fairly wide-ranging contacts in the Middle Bronze Age. The fact that it is also mentioned in the Egyptian Execration Texts corroborates its international status. To this same period (the second half of the eighteenth century B.C.) dates the building of the fortification system, consisting mainly of a wall from twelve to twenty feet thick which surrounded the city. Earthen ramparts were built both inside and outside of the wall. These too suggest a city with something worth defending.

The Israelite phase of the tell provides the greatest interest, however. The Bible (Josh. 19:47; Judg. 1:34; 18) states that the tribe of Dan, unable to take possession of the territory in southwestern Palestine assigned to it, moved to the north and conquered the city of Laish, settling it and renaming it Dan. The archaeological evidence does indeed indicate some destruction and a definite change in material culture at the beginning of the Iron Age, though no great conflagration in the area excavated. The new culture persists through the twelfth to the middle of the eleventh century B.C. Biran relates this to Judges 18:30, 31, which places the beginning of the Danite occupation in the second generation after Moses, and the use of Micah's idol at Dan in the period "when the house of God was at Shiloh." This would indeed correspond to the period from the beginning of the twelfth century to the mid-eleventh century; but whether this equation is correct or not remains to be seen.

The outstanding feature of the Israelite city of Dan, from the biblical point of view, was its function as a cult center. It was the site of a shrine or high place (*bamah*) with attendant priests and

The inscription discovered at Dan in 1976.

Cobblestone roadway curving up over the rampart of Dan.

The gate complex of Dan viewed from the south.

paraphernalia, first for the tribe of Dan (Judg. 18) and later for the Northern Kingdom of Israel under Jeroboam I and his successors (I Kings 12:26ff.; II Kings 10:29; Amos 8:14). Biran and his excavators discovered the high place at Dan in the northwest part of the city, in an area abundant with springs. The tenth-century pottery found with it correlates well with the date of its construction by Jeroboam (ca. 920 B.C.). It consists basically of a platform of ashlar stones, about 160 feet long in its first stage of construction. This high place was destroyed by fire and replaced in the mid-ninth century by another, now surrounded on three sides by a wide courtyard and enclosure walls. At a later stage, a flight of monumental steps was added to the south side of the *bamah*. One of these reconstruction phases may likely be assigned to the reign of King Ahab. The cult tradition at this spot in the city of Dan was continued as late as the Hellenistic and Roman periods.

Jeroboam had two golden calves set up, one at Dan and one at Beth-el. Why did he pick these two cities instead of some single central point? Dan and Beth-el both had long traditions as centers of worship—extending back to the time of the judges for Dan and to that of the patriarchs for Beth-el—but so did such places as Shechem and Gilgal. Why then were Dan and Beth-el selected as the sites for Jeroboam's centers?

According to Yohanan Aharoni, it may have been customary in ancient times to erect sanctuaries *on the borders* of a country. Thus, he himself has excavated an Israelite temple at Arad, on Judah's southern border, which goes back to the time of Solomon, and another sanctuary at Beer-sheba. It would make sense, then, for Jeroboam to establish two main centers of his reorganized cult, one at either end of his kingdom's north-south axis.

The cult itself is thought to have maintained the worship of Yahweh, but with an entirely revised apparatus: not only did the king himself officiate at the altar, but there were a different priesthood, a different calendar, and a golden calf instead of the two cherubim of the Jerusalem temple. The calf may have been conceived of as the throne or pedestal of the invisible Yahweh, just as were the ark and attendant cherubim in Jerusalem. This would be similar to Syrian representations of storm gods standing on bulls.

While Beth-el was the chief center of this cult, it seems that Jeroboam may have felt it necessary to make some improvements at Dan befitting its new official status, for the unusually large city gate excavated by Biran dates to the end of the ninth century. This gate, built into a city wall *outside* the earlier rampart, includes a broad basalt pavement which leads through it and into the city. There is an inner gate and an outer gate, and between the two the pavement broadens to form the "entrance to the gate" where the city's elders conducted its business. Biran found this space equipped with a stone bench for the elders, and facing the outer entrance there was a canopied seat for the local ruler. The gate was destroyed in the first half of the ninth century B.C., perhaps by Ben-Hadad of Aram, who attacked Israel from the north at the instigation of King Asa of Judah (I Kings 15:16–21).

The horned altar discovered at Dan.

Later constructions at Dan show evidence of an occupation in the eighth century, no doubt brought to an end by the Assyrians in 732 B.C., and of a still later occupation lasting perhaps to the early sixth century, a period when the prophet Jeremiah made mention of Dan (Jer. 4:15; 8:16).

Two of the most exciting finds at Tell Dan were a horned altar discovered in 1974, and a plaque with a bilingual inscription found in 1975. Unlike the horned altar discovered in 1973 by Aharoni at Beer-sheba, which consisted of several stones, the Tell Dan altar was cut from a single limestone block. It measures approximately sixteen by sixteen inches. Biran has dated the Dan altar to the ninth century or earlier. Such altars were used primarily for burning incense. As for the second find, on the small limestone plaque, which is approximately six by twelve inches, there is a Greek inscription, dated to the second century B.C. on the basis of epigraphy, which states, "The vow of Zilas to the god of Dan." The vow is repeated in Aramaic; although some letters are broken off, the content of the inscription is apparent. Both of these discoveries were made in the area directly to the south of the monumental steps which lead up to the high place at Dan. The inscription is of singular importance because it establishes the identity of the mound as Dan, at least in the time in which Zilas' votive offering was made, and there can be little doubt that name is simply the continuation of the Early Iron Age designation of the site.

SUGGESTED TOPICS FOR FURTHER STUDY

1. The golden calf—the religious reorganization of Jeroboam I.
2. Dan and Beth-el—the question of border sanctuaries.
3. Israelite religion in the time of the judges.
4. The history of the fortification system at Tell Dan.

RECOMMENDED READING

Aharoni, Yohanan, "The Israelite Sanctuary at Arad" in *New Directions in Biblical Archaeology,* ed. D. N. Freedman and J. C. Greenfield (Garden City, NY: Doubleday, 1969), pp. 25–39.

Albright, W. F., *From the Stone Age to Christianity,* second edition (Garden City, NY: Doubleday, 1957).

Biran, Avraham, "Tel Dan," *Biblical Archaeologist* 37 (1974), pp. 26–51.

Kaufmann, Y., *The Religion of Israel* (Chicago: University of Chicago Press, 1960).

Malamat, A., "Syro-Palestinian Destinations in a Mari Tin Inventory," *Israel Exploration Journal* 21 (1971), pp. 31–38.

Negev, A., "Soundings at Tel Dan," *Ariel* 16 (Autumn 1966), pp. 71–75.

Van Beek, G. W., "Dan" in *The Interpreter's Dictionary of the Bible,* ed. G. A. Buttrick (New York: Abingdon Press, 1962), vol. 1, pp. 759–60.

FOR FURTHER READING

Avi-Yonah, Michael, "Dan" in *Encyclopedia Judaica* (Jerusalem: Keter, 1971), vol. 5, cols. 1259–60.

Biran, Avraham, *The Archaeological Excavations at Tel Dan: Summer, 1974* (Jerusalem: Hebrew Union College—Jewish Institute of Religion, Nelson Glueck School of Biblical Archaeology, 1974).

______, "Tel Dan," *Israel Exploration Journal* 19 (1969), pp. 239–41; 20 (1970), pp. 118–19; 22 (1972), pp. 164–66; 23 (1973), pp. 110–12.

Malamat, A., *Near Eastern Archaeology in the Twentieth Century,* ed. G. E. Wright (New York: Doubleday, 1970), pp. 168–72.

19

Gezer

Tell Gezer is located five miles southeast of modern Ramla, more than halfway to Jerusalem on the road from Tel Aviv that runs through the Shephelah, the low hills directly adjacent to the coastal plain before one begins the ascent into the central highlands. Here the city rose atop a height great enough to command an impressive view along the coast. From this vantage point an enemy force could be spotted well in advance, and a watch set on a nearby hill could guard the entrance to the Valley of Aijalon leading towards Jerusalem. The strategic advantages of Gezer's location are important in accounting for its virtually continuous occupation from Chalcolithic to Roman times, and the site currently retains its military significance as an observation post. There are additional reasons for its long history of occupation. The marginal position between highland and plain provides access to flat, fertile fields on two sides of the tell and to hills for grazing on the other two sides. The site is also supplied with adequate water resources. Springs are located adjacent to the eastern and southern slopes of the tell.

The identification of the site was fixed when Clermont-Ganneau located a boundary stone on a nearby hill. The name *Gezer* was inscribed on the stone. Rarely is identification so simple. His discovery, made almost a century ago, was substantiated by six additional boundary stones found in the area, all dating from the Roman period. Five of them bear the words, "the boundary of Gezer."

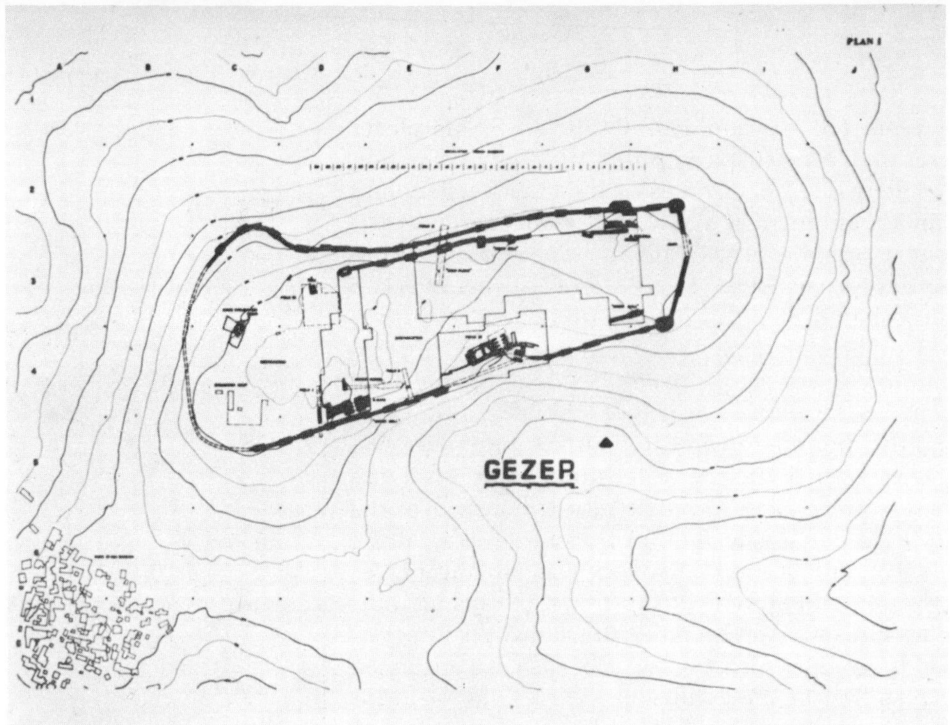

Isometric plan of Gezer and the excavations.

Royal Judean stamped jar handles discovered at Gezer.

The Solomonic gate at Gezer.

During the years 1902–05 and 1907–09, R. A. S. Macalister excavated Gezer under the auspices of the Palestine Exploration Fund. He had interrupted his studies of Irish archaeology and language for an appointment at age twenty-eight as the Assistant Field Secretary of the fund. After a brief apprenticeship with the American archaeologist, F. J. Bliss, Macalister attacked Gezer. There can be no doubt of his determination and drive. With the help of only one Egyptian foreman, he directed approximately two hundred workmen, mainly residents of the local Arab village, in an enormous excavation. He dug numerous trenches across the mound—always to bedrock, built a protective wall that was washed into the water tunnel, and even dug one tunnel of his own design in an attempt to "turn over the whole mound." He was easily the most prolific writer of the early archaeologists in Palestine. His work was significant, revealing several important structures and finds, but his identification of the structures was rarely correct. It was simply impossible for one man to conduct such a massive project at a sustained pace without resulting in the confusion that is evident in his reports and interpretations. Very little of his material could be used to reconstruct the history of the site.

In order to determine if excavations should be renewed on the tell, Alan Rowe spent six weeks at Gezer in 1934, under the auspices of the Palestine Exploration Fund. He chose a spot for sounding, however, that produced only a small amount of Early Bronze and Middle Bronze material, so full-scale excavations were not reopened.

Interest in Gezer did not revive until G. Ernest Wright conducted three small campaigns there in 1964–65. These proved successful enough to launch a new series of massive excavations at Gezer, this time with a large, well-trained staff and numerous volunteers. The new effort was conducted jointly by Hebrew Union College and the Harvard Semitic Museum, with Wright and Nelson Glueck as advisors. William G. Dever directed the excavations from 1966 to 1971. He was succeeded by Joe D. Seger in 1972 and in 1973, the final season of the recent excavations. The Gezer dig has become known for its careful techniques, its training program, and its inclusion of nonarchaeological experts on the staff, such as a geologist. The coordination of the archaeological efforts with an independent paleo-ecological survey of the site marked a further innovation at Gezer.

The excavations have indicated a long period of calm prosperity for Gezer, culminating in the building of the "South Gate" and an enormous tower about 1600 B.C. To these was added a glacis, a steep plastered slope to the outside of the wall, about fifty years later. This entire phase was brought to an end in the fifteenth century B.C., as shown by a thick layer of ashes and rubble, probably to be attributed to an attack by Pharaoh Thutmosis III about 1468.

An interesting highlight of the recent Gezer excavations centers on the rediscovery of the Gezer "high place." Originally

The Gezer high place.

discovered by Macalister, it consists of a row of ten monoliths of varying size, standing on end and oriented approximately north-south. In the middle of the row of stones is a large rectangular stone block with a hole fifteen inches deep cut into the top of it. Macalister gave the complex the name *high place,* and reburied it against the possibility of depredations by the superstitious local populace. The re-excavation took place in 1968, following a series of surface probes. The initial removal of large amounts of Macalister's dump by means of a bulldozer was an extraordinary innovation in Palestinian archaeology; it was followed by a painstaking investigation of the installation in order to solve problems of date, construction, and function that still remained from Macalister's excavations. The installation is now dated to Middle Bronze II C, circa 1600 B.C.—the same period as the construction of the massive tower on the city's south side. The function of the "high place" is still problematical. A reasonable hypothesis is that the complex was erected to commemorate an event, quite possibly the witnessing of a contract (covenant) between individuals or groups.

The current excavations have shown that the city was a strong Philistine fortress at a time when Philistine power had expanded well beyond their five major cities. The Bible speaks of the "Canaanites" of Gezer, and relates that Joshua defeated their king, but that the Israelites were never able to capture the city, merely reducing its inhabitants to forced labor. Despite this reference to "Canaanites," the evidence of Philistines on the site is abundantly clear. The Philistines, however, may only have been the rulers there. The existence of a Philistine stronghold at Gezer would help to explain David's frequent battles in the area. Gezer, nevertheless, remained in Philistine hands in David's time as well.

According to I Kings 9:15, 16, a pharaoh had conquered Gezer and had given it as a dowry to his daughter, who married Solomon. It is possible that this peculiar incident, which violates known Egyptian custom in involving a daughter of a pharaoh in a diplomatic marriage, may represent an Egyptian incursion in order to try the strength of the new Israelite monarch after the death of the powerful King David. Solomon apparently proved his strength, and the Egyptians arranged a peace treaty sealed by the gift of at least one city and the pharaoh's daughter. During Solomon's reign, then, Gezer passed under the control of Israel. Its destruction by the pharaoh is attested in the excavated remains by a destruction level twenty inches thick.

Solomon turned Gezer into one of his main fortresses, a sister city to Jerusalem, Hazor, and Megiddo. The Solomonic gate located at Gezer became the key to the answer to a great controversy surrounding the chronological sequence and relative stratigraphical positions of the walls and gates constructed during the United Kingdom. Macalister had come across one corner of the gate, but in his confusion he pronounced it a Maccabean castle. Yigael Yadin, struck by its similarities to the Solomonic gate structures uncovered previously at Megiddo and at Hazor, studied the plans of the structure in Macalister's publications and perceived its real nature. Subsequent excavations substantiated the detective work of Yadin, revealing the Gezer gate to be almost identical to the two already uncovered at Hazor and Megiddo. All three structures are now known to have been associated with casemate walls. This firmly identified the style of Solomonic fortifications since Gezer did not belong to the Israelites before Solomon's time. One of the astounding results of modern biblical archaeology is that in three of the four cities fortified by Solomon, the gate structures have been laid bare once more to human eyes. Presumably Jerusalem contains the ruins of similar structures.

The Gezer Calendar, discovered by Macalister, is an invaluable object dating from Gezer's Israelite days. The hand-sized tablet of soft limestone is inscribed in a paleo-Hebrew script and

Sketch of the Gezer Calendar.

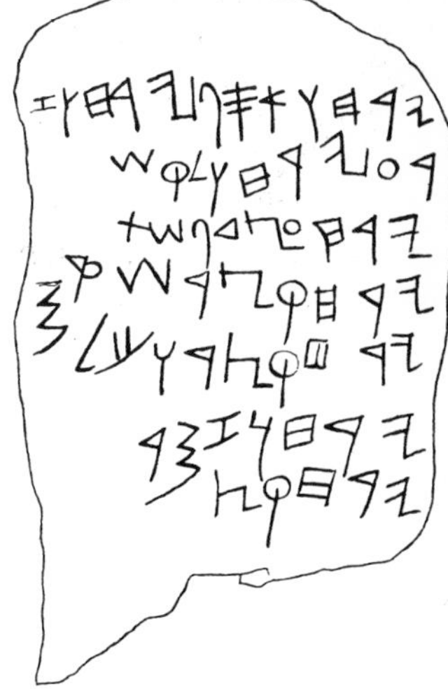

contains a sequence of the normal agricultural activities for the area. W. F. Albright has translated the text as follows:

> His two months are (olive) harvest,
> His two months are planting (grain),
> His two months are late planting;
> His month is hoeing up of flax,
> His month is harvest of barley,
> His month is harvest and *feasting;*
> His two months are vine-tending,
> His month is summer fruit.

This early example of Israelite writing has helped to date developments in the Hebrew language and script.

Another problem presented by the excavations concerns the jar handles stamped with the signs of the late Judean monarchy that have been discovered at Gezer. These have been found at many Judean sites, but Gezer was a city on the southern boundary of the Northern Kingdom. The occupation of Gezer by the Assyrians during the later period of the Judean monarchy is well attested by cuneiform documents found on the site. This may have begun with the campaigns of Tiglath-pileser III in 734–733 B.C., since a relief from his palace depicts the capture of a city called *Gazru*. Gezer probably contained an Assyrian garrison following the destruction of Samaria. The jar handles, quite possibly from the days of King Josiah, may have appeared after that monarch's expansion into the north, but similar handles have not been found at Beth-el, which Josiah also took. The problem is still not solved.

Fragment of a seventh-century B.C. Hebrew ostracon discovered at Gezer.

Recent excavations have shown that the Babylonians destroyed Gezer when they took the Judean kingdom, and that it was reoccupied in Persian times. According to I Maccabees 9:52, the city was fortified by the Seleucid general Bacchides, but it was captured by Simon, the brother of Judah the Maccabee. Simon banished the unsympathetic, strengthened the fortress, and built within it a palace for himself. A line of graffiti may date from that specific event. It curses Simon's palace in these words: "(Says) Pampras, to blazes with Simon's palace."

Further problems still remain unsolved at Gezer. The real function of the boundary stones is yet unknown. They date from about A.D. 100, and read in Hebrew, "boundary of Gezer," and in Greek, "belonging to Alkios." Who was Alkios? Was he a local official, or did all of Gezer by that time perhaps belong to him as a private estate? The date and the exact character of the water tunnel, and the location of a possible Solomonic palace, are also questions awaiting solutions. With the cessation of excavations at Gezer at the close of the 1973 season, it is unlikely that these problems will find further solutions, unless and until future archaeologists return to Tell Gezer.

SUGGESTED TOPICS FOR FURTHER STUDY

1. The evidence for the Philistine occupation of Gezer.
2. Literary references to Gezer in the light of archaeological excavation.
3. The significance of the Gezer Calendar.
4. The nature and meaning of the mysterious Gezer "high place."
5. The evidence of architectural uniformity in Solomonic structures.
6. The Gezer excavations, old and new—a comparison of archaeological techniques.
7. Gezer in the Bible—the historical setting of the biblical references.
8. The location of Gezer—its commercial and military significance.
9. Gezer in prehistory—the archaeological evidence.

RECOMMENDED READING

Biblical Archaeologist 30, no. 2 (May 1967); 34, no. 4 (Dec. 1971).

Dever, W. G., H. D. Lance, and G. E. Wright, *Gezer I: Preliminary Report of the 1964-1966 Seasons* (*HUCBASJ Annual*, vol. 1 [Jerusalem: Keter, 1970]).

Hamilton, R. W., "Gezer" in *The Interpreter's Dictionary of the Bible*, ed. G. A. Buttrick (New York: Abingdon Press, 1962), vol. 2, pp. 388–89.

FOR FURTHER READING

The Biblical World, ed. Charles F. Pfeiffer (Grand Rapids: Baker, 1966), pp. 254–59.

Dever, W. G., "Excavations at Gezer," *Biblical Archaeologist* 30 (1967), pp. 47–62, figs. 7–12.

Lance, H. D., "Gezer in the Land and in History," *Biblical Archaeologist* 30 (1967), pp. 34–47, figs. 1–6.

Macalister, R. A. S., *The Excavation of Gezer, 1902-1905 and 1907, 1909*, three volumes (London: Palestine Exploration Fund, 1912).

Rowe, A., "The 1934 Excavations at Gezer," *Palestine Exploration Quarterly* 67 (1935), pp. 19–33, 2 plans, pls. 1–6.

Ussishkin, D., and G. E. Wright, "Gezer," *Encyclopedia of Archaeological Excavations in the Holy Land* (London: Oxford University Press, I–IV, 1975–77), pp. 11–117 and figs.

Wright, G. E., "Gezer," *Israel Exploration Journal* 15 (1965), pp. 252–53.

______, "The Troglodytes of Gezer," *Palestine Exploration Quarterly* 69 (1937), pp. 67–68, fig. 1.

Yadin, Y., *Hazor* (London: Oxford, 1972), pp. 147–50, figs. 35–36.

20

Gibeon

The name *Gibeon* suggests height. The site is situated on an outcropping in the Judean hills about five miles north-northwest of Jerusalem and three miles south of Ramallah on a tell called el-Jib. It is at almost the same latitude as Tell Gezer, but it lies at the eastern end of the Valley of Aijalon, whereas Gezer lies at the western end of the valley.

After a brief visit to the site in 1838, Edward Robinson proposed identifying el-Jib with Gibeon on the basis of the similarity of the names and the biblical references to its location. The identification was not universally accepted, since Eusebius' *Onomasticon* had placed it elsewhere. Opposition was led by Albrecht Alt, who sought to place the site of Gibeon on another tell. The identification was still debated until W. F. Albright studied the jar handles found in the excavation and pronounced that they were indeed inscribed "Gibeon," as the excavators had claimed. It could still be argued that the jars came from a different site, but the discovery of the wineries enhanced the view that the jars were of local manufacture. If the jars had been distributed to other cities, they had been, in modern terminology, recycled. Jar handles inscribed with the name *Gibeon* have not yet been found on other excavated sites. The identification of the city can therefore now be considered secure.

Jar handle with royal seal from Gibeon (seventh-sixth century, B.C.).

A. K. Dajani had conducted surface explorations and had investigated a tomb at Gibeon in 1950 on behalf of the Jordanian Department of Antiquities, but it wasn't until 1956 that excavations were opened on the site. The project was the result of a decision on the part of James B. Pritchard to excavate a virgin site. The excavation, sponsored by the American Schools of Oriental Research, the University Museum of the University of Pennsylvania, the Church Divinity School of the Pacific, and the Department of Antiquities of Jordan, was carried on in the years 1956, 1957, 1959, 1960, and 1962. Gibeon, as a significant site that was first excavated in the latter half of this century by a well-organized excavation using modern methods, therefore bypassed many of the problems inherent in re-excavating a site that has been worked earlier. The factor of earlier interpretations, sometimes erroneous due to primitive methodology, was eliminated at Gibeon.

The city was certainly unique among biblical sites. It was a large city existing over three millennia, from the Early Bronze period to the Roman-Byzantine era. The fact that it contains no full destruction layers in the Late Bronze to Iron II periods is significant; the city provides the best available example of occupational continuity for that period. Whatever the true story behind Gibeon's peaceful assimilation with the Israelites (a problem for which the excavation could not provide the answer), it seems that the "elders" of Gibeon were adept at keeping the

Air view of Gibeon.

ravages of war away from their city and their vineyards. The record of continuous occupation which they wrote can now be employed by Palestinian archaeologists as a control when it is compared with other sites which show successive destructions in the same time period.

The wealth of the city predated the Israelite settlement. It was apparently based on the vineyards which provided the raw material for the major industry—wine-making. When the "industrial area" was first found, its purpose was uncertain. The area was a large complex of more than 1,100 square yards containing numerous pits cut into the limestone. Further excavation produced wine jars, a ceramic funnel, and stoppers for the jars. The purpose of the area was determined when the installation and equipment were compared with the wine-making facilities operated by the Trappists in the nearby Latrun Monastery. Wine presses, fermenters, and sixty-three cellars were identified in the Gibeon winery. The cellars had been cut in limestone, which is a good aquifer, and had been left unplastered. The excavators were mystified by the apparent inability of the cellars to hold a liquid. They hired a rather confused villager and his donkey to bring vast loads of water which were poured into one of the cellars to test its ability to hold a liquid. The water rapidly disappeared through the rock. It was not until they found a cellar containing a pile of smashed storage jars that they understood that the wine was not stored in bulk, but in jars. Some of the cellars were more than seven feet deep and had stone covers. All together, they were capable of holding twenty-five thousand U.S. gallons of wine in jars.

The other notable structures at Gibeon were those used for procuring water. Pritchard's excavation was fortunate to come upon a "pool" of enormous proportions. This is a cylindrical shaft, thirty-seven feet in diameter and thirty-five feet deep, which housed a spiral staircase winding down the sides of the shaft. The stairs lead to a curving tunnel which winds downward to a depth of forty-five feet below the stairs and the floor of the "pool." There it opens onto a chamber of about twenty-three feet by eleven feet. At this depth the ground water level has been reached and a spring fills the chamber with water. The pool was probably constructed in the twelfth or eleventh century B.C. It is not known why such tremendous labor, as must have been used to carve this great hole out of limestone, was delegated to such seemingly unnecessary work. Why did they not build a simple tunnel like those at other sites? Perhaps the Gibeonites asked themselves the same question, for in the tenth century they built a more conservative water tunnel, like the ones at other sites. It is possible that the pool did not provide enough water and a spring on the side of the tell had to be used. The tunnel followed the incline of the hill under the city wall and continued directly under the surface until it reached a cave. A trough helped carry the water to this cave from the spring, which was located just inside the tell. A front door to the cave led to the side of the tell and could be blocked in case an enemy approached. The tunnel and its ninety-three steps also took many man-hours to carve out of the rock, but it was evidently more practical than the pool and was used for several centuries.

Pritchard's excavation could investigate only a small fraction of the tell, which still remains partially undisturbed under a small orchard, yet it located the important installations listed above, the epigraphic materials, the fortifications, and evidences of the long occupation. It was able to illuminate some biblical passages concerning Gibeon, but the references are to particular events of the sort that archaeological investigation is unable to confirm. For the most part, the excavations merely open new lines of speculation about the biblical events.

The first appearance of the Gibeonites in the Bible is when they fooled Joshua in order to achieve peaceful assimilation with the Israelites (Josh. 9:3–15). At first glance, this seems to be a rather peculiar story, but the excavation has demonstrated that Gibeon was not destroyed during the period of the conquest. The culture of the city shows no definite break between pre-Israelite and Israelite times but rather a gradual transition. The same structures continued to be used. The story in the Book of Joshua may in some way reflect long-standing Gibeonite policies. Among the worn articles the Gibeonites showed Joshua were old wineskins; thus the first time the Gibeonites appear in the Bible they are connected with wine. It is impossible to determine if this is a coincidence. Joshua soon learned that the men who told him that they had come from far away were in fact Gibeonites. He did not break his covenant with them, but proclaimed that they would be "hewers of wood and drawers of water." It is possible that yet another famous aspect of Gibeon is referred to here. The inhabitants of Gibeon certainly had complex and peculiar methods of drawing their water, and the "pool" at Gibeon was well known.

Nothing is said of Gibeon in the Bible thereafter for almost two centuries. Then early in the reign of David, Joab is said to have met Abner in battle there (II Sam. 2:13–17). Twelve champions from each side fought by the "pool of Gibeon." When the contestants killed each other, a full-scale battle erupted. Nothing further is said about the location, but behind the passage lies the assumption that the pool was a well-known place that could

The "pool" of Gibeon after excavation.

identify the scene of an event without further explanation. The two forces most likely agreed to meet at a place they both knew well. The great cylindrical shaft with the stairs is, as has been shown, an impressive structure likely to be remembered. A wide open space around it would have been a suitable location for the battle. There is no other candidate for the "pool of Gibeon" yet known, and it seems quite probable that this shaft was the very site of that affair.

Later, Joab killed Amasa on the highway at "the great stone which is in Gibeon." The excavators did not discover anything that might be called a "great stone." A third gruesome tale involves David's surrender of seven of Saul's sons to the Gibeonites for hanging (II Sam. 21:1–6; 8–10). Atonement for Saul's murder of several Gibeonites was necessary in order to halt a famine. It is clear that the Gibeonites were still unassimilated in David's time. The passage explicitly states, "Now the Gibeonites were not of the people of Israel, but of the remnant of the Amorites, although the people of Israel had sworn to spare them." Furthermore, the Gibeonites would have taken blood revenge of their own volition if they had followed Israelite custom.

Yet, by about 960 B.C., at the start of Solomon's reign, the city was considered Israelite and the Israelites sacrificed on its high place. The Gibeon altar seems to have been a favorite one of Solomon's before the temple was built, and it was there that he was granted his wisdom (I Kings 3:4–6; 9–13). It was conveniently located not far from Jerusalem. It is quite possible that this same high place was once used for Canaanite purposes, but it has not been located and therefore cannot be checked. The high place may be near to Gibeon, on the mountain Nebi Samwil, and not on the tell proper. The importance of the story is in its correlation with the archaeological record about the gradual transition of Gibeon from Canaanite to Israelite. The chronicler states that Gibeon had once housed the tent of meeting (II Chron. 1:3, 13), the ark, and the altar of burnt offering (I Chron. 16:39). Apparently its non-Israelite aspect had been forgotten, or deserved no mention in the fifth century B.C. when the chronicler was writing.

There is no further biblical report of Gibeon for the next four centuries. The adage "no news is good news" seems to hold true in this case, for Gibeon was flourishing at the time. Fortunately, the archaeological record has been able to fill in the gap where the historic accounts are silent. The dating of the winery revealed that this period witnessed the height of Gibeon's wine production.

Finally, a Gibeonite prophet is reported in the days of Nebuchadnezzar (Jer. 28:17). This is the false prophet Hananiah who opposed Jeremiah. "Hananiah ben Nera" was one of the most common names inscribed on the jar handles found on the site. Jeremiah supported the Rechabites who abstained from drinking wine. W. L. Reed suggests that in view of Gibeon's interest in wine, perhaps there were more motives than the obvious ones for the enmity between Hananiah and Jeremiah!

After the fall of Jerusalem, Ishmael's forces met Johanan's at "the great waters that are in Gibeon" (Jer. 41:12). This reference to a body or container of water in the city and other references to Gibeon and Gibeonites cannot be related to the results of the excavation.

SUGGESTED TOPICS FOR FURTHER STUDY

1. The stamped and inscribed jar handles from Gibeon.
2. The water systems of Gibeon and Megiddo.
3. Industrial Gibeon.

RECOMMENDED READING

"Gibeon" in *The Biblical World,* ed. Charles F. Pfeiffer (Grand Rapids: Baker, 1966), pp. 261–68.

Pritchard, J. B., "Gibeon" in *The Interpreter's Dictionary of the Bible,* ed. G. A. Buttrick (New York: Abingdon Press, 1962), vol. 2, pp. 392–93.

———, *Gibeon: Where the Sun Stood Still* (Princeton: Princeton University, Press, 1962).

———, "Gibeon: Where the Sun Stood Still" in *Archaeological Discoveries in the Holy Land* (New York: Crowell, 1967), pp. 139–46.

———, "Industry and Trade at Biblical Gibeon," *Biblical Archaeologist* 23 (1960), pp. 23–29.

Reed, W. L., "Gibeon" in *Archaeology and Old Testament Study*, ed. D. W. Thomas (Oxford: Clarendon, 1967), pp. 231–43.

FOR FURTHER READING

Dajani, A. K., *Annual of the Department of Antiquities of Jordan*, nos. 1 and 2.

Pritchard, J. B., *The Bronze Age Cemetery at Gibeon* (Philadelphia: University of Pennsylvania Museum Monograph, 1963).

———, *Hebrew Inscriptions and Stamps from Gibeon* (Philadelphia: University of Pennsylvania Museum Monograph, 1959).

———, *The Water System of Gibeon* (Philadelphia: University of Pennsylvania Museum Monograph, 1961).

———, *Winery, Defenses and Soundings at Gibeon* (Philadelphia: University of Pennsylvania Museum Monograph, 1964).

21

Hazor

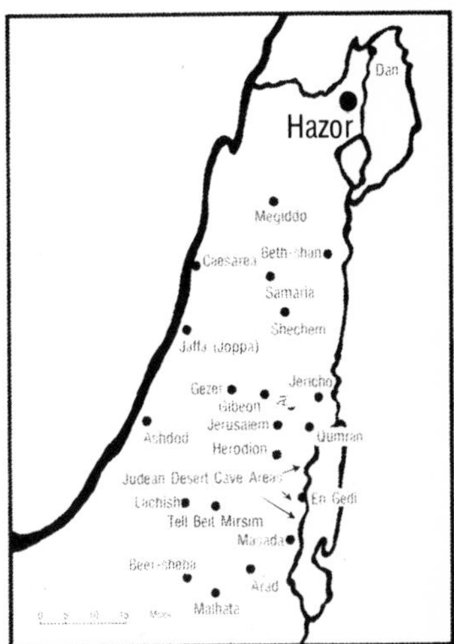

Tell el-Qedah is a hill in Upper Galilee that contains the ruins of the city of Hazor, located five miles northwest of Safed and almost ten miles due north of Capernaum. Kibbutz Ayelet Hashahar lies at the foot of the tell. The tell commands the Huleh Valley, an important military and caravan route.

Hazor was first identified by J. L. Porter. The tell was again proposed as the site of Hazor by J. Garstang in 1926, and the identification has been generally accepted since then. Final proof has come from the recent discovery of a cuneiform tablet on the site. The tablet deals with local real estate and names the town.

Garstang conducted soundings at Hazor in 1928, under the sponsorship of the Palestine Exploration Fund, but it was not until 1955 that full-scale excavation was started. This was the J. A. de Rothschild expedition, which was co-sponsored by the Hebrew University. It was led by Yigael Yadin and on its staff were included many people now famous in Israeli archaeology. The excavation was conducted in the years 1955–58, and again in 1968–69.

There is no doubt that Hazor was the most outstanding city in Palestine during the Middle and Late Bronze periods. An earthen rampart was built during Hyksos times, about 1750 B.C., to create a great lower city of 175 acres at the foot of the tell. The lower city supplemented an upper city which alone stretches over some thirty acres. After the rampart was built, Hazor

Section of the casemate wall at Hazor with pillared warehouse in the background.

rivaled the greatest cities of the Near East in size and commercial importance, with a population estimated at forty-thousand people. As a result, there are many extrabiblical literary references to the city. These include the Posener Execration Texts (nineteenth century B.C.?), the Mari letters (eighteenth century B.C.), four Amarna letters, and the city lists of Thutmosis III (1504–1450), Amenophis II (1450–1425), and Sethos I (1318–1304). Therefore the chronological problems of Hazor are related to the history of areas outside of Palestine. Yadin believes that by fixing the approximate date of the construction of the lower city, he has helped to fix the date of the Mari letters.

Among the most significant finds are several Canaanite temples of the peak period of Hazor's prosperity. Three temple sites were located in the lower city: a large building using an extensive drain system (for sacrificial blood?) was constructed in Middle Bronze II C and continued in use, with improvements, through the fourteenth century; on another site was found an important group of stelae and statuettes of the fourteenth and thirteenth centuries, with representations of male deities and of hands stretched toward a moon symbol; and a succession of temples was found on one spot in Area H. These series of temples began in Middle Bronze II C (seventeenth-sixteenth centuries B.C.) as a broad hall with a raised platform to the south. In succeeding periods it was expanded and remodeled till in Late Bronze II A and B (fourteenth and thirteenth centuries) it resembled temples unearthed at Alalakh and the biblical description of Solomon's temple (with a porch, a hall, and a "Holy of Holies"). The upper city yielded a palace of the Late Bronze Age which contained orthostats, including one with a relief of a lioness, similar to those found in the contemporary temple in Area H.

A Canaanite cult mask unearthed at Hazor.

It is important to understand the greatness of Hazor in the Middle and Late Bronze Ages in order to grasp the full significance of its destruction. The Rothschild expedition has shown that Hazor maintained its size and strength until it was completely demolished some time in the thirteenth century. The lower city was never used again and the upper city was inhabited by a new group of people who rarely reused anything from the former city. Because of the clear evidence of a violent destruction and the numerous references to Hazor in the Bible, the excavation of the city has provided information extremely important in understanding the Israelite conquest.

The biblical references to the conquest of Hazor and its king are to be found in Joshua 11:10–13 and Judges 4–5. Arguments in interpretation have surrounded the correlation of these two descriptions, but it is the story in Joshua that tells of the burning of the city. Yadin feels that the archaeological record of the destruction fits the biblical account so well that he describes it as a serious challenge to those who doubt the historicity of Joshua 11. The account in Judges 4–5 of a second Israelite campaign against the forces of "Jabin king of Hazor" must now be carefully reconsidered. Sisera is evidently the real foe in these chapters, yet if he is connected with a still existing kingship at Hazor, then the destruction of Hazor should *follow* the Israelite settlement of Galilee. The archaeological evidence is against this (cf. below).

The Joshua account refers to Hazor as "the head of all those kingdoms." While the excavation was unable to define this position more clearly, it is evident that a city of such dimensions would control a vast area around it.

After the destruction layer mentioned above, there is a layer clearly showing occupation by seminomadic people. There are no city walls and no public buildings, but only evidence of the foundations of huts or tents, cooking installations, and storage pits. This is an extremely significant layer, since it is undoubtedly a sign of the first settling down of the nomadic Israelites. The pottery is similar to examples found in small Iron Age settlements in Upper Galilee, excavated by Aharoni, who claims they represent this early Israelite phase. The relative chronology given by the Hazor excavation is crucial: the destruction precedes the settlement. Those who maintain the concept of the peaceful infiltration of the Israelites into the land will now have to contend with the Hazor evidence.

The unwalled village was replaced by a well-fortified Solomonic city. I Kings 9:15f. reports that Solomon built Hazor, Megiddo, Gezer, and Jerusalem, and explains how he acquired Gezer. Since no explanation is given for Hazor and Megiddo, it is presumed that Solomon was in control of them already. This is in accord with the evidence for the Israelite conquest given earlier. Yadin found that there were matching Solomonic gates at Gezer and Hazor, but the excavation of Megiddo had confused the stratigraphy there. Therefore, in 1960 and again in 1966 and 1967, he conducted brief soundings at Megiddo in order to reinvestigate the problem. This effort has definitely proven the similarity among the three cities. At Hazor, the Solomonic level is now known to have been confined to a relatively small settlement on the western side of the main (upper) tell.

Solomonic Hazor is clearly separated from the next period of rebuilding, the time of Ahab. Ahab's city differed greatly from Solomon's. The new city had much stronger fortifications and

View northward up the Huleh Valley from atop the mound of Hazor.

Water shaft at Hazor.

Stelae and statuettes from the Late Bronze Canaanite temple at Hazor.

Ruins of one of the Canaanite temples at Hazor.

STRATA AND PERIODS OF ARCHAEOLOGICAL EXCAVATIONS AT HAZOR

General Strata				
Upper City	Lower City	Period	Principal Features	Excavation Areas
I	—	Hellenistic — 2nd cent. BCE	Citadel	B, (A)
II	—	Persian — 4th cent. BCE	Citadel & settlement	B, b
III	—	Assyrian — 7th cent. BCE	Citadel	B
IV	—	Israelite — 8th cent. BCE	Unfortified village	B, G
V	—	Israelite — 8th cent. BCE	Destroyed by Tiglath-Pileser III in 732 BCE	A, B, b
VI	—	Israelite — 8th cent. BCE	Jeroboam II — destruction by earthquake	A, B, b
VII	—	Israelite — 9th cent. BCE	Partial restoration of stratum VIII	A, B, b
VIII	—	Israelite — 9th cent. BCE	Omrid dynasty	A, B, b
IX	—	Israelite — end of 10th begin. of 9th cent. BCE	Destroyed by Ben-Hadad I	A, B, b(2)
X	—	Israelite — middle 10th century BCE	City of Solomon	A, B, b(2)
XI	—	Israelite — 11th cent. BCE	Limited unfortified settlement	B
XII	—	Israelite — 12th cent. BCE	Beginning of Israelite semi-nomadic settlement	A, B
XIII	1a	Canaanite — 13th cent. BCE	Destruction by Joshua	A, B, C, D, E, F, H, K, 210
XIV	1b	Canaanite — 14th cent. BCE	El-Amarna period	" " " "
XV	2	Canaanite — 15th cent. BCE	Thutmose III — Amenhotep II	" " " "
XVI	3	17th—16th centuries BCE	Destruction by Amosis	A, B, C, D, E, F, G, H, K, 210
XVII	4	18th—17th centuries BCE	Foundation of Lower City	" " " " "
XVIII	—	21st—20th centuries BCE	Semi-nomadic settlement	A, B
XIX XX	— —	26th—24th centuries BCE	Early Bronze III (Khirbet Kerak culture)	A
XXI	—	27th century BCE	End of Early Bronze II	A

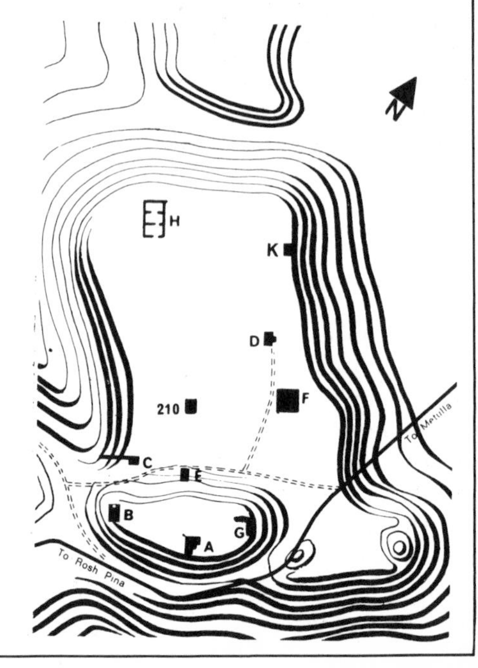

was basically a citadel covering the entire main tell, while Solomon's had been more of an administrative center than a fortress. An enormous underground water system and storehouses were created as preparations for periods of siege, and the size of the city was doubled. The huge water system, including a pool and its shaft, was found after a search inspired by the parallels between Ahab's Hazor and the Megiddo of his time. The shaft of the Hazor water system is about fifty by sixty feet at its entrance and goes down through the mound and the bedrock below nearly a hundred feet. A ten-foot-wide staircase is cut into the sides of the shaft, which culminates in a sloping tunnel leading over eighty feet further through the rock. The tunnel ends where water is reached, 140 feet below the surface of the tell. The tunnel's west-southwesterly orientation surprised the excavators, who had expected it to make straight for the springs to the south of the mound. Evidently the original architects were aware that they would strike water *within* the mound, and with a shorter tunnel, once they reached the level of the springs outside the city.

II Kings 15:29 tells of the fall of Hazor in 732 B.C. Excavation has shown that in the period before this destruction, the inhabitants of Hazor tried desperately to alter their city to be better able to meet the enemy. Many changes in the city date from this time. Above a layer showing the terrible destruction wrought by the Assyrians in 732 is a phase containing very poor structures. Eventually a large Assyrian or Babylonian fortress was built on one side; this was reused in the Persian period and rebuilt in Hellenistic times. There may be some connection between the fort and the battles of the Hasmonean Jonathan against the forces of the Syrian king Demetrius on the plain of Hazor mentioned in I Maccabees 11. Before the excavation, it was not known if the passage referred to a settlement that existed at Hazor at the time, but now evidence indicates that the site was occupied in the Maccabean period.

SUGGESTED TOPICS FOR FURTHER STUDY

1. References to Hazor in the Mari letters.
2. The Hyksos ramparts in Palestine.
3. Canaanite temples at Hazor.
4. Evidence for the earliest Israelite settlement in Palestine.
5. The Hazor water system.
6. Hazor and Megiddo: two cities rebuilt by Ahab.
7. The Solomonic gateways at Hazor, Gezer, and Megiddo.

RECOMMENDED READING

"Hazor" in *The Biblical World,* ed. Charles F. Pfeiffer (Grand Rapids: Baker, 1966), pp. 283–86.

"Hazor" in *Encyclopedia Judaica* (Jerusalem: Keter, 1971), vol. 7, cols. 1535–39.

Yadin, Yigael, "Excavations at Hazor" in *The Biblical Archaeologist Reader,* ed. E. F. Campbell, Jr., and D. N. Freedman (Garden City, NY: Doubleday, 1964), vol. 2, pp. 191–224.

———, "The Fifth Season of Excavations at Hazor, 1968–1969," *Biblical Archaeologist* 32 (1969), pp. 50–71.

———, *Hazor* (London: Oxford, 1972).

———, "Hazor" in *Archaeology and Old Testament Study,* ed. D. Winton Thomas (Oxford: Clarendon, 1967), pp. 224–63.

———, *Hazor: The Rediscovery of a Great Citadel of the Bible* (New York: Random House, 1975).

———, "The Rise and Fall of Hazor" in *Archaeological Discoveries in the Holy Land* (New York: Thomas Crowell, 1967), pp. 57–66.

FOR FURTHER READING

Garstang, J., *Foundations of Biblical History: Joshua, Judges* (London: Constable & Co., Ltd., 1931).

Yadin, Yigael, "Excavations at Hazor," *Israel Exploration Journal* 6 (1956), pp. 120–25; 7 (1957), pp. 118–23; 8 (1958), pp. 1–14; 9 (1959), pp. 74–88; 19 (1969), pp. 1–19.

———, "The Fifth Season of Excavations at Hazor," *Biblical Archaeologist* 32 (1969), pp. 50–71.

Yadin, Yigael, et al., *Hazor I: An Account of the First Season of Excavations, 1955* (Jerusalem: Magnes Press, 1956).

———, *Hazor II: An Account of the Second Season of Excavations, 1956* (Jerusalem: Magnes Press, 1960).

———, *Hazor III–IV: An Account of the Third and Fourth Seasons of Excavations, 1957–1958* (Jerusalem: Magnes Press, 1961).

22

Herodion

Herodion is the site of a fortress complex which Herod the Great began to construct in 24 B.C. It was completed by 15 B.C., for Josephus reports that Herod showed off the palace to his friend, Marcus Agrippas, upon his visit to Palestine at that time (*Wars* I.21.10; *Ant.* XV.9.4). Herodion was but one of a chain of such palatial fortresses, which also included Masada, Alexandrium, Hyrcania, Machaerus, and Cypros. Its location in the Judean desert seven miles south of Jerusalem and approximately three miles southeast of Bethlehem placed it in an extremely strategic location as a refuge and a retreat.

An incident earlier in Herod's life may have influenced his selection of the site. During a Parthian invasion of the Syro-Palestinian area, Herod was forced to flee Jerusalem (40 B.C.). In his flight he encountered hostile Jewish troops near the place where Herodion was later built. Upon defeating this resistance, he made his way to Rome where he received military aid and was named king of Judea, a fiction that became a fact in 37 B.C. with the assistance of Rome.

Near Bethlehem, a Taamira Bedouin encampment with the Herodion in the background.

The Arabic name of the site is Jebel el-Fureidis ("the Hill of Paradise"). C. R. Conder discovered an Idumean royal tomb with the inscription, *kabr el melek fordus* ("tomb of King Paradise"), but he noted that Ferdus was a common Idumean name equivalent to "Herodus." Accordingly, the name is probably a corruption of the name *Herod.* Herodion has also been called Frankenburg ("Hill of the Franks"), because many Euro-

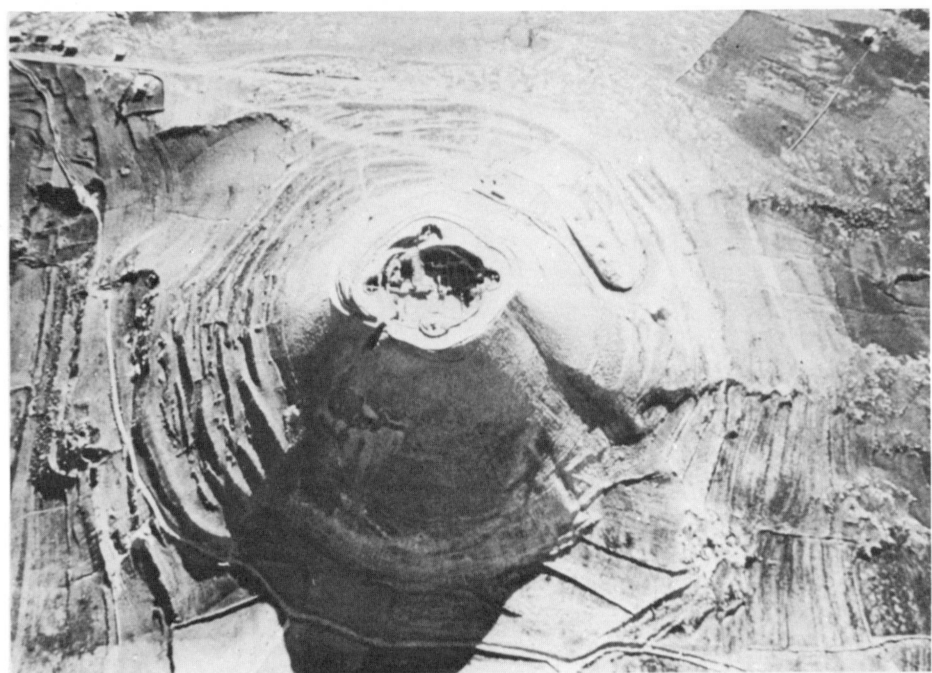

Air view of the Herodion.

Closeup view of the Herodion excavation.

pean travelers in the Holy Land mistook the ruins for a Crusader castle.

Herodion was designated by Herod to be the site of his tomb (Josephus, *Ant.* XVII.8.3), and he is reported to have been buried in a full-size golden coffin rather than having his bones placed in an ossuary, as was the custom at the turn of the era. The location of the tomb in the complex was not specified by Josephus, and the recent excavations discussed below have not led to its discovery.

Nineteenth-century travelers visited and described the site, but actual excavations were first carried out from 1962 to 1967 by an expedition jointly sponsored by the Department for Cultural Relations of the Government of Italy and the Custodia di Terre Sancta (Franciscan Order). Vergilio Corbo directed these excavations. In the winter and spring of 1968–69, Gideon Foerster was commissioned by the Department of Antiquities and National Parks to further excavate and clear the site. As a result, three occupational levels have been discerned: the fortress palace built by Herod and used until the end of the first Jewish revolt against the Romans; a phase during the second (Bar Kochba) revolt; and a minor occupation by Christian monks.

The fortress palace was built atop a mountain which is 2489 feet above sea level today. Herod's engineers built massive earthen ramparts 150 feet high, artificially elevating the mountain. The citadel was protected by double walls with four towers at the major compass points. The eastern tower is completely round. Foerster believes that Herod's coffin reposes somewhere within its sixty-foot diameter, but the entrance to the tower was not discovered, and there are no plans at the moment for further excavations. The other three towers are semicircular in form.

Within the walls the eastern sector was constructed as a court with three rows of free-standing columns and another row of half-columns attached to the wall. An entrance room to the palace had fine plastering and dado panels painted in red, green, and black. This room showed signs of a conflagration which probably occurred in A.D. 72. The western half of the palace included a large dining hall (triclinium) with adjoining rooms and a Roman-style bath. The walls of the bath were made of stucco and were painted so that they would resemble marble. The floors were inlaid with mosaic tile, and the whole bath installation included an *apodyterium* ("dressing room"), a *frigidarium* ("cold bath"), and a *tepidarium* ("hot bath").

On the northern side of the palace, Corbo uncovered numerous examples of graffiti. These were written in Hebrew, Aramaic, Greek, and Latin and date from the Herodian, Zealot,

Bar Kochba, and Byzantium periods. A number of ostraca were also recovered. These writings include people's names, messages, witticisms, and pornographic expressions.

The corridor between the walls provided access to the guard towers and to underground storerooms and reservoirs. All these features bear similarities to the complex which Yadin excavated at Masada, and scholars believe that the architects who built Herodion were also involved in the construction of Masada and, possibly, with the work done at the temple mount.

According to Josephus, surrounding the foot of the hill upon which the acropolis was built were numerous apartments, gardens, baths, storehouses, terraces, and pools (*Ant.* XV.9.4.). The pools particularly impressed the historian, for there is no water nearby; it was supplied from Solomon's Pools and Artas (both near Bethlehem) via aqueducts. Vaulted channels measuring three meters high have been uncovered; they were designed to feed into four huge plastered cisterns located fifty feet beneath the palace. It is probable that donkeys loaded with water jugs brought the water up to the fortress, as at Masada.

Some of the evidence from the Herodian period was obliterated by later occupation, although some small items such as sherds, glass, ostraca, coins, and an inkwell which is similar to those uncovered at Qumran were found. Herodion provided a defensive fortress for Zealot forces during the first revolt (A.D. 66–73). After the destruction of the temple in A.D. 70, it was a stronghold of Jewish resistance that Rome was compelled to eradicate. In A.D. 72 the Roman general, Lucilius Bassus, captured Herodion. The excavators found evidence of the power of Roman siege machines in the battered walls of the fortress.

During the Bar Kochba revolt (A.D. 132–35), Herodion was reoccupied as a major military fortress of the revolutionaries. The Bar Kochba letters recovered from the Wadi Murabbaat indicate that the site was used as a center for collecting grain and as a treasury seat to which the annual tithe was sent. The excavations recovered coins, ostraca, and graffiti, and evidence of structural modifications of a minor nature. The eastern hall was converted into an assembly hall or a synagogue, and in an adjoining room were discovered facilities for what archaeologists believe was a ritual bath (*mikveh*). At the close of the revolt, Herodion was abandoned.

In the course of the fifth century Christian monks came into the Judean desert and established a chapel among the ruins. This was also the case at Masada and at Khirbet Mird. The chief finds from this Byzantine period include inscriptions, coins, and some evidence of the adaptation of one of Herod's halls for use as a chapel. The Muslim conquest in the seventh century ended this occupation, and the ruins lay undisturbed until the recent excavations.

SUGGESTED TOPICS FOR FURTHER STUDY

1. A survey of Herod's desert fortresses.
2. The epigraphic materials from Herodion.
3. Herodion according to Josephus and according to archaeology.
4. Architectural styles of the Herodian period.
5. Solomon's Pools and the aqueducts.

RECOMMENDED READING

Flavius Josephus: The Second Jewish Commonwealth, ed. Nahum Glatzer (New York: Schocken Books, 1971).

"Herodion" in *The Biblical World,* ed. Charles F. Pfeiffer (Grand Rapids: Baker, 1966), pp. 287–89.

"Herodion" in *Encyclopedia Judaica* (Jerusalem: Keter, 1971), vol. 8, cols. 388–90.

"Herodium" in *The Interpreter's Dictionary of the Bible,* ed. G. A. Buttrick (New York: Abingdon Press, 1962), vol. 2, pp. 595–96.

Josephus (New York: Washington Square Press, 1965).

Rabinowitz, M., "Herodion," *Hadassah,* Sept. 1972, p. 20f.

FOR FURTHER READING

Conder, C. R., "Herodium," *Palestine Exploration Fund Quarterly Statement* (1877).

Corbo, V., "Gebal Fureidis: Risultati della prime campagne di scava all' Herodion," *La Terre Santa* (Aug.-Oct. 1962), pp. 231–35.

Foerster, G., "Herodion," *Israel Exploration Journal* 19 (1969), pp. 123–24.

23

Jaffa

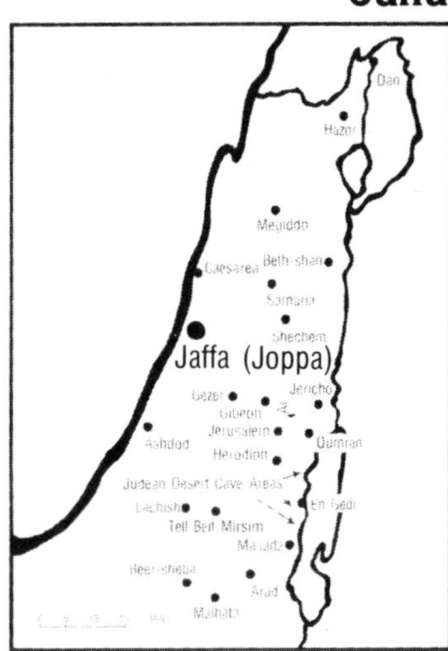

Jaffa (often referred to as Joppa) is an ancient port city situated in the central sector of the coastal plain. Today Jaffa is a part of the city of Tel Aviv. The ancient city was built on a rock hill 116 feet high which juts out westward into the Mediterranean Sea. A natural breakwater of rocks formed a shallow harbor on the northern side of the cape, and this harbor gave ancient Joppa its reason for existence. The name *Jaffa* is derived from the Hebrew word *yapo* meaning "pretty or lovely." Until quite recently most of the history of ancient Jaffa was derived from historical and literary sources. Modern Jaffa is built on the ruins of previous settlements which date back into the Bronze Age. Because the site was densely populated, excavations in the area were not possible. But beginning in the early 1950s the town of Jaffa underwent a massive reconstruction program which has permitted excavations. In 1949–50 P. L. O. Guy of the Israeli Department of Antiquities took a sounding of the site. A more intensive investigation at the site was conducted by J. Kaplan of the Museum of Antiquities, Tel Aviv-Jaffa, from 1955 to 1966. The three areas under investigation were: Area A—the eastern part of the citadel; Area B—the Hamman or Turkish Bath area, and Area C—the area around the Church of St. Peter.

Jaffa was an important port city located on the Via Maris, the trade route from Mesopotamia to Egypt. During the Hyksos period (eighteenth century B.C.) a walled fortress was built to protect the city. Kaplan has uncovered a square enclosure with a rampart built of beaten earth which can be dated to this period. Excavations at Area A (the eastern part of the citadel) have uncovered pieces of sun-dried clay bricks which date back to the sixteenth century B.C. Ancient documents indicate that Egypt maintained military control over this area from the fifteenth to the thirteenth century B.C. The Harris Papyrus, which was uncovered at Thebes, relates that during the reign of Thutmosis III Jaffa was besieged by the Egyptian general Thoth (or Thuti). Thoth eventually conquered the city by tricking the prince of Jaffa into allowing the Egyptians to "surrender" to the prince. Five hundred Egyptian soldiers brought into Jaffa two hundred baskets which were to be part of the tribute to the victorious prince. À lá the Trojan Horse and Ali Baba, two hundred Egyptian soldiers leaped out of the baskets and conquered the city. On the walls of the temple of Karnak the name of Jaffa was included in the list of Canaanite cities conquered by Thutmosis III. Among the Tell el-Amarna letters (ca. 1350 B.C.) Jaffa is mentioned as being one of the important Egyptian military outposts in the area. One of the letters relates that the city was ruled by a native prince who had received Egyptian training. This document revealed that the prince of Jaffa wrote to Abdu-heba, prince of Jerusalem, requesting military support. In another letter, Hori, an Egyptian official stationed in Jaffa, wrote to the scribe Amen-em-opet, describing the beauties of Jaffa's gardens and the skill of its leather, wood, and metal artisans.

Excavations have uncovered three stones which were part of the citadel gate located on stratum V. They were inscribed with various titles of Ramses II, such as "Horus the mighty bull, beloved of the goddess Maat, King of Upper and Lower Egypt." Kaplan also uncovered a road two to four meters wide which extended eighteen meters from the citadel gate. The walls of ancient Jaffa were built of sun-dried bricks which bore signs of being destroyed by fire. It is believed that the city of stratum V was destroyed sometime near the end of the reign of Ramses II. Stratum IV (dated sometime in the twelfth century B.C.) was built during the reign of Ramses III (ca. 1198–1166) two meters above the ruins of stratum V. The walls of stratum IV were built upon the exact lines of the burnt walls of stratum V. This city was also violently destroyed, supposedly by the Sea Peoples who invaded the coastal shores in the twelfth century B.C. These invaders included the Philistines who came from the Aegean isles and maintained control over the coastal region of Palestine from the twelfth to the tenth century B.C. The supposition that stratum IV was conquered by the Sea People-Philistines is strengthened by the discovery of Philistine ash pots and pot-

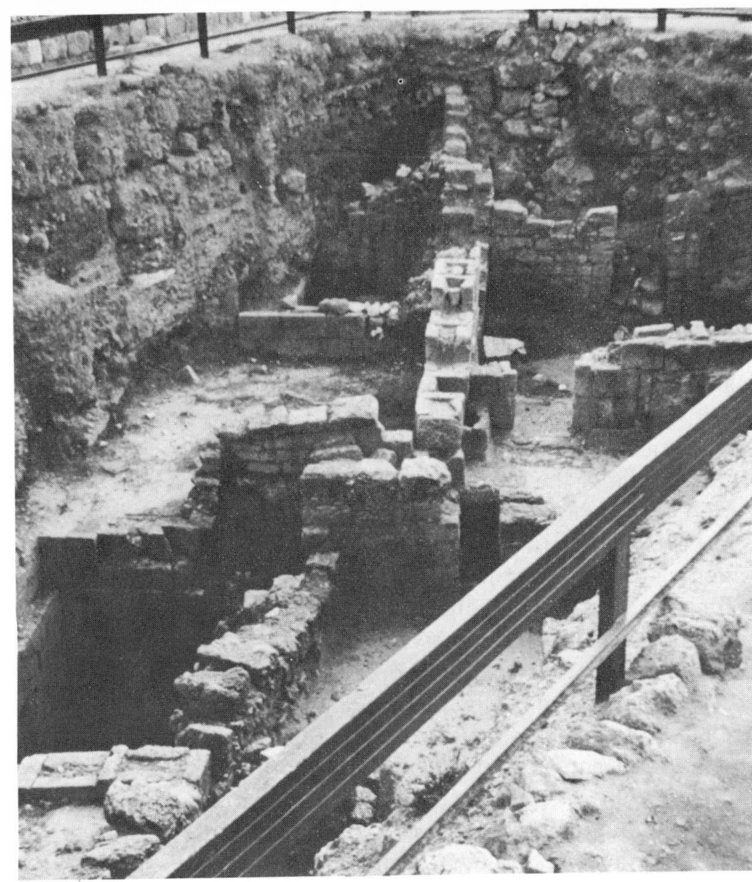

General view of excavations at Jaffa.

sherds among the debris found in the ruins of the city. It is quite possible that it was during this period that Jaffa became identified with a geographical site in Greek mythology. According to Greek legend, the city was founded by King Cepheus who named it after his wife Iopia (Cassiopeia). As part of a sacrifice to a sea monster the couple's daughter, Andromeda, was chained to a rock located in the harbor. Andromeda was saved from a sure death by the hero Perseus, who slew the monster and freed the maiden.

In Joshua 19:46 it is reported that the city was given to the tribe of Dan, but it is doubtful that they controlled the city. Two centuries later David crushed the Philistine domination of the coastal area. During Solomon's construction of the temple in Jerusalem, Jaffa was the port to which King Hiram of Tyre sent the cedars of Lebanon which were used in its construction. (Jaffa was used again for this purpose in the building of the second temple; cf. Ezra 3:7). It was from the port of Jaffa that the prophet Jonah boarded a ship in hope of escaping the calling of the Lord (Jonah 1:3).

Excavations have revealed part of a fortification from the ninth century B.C. The fortifications uncovered at Area B (Turkish Bath area) included a glacis which had a width of four to five meters; its exterior was made of stone while its interior was constructed of alternate layers of earth and sun-dried bricks. After the Assyrian invasion of Judah in the eighth century B.C., Jaffa was included in the list of conquered cities inscribed on the prism stele located in Sennacherib's palace at Nineveh. The Eshmunazar and Ben Abdun inscriptions of the fifth century B.C. indicate that the cities of Jaffa and Dor were given to Eshmunazar, king of Sidon, as a gift from the king of Persia (probably Artaxerxes II—404–358 B.C.). In 1892 a Sidonian stone which mentions the establishment of a Sidonian temple in Jaffa was uncovered. It also describes how the worship of Eshmun (Egyptian Osiris or Greek Adonis) and Baal Gad had been established in the city. Jaffa became an independent city after the destruction of Sidon by Artaxerxes III (358–338 B.C.).

The city was conquered in 332 B.C. by Alexander the Great. He established a mint in the city. Shortly after his death in 323 B.C., his empire was divided among his generals. Control of Jaffa repeatedly switched hands between the Egyptian Ptolemies and the Syrian Seleucids. After the battle of Ipsus in 301 B.C., Jaffa fell under the control of Ptolemy I (323–283 B.C.). The Greeks altered the name of the city to Ioppe. Under the reign of Ptolemy II and Ptolemy III coins bearing the name *Ioppe* were minted in the city. In 1961 a third-century B.C. catacomb dedicated to Ptolemy Philopator (221–203 B.C.) and his wife Bernice was discovered. In 198 B.C. Jaffa was annexed to Syria after the victory of Antiochus III at the battle of Panean (Banias).

During the Maccabean revolt the city was annexed to the Jewish state. In 138 B.C. the Syrians tried to regain control of the city but they were defeated by Jewish forces under the leadership of the Hasmonean king, Simon (I Macc. 15:25–35 and 16:1–10). In 1949 P. L. O. Guy uncovered a hoard of coins from the reign of Alexander Jannaeus (103–76 B.C.). Kaplan's excavations have uncovered the remains of a Hasmonean fortress wall; the floors of the fortress were paved with sea shells. In 66 B.C. the Romans under Pompey occupied Jaffa and made it into an autonomous city in the subprovince of Phoenicia. The city was conquered by Herod in 37 B.C., but the city's populace was so hostile to his rule that he was forced to transfer the site of his main port to Caesarea to the north. Excavations in Area C near the Church of St. Peter have uncovered a house from this period which included an entrance yard, water cistern, and a few rooms.

During the first Jewish revolt (A.D. 66–73) the city was attacked and conquered by the Romans. Vespasian razed the city and stationed a garrison of Roman soldiers there. This victory was commemorated in coins which were minted shortly after the victory. One of them depicted a woman sitting under a palm tree with the inscription *Judea Navalis;* another coin depicted Titus trampling the prow of a ship. The inscription read *Victoria Navalis.* Vespasian erected a fortress and renamed the city Flavia Ioppe. Despite this defeat, the Jewish community in the city slowly grew. A number of tombs which date to the period A.D. 70–126 have been discovered. Included in the discovery were three inscriptions bearing the name *Judah,* an official who was the inspector of weights and measures during the reign of Trajan (A.D. 98–117). Other finds which may date from this period are mostly coins and pieces of pottery. The Talmud mentions a thriving Jewish community in the port of Jaffa. In the New Testament, Peter came to Jaffa upon the request of some Christians. After arriving in the city he revived Tabitha (or Dorcas) from the dead (Acts 9:36–43). Peter stayed in Jaffa for many days at the house of Simon the tanner, where he received a vision which told him that it was now permissible for Christians to eat ritually unclean foods (Acts 10:9–16).

SUGGESTED TOPICS FOR FURTHER STUDY

1. The importance of Jaffa as a port city.
2. Jaffa under Egyptian rule.
3. The history of Jaffa as revealed in ancient documents.
4. The biblical references to Jaffa.
5. Jaffa in the intertestamental period.

RECOMMENDED READING

Abramsky, Samuel, *Ancient Towns in Israel* (Jerusalem: Youth and Hechalutz Department of the World Zionist Organization, 1963), pp. 151–58.

Doudayi, Naomi, "Jaffa Resurgent," *Ariel* 20 (1967), pp. 17–32.

"Jaffa" in *Encyclopedia Judaica* (Jerusalem: Keter, 1971), vol. 9, cols. 1249–51.

"Joppa" in *The Interpreter's Dictionary of the Bible,* ed. G. A. Buttrick (New York: Abingdon Press, 1962), vol. 2, pp. 970–71.

Kaplan, J., "Jaffa's History Revealed by the Spade," *Archaeology* 17 (1964), pp. 270–76.

Charles F. Pfeiffer, ed., *Baker's Bible Atlas* (Grand Rapids: Baker, 1972), pp. 80, 144, 209.

———, *The Biblical World* (Grand Rapids: Baker, 1966), p. 332.

Pritchard, James A., *Ancient Near Eastern Texts* (Princeton: Princeton University Press, 1955), pp. 22–23, 242, 287, 478.

———, *Archaeology and the Old Testament* (Princeton: Princeton University Press, 1958), pp. 70–74, 97, 156.

Tolkowsky, S., *The Gateway of Palestine: A History of Jaffa* (London: G. Routledge & Sons, Ltd., 1924).

FOR FURTHER READING

Kaplan, J., "Jaffa," *Israel Exploration Journal* 6 (1956), pp. 259–60; 10 (1960), pp. 121–22; 11 (1961), pp. 191–92.

Kindler, A., "The Jaffa Hoard of Alexander Jannaeus," *Israel Exploration Journal* 4 (1954), pp. 170–85.

24

Jericho

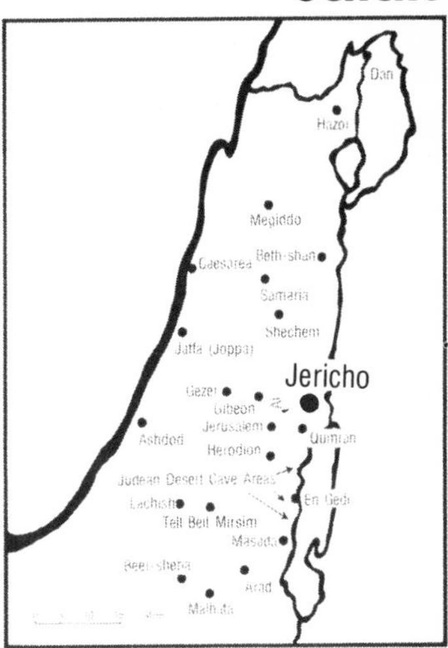

Ancient Jericho, considered by archaeologists to be the oldest town in the world, has emerged slowly, over the last century, from the mound known as Tell es Sultan. Its ruins have yielded meager confirmation of biblical accounts; on the other hand, a fascinating picture of over six millennia of prehistory has unfolded before the eyes of scholars.

Tell es Sultan lies one mile to the northwest of modern Jericho, four-and-a-half miles west of the Jordan River, twelve miles north of the Dead Sea. Adjacent to the site is Ain es Sultan, also known as the Spring of Elisha, the source of water supply for the most ancient settlements as well as for the modern town of Eriha to the southeast. Because of this copious spring, Jericho has been throughout the centuries an oasis in the Dead Sea area. In the Bible it is sometimes called the "city of

The mound of ancient Jericho, looking eastward across the Jordan Valley.

palm trees" (Judg. 3:13; II Chron. 28:15). However, the temperature in this semitropical oasis can reach 120° Fahrenheit in the summer. Jericho's importance was also enhanced by its geographical position, thanks to which it dominated the trade in salt, sulphur, and bitumen from the Dead Sea and controlled the entrance to the hill country of Palestine. The city also dominated the major east-west trade route which provided access to Transjordan and points eastward.

The name *Jericho* is derived from the word *yareah* ("moon"); scholars believe that the city may have been dedicated to the moon goddess Yarih or Yerah, but to readers of the Bible the name *Jericho* immediately calls to mind the account in Joshua according to which "the walls came tumbling down." Joshua, so the story goes, sent two spies to inspect the city and report on the prospects of victory. Upon the return of the spies, the Lord commanded the Israelites to march around the city once each day for six days, and on the seventh to march around it seven times. The people did as commanded, and on the seventh day the walls miraculously collapsed. The Israelite army entered the city, burned it to the ground, and killed all its inhabitants except Rahab and her family, who had protected Joshua's spies during their previous visit to Jericho. Joshua then laid a curse on anyone who would rebuild the city.

The first major excavator of Jericho, John Garstang, caused a considerable stir in the 1930s when he claimed to have found the wall destroyed by the Israelite conquest. He found the remains of two parallel walls, which he associated with a layer of ash which indicated deliberate burning of the city, and with tomb scarabs which seemed to date this stratum to the time of Amenhotep (previous to 1385 B.C.). The immediate cause of the walls' collapse, he said, had been an earthquake.

Eagerly welcomed in some quarters as "proof" of the Bible, Garstang's reconstruction was disproved by Kathleen Kenyon, who, using the precise stratigraphic methods she had perfected, excavated the site in the 1950s. The walls were Early Bronze, a millennium older than the Israelite conquest, and the layer of ashes belonged to an entirely different episode, to the destruction of the city by the Egyptians in the mid-sixteenth century B.C. From the Late Bronze period (1550–1200), when the conquest took place, very few remains have been found, and no traces of any city wall. It is probable that the mud-brick disappeared in a long period when the site was unoccupied and suffered what Miss Kenyon described as the "tremendous denudation" of the upper strata. It is believed that from 1550 to 1400 the site was unoccupied; a small part of the site was reoccupied from

1400 to 1300, since some tombs and pottery which can be attributed to this period have been found. But the surviving evidence suggests that during the actual epoch of the invasion, if it occurred in the thirteenth century as the archaeological evidence indicates, the site was abandoned or sparsely occupied.

As noted above, it has been suggested that erosion removed the city walls of this period; alternatively, the Canaanites of the time may not have built their own walls, but rather reused the defense system of an earlier city. A number of scholars, however, now look for the origin of the story of the "fall of Jericho" in the poetic process of legend formation. They suggest that the biblical account is perhaps etiological—invented centuries later to explain the ruins of the city. The conquest was attributed to Joshua, who some believe was originally the leader of the tribe of Joseph (Ephraim and Manasseh), later adopted as a national folk hero. Jericho was listed as the first city to be conquered because it was geographically a natural point of entry into Canaan from Transjordan; hence the biblical account of Joshua telling the spies to "go view the land, even Jericho" (Josh. 2:1).

Later biblical accounts suggest that, despite Joshua's curse, there was a continuous Israelite occupation at or near the site of Jericho. David sent his servants to recuperate in Jericho after their humiliation by Hanon, king of Amon (II Sam. 10:15; I Chron. 19:5). During the reign of King Ahab, Hiel the Bethelite began building at the site of Jericho, but here the curse took its toll and the oldest and youngest children of Hiel died (I Kings 16:34). Apparently the city was inhabited in the time of Elijah and Elisha, since it is related that the two passed through Jericho before Elijah's ascension (II Kings 2:4–14), and that they were greeted by the "sons of the prophets that were at Jericho" (II Kings 2:5). After the ascension of Elijah, Elisha returned to Jericho, where the people complained to him that their water supply had gone bad; Elisha threw salt into the water and the water sweetened (II Kings 2:21, 22); hence his name was given to the area's major spring. During the Judean revolt against Babylonia, King Zedekiah of Judea was captured by the Babylonians at Jericho while he was fleeing from Jerusalem (II Kings 25:5; Jer. 39:5). Among the Jews who returned to Zion were 345 men who settled in Jericho and who helped in the rebuilding of the walls of Jerusalem (Ezra 2:34; Neh. 3:2; 7:36). Archaeologists have uncovered the remains of a storehouse dating to the reign of King David in the tenth century, and the ruins of an extensive unfortified settlement of the eighth and seventh centuries B.C. This occupation probably continued until the Babylonian destruction in 587 B.C.

The excavation of ancient Jericho began in 1868, when Charles Warren excavated the site for the Palestine Exploration Fund. Unfortunately, the shaft which he dropped into a section of the southern end of the mound hit an Early Bronze mud-brick wall which did not appear to be significant, and so he gave up his excavation. Between 1901 and 1909 Ernst Sellin and Carl Watzinger excavated the site for the Kaiserliche Academie der Wissenschaften in Vienna and the Deutsche Orient-Gesellschaft. They uncovered some of the Neolithic site and unearthed many pieces of pottery; but because the science of archaeology was still in its early stages they gave minimal attention to these valuable finds. Like many early excavators, they were looking for striking individual objects rather than a picture of the total development. A city which Sellin identified with the Israelite city conquered by Joshua was later reassigned to the Middle Bronze period.

John Garstang's excavations, carried out in 1930–36 for the Marston-Melchett expedition, the University of Liverpool, and the British School of Archaeology in Jerusalem, uncovered four stages of mud-brick town walls, two from the Early Bronze, one from the Middle Bronze, and one from the Late Bronze Age. He also discovered twenty-five tombs which he dated to the Early Bronze Age, brought to light the first evidence of occupation in the prepottery Neolithic period, and made the first attempt at establishing a sequence of occupation layers for the site. Level IV was the city which he thought had been destroyed by earthquake and fire at the time of Joshua's invasion.

As stated previously, this conclusion was disproved by the work of Kathleen Kenyon. Her investigations were carried out from 1952 to 1961 for the British School of Archaeology in Jerusalem, the Palestine Exploration Fund, the British Academy, the American Schools of Oriental Research, and the Department of Antiquities of Jordan. The primary interest of Jericho now lies in the previously unknown world of prehistorical civilization which the diggings have revealed.

The earliest evidence of occupation found by Miss Kenyon was discovered on bedrock near the spring. The natural clay at this spot had been removed except in one area, where it was left in place and edged with a stone wall in which two stone sockets had been set. Associated with this curious structure were flints of Mesolithic origin and the remains of timbers which must have been destroyed by fire around 7800 B.C., according to radiocarbon analysis. Kenyon believes that this structure was a shrine erected by Mesolithic hunters visiting the spring. Their descendants—the continuity can be traced in the types of bone and flint artifacts—gradually underwent the transition from nomadic to sedentary and finally to urban existence.

In the core of the mound there remain thirteen feet of tramped-earth surfaces, with humps apparently representing bases on which round superstructures of perishable materials had presumably been erected. Miss Kenyon calls this stage of incipient settlement Proto-Neolithic. The Neolithic settlement at Jericho can be divided into four periods, each with its distinctive culture. In prepottery Neolithic A, the inhabitants lived in rounded houses—a transformation perhaps of the earlier shelters—made of plano-convex mud-bricks. As soon as these houses appeared, the area of the settlement expanded rapidly, until it covered ten acres. Then a free-standing stone wall was built around the city. The wall is believed to have reached a height of twenty-three feet. It was six-and-a-half feet thick and had a circumference of half a mile. A moat was built outside the wall, cut twenty-seven feet wide and nine feet deep into bed-

East-west trench in which the earliest remains of a walled village were uncovered at Jericho.

rock. Inside the eastern wall of the city a circular stone tower, thirty feet high and twenty-eight feet in diameter, was uncovered. Inside the tower was a stairway which led to the top of the wall. The coordinated effort needed to build such fortifications, without the use of metal tools, is rather impressive; it suggests that the town must have possessed a high degree of social organization and control. The extent of the settlement also suggests that a system of irrigation must have been in operation in order to provide a sufficient food supply. The town walls were completely rebuilt three times; after the final stage the level of the ground inside the walls continued to rise with succeeding occupations, until the top of the tower was almost covered. A house destroyed by fire at this point gives a radiocarbon date of 6800 B.C. Thus it is likely that this oldest known city of the ancient world, with its massive fortifications and public works, was in existence before 7000 B.C.

How this first urban civilization came to an end is not known; there is a hard-to-date occupation gap marked by erosion. The artifacts and houses of prepottery Neolithic B (ca. 6250 B.C.) point to an entirely different people who probably shared a common ancestor with the Catal Hüyük people of Anatolia. From this civilization archaeologists have uncovered eleven building phases, and twenty-two stages of superimposed plastered floors. The houses of these people were rectangular, built of mud-brick. The plaster floors were painted red and yellow and burnished with a glossy finish. Impressions of rush mats were found on them. The inhabitants excelled especially in sculpture: they made clay figurines of goats and sheep, a clay model house forty inches long and thirty inches wide, and clay masks. Everything points to a civilization with very elaborate cultic and funerary practices. The dead were buried beneath the floors of the houses; from many of the skeletons the crania were missing. A number of skulls were found, plastered apparently in imitation of the living person's features, probably in connection with an ancestor cult. Some of the skulls had seashells for eyes; their lips were painted, and they may have had wigs or headdresses. However, these people had no knowledge of the art of pottery-making.

The art of pottery-making was known to the next occupants, who arrived, after an indefinite period marked again by abandonment and erosion, perhaps around 4500 B.C.; these strata are accordingly called pottery Neolithic. In other respects, however, this new culture was more primitive than the preceding. Their dwellings were huts constructed over pits cut into the ruins of the prepottery town. The pottery was handmade and mostly very coarse, but some finer vessels were decorated with red chevrons on a cream slip. Sometime before 4000 B.C. came the division between pottery Neolithic A and pottery Neolithic B, which is marked by the appearance of permanent structures made of bun-shaped plano-convex bricks and a new type of pottery covered with a matte red slip and decorated with herringbone incisions.

When the pottery Neolithic stage ended is not certain. Jericho did not share in the cultural flowering of the Chalcolithic period, though the type site for this period (Teleilat el-Ghassul) was only a few miles distant. The pottery Neolithic B people had some contacts with the Ghassulians, and the latter overlapped in time the arrival, dated by radiocarbon at about 3300 B.C., of the groups which Kenyon calls Proto-Urban. One must reckon with an occupation gap of several centuries in the fourth millennium B.C. The question arises how an oasis like Jericho could remain unoccupied for such a long period of time. Kenyon has pointed out that the oasis of Jericho depended on the upkeep of its irrigation system. After a cataclysm such as an invasion the irrigation system was usually destroyed. Within the span of a year the oasis could once again become a desert except for the immediate area surrounding the spring.

The most striking feature of Proto-Urban culture was the burial of the dead in tombs cut out of rocks. Some of these tombs contained the remains of several hundred individuals, the bones having been stacked in the tombs after the flesh decayed. This was a burial practice which was destined to continue in one form or another into the common era. In the Early Bronze Age (ca. 3250–2200 B.C.) the city was protected by a wall of unbaked mud-brick which was built almost exactly over the walls of the Neolithic city. There was also a semicircular tower, a type of structure rare in Palestine during this period. In one area, seventeen different stages of the rebuilding of the town wall have been identified, reflecting repeated destruction through war and earthquake. It is believed that earthquakes occurred as often as once every twenty-five years.

The Early Bronze town was violently destroyed by fire, probably around 2300 B.C. The invaders were nomads, whom Kenyon identifies as Amorites. From the kinds of tombs which were constructed and the kinds of offerings which were placed in them, a picture emerges of a nomadic population with a tribal structure. The town itself was little more than a campsite, yet four hundred tombs were found in which bodies were buried singly, with offerings of copper daggers, pottery, and jewelry.

About 1900 B.C., in the Middle Bronze Age, a population arrived which seems to have been related to the Canaanites of coastal Syria, and urban life resumed. At first the town was fortified with a mud-brick wall, similar to that of the Early Bronze town, but then around the middle of the eighteenth century B.C. a new type of fortification was constructed, consisting of a glacis of beaten earth reinforced with a stone retaining wall twenty feet high. On top of the glacis stood the town wall proper. This type of defense was common during the Hyksos period—the glacis was probably used as a means of defense against the recently developed battering ram.

The connection between Jericho and Egypt in the Middle Bronze period, implied by the Hyksos fortifications, is confirmed by the contents of the rock-hewn tombs in which many

A tomb at ancient Jericho. To the right, an inhabitant of Jericho, ca. 1600 B.C., lying on a bed, beside a table, loaded (removed before the picture was taken) with food. Also in the tomb were the skeletons of (probably) his wife and children.

corpses, apparently of family members, were deposited. In these tombs were found not only objects of bronze and alabaster, scarabs, and jewelry, but also wooden furniture and utensils, reed mattings and baskets, and the remains of offerings of food—ostrich eggs, trays of pomegranates, and platters of roasted sheep. The partial preservation of these perishable objects is due to unique climatic factors in these tombs.

This city was violently destroyed by fire sometime early in the sixteenth century, either by the Egyptians when they expelled the Hyksos from Egypt, or perhaps by the Hyksos themselves. Tell es Sultan was never again a fortified site, although, as previously mentioned, it had a history of sporadic settlement lasting probably until the Babylonian destruction. When Herod rebuilt "Jericho," he chose a site within the oasis south of the mound near the mouth of the Wadi el-Qilt, and it is this city which figures in the New Testament.

SUGGESTED TOPICS FOR FURTHER STUDY

1. Legend and history in the Book of Joshua.
2. Fortifications in prepottery Neolithic A.
3. The oldest towns: a comparative study.

4. Neolithic religious beliefs, as suggested by the evidence from prepottery Neolithic B.
5. Tombs of the Amorite invaders.
6. Tomb-offerings of the Hyksos period.
7. The development of agriculture in the ancient Near East.
8. The development of animal husbandry in the ancient Near East.
9. Herod's Jericho.

RECOMMENDED READING

Avidgad, N., "Jericho," in *Archaeology* (Jerusalem: Keter, 1974), pp. 113–21.

Kelso, J. L., "Jericho" in *The Interpreter's Dictionary of the Bible,* ed. G. A. Buttrick (New York: Abingdon Press, 1962), vol. 2, pp. 835–39.

Kenyon, Kathleen, *Digging Up Jericho* (London: Ernest Benn, Ltd., 1957).

______, *Excavations at Jericho,* vol. I (London: British School of Archaeology in Jerusalem, 1960), vol. II (1965).

______, "Jericho" in *Archaeology and Old Testament Study,* ed. D. Winton Thomas (London: Oxford University Press, 1967), pp. 264–75.

FOR FURTHER READING

Garstang, J. and J. B. E., *The Story of Jericho* (London: Marshall, Morgan & Scott, 1948).

Hawkes, Jacquette, *Atlas of Ancient Archaeology* (London: Heinemann, 1974), p. 198.

"Jericho" in *The Biblical World,* ed. Charles F. Pfeiffer (Grand Rapids: Baker, 1966), pp. 305–09.

"Jericho" in *Encyclopedia Judaica* (Jerusalem: Keter, 1971), vol. 9, cols. 1365–71.

"Jericho" in *The New Bible Dictionary,* ed. J. O. Douglas (Grand Rapids: Eerdmans, 1962), pp. 611–14.

Sellin. E., and C. Watzinger, *Jericho* (Leipzig: J. C. Heinrichs, 1913).

The reports of the various excavators are to be found in *PEFQS (PEQ)* and *QDAP* as follows:

C. Warren, *PEFQS* 1869.

J. Garstang, *PEFQS* 1930, 1931, 1932, 1935; *QDAP* 1934.

K. Kenyon, *PEQ* 1951, 1952, 1953, 1954, 1955, 1956, 1957, 1960.

25

Jerusalem

In contrast to many of the other sites mentioned in the Bible, there has never been any question about the location of Jerusalem, the city that is holy to the three major monotheistic religions—Judaism, Christianity, and Islam. Set in the midst of the central highlands, the city has been occupied continuously throughout its long history. Thus, when archaeologists turned their attention to the Holy Land in the nineteenth century, there was great interest in investigating Jerusalem because of its unique religious and historical significance.

The Bible is replete with explicit references to Jerusalem, beginning with Joshua 10:1, the earliest text containing the name. The Bible is also filled with obvious allusions to it, beginning with the reference to Salem in Genesis 14. In texts already published, the earliest mention of the city outside the Bible is probably the name *Urushalim,* which occurs in the Egyptian Execration Texts of the nineteenth century B.C., but an even earlier reference, dating to the twenty-third century B.C., has been reported in the yet unpublished tablets from Tell Mardikh (Ebla) in Syria. The Amarna letters of the Late Bronze Age discovered in Egypt record the name as *Urusalim,* and Assyrian documents of several centuries later employ the name *Urusilimmu.* From the perspective of biblical history, however, Jerusalem was little more than the citadel of a Canaanite clan, the Jebusites, until its conquest by King David in the tenth century B.C. That astute monarch made the city not only the political and religious capital of Israel, but his own personal possession. Thereafter it has frequently borne the title *City of David*.

The Babylonian exile provided the environment in which the Judean city, which lay desolate in ruins, was transformed into a spiritual entity for the dispersed Jews. The city has since undergone a series of destructions and reconstructions which have changed markedly its material appearance, and in the process destruction debris has been deposited in places up to seventy feet deep. But Jerusalem has always retained the spiritual connotations which have made it *El Quds* ("the Holy City") to the Islamic world, the expression of hope for countless Jews of the Diaspora, reflected in the phrase "next year in Jerusalem," and the focus of pilgrimage for devout Christians through the centuries.

The combination of continual occupation and sacred associations has made archaeological research in Jerusalem incredibly difficult. The repeated destructions and reconstructions of the city have both destroyed ancient remains and impeded an objective study of those that survive. The topography has been altered to a considerable degree by the building programs of past rulers, especially those of Solomon and of Herod, and erosion has affected the city at certain points in its history. The inhabitants of the city have displaced parts of older buildings and reused them in newer structures, and the existing medieval and modern buildings leave a minimal number of areas available for excavation.

The earliest investigations were essentially observations of ancient remains on the surface. These were carried out in the first half of the nineteenth century by E. Robinson, T. Tobler, and C. J. M. deVogue. Their sketches and descriptions record some materials subsequently lost due to modern building activities. The first detailed survey of the city was carried out by Charles Wilson (1864–66), and the first excavation was the work of F. De Saulcy, a French scholar who cleared the so-called Tombs of the Kings, the burial chambers of the house of Adiabene dating to the first century A.D. The British Palestine Exploration Fund was established in 1865 and has since been the most active organization in investigating Jerusalem. From 1867 to 1870 Charles Warren excavated under the fund's auspices. He was restricted by the Turks to digging small pits, but by clandestine tunneling he attempted to trace the line of the ancient walls and the platform of the temple mount.

From this beginning, subsequent investigators have attempted to recover information about the city and its fortifications in the pre-exilic period, to find evidence for the expansion

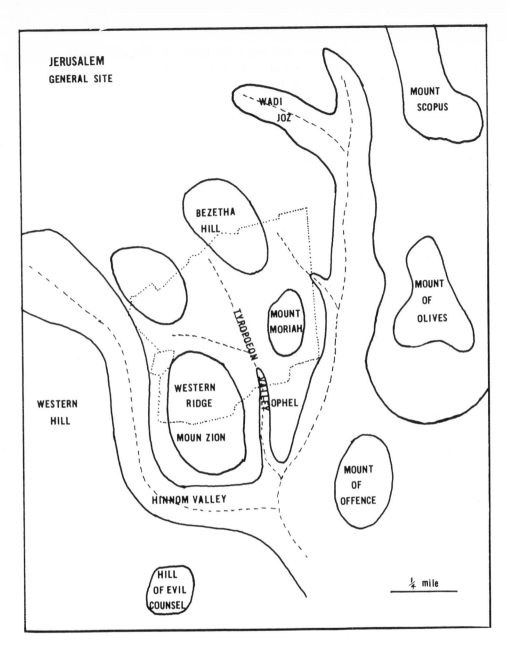

JERUSALEM
GENERAL SITE

WADI JOZ
MOUNT SCOPUS
BEZETHA HILL
MOUNT OF OLIVES
TYROPOEON VALLEY
MOUNT MORIAH
WESTERN RIDGE
OPHEL
WESTERN HILL
MOUN ZION
MOUNT OF OFFENCE
HINNOM VALLEY
HILL OF EVIL COUNSEL
¼ mile

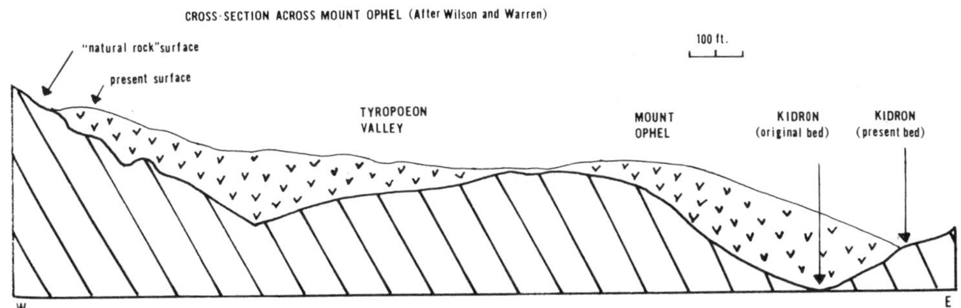

CROSS-SECTION ACROSS MOUNT OPHEL (After Wilson and Warren)

of the city and its fortifications to the western hill, to uncover the extent and nature of the city in the Herodian and Early Roman periods, and to investigate the ancient cemeteries in the vicinity. (Archaeological research, of course, has illuminated subsequent occupational periods—Byzantine, Early Arab, Crusader, etc.—but these are beyond the scope of our present study.)

A stream of investigators worked in Jerusalem from Warren's time until the outbreak of World War I, but all were hampered to some degree by the factors listed previously, as well as by political interference and by the adolescent stage of archaeological research at that time. Conrad Schick, a German architect, made an extended and important topographical study of the city during this period, and the French scholar, C. Clermont-Ganneau, recovered the famous Greek inscription from the Herodian temple period which warned Gentiles not to enter the forbidden inner courts of the temple. Between 1894 and 1897 F. J. Bliss and A. C. Dickie excavated in the area of the Siloam Pool, uncovering the remains of the southern walls of the city. Father L. H. Vincent excavated near the Gihon spring and found caves with pottery dating to the Early Bronze I period, and on the basis of his collection and analysis of all the archaeological data recovered by others, he was able to establish that the southeastern area of the hill Ophel was the site of the original Jebusite city of Jerusalem.

After the establishment of British rule under the mandate in 1920, archaeological work began anew under more favorable circumstances than those imposed by the Turks. R. A. S. Macalister and J. G. Duncan uncovered ancient walls high on the slope of Ophel from 1923 to 1926, attributing them to the Jebusites and the earliest period of Jerusalem; and in nearby excavations in the Tyropoeon Valley that ceased in 1928 J. W. Crowfoot recovered remains from the second temple and Byzantine periods. These excavations in the area of Ophel were the last until Kathleen Kenyon returned to the site in 1961 and continued a series of excavations until 1967.

Miss Kenyon concentrated primarily on the eastern side of Ophel, attempting to clarify the walls and architecture. The excavations revealed the Middle Bronze II city wall some 160 feet *below* the crest of the ridge and slightly above the spring Gihon, the major source of water for ancient Jerusalem. The waters of the spring were made available to the inhabitants within the walls by means of a water shaft (biblical *tzinnor*) which descended to a cave behind the spring. II Samuel 23:14ff. and I Chronicles 11:4ff. tell how David's commander, Joab, exploited

Kathleen Kenyon discovered the remains of King David's Jerusalem in this trench on the eastern slope of Ophel.

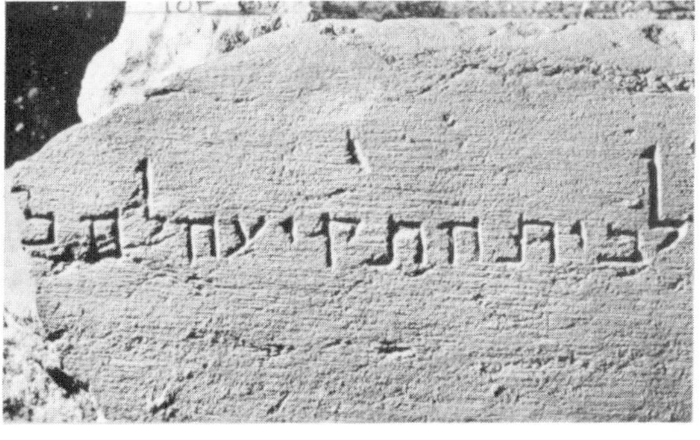

Inscription from top of the southwestern corner of the temple mount: "to the place of trumpeting."

this shaft as an access to the city. The Kenyon excavations thus disproved Macalister's dating of the wall at the crest of the eastern slope; that wall is now considered to have been constructed after the destruction of the first temple, for it was built upon the ruins of houses from that period. Clear signs and physical evidence of the conquest of Jerusalem by the Babylonian army of Nebuchadnezzar were also revealed by Miss Kenyon's research.

Inside Hezekiah's water tunnel.

An interesting insight into the city plan of David's Jerusalem has also resulted from the British excavations on Ophel. The Bible mentions the "Millo" and its reconstruction several times. Since the word signifies "a filling," it has now been established that the Millo was a series of terraces along the eastern slope of Ophel upon which houses were constructed. By means of this innovation, the residential area of the city could be considerably expanded. The walls of the terraces, however, required frequent repairs and rebuilding, a process which continued at least until the time of King Joash (II Kings 12:20).

The Gihon spring, the primary source of water supply for the city, was outside the city walls, although from within the walls access to the cave from which the waters flowed was possible through the water shaft. This shaft was abandoned in time, however, and the Israelites dug a channel along the eastern slopes of the Kidron Valley so as to bring the water to the old Pool of Siloam. This pool lay outside the city walls, though, so it was useless to the inhabitants of the city in time of siege. Thus, in the days of the prophet Isaiah, King Hezekiah constructed the now famous tunnel which brought the water under the hill on which the city was built to the new Pool of Siloam. The construction of Hezekiah's water tunnel was carried out in haste under the threat of the approaching armies of the Assyrian monarch, Sennacherib.

II Kings 20:20 and II Chronicles 32:30 give some details about this remarkable feat of hydraulic engineering, but the biblical record was supplemented in 1880 by the discovery of an inscription written in Hebrew which details dramatically the completion of the tunnel. The text describes how ". . . on the day of the piercing through, the stonecutters struck through each to meet his fellow, axe against axe. Then ran the water from the Spring to the Pool for twelve hundred cubits. . . ."

The archaeological evidence for the beginning of the expansion of the city to the western hill (modern Mount Zion) points to the time of Hezekiah. Fragments of a wall which crossed the upper ridge of the Valley of Hinnom were discovered by F. J. Bliss and A. C. Dickie in 1894–95. N. Avigad believes these fragments were part of a wall built by Hezekiah. This wall is to be identified with the "first wall" mentioned by Josephus; it encircled present-day Mount Zion and probably connected with the segment of wall uncovered by Avigad in 1970 in the modern Jewish Quarter. The wall is twenty-three feet thick and built of large natural stones without mortar. The remnant found by Avigad still stands up to ten feet in height and extends for 128 feet. This expansion of the city into the western hill toward the close of the Judean monarchy may have been required by an influx of Israelite refugees when the Assyrians overran Samaria, the capital of Israel, in 722 B.C.

The memoirs of Nehemiah describe the rebuilding of Jerusalem's defensive walls in the middle of the fifth century B.C. It appears that the reconstruction did not include the western hill, but was restricted to the eastern hill and Mount Moriah, the environs of the temple area. The recent excavations of N. Avigad in the Jewish Quarter, of R. Amiran and A. Eitan at the citadel near the Jaffa Gate, of D. Bahat and M. Broshi in the Armenian Garden south of the citadel, and of Broshi just south of the Zion Gate, all of these since 1968, have shown that the western hill was not occupied and defended after the Babylonian exile until the late second temple period, probably beginning with the activities of the Hasmonean kings. It seems likely, as B. Mazar has suggested, that Nehemiah did not fortify the entire populated area of the city; rather occupied areas to the west and north remained outside the reconstructed walls.

Little evidence for the Early Hellenistic period has been recovered. According to the writer of Ecclesiasticus, one of the books of the Apocrypha, the high priest, Simon the Righteous, strengthened the city walls and the temple fortifications and built the reservoir which is mentioned in the New Testament as the Pool of Bethesda. This pool has been partially uncovered by the White Fathers of St. Anne's Church, to which the pool is adjacent, just inside St. Stephen's Gate. A number of jar handles and coins of unknown provenance have also come to light in recent years, bearing the inscription YHDY (Judah) and a portrait of Ptolemy I; these can now be attributed to the Early Hellenistic era.

The Pool of Siloam and the mouth of Hezekiah's water tunnel.

The Hasmoneans have left evidence of their building activities at the citadel, adjacent to the Jaffa Gate. A massive tower had been built as a part of the wall (which itself had an earlier Hellenistic phase) by the successors of the leaders of the Maccabean revolt. A house dated to the late Hasmonean period on the basis of numismatic evidence was discovered by Avigad in the Jewish Quarter excavations. It had been built directly atop the earlier Israelite city wall.

Information gained from post-1968 excavations has particularly illuminated Herodian Jerusalem, one of the most glorious periods in the history of the city from the standpoint of material culture. In the Jewish Quarter evidence of a wealthy residential area has been uncovered. One of the houses, showing evidence of destruction in A.D. 70, provided many coins and ceramic materials in sealed loci beneath fallen stones, carbonized wooden beams, and layers of ash. Another large building contained a fine mosaic floor paved with geometric patterns in black and red, and quite similar in design to mosaic pavements discovered at Masada. Among the small finds recovered in the Jewish Quarter excavations are a relief with a cornucopia and pomegranate, a motif known previously only on Hasmonean coins, and a depiction of a seven-branched menorah incised on the back of some fragments of plaster. Depictions of the menorah from this period are quite rare. Many fragments of painted plaster were also found in the ruins of one of the houses. The excellence of workmanship and diversity of motifs point to the high art of the craftsmen of the period; their art is on a par with similar frescoes discovered at Masada. Hellenistic influence was particularly indicated in the form of column bases, capitals, and segments carved from local limestone. One of the columns was originally at least thirty-six feet high.

The excavations in the citadel have revealed how Herod modified the preceding Hasmonean structures in order to build here the three strong towers, Phasael, Hippicus, and Mariamne. These were a part of his palace complex which covered some four-and-a-half acres in the area south and east of the citadel. Nothing of the superstructure remains, except the base of the tower Phasael; of the palace only some of the foundational walls remain. These excavations, along with those in the Armenian Garden and further south on Mount Zion, reveal the opulence of the wealthy upper classes who resided in the upper city toward the close of the second temple period.

The most remarkable finds of Herodian Jerusalem have resulted from the excavations near the temple mount which have been carried out under the direction of Benjamin Mazar, beginning in 1968, since the reunification of the city. Mazar has worked on behalf of the Israel Exploration Society and the Institute of Archaeology of the Hebrew University; among the scholars who have assisted him are N. Avigad, M. Avi-Yonah, Y. Yadin, M. Ben-Dor, and A. Biran.

The second temple as it was first built in 515 B.C. was small and insignificant in comparision to the earlier structure built by Solomon. Herod, who is known as one of the greatest builders of antiquity, began the rebuilding of the structure in 20 B.C. He was careful not to alter the size of the inner temple, but he doubled the area of the outer courts by smoothing the rock surface, filling in the steep southeastern slope, and expanding

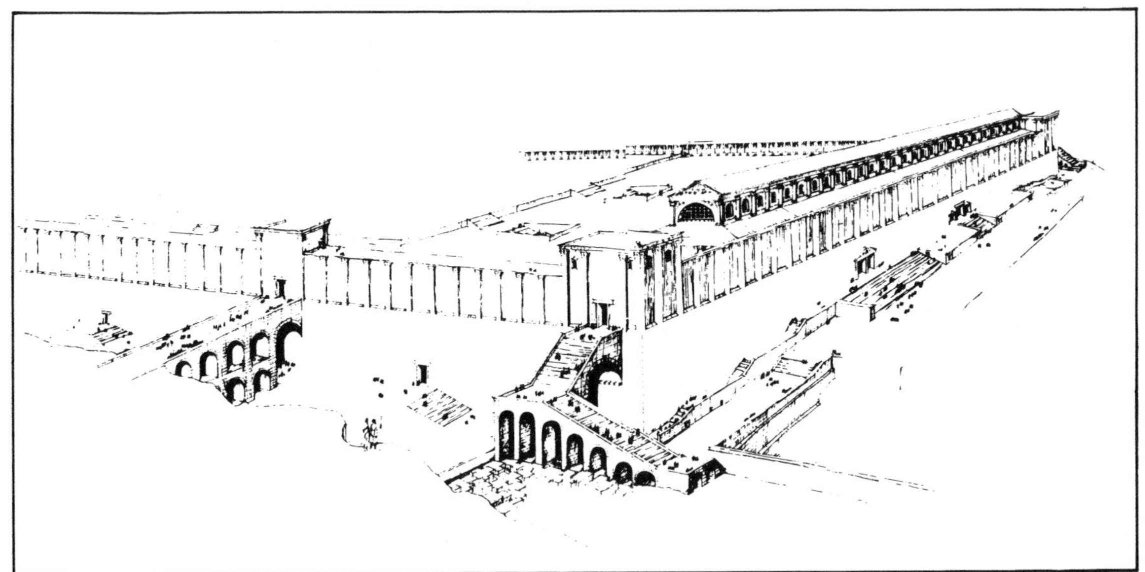

Artist's depiction of the southern and western walls of the Herodian temple.

the platform around the temple with massive retaining walls. He leveled the area between the Tyropoeon Valley and the temple mount at the southwestern corner of the temple area and built there a royal portico, or stoa, of which the historian Josephus states: ". . . it was a structure more noteworthy than any under the sun, for while the depth of the Tyropoeon Valley was great . . . the height of the portico over it was greater." He also mentioned that the capitals of the stoa were in the Corinthian style, with gold plating which covered the exterior of the temple and which "at the first rising of the sun reflected a very fiery splendor." The Mishna also describes the temple as overlaid with gold. The excavations produced fragments confirming the Corinthian style, and four of the fragments retained traces of gold leaf overlay.

In 1838 Robinson had noted the base of an arch along the southwestern edge of the platform of the temple complex. "Robinson's Arch" was once believed to be a part of a bridge across the Tyropoeon Valley to the upper city to the west, but the theory has been disproved. The arch was once a part of a monumental stairway that provided access to the temple courts from the north-south street that passed adjacent to the wall along the Tyropoeon. Further north along this street was Wilson's Arch, which was a part of a viaduct connecting the temple mount with the upper city.

The excavations also revealed an east-west street that ran along the base of the southern wall of the temple platform. It led eastward to provide access to the Hulda Gates, the western a double gate and the eastern a triple portal. To the south of the wall bordering this street was a large area (about thirteen meters wide) paved with flagstones. A broad monumental stairway led up to the double gate, and a large vault before the triple gate suggested that it, too, carried a stairway to the entrance of the temple. In this area, near the eastern end of the wall, were many plastered pools and cisterns which had been hewn into the rock. All in all, the pavement and water installations, among other features, suggested facilities for ritual purification and entry into the temple area by the large numbers of worshipers who annually made the pilgrimage to worship in Jerusalem, particularly at the feasts of Passover, Pentecost, and Tabernacles.

The paved streets were covered with heaps of debris, including sundry Herodian-style building stones and decorated architectural fragments which had crashed from the top of the wall 120 feet above when the Roman legions destroyed the city and its temple. In the southwestern area was found a stone which bore a Hebrew inscription in a script similar to that known from the Dead Sea Scrolls. It had apparently been a part of the corner parapet from which the trumpet blast sounded the approach and close of the Sabbath, for the inscription translates, "To the place of trumpeting. . . . " The stone contained a niche in which a man might stand. The inscription seems to confirm Josephus' report of the defensive measures taken at the temple mount as the Romans laid siege to the city during the first Jewish revolt. He described how the Jewish Zealots built a tower "over the roof of the priests' chambers, where one of the priests invariably stood to proclaim by trumpet blast in the late afternoon the approach of the Sabbath, and on the next evening its close, calling on the people in the first to cease work, in the second to resume it." The stone was found below the place where one of the four towers erected on the walls by the Zealots is said to have stood.

Other fragmentary inscriptions were found along with pottery, stoneware, glassware (almost all fragmentary) and bone objects—all from the Herodian period. A fragment of a stone vessel was inscribed with the Hebrew word *korban*. Several hundreds of coins were also recovered in Mazar's excavations, with a significant majority coming from the Herodian dynasty.

Excavations in progress along the southwestern wall of the temple mount.

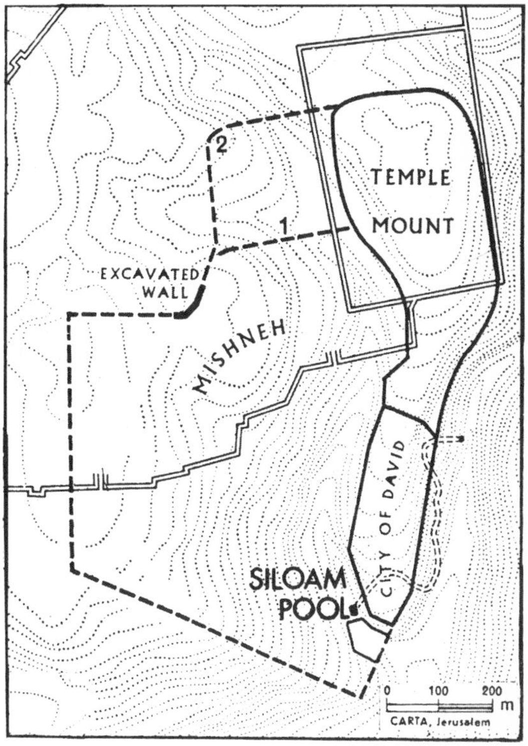

Jerusalem of the late Judean monarchy.

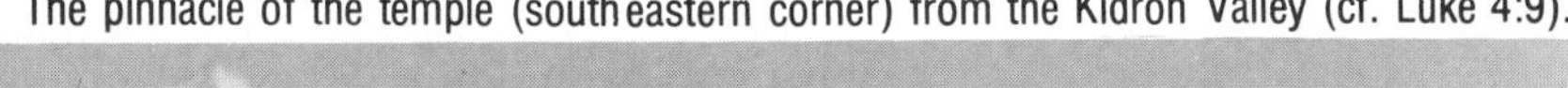

The pinnacle of the temple (southeastern corner) from the Kidron Valley (cf. Luke 4:9).

Only a few coins came from the time of Herod himself and his son, Archelaus; many belong to the time of Agrippa I and several of the Roman procurators. Coins of the first Jewish revolt were also found, with coins of the second year most plentiful. No coins of the fifth year were found at all. Finally, a number of foreign coins were recovered, primarily Tyrian and Nabatean in origin.

A Roman decision to rebuild Jerusalem as a Roman colony named Aelia Capitolina followed a Jewish uprising in A.D. 115 and the subsequent visit of the Emperor Hadrian to the city in A.D. 130. The recent excavations have produced evidence of public buildings and occupational debris connected with that phase of the city's history. The Romans reused stones that had been toppled from the supporting walls of the temple mount and from the buildings and pavements of the destroyed city. The building activities of the Tenth Legion were in evidence in the form of bricks and roof tiles bearing the legion's stamp; other bricks were stamped C AEL C; that is, C(olonia) AEL(ia) C(apitolina). Other material remains from this period include pottery, decorated lamps, coins, statuary, and dice.

The Roman decision helped spark the Bar Kochba revolt, which began in 132. While Bar Kochba was able to regain Jewish control of the city for a short time, the excavators found nothing which could be attributed with certainty to his rule except two coins with the legend "To the Liberation of Jerusalem." This suggests that his rule in Jerusalem was short and that little if any reconstruction took place during that time. Thereafter, Jews were forbidden by Hadrian to live in the city and, although local authorities relaxed the restrictions as early as the middle of the second century A.D., the western wall (Wailing Wall) became the focus of Jewish pilgrimage and prayer, a memorial to the past and a hope for the future.

The walls of the city of Jerusalem at the time of its destruction by the Romans in A.D. 70 have been an important focus of investigation. Josephus mentions three such walls: (1) the first wall surrounded the upper and lower cities; (2) the second wall extended the city northward, encircling a commercial quarter; and (3) the third wall was built to protect an extension of the city even further to the north.

Remnants of the first wall have been traced from the citadel southward to Mount Zion and from Mount Zion along the Valley of Hinnom to the Kidron Valley; and, as a result of Kenyon's excavations, the wall at the crest of the eastern hill, which connected to the southeastern corner of the temple mount, is now known to have been built in the Hasmonean period. From the citadel eastward to the temple mount, sections of the wall have been charted by Warren, Bliss, and Johns.

The second wall is the most problematic because it has been tentatively reconstructed on the basis of written sources rather than on archaeological data. The line of the second wall began at the first wall near the citadel, passed near the Church of the Holy Sepulchre, reached the Damascus Gate, then somewhat to the east of that gate turned south to link up with the Tower of Antonia at the north end of the temple mount. The wall has been assigned to both the Hasmoneans and to Herod, with the archaeological evidence from excavations at the Damascus Gate supporting the latter. The location of the second wall has an important bearing on the authenticity of the traditional site of Calvary (adjacent to the Church of the Holy Sepulchre), since the Gospel accounts place the crucifixion of Jesus outside the city walls. Although the exact line of the walls is not known, the excavations of Kenyon and Ute Lux in the Muristan market and beneath the Church of the Redeemer have indicated that the area was outside the walled city in second temple times.

The third wall was begun in the time of Agrippa I (ca. A.D. 37) and was intended to encircle and to protect the expansion of the city northward into a sector known as Bezetha. The wall started at the Hippicus Tower of the citadel and extended northward to the Psephinus Tower (the area of the Russian compound in modern Jerusalem). The wall then extended eastward to the Kidron, then southward to join the northeastern corner of the temple mount. The course of this wall is still in dispute. The description above is based upon the work of E. L. Sukenik, L. A. Meyer, and S. ben-Aryeh, who have followed the line of the wall some 1600 feet from the Italian Hospital to the W. F. Albright Institute of Archaeological Research. This wall lies about 1600 feet north of the present northern wall of the Old City. Agrippa was unable to complete the third wall, according to Josephus, but it was rushed to completion by Jerusalem's defenders at the outbreak of the first revolt.

A remarkable aspect of the archaeology of Jerusalem has been the investigation of its necropolis, a ring of cemeteries that encircled the city. The biblical record (I Kings 2:10; 11:43; II Chron. 21:20; 26:23, etc.) indicates that the royal cemetery of the Davidic dynasty was located within the city walls, probably in the southeastern sector. R. Weill's excavations in 1913–14 may have located the royal burial place. He discovered three main tombs which had, unfortunately, suffered considerable damage by subsequent quarrying. (The view that the tomb of David is on the present Mount Zion developed centuries after the destruction of Jerusalem by the Romans.)

It is known that some of the kings, Joram and Uzziah, for example, were buried in the city of David, but not in the tombs of the kings. Mazar believes the place of these burials may be the necropolis which his excavations uncovered on the eastern slope of the western hill, just opposite the western wall of the Herodian temple. The tombs found by Weill and those discovered by Mazar bear resemblances to Phoenician tombs, a factor to be expected in light of the influence Phoenicia had upon Israelite art and architecture in the period of the Davidic monarchy.

Most of the hundreds of rock-hewn tombs at the northern edge of the city, along Mount Scopus and the Mount of Olives, on the hill occupied by the U.N. headquarters, and in the Talpiyyot and Ramat Rachel sectors to the south belong to the Hasmonean and Herodian periods. Bodies of the deceased were placed in chambers off a central room in most of these tombs, and since these tombs were often reused, the bones of earlier burials would be collected into small limestone caskets called ossuaries. The façades of some of the tombs, including the striking "Absalom's Tomb" in the Kidron Valley, reflect a mixture of eastern Hellenistic and western influence.

A number of inscriptions have been found in connection with the tombs around the city, particularly in the area of the modern village of Silwan along the lower western slopes of the Mount of Olives. C. Clermont-Ganneau discovered one such inscription in 1872 which he partially translated; a more definitive translation was done by N. Avigad in 1954: "This [is the burial . . .] of . . . yahu who is over the house. There is no silver and no gold here but [his bones] and the bones of his handmaiden [slave-wife] with him. Cursed is the one who opens this [tomb]!" The inscription was written in archaic Hebrew script, and the tomb probably was that of Shebna, one of King Hezekiah's staff who was "over the house" (Isa. 22:15ff.).

Jewish ossuary from Jerusalem.

King Uzziah was buried in the "burial field which belonged to the Kings" (cf. II Chron. 26:23 RSV—see above), rather than in the "Tombs of the Kings," because he was a leper. His remains were subsequently moved, however, for an Aramaic inscription on a limestone plaque which was discovered in the collection of antiquities in the Russian church on the Mount of Olives reads: "Hither were brought the bones of Uzziah, king of Judah; do not open." The provenance of the inscription is unknown.

From 1926 to 1940 E. L. Sukenik studied Jewish tombs of the turn of the era. In the process he became an expert on the Jewish scripts of the period, and this knowledge enabled him to recognize the authenticity of the Dead Sea Scrolls when they came into his possession for an initial appraisal.

One other tomb discovery of extraordinary interest was made by V. Tsaferis in 1968 during his excavation of several tombs at Givat ha-Mivtar, northeast of the city. In one tomb there had been thirty-five burials, including one of a young man named Yohanan, who had been crucified. This was the first material evidence of crucifixion thus far discovered, a fact which is all the more remarkable in view of records that thousands of individuals suffered crucifixion in the ancient world.

Excavations by Kathleen Kenyon on the hill of Ophel. This is a view south along Nehemiah's wall.

SUGGESTED TOPICS FOR FURTHER STUDY

1. The conquest of Jerusalem by David—historical and archaeological evidence.
2. The temple of Solomon and the temples of Canaan.
3. Historical and archaeological evidence for Nebuchadnezzar's conquest and destruction of Jerusalem.
4. Jerusalem in the Persian period.
5. The topography of Jerusalem at the time of the Maccabean revolt.
6. A descriptive analysis of the Herodian temple.
7. The problem of the location of Calvary and the second wall.

8. Tales tombs tell—the results of tomb research in the environs of Jerusalem.
9. The archaeological evidence for the location of the city of David.
10. The discoveries of C. Clermont-Ganneau in Jerusalem.
11. The investigation of Jerusalem by C. Warren and C. Wilson.
12. British excavations in Jerusalem—1947–1967.
13. Excavations at the temple mount—1968–1977.
14. The archaeological history of the citadel.
15. Excavations in the Jewish and Armenian Quarters since 1967.
16. The walls of Jerusalem—their sequential story.

RECOMMENDED READING

Ap-Thomas, D. R., "Jerusalem" in *Archaeology and Old Testament Study*, ed. D. Winton Thomas (London: Oxford University Press, 1967), pp. 276–95.

Avi-Yonah, Michael, "Jerusalem" in *Archaeology* (Jerusalem: Keter, 1974), pp. 121–42.

Burrows, Millar, "Jerusalem" in *The Interpreter's Dictionary of the Bible*, ed. G. A. Buttrick (New York: Abingdon Press, 1962), vol. 2, pp. 843–66.

Kenyon, Kathleen, *Archaeology in the Holy Land*, third edition (New York: Praeger Publishers, 1970), pp. 240–304.

———, *Digging Up Jerusalem* (New York: Praeger Publishers, 1974).

May, H. G., ed., *Oxford Bible Atlas* (New York: Oxford University Press, 1962), pp. 80–81 and 88–89.

Mazar, Benjamin, *The Mountain of the Lord: Excavating in Jerusalem* (Garden City, NY: Doubleday, 1975).

Yadin, Y., ed., *Jerusalem Revealed* (Jerusalem: Israel Exploration Society, 1975).

FOR FURTHER READING

Scholarly and popular works on Jerusalem are so numerous that we have chosen to include here only a few important titles. Among them are books containing extensive bibliographies which the reader may wish to consult for particular topics. (Note also the books listed above under *Recommended Reading*.)

Callaway, J. A., "Jerusalem" in *The Biblical World*, ed. Charles F. Pfeiffer (Grand Rapids: Baker, 1966), pp. 309–23.

Clermont-Ganneau, C., *Archaeological Researches in Palestine, 1873–74* (London: The Committee of the Palestine Exploration Fund, 1899).

"Concise Bibliography of Excavations in Palestine—Jerusalem," *The Quarterly of the Department of Antiquities of Palestine* I (1932), pp. 163–99.

Israel Exploration Society, *The Twenty-fifth Archaeological Convention: Jerusalem Through the Ages* (1968).

Simons, J., *Jerusalem in the Old Testament: Researches and Theories* (Leiden: Brill, 1952).

Vogel, Eleanor K., *Bibliography of Holy Land Sites* (offprint of *Hebrew Union College Annual* XLII [1971]).

Warren, C., and C. R. Conder, *The Survey of Western Palestine: Jerusalem* (London: The Committee of the Palestine Exploration Fund, 1884).

Wilson, C. W., and C. Warren, *The Recovery of Jerusalem* (London: R. Bentley, 1871).

For excavation reports consult the indices and specific numbers of the following journals:

Annual of the Department of Antiquities of Jordan
Biblical Archaeologist
Bulletin of the American Schools of Oriental Research
Christian News from Israel
Israel Exploration Journal
Palestine Exploration Fund Annual
Palestine Exploration Quarterly (Quarterly Statement)
Qadmoniot
Quarterly of the Department of Antiquities of Palestine
Revue Biblique

26

Lachish

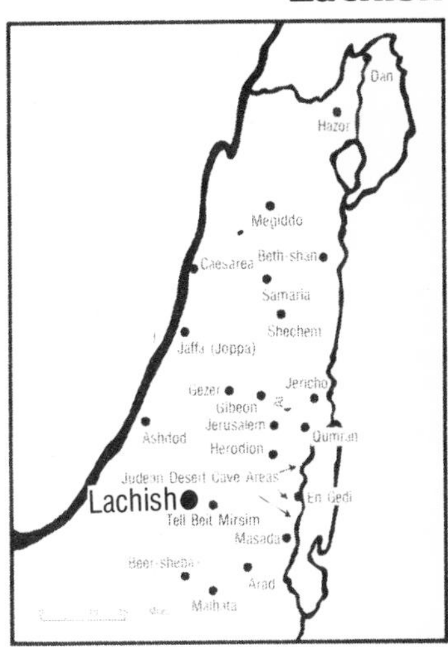

Lachish, mentioned a number of times in the Bible as an important fortified city of Judah, lay nestled in the lower western slopes of the Judean hills. The site, now known as Tell ed-Duweir, is situated about thirty miles southwest of Jerusalem and fifteen miles west of Hebron. Plentiful water near the surface favors the site, and the tell is one of the largest in Palestine.

During the nineteenth century, C. F. Conder, W. M. F. Petrie, and F. J. Bliss had placed biblical Lachish at the site known as Tell el-Hesi, but in 1929 W. F. Albright identified Tell ed-Duweir with Lachish. His identification was based upon its prominence and location, which corresponds well with the fourth-century village of Lakeis, which Eusebius placed in the seventh Roman mile from Eleutheropolis. Excavation has borne out Albright's thesis. The remains of the fortification system at Tell ed-Duweir strikingly parallel the defenses of Lachish as portrayed in Assyrian art, and there is close correspondence between the mound's stratigraphical evidence and what is known of Lachish from literary sources. An ostracon found at the site mentions Lachish by name; though not definitely proving the identification, the ostracon does add to its strength.

The excavation of Lachish was begun in 1932 under the auspices of the Wellcome-Colt (later the Wellcome-Marston) archaeological research expedition. It was directed by J. L. Starkey until his tragic murder by brigands in early 1938. C. H. Inge and G. Lankester Harding thereupon took over direction of the dig

The mound of Lachish, from atop Lachish.

Current excavations in progress in the area of the city gate at Lachish.

Lachish, as seen from the base of the mound.

and continued it for a brief period. Although many important discoveries were made at Tell ed-Duweir, a complete stratigraphical excavation was not carried out, and as a result not all of the city's occupational levels are clearly understood. Differences of opinion persist among scholars concerning the relationship between the finds at some levels and historical events to be associated with them.

Human occupation of the Lachish area stretches back as far as 8000 B.C. People lived in caves adjacent to the site during the Chalcolithic (before 3000) and Early Bronze I periods. Sometime in the third millennium B.C. they transferred their habitations to the site itself, and began using the caves for burials.

Middle and Late Bronze Age Lachish knew the strong influence of Egypt. By about 1750 B.C. the tell had been surrounded by a defensive bank or glacis rising a hundred feet above the valley floor. At its base was a moat or fosse. These defenses fell into disuse with the expulsion of the Hyksos and the reestablishment of Egyptian power in the area in the sixteenth century. Scarab seals of a number of Middle and Late Bronze Age pharaohs have been discovered at the site. The city's position and standard of living improved during the Late Bronze Age as a result of its Egyptian contacts. The founding of a small temple on the rubbish filling in the fosse dates to the sixteenth century (see below). The Tell el-Amarna letters of the fourteenth century relate that the rulers of Lachish favored the Habiru who were upsetting conditions in Egyptian-dominated Canaan. A number of inscriptional finds of the Late Bronze Age were also made at Lachish. The city was destroyed sometime early in the twelfth century B.C., perhaps by Joshua and the invading Israelites (cf. Josh. 10), although some attribute the destruction to the disruptions accompanying the invasions of the Sea Peoples, including the Philistines, at nearly the same time. The site was abandoned during the twelfth and eleventh centuries, the period of the biblical judges.

Lachish under Israelite rule was an important city. A palace, built on a 105-foot-square platform, may date to King David's time in the tenth century B.C. The platform itself, consisting of an earth and rubble filling enclosed by walls twenty-three feet high, is thought by many to represent the type of structure called in the Bible a *millo* ("filling"). The palace, probably that of the provincial governor, remained in use for several centuries. The defenses of the city were first constructed by Rehoboam sometime before 900 B.C. They consisted of a brick wall nineteen feet thick surrounding the top of the mound and an outer or revetment wall of stone about fifty feet lower down the slope.

A view from atop Lachish.

Rising in the center of Lachish are the ruins of a palatial building.

Assyrian relief depicting Sennacherib on his throne at the siege of Lachish.

The Lachish letters were discovered just beyond this threshold.

Both walls were made with alternating salients and recessed panels, and both had towers, the upper wall at regular intervals and the lower wherever most needed. The city gate was on the west side, and to the southwest was a free-standing square structure defending the roadway leading to the city. At a later date, this outwork was incorporated into the lower wall. The two walls, the recesses and salients, the towers and the square bastion are all represented in a relief discovered at Nineveh which commemorates the Assyrian emperor Sennacherib's siege and capture of Lachish about 700 B.C. (II Kings 18:13–17; Isa. 36:1ff.).

Probably the clearance of the city after this battle produced the mass burial pit discovered on the northwest side of the tell. The jumbled remains of over fifteen hundred human bodies were found in this pit, many showing evidence of burning. The age and kinds of pottery found mixed with the bones, the burning, and the fact that few old people's skeletons are included all suggest that these were not ordinary burials, but the result of the siege of Sennacherib. Strikingly, a layer of animal bones lay atop the human skeletons, and most of them were pig bones! Since Jewish dietary law forbids all contact with swine, it has been suggested that the animal bones derive from the Assyrian army's commissary. Three of the skulls from the pit show evidence of trephining, the removal of a circular section from the skull to relieve pressure on the brain. One of the patients evidently lived long enough for the saw marks on the bone to begin healing.

At some point Lachish passed back into Judean hands and was rebuilt, perhaps by Manasseh (II Chron. 33:14). It was taken again by Nebuchadnezzar in 598 B.C. To this capture most scholars relate the destruction of Level III of the city, for it involved a violent conflagration and the collapse of the palace. (Others, however, including O. Tufnell, who did much of the work on Lachish, attribute this destruction level to Sennacherib.) The upper wall was badly damaged and had to be at least partly replaced with a thinner stone wall. The ruined palace was never rebuilt, and the city must have been much weakened when Nebuchadnezzar launched his second attack against Judah ten years later. Again Lachish was utterly destroyed, this time with a fire so fierce that the masonry of the city disintegrated. The city was abandoned until the Persian period (ca. 450 B.C.), when it was rebuilt with a residence for a provincial governor, probably Geshem the Arab and his line (Neh. 6:1). A small temple, thought by the first excavators to be a solar shrine, was built during the Hellenistic period. A recent reinvestigation by Y. Aharoni, B. Boyd, and G. D. Young, however, suggests, on the basis of the shrine's striking similarity to the Israelite sanctuary found at Arad, that it was in fact Jewish. Other shrines were built outside Jerusalem during the Persian and Hellenistic periods at Elephantine, Leontopolis, by the Tobiad family at 'Araq el-Amir, and by the Samaritans at Mount Gerizim. In fact, among a collection of Persian-period incense altars found at Lachish itself was one inscribed with an Aramaic dedication to "Yah (our) Lord," showing Jewish cultic activity at Lachish before the building of the "solar" shrine.

Certain of the discoveries at Lachish deserve fuller mention. One of these is the Canaanite temple of the Late Bronze Age discovered in the fosse at the base of the tell. In Tufnell's opinion it was not the main religious center of the city—if it had been, it would have been more prominently located. Nevertheless it apparently enjoyed considerable popularity. It was first built about 1550 B.C., with the main cult room about thirty-three feet long (north-south) and sixteen-and-a-half feet wide (east-west). It was widened to form a square about 1450 B.C., when additional rooms were added to the complex as well. Further additions were made about 1350. The shrine of the temple was always on the south side of the main room. In the first phase, it was merely a low clay bench with three projections. The second phase had only one projection, and was made of unhewn stones (cf. Exod. 20:24f.). At this time, too, a hearth was placed in front of the altar, and brick benches to receive offerings were built along the other three walls. The third shrine began as a large, white-plastered platform, at the front of which was later added an altar of brick with three steps leading up to it (contrast Exod. 20:26). The hearth and benches remained, and an earthenware bin, found filled with animal bones, was added to the left (east) of the altar, with a libation stand or laver to the right. Some information about the nature of the cult observed in this temple can be derived from the finds associated with it, though no statue of a deity was found. A vast quantity of pottery bowls was found on the offering benches, around the shrine, and stored in cupboards and anterooms. Presumably these bowls were intended for offerings brought to the temple. More precious offerings, such as vessels, ornaments, and beads, made of ivory, glass, faience, or metal, were found on the platform of the third phase of the temple, and even in the many refuse pits which surrounded it. The animal bones found in these pits, in the earthenware bin, and in the soil in the area included bones of oxen, gazelles, ibex, and fish and birds, but consisted mostly of the right forelegs of sheep or goats. This corresponds to the priests' portion of the "peace offerings" mentioned in Leviticus 7:32.

The other significant discovery of the Lachish excavation was a large quantity of inscriptional material, more than from any other Palestinian site. This includes Egyptian seals, scarabs, and tax records written on fragments of a bowl; several pottery fragments with inscriptions in the "proto-Sinaitic" alphabet which form something of a chronological link between the Sinai inscriptions and the earliest Phoenician writings; a number of Hebrew seals, weights, and inscribed jar handles, most of the last-mentioned reading "to [of] the king," followed by the name of one of the towns (Hebron, Socoh, Ziph, or Mmsht—a previously unknown town); and the first five letters of the Hebrew alphabet, in the same order known from later tradition, carved in a step and dated about 800 B.C. But far more important than any of these is the group of eighteen ostraca found in a guardroom in the outer gate that was destroyed by Nebuchadnezzar in 587/6 B.C. Known as the Lachish letters, they are one of the most important extrabiblical sources available for the Hebrew language and handwriting, and for the history of Judah in the days of Jeremiah.

Lachish Letter 4 contains correspondence in Hebrew between Lachish and its military outpost during the time of the Babylonian invasion of Judah (ca. 588 B.C.).

The letters, which date apparently to the time just before Lachish fell to Nebuchadnezzar, form part of a single group of correspondence. The language is essentially the same as the biblical Hebrew of Jeremiah and his contemporaries. All the letters seem to have been addressed to an official, perhaps the governor of the city, named Ya'osh. They are from a subordinate of his whose name, Hoshaiah, is given in letter three. Not all the letters are completely or even mostly legible. While in some of them Hoshaiah seems to be trying to extricate himself from a difficult situation relative to his commander, perhaps regarding some letters, the overall interpretation of the ostraca is not entirely settled.

In letter three, Hoshaiah reports on the journey of one Koniah son of Elnathan to Egypt. He refers also to a letter from a royal official named Tobiah containing a warning from a prophet. (This is the first occurrence of the Hebrew word for prophet, *naḇi'*, in nonbiblical texts from before the exile of Judah.) Letter four, after acknowledging orders and giving reports, ends "and let (my lord) know that we are watching for the signals of Lachish, according to all the indications which my Lord hath given, for we cannot see Azekah." Evidently the end was near for the Judean soldiers; according to Jeremiah 34:7, Jerusalem, Lachish, and Azekah were the last of the fortified cities of Judah to be taken. This letter interestingly confirms the use of fire signals in ancient Israel, using a word for them which is also found in the Talmud. Letter six, commenting on a letter from the king and the demoralizing activities of certain persons in Jerusalem, refers to "weakening the hands" of the people (cf. Jer. 38:4).

Thus, while they present valuable material for the study of the grammar and script of the ordinary Hebrew of this period, the light shed by the Lachish letters on the details of Judean history near its end is probably their most important contribution to modern biblical studies.

Excavations at Lachish have resumed in recent years under the direction of David Ussishkin of Tel Aviv University. The excavations have already illuminated and clarified the destructions of the great city gateway in 701 B.C., when the Assyrian monarch, Sennacherib, captured Lachish, and in 598/7 B.C., when it fell to the forces of Nebuchadnezzar. The Tel Aviv University effort will be a continuing project, on a modest scale, for another decade or more.

SUGGESTED TOPICS FOR FURTHER STUDY

1. The "fosse temple" at Lachish and Canaanite religion.
2. Problems in the archaeological history of Lachish.
3. The Lachish letters and biblical Hebrew.
4. The Lachish letters and the late history of Judah.
5. Evidence on the siege of Lachish from Assyrian ruins.

RECOMMENDED READING

Albright, W. F., "The Lachish Ostraca" in *Ancient Near Eastern Texts Relating to the Old Testament,* ed. James B. Pritchard (Princeton: Princeton University Press, 1955), pp. 321–22.

Gibson, John C. L., *Textbook of Syrian Semitic Inscriptions* (Oxford: Clarendon Press, 1971).

Hamilton, R. W., "Lachish" in *The Interpreter's Dictionary of the Bible,* ed. G. A. Buttrick (New York: Abingdon Press, 1962), vol. 3, pp. 53–57.

"Lachish" in *The Biblical World,* ed. Charles F. Pfeiffer (Grand Rapids: Baker, 1966), pp. 343–49.

Torczyner, H., O. Tufnell, C. H. Inge, G. L. Harding, et al., *Lachish,* vol. I, *The Lachish Letters* (London: Oxford University Press, 1938); vol. II, *The Fosse Temple* (London: Oxford, 1940); vol. III, *The Iron Age* (London: Oxford, 1953); vol. IV, *The Bronze Age* (London: Oxford, 1958).

Tufnell, Olga, "Excavations at Tell ed-Duweir, Palestine, Directed by the Late J. L. Starkey, 1932–1938," *Palestine Exploration Quarterly* 80 (1950), pp. 65–80.

______, "Lachish" in *Archaeology and Old Testament Study,* ed. D. Winton Thomas (Oxford: Clarendon, 1967), pp. 296–308.

Wright, G. Ernest, "Judean Lachish," *Biblical Archaeologist* 18 (1955), pp. 9–17.

FOR FURTHER READING

Aharoni, Y., "Trial Excavation in the 'Solar Shrine' at Lachish," *Israel Exploration Journal* 18 (1968), pp. 157–69.

Hamilton, R. W., "Lachish" in *The Interpreter's Dictionary of the Bible,* ed. G. A. Buttrick (New York: Abingdon Press, 1962), vol. 3, pp. 53–57.

Tufnell, Olga, "Excavations at Tell ed-Duweir, Palestine, Directed by the Late J. L. Starkey, 1932–1938," *Palestine Exploration Quarterly* 80 (1950), pp. 65–80.

———, "Lachish" in *Archaeology and Old Testament Study,* ed. D. Winton Thomas (Oxford: Clarendon, 1967), pp. 296–308.

Wright, G. Ernest, "Judean Lachish," *Biblical Archaeologist* 18 (1955), pp. 9–17.

27

Masada

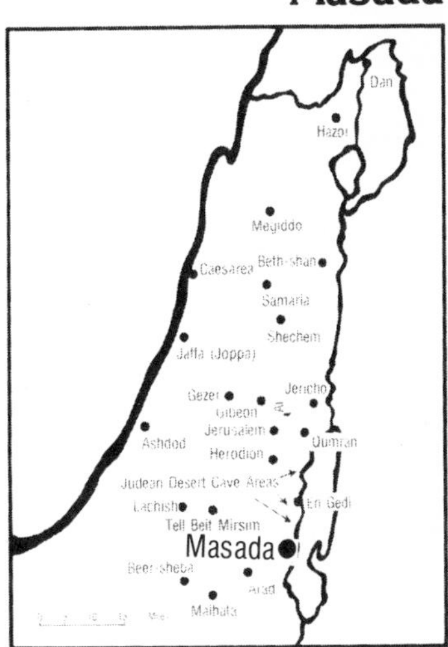

Masada, whose name in Aramaic means "fortress-stronghold," is built on an isolated rock 1300 feet above the Judean desert near the southwestern shores of the Dead Sea. Until 1963 it was perhaps the best-known unexcavated site of antiquity in Israel. It was known to classical archaeologists as the site where Herod the Great constructed his famous fortifications, palaces, and storerooms. It was known also to the youth of Israel as a place of national pilgrimage to commemorate the tragic and heroic death of its 960 Zealot Jewish defenders, who in A.D. 73 preferred to end their lives at their own hands rather than become slaves—both physically and spiritually—to the Romans.

In 1963, an archaeological expedition under the leadership of Yigael Yadin, one of the most renowned archaeologists in Israel, set out to determine what archaeological discovery could lend to the prevailing myth and legend of Masada's history. The excavation substantiated, for the most part, the sole contemporary account of Masada—that of Josephus, a first-century Jewish historian. The ornate mosaics of luxurious palaces discovered side by side with crude living quarters showed the sharp contrast between Herod's life at Masada in 30 B.C. and that of the Zealots in A.D. 66. Masada is also a historical catalogue of the nature of art and architecture from Herod's time to the Byzantine period.

The major fortifications at Masada were completed by Herod the Great, an Edomite appointed by the Romans as king over Judea. He was disliked by his Jewish subjects for his cruel treat-

Left, top: Air view of Masada. In the center is Herod's trilevel northern palace and to the right of center is the Roman ramp. Left, middle: View from Herod's northern palace looking down on ruins of a Roman camp. Left, bottom: Northwest face of Masada with Herod's trilevel palace at top center. Beneath are a series of cisterns. Above: Interior of a Masada cistern.

ment of them; he therefore feared the multitudes lest they overthrow him and restore their former Maccabean kings to the throne. According to Josephus, Herod also faced the danger of foreign attack from Cleopatra, the powerful queen of Egypt who did not conceal her intentions to rule over Judea. With the help of her lover Antony, she was a formidable threat. The fortress of Masada was built as a personal refuge for Herod and his family. Situated above the surrounding lands, it was an ideal spot for a small number of determined defenders to hold off the superior forces of attacking armies. The 1900 by 650 foot surface of Masada was ringed with a protective casemate wall—a double wall with the intervening space partitioned into chambers to serve as storerooms, barracks, and arsenals. A watercourse was constructed to catch the winter rains and a large number of cisterns were hewn out of the rock. Herod also built himself a luxurious palace hanging on a precipice on the northern shaded cliff; this palace was equipped with large storerooms, baths, and a swimming pool. Here he could entertain his guests lavishly for Masada also served the royal family as a winter palace.

After Herod's death in 4 B.C., Palestine was occupied by the Romans and a Roman garrison took control of Masada. In an effort to regain their freedom and independence, the Jewish inhabitants organized sporadic rebellions. Open revolt finally flared up into a full-scale war in A.D. 66 and raged with fierce bitterness for four years. At the beginning of the war, a group of Jewish Zealots, an orthodox sect which fought against foreign rule at all costs, destroyed the Roman garrison and captured Masada. The Romans brought legion after legion of reinforcements into Palestine to suppress the rebels. Finally, in A.D. 70, after fierce battles, the Roman general Titus conquered Jerusalem, sacked the city, destroyed the temple, and expelled the bulk of the Jewish inhabitants from the country. Only one stronghold remained until A.D. 73—the fortress of Masada.

The few surviving patriots who evaded Roman capture after the fall of Jerusalem made their way to Masada and rejoined the battle for freedom. These Zealots, numbering less than one thousand, used the advantageous position of Masada to harass and attack Roman garrisons for over two years. The Roman general, Flavius Silva, was determined to crush at all costs this last outpost of resistance. With five thousand soldiers and over nine thousand slaves and prisoners of war carrying water, timber, and provisions, he stationed himself along the slopes of Masada. The remains of at least nine Roman camps at the base of the rock are still clearly visible today. At the western approach to Masada, Silva's men constructed a ramp of beaten earth and stones. They erected a siege tower on this ramp; and under covering fire from the top of the tower, they directed a battering ram against the fortress wall. Finally, in A.D. 73, the Roman forces succeeded in making a breach in the Zealots' fortifications at the top of Masada. Assured of their imminent victory, they retreated to their camps to prepare for an all-out attack the next day. Josephus relates that at this point, Eleazar Ben Ya'ir, the leader of the Jewish defenders, delivered a stirring speech to his fellow Jews. "Daybreak will end our resistance," he told them. "But we are free to choose an honorable death with our loved ones. Let us leave this world unenslaved by our enemies, free men, in company with our wives and children. But before we die," Ben Ya'ir ordered, "let the whole fortress go up in flames: it will be a bitter blow to the Romans to find our persons beyond their reach and nothing for them to loot. One thing only let us spare; let us spare our store of food: it will bear witness that we perished not through hunger, but because we chose death rather than slavery." Josephus relates that each man killed his own wife and children and then lay down beside them to be killed by one of ten men chosen by lot. When these ten had slain all the other men, they cast lots among themselves and one was chosen to slay the rest, then take his own life. The next morning, as the Romans launched their confident assault, they met smoldering ruins and silence. Only two women with several children emerged from their hiding place to tell the story of the 960 Jews who had died. Josephus writes that after viewing "the multitude of the slain, the Romans could take no pleasure in the fact, though it were done to their enemies. Nor could they do other than wonder at the courage of their resolution, and at the immovable contempt of death which so great a number of them had shown, when they went through with such an action as that was."

After the deaths of the Jewish defenders, a Roman garrison was again stationed at the fortress for some time. The last inhabitants of Masada were Byzantine monks during the fifth and sixth centuries A.D. They lived in humble cells and caves and built themselves a chapel with a mosaic floor. It is assumed that they were forced to leave with the Persian or Moslem conquest of the early seventh century. Since then, Masada has been unoccupied.

In 1963, Yigael Yadin and a company of professional archaeologists set out to verify the events at Masada as recorded by Josephus. Such was the magnetic appeal of Masada and its archaeologist that Yadin was flooded with over five thousand applications from prospective volunteer workers. Their help and devotion enabled Yadin to run twenty-three two-week shifts averaging over three hundred workers each shift. The archaeological expedition worked a total of eleven months through two seasons (1963–64 and 1964–65), excavating 97 percent of the area. These volunteers sifted fifty thousand cubic yards of earth and accomplished what normally would have been the work of twenty-five archaeological seasons. The results of the excavations have excited the public more than any other discovery ever made in Israel. Moreover, the scholarly world now possesses a rich harvest of one of the most highly organized archaeological explorations in the Middle East.

The major finds can be divided into the two distinct periods to which they belong—the Herodian period of about 30 B.C. and that of the Zealots, A.D. 70–73. The true location of Herod's famous northern palace-villa was unclear until archaeological soundings were completed in the 1950s and Yadin's excavations further confirmed Josephus' detailed description. It was a triple-terraced hanging palace, built on the very edge of the precipice, 900 feet above the Dead Sea. The upper terrace is the highest point on Masada and contained no more than four rooms, comprising the living quarters of the palace. These chambers, adorned with white and black mosaics and wall paintings, were most probably intended for Herod's personal use. On the middle terrace, sixty feet lower down, are the remains of two concentric walls which formed a circular building for leisure and relaxation in Herod's time. Best preserved was the bottom terrace with its multicolored wall painting adorning the double colonnade which surrounded a large balcony overlooking the sea. Not only is this luxurious palace strategically positioned, but it is also the only spot on Masada that enjoys both constant shade and shelter from the desert winds.

Interior of Roman bath at Masada.

One of the biggest and most ancient Roman public baths ever discovered in this part of the world was found complete with all its installations and lavish adornments. In the typical Roman style, it contained four rooms—the *caldarium* or "hot room," which was the largest and was heated by an underground chamber beneath the floor; adjoining it, the *tepidarium* or "tepid room," the *frigidarium* or "cold room," and the *apodyterium,* which was the "disrobing room." The walls of these rooms were covered with Roman frescoes and their floors with beautiful mosaics.

Yadin's excavations also uncovered the western palace, which was the largest building on Masada, covering 36,000 square feet. It served King Herod's ceremonial functions and included service rooms and dwelling quarters in addition to large storerooms

Mosaic from the western palace, damaged by later Zealot rebuilding activities.

which made the palace completely self-sufficient. The main storerooms on Masada, however, were located in the north and the south. They were built of large dolomite stone slabs quarried on the site and weighing up to five hundred pounds each. Seven storerooms yielded hundreds of jars containing remnants of food with labels in Aramaic and Hebrew clearly describing their contents. These sherds are of great significance to the archaeologist for they mark the development in pottery style and shape from the time of Herod to that of the Zealots—about seventy years.

Some of the exciting inscriptions were on jars belonging to the Herodian period. The discovery of wine jars bearing exact dates was a rare find. The dating of these jars followed the standard Roman system of indicating the name of the Roman consul for that particular year. Most of the jars bear the name *Sentius Saturninus*—consul in the year 19 B.C. For the first time, scholars discovered an inscription with Herod's actual name. The last line on some of the wine jars reads, "To King Herod of Judea." More than one thousand coins were also found in the storerooms. One container held thirty-eight silver shekels of the time of the revolt; they bear the inscription "Jerusalem the Holy" and on the reverse side "Shekel of Israel" and the date—the year the rebellion began (A.D. 66). Other important inscriptions were found on ostraca or inscribed pieces of pottery. These were common writing material for everyday use since papyrus and parchment were too costly. Over seven hundred such inscriptions have been uncovered at Masada. Eleven of the potsherds were inscribed with Jewish names, one in particular with

Excavated storerooms at Masada.

the name of the Zealot leader, Ben Ya'ir. This has been described by Yadin as his most exciting discovery. Could these possibly have been the lots cast by those last few defenders, as related by Josephus, or did they simply serve as "identity" documents? The ostraca from Masada have also been important to scholars for the study of the history of the Hebrew script.

Yadin's most significant discoveries were made in the fortress casemate wall, discoveries which revealed the Zealots' pattern of life at Masada. Although the Zealots used several of Herod's public buildings for administrative purposes, the palaces proved to be impractical and could house only a few families. For the most part, the Zealots lived in the partitioned chambers of the casemate wall which was eighteen feet high, thirteen feet thick, and extended 4200 feet around the mountain-top perimeter. The intervening space between this double wall contained seventy rooms, thirty towers, and four gates. Excavations of these chambers yielded cupboards, ovens, domestic utensils, cosmetic items, and bits of clothing—all in contrast with the luxury and opulence of the palaces and other Herodian structures.

The religious life of Masada's inhabitants was revealed with the discovery of two buildings. One chamber of the casemate wall had been converted into a ritual bath (*mikveh*) by the Zealots. Constructed according to the strict requirements of the Halakah (rabbinic religious law), it contained three basins or baths which were supplied by rain water. The discovery created quite a stir in the orthodox religious circles because it is the only ritual bath to survive from this period. Located near the casemate wall is a second structure which Yadin believes to have been a synagogue. The hall is rectangular in shape with two rows of columns and mud benches all around. The entrance of the structure faces east, oriented toward Jerusalem. If this was indeed a synagogue, it is not only the earliest known synagogue but also the only one to survive from the time of the second temple.

The synagogue at Masada.

Other very exciting discoveries were made in the synagogue and in one of the chambers of the casemate wall, close to the synagogue. Here, Yadin found his greatest prize—scrolls. Portions of fourteen biblical, sectarian, and apocryphal scrolls have been found at Masada. These include five chapters of the Book of Psalms, identical in wording and spelling with the traditional Hebrew text. Fragments from Genesis, Leviticus, and Ezekiel were also uncovered and examined. Additional fragments were found of a first-century Hebrew text of the apocryphal Book of Ecclesiasticus, also known as the Wisdom of Jesus the Son of Sirach or, in Hebrew, Ben Sira. This find was very important because the Hebrew original of the book, composed about 200 B.C., was lost and existed only in translation. In 1896, a few chapters had been discovered in the *geniza* (storage place for sacred manuscripts) of an old Cairo synagogue. The excavations at Masada uncovered more chapters and verified that the copy from the Cairo *geniza* contained the authentic Hebrew text of the book, a point long disputed by scholars. Another scroll fragment containing a passage whose Hebrew form had completely disappeared was discovered and found to belong to the pseudepigraphical *Book of Jubilees*. Available to scholars only in translation before the excavations, it describes the journeys of the patriarchs from the Book of Genesis in accordance with the special calendar of the Qumran sect.

The fragment known as "The Scroll of the Sabbath Sacrifices" is identical in liturgy and terminology with one found in Qumran Cave 4 of the famous Dead Sea Scrolls. This discovery provides another link between the Essene sect of Qumran and the Zealots of Masada. It has also caused a new and heated debate among scholars who wonder why literature belonging to the Essene sect—regarded as a mystical, pacifist, and celibate group—was found at Masada, the stronghold of the fierce, orthodox Zealots. Yadin feels that the Essenes joined the last Jewish outpost at Masada after the destruction of their communities by the Romans in A.D. 68 and that they brought some of their scrolls with them. To support his thesis, Yadin notes that Josephus writes of a leader at Masada named "John the Essene." It is even probable that there were a large number of Essenes under his command. This is important because it shows that the revolt against the Romans was nonsectarian, including both Zealots and Essenes.

As mentioned earlier, the third major settlement of Masada occurred between the fifth and seventh centuries A.D. when Byzantine monks occupied the site. They lived in small cells and caves and built one structure—a chapel with a beautiful mosaic floor. The patient and delicate work of Yadin's volunteers uncovered sixteen round medallions in this floor, containing representations of plants, fruits, and flowers.

In addition to the question of the Essenes' presence at Masada, a second issue has caused debate among scholars. The noted writer, Trude Weiss-Rosmarin, editor of *The Jewish Spectator,* claims that the final heroic action of Masada's defenders was not heroism at all since self-annihilation is contrary to basic Jewish doctrine. Weiss-Rosmarin also questions the reliability of Josephus as a historian. Apparently, Josephus was already in

Rome enjoying the protection of Flavius when Masada fell and could not have quoted the Jewish heroes verbatim.

Although it is true that Jewish law does not condone suicide, we know that Jews are told to trust in God's omnipotent help even on the threshold of death. Weiss-Rosmarin objects to Yadin's view that the Zealots were devout Jews and yet committed suicide. However, as the eminent scholar Salo Baron notes, religious martyrdom dominated the minds of Jews and Christians for countless generations. There is warrant in Jewish tradition for condoning and even justifying the taking of one's own life in order to avoid the agony of torture or the exposure to indignity and dishonor at the hands of foes. The Zealots must have been inspired by the heroic example of the Maccabees two hundred years before Masada.

Today, Masada is visited by countless people in memory of those Zealots who chose death over slavery. The courageous spirit of Ben Ya'ir and his comrades has endured and remains an inspiration for modern youth and for the defense forces of Israel who in their oath of allegiance taken on Masada's summit proclaim—"Masada shall not fall again!"

SUGGESTED TOPICS FOR FURTHER STUDY

1. Review the three main stages of habitation at Masada.
2. Give the background for Herod's construction of Masada as a fortress.
3. Contrast the life of the Zealots at Masada with life there during Herod's time in light of the major finds of the excavation.
4. Discuss the significance of the scrolls discovered at Masada to biblical study.
5. Describe the relationship between the Zealots and the Essenes of Qumran and the evidence which substantiates this relationship.
6. What were the main issues raised by the finds of Masada? Why were they raised?

RECOMMENDED READING

Josephus, *Jewish Antiquities* XIV.358–63 (pp. 639–40 in Loeb Classical Library edition); *Jewish Wars* I.265–67 (same as *Jewish Antiquities* XIV.358–63—Loeb: p. 125); II.408–10 (Loeb: p. 193); IV.398–410 (Loeb: pp. 117–21); VII.252–408 (Loeb: pp. 577–619).

Yadin, Yigael, "The Excavations of Masada" (1963–64, Preliminary Report), *Israel Exploration Journal* 15 (1965).

———, *Masada, Herod's Fortress and the Zealots' Last Stand* (New York: Random House, 1966).

FOR FURTHER READING

Avi-Yonah, M., N. Airgred, Y. Aharoni, I. Dunayevsky, and S. Guttman, "Masada, Survey and Excavations, 1955–1956," *Israel Exploration Journal* 7 (1957), pp. 1–60.

Farmer, William Reuben, *Maccabees, Zealots, and Josephus, An Inquiry into Jewish Nationalism in the Graeco-Roman Period* (New York: Columbia University Press, 1956).

Furneaux, Rupert, *The Roman Siege of Jerusalem* (New York: David McKay Company, Inc., 1972).

Guttman, S., *With Masada* (Tel Aviv, 1965)—in Hebrew.

Hawkes, C., "The Roman Siege of Masada," *Antiquity* 3 (1929), pp. 195–260.

Keller, Werner, *Diaspora, The Post Biblical History of the Jews* (New York: Harcourt Brace and World, 1969), pp. 58–59.

Margolis, Max, and Alexander Marx, *A History of the Jewish People* (New York: Harper and Row, 1965), pp. 203–04.

Pearlman, Moshe, *The Zealots of Masada* (London: Hamish Hamilton, 1967).

Richmond, I. A., "The Roman Siege Works of Masada, Israel," *Journal of Roman Studies* 52 (1962).

Yadin, Yigael, "The Ben Sira Scroll from Masada," The Israel Exploration Society and The Shrine of the Book (Jerusalem, 1965).

28

Megiddo

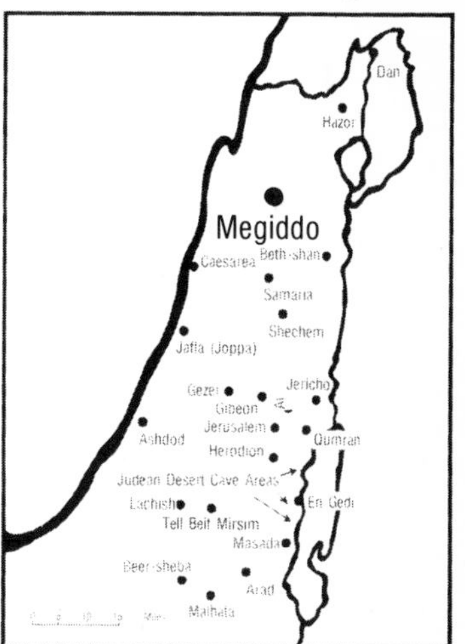

Megiddo, one of the most famous of ancient Palestinian sites, can be found on the mound Tell el-Mutesellim. It is situated on a spur of the Carmel ridge near its southern extremity, with Haifa lying sixteen miles to the northwest and Afula six miles to the northeast.

The tell commands a view of almost the entire Esdraelon Valley, and it overlooks the intersection of two ancient routes—the road connecting central and eastern Palestine with the Mediterranean coast and the ancient port of Acco, and the route (Via Maris) connecting Egypt with the Fertile Crescent. The latter road penetrates the Carmel range through the pass of the Wadi 'Arah, adjacent to Megiddo, providing access from the Plain of Esdraelon to the Plain of Sharon. Due to this strategic location, it is not surprising that occupational debris at Megiddo spans a period from the fourth millennium to the fourth century B.C. with hardly a break.

G. Schumacher led the first excavation at Megiddo (1903–05), along with C. Steuernagel and C. Watzinger, for the Deutsche Orient-Gesellschaft and the Deutsche Palästinaverein. This excavation, which cut a north-south trench across the center of the mound, was essentially a destructive one. A Harvard University excavation under G. A. Reisner dug on the tell for two more years (1908–10). They were succeeded by the Oriental Institute of Chicago, which sent J. H. Breasted to the tell in 1925. The American excavation was an extravagant affair, thanks to the generous support of John D. Rockefeller. The plan was to strip the top of the mound layer by layer while using the most impressive scientific equipment available, including balloons for air photographs. Breasted left the work after a trial dig, and C. S. Fisher took over (1925–27). He in turn was followed by P. L. O. Guy (1927–35) and subsequently by G. Loud (1935–39). Their work was highly methodical in its treatment of the stratigraphy, which makes their reports particularly useful to present-day archaeologists. Due to the long, almost continuous habitation of the site, the importance of the city, and the fact that the Oriental Institute excavation was one of the earliest excavations to be done in a systematic manner, the Megiddo reports become vital in the interpretation of subsequent excavations in the region. The work of the excavators, however, still predated modern techniques and the accurate refinement of the pottery chronology. The stratigraphy is fairly complicated at Megiddo. This in addition to the constant turnover of directors damaged the unity of the work, causing some confusion in the stratigraphical interpretation. While the reports of the excavation greatly affected the evaluation of other sites, all too often the Megiddo evidence conflicts with the results of more recent excavations. It is because of these problems that such an important site as Megiddo is beset with unending controversies.

It was in the hope of resolving one of these controversies, that of the stratigraphical location of Solomon's Megiddo, that Yadin initiated an exploratory probe at Megiddo in 1960, returning to the problem again in 1965–67 (see below). The success of his small-scale excavation underlined the advances made in excava-

Airview of Megiddo and excavated area.

tion techniques and methodology since the days of the Oriental Institute excavation.

Late Bronze Age Megiddo produced many impressive finds, including a cuneiform tablet containing a part of the *Gilgamesh Epic*. The discovery was not made, however, by the American excavators, but by a shepherd wandering over the mound in 1955. Canaanite Megiddo was quite wealthy, and large numbers of impressive articles, including imports from Egypt and the Aegean area, carved ivories, and a temple with a *bamah,* or high place, were found. Either Israelites, Egyptians, or Philistines finally defeated the city between 1150 and 1120 B.C. The fortified Canaanite city of Megiddo was replaced by a Canaanite-Philistine town. New objects were introduced, including Philistine pottery, without the rejection of older elements. It is probable that the Philistines merely maintained a garrison in a city that remained basically Canaanite. The city was poorly built and not well fortified. The temple and sacred area had been destroyed by the conquerors, but numerous cult objects indicate a religious continuity between the two periods of occupation. This stratum probably reflects the situation in Judges 1:27f., where it states that Megiddo remained Canaanite until Israel became stronger.

Stratum VI A was replaced by one without the Canaanite material culture and with an entirely different type of pottery. The structures are poorly built and there is a lack of fortifications and public buildings. Stratum V B probably represents an Israelite occupation from the start of David's reign. As usual, impressive structures are an innovation of Solomon's time. The story of

Model of ancient Megiddo in the Solomonic period.

Base of Canaanite gate and wall at bottom.

the investigations of the Solomonic level is typical of the Megiddo controversies, but with a happy ending; the solutions have been satisfactorily worked out.

The excavators had correctly attributed the six-chambered gate to the Solomonic level; since then the Solomonic gates at Hazor and Gezer were found to match it (see the "Gezer" and "Hazor" entries). At the other sites the gates were integrated with casemate walls, comprising distinctive Solomonic fortifications, but the Megiddo excavators had associated their gate with an offsets-insets wall (a solid wall with sections alternately protruding from the center line of the wall). It is unlikely that Solomon would have fortified his cities in two different ways. Since Hazor to the north and Gezer to the south were fortified similarly, why would the city between them differ in its fortifications? This was not the only problem in the reports on Solomonic Megiddo. The excavators had attributed structures identified as stables to Solomon's reign. This fitted well with the biblical reports of Solomon's chariot cities (I Kings 10:26). The stables were clearly associated with the offsets-insets wall, but later the excavators found the ruins of a magnificent palace and another large building *under* the offsets-insets wall. These buildings were constructed of large ashlar blocks that matched the style of the gate, and they were definitely of Solomonic architecture. Could Solomon have demolished these two elegant buildings so as to build the offsets-insets wall later in his reign?

For decades biblical archaeologists debated the discrepancies inherent in the reports of Solomonic Megiddo. The excavators' stratigraphy was suspect. There were clearly too many pieces that did not fit properly together. It was after connecting the Gezer gate and wall complexes with those at Hazor that Yadin felt it was time to reinvestigate Megiddo. With the help of the architect I. Dunayevsky, he examined a section of the offsets-insets wall that had not been touched in the previous excavations. A new Solomonic palace was uncovered, and it was clearly *underlying* the offsets-insets wall and the stables. Finally, another wall was discovered underneath the offsets-insets wall. Yadin demonstrated that the lower wall had been built at the same time as the gate, but that it had been "robbed" in many places; this is the reason earlier excavators had not found it. (The "robbing" of older materials for reuse in later building was a common practice in ancient Palestine.) The lower wall is a casemate wall like the ones at Hazor and Gezer. Yadin found that the offsets-insets wall had been attached to the gate at a higher level after the bottom of the gate was blocked up.

This means that there is at Megiddo a Solomonic level (IV B–

Remains of the Solomonic gate.

Remains of Canaanite temple.

V A) similar to those at Gezer and Hazor, and that above it there is another level which includes the stables and the offsets-insets wall. The stratigraphy now follows a logical pattern, and the correlation of the three cities that Solomon had built at the same time is now corroborated by substantial evidence.

A proto-Ionic capital about 7′3″ long from the southern palace of Megiddo.

The stratum directly above the Solomonic city belongs to a rebuilding period in the time of the house of Omri, probably Ahab's reign. At that point the city plan was revised and it was made into a "siege city" (a city capable of withstanding a siege) equipped with great fortifications and a protected water system. It now seems that the Megiddo water tunnel, previously thought to be Canaanite, belongs to this period. It had been dated by Lamon in relation to the other strata. The relative chronology was not incorrect, but the reidentification of the levels above it demanded a revision of the date. Now that the questions have been answered, Y. Aharoni has raised a new one: are the famous Megiddo stables really stables? No equestrian equipment has been found in them. Instead, he would see them as storehouses analogous to those discovered in his Beer-sheba excavations.

Megiddo maintained its importance as an Israelite fortified city until it was conquered by Tiglath-pileser in 733. It is worth noting that a phenomenon common to all Israelite levels at Megiddo is an abundance of cult objects, especially ceramic figurines, along with objects for normal use bearing foreign cultic designs. The last reference in the Bible to Megiddo alludes to such religious syncretism (Zech. 12:11).

The water tunnel at Megiddo.

The Assyrians rebuilt the city according to a new plan containing several large buildings with a central court, a common feature of the Assyrian style. Megiddo became an important military-administrative center. There are only scattered remains from the Babylonian and Persian periods. The Romans, scorning the abandoned tell of Megiddo, built a camp nearby in the second-third centuries A.D. Today the abandoned ruins of an Arab village mark the site, and the name (Lejjun) reflects a corruption of the Latin word *legion*. As for Megiddo, the name has been retained in the final book of the New Testament in the form *Armageddon,* derived from the Hebrew *har megiddo* ("the Mountain of Megiddo"—Rev. 16:16, LB). The seer of the Apocalypse chose to describe the battle of the end of days with the figure of Megiddo—the city of the Bible that above all others had known the clash of armies and the clangor of battle.

SUGGESTED TOPICS FOR FURTHER STUDY

1. Middle Bronze-Late Bronze Megiddo and Canaanite culture.
2. Extrabiblical evidence for the history of Megiddo.

3. The Megiddo water system and the problem of water in Palestine.
4. The non-Israelite influences on the architecture of King Solomon.
5. The Canaanite temple at Megiddo and Solomon's temple in Jerusalem.
6. Megiddo in the Bible.
7. The reign of King Ahab and the Megiddo stables.
8. The Megiddo excavations and James Michener's *The Source.*

RECOMMENDED READING

Kenyon, K. M., *Royal Cities of the Old Testament* (London: Barrie and Jenkins, 1971).

Schofield, J. N., "Megiddo" in *Archaeology and Old Testament Study,* ed. D. W. Thomas (Oxford: Clarendon, 1967), pp. 309–28.

Van Beek, G. W., "Megiddo" in *The Interpreter's Dictionary of the Bible,* ed. G. A. Buttrick (New York: Abingdon Press, 1962), vol. 3, pp. 335–42.

Wright, G. E., "The Discoveries at Megiddo, 1935–1939" in *The Biblical Archeologist Reader,* ed. E. F. Campbell, Jr., and D. N. Freedman (Garden City, NY: Doubleday, 1964), vol. 2, pp. 225–40.

Yadin, Y., "Megiddo of the Kings of Israel," *Biblical Archaeologist* 33 (1970), pp. 66–96.

———, "New Light on Solomon's Megiddo," *Biblical Archaeologist* 23 (1960), pp. 240–47.

FOR FURTHER READING

Dunayevsky, I., and A. Kempinski, "Megiddo," *Israel Exploration Journal* 15 (1965), p. 142.

Fisher, C. S., *The Excavation of Armageddon* (Chicago: University of Chicago Press, 1929).

Guy, P. L. O., *New Light from Armageddon* (Chicago: University of Chicago Press, 1931).

Lamon, R. S., *The Megiddo Water System* (Chicago: University of Chicago Press, 1935).

———, and G. M. Shipton, *Megiddo I* (Chicago: University of Chicago Press, 1948).

Schumacher, G., *Tell el-Mutsellim I,* two volumes (Leipzig, 1908).

Yadin, Y., "Megiddo," *Israel Exploration Journal* 17 (1967), pp. 119–21.

29

The Dead Sea Scrolls and Qumran

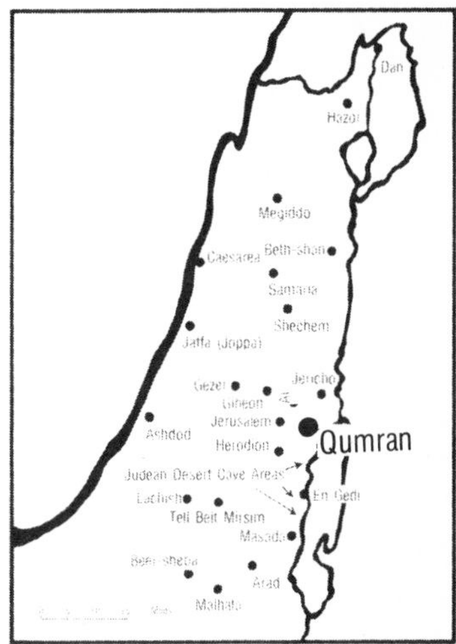

The Discovery

In the spring of 1947, two Bedouin shepherds were searching for a stray goat in the vicinity of Qumran northwest of the Dead Sea. During their search they stumbled upon a cave, and in the cave they found several earthenware jars, one of which contained decaying bundles of leather scrolls which proved to be of great significance to biblical studies and to the background of Christianity. The Bedouin brought the leather bundles to the market place in Bethlehem where they were bought by an antique dealer. Upon closer inspection, the bundles were found to comprise seven large scrolls and several fragments, all wrapped in linen and written in Hebrew and Aramaic. All seven of the scrolls are now owned by the Hebrew University in Jerusalem.

After the discovery of the first cave in 1947, the Bedouin and the archaeologists excavated about three hundred caves in the Dead Sea region and eleven caves yielded additional written material. The many different types of manuscripts consisted chiefly of biblical writings, commentaries on biblical books, apocryphal manuscripts, Old Testament pseudepigrapha, and sectarian literature—a total of several more or less complete scrolls in addition to tens of thousands of fragments, estimated by some to number about forty thousand. These finds are now generally known as "The Dead Sea Scrolls," "Qumran Scrolls," or "Qumran Writings"—Qumran being the name of the nearby

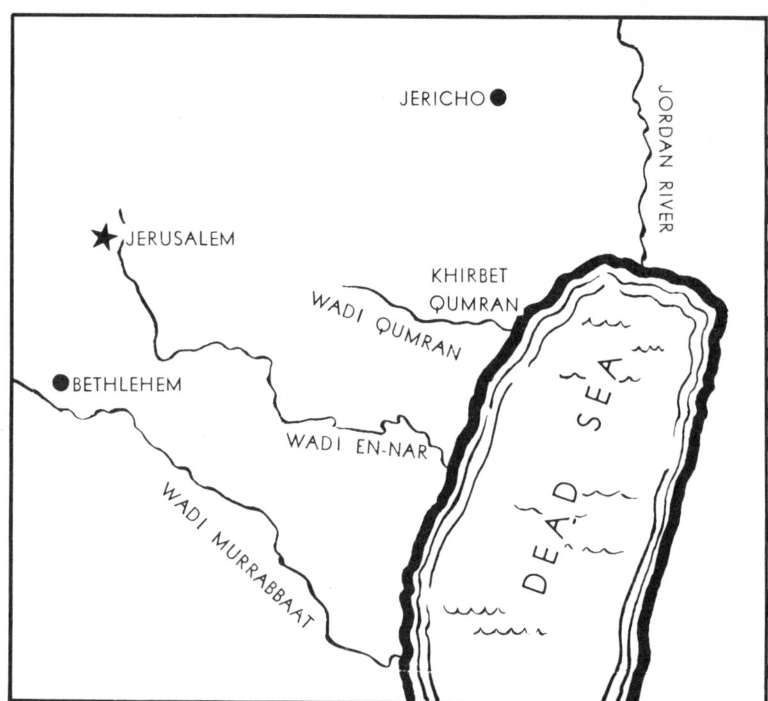

Map of the Qumran region.

site where the Qumran sect is believed to have lived. References to the individual scrolls often appear with a number (the number assigned the cave of its discovery), the letter "Q" (for Qumran), and the first letter of the Hebrew title of the scroll. For example, the *Hodayot Scroll (Thanksgiving Hymns)* is referred to as IQH.

Following is a description of the seven scrolls originally discovered in the first cave.

(1) There is a complete scroll of Isaiah, twenty-four feet long, written in Hebrew and almost identical with the Masoretic text of the Book of Isaiah in the Hebrew Bible. This scroll is sometimes known as the *St. Mark's Monastery Isaiah Scroll,* as it was previously owned by the monastery.

(2) The *Manual of Discipline* is a scroll containing rules and regulations by which members of the sect along the Dead Sea were governed.

(3) The *Commentary on the Book of Habakkuk,* the text of the first two chapters of the Book of Habakkuk with a running commentary and interpretation, contains some interesting historical allusions to figures believed to have lived at the time the scroll was written.

(4) The *Genesis Apocryphon,* first known as the *Lamech Scroll,*

contains apocryphal accounts of some of the patriarchs of Genesis; for example, Lamech, Enoch, Noah, Abraham, and Sarah. This scroll is written in Aramaic.

(5) Then there is an incomplete scroll of Isaiah, also known as the *Hebrew University Isaiah Scroll.*

(6) The *War Scroll* (the full title of which is the *Scroll of the War of the Sons of Light Against the Sons of Darkness*) gives directions for the conduct of an actual or eschatological war between members of the sect and their enemies.

(7) The last of the original seven scrolls found in the first cave is the *Scroll of the Thanksgiving Hymns,* containing about thirty hymns resembling the psalms in the Old Testament.

The Dating of the Scrolls

In 1947–48 when the scrolls were first found, there was considerable controversy among scholars as to their authenticity and the date of their composition. A few scholars suggested that the scrolls were a forgery and a hoax, and others felt that they were authentic but not very old. A whole series of dates was offered—from the third century B.C. to the Middle Ages and even to the twentieth century. Most scholars are now generally

Manual of Discipline.

agreed in dating the manuscripts between the second century B.C. and the first century A.D.

The problem in dating the scrolls revolves around the question of when the original sectarian works (like the *Manual of Discipline* and the *Thanksgiving Hymns*) were composed and when the biblical scrolls were copied. The evidence which determined the date of the scrolls was based on studies made by scholars in the fields of archaeology, paleography, orthography and linguistics, history, and science. Archaeologists studied the context in which the manuscripts were found—the pottery, the coins, and the linens that were found with the scrolls. The pottery found was clearly Roman, dating approximately from the second century B.C. to the first century A.D. The coins found in the caves were also from the same period. Nobel prize winner W. F. Libby, the atomic energy expert, administered a carbon-14 test on the fragments of linen textiles in which the scrolls were wrapped. He reported that the fabric could be dated to the year A.D. 33, with a possible error margin of two hundred years either way. This would place the date of the linen wrapping roughly between 200 B.C. and A.D. 200. Thus the dates accepted by most scholars were confirmed by the physical scientists. The evidence provided by the scholars who studied the orthography

Habakkuk Commentary.

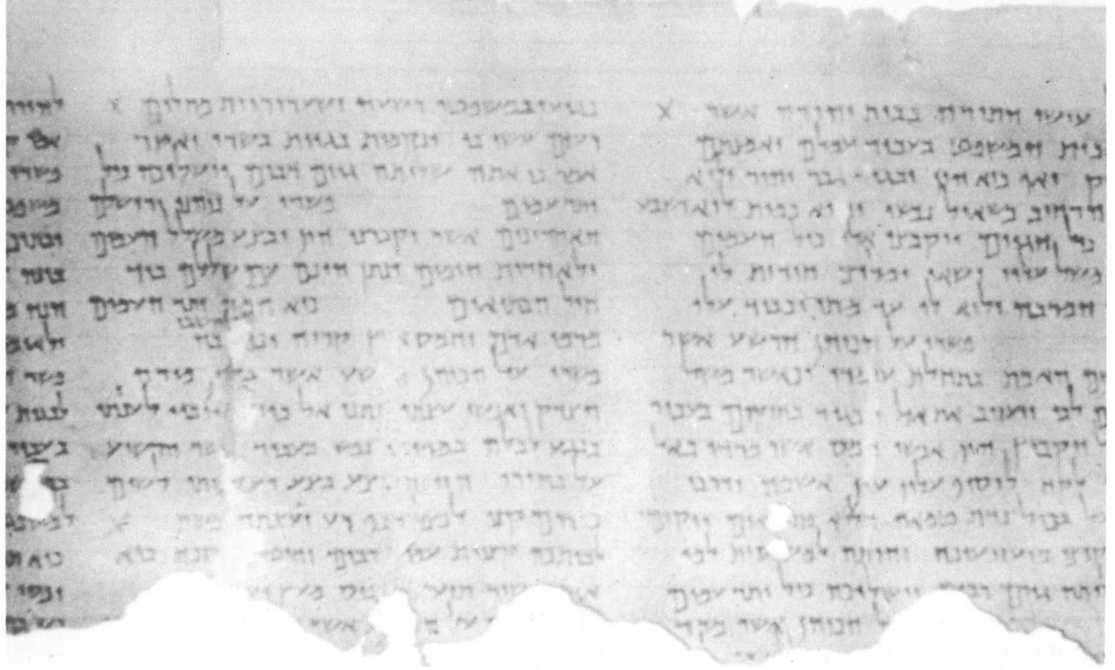

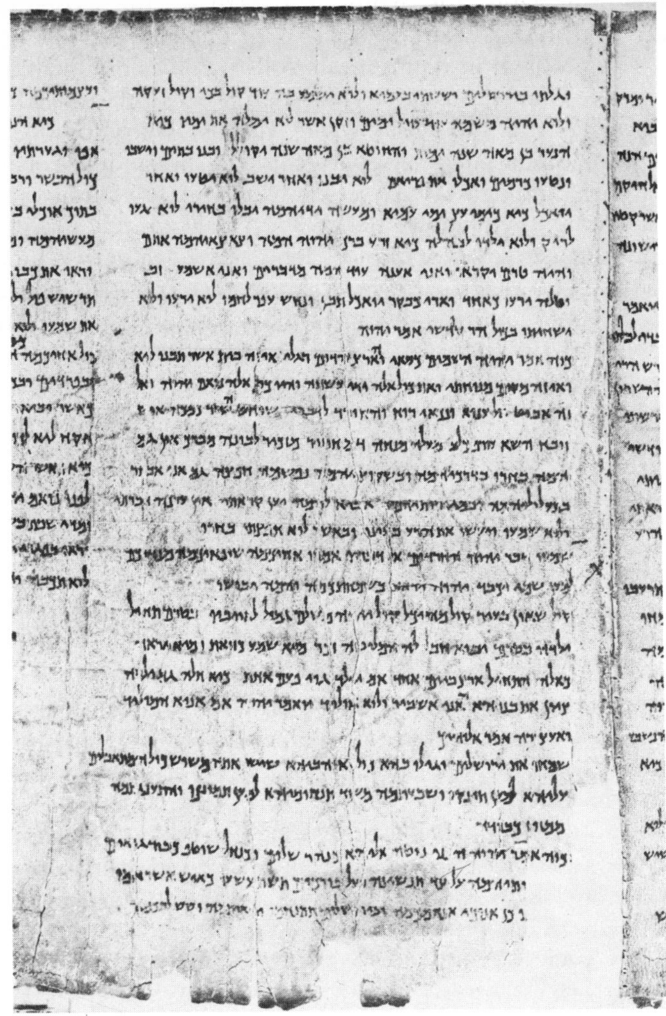

A column of the Isaiah Scroll.

and language of the scrolls showed that the language, based solidly on biblical Hebrew, is strongly flavored with pre-Christian Aramaic, late Hebrew, and, to some extent, Samaritan, and that the orthography and other linguistic features support a date between 200 B.C. and A.D. 100.

It is generally agreed that the scrolls were all written before A.D. 68 as the caves in which they were found showed no signs of habitation after that date. It is testified by Josephus, the Jewish historian of the time, that 68 was the year the Roman legions swept down on Jerusalem, having passed through the Qumran area. It appears that the inhabitants of Qumran temporarily stored away their documents, some with great care and others in haste, in earthenware jars in the caves; apparently they were never able to return to reclaim them.

General Contents of the Scrolls

After the inital discovery in 1947, research showed that the materials found were parts of some four hundred manuscripts, including biblical books. Every book in the Hebrew Bible except the Book of Esther is attested. The scrolls were written in Hebrew and Aramaic, some in an ancient Hebrew (Phoenician) script similar to the ancient scripts still in use by the Samaritans today. About ten scrolls have been well preserved; on the other hand, some texts are represented by only one fragment. Scholars all over the world are currently working on these fragments.

Biblical Scrolls

The biblical scrolls of Qumran have yielded a great deal of data that is enabling scholars to reconstruct the textual history of the Old Testament. In general, those scrolls indicate that the standard text of the Hebrew Bible, known today as the Masoretic text, was prevalent in the first century A.D. Some of the biblical scrolls, however, have proven that a variety of biblical texts was in circulation at the same time, at least up to the year A.D. 70. The material from different caves, and especially from Cave 4, has produced different textual traditions for the same book. These variant readings have helped clarify certain biblical passages that had before been obscure, and it is believed that in some cases the variations found are closer to the original words of the books as they were written. On the basis of belief in the authenticity of these variant texts, the Revised Standard Version of the Bible in its newest edition, after careful deliberation on the part of a committee of biblical scholars, has followed the St. Mark's Isaiah in thirteen variant readings.

About a quarter of the total manuscripts and fragments found in the Qumran caves consists of copies of books of the Bible, every book of the Hebrew Bible being represented except the Book of Esther, while parts of books such as Deuteronomy, Psalms, Isaiah, and the Minor Prophets are represented by more than ten copies. Some of the scrolls bring us closer to the original of some of the books of the Old Testament than do any other biblical writings in existence. The Book of Daniel is believed by many scholars to have been written about 165 B.C.; it is possible that the Qumran manuscripts of Daniel were transcribed within one hundred years after the original composition of the book.

Before the discovery of the Dead Sea Scrolls, the oldest known biblical manuscript was the Codex Petropolitanus, which dates from A.D. 916. Thus the biblical manuscripts from the Dead Sea caves are of utmost significance, since the Isaiah manuscripts bring us a thousand years closer to the original than does any other copy of that book.

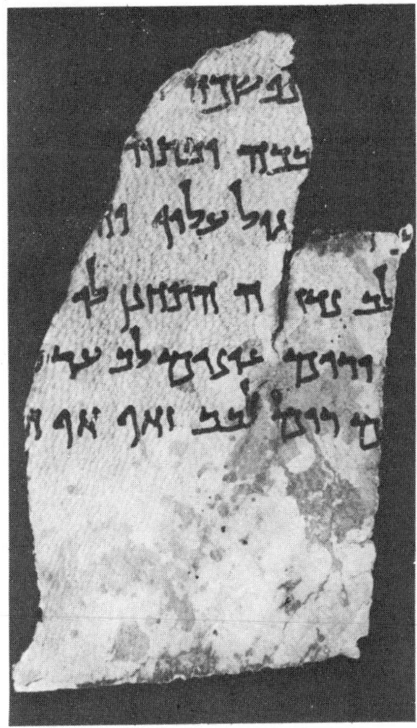

Fragment of a scroll containing the Thanksgiving hymns.

Apocryphal and Pseudepigraphical Literature

The popularity of apocryphal and pseudepigraphal works during intertestamental times is reflected in the sizable amount of these kinds of literature found at Qumran. Examples of three apocryphal (sacred writings included in the Greek Septuagint but not in the Hebrew Bible) books—Tobit, Ecclesiasticus (Ben Sira) and the Epistle of Jeremiah—have been found among the Dead Sea Scrolls. In addition, the caves have yielded a significant amount of literature described as pseudepigraphical; that is, a noncanonical writing ascribed to a famous historical personage in order to enhance the book's spiritual nature. Most of the Qumran pseudepigraphical works are considered to be of pre-Christian origin, though some of the non-Qumran works reflect evidence of Christian interpolation.

Fragments of about ten different manuscripts of the pseudepigraphical works have been found. The *Book of Jubilees* is an account of the origins of the chosen people. It insists on the solar calendar spoken of in other Qumran writings. The *Book of Enoch,* written in Aramaic, was previously known from an Ethiopic version and from a section of a Greek text. The *Testament of the Twelve Patriarchs,* written in Greek, seems to be an adaptation and compilation of other pseudepigraphical testaments, two of which, the *Testament of Naphtali* (in Hebrew) and the *Testament of Levi* (in Aramaic), were among Qumran fragments. Other pseudepigraphical works from Qumran include a pseudo-Jeremiah work (which has only loose connections with the rest of the known literature attributed to the prophet or his secretary, Baruch), the *Psalms of Joshua,* the *Vision of Amram* (the father of Moses and Aaron), and the beginnings of a small Aramaic scroll entitled the *Prayer of Nabonidus,* which seems to be the source (whether in written or oral form) used by the author of the Book of Daniel when he wrote of Nebuchadnezzar's illness.

Biblical Commentaries

The books of the Bible were the most important sources for study for the Qumran community, and like other teachers in

Israel, the teachers of the sect believed that the words of the Scripture could be applied to the events of their own lives. Generally, the commentaries quote the biblical text, a verse or a few words from a verse at a time. Immediately after the quotation, the author adds his commentary, explaining the biblical text in the perspective of his own day. The *Commentary on the Book of Habakkuk,* one of the seven original scrolls of the first discovery, is the most complete of the Qumran commentaries, containing nearly all of a text of Habakkuk which is one thousand years older than any other Hebrew text of Habakkuk so far known. It is also important in that it enables us to learn about the problems of the members of the sect who wrote the scroll, and to learn that the Teacher of Righteousness was clearly the leader and perhaps the founder of the community.

The *Nahum Commentary* generally follows the pattern of the *Commentary on the Book of Habakkuk,* and like the other commentaries, speaks of conflict and the sect's enemies. It is the only one which gives the names of actual historical personages. The historical allusions are helpful in determining the date when the scrolls were written and in telling us more about the sect, its history, and the history of the period in which its members lived.

The *Psalms Commentary* from Cave 4 is similar in style to the other commentaries and in all probability was written about the same time. It contains fragments from Psalms 37, 45, 57, and 68, the commentary on Psalm 37 being important for its biographical data about the Teacher of Righteousness. In addition, fragments have been found of commentaries on Genesis 49, Isaiah (one in Cave 3 and another in Cave 4), Hosea, Micah, Nahum, and Zephaniah. The *War Scroll* contains a commentary on a passage from Ezekiel.

Sectarian Literature

Some of the most interesting nonbiblical and hitherto unknown scrolls found at Qumran can be conveniently included under the heading of "Sectarian Literature"; they are obviously the writings of a religious sect that occupied the Qumran region. That such a sect occupied that region has been proved by the excavation of ruins called Khirbet Qumran in the vicinity of the caves. It has also been established through archaeological evidence (such as jars and coins) that the religious community that occupied the buildings at Khirbet Qumran from the second century B.C. to A.D. 68 was the same community that copied the biblical manuscripts found there and wrote the manuscripts that have been classified as "Sectarian Literature."

The scroll of the war of the Sons of Light against the Sons of Darkness.

General view of the Qumran ruins, looking south toward Ain Feshka.

The Temple Scroll as it was found.

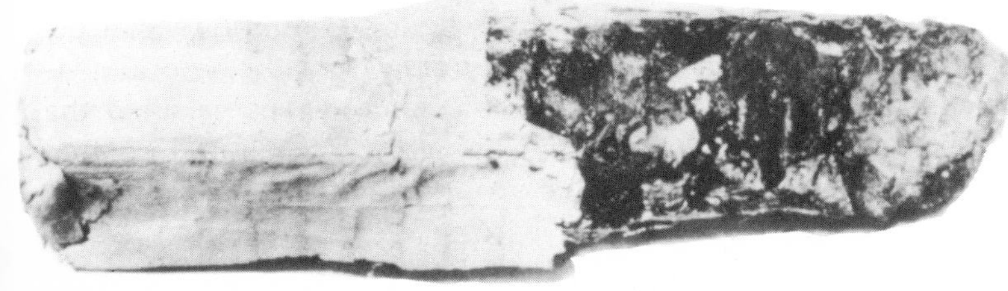

The *Scroll of the Thanksgiving Hymns* is one of the most interesting scrolls, its hymns being important for the study of the religious ideas of the sect which preserved them. This collection of hymns seems to be the product of a single author whose experiences and feelings they vividly reflect. It is also an invaluable document for research on the comparative study of the doctrines of the sect and the background of Christianity. Some of the doctrines contained in this scroll are dualism, predestination, salvation through election, divine knowledge, and immortality.

The scroll called the *Manual of Discipline* describes the doctrine of the sect and the rules and regulations by which its daily life was governed. The scroll discusses the three-stage probation period through which each initiate had to pass, the initiation ceremony, the daily life of the members, and their disciplinary code. It tells us that the members of the sect were volunteers who pledged themselves to do what was good and right before God. We learn that the members sought to separate themselves from the society of wicked men, to love all sons of light and to hate all the sons of darkness, to practice in community truth and modesty, to act righteously and justly, to love mercy and walk humbly in all their ways. The scroll implies that the members were celibate, although there must have been women and children in the community, since skeletons of females and children were found in the cemetery next to Khirbet Qumran. We may therefore assume that some of the members did marry. It is also possible that the members who volunteered to join the community brought their wives and children with them.

The *War Scroll* is unlike any known so far in either the Jewish or Christian literature of the time, and no work like it has been found among the sect's other books. This scroll is important for several reasons. For the first time we have comprehensive data on military regulations of the Jewish armies during the late period of the second temple. The scroll contains military and technical terms hitherto unknown, and is the oldest extant record of Hebrew military craft.

The Temple Scroll

In 1967 Yadin announced the acquisition of another Qumran scroll—the *Temple Scroll*. It is the longest scroll found thus far near the Dead Sea—over twenty-eight feet long (the Qumran *Isaiah Scroll* being twenty-four feet). It is also unique in its content which is concerned with four groups of subjects: (1) a large collection of Halakoth—religious rules and regulations—on various topics including ritual cleanliness; (2) sacrifices and offer-

A jar and other artifacts from Qumran.

Pottery *in situ* in the Qumran pantry.

The Copper Scroll *in situ*.

One of the large meeting halls in the Qumran center.

ings associated with the festivals; (3) statutes of the king and of the army; and (4) a detailed description of the temple. It was because of this last section of the scroll that Yadin arbitrarily called it the *Temple Scroll*.

The Copper Scroll

Cave 3 of Qumran yielded two copper scrolls which actually form a single scroll. The scroll contains a long list of hidden treasures in the amount of some six thousand gold and silver talents. Many of the hidden items described in the *Copper Scroll* had been collected as "tithes" for the temple and its priests. The *Copper Scroll* was probably intended to tell the Jewish survivors of the war then raging where this sacred material lay buried, so that if any should be found, it would never be desecrated by profane use. The scroll would also act as a guide to the recovery of the treasure, should it be needed to carry on the war. The present value of the treasure described in this scroll would be about a million U.S. dollars.

The Sect of the Scrolls

There has been considerable controversy as to the identity of the sect that produced the Dead Sea Scrolls. Influenced by a description of contemporary Jewish sects in the writings of Josephus, many scholars have identified the Qumran sect with the Essenes, a group which flourished mainly in Palestine during the second Jewish commonwealth. Here the Essenes lived in monastic communities from which women were excluded, although there are records of women in some other Essene communities.

The Qumran sect stressed priesthood. Its leader and its most hated enemy were both priests, and in their sectarian literature, the members often refer to themselves as the "sons of Zadok." They upheld rigid rules of Levitical purity, and though they recognized temple service as obligatory, they disassociated themselves from the Jerusalem temple because, in their opinion, its priests were defiled and its liturgical calendar was incorrect.

The sect of Qumran was part of a Jewish apocalyptic movement of the day. Its basic doctrine, institutions, and practices were in anticipation of the end of days when God would raise this sect to be the ruling class. Thus they dedicated themselves to a strict way of life in zealous preparation for the times when they, the "Sons of Light," that is, members of the sect, would triumph over their enemies, the "Sons of Darkness."

The sectarian literature of Qumran reflects the important position of the community's spiritual leader, the Teacher of Righteousness. He was the prime example of one who had been given a secret, profound knowledge, shared to a certain extent by the other members of the sect, but lacking in persons outside the sect. A basic attitude of thankfulness for this gift is expressed in the *Thanksgiving Hymns.* The members of the Qumran sect led an austere, presumably celibate, life of shared goods, spending their time in study and writing, in crafts, and in agricultural works which helped support the community.

Points of contact have been found between the way of life, practices, and doctrines of the Qumran sect and those of the early Christians. Both the Qumran community and the early Christian community were eschatological and both practiced a policy of shared goods. Charles Fritsch of Princeton Theological Seminary estimated that there are over five hundred verbal parallels between the Qumran scrolls and the New Testament, especially in John's Gospel. Both John and the Essenes were products of the same Jewish milieu, and thus it is not surprising that the two groups of writings should bear similarities. Parallels have been drawn between the leader of the Qumran sect, the Teacher of Righteousness, and Jesus of Nazareth, but closer inspection of their ways of life and doctrines clearly shows the two to be distinct from one another. It is possible that both Jesus and John the Baptist did come into contact with the sect. In fact, some writers have suggested the possibility that the unknown years in the life of Jesus, from the age of twelve to about thirty, might have been spent with the Essenes. There is, however, no reference whatsoever in the texts to this. The differences between Jesus and the Qumran sect are very significant: Jesus' objective was not to form a community of solitaries as the Qumran community seems to have been. The universality of his message stands in sharp contrast to the exclusiveness of Qumran. The Qumran sect was ritualistic and legalistic whereas Jesus stressed concern for one's fellow man. The Qumran doctrines can be understood without their leader, but Christianity is unthinkable without its leader.

Importance of the Scrolls

The Dead Sea Scrolls have proved to be valuable and unique for many important areas of study. They have provided us with new information about life in Palestine from the second century B.C. to the first century A.D. They have increased our knowledge of the history of the developments of the Bible and of the Hebrew language and script. They have also shed new light on the history of the Jewish religion and Jewish religious life and thought in Palestine at the most fateful period in religious history, namely, the birth of Christianity. They give us more precise insight into the life and faith of one of the Jewish dissident sects of brotherhood which existed during the intertestamental period.

The paramount importance of the scrolls to New Testament studies is their contribution toward knowledge of the immediate pre-Christian era. In bringing greater clarity to our understanding of the setting in which Christianity was born, they show us not only the roots of some of its ideas, but also its unique and distinct character.

Excavations at Khirbet Qumran

Roland de Vaux, O.P. at Qumran.

While excavating Cave 1 in 1949, Father Roland de Vaux and G. L. Harding searched for evidence of human habitation which might explain the deposit of the scrolls in the cave. They spotted the ruins of a building standing on a plateau halfway between the sea and the cliffs about a thousand yards to the southeast of Cave 1. The ruins were not a new find, having been mentioned nearly a century earlier in an 1851 report by F. De Saulcy, who conjectured that the site might have been the biblical Gomorrah.

In 1951 serious excavations at Khirbet Qumran began, and this campaign led to the discovery of pottery and cloth as well as hundreds of tiny manuscript fragments. According to archaeologists, the pottery finds were of two main groups, one coming from the Hellenistic period and the other, only a few fragments of two lamps and a pot, coming from the Roman period. The fragments of cloth found in the cave were obviously used as envelopes for the scrolls. In 1949 a cemetery had been uncovered, and in the following year the rubble was cleared out from the walls to expose the main outline of a building. Since the building had large meeting rooms with plaster benches along the walls and a water cistern much larger than would be needed for a family, it was assumed that the building was not a dwelling but rather a community center of some sort. One of the most important finds amid the ruins was a jar, still intact, of exactly the same shape as those found in Cave 1. This allowed archaeologists to link with certainty the people of the scrolls and the inhabitants of Khirbet Qumran. During this time, three occupation levels covering a period of 250 years were found, the lowest (oldest) being 135 B.C. Later, evidence of occupation in the eighth and seventh centuries B.C. was found. The excavations at Khirbet Qumran continued until 1956.

At the lowest level were found remains of walls and pottery which belonged to Iron Age II (eighth and seventh century B.C.). One of the potsherds found at this level was inscribed with Phoenician characters of the kind used to write Hebrew at that time. Also found at this level was a royal seal stamped on a jar handle and a fragmentary ostracon. While there is interesting speculation whether this building comes from the time of Uzziah, king of Judah (780–740 B.C.), who according to II Chronicles 26:10 "built towers in the desert," the chief interest is in the 250 years covering the Greco-Roman period.

The first stage in this period is from the end of the second century B.C. to A.D. 68, and is divided into two parts. The community appears to have abandoned the building for thirty or forty years at the end of the first century B.C. Not long after they abandoned the building, it was severely damaged by an earthquake, and as a result, extensive reconstruction was necessary when the sect returned to occupy it once again. On the basis of evidence supplied to us by the historian Flavius Josephus writing in the first century A.D. we can date the earthquake to the spring of 31 B.C. The earthquake left the cisterns cracked and caused plaster to crack and ceilings to cave in. It is possible that in fact the inhabitants of the sect left because of the earthquake, and not before it. This question has not yet been resolved. About thirty years after the earthquake, the sectarians returned, cleared the rubble, and rebuilt the walls. This part of the first stage lasted until the fall of the monastery in A.D. 68.

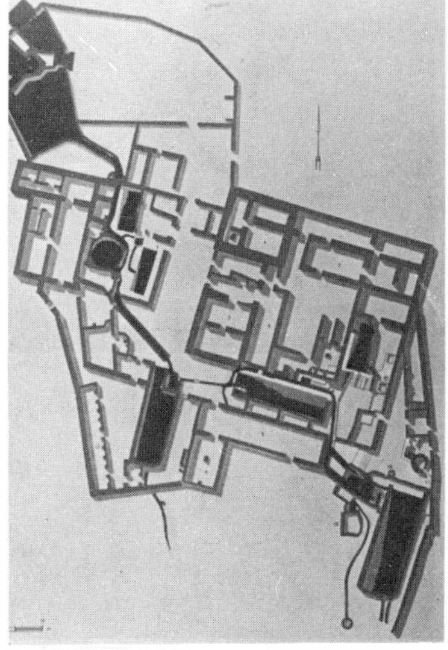

Plan of the Qumran complex highlighting the water system.

The second stage was an occupation by a Roman garrison between A.D. 68 and 86. Josephus tells us that in the spring of A.D. 68, the Emperor Vespasian brought his Tenth Legion down the Jordan Valley to Jericho. The Roman approach was met with general panic, and much of the population fled into "those mountainous parts which lay over against Jerusalem." The Roman victors did not leave immediately, and the rest of this period is marked by a reutilization of the building's defense works, the leveling of debris, and the division of the larger meeting rooms into smaller living quarters.

Following the Roman occupation, the building remained empty until A.D. 132 when the second revolt against Rome by Jewish insurgents broke out in Judea. After three years of bitter fighting the revolt was finally crushed, and Khirbet Qumran, which had been used because of its strategic location, was completely demolished.

The major archaeological evidence of these three stages of occupation lies in coins and in pottery. Several hundred coins from five different periods have been found, the earliest being a group from the reign of John Hyrcanus in 135–104 B.C. The next group of coins runs continuously until the time of Herod the Great in 37–34 B.C.—a period for which only one coin was found. The third series of coins begins with Herod Archelaus (4 B.C.-A.D. 6) and continues until A.D. 68. Seventy-three coins from this year have been found. The fourth period is marked by only a very few coins ranging in date from the last two years in Nero's reign to the reign of Titus (A.D. 79–81). The last large group of coins from the building comes from the time of the second Jewish revolt in A.D. 132–35.

The pottery remains have been analyzed by Father de Vaux, and he suggests that, to begin with, Level I belongs to the end of the Hellenistic period. Level II he dates from the beginning of the Roman period, and Level III is only slightly more recent than Level II. According to Father de Vaux, the use of the caves was contemporary with Levels I and II of Khirbet Qumran, the material corresponding to Level II being predominant.

STUDY QUESTIONS

1. Name the main types of literature discovered in the Qumran caves and describe one specific text representing each type.
2. List some of the main doctrines of the Qumran sect which are reflected in their sectarian literature.
3. Cite the evidence by which scholars have determined the date of the scrolls.
4. Describe the lifestyle of the Qumran sect.
5. Compare ideas and practices of the Qumran sect with those of the early Christians.
6. Name one or two Qumran documents which you find most interesting and discuss their significance.

FOR FURTHER READING ON THE SCROLLS

Allegro, J. M., *The Dead Sea Scrolls* (Baltimore: Penguin Books, 1964).

———, *The Treasure of the Copper Scroll* (London, Routledge & K. Paul, 1964).

Avigad, N., and Y. Yadin, *A Genesis Apocryphon* (Jerusalem: Magnes, 1956).

Black, M., *The Scrolls and Christian Origins* (London, 1961).

Burrows, M., *The Dead Sea Scrolls* (New York: Viking Press, 1955).

———, *More Light on the Dead Sea Scrolls* (New York: Viking Press, 1955).

Cross, Frank M., Jr., *The Ancient Library of Qumran* (London: G. Duckworth, 1958; paperback—Garden City, N.Y.: Doubleday, 1961).

Dupont-Sommer, A., *The Essene Writings from Qumran* (Oxford: B. Blackwell, 1961).

———, *The Jewish Sect of Qumran and the Essenes* (London: Valentine, Mitchell, 1954).

Fitzmyer, J. A., *The Dead Sea Scrolls: Major Publications and Tools for Study* (Missoula, MT: Scholars Press, 1975).

Fritsch, C. T., *The Qumran Community* (New York: Macmillan, 1956).

Gaster, T. H., *The Dead Sea Scriptures* (Garden City, N.Y.: Doubleday, 1956).

Mansoor, M., *The Dead Sea Scrolls: College Textbook and Guide* (Grand Rapids: Eerdmans; and Leiden: E. J. Brill, 1964; second printing, 1967).

———, *The Thanksgiving Hymns* (Leiden: E. J. Brill, 1961).

Milik, J. T., *Ten Years of Discovery in the Wilderness of Judea* (Naperville, IL: A. R. Allenson, 1959).

Murphy-O'Connor, J., *Paul and Qumran* (London: Geoffrey Chapman, 1968).

Rabin, Chaim, *Qumran Studies* (New York: Schocken Books, 1975).

Ringgren, Hilmer, *The Faith of Qumran* (Philadelphia: Fortress Press, 1963).

Rowley, H. H., *The Dead Sea Scrolls and the New Testament* (London: V. S. P. Cok, 1959).

Siegel, J. P., *The Severus Scroll in 1QIs*[a] (Missoula, MT: Scholars Press, 1975).

Van der Ploeg, J., *The Excavations at Qumran* (New York: Longmans, Green, 1958).

Vermes, G., *The Dead Sea Scrolls in English* (Baltimore: Penguin Books, 1962; revised edition, 1968).

———, *Discoveries in the Judean Desert* (New York: Deselee Co., 1956).

Wilson, E., *The Dead Sea Scrolls, 1947–1969* (Oxford University Press, 1969).

———, *The Scrolls from the Dead Sea* (New York: Meridian Press, 1955).

Yadin, Y., *The Message of the Scrolls* (New York, London: Universal Library, 1957).

———, *The Scroll of the War* (London: Oxford University Press, 1962).

30

Samaria

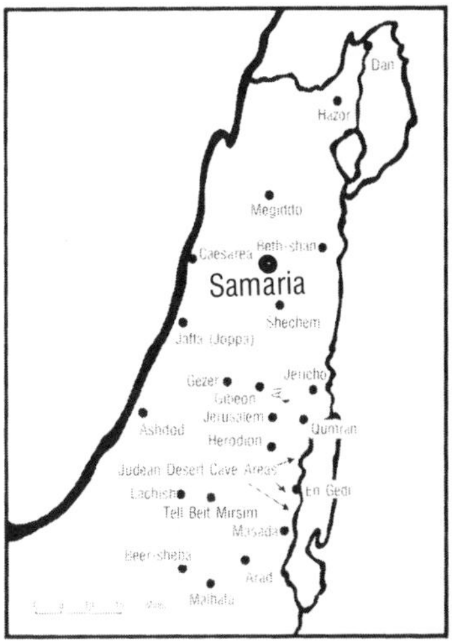

Samaria, the ancient capital of the Northern Kingdom of Israel, occupied a hill which protrudes from the floor of a broad valley cutting across the central highlands of Palestine between Shechem and the seacoast. Samaria (*Shomron* in Hebrew) was the town's name until Herod the Great rebuilt it and renamed it Sebaste, after his patron, the Emperor Augustus (Greek *sebastos* = Augustus). The modern village near the site is still called Sebastiyeh. The hill itself, although relatively low, is far enough from the surrounding heights to be easily defended. It guarded the main trade route from the south to the north and west and gave easy access to Israel's rich western territory and to the Phoenician cities on the coast. All in all, it was an excellent site for the capital.

The site, if well-favored, has also been well excavated. In 1908–10, Harvard University sent to the site an expedition directed by G. A. Reisner. In 1931–35, J. W. Crowfoot directed a joint expedition sponsored by Harvard, the Hebrew University, the Palestine Exploration Fund, the British Academy, and the British School of Archaeology in Jerusalem. E. L. Sukenik, K. M. Kenyon, and others participated in that dig. In 1965–67, F. Zayadine and P. W. Lapp worked at Samaria for the Jordanian Department of Antiquities, and in 1968, J. B. Hennessey excavated for the British School of Archaeology.

All the excavators at Samaria have been frustrated by the fact that Samaria was built of stone rather than mud-brick, and that it was thoroughly rebuilt in Hellenistic and Roman times. A destroyed mud-brick city serves later builders as ground level; a stone city serves as their quarry. Some of the stones of destroyed buildings are dug from the ground to be reused in later constructions. As a result of this and of the deep foundation trenches dug by Greek and Roman builders, little of the earliest Israelite city was left to be excavated.

Samaria, nevertheless, is of unique archaeological importance. It is the only major city known to have been *founded* by the Israelites. Its earliest strata therefore contain artifactual materials securely datable to the Iron Age II period.

According to I Kings 16, when Omri had established his rule over Israel, about 800 B.C., he moved the capital from Tirzah to the hill of Shemer, upon which he had the city of Samaria built. Excavations at Tirzah have shown that Omri began a building program there which was abandoned before it could be completed. The rebuilding of Tirzah ends chronologically exactly where the construction of Samaria begins. The new site had all the advantages listed earlier, including easy accessibility to the rich Phoenician coastal cities. With these cities Omri established cordial relations. The new site also afforded an opportunity to design and construct a city without the interference posed by the remnants of earlier structures. Excavations at Samaria suggest, too, that Omri wished to build himself something unprecedented in Palestine, an exclusively royal quarter atop the hill, luxurious and separate from the other people. It has yet to be shown that any common dwellings existed at Samaria during the Israelite period. Hennessey could find no occupation on the lower slopes to the west before the Persians. If there were ordinary houses, they must have been located on the eastern side of the hill, an area as yet unexcavated.

The main outlines of the Israelite building phases are clear. Omri and his son Ahab built a royal quarter with spacious courtyards, a pool (cf. I Kings 22:38), a palace, and an "ivory house" (I Kings 33:39; Amos 3:15), that is, a house whose furnishings and walls were elaborately overlaid with beautifully carved ivory panels. The remnants of these have been found, broken and burned, among the evidences of the Assyrian destruction of the city. For the ivory panels and for the construction of walls and buildings, skilled Phoenician craftsmen were employed, so that the masonry work of the first enclosure wall of the royal quarter is of a quality unexcelled in the history of Palestine. In a second phase, this quarter was made more definitely a fortifica-

An airview of the hill of Samaria.

Remains of the city gate of Samaria.

tion by the addition of a thick casemate wall outside the enclosure wall. Period III saw a great deal of rebuilding, in a much poorer style than before; evidently the Phoenicians were no longer present. Along with repairs to earlier walls and terraces, the final three periods (IV, V, and VI) continued the trend of reducing the courtyard space by adding poorly-built new structures.

Though this outline is clear, fitting it exactly to fixed historical points is another matter. An interesting debate over archaeological methods arose between Kenyon on the one hand, and G. E. Wright, Y. Aharoni, and others, on the other hand. Kenyon had departed from the usual practice of dating floor levels by the pottery found *on* them, and had used instead that found *under* them. She had thus arrived at six pottery periods corresponding to her six building periods. Period I she assigned to Omri, II to Ahab, III to the later Jehu, and so on. Aharoni, R. Amiran, and Wright found fault with this method, pointing to the virtual identity of Kenyon's first two pottery periods and their tenth century (pre-Omri) character. They suggested that these two pottery periods belong in fact to a small village which existed on the site before Omri, and which was obliterated by him. In this view Kenyon's Pottery III equals her Building I, the Omri-Ahab venture, and Building II (= Pottery IV) is assigned to Jehu. Kenyon has maintained her former view, and the question is still open.

In one room of the royal quarter were found over sixty ostraca, evidently recording the receipt of various goods (oil, wine, barley, etc.) from different places and individuals. The most widely-held opinion is that they are tax records, a rather unexciting subject, but their importance for the history of the Hebrew script is great indeed. Their date is disputed; most scholars have interpreted the numerals on them (such as 9, 10, 15, and 17) as the regnal years of some king, and have dated them to the seventeen-year reign of Jehoahaz (ca. 814–798 B.C.), or to Jeroboam II (ca. 782–743). Yadin, however, has persuasively argued that the numerals read only 9 and 10. He dates the ostraca to Menahem (ca. 752–742), who reigned just ten years. Menahem became tributary to Assyria in his ninth year and levied a heavy tax on his own subjects in order to pay the tribute (II Kings 15:19, 20).

Samaria was destroyed by the Assyrians in 722 B.C., after resisting the finest army of that era in a three-year siege. The conquerors undoubtedly carted off the best of the ivories and other rich furnishings (ivories in a style very similar to those of Samaria have been found at the Assyrian sites of Arslan Tash and Nimrud). They deported much of the population, and Samaria became an Assyrian military colony. Excavation shows that the city was burned, and in the next layer alien pottery forms appear. The city remained an administrative center under the Babylonians and Persians, likely controlling Judah as well; hence the friction when returning Judean exiles began restoring Jerusalem.

Samaria's residents made the mistake of resisting Alexander the Great, and were deported to Shechem about 331 B.C. Samaria was resettled with Greeks and became a Hellenistic city. It was heavily fortified, with well-built round towers, around 300 B.C., and strengthened further in the second century. The Hasmonean John Hyrcanus destroyed it, however, probably because of its Hellenistic culture, and for a time it was uninhabited.

The Romans removed the city from Judean hegemony and began restoring it under Pompey (63 B.C.) and Gabinius (57 B.C.). Finally Herod the Great obtained Samaria in 30 B.C. and made it one of his chief cities, resettling it with mercenaries from

Round tower of the Hellenistic era, built over Israelite remains.

Europe. He built there a temple for his patron, Caesar Augustus, a stadium, a forum, an aqueduct, and a long colonnaded street. Sebaste, as Herod renamed the city, was destroyed early in the first Jewish revolt against Rome between A.D. 66 and 70. It was later rebuilt by the Romans.

Oddly enough, Samaria has little to do with the Samaritans, the sect so hostile to, and regarded with such hostility by, orthodox Judaism in antiquity. The sect probably originated with the Israelites left in the district of Samaria by the Assyrians, not with the foreigners imported by the latter. It was apparently only in the period after they had been expelled to Shechem that the "Samaritan" conflicts with Judaism became irreconcilable; Shechem, not Samaria, was the center of dissident Samaritanism.

Nevertheless, Samaria-Sebaste seems to have stood in opposition to normative Israelite religion throughout most of its history, first as the "Phoenicianizing" capital city, where Baal worship was prominent (in the ostraca the ratio of personal names compounded with "Baal" to those compounded with "Yahweh" is about 7:11); then as a foreign colony and administrative center; and later as a center of Hellenistic and Roman culture. Furthermore it was Samaria, with her calf-gods, ivory-laden palaces, and opulent banquets, that prophets like Amos and Hosea zeroed in on, saying her wealth had been acquired at the

The Roman amphitheatre at Samaria.

The forum of Herod's Samaria.

cost of perverting the religion of Yahweh and riding roughshod over the poor. These diatribes, and the layers of blackened ash, must give one pause in contemplating the admirable beauty of the architecture and ivories found by the excavators.

SUGGESTED TOPICS FOR FURTHER STUDY

1. The Samaria ostraca.
2. The Samaria ivories.
3. Archaeological method and the history of Samaria.
4. Samaria and the prophets.
5. Omri and Phoenician influence in Israel.

RECOMMENDED READING

Aharoni, Y., and R. Amiran, "A New Scheme for the Sub-division of the Iron Age in Palestine," *Israel Exploration Journal* 8 (1958), pp. 171–84.

Crowfoot, J. W., et al., *Samaria-Sebaste*—J. W. Crowfoot, K. M. Kenyon, and E. L. Sukenik, vol. I, *The Buildings* (Palestine Exploration Fund, 1942); J. W. and G. M. Crowfoot, vol. II, *Early Ivories from Samaria* (London: Palestine Exploration Fund, 1938); J. W. and G. M. Crowfoot, and K. M. Kenyon, vol. III, *The Objects* (Palestine Exploration Fund, 1957).

Hennessey, J. B., "Excavations at Samaria-Sebaste, 1968," *Levant* 2 (1970), pp. iv–v, 1–21.

Kenyon, K. M., *Archaeology in the Holy Land* (New York: Praeger, 1970).

______, *Royal Cities of the Old Testament* (London: Barrie and Jenkins, 1971).

Reisner, G. A., C. S. Fisher, and D. G. Lyon, *Harvard Excavations at Samaria, 1908–1910* (Cambridge, MA: Harvard University Press, 1924).

Van Beek, G. W., "Samaria" in *The Interpreter's Dictionary of the Bible,* ed. G. A. Buttrick (New York: Abingdon Press, 1962), vol. 4, pp. 182–88.

Wright, G. E., "Israelite Samaria and Iron Age Chronology," *Bulletin of the American Schools of Oriental Research* 155 (1959), pp. 13–29.

———, "Samaria," *Biblical Archaeologist* 22 (1959), pp. 67–68.

Yadin, Y., "Ancient Judean Weights and the Date of the Samaria Ostraca," *Scripta Hierosolymitana* 8 (1961), pp. 9–25.

FOR FURTHER READING

Ackroyd, P. R., "Samaria" in *Archaeology and Old Testament Study,* ed. D. Winton Thomas (Oxford: Clarendon, 1967), pp. 343–54.

Cross, F. M., "Papyri of the Fourth Century B.C. from Daliyeh" in *New Directions in Biblical Archaeology,* ed. D. N. Freedman and J. C. Greenfield (Garden City, NY: Doubleday, 1969), pp. 41–62.

Pfeiffer, Charles F., ed., *The Biblical World* Grand Rapids: Baker, 1966), pp. 493–96.

31

Shechem

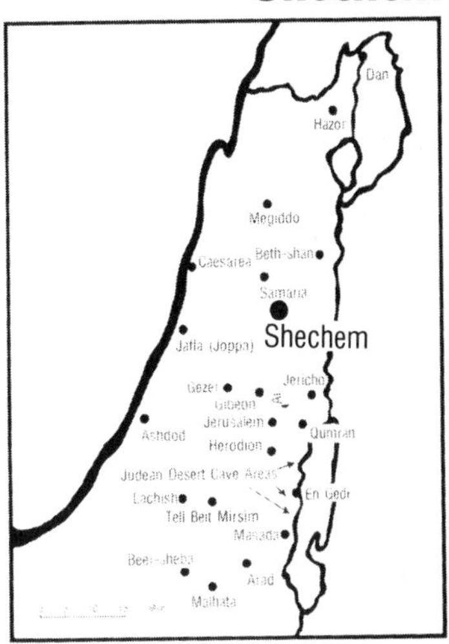

Shechem lies in the central highlands of the country at the foot of the eastern end of Mount Gerizim, near the pass that separates that massif from Mount Ebal. Directly north of the village of Balatah, one mile east of Nablus, is a low mound of about ten to twelve acres that contains the ruins of the ancient city of Shechem. Routes from several directions meet at this point, so that a great fort in this location could control all the main roads in northern central Palestine. The name *Shechem,* meaning "shoulder," suggests the slight elevation on which the mound was built at the mouth of the pass between Mount Gerizim and Mount Ebal. The plain in front provided the city with plenty of rich soil to support its population. The place is associated with the patriarchs by popular tradition, for a nearby Greek Orthodox church marks the place called "Jacob's Well," and a local Moslem shrine is the "Tomb of Joseph."

The knowledge of the general location of Shechem was insured by the survival of the Roman city Neapolis ("new city"—the modern Nablus), and by the continuing presence of the Samaritans in the area. Debates were carried on for a considerable time, however, about whether the biblical Shechem was to be found under Nablus or at the mound of Balatah. The *Onomasticon* of Eusebius and other early traditions placed Shechem east of Nablus, between Jacob's Well and the village of 'Askar. Jerome, Edward Robinson, and later scholars rejected this location as a vague speculation, and believed the site to be underneath Nablus. The discovery of a bronze hoard during construction work on Balatah attracted Ernst Sellin's attention to the site. The place was recognized as Shechem when a city with great fortifications was uncovered. Even then, it was not until many years later that all arguments concerning the identity of the site ceased.

The first work on Shechem was done by Professor Sellin in 1913. The excavation was sponsored by the Vienna Academy of Science, the Vorderasiatischaegyptische Gesellschaft, the German Archaeological Institute for the Notgemeinschaft der Deutschen Wissenschaft, and the Deutsche Evangelischen Institut für Altertumswissenschaft des Heiliges Landes, and was carried out in the years 1913–14, 1926–27, 1928, 1931, and 1934. Sellin uncovered many important structures, but since he had no training in archaeological techniques, these structures often had to be relabeled in later times. The German Archaeological Institute removed Sellin and replaced him with G. Welter. Welter's work was short and not much is known of it. His views are better known, and they usually opposed Sellin's. Welter even doubted that Shechem was at Balatah, and eventually he too was removed. A rather interesting arrangement was created next: Sellin was reinstated as the "Theological Director," with Hans Steckeweh, who had previously worked in Egypt, as the archaeological expert. The German excavation never quite acquired the right combination of people to make it work properly, but was continually plagued with problems and quarrels.

Starting in 1954, the Drew-McCormick archaeological excavation reopened work at Shechem under the sponsorship of the American Schools of Oriental Research; Austin, Drew, Garrett, and McCormick Theological Seminaries; and the Department of Antiquities of Jordan. The excavation, which was carried on in

The eastern gate of Shechem.

1956, 1957, 1960, 1962, 1964, 1966, and 1968, was directed by several people. G. Ernest Wright was called the Archaeological Director and Dean Anderson started as Administrative Director. After Anderson left, Lawrence E. Toombs of Drew was made Associate Director and Edward F. Campbell, Jr., of McCormick became Assistant Director. The excavation was partly aimed at training a new generation and type of biblical archaeologist, and in this it can be considered successful.

In the Bible Shechem is associated with the patriarchs Abraham and Jacob, of whom the former erects an altar (Gen. 12:7) and the latter a standing stone (Gen. 33:18–20). Both seem to claim Shechem in some way. The history of covenants at Shechem dates back to patriarchal times, that is, to the treaty between Shechem and Jacob. There is certainly an early Israelite claim on the city (Gen. 44:22). It is clear that when Joshua did not bother to conquer Shechem but made it the center for the great tribal covenant, the city must have already had some relationship with the Israelites (Josh. 24). This alliance was not perfect; Abimelech later destroyed the city and its temple (Judg. 9).

The position of Shechem in the Israelite tribal system is a social situation not easily clarified by material remains, but the archaeological excavations have thrown some light on the traditions of the city. Early in the Middle Bronze Age, a sacred area was built on a platform near the city. This remained the sacred area until it was destroyed at the end of the Bronze Age. During the period of its use, the sacred area acquired *maṣṣebot* and temples, and was incorporated by the growing city. Wright has seen a continuity in the covenant and cultic traditions of Shechem throughout this period, marked by the constant features of the sanctuary, the covenant, the particular name of God used there, the tree, and the pillar. The fact that these features are repeated so often in the Bible in relation to Shechem points to longstanding traditions, as does the existence of the Middle Bronze II A and Late Bronze II sacred area. The sacred area can therefore be interpreted as housing the important cultic places in Shechem mentioned in the Bible, and each event can be better understood in view of the correlative archaeological evidence.

This problem is extremely important in the identification of the "Temple of El-Brith" and the "Migdal Shechem" (KJV, "Tower of Shechem"). Wright has tried to show that the two were one and the same and could be identified with a temple in the sacred area. This is an impressive structure first built in the Middle Bronze II C period when security needs were dominant. The building was a fortress-temple, that is, both a fortress and a temple at the same time. Since the excavation of the Shechem

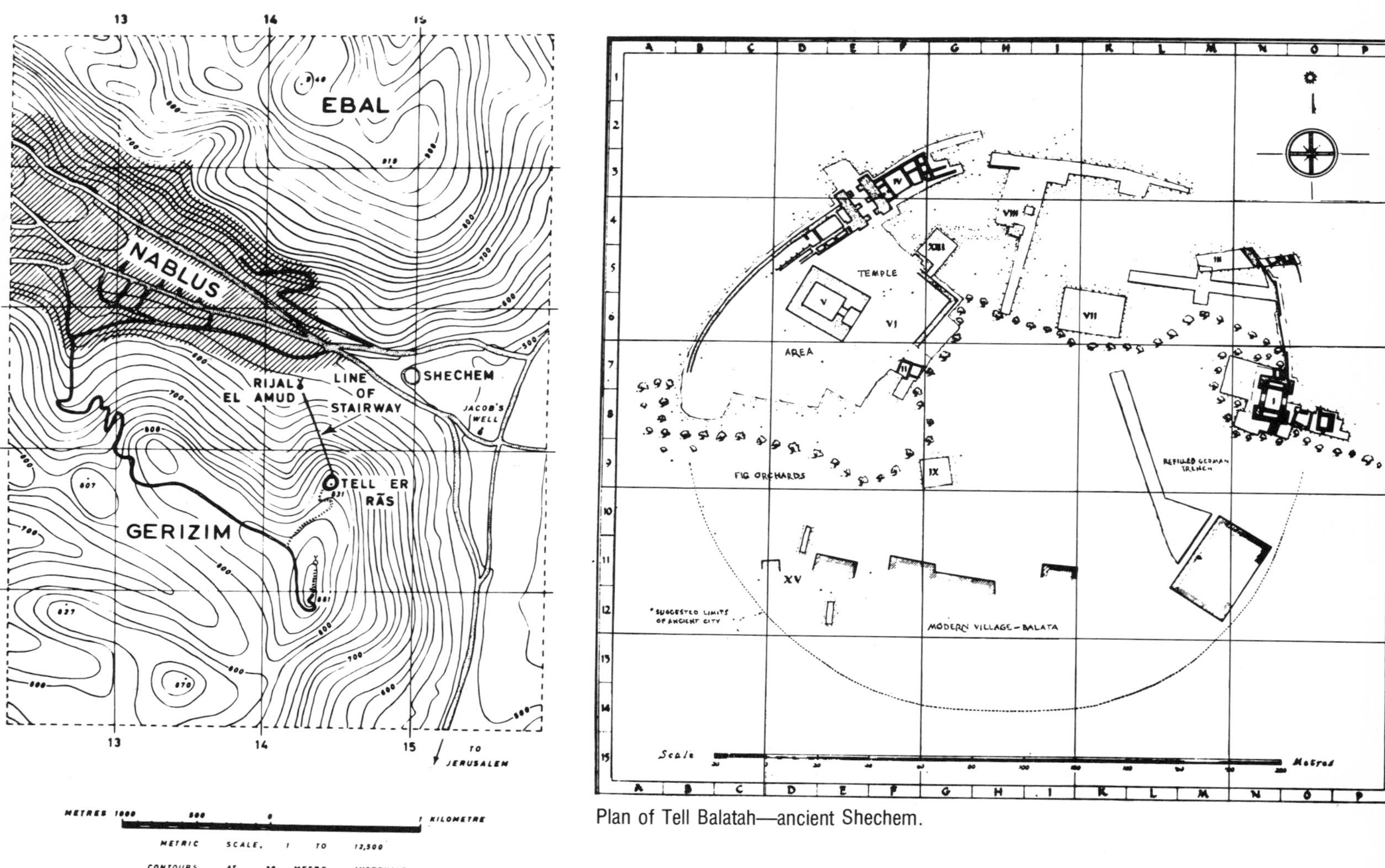

Map of the Nablus regions with Tell er-Ras atop Mount Gerizim and Shechem in the valley.

Plan of Tell Balatah—ancient Shechem.

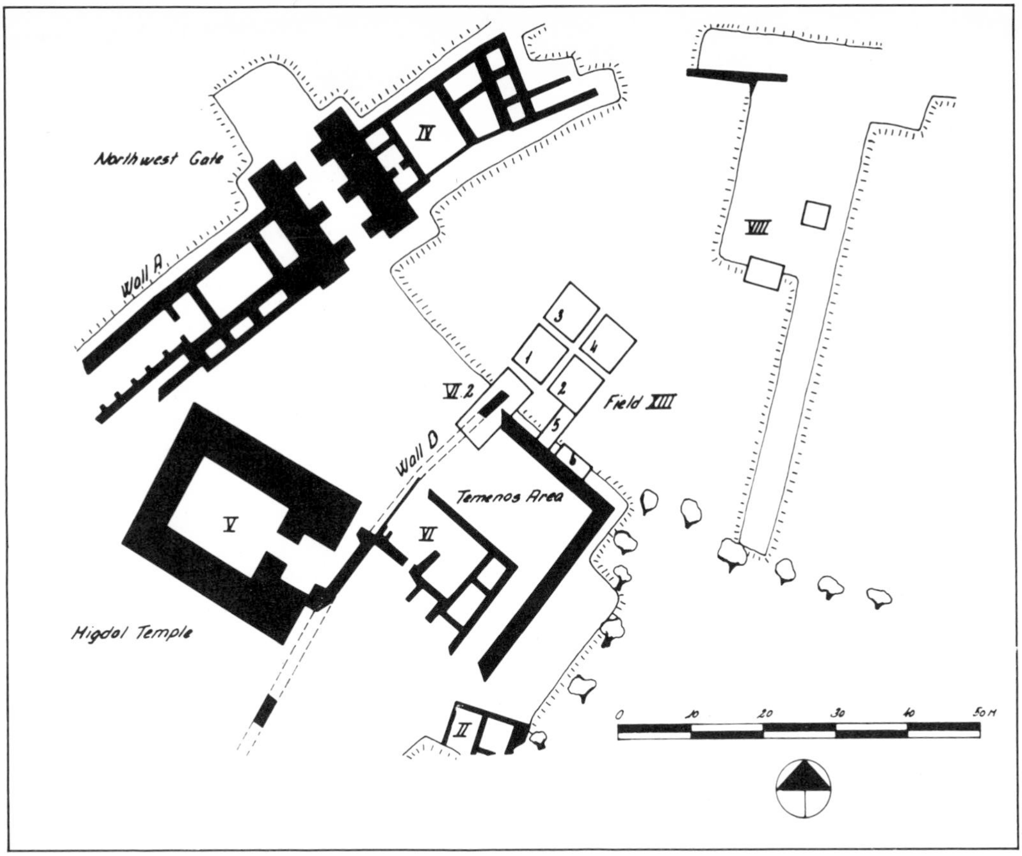

Plan of the northwest gate area temple structures at Shechem.

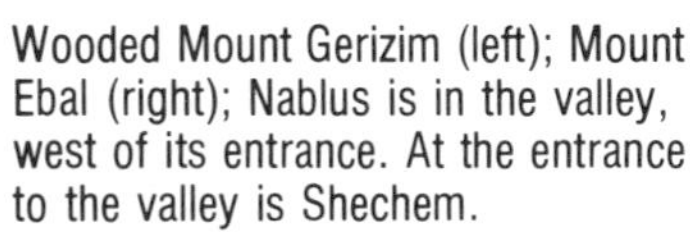

Wooded Mount Gerizim (left); Mount Ebal (right); Nablus is in the valley, west of its entrance. At the entrance to the valley is Shechem.

fortress-temple, parallel examples have been found in other cities. This has given Mazar the basis for his theory that the fortress-temple was a widespread phenomenon. The Shechem temple was rebuilt several times and remained in use until its destruction some time in the twelfth century. It would therefore fit the description of the Temple of El-Brith (which means "God of the Covenant") and the Migdal, which were both supposed to have been destroyed by Abimelech the son of Gideon. If the identification of the building is correct, the Migdal would have been inside the city and not outside as some hold that it was. Above the temple's twelfth-century destruction layer, the whole building was sealed under an Israelite warehouse. There is rarely any final proof for an identification of this sort, but Wright and Mazar have presented rather persuasive arguments.

At the close of Iron Age I, the city functioned under King Solomon's rule as the administrative center of the district of Mount Ephraim. It served in this period also as both a Levitical city and a city of refuge. Rehoboam came to the city seeking the validation of his succession to the throne of his father, but his rule was rejected and instead Jeroboam I began his reign as the first king of the Northern Kingdom of Israel. Jeroboam established his first capital at Shechem. Archaeological evidence for this period includes the ruins of a large government warehouse erected on the site of the former fortress-temple, and a casemate wall.

The checkered history of Shechem until the time of Alexander the Great has been pieced together from the remains of strata V-IX. Correlations with the textual evidence in the Bible have made it possible to trace the destructions wrought by Israel's wars with the Arameans (I Kings 20; II Kings 12), the conquest of Israel by the Assyrians, and the weakness of the city in the days of King Josiah (II Chron. 34:6f.) and the prophet Jeremiah (Jer. 41:5).

Shechem seems to have been unoccupied through the fifth and fourth centuries B.C.; then it was resettled for a period in the third and second centuries. This renaissance involved a sudden population boom accompanied by a building campaign of enormous proportions. Following the third- and second-century occupation, all habitation stopped abruptly. This odd demographic pattern fits the picture that can be pieced together from the historical sources about the Samaritan establishment of a new capital in Shechem after their expulsion from Samaria by Alexander about 330 B.C. The life of the new capital was probably cut short by the campaigns of John Hyrcanus when, about 128 B.C., he destroyed the temple the Samaritans had built on Mount Gerizim.

After Nablus was established, the center of the life of the Samaritan sect shifted there, and the dust of the centuries settled over the historic site of Shechem, until it was disturbed by the archaeologists' spade in this century.

To the south of Balatah, a spur of Mount Gerizim rises steeply about a thousand feet above the floor of the pass. At its top, at the end of a ridge which runs back to the highest peak of the mountain, is a site called Tell er-Ras. The presence on Tell er-Ras of quantities of limestone, marble, and granite architectural fragments led members of the Shechem expedition to suspect that it was the location of the temple of Zeus built by the Emperor Hadrian about A.D. 130 and reported in ancient sources as connected by a stairway of fifteen hundred steps with the village below. A probe in 1964 was followed by full-scale excavations in 1966 and 1968, under the direction of R. J. Bull.

The temple and the line of the stairway were in fact located by the expedition. The identification of the temple was made certain by fragmentary dedicatory inscriptions in Greek, "To Zeus Olympus." It was a huge affair, the podium being about sixty-six by forty-six feet, built on a platform twenty-five feet high. This platform consisted of thick retaining walls forming a rectangle 213 by 148 feet, and filled in with thousands of tons of earth, rock, and cement. In the center, directly beneath the Zeus temple, was another building, which the Roman builders used as the core of the enormous platform. The foundations of this other building were associated with Hellenistic pottery.

It is the excavators' belief that this earlier structure is the temple built by the Samaritans after their removal to Shechem by Alexander. Its location on Mount Gerizim, its size, and Hellenistic date point to this conclusion. Samaritan tradition places the temple site on the highest peak of Gerizim, but other than the structure on Tell er-Ras there are in fact no building remains on the mountain which accord with the date and presumed size of the temple. The building is made of unhewn stones, suggesting that, like the Jerusalem temple (I Kings 6:7), it was built without the sound of tools. It measures about sixty-six feet square and in sixteen courses of stone rises to a height of about twenty-five feet.

SUGGESTED TOPICS FOR FURTHER STUDY

1. Theories of covenant traditions in ancient Israel.
2. Evidence for fortress-temples in Palestine.
3. Historic evidence for the Samaritan occupation of Shechem.
4. The courtyard temples at Shechem.
5. Traditions associated with Mount Gerizim and Mount Ebal.

RECOMMENDED READING

Biblical Archaeologist 20 (1957), pp. 2–23, figs. 1–10; pp. 82–105, figs. 1–13.

Campbell, E. F., Jr., and J. F. Ross, "The Excavation of Shechem and the Biblical Tradition," *Biblical Archaeologist* 26 (1963), pp. 1–27, figs. 1–10.

Ross, J. F., and L. E. Toombs, "Six Campaigns at Biblical Shechem" in *Archaeological Discoveries in the Holy Land* (New York: Crowell, 1968), pp. 19–41, figs. 1–17.

———, "Three Campaigns at Biblical Shechem," *Archaeology* 14 (1961), pp. 171–79.

"Shechem" in *The Biblical World,* ed. Charles F. Pfeiffer (Grand Rapids: Baker, 1972), pp. 518–22.

Wright, G. Ernest, "Shechem" in *Archaeology and Old Testament Study,* ed. D. Winton Thomas (Oxford: University Press, 1967), pp. 353–70.

———, *Shechem: The Biography of a Biblical City* (New York: McGraw Hill, 1965).

FOR FURTHER READING

Bull, R. J., "The Excavation of Tell er-Ras on Mt. Gerizim," *Biblical Archaeologist* 31 (1968), pp. 58–72.

———, "The Hadrianic and Samaritan Temples," *American Schools of Oriental Research Newsletter* 10 (Jan. 1969), pp. 5–8.

———, J. A. Calloway, E. F. Campbell, J. F. Ross, and G. E. Wright, "The Fifth Campaign at Balatah (Shechem)," *Bulletin of the American Schools of Oriental Research* 180 (1963), pp. 7–41, figs. 1–20.

Campbell, E. F., Jr., J. F. Ross, and L. E. Toombs, "The Eighth Campaign at Balatah (Shechem)," *Bulletin of the American Schools of Oriental Research* 205 (1971), pp. 2–16.

Sellin, E., "Die Ausgrabung von Sichem," *Zeitschrift des deutschen Palastina-vereins* 49 (1926), pp. 229–36, pls. 29–31; pp. 304–20, pls. 32–43; 50 (1927), pp. 205–11, pls. 11–21; pp. 265–74, pls. 22–30.

———, and H. Steckeweh, "Sichem," *Zeitschrift des deutschen Palastina-vereins* 64 (1941), pp. 1–20, fig. 1, pls. 1–4.

Toombs, L. E., and G. E. Wright, "The Third Campaign at Balatah (Shechem)," *Bulletin of the American Schools of Oriental Research* 161 (1961), pp. 11–54, figs. 1–20; "The Fourth Campaign at Balatah (Shechem)," *BASOR* 169 (1963), pp. 1–60, figs. 1–26.

Wright, G. E., "The First Campaign at Tell Balatah (Shechem)," *Bulletin of the American Schools of Oriental Research* 144 (1956), pp. 9–20, figs. 1–6; "The Second Campaign at Tell Balatah," *BASOR* 148 (1957), pp. 11–28, figs. 1–15.

32

Transjordan

The biblical writers knew Transjordan as "the other side of Jordan toward the rising of the sun" (Josh. 12:1). The upland plateau east of the river is divided into regions by the major east-west wadis: north of the Yarmuk lies the region of Bashan and the area known as the Golan Heights; south of the Yarmuk to the Wadi Zerqa (Nahr ez-Zarqa, biblical Jabbok) is the area of north Gilead; Gilead then extends southward to the Wadi el-Mujib (biblical Arnon) while east of Gilead lies the area formerly occupied by the Ammonites. Moab possessed the territory south of the Wadi el-Mujib to the Wadi el-Hasa (biblical Zered), and from the Zered south to the Gulf of Eilat was Edomite territory.

The recovery of the history and prehistory of Transjordan can be traced back to the travels of Ulrich Seetzen in the first decade of the nineteenth century. He discovered Caesarea Philippi (Banias), Amman, and Gerasa (Jerash). A few years later Johann Burckhardt discovered Petra, then C. L. Irby and James Mangles discovered 'Araq el-Amir in 1818. The work of Edward Robinson in 1838 included a survey of a part of Transjordan. In 1884 Gottlieb Schumacher, who was later to excavate at Megiddo, began a cartographic and archaeological survey of the Hauran and northern Transjordan, and the British survey of Palestine included eastern Palestine.

In the years from 1932 to 1947, Nelson Glueck completed an extensive surface survey of archaeological sites throughout the region. More recently John Peterson has made a survey of suggested sites of Transjordanian Levitical cities, and James Sauer of the Amman Center of Oriental Research has been engaged in a survey of all sites of antiquities in Jordan.

The prehistoric remains in Transjordan include dolmens, megalithic constructions in which two large upright stones are capped by a massive lintel. About twenty thousand dolmens have been found in Transjordan. They occur in fields (or groups) of three hundred to a thousand, primarily in the northern area of Transjordan. Glueck dated them to as early as the sixth millennium B.C., but others suggest the Chalcolithic and Early Bronze Age. They have been interpreted as funerary installations. A somewhat similar undated prehistoric feature is the standing stone pillars known as *menhirs.* These are monoliths, similar in some respects to the *maṣṣebot* of Gezer. They are assumed to date to the Middle Bronze Age or somewhat earlier.

The 1960 excavations at Teleilat Ghassul.

Teleilat el-Ghassul

Teleilat el-Ghassul is a Chalcolithic site consisting of a few low mounds which are located about two miles northeast of the Dead Sea. The seven-acre site was excavated in the years 1929–38 by an expedition from the Pontifical Biblical Institute in Jerusalem; subsequent expeditions by R. North in 1960 and J. B.

Dolmens in the hills of Jordan.

Hennessey in 1967–68 were sponsored by the British School of Archaeology in Jerusalem. The site has been particularly illuminating for the culture of the period. The houses were decorated with beautifully painted walls in black, white, red, and brown tones, including geometric designs, stars, and stylized imagery. The pottery was handmade and included a ceramic jug that has been identified as a churn. In form it is reminiscent of a goatskin water bag. Such containers are still used occasionally as butter churns among the Bedouin.

The recovered items included ceramic forms, stone implements and flints, and a small number of copper artifacts. The site has given its name to the contemporary cultural phase in Palestine, and artifacts of the Ghassulian culture have been recovered from a number of widely scattered sites in the land.

Early Bronze IV pottery from Tomb A54.

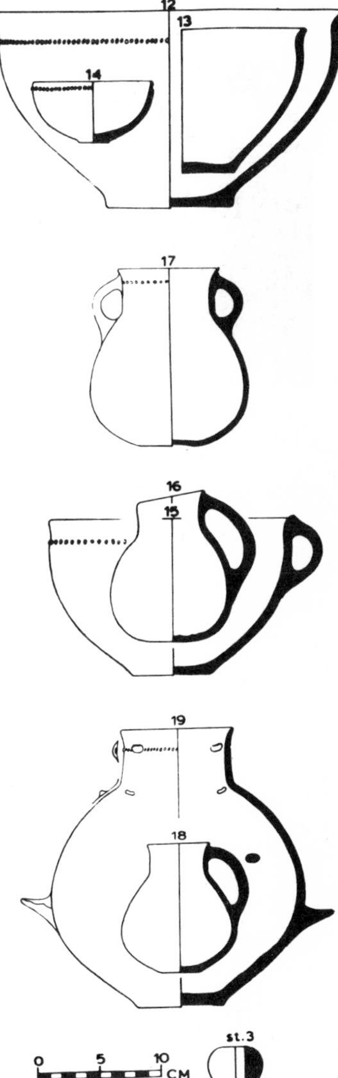

Bab edh-Dhra'

In 1924 W. F. Albright and M. G. Kyle surveyed the eastern shore of the Dead Sea along the Lisan and the area to the south. One of their discoveries was the Early Bronze IV town and cemetery at Bab edh-Dhra' which is located west of Kerak on the Lisan. During 1965–67 Paul W. Lapp investigated the cemetery and upon the basis of his excavations estimated that it had once held as many as fifty thousand bodies. Three types of burial were found. The earliest was associated with the preurban period of Early Bronze I, and consisted of burials in round pits; the second type was dated to Early Bronze III, and the bodies were placed in large rectangular mud-brick tombs constructed for multiple burials. A third type was associated with the latest phase of habitation, Early Bronze IV, and consisted of burials in narrow, shallow pits over which a rounded heap of stones was placed.

Walter Rast and Thomas Schaub, who had worked with Lapp, returned to the area in 1973 and surveyed the valleys south of the Lisan. They discovered a number of important Early Bronze sites, and they returned to excavate the ruins of Bab edh-Dhra' in 1974–76 and to make soundings at some of the other locations. These investigations continue and hold promise of illuminating the fascinating reports about the Cities of the Plain in Genesis 13 and about Sodom and Gomorrah in Genesis 19.

Petra

The work of Nelson Glueck has established that a major gap in the history of the occupation of Transjordan occurred from the

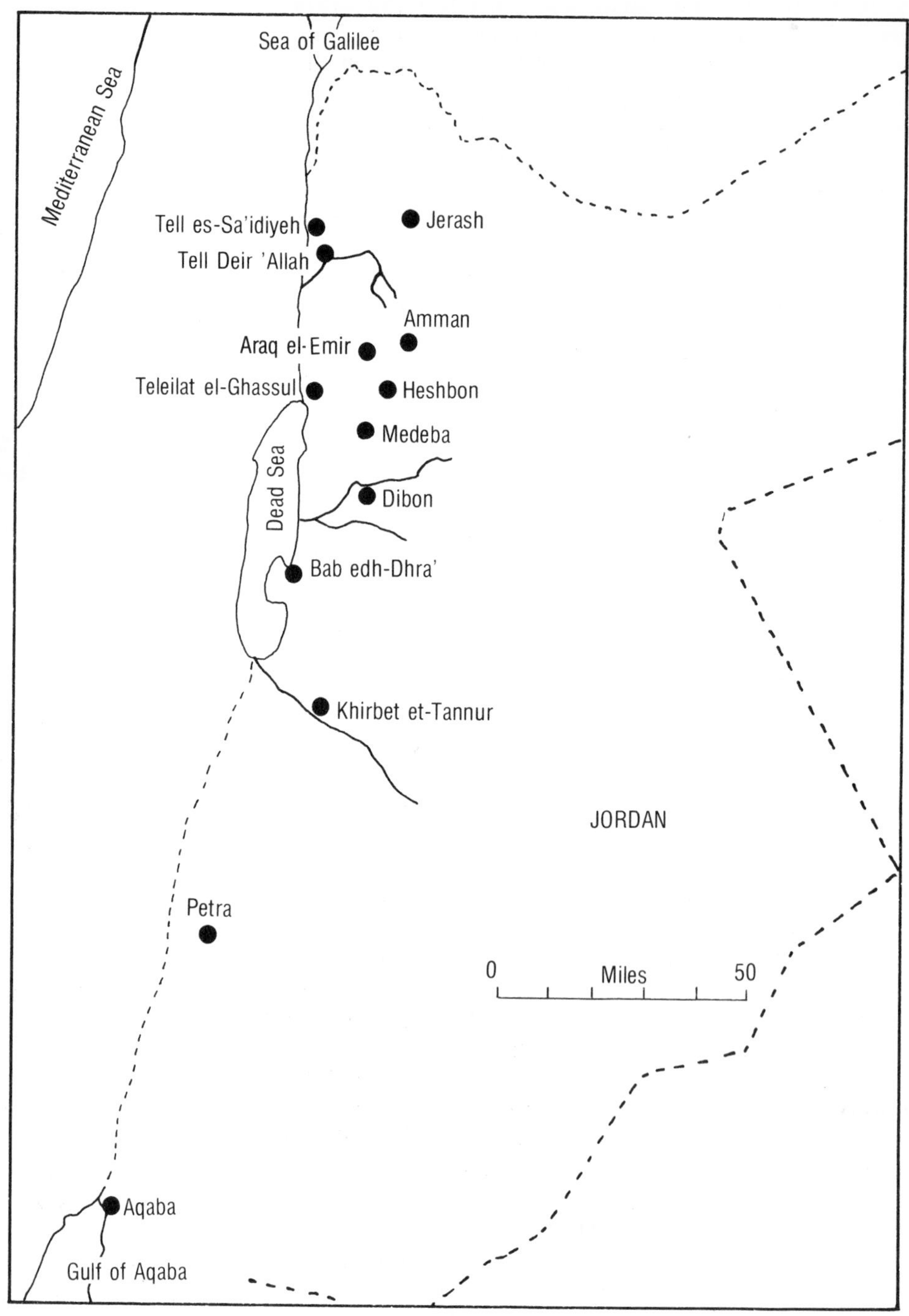

Archaeological Excavations in Jordan

end of Middle Bronze I to the beginning of the Iron Age. It is probable that the destruction of the major fortified cities along the King's Highway, the major north-south route through the area in antiquity, by the forces of Chedorlaomer and his allies contributed to the depopulation. It was a long time before the reestablishment of sedentary populations, particularly in the southern area. But Glueck found that during the period between the thirteenth and the sixth centuries B.C., in Iron Age I-II, Edom, Moab, Ammon, and the Amorite kingdoms of Gilead were strongly organized and had developed an advanced material culture. The borders of these kingdoms were protected by a series of strong fortresses (charted by Glueck) that were powerful enough to hinder the movement of the wandering Israelites through the territories of Edom and Moab (cf. Num. 20:14ff.).

The kingdoms of Edom, Moab, and Ammon later experienced sporadic warfare with Israel and with Judah. An account in II Kings 3:4ff. describes the conflict between the Moabites, led by King Mesha, and the Israelites following the death of King Ahab. The discovery in 1868 of the extraordinary Moabite Stone has provided substantial confirmation of the biblical account. At Dibon east of the Dead Sea, F. A. Klein, a missionary, discovered the stone which commemorates Mesha's victory over Israel. The interest of Westerners in the stone led local natives to break it into pieces as talismans for good luck, but not before a squeeze had been made of the inscription. The remains of the stone were later collected by Clermont-Ganneau, and the reconstructed stone has been in the Louvre since 1873.

The Moabite Stone.

All the peoples of Transjordan suffered to a degree the depredations and conquests of Assyria and Babylon that Israel and Judah knew. In the aftermath of the Babylonian conquest, Edom and Moab in particular lacked a widespread sedentary population. Then the Edomites gradually shifted across the Arabah into the region at the northern fringe of the Negev and into southern Judah where they came to be known as the Idumeans. By the fourth century B.C., the traditional Edomite territory south of the Wadi Arnon had come under the domination of a new group, the Nabataeans, who were a seminomadic Arab people. They adopted a settled way of life and developed important commercial relationships with Damascus to the north, with Arabia to the south, and with Egypt and the southern Palestinian seaports of Gaza and Ashkelon to the west. From Petra, "the rose-red city half as old as time," the Nabataeans controlled a powerful kingdom that extended northward to Damascus and westward to the seacoast across the Negev. Only in A.D. 106 did Rome choose to absorb the Nabataeans as a part of the empire.

Petra Acropolis. The cliff-top at the left of center contained early Edomite remains.

Glueck identified over five hundred Nabataean sites in southern Transjordan; among them Petra drew his particular interest, but his major excavation was of a Nabataean temple at Khirbet Tannur. Excavations in Petra began only in 1929, under the direction of George Horsfield with A. Conway and W. F. Albright, despite the fact that the fabled place had been rediscovered by J. L. Burckhardt in 1812 after it had been lost for over half a millennium. The excavations continued until 1936. Subsequent excavations were carried out by M. A. Murray in 1937; by Diana Kirkbride, P. J. Parr, and G. L. Harding from 1955 to 1957; by Parr, Kirkbride, G. R. H. Wright, and C. M. Bennett from 1958 to 1968; and by P. C. Hammond in 1961–62. Since that time the Department of Antiquities of the Hashemite Kingdom of Jordan has carried out a number of clearing operations and reconstructions which enhance Petra as a major attraction for visitors in Jordan.

The Treasury (Khazneh in Arabic) is an imposing royal tomb cut out of the rose-red rock at Petra by the Nabataeans.

One of the most active archaeologists in Transjordan is Crystal Bennett of the British School in Jerusalem. She excavated Umm el Biyara, the Edomite stronghold in Petra, and Tawilan near the village of Elji just outside Petra. In 1971 she dug at Buseira where she found a veritable storeroom of Edomite pottery from between the ninth and seventh centuries B.C.

In 1968–70 Miss Bennett completed her excavations at Tawilan. She found no evidence of a fortified Iron Age I settlement at the site, but there had been a large Iron Age II settlement. Excellent painted Edomite pottery was recovered from the seventh-century levels. No structures were found that could be associated with later Nabataean or Roman occupations. It is very doubtful, in the view of Miss Bennett, that Tawilan should be equated with biblical Teman, for there is no trace of the fortifications which would be expected in a major Edomite town. There is no sign, either, of a Roman military post which, according to Eusebius' *Onomasticon,* existed there. Bennett has suggested that Teman (cf. Amos 1:12) is a region rather than a town and that the identification with Tawilan is erroneous.

Heshbon

Tell Ḥesbân is a fifty-acre site located seventeen miles southeast of Amman and six miles north of Medeba. It probably contains the ruins of biblical Heshbon. Heshbon was the capital of Sihon, king of the Amorites, and the first major city conquered by the Israelites under Moses (Num. 21:12–30). The city was allotted to the tribe of Reuben, but it later became a possession of the tribe of Gad. By the time of Isaiah (15:2, 4; 16:8, 9) it was a Moabite city; Moab probably had acquired it earlier during the war with Israel in the days of Ahab. Jeremiah 49:2, 3 identifies Heshbon as an Ammonite city. The Hasmoneans made the city a part of their territory in the days of John Hyrcanus, an act concurrent with the development of a substantial Jewish population in Transjordan in the Hellenistic period. In the early Christian centuries Heshbon was the seat of a bishop; Bishop Gennadius is mentioned frequently in the records of the Council of Nicaea which assembled in 325. Later it was little more than an Arab village, finally to lie desolate for several centuries. The modern village of Ḥesbân was established on the eastern slopes of the tell only in the closing decades of the nineteenth century.

The first season of excavations at Heshbon was planned for the summer of 1967, but the Six Day War forced cancellation. A renewed effort in 1968 brought a crew of 186 men and women to the site for a seven-week season under the direction of Siegfried H. Horn. The excavations of the first and subsequent seasons have been sponsored by Andrews University, Berrien Springs, Michigan, with the cooperation of the American Schools of Oriental Research. Horn directed the work until his retirement when he was succeeded by Lawrence T. Geraty.

Atop the acropolis of Heshbon a Byzantine church with a mosaic floor came to light in the first season. The latest phase of the church was dated to the last half of the sixth century, but it had undergone a number of earlier rebuildings. The first season also established the sequence of occupation extending from the Arab period back through Byzantine, Roman, Iron III, II, and I, and Late Bronze. A Hebrew ostracon of the sixth to fourth century B.C. was found, but the five broken lines of text seem to be simply a list of names.

A second season was planned for 1970, but it was aborted due to civil strife in Jordan. A six-week season was carried out in 1971. There were additional campaigns in 1973, 1974, and 1976. These efforts have established a sequence of Ammonite pottery forms (which had heretofore been found only in tombs) in a stratigraphical context. A survey of the area within a six-mile radius of the site has resulted in the identification of 125 archaeological sites. A sounding was made at one of the sites, Umm es-Sarab, in an effort to check the validity of surface surveys for determining the outline of a site's occupational history. The procedure was found to be valid provided the surface sherds are collected with sufficient thoroughness.

The Heshbon expedition has collected seed, pollen, organic materials, shells, soil and rock samples for analysis in the United States, and a zooarchaeologist, A. S. LaBianca, has processed and analyzed more than ten thousand pieces of bone in the field. These efforts are aimed at comprehending the total bioethnic context of the occupational periods. A huge reservoir measuring fifty by forty by fifteen feet has been discovered. The installation was built in the ninth-eighth centuries; it may be "the fishpools of Heshbon, by the gate of Bath-rabbim" mentioned in the Song of Songs 7:4. Two examples of Early Roman tombs with rolling stone closures have been discovered. These are the first of this type thus far discovered east of the Jordan River. But surprisingly, no evidence of the Late Bronze city which the Israelites conquered has been discovered on the site. It may be that Sihon's capital was located nearby, and the Israelites shifted the name to the site when it was built up again in the period of the judges, or, more likely, it may be that the evidence is there but has been missed thus far due to the accidents in preservation and discovery.

Dibon

The site of biblical Dibon, which is a part of the territory conquired by Israel under Moses (Num. 21:26–30), is the ruin Dhîbân located forty miles south of Amman, thirteen miles east of the Dead Sea, and a few miles north of the Wadi el-Mujib. In the Moabite Stone, which was found at Dibon, King Mesha describes his building activities at Dibon. He constructed the city walls, gates, towers, a palace, and two reservoirs for water. The subsequent history of the site is connected with the history of the general region which was sketched briefly in our discussion of Heshbon.

The excavation of Dibon began in 1950 under the auspices of the American Schools of Oriental Research in Jerusalem. F. V. Winnett, A. D. Tushingham, W. L. Reed, and W. H. Morton worked as a team on the site, except for the 1953–54 season, until the end of the expedition in 1956. In some respects the results of the Dibon excavations have been disappointing, due to the extremely difficult stratigraphical problems, but its occupational history has been generally established.

A few Early Bronze sherds have been recovered, but there is no evidence of prolonged sedentary habitation on the site in the Bronze Age. The earliest concentrated occupation began in Iron Age I and continued in Iron Age II. The latter is the period of King Mesha whose reign coincided in part with that of King Ahab of Israel. This Moabite period was brought to a close by the conquest of the area in 582, five years after the destruction of Jerusalem by the same Babylonian enemy. There followed a long gap in occupation which ended with the establishment of a Nabataean settlement at the site over half a millennium later, near the beginning of the first century A.D. This occupation ended with the downfall of the Nabataean kingdom in A.D. 106. A few scraps of evidence in the form of building inscriptions and coins indicate a Roman occupation of the site from about A.D. 200, but by the middle of the fourth century the historian Eusebius spoke of it only as an "unwalled town." In the fifth and sixth centuries the city underwent a period of gradual development; the ruins of two Byzantine churches from the period were discovered in the 1950–53 seasons.

The most interesting discovery at Dibon was the foundation of a building that has been interpreted as a temple or a palace-temple. Extremely thin pottery fragments of excellent quality were found in it, and in a central sector of the building were found a very fine incense stand and several fertility figurines. No plans have been published for further excavations at Dibon, although further investigation is warranted.

Amman

The modern city of Amman is built upon the ruins of biblical Rabbath-Ammon, Rabbah of the Ammonites. Here David had Joab set Uriah the Hittite in the forefront of the battle in the face of certain death so that he might take Bathsheba, Uriah's widow, as his wife (II Sam. 11). The relations between ancient Israel and the Ammonites were frequently antagonistic so that the prophets Amos and Jeremiah both proclaimed judgment on the Ammonites. In the Hellenistic period the city was renamed Philadelphia, after Ptolemy Philadelphus (285–247 B.C.), and it became one of the ten Greek cities known as the Decapolis. In the Roman period Philadelphia flourished, but a long period of decline followed so that it was almost totally deserted when it was resettled in the last quarter of the nineteenth century by Circassians from Russia. It grew from village to town to city until in 1922 it became the capital of the territory that now comprises the Hashemite Kingdom of Jordan. The rapid incursions of ref-

The acropolis of Uriah at Amman (cf. II Sam. 11:15).

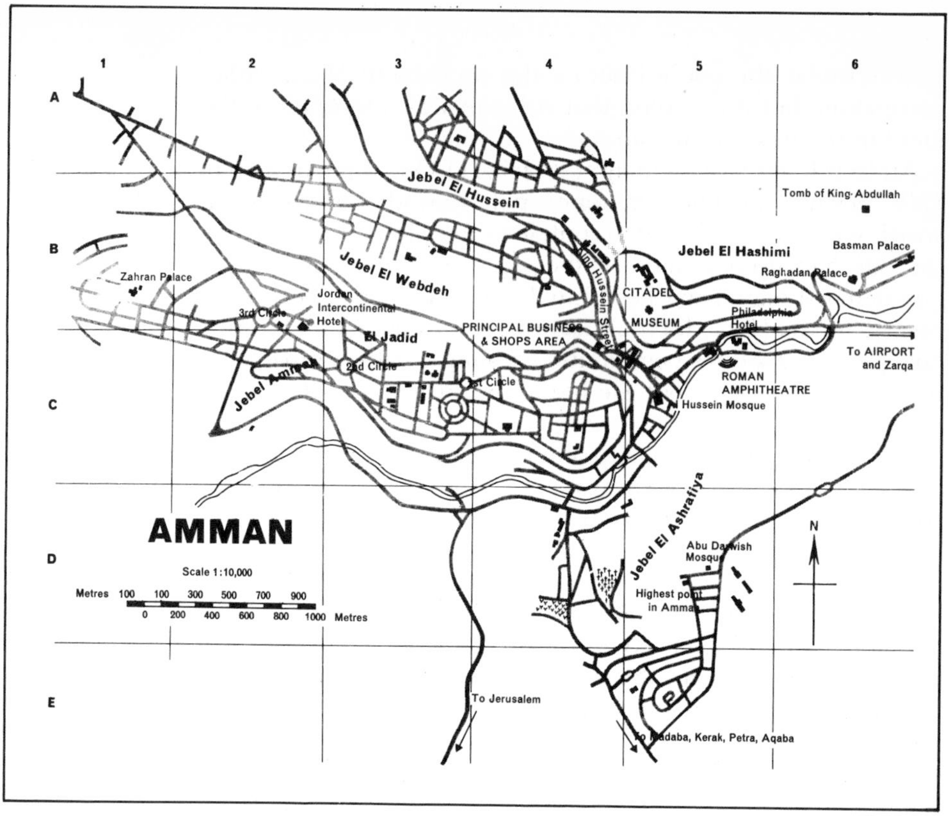

AMMAN

Scale 1:10,000

Metres 100 100 300 500 700 900

0 200 400 600 800 1000 Metres

Jebel El Hussein

Tomb of King Abdullah

Jebel El Hashimi

Basman Palace

Raghadan Palace

Zahran Palace

Jebel El Webdeh

Jordan Intercontinental Hotel

3rd Circle

El Jadid

2nd Circle

1st Circle

Jebel Amman

PRINCIPAL BUSINESS & SHOPS AREA

King Hussein Street

CITADEL

MUSEUM

Philadelphia Hotel

To AIRPORT and Zarqa

ROMAN AMPHITHEATRE

Hussein Mosque

Jebel El Ashrafiya

Abu Darwish Mosque

Highest point in Amman

To Jerusalem

To Madaba, Kerak, Petra, Aqaba

Modern Amman, with the location of the citadel and other antiquities.

ugees in recent years, as a result of Israeli-Jordanian conflicts, has led to a tenfold increase in Amman's population in a period of twenty years. Amman now numbers in excess of four hundred thousand people.

Ruins of the Roman theater of Philadelphia (Amman).

The most impressive ancient structure in Amman is the Roman theater in the center of the modern city, in the area that also comprised the center of Philadelphia. The theater had a seating capacity of six thousand. The Department of Antiquities has partially restored the theater and has been clearing a part of the forum that was contiguous with it on the north and west.

The center of the American Schools of Oriental Research in Amman, which is more properly known as the Amman Center of Oriental Research, has excavated on the citadel, Jebel el-Qala'. The joint expedition included the University of Jordan and the Department of Antiquities. Work began in 1968 with Rudolph H. Dornemann in charge, and occupational debris indicated Byzantine, Roman, Hellenistic, Late Iron, Late Bronze, and Middle Bronze phases. The Middle Bronze walls were protected by a sloping glacis typical of the period. Early Bronze sherds under the glacis indicate the probability of an earlier occupation, but it is certain that Amman was a fortified settlement in the time of the patriarchs.

An Iron II tomb came to light on Jebel el-Qusur in Amman in 1966. Besides the fine Ammonite pottery and a bronze lamp which were found, the tomb contained five clay coffins. Two of the lids had been formed in the shape of human faces, and outstretched hands had been molded into the sides of the coffins. The two lids did not feature the traditional Philistine headgear such as has been found on similar coffins discovered in western Palestine, but the burial practices are evidently the same.

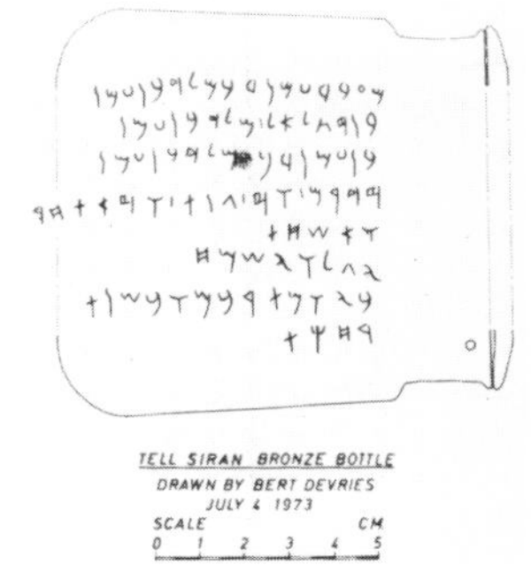

Tell Siran Bronze Bottle.

Tell Siran is a small site adjacent to the campus of the University of Jordan which was excavated by students from the university in 1972 under the direction of Henry O. Thompson as a part of their course work. On bedrock they made the extraordinary discovery of a small bronze bottle ten centimeters in length. On it was inscribed in Phoenician-type script the first complete Ammonite inscription to come to light. The eight lines contained ninety-two letters, and the text described how a king had ordered the construction of an irrigated royal garden. The king, named Ba'lay, mentioned his father's name, Aminadab, whose father was Hisser-'el, whose father was Aminadab. Apparently the Ammonite royal family followed the practice of naming children after the grandfather. Scholars now identify three Aminadabs: Aminadab I, mentioned in Assyrian records about 667 B.C.; a grandson, Aminadab II; and another grandson, Aminadab III, the father of Ba'lay, circa 600 B.C. On the basis of the inscription, F. M. Cross, Jr., has concluded that the Ammonite language was akin to Canaanite rather than to Aramaic and that the Ammonite royal house was Canaanite from the tenth century on.

The Amman citadel inscription, discovered in 1961 by R. Dajani of the Jordanian Department of Antiquities.

Jerash

As an historical attraction, the ruins of Jerash are second only to Petra. The Jordanian Department of Antiquities has pursued an active program of conservation and restoration at the site in recent years, a program that was initiated by the British during the period of the mandate. Located some thirty miles north of Amman and twenty miles east of the Jordan River, in the hills of Gilead, Jerash was also a city of the Decapolis.

By the time the inveterate explorer, Burckhardt, had arrived in the area, Jerash had long lain in ruins so that only a few columns were visible on the surface to mark the location of the city.

Charles Warren visited the site in 1867, and he was followed by others including two princes of Wales. Reconstruction and restoration were carried out by J. Garstang, G. Horsfield, and P. A. Ricci from 1925 to 1928 on behalf of the British School of Archaeology in Jerusalem and the Department of Antiquities of Palestine. Further work at Jerash was carried on by a sequence of British and American expeditions between 1928 and 1934. In the aftermath of World War II additional excavations and restoration were accomplished by the Jordanian Department of Antiquities so that today one can walk the colonnaded streets and sit in the remarkably preserved theaters of ancient Jerash.

The archaeological evidence indicated that Jerash was founded in the Hellenistic period, but in 1938 Nelson Glueck was able to identify an Early Bronze Age location just 200 meters to the north of the city wall. The earlier occupation ended early in the Middle Bronze era, however, and the only Iron Age site is several kilometers away.

The monumental structures at the site include a temple of Artemis with forty-five-foot columns still standing; an oval-shaped, colonnaded forum from the late first century A.D.; the south theater, from the same period, with thirty-two tiers of seats for audiences up to five thousand in number; and a triumphal arch consisting of a monumental triple-entry gate which was erected to honor the visit of the Emperor Hadrian who traveled through the area in the winter of A.D. 129–30. These ruins reflect the wealth and sophistication of a largely pagan city in the heyday of Rome's domination of Palestine.

The excavations have uncovered numerous inscriptions which illuminate the history of the city, since many are dedicatory inscriptions to individuals or funerary inscriptions. The earliest inscription honors a Nabataean king. In 1974, while restoration work was underway along the east wall of the south theater, two Greek inscriptions were uncovered. Bastiaan Van Elderen has translated the more significant of the two as follows:

> Good Tyche Year 153
> For the Emperor Caesar, (son of) divine Vespasian,
> [Domitian], Augustus, Germanicus
> pontifex maximus, tribuniciae potestatis,
> father of the fatherland, the theater was dedicated
> according to the decree of Lappius Maximus, legatus
> pro praetore of Augustus.

More than a dozen churches have been discovered at Jerash; the oldest is Cathedral Church which dates to the fourth century. By the close of that century Jerash could boast a bishop.

Panoramic view of Jerash.

From the same period are the ruins of a synagogue. The mosaic floor depicts animals disembarking from Noah's ark. Many of the churches also possessed mosaic floors. In fact, an outstanding feature of archaeological discovery in Jordan over the past decade has been the dramatic increase in the number of churches dating to the Byzantine period that have come to light. In Medeba alone fourteen churches with mosaic floors have been identified. So many Christian churches have been discovered in Jordan that they exceed in number the churches of any other comparable area in the same period. Transjordan was a leading center of Christianity prior to the Arab conquest.

Zarethan

Tell es-Sa'idiyeh is a large mound to the east of the River Jordan, halfway between the Sea of Galilee and the Dead Sea. The tell has been tentatively identified as the site of ancient Zarethan, which is mentioned in the Bible in connection with the Israelite crossing of the Jordan (Josh. 3:16). In I Kings 7:46 Zarethan is also mentioned as the place near which the bronze vessels were cast for the temple of Solomon. The tell was excavated in 1964–67 by J. B. Pritchard for the Museum of the University of Pennsylvania.

The earliest occupational period of the site was determined by the surface survey of Nelson Glueck. It began in the Chalcolithic era and continued into the Early Bronze II period. Pritchard's excavations on the upper level of the mound revealed an occupation in the Iron Age, with the latest phase assigned to the ninth-eighth centuries B.C. Only a casemate wall remained of this occupation. In the preceding city a residential area was uncovered, with twelve houses arranged along a street five feet wide, with six houses on each side of the street. The houses were all built according to the same floor plan—there was a large hall with four pillars and a courtyard. The numerous spindle whorls that were found in the houses may be interpreted as evidence that the occupants were engaged in spinning and weaving. Storerooms, ovens, cooking pots, and similar household ware were a part of the complex.

An interesting feature of the city was the double flight of stairs which led down to a spring at the foot of the mound, about 300 feet away. Protective walls encased the stairs, and a divider wall of bricks separated the traffic on the stairs. The installation was dated to the ninth century B.C.

The lower mound contained large buildings of the Persian period which were probably administrative in nature. Hellenistic and Roman remains were also found in the lower area. A local cemetery yielded imported pottery, jugs, lamps, and bronze bowls of the thirteenth-twelfth centuries. All this evidence points to commerical and cultural relations between the inhabitants of Zarethan and Egypt, Cyprus, and Syria in the Late Bronze Age.

Succoth

Northeast of the Zerqa River (biblical Jabbok) lies Tell Deir'Alla which was identified with biblical Succoth by Nelson Glueck in the 1930s. The vessels for Solomon's temple were cast between Succoth and Zarethan (I Kings 7:46).

A Dutch expedition led by H. J. Franken began excavations on the ten-acre site in 1960 with the purpose of establishing the sequence of pottery types on the basis of careful stratigraphic excavation rather than on a typological comparison with materials from earlier Palestinian excavations. The occupational sequence included the Chalcolithic, Late Bronze, Iron I and II, and Persian eras. The primary purpose of the expedition was broadened, however, when a temple complex of the Late Bronze Age was discovered.

The temple and adjacent structures revealed a broad variety of ceramic artifacts a large quantity of which were plain wares of the type that would be used in daily domestic life, but one section of the facility contained a finer collection of pottery, including Mycenaean and other decorated imports. Other objects discovered in this "treasury" of the temple included cylinder seals, scarabs, and juglets, but the most important find was of three clay tablets that were inscribed in an unknown script. Since the sanctuary also contained a vase that bore the cartouche of Tausert, the wife of Pharaoh Seti II, who ruled near 1200 B.C., the destruction of the temple has been dated. Beneath the temple several earlier phases were identified. The earliest sanctuary had been built in the sixteenth century B.C. atop a man-made platform. Above the ruins of the Late Bronze sanctuary was evidence of a camplike occupation, similar to that discovered by Y. Yadin at Hazor and attributed by him to the first Israelite occupation after Joshua's conquest. Above this at Tell Deir 'Alla was occupational debris containing Philistine ware.

Two other discoveries are worthy of mention. In 1967 Franken discovered frescoed walls of the Persian period that were covered with Aramaic religious texts. These have not yet been published. Evidence was also discovered of a metallurgical industry for the smelting and casting of iron and copper.

The identification of the site with biblical Succoth has not been proved by the excavations, but the possibility that Tell Deir 'Alla is either the Gilgal to which Saul went with the men of Jabesh-Gilead (cf. I Sam. 13:15) or Succoth is very strong.

The archaeological sites of Transjordan hold tremendous potential for illuminating biblical history, for few of the known sites have been excavated and recent surveys are only now revealing the extraordinary quantity of sites that await present and future archaeologists. Progress should be substantial in the future under the encouraging policies of the Department of Antiquities of the Hashemite Kingdom of Jordan.

SUGGESTED TOPICS FOR FURTHER STUDY

1. The adventures of Johann Burckhardt in Transjordan.
2. The influence of topography upon the route of the King's Highway.
3. Surface survey—the methods of Nelson Glueck.
4. The Cities of the Plain (Gen. 13:12) and the Bab edh-Dhra' excavations.
5. The history of Edom in the light of archaeological research.
6. The history of Moab in the light of archaeological research.
7. The Ammonite kingdom in the light of archaeological research.
8. Petra and the Nabataeans.
9. Avdat—A Nabataean city in the Negev.
10. The route of the Israelites through Transjordan.
11. Byzantine churches in Transjordan.
12. The cities of the Decapolis.
13. The antiquities of Jerash.
14. The excavation of Pella.
15. The expedition to Machaerus.
16. A survey of inscriptions discovered in Transjordan.

RECOMMENDED READING

Aharoni, Y., *The Land of the Bible: A Historical Geography*, tr. A. F. Rainey (Philadelphia: Westminster Press, 1967), pp. 33–57; 305–09.

Glueck, Nelson, "The Civilization of the Edomites" in *The Biblical Archaeologist Reader*, ed. E. F. Campbell, Jr., and D. N. Freedman (Garden City, NY: Anchor Books, 1964), vol. 2, pp. 51–58.

———, *The Other Side of the Jordan* (Cambridge, MA: American Schools of Oriental Research, 1970).

Harding, G. L., *The Antiquities of Jordan* (New York: F. A. Praeger, 1967).

Landes, George M., "The Material Civilization of the Ammonites" in

The Biblical Archaeologist Reader, ed. E. F. Campbell, Jr., and D. N. Freedman (Garden City, NY: Anchor Books, 1964), vol. 2, pp. 69–88.

van Zyl, A. H., *The Moabites* (Leiden: E. J. Brill, 1960).

FOR FURTHER READING

General works of recent date that specifically treat Transjordan are very rare; older works deal with Cisjordan and Transjordan as a unit, that is, as Palestine. The following works, in addition to those listed above in *Recommended Reading,* should prove useful.

Albright, William F., *The Archaeology of Palestine,* fourth edition (Baltimore: Penguin Books, 1960).

Archaeological Discoveries in the Holy Land, Archaeological Institute of America (New York: Crowell, 1969).

Encyclopedia of Archaeological Excavations in the Holy Land, Avi-Jonah, ed. (Jerusalem: Israel Exploration Society and Masada Ltd., 1975).

Glueck, Nelson, *Deities and Dolphins: The Story of the Nabataeans* (New York: Farrar, Strauss, 1965).

______, *Explorations in Eastern Palestine I–IV = Annual of the American Schools of Oriental Research* xiv (1934), xv (1935), xviii–xix (1939), xxv–xxviii (1951).

______, *The River Jordan* (New York: McGraw-Hill, 1968).

Kenyon, Kathleen M., *Amorites and Canaanites* (London: Oxford University Press, 1965).

Negev, Avraham, *Archaeological Encyclopedia of the Holy Land* (Jerusalem: Hebrew University Department of Archaeology, 1972).

Pfeiffer, Charles F., ed., *The Biblical World* (Grand Rapids: Baker, 1966).

Vogel, Eleanor K., *Bibliography of Holy Land Sites* (offprint of *Hebrew Union College Annual* XLII [1971]).

Listed below are the principal journals in which reports of discoveries in Transjordan are published.

Annual of the Department of Antiquities of Jordan (Amman)

Biblical Archaeologist

Bulletin of the American Schools of Oriental Research

Journal of the Palestine Oriental Society (Jerusalem)

Levant. Journal of the British School of Archaeology in Jerusalem (London)

Newsletter of the American Schools of Oriental Research

Palestine Exploration Fund Annual (London)

Palestine Exploration Quarterly (Quarterly Statement) (London)

Quarterly of the Department of Antiquities of Palestine (London)

Revue Biblique (Paris)

Vetus Testamentum (Leiden)

Index

Abdashtart, 337
Abdu-heba, 386
Abimelech, 315, 475, 478
Abner, 336
Abraham (Abram), 39, 167, 173–74, 181, 194, 219, 256, 277, 315, 317, 475
  covenant with, 227
Abram. *See* Abraham
"Absalom's Tomb," 414
Abu-Simbel, 44
  temple of, 262
Achaemenes, 209
Achaeans, country of the, 225
Acropolis, 213, 214
Adad, 247
Adad-nirari III, 174, 196–97
Adam, 18
Adiabene, 402
Adonis. *See* Eshmun
Aegean area, 46, 49
Aelia Capitolina, 65, 305, 412. *See also* Jerusalem
Agade, 180
Ahab, 53, 196, 351, 393, 444, 466, 468, 485, 487
Aharoni, Yohanan, 40, 287, 307, 308, 315, 318, 320, 351, 374, 425, 444, 468
Ahaziah, 54, 202
Ahhiyā. *See* Ahhiyawā
Ahhiyawā (Ahhiyā), 225
Ahimelech, 219
Ahiram, 250
Ahmose, 256
Ahura Mazda, 209, 211, 214
Ai (Aiath, A-i'ja, et-Tell, Ha'ai), 45, 224, 277–83
Aiath. *See* Ai
A-i'ja. *See* Ai
Ain es Sultan (Spring of Elisha), 391
Ain Shems, 99
Akawasha, 47
Akhenaten, 260. *See also* Amenophis IV
Akhetaten. *See* Tell el-Amarna
Akiba ben Joseph, 305, 340
Akkad, 179–80, 243
Akkadian, 259
  language, 42
  texts, 177
Alaja Hüyük, 220
Albright, William F., 26, 40, 69, 86, 90, 106, 115, 158, 162, 163, 165, 280, 323, 326, 360, 363, 419, 483, 486
Aleppo, 220, 234
Alexander the Great, 58, 189, 209, 211, 388, 469, 478, 479
Alexandria, 18, 61
Alishar, 195, 222
Alkios, 360
alphabetic writing, 139–50

alphabets, 127
  Canaanite, 139, 141, 142
  Etruscan, 150
  Greek, 145–50
  Phoenician, 142, 145
  Semitic, 145–50
  Ugaritic, 141
Alt, Albrecht, 363
Alulim, 178
Amarna letters, 220, 236, 258–60, 286, 373, 401, 421
Amasa, 367
Amen-em-opet, 386
Amenophis II, city lists of, 373
Amenophis IV (Akhenaten, Amenhotep IV), 196
Amenemhet, 254
Amenhotep III, 43
Amenhotep IV (Akhenaten), 43, 258. *See also* Amenophis IV
American excavations, 96
Amiran, Ruth, 91, 285, 407, 468
Amman (Philadelphia, Rabbath-Ammon), 75, 481, 489–91
Ammon, 485
Ammonites, 48, 49, 75
Amorites, 46, 175, 180, 195, 248, 295, 397
Amos, 22, 54, 197, 320, 471
Amosis, 42
Amun, 258
  temple of, 265
Anderson, Dean, 475
Andrae, Walter, 207
Andromeda, 387
Anittas, 223
Ankhesenamun, 224
Antiochus III, 388
Antiochus IV Epiphanes, 59
Antony, 431
Anu, 247
Anu-adad temple, 207
Apadana, the, 211, 213, 214
'Apiru. *See* Habiru
Apocrypha, 17, 18, 23, 24, 26, 210
Applebaum, S., 331
Arabah, 52, 74
Arad, 54, 254, 285–91
  documents, 318
Aramaic, 210
Arameans, 48. See also *Aramu*
Aramu (Arameans), 235
'Araq el-Amir, 481
archaeological sites, selection of, 98–100
archaeology, definition of, 16
  history of the word, 79
  limitations of, 156–59
Armenia, 223
Armenian Garden, 407
Arslan Tash, 468
Artaxerxes III, 388
Artemis, temple of, 492
Artisan's City, the, 213
Asa, 352
Ashdod (Azotus, Tell Ashdod), 293–301
  capture of, 204
asherim, 233
Ashtaroth, 297
Ashur (Qalat Sharqat), 195, 204, 207–208
Ashurbanipal, 54, 80, 197, 202, 265
  library of, 80, 198
Ashurnasirpal, 202, 204
Ashurnasirpal II, 84, 199, 200
Asia Minor, 219–29
Asshur-uballit I, 196
Astyages, 209
Aswan, 58
Atarhasis. *See* Ubar-Tutu
Aten, 258
Augustus, 465
Avaris. *See* San el-Hagar
Avigad, N., 308, 310, 406, 407, 408, 414
Avi-Yonah, M., 340, 408
Ayelet Hashahar, 371
Azariah, 197
Azotus. *See* Ashdod

Baalat Gebal, 248
Baal Gad, 388
Baal, temple of, 240
  worship, 470–71
Baal-zebub, 297
Bab edh-Dhra', 483
Babel, tower of, 188
Babylon, 22, 55, 180, 182, 188–92, 197, 208, 209, 223
Babylonian captivity, 53, 56, 174
Babylonian Chronicle, 190
Bacchides, 360
Bahat, D., 407
Balatah, Mound of, 473, 474
Banias. *See* Caesarea Philippi
Bar-Adon, P., 308, 311
Bar Kochba, Simon (Bar Kosiba, Shimon), 303–13
  era, 34
  letters, 308–10, 382
  revolt, 65, 340, 382, 412
Bar Kosiba, Shimon. *See* Bar Kochba, Simon
Bar Miasa, Botniya, 312
Baron, Salo, 437
Barthelemy, P., 311
Bashan, 74
Bassus, Lucilius, 382

Bathsheba, 489
Bauer, Hans, 237, 238
Beer-sheba (Tell as-Sabʿ, Tell Beer-sheba), 34, 99, 315–21
Behistun Inscription, 85, 137
Bel-shar-usur, 189
Ben Abdun inscription, 388
ben-Aryeh, S., 413
Ben-Dor, M., 408
Bene-Yamina (Benjaminites, Sons of the South), 235
Ben-Hadad, 352
Beni Hasan, tomb of, 254
Benjaminites. See *Bene-Yamina*
Bennett, Crystal M., 486
Ben Sira, 61
Bethar, 305
Beth-el, 45, 48, 277, 280, 351
Beth-shan (Scythopolis, Tell el-Husn), 329–35
Beth-shemesh, 99
Beth-zur, 57, 61, 101
Bible, limitations of the, 154, 156
  versions, 19–20
biblical, definition of, 16–17, 65, 69
biblical archaeology, use of the term, 164–65
Biran, Avraham, 341, 347, 351, 352, 408
Bittel, K., 220
Black Obelisk of Shalmaneser III, 196, 202
Bliss, Frank J., 88, 89, 357, 404, 406, 413, 419
Boghazköy (Hattusas), 195, 220, 224, 225, 227, 295
Book of Enoch, the, 453
Book of Jubilees, the, 453
Book of the Dead, 139
Borchardt, Ludwig, 260
Bossert, H. T., 221
Botta, Paul E., 84, 198, 205
Boyd, B., 425
Breasted, James Henry, 69, 257, 439, 440
British excavations, 96
Broshi, M., 407
Brugsch, Emil, 262
Bull, Robert J., 341
Burckhardt, Johann Ludwig, 85, 481, 486, 491
Buseira, 486
Byblos (Gebal), 17, 141, 234, 247–50

Caesar Augustus, 337–38, 470
Caesarea, 99, 337–45
  aqueduct, 338
Caesarea Maritima, 102
  Joint Expedition to, 341
Caesarea Philippi (Banias), 481
Calah, 196, 198. *See also* Nimrud
Callaway, Joseph A., 277, 279, 280
Campbell, Edward F., Jr., 475
Cambyses, 268
Cambyses II, 211
Campbell, Edward F., Jr., 475
Canaanite Age. *See* Early Bronze Age
Canaanite temple, 240, 373
Capernaum (Tell Hum), 343–44
Caphtor, 49. *See also* Crete
Cappadocia, 222
Cappadocian texts, 195, 222–23
carbon-14 dating, 91, 115
Carchemish, 225
  battle of, 197
Carter, Howard, 260
Cassiopeia. *See* Iopei
Cassites, 189
Catal Hüyük, 396
Cepheus, 387
Chalcolithic Period, 34–36
Chaldean regime, 56
Champollion, Jean François, 83, 137–39
Chantre, Ernest, 220
Chedorlaomer, 485
Chenoboskion papyri, 272
Chiera, Edward, 192, 205
Cilicia, 225
City of David, 402. *See also* Jerusalem
Cleopatra, 431
Clermont-Ganneau, Charles, 86, 355, 404, 414, 487
Codex Petropolitanus, 453
Commentary on the Book of Habakkuk, 448, 454
Conder, C. R., 86, 96, 161, 379, 419
Conder-Kitchener survey, 340
Conway, A., 486
Conze, Alexander, 89
Copper Scroll. *See* Dead Sea Scrolls, the
Corbo, Vergilio, 381
Cornelius, 338
Cotovicus, Johann van. *See* Kootwyck, Johann van
Cowley, A. E., 268
creation, the, 167
Cretan script, 141
Crete (Caphtor), 295
Crocodile River dam, 338
Cross, F. M., Jr., 491
Crowfoot, J. W., 90, 404, 465
Crusades, 65, 81
Crusaders, 340, 341
cuneiform, 136–39, 175

Cyprus, 43
Cyril, Bishop, 81
Cyrus, 55, 56, 186, 189, 192, 209, 210, 211
Cyrus Cylinder, 192

Dagon, 233, 235, 297
  gate of, 244
  temple of, 240
Dajani, A. K., 363
Dan (Laish, Tell Dan, Tell el-Qadi) 42, 234, 347–53
Dan, tribe of, 349, 351, 387
Daniel, coffin of, 214
Danuna, 47
Darius I, 85, 211, 214
Darwin, Charles, 84
David, 22, 48, 49, 51, 53, 56, 297, 333, 359, 366, 367, 387, 393, 421, 489
  tomb of, 413
Dead Sea (Salt Sea, Sea of Asphalt), 34, 64, 74
Dead Sea Caves, 18
Dead Sea Scrolls, the (Qumran Scrolls, Qumran Writings), 17, 21, 24, 61, 72, 97, 447–63
  apocryphal and pseudepigraphical literature, 453
  biblical commentaries, 453–54
  Copper Scroll, 458
  dating of the, 449–52
  discovery of the, 447–49
  importance of the, 459–60
  Sect of the, 458–59
  Sectarian literature, 454–56
  Temple Scroll, 24, 456, 458
de Beauchamp, J., 188
Debir (Kirjath-sepher, Tell Beit Mirsim), 45, 323
Decalogue, 226–27
Deetz, James, 119
de Garis Davies, N., 260
Deir 'Alla, 298
Demetrius, Syrian king, 377
de Morgan, Jacques, 213, 214
dendrochronology, 119
de Perthes, Boucher, 83
de Saulcy, F., 86, 161, 402, 460
deVaux, Roland, 79, 460, 462
Dever, William G., 38, 91, 164, 357
deVogue, C. J. M., 402
Dhîbân. *See* Dibon
Dharme, Edouard, 238
Diaspora, 64, 65, 270, 402
Dibon (Dhîbân), 488–89
Dickie, A. C., 404, 406
Dieulafoy, Marcel and Jane, 213
dolmens, 482
Dorcas. *See* Tabitha
Dornemann, Rudolph H., 490
Dorpfeld, Wilhelm, 87
Dothan, Moshe, 204, 293
Douglas, A. E., 119
Drew-McCormick excavation, 474
Dumuzi, 178
Dunand, Maurice, 247, 248, 250
Dunayevsky, I., 442
Duncan, J. G., 404
Dur-Sharrukin. *See* Khorsabad

Early Bronze Age (Canaanite Age), 36–38
Ebla (Tell Mardikh), 242–46
  tablets, 243, 244–45
Eblaite, 245–46
Ecbatana, 211. *See also* Hamadan
Ecclesiastical History, 340
Edom, 45, 75, 485
Edomites (Idumeans), 485
Egypt, 253–74
Egyptian Execration Texts, 39, 248, 256, 349, 401
Eitan, A., 407
Ekron, 99
El, 247
Elamites, 175, 180
  citadel of the, 214
El-Brith, Temple of, 475, 478
Eleazar Ben Ya'ir, 432, 435, 437
Elephantine, 268–73
Elephantine Papyri, 58, 268
Eliezer, heir of Abraham, 194
Elijah, 383
Elisha, 54, 393
el-Jib, 363. *See also* Gibeon
El Quds, 402. *See also* Jerusalem
En Gedi, 36, 303, 309, 310, 312
Enoch, 18
Enlil temple, 176, 180, 207
Enuma elish, 188, 199, 208
Ephron the Hittite, 219
eponym list, 207–208
Erech, 186. *See also* Uruk
Eridu, 178
Erman, Adolf, 257
Esangila, 188
Esarhaddon, 80, 197, 202
Esau, 194, 219
Eshmun (Adonis, Osiris), 388
Eshmunazar, 145
  inscription, 388
Essenes, 61, 436, 458
Esther, 214
  tomb of, 213
Etana, 179
et-Tell. *See* Ai, 277
Evans, Sir John, 83
Evil-Merodach, 55

excavation methods, 103–12
Ezekiel, 55
Ezida, 202
Ezion Geber, 52
Ezra, 23, 57

Fabri. *See* Schmidt, Felix
Fertile Crescent. *See* Mesopotamian Valley
Fisher, Clarence S., 89, 106, 323, 329, 440
FitzGerald, G. M., 329
Flood, the, 167
Foerster, Gideon, 381
Fort Shalmaneser, 200, 204
Franken, H. J., 495
Frankenburg, 379. *See also* Herodion
Freedman, David Noel, 293
Frere, John, 83
Fritsch, Charles, 459
Frova, Antonio, 340
Funding expeditions, 95–97

Gabinius, 469
Galilee, 62
  Sea of, 73
Garrod, Dorothy, 90
Garstang, John, 90, 280, 371, 392, 394, 492
Gasur. *See* Nuzi
Gath, 99
Gazru, 360. *See also* Gezer
Gebal, 17. *See also* Byblos
Genesis Apocryphon (Lamech Scroll), 448
Gennadius, 487
Gerasa (Jerash), 481
Geraty, Lawrence, T., 487
German expeditions, 96
Geshem, 57
Gezer (Gazru, Tell Gezer) 40, 42, 52, 61, 89, 101, 141, 157, 355–61
  calendar, 359
  high place, 358
  south gate of, 357
Ghassul, 34
Ghassulian culture, 90
Gibeah, 48
Gibeon (el-Jib), 99, 363–69
  pool of, 365, 366, 367
Gihon spring, 54, 404, 406
Gilead, 74, 75
Gilgamesh, 179
Gilgamesh Epic, 186, 199, 441
Girshman, Roman, 214
Givat ha-Mivtar, 415
Gizeh, 87
Glueck, Nelson, 40, 44, 91, 156, 162–63, 261, 357, 481, 482, 483, 485, 486, 492, 494, 495
Godard, André, 213
Goldman, Hetty, 222
Goliath, 297
Gophna, R., 315
Grotefend, Georg Friedrich, 85, 136
Great Family, the, 225
Grenfell, B. P., 272
Griffith, F. L., 260
Gudea, 180
Gurob, 272
Gutenberg Bible, 20
Gutians, 180
Guy, P. L. O., 385, 388, 440

Ha'ai. *See* Ai
Habiru ('Apiru), 195, 227, 240, 259–60, 331, 421
Hadrian, 65, 305, 312, 412, 479, 492
Haggai, 57
Hall, H. R., 182
Hama, 220
Hamadan (Ecbatana), 213
Hammond, P. C., 486
Hammurabi, 179, 180, 189, 233, 234
  Code of, 192, 199, 208, 214
Hananiah ben Nera, 368
Hanon, king of Amon, 393
Hantilis, 223
Hapiru, 258
Haran, 39, 223, 235
Harding, G. Lankester, 306, 419, 460, 486
Harris Papyrus, 386
Hasidim, 61
Hasmonean Kingdom, 61, 63
Hathor, temple of, 261
Hatti, 223
Hattic peoples, 195, 222
Hattusas, 46, 221, 223, 225. *See also* Boghazköy
Hattusilis I, 223, 224
Hattusilis II, 225
Hawkes, Jacquetta, 80
Hayes, John H., 176
Hazor (Tell el-Qedah), 40, 41, 42, 45, 52, 96, 122, 234, 371–78
Hebrew Bible, 20
Hebrew University, Isaiah Scroll, 449, 450
Hellenistic Period, 58–63
Hennessey, J. B., 465, 466, 482
Herbert, Thomas, 82
Herculaneum, 83

Herod Agrippa I, 63, 412, 413
Herod, Antipas, 63
Herod Archelaus, 63, 412, 462
Herod Philip, 63
Herod the Great, 63, 379, 381, 402, 408, 412, 429, 430, 462, 469, 470
his palace, 433–34
Herodion (Frankenburg, Jebel el-Fureidis), 379–83
Herodotus, 128
Herzfeld, Ernst, 210, 213
Heshbon (Tell Ḥesbân), 487–88
Hezekiah, 54, 197, 290, 317, 318, 406, 414
Hiel, the Bethelite, 393
hieroglyphics, 136–39
Hillah, 188
Hilprecht, Herman V., 176
Hincks, Edward, 85
Hiram, 51, 141–42, 387
Hippicus tower, 408
Hittites, 194, 219–29, 226–27
Hodayot Scroll (Thanksgiving Hymns), 448, 450, 456, 459
Hor-Åha. *See* Menes
Hori, 386
Horites. *See* Hurrians
Horn, Siegfried H., 487
Horsfield, George, 486, 492
Hosea, 471
Hrozný, B., 221
Hulda Gates, 410
Huleh Valley, 73
Hurrians (Horites), 194, 223, 295
Hüyük, Alaja, 222
Hyksos, 41, 42, 43, 243, 263, 293, 295, 324
expulsion of, 421
period, 256
Hyrcanus, John, 62, 334, 461, 469, 478, 487

Ibbit-Lim, 243
ideograms, 131–36
Idumea, 62
Idumeans. *See* Edomites
Inanna, 177, 199
Inge, C. H., 419
inscriptions, Proto-Sinaitic, 261
"Instruction of Amenemope," 271–72
Iopei (Cassiopeia), 387
Ipsus, battle of, 388
Iran. *See* Persia
Irby, C. L., 481
Iron Age I, 46–52
Iron Age II, 52–56
Iron Age III, (Persian period), 56–58
Isdud, 293
Ishmael, 368
Ishtar, 199, 207, 233, 244
Gate, 190, 191
Temple, 190
Isin, 180
Isin-Larsa, 41
Ittebaal, 250
Ivriz, 220

Jacob, 194, 256, 475
Well of, 473
Jaffa (Joppa), 47, 385–90
Gate, 407
James, 19
James, Frances, 331, 332
Jamnia, 64
Jannaeus, Alexander, 388
Japheth, descendants of, 208
Jebel el-Fureidis, 379. *See also* Herodion
Jebel el-Qalá, 490
Jebel el-Qusur, 491
Jebusites, 223, 401
Jehoahaz, 468
Jehoash, 197
Jehoiachin, 55, 192
Tablets, 55
Jehoram, 54, 142
Jehu, 54, 167, 196, 202, 468
Jerash, 491–94. *See also* Gerasa
Jeremiah, 55, 197, 368
Jericho (Tell es Sultan), 33, 42, 45, 99, 157, 175, 391–99
Jeroboam I, 53, 351, 478
Jeroboam II, 54, 197, 468
Jerusalem (Aelia Capitolina, City of David, El Quds, Urusalim, Urushalim, Urusilimmu), 22, 24, 49, 52, 57, 99, 161, 174, 197, 305, 306
fall of, 190, 191, 368
first capture of, 167
location of, 69, 72
map of, 403
Jewish Quarter excavations, 407, 408
Jezebel, 53
Joab, 366, 367, 404, 406, 489
Joash, 406
Johanan, 368
Johanan ben Zakkai, 64
John, the apostle, 19
John the Baptist, 459
Jemdet Nasr, 178
Joppa, 64, 385. *See also* Jaffa
Joram, 202, 414
Jordan River, 73–74
Joseph, 256

Joshua, 56, 279, 358, 366, 392, 393, 394, 475, 495
Josiah, 22, 54, 197, 290, 318, 360, 478
Jude, 19
Judea, 62, 219
  conquest of, 190

Kadesh, battle of, 224
Kanesh, 223
Kaplan, J., 385, 386, 388
Karahüyük, 222
Karatepe, 222
Karnak, temple of, 257, 386
Kaufmann, Yehezkel, 280
Kenites, 288, 290
Kenyon, Kathleen, 27, 31, 33, 52, 91, 97, 100, 106, 158, 392, 394, 395, 397, 404, 406, 412, 413, 465, 468
Keret, 240
kernoi, 300
Kheta, 219
Khirbet Haiyan, 279, 280
Khirbet Kerak ware, 239
Khirbet Khudriya, 279
Khirbet Qumran. *See* Qumran
Kirjath-sepher. *See* Debir
Kirkbride, Diana, 486
Khorsabad (Dur-Sharrukin), 84, 204–207
King's Highway, the, 75
Kish, 178–79, 186
Kitchener, H. H., 86, 96, 161
Kizzuwatna province, 225
Klein, F. A., 485
Knudtzon, J. A., 221
Kochavi, M., 323
Koldewey, Robert, 55, 123, 188, 192, 207
Kootwyck (Cotovicus), Johann van, 82
Kosay, Hamit, 222
Kraeling, Emil G., 268
Kramer, Samuel N., 175, 176, 181
Kültepe, 195, 222, 223
Kummukhi, 225
Kurustamma, 227
Kuyunjik, 198, 199
Kyle, M. G., 323, 483

Laban, 235
Labarnas, 223
Labayu, 260
LaBianca, A. S., 488
Lachish (Lakeis, Tell ed-Duweir), 40, 45, 54, 90, 419–28
  letters, 426, 427
Ladder of Tyre, 72
Lagash, 180
Laish, 234, 347, 349. *See also* Dan
Lakeis, 419. *See also* Lachish
lamassu, 202
Lamech Scroll. See *Genesis Apocryphon*
Lamon, 444
Landes, A. Daulier des, 82
Lapp, Paul W., 38, 156, 164, 465, 483
Larsa, 180
Late Bronze Age, 42–46
Layard, Austen Henry, 84, 188, 198–99, 200, 202, 207
Leakey, Louis, 73
Lebanon, 231–52
  cedars of, 247, 284
Lejjun, 444. *See also* Megiddo
Lenzen, Heinrich, 188
Libby, Willard F., 115, 450
Libyans, 46
Link, E., 341
Lisan, 74
Loftus, W. K., 181–82, 186, 200, 213
Logia (Sayings of Jesus), 272
Loud, G., 440
Lubbock, Sir John, 84
Lugalzagesi, 179
Luka, 47
Luwian, 222, 225
Lux, Ute, 413
Luz, 219
Lyell, Sir Charles, 84

Macalister, R. A. S., 89, 357, 358, 359, 404, 406
Maccabean revolt, 23, 58, 59, 61
Maccabees, 59–61
Machpelah, cave of, 219
Mahmud Hamza, 262
Mallowan, M. E. L., 202
Manasseh, 54, 197, 424
Manetho, 253
Mangles, James, 481
Manual of Discipline, 448, 450, 456
Marduk, 188, 208, 245
  temple complex of, 190
Mari (Tell Hariri), 232–36
  documents, 39, 373
Mariamne, 408
Mariette, August E., 257
Marisa, 61
Marquet-Krause, Judith, 277, 278–79, 280
Masabala bar Shimon, 309
Masada, 64, 100, 382, 429–43
Masoretic Text, 20–21
Maspero, Gaston, 257
maṣṣebab, 233

Matthiae, Paolo, 243
Maundrell, Henry, 82
Mazar, Benjamin, 91, 344, 407, 408, 410, 414, 478
McCown, Donald E., 176
Medes, 208, 209
Media, 209
Medinet Habu, 47, 264, 296
Megiddo (Lejjun, Tell el-Mutesellim), 40, 42, 52, 90, 96, 99, 157, 265, 374, 377, 439–45
  battle of, 197
Mekal, 332
Menahem, 197, 204, 468
Menes (Hor-Aha), 253
Menhirs, 482
Merneptah, 44, 46, 262, 264
  Stele, 44
Mesha, 142, 485
Mesha Stone. *See* Moabite Stone
Mesolithic period (Middle Stone Age), 31
Mesopotamia, 173–217
Mesopotamian Valley, 42, 69
Meyer, L. A., 413
Middle Bronze Age, 38–42
Middle Stone Age (*See* Mesolithic period)
Midianites, 48
Midgal Shechem (Shechem, Tower of), 475
Millo, 406
Minet el-Beida, 236
Mitanni, 42, 43, 194, 196
  kingdom, 223, 224
Mithra, 342
Mithraeum, 342
Moab, 45, 75, 485
Moabite (Mesha) Stone, 87, 142, 485
Moabites, 48
Montet, Pierre, 247, 263
Moorey, P. R. S., 16
Mordecai, tomb of, 213
Morton, W. H., 488
Moses, 18, 22, 44, 487, 488
Moslems, 340
Mosul, 198
Mount Carmel, 31
Mount Zion, 407, 408
Murray, M. A., 486
Mursilis I, 189, 223
Mursilis II, 227

Nabataeans, 485
Nablus (Neapolis), 473–74, 478
Nabonidus, 182, 189
Nabopolassar, 189, 197
Nabu, 199, 202, 207, 245
Nag Hammadi Texts, 272
Nahal Hever, 307
Nahal Mishmar, 34
Nahor, 235
Nahum Commentary, the, 454
Napoleon, 137, 138, 257
Naram-Sin, 180, 243
  inscription, 199
Narmer, 253, 254
  Palette of, 131, 134, 253
Natufian culture, 31, 90
Nau, Michael, 82
Naville, Edouard, 264
Neapolis. *See* Nablus
Nebi Samwil, 368
Nebi-Yunus, 198
Nebuchadnezzar, 54–55, 57, 192, 424, 426, 427
  army, 406
  palace of, 80
Nebuchadnezzar II, 189, 190, 197
Necho, 197
Negev, A., 341
Nehemiah, 57
Nelson, H. H., 257
Neolithic period (New Stone Age), 31–34
Nero, 462
New Kingdom period (Egyptian), 257
New Stone Age. *See* Neolithic period
New Testament archaeology, definition of, 343
Newton, F. G., 260
Nile, 26
Nimrud (Calah), 198, 200–204, 469
Nimurta. *See* Ninurta
Nineveh, 80, 198–200, 204, 209,
  fall of, 208
Ninlil temple, 180
Ninni-Zaza, temple of, 233
Ninurta (Nimurta), 200
  temple of, 190
Nippur (Nuffar), 175–81
Niqmad II, 239–40
North, R., 482
Nuffar. *See* Nippur
Nuzi (Gasur, Yorghan Tepe), 39, 192–95, 224

Olduvai Gorge, 73
Olmstead, A. T., 80
Omri, 53, 142, 466, 468
Ophel, hill, 404
Oppert, Jules, 85, 177
Orfali, G., 343
Origen, 340
Osiris. *See* Eshmun

Osten, H. H. von der, 222
Oxyrhynchus, 272
Özgüç, Tahsin, 222

Paddan-Aram, 39
Palaic, 222
Palermo Stone, 248
Palestine
  climate of, 75–76
  geography of, 69–75
papyrus, 17
Parrot, André, 233
Parr, P. J., 486
Pasargadae, 210–11
Paul, 19, 344
  trial before Felix, 338
Peet, T. Eric, 260
Pekah, 197
Peleset, 47, 264
Pella, 344
Pentateuch (Torah), 17, 20, 26
Pe-Rameses, 262–64
Perea, 62
Perrot, J., 315
Persepolis, 211–13
Perseus, 387
Persia (Iran), 58, 208–10
Persian period. *See* Iron Age III
Peter, 19, 338
Peters, John, 176
Petra, 481, 483–86
Petrie, Sir W. M. Flinders, 87–89, 95, 106, 161, 162, 257, 260, 263, 264, 272, 419
Pettinato, Giovanni, 153, 246
Pfeiffer, Robert H., 192
Pharisees, 61
Phasael tower, 408
Philadelphia, 489. *See also* Amman
Philip, 338
Philistia, 300
Philistines, 48, 49, 225, 264, 295, 297–98, 331–32, 358–59, 386–87, 441
Phoenicians, 48, 52, 57, 337
pictograms, 131–35
picture writing, 129–36
Pilate, Pontius, 62, 338
  inscription, 340–41
Pilgrim of Bordeaux, 81
Pithom, 44, 262–64
Pitkanas, 223
Pizzicolli, Cyriac de, 81
Place, Victor, 205, 207
Pompeii, 83
Pompey, 61, 62, 334, 469
  conquest of, 337
Porter, J. L., 371
Posener Execration Texts, 373
potassium-argon dating, 118
pottery, 33, 37, 43, 48–49, 55, 61–62
  chronology of Palestinian, 90
  dating, 113–15, 119
  Halafian, 238
  Hassuna, 199
  Late Helladic III C, 49
  Neolithic, 33
  Philistine, 298, 299
  Ubaidian, 199
Prayer of Nabonidus, the, 453
Pre-Cave Culture, 30–31
Prepottery Neolithic era, 33
Prestwich, Sir Joseph, 83
Pritchard, James B., 364, 366, 494
Psalms Commentary, the, 454
Psalms of Joshua, the, 453
Pseudepigrapha, 17, 18
Ptolemy I, 59, 388
  portrait of, 407
Ptolemy II, Philadelphus, 61, 388, 489
  army of, 334
Ptolemy III, 388
Ptolemy IV, Philopator, 388
Pul. *See* Tiglath-pileser III
pyramids, 257

Qalat Sharqat. *See* Ashur
Qantir, 44, 262
Qarqar, battle of, 54, 196
Quietus, war of, 65
Qumran (Khirbet Qumran), 65, 447–63
Qumran Scrolls. *See* Dead Sea Scrolls
Qumran Sect, 24
Qumran Writings. *See* Dead Sea Scrolls

Rabbath-Ammon. *See* Amman
Rahab, 392
Ramesseum, the, 262
Ramses (city), 44
Ramses I, 44
Ramses II, 44, 46, 220, 261, 262, 263, 264, 386
Ramses III, 47, 265, 296, 386
  mortuary temple of, 264
  statue of, 331
  stele of, 330, 331
Ramses-Wesr-Khepesh, inscription of, 331, 333
Rasap, gate of, 244
Rassam, Hormuzd, 198, 202, 207
Ras Shamra, 43, 236, 238
  texts, 241–42
Rast, Walter, 483

Rauchwolff (Rauwolf), Leonhard, 82
Rauwolf, Leonhard. *See* Rauchwolff, Leonhard
Rawlinson, Henry Creswicke, 85, 137, 182, 186
Rechabites, 368
Reed, W. L., 368, 488
Rehoboam, 264, 478
Reisner, George A., 89, 106, 158, 257, 439, 465
Reland, Adrian, 82
Renan, Ernest, 247
"Report of Wenamon," 271
Resheph, 248
Rib-Addi, 248
Ricci, P. A., 492
Rich, Claudius J., 84, 174, 188, 195, 198
Rift Valley, 69, 72–73
Robinson, Edward, 85–86, 95, 99, 161, 347, 363, 402, 409, 473, 481
  Arch, 409
Roman Period, the, 62–65
Rosetta Stone, 83, 137, 138, 139, 257
Rothenberg, Beno, 40, 261
Rothschild Expedition, 371, 373
Rowe, Alan, 329, 357
Royal City, the, 213, 214

Sachau, Eduard, 268
St. Catherine's Monastery, 72
St. Helena, 81
St. Mark's Monastery Isaiah Scroll, 448, 449
St. Peter, Church of, 388–89
St. Stephen's Gate, 407
Salt Sea. *See* Dead Sea
Samaria (Sebaste, Sebastiyeh, Shomron), 54, 56, 57, 61, 62, 99, 465–72
  fall of, 167
Sami, Ali, 210, 213
Samuel, 49, 52
Sanballat, 57, 58
San el-Hagar (Avaris, Zoan), 263
Saqqara, 257
Sargon, 179–80, 184, 194, 195, 204
  palace of, 205
Sargon II, 54, 80, 84, 197, 199, 204, 209, 300
Sauer, James, 482
Saul, 47, 49, 51, 496
  death of, 332, 333
  sons of, 367
Sayce, A. H., 220, 268
Sayings of Jesus. See *Logia*
Schaeffer, Claude F. A., 236, 237, 238
Schaub, Thomas, 483
Schick, Conrad, 404
Schliemann, Heinrich, 87, 95, 102, 161
Schmidt, Felix (Fabri), 81
Schmidt, E. F., 210, 213
Schumacher, Gottlieb, 161, 439, 481
Scroll of the War of the Sons of Light Against the Sons of Darkness. See *War Scroll*, the
Scythians, 209
Scythopolis, 334, 335. *See also* Beth-shan
Sdot Yam, 340
Sea of Asphalt. *See* Dead Sea, 74
Sea Peoples, 45, 46, 47, 225, 239, 264, 295–96, 297, 298, 331, 332, 386, 421
Sebaste, 465, 470. *See also* Samaria
Sebastiyeh, 465. *See also* Samaria
Seetzen, Ulrich, 85, 481
Seger, J. D., 91, 357
Seleucia, 189
Seleucus I, 59, 189
Seleucus III, 59
Seller, Ovid R., 101
Sellin, Ernst, 89, 394, 474
Semites, 38, 41
Sennacherib, 54, 80, 197, 198, 199, 317, 388, 406, 427
  siege of Lachish, 424
Septuagint, 18, 61
Serbit el-Khadim, 141, 261
Sethos I, 331
  city lists of, 373
Seti I, 44, 46, 261
Seti II, 262
Severus, Julius, 305, 312
Shalmaneser III, 54, 202, 209
  inscriptions of, 174, 196
Shalmaneser V, 197, 204
Shamash, 192, 207
Sharkali-sharri, 189
Shechem, 39, 40, 42, 53, 61, 157, 227, 469, 470, 473–80
Shechem, Tower of. *See* Migdal Shechem
Sheklesh, 47
Sherden, 47
Sheshbazzar, 56
Sheshonq I. *See* Shishak
Shiloh, 48
Shinar, 175
Shishak (Sheshonq I), 264, 265, 317, 325, 333
Shomron, 465. *See also* Samaria

Shulgi, 185
Shuruppak, 178, 186
Shushan, 214, 216. *See also* Susa
Sidon, destruction of, 388
Sihon, 487
Siloam Pool, 54, 404, 406
Silva, Flavius, 431
Simon, Hasmonean king, 360, 388
Simon the Righteous, 407
Simons, J., 280
Simonsen, L. S. Vedel, 84
Sinai, 41, 48, 227, 261–62
Sinaiticus, 19
Sin, the god, 235
Sipiš, gate of, 244
Sippar, 192
Sisera, 374
Six Day War, 100
Smith, Eli, 85–86, 99, 161
Smith, George, 199, 202
Solomon, 22, 49, 52, 53, 115, 167, 202, 204, 219, 240, 247, 288, 333, 359, 387, 402, 408, 442, 444, 478
  palace of, 265
  pillars, 261
  temple, 289
Sommer, F., 221
Sons of the South. See *Bene-Yamina*
Speiser, E. A., 26
Spring of Elisha. *See* Ain es Sultan
Starkey, J. L., 90, 419
Star, Richard F. S., 192
Steckeweh, Hans, 474
Stein, Sir Aurel, 210
step-trench method, 106
Steuernagel, C., 439
Stonach, David, 211
"Story of Sinuhe," 270
Strato's Tower, 337, 342
Subarians, 175
Succoth (Tell Deir 'Alla), 495–96
Suhm, P. F., 84
Sukenik, E. L., 97, 413, 414, 465
Sultan Sanjar, 214
Sumer, 176, 179
Sumerian King List, 178, 179, 183, 185–86
Sumerian literature, 181
Sumerians, 175
Sumerology, 178
Suppiluliumas, 196, 224, 240
Susa (Shushan), 192, 213–16
Swauger, James L., 293
Syria, 36, 225, 231–52

Tabitha (Dorcas), 389
"Tale of Two Brothers," 271
Talmud, 210
Tanis, 41, 44, 262
  temple, 262
Tarsus, 225
  Mountains, 48
Tausert, wife of Seti II, 495
Tavernier, Jean-Baptiste, 82
Tawilan, 486
Taylor, J. E., 182
Taylor Prism, 198, 388
Teacher of Righteousness, 459
Tekoa, 57
Tel Aviv, 385
Teleilat el-Ghassul, 90, 482–83
Telepinus, 224
tell, definition of, 98
Tell Abu Matar, 34, 315
Tell Ajjul, 43
Tell Arad, 317
Tell Ashdod. *See* Ashdod
Tell as-Sab'. *See* Beer-sheba
Tell Beer-sheba, 99. *See also* Beer-sheba
Tell Beit Mirsim, 40, 48, 90, 158, 162, 323–27. *See also* Debir
Tell Dan, 347, 349, 352. *See also* Dan
Tell Deir 'Alla. *See* Succoth
Tell ed-Duweir, 90, 419, 423. *See also* Lachish
Tell el-Amarna (Akhetaten), 44, 258–60
Tell el-Farah. *See* Tirzah
Tell el-Hesi, 88, 106, 157–58, 161, 419
Tell el-Husn. *See* Beth-shan
Tell el-Jib, 99
Tell el-Maskhuta, 264
Tell el-Milh, 288
Tell el-Muqayyar, 182. *See also* Ur
Tell el-Mutesellim, 439. *See also* Megiddo
Tell el-Qadi, 347. *See also* Dan
Tell el-Qedah, 371. *See also* Hazor
Tell er-Retabah, 264
Tell er-Ras, 479
Tell er-Rumeilah, 99
Tell es-Sa'idiyeh. *See* Zarethan
Tell es Sultan, 391, 398. *See also* Jericho
Tell Gezer, 355. *See also* Gezer
Tell Halaf, 34
Tell Hariri. *See* Mari
Tell Ḥesbân, 487. *See also* Heshbon
Tell Hum. *See* Capernaum
Tell Malhata, 317
Tell Mor, 293

Tell Mardikh, 153. *See also* Ebla tablets, 401
Tell Masos, 99
Tell Siran, 100, 491
Teman, 486
Temple Scroll. *See* Dead Sea Scrolls, the
temple, the, 56
  temple, the second, 210
Testament of Levi, the, 453
Testament of Naphtali, the, 453
Testament of the Twelve Patriarchs, the, 453
Texier, Charles, 220
Thanksgiving Hymns. See *Hodayot Scroll*
Thebes, 46, 256, 257, 258, 264–68
thermoluminescence dating, 118
Thompson, Henry O., 491
Thompson, R. Campbell, 182, 199
Thorlacius, S., 84
Thoth (Thuti), 286
Thuti. *See* Thoth
Thutmosis I, 43
Thutmosis III, 257, 264, 331, 358, 386
  city lists of, 373
Tiamat, 245
Tiberias, 20
Tiglath-pileser I, 196, 199, 220, 247
  cylinders of, 207
Tiglath-pileser III (Pul), 80, 174, 197, 202, 204, 360, 444
Tilia, Giuseppe and Ann Gritt, 213
Timna, 261
Tirzah (Tell el-Farah), 40, 53, 466
Titus, son of Vespasian, 64, 431, 462
Tobiah, 57
Tobler, T., 402
Tomb of the Kings, 402
tools, 102–103
Toombs, Lawrence E., 475
Torah, 23, 24, 59. *See also* Pentateuch
Transjordan, 44, 56, 57, 481–97
Troy, 87, 161, 225
Tudhaliyas II, 224
Tufnell, O., 424, 425
Turk period, 65
Tursha, 47
Tushingham, A. D., 488
Tutankhamun (Tutankhaten), 44, 224, 260
Tyanitis, 225
Tyche, statues of, 342
Tyre, siege of, 204
Tyropoeon Valley, 404, 409, 410

Ubaid, 183
Ubadians, 175
Ubaidiyah, 30
Ubar-Tutu (Atarhasis, Utnapishtim, Ziusudra), 178
Ugarit, 42, 46, 224, 227, 236–42, 264, 298
  alphabet, 141
  myths of, 240
Umm el Biyara, 486
Umm es-Sarab, 488
Upper Mesolithic period, 31
Ur (Tell el-Muqayyar), 41, 180, 181–86, 195
Urarti, 223
Urhi-Teshub, 224
Uriah, 219, 228, 489
Ur-Nammu, 180, 182, 185
Uruk (Erech), 130, 179, 186–88
Urusalim, 401. *See also* Jerusalem
Urushalim, 401. *See also* Jerusalem
Urusilimmu, 401. *See also* Jerusalem
Ussishkin, David, 430
Utnapishtim, 199. *See also* Ubar-Tutu
Uzziah, 54, 317–18, 414, 461

Valle, Pietro della, 82, 188
Van Elderen, Bastiaan, 492
Vaticanus, 19
Ventris, Michael, 141
Vespasian, 340, 389, 461
Via Maris, 385
Vincent, L. Hugues, 280, 404
Virolleaud, Charles, 236, 237, 238
Vision of Amram, the, 453

Wadi al-Ṣarar, 99
Wadi el-Hasa (Zered), 75
Wadi en-Natuf, 31
Wadi-Murabbaat caves, 303, 306
Wailing Wall, 412
Warka, 186
Warren, Charles, 86, 161, 394, 402, 404, 413, 492
War Scroll, the (*Scroll of the War of the Sons of Light Against the Sons of Darkness*), 449, 454, 456
Watzinger, Carl, 89, 394, 439
Weill, R., 413, 414
Weiss-Rosmarin, Trude, 436–37
Wellcome-Colt expedition (Wellcome-Marston expedition), 419
Wellcome-Marston expedition. *See* Wellcome-Colt expedition
Welter, G., 474
Weshesh, 47

Wheeler, Sir Mortimer, 79, 91, 106, 268
Wheeler-Kenyon method, 106–107, 112
Wilbour, Charles E., 268
Wilson, Charles, 402
  Arch, 410
Winckler, Hugo, 220, 221
Winckelmann, Johann J., 82
Winnett, F. V., 488
Woolley, Sir Leonard, 183–84, 260
Wright, G. Ernest, 38, 55, 90, 91, 97, 101, 106, 162–63, 164, 357, 468, 475, 478
Wright, G. R. H., 486
writing, development of, 127–51

Yadin, Yigael, 45, 91, 96, 97, 122, 305, 308, 312, 359, 371, 374, 382, 408, 429, 432–33, 435, 436, 437, 440, 442, 456, 458, 468, 495
Yahu, temple of. *See* Yahweh, temple of
Yahweh, temple of, 268, 269
Yamhad, 234, 243
Yazilikaya, 220
  shrine of, 221
Yehonatan bar Ba'yah, 309
Yehoshua ben Galgola, 306
Yeivin, Samuel, 277, 279
Yorghan Tepe. *See* Nuzi
Young, G. D., 425
Young, Sir Thomas, 137

Zadok, sons of, 458
Zannanza, 224
Zarethan (Tell es-Sa'idiyeh), 494–95
Zayadine, F., 465
Zealots, 340, 410, 429, 431, 432, 433, 434, 435, 436, 437
  death of the, 432
Zechariah, 57
Zedekiah, 393
Zered, 75. *See* Wadi el-Hasa
Zerqa, 338
Zeus, temple of, 479
Zilas, 352
Zimri-Lim, palace of, 234
Zion Gate, 407
Ziusudra. *See* Ubar-Tutu
Zoan. *See* San el-Hagar
Zori, N., 331
Zoroastrianism, 209
Zuallart, Johann, 82